Cambridge Guide to Fiction in English

The *Cambridge Guide to Fiction in English* offers a comprehensive span of information about the novel from its inception to the present day. The novel form encompasses a range of expression from fantasy to faction, from the classics to dirty realism and in an authoritative and thought-provoking Introduction Ian Ousby looks at all the manifestations of this genre. He places the novel in the context of English literature in general and looks at its history, development and diversity. He considers the theory of the novel and various forms of related writing such as historical novels, short stories, novellas.

The range of creative writing in English extends worldwide, and this book incorporates A–Z entries on novelists and works from all those countries where English is written: Britain, USA, Canada, the Caribbean, Australia, New Zealand, South Africa, Africa, India. Additionally, the book includes a wide range of thematic entries. Particular types of novels – from the Gothic to the campus novel – receive detailed coverage as do trends in fiction – from realism to naturalism. Popular genres such as detective fiction, spy fiction, science fiction, are generously represented. This is the first general reference work on the novel to include Chicano and Quebecois writing. Readers of the novel looking for abstruse references will not be disappointed, nor will those who want information on contemporary fiction. A selective bibliography indicates areas for further reading in each of the main areas of the novel form.

Ian Ousby was educated at Cambridge and Harvard, and he taught in Britain and the USA before becoming a professional writer. His books on literature include the prestigious *Cambridge Guide to Literature in English*, *Bloodhounds of Heaven: The Detective in English Fiction from Godwin to Doyle*, *The Blue Guide to Literary Britain and Ireland*, *The Correspondence of John Ruskin and Charles Eliot Norton* (with John Bradley) and *The Crime and Mystery Book: A Reader's Companion*. Ian Ousby's interest in history has produced *Occupation: The Ordeal of France, 1940–1944*. He is also a well-known travel writer whose publications include *The Englishman's England: Taste, Travel and the Rise of Tourism*, *The Blue Guide to England*, *The Blue Guide to Burgundy* and *James Plumptre's Britain: The Journals of a Tourist in the 1790s*.

Cambridge Guide to Fiction in English

IAN OUSBY

CAMBRIDGE
UNIVERSITY PRESS

PUBLISHED BY THE PRESS SYNDICATE OF THE UNIVERSITY OF CAMBRIDGE
The Pitt Building, Trumpington Street, Cambridge CB2 1RP, United Kingdom

CAMBRIDGE UNIVERSITY PRESS
The Edinburgh Building, Cambridge, CB2 2RU, UK http://www.cup.cam.ac.uk
40 West 20th Street, New York, NY 10011–4211, USA http://www.cup.org
10 Stamford Road, Oakleigh, Melbourne 3166, Australia

First published 1998

Printed in Great Britain at the University Press, Cambridge

Typeset in Swift 9/9.25pt

A catalogue record for this book is available from the British Library

Library of Congress cataloging in publication data
Ousby, Ian 1947–
Cambridge guide to fiction in English / Ian Ousby.
p.   cm.
Includes bibliographical references
ISBN 0 521 63138 6 (hardback) ISBN 0 521 57617 2 (paperback)
1. English fiction – Encyclopedias.   2. English-speaking countries –
In literature – Encyclopedias.   3. American fiction – Encyclopedias.
I. Title.
PR821.O97   1998
823.003–dc21   98-13753 CIP

ISBN 0 521 63138 6 Hardback
ISBN 0 521 57617 2 Paperback

Contents

Consultants

RUTH BROWN (New Zealand)   ANN DRY (South Africa)   ALISON HENNEGAN (UK)
JOHN HOEY (French Canada)   BRIAN KIERNAN (Australia)   DAVID W. MADDEN
and PATRICK O'DONNELL (US)   JOHN SKINNER (Africa, India and South Asia)
BRIAN STABLEFORD (Science Fiction)   JOHN THIEME (Canada and the Caribbean)

Contributors

ALISON BLAIR-UNDERWOOD
JOHN L. BRADLEY
ANDREW BROWN
RUTH BROWN
GLEN CAVALIERO
HENRY CLARIDGE
PAULETTE COETZEE
GRAHAM COSTER
DOROTHY DRIVER
ANN DRY
ROD EDMOND
JOHN ELSOM
JEANETTE EVE
JEREMY FOGG
COLIN GARDNER
CAROLINE GONDA
VALERIE GROSVENOR MYER
ALISON HENNEGAN

ANNA HODSON
JOHN HOEY
C. L. INNES
MAYA JAGGI
BRIAN KIERNAN
DOUGLAS KILLAM
ANDREW LOWNIE
JAMES LYNN
DAVID W. MADDEN
ALASTAIR NIVEN
PATRICK O'DONNELL
IAN OUSBY
FIONA PATERSON
GAY RAINES
JOHN SKINNER
BRIAN STABLEFORD
JOHN THIEME
NICHOLAS TUCKER

Acknowledgements

In compiling and writing this book my first debt has been to its consultants and contributors, and particularly to Alison Hennegan, David Madden, Patrick O'Donnell and John Skinner, who landed up being consulted more often and contributing rather more than they had originally bargained. My editor Caroline Bundy has generously drawn on her considerable reserves of patience and understanding. My thanks also go to Andrew Lownie and Anna Saunders for their encouragement.

Note to the reader

The entries in this *Guide* are listed in alphabetical word-by-word order. Headings for writers, movements, literary terms and so forth appear in **bold face** and headings for the titles of books in ***bold face italics***. The appearance of SMALL CAPITALS or, for a book title, *SMALL CAPITAL ITALICS* in the course of an entry indicates that the topic receives an entry of its own elsewhere.

In the case of writers who published under a distinctively abbreviated version of their full name, the heading supplies the unused part in brackets; thus E. M. Forster appears as **Forster, E(dward) M(organ)** and F. Scott Fitzgerald as **Fitzgerald, F(rancis) Scott (Key)**. Writers who are remembered by the pseudonyms under which they commonly wrote, such as George Eliot and Mark Twain, are listed under their pseudonyms with their real names given in square brackets afterwards. People who used more than one pseudonym, or adopted an obviously fanciful pseudonym (such as 'Q'), or published under their real names as well, appear under their real names. Names beginning 'Mc' have been put with those beginning 'Mac'. Works commonly known by the name of the protagonist which appears in their title are listed under that name: ***Huckleberry Finn, The Adventures of*** not *Adventures of Huckleberry Finn, The*.

Introduction
'A Large Diffused Picture'

A novel is a living thing, all one and continuous, like every other organism, and in proportion as it lives will it be found, I think, that in each of the parts there is something of each of the other parts. The critic who over the close texture of a finished work will pretend to trace a geography of items will mark some frontiers as artificial, I fear, as any that have been known to history.

Henry James, 'The Art of Fiction' (1884)

The present Introduction apart, this book consists of several thousand entries dealing with literary movements, tendencies, types and devices but mainly with particular authors and books from the Renaissance to the present day. The criterion determining their scope is indicated in the title by the phrase 'fiction in English'. The choice of the word 'fiction' is cautious; indeed, it is doubly so. Most simply, it stands in implicit reminder that this book embraces short stories and novellas, or long short stories, as well as full-length novels. It is well to remind ourselves of their claims. The novel, however, has not just dominated these apparently lesser forms. Historically, it has dominated our approach to narrative fiction in general. For a long time criticism remained, in the current jargon of rebellion, 'novel-centred'. To give some idea of what this involved I need only offer and then examine the sort of preliminary definition which an introductory essay would have attempted three or four decades ago, in the days when the book it introduced would have been roundly entitled a 'Guide to the English Novel'.

The novel, it would then have been proposed, is 'a long fictional narrative in prose'. This definition would have been offered with slight embarrassment: unease at the blandness of its results, given the richness and significance of its subject, used to be a recurrent feature of novel criticism. But the advantages of the definition would also have been insisted on. The simple qualification 'in prose' excluded the tradition of verse epic from Homer and Virgil to Milton and Blake and beyond, all of it undoubtedly long and undoubtedly fictional and undoubtedly narrative. By the same token, verse romances from medieval tales of Arthurian chivalry to Edmund Spenser's *The Faerie Queene* (1590–6) were also ruled out of consideration. Yet, of course, it had to be conceded that the term 'novel' could not always be limited to works in prose. Rare and eccentric though they might be, novels in verse did exist too: Elizabeth Barrett Browning's *Aurora Leigh* (1856) was the instance usually cited, though some critics also remembered to mention another work by a fellow-Victorian, Arthur Hugh Clough's *Amours de Voyage* (1858). (Vikram Seth has since provided another example, *The Golden Gate* [1986].)

My purpose in hinting at these quibbles is not to laugh the old-school definition out of court. It is the business of any definition to be exclusive and yet, however tightly it draws its lines, it will still need to admit exceptions. As definitions of literary forms go, this one has proved frustratingly durable. The real problems it presented stemmed not so much from the terms in which it was stated – safe, unchallengeable, if only offering modest guidance – as from the disparity between these terms and the fashion in which it was usual to apply them.

As soon as critical discussion turned to a review of the history of the novel, and hence to particular examples, a surprisingly narrow and exclusive approach declared itself.

A lot of long fictional narratives in prose, it turned out, were not quite novels or not really novels, not proper novels or not novels at all. What about Elizabethan prose romances such as Philip Sidney's *Arcadia* (1590 and 1593) or Thomas Lodge's *Rosalynde* (1590)? Romances, it seemed, were not novels because of their fascination with the marvellous. What about Thomas Nashe's *The Unfortunate Traveller* (1594), the only one of the many Elizabethan tales of low life which criticism regularly bothered to rescue from oblivion? *The Unfortunate Traveller* was almost a novel but not quite, largely because its crudely episodic form did not even aspire to the unity of action expected of novels. And what about John Bunyan's *The Pilgrim's Progress* (1678–84)? Bunyan was praised for the simple strength of his story, the naturalism of his dialogue and a host of 'novelistic' qualities, but of course *The Pilgrim's Progress* could not really be a novel: it was an allegory with openly didactic intent.

And so, as the discussion continued, it left in its wake a lengthening list of works rejected or ignored. Jonathan Swift's *Gulliver's Travels* (1726) was regularly discussed, but as a work by a contemporary of Alexander Pope rather than of Daniel Defoe and hence discussed by students of Augustan satire rather than by students of the novel. A long tradition of utopian and dystopian fiction – embracing not just Thomas More's own *Utopia* (in Latin, 1516; in English, 1551) and the prose fables of Sir Francis Bacon but, in our own century, Aldous Huxley's *Brave New World* (1932) and George Orwell's *Animal Farm* (1945) – was quietly sidelined. So, too, for a variety of reasons were Thomas Love Peacock's country-house conversation novels, the unreliably autobiographical fictions of George Borrow and the socialist fables and pseudo-medieval romances of William Morris. Laurence Sterne's *Tristram Shandy* (1760–7), conspicuous at once for its determination to settle down to telling a story and its perverse inability to do so, could not be sidelined, despite Samuel Johnson's confident belief that its oddity would stop its reputation lasting. Instead, *Tristram Shandy* became a notorious test case – a status that a good deal of recent criticism has affirmed, albeit in a different and altogether more admiring spirit.

Even from this short list of examples, it is not hard to reconstruct the larger assumptions and the particular arguments which operated to produce these judgements. They were partly historical and partly theoretical. The historical argument was that in Britain, at least, the novel had a reasonably precise point of origin in the eighteenth century. It was brought to birth by a generation of writers – Daniel Defoe, Samuel Richardson and Henry Fielding – whose work covered a span of some thirty years, from Defoe's first novel, *Robinson Crusoe*, in 1719 to Fielding's last novel, *Amelia*, in 1751. Defoe's *Moll Flanders* (1722) was often signalled out for particular attention, while Richardson's *Clarissa* (1747–8) and Fielding's *Tom Jones* (1749) were usually cited as the first masterpieces signalling the full importance of what could be achieved. This achievement (so the argument ran) was not just stimulated but, in a crucial sense, made possible by a combination of social, economic and cultural circumstances. In brief, they had created a middle-class public literate enough to seek, confident enough to require, and affluent enough to pay for a new literary form. The form inevitably reflected the tastes, interests and values of the audience which had summoned it into being.

From such a perspective – interpreting literary history in terms which are, at root, evolutionary in their insistence on notions of origin and development – earlier work could be acknowledged only as the first stirrings of a form which could not yet properly emerge. Nashe, the Elizabethan prose romancers and Bunyan lived at the wrong time and in the wrong culture; they lacked the environment which could have made them novelists. The middle-class public of the Augustan era did provide that environment, and its taste gave the new form its proper and most fitting identity. It created what later critics, though not original readers, often called 'classic realism'.

Classic realism required two things in particular of the novel. It required an avoidance of the remote and unspecific settings of romance, where the marvellous and the impossible could flourish, in favour of a representation of life which, if not necessarily contemporary, was still life depicted in terms which the middle-class public could recognize as the terms of its own life. And, increasingly, classic realism required that prose narrative avoid the episodic, the anecdotal or the merely haphazard in favour of an order and shape which bore some relation to the order and shape which the middle-class public detected in their own lives, as members of families, as economic units, as souls answerable to their own Protestant consciences, but perhaps above all as individual beings in a society which increasingly promoted individualism.

The literary historians who endorsed this view were not much given to quoting Smollett (though not a test case like Sterne, he was hardly the most respected of the early novelists), but they would have found little to disagree with in the account he gave of the novelist's task in the dedication to *The Adventures of Ferdinand Count Fathom* (1753):

A novel is a large diffused picture, comprehending the characters of life, disposed in different groups, and exhibited in various attitudes, for the purposes of a uniform plan, and general occurrence, to which every individual figure is subservient.*

By and large they would have applauded, too, the immediate qualification Smollett added, that the necessary key to both the picture of life and the uniform plan is the fortunes of one particular person: a hero, or 'principal personage to attract the attention, unite the incidents, unwind the clue of the labyrinth, and at last close the scene by virtue of his own importance'.

It was, virtually, the destiny of fictional narrative to be the novel, and of the novel to be classic realism. So ran an argument at once historical and critical, never more persuasively or influentially stated than by Ian Watt in *The Rise of the Novel* (1957). And because the argument was evolutionary in its assumptions, it could go on to read the subsequent history of the form which had established itself in the first half of the eighteenth century in terms of consolidation, expansion and refinement. Certainly, there can be little doubt that the audience for the novel grew vastly during the next one hundred and fifty years in its size, its literacy and its buying power, as well as in the confidence with which it stated its requirements of art. In the nineteenth century the novel assumed a position in culture and society which it still to some extent occupies: at once constrained by popular taste, dictating which aspects of the available contemporary reality were proper to depict, and served by mass distribution in the form of libraries and cheap methods of publication.

The novel, then, was not just created for and in a sense by a bourgeois audience. It became inextricably involved with, if not dependent on, an audience which Frank Kermode has described as 'not ordinarily very interested in art, and quite ready to judge fiction by standards that might seem, to those engaged in technical research, tediously or even lethally conventional'.† His phrasing aptly suggests how popularity brought with it a price to pay. Certainly there has been no lack of those willing to spell out the price. Thackeray memorably grumbled about censorship, or rather about the self-censorship which a writer like himself had to practise if he wished to reach the available audience, when he complained in his preface to *Pendennis* (1848–50) that since Fielding's death it had been impossible for the novelist 'to depict to his utmost power a MAN'. Sex would often prove the trickiest aspect of the individual's life for the novel to tackle, and not just in the Victorian period. As for the subtler constraints limiting the Victorian novel, it used to be something of a commonplace among critics to lament in a more general way that, in the hour of its first great triumph, the novel had lost a measure of the happy freedom it had enjoyed a century before.

Yet the dominance that the novel had achieved brought advantages, and advantages more subtle than commercial success. Dickens, Thackeray and George Eliot – to take the list no further – are not just the names of major Victorian writers: they are, in a real sense, the names of *the* major Victorian writers. The novel dominates (perhaps one should say swamps?) critical

---

* Spelling and capitalization in all quotations from early texts have been modernized. The books by Geoffrey Day and Ioan Williams in the Suggested Reading (pages 308–12) provide useful anthologies of the eighteenth-century discussion of fiction; Miriam Allott's useful work has a wider scope.

† *Essays on Fiction 1971–82* (1983).

appreciation of what the possibilities of nineteenth-century art were, quite as thoroughly as the achievement of Shakespeare and his contemporary dramatists dominates any approach to the Renaissance in Britain. Narrative, and more specifically the novel conceived according to the doctrine of classic realism, became in the nineteenth century a condition to which other types of literature and art aspired.

One obvious way of explaining the appearance of novels in verse such as Elizabeth Barrett Browning's *Aurora Leigh* and Clough's *Amours de Voyage* is simply to say that poetry wanted to be as much like fiction as it could. The aspiration had arguably first made itself felt in the Romantic period with Byron's *Don Juan*, and it asserted itself again in the Victorian period when Tennyson reserved his major poetic energy for *The Idylls of the King* and Browning his for *The Ring and the Book*. Victorian painting and even music wanted to be like fiction as well. Canvases by, for example, the Pre-Raphaelites are deliberately strewn with narrative detail: visual clues to be deciphered in working out the past history and the future fate of the lovers, or the husband and wife, or the soldier returning from the wars. 'Programme music' by Berlioz or Mendelssohn invited the listener to 'read' the symphony or concert overture not as an abstract pattern of sound but, in some fashion, as a narrative about flesh-and-blood characters and stirring events set against a backdrop of almost palpably visual scenery. Sometimes, indeed, the painting or music bore a title specifically invoking the particular work of literature which it sought to translate. And when it did so, as often or not the work was a play by Shakespeare or a poem by Byron or a novel by Sir Walter Scott.

Scott's name, once hugely admired but now faded apparently beyond repair, is pertinent to invoke in asking where the Victorian achievement stood in relation to the doctrine of classic realism which later critics would elaborate. Scott himself, of course, wrote before the Victorian era: his first novel, *Waverley*, appeared in 1814 and his last two, *Count Robert of Paris* and *Castle Dangerous*, jointly in 1832. With the solitary exception of *St Ronan's Well* (1823), they are all historical fiction taking the past conflicts of Scotland or the medieval history of England and casting them into shapes which, if only by the sheer amplitude of the stories, satisfied Smollett's prescription of 'a large diffused picture' virtually to the letter. Their admiration for Scott encouraged all the major Victorians and most of the minor ones to attempt historical novels, usually without his success but always in the belief that they were venturing on the most respectable and exacting task a novelist could undertake. Even when they were not writing historical fiction, Scott's example confirmed their belief that a novel's ambition corresponded to its sheer size. Thackeray's *Vanity Fair* (1847–8), Dickens's *Bleak House* (1852–3) and George Eliot's *Middlemarch* (1871–2) all make a fundamental assertion, not vulgarly but emphatically, through the sheer thickness of their pages in the reader's hand. If the novel was to be realistic, the goal was most obviously to be achieved through a large inclusiveness, an epic inclusiveness of detail and variety. In every sense, it should seek to comprehend the world.

Yet Scott himself, modest about his own achievement and generous in acknowledging his fellow-novelists, could also point in a different direction, toward a different definition of classic realism. He did so most clearly when re-reading Jane Austen's *Pride and Prejudice* (1813) prompted him, in 1827, to pay tribute to her

talent for describing the involvements, and feelings, and characters of ordinary life, which is to me the most wonderful I ever met with. The Big Bow-wow strain I can do myself like any now going; but the exquisite touch, which renders ordinary commonplace things and characters interesting, from the truth of the description and the sentiments is denied to me.

So the novel could aim instead at something strikingly different from the 'Big Bow-wow strain' and look suspiciously as if it were fulfilling its natural destiny when it did so. It could confine itself to the narrowest of compasses – did not Jane Austen herself speak memorably of her 'little bit (two inches wide) of ivory'? – and concentrate on what most immediately reflected the life, inner and outer, of its most ordinary reader.

In an important sense, both these possibilities inform the Victorian novel. Indeed it is often the tension between them which generates their distinctive shape and atmosphere. Inside those bulky forms that speak unmistakably of Scott's influence there operates, with as much power but less open acknowledgement, the influence of Austen, or at least the influence of Austen as Scott had read her. Characteristically, the Victorian novel defines its power and its purpose as being to explain history to those who have inherited it and now live among its consequences, to explain the increasingly intricate operations of society to those who live within its great web. The very titles of Dickens's *Hard Times, For These Times* (1854) and Trollope's *The Way We Live Now* (1874–5) announce the confidence with which such novels addressed contemporary life at all its levels. At times, indeed, they seem to assert their ability not just to reflect reality but to embody it, their characters escaping the limits of the printed page and claiming a life of their own. Such a moment occurs when Dickens mourns and protests the death of Jo, the crossing sweeper in *Bleak House*:

Dead, your Majesty. Dead, my lords and gentlemen, Dead, Right Reverends and Wrong Reverends of every order. Dead, men and women, born with heavenly compassion in your hearts. And dying thus around us every day.

This is 'realism of character' with such a vengeance that it makes most modern readers uncomfortable, reluctant as we now are to allow our emotions to be manipulated in the name of such naive aesthetic assumptions. Yet, by definition, novels such as *Bleak House* would not even have attempted such effects unless they balanced their larger ambition with an equally powerful belief in the significance of ordinary and indeed insignificant people like Jo. Victorian fiction insists that its purpose would be incomplete unless, scene by scene and page by page, it also dwelt on all those aspects of life which the Victorians usually sought to comprise in the adjective 'humble'. It celebrates the private affections which keep marriages and families together, the small gestures of kindness or charity which palliate the larger harshness of society, the lifetimes of unglamorous work which show the value of service and duty.

In the process a dual purpose is served, of reconciling the individual both to the larger framework of society and to the limits of any single position inside it. If, thus stated, the task sounds a little too conveniently attractive to the bourgeois liberal conscience, then that (some critics would claim) is yet more evidence that the novel always bore the mark of its origins in the tastes and requirements of a particular audience. To gauge the finest nuances which performance of its task could assume, one need only turn to the closing paragraphs of *Middlemarch*, where the account of the eventual fate of the characters – notably Dorothea Brooke and Dr Lydgate – assesses what such a reconciliation involves with the most deliberate and painstaking clarity.

By common consent *Middlemarch* marks a summit, if not the summit, of classic realism in its Victorian phase. Or, as one of its first reviewers put it, 'it sets a limit . . . to the development of the old-fashioned English novel'. The reviewer was Henry James, who took upon himself the task of refining the form which the eighteenth century had established and the high Victorian era so generously expanded. More than any other single writer from the next generation, he was responsible for developing the definition of 'realism', a term the English language was then in the process of borrowing from French, which had in turn borrowed it from philosophy. And the manner in which James developed the concept of realism directly paved the way for the generation of modernists who emerged in the early decades of the twentieth century.

'There is no impression of life, no manner of seeing it and feeling it, to which the plan of the novel may not offer a place', James wrote in 'The Art of Fiction' (1884) with a large confidence which shows the debt he owed the Victorian achievement in exploring the potentialities that fiction held. Yet he always viewed this legacy ambivalently. There was, on the one hand, the 'impression of life' which the novel could render; on the other, there was the 'plan' or formal design through which it rendered the impression. And, by and large, the Victorian novel had not mediated successfully between the two. Its sheer energy, its determination to bring the abundance and variety of life before the reader, had brought aesthetic dangers. Of the never-ending web of relations which make up life it had given at times an adequate idea, but without satisfactorily addressing itself to the delicate task of selecting from this mass its own particular subject and focus, its own 'figure in the carpet'.

Even *Middlemarch*, though 'a treasure-house of details', James found 'an indifferent whole'. Despite this larger failure, he still regarded it with proper respect. He was not so respectful toward other novels and other novelists. The intricate multi-layered plotting which held together the fabric of a late Dickens novel like *Our Mutual Friend* (1864–5) he contemptuously dismissed as 'the manufacture of fiction'. The word 'manufacture' is (like all James's words) precisely chosen. The Victorian novel had been a commodity offered to a mass public and the price it had paid for its position in the marketplace had gone far beyond submitting itself to prudish self-censorship (though James was willing to follow Thackeray in complaining of this result). It had given the novel a crudity in its very system of organization, at worst a preference for the pot-boiling plot

full of incident and movement, so that we shall wish to jump ahead, to see who was the mysterious stranger, and if the stolen will was ever found, and shall not be distracted from this pleasure by any tiresome analysis or 'description'.

The ending of such novels, when the breathless reader does reach them, turns out to be matter of contrivance and complacency. James is memorably savage on those Victorian last chapters which consist of 'a distribution of prizes, pensions, husbands, wives, babies, millions, appended paragraphs, and cheerful remarks'. The satisfactions they offered had proved an inescapably powerful requirement in the case, for instance, of Dickens's *Great Expectations* (1860–1). His original ending had left the hero and heroine, Pip and Estella, apart but in sympathetic agreement over the lessons which experience had taught them in humbling their youthful arrogance. On the advice of Bulwer Lytton (a novelist with unrivalled understanding of the demands made by the reading public) Dickens had substituted an ending which brought the couple together, albeit in a chastened and melancholy spirit.

Fundamental to James's critique, then, was a suspicion of the audience which the novel had previously enjoyed and of what writers had allowed this audience to do to their art. He was not the only novelist to reach this conclusion, nor was his route toward it the only one a novelist of his time could tread. Thomas Hardy, whose approach to fiction is at virtually every point markedly different from James's, gave up novels for poetry after public outcry against the supposed immorality of *Tess of the d'Urbervilles* (1891) and *Jude the Obscure* (1895). Among his reasons, he cited the greater aesthetic freedom that came with writing for the smaller audience which poetry enjoyed.

James's prescription was, in effect, that the novel should distance itself from the marketplace, actually begin to refuse the pressures that went with popularity in order to benefit from the opportunity such freedom would bring. In this, as much as in the specifics of his commentary on how exactly novelists should use their freedom, he was profoundly influential. Before him, novelists had taken it as axiomatic that they had access to a large and varied audience, and they had welcomed the chances it gave them. Dickens's relish at knowing his words reached out to a crowded auditorium is quite palpable; indeed, the public readings of his last years made the crowded auditorium no metaphor but a literal fact. After James, novelists were as likely to take it as axiomatic that they had a choice to make between being 'serious' and being 'popular'. A great deal of the history of fiction, and its attendant criticism, from the later years of the nineteenth century up to the present day hinges on the increasingly sharp definition, as well as the powerful connotations, these terms would assume.

For James, the purpose of withdrawing the novel from the position it had occupied in the culture, or at least of retrenching its position, went far beyond the need to purge it item by item of the various faults he detected in the work of his predecessors: enforced prudery, over-plotting, vacuously happy endings and so forth. It was, quite simply, to reflect and so to break with the energetic unself-consciousness the novel had possessed in the days when it

had no air of having a theory, a conviction, a consciousness of itself behind it – of being the expression of an artistic faith, the result of choice and comparison ... There was a comfortable, good-humoured feeling abroad that a novel is a novel, as a pudding is a pudding, and that our only business with it, could be to swallow it.

This picture of Victorian simplicity might be deliberately overstated, but that did not prevent its colouring the reading of Victorian fiction for several generations. Nor does it invalidate the obvious truth that James himself marked a dividing-line between those novelists who had worked without the need to set down a critical theory and those who did feel the need, as an inevitable part of their artistic decision to be 'serious'.

Major novelists since James have often been major critics of the novel as well. Virginia Woolf and D. H. Lawrence are the first examples which spring to mind. They are also the most pertinent, since as members of the generation which flourished in the first three or four decades of this century their criticism – particularly Virginia Woolf's – stands in a clear line of descent from James's precept and example. The new realism he proposed to substitute for the 'old-fashioned English novel' shaded into modernism. 'Modernism' is, of course, a label not so much for a single theoretical stance as for a loose collection of tendencies which affected virtually all forms of literature and the arts; even as it applies just to the novel, it is various and sometimes conflicting in its manifestations. Yet in at least two respects the modernist novel is consistent and consistent in its debt to what James had advocated and James had done.

The first hinges on the question of whether the reality which the novels render is conceived of as something external or internal: very crudely put, as something to be seen from the outside or something to be felt from the inside. Of course, some approaches would deny the suggestion of a dichotomy altogether, just as very few would reject the notion of a significant internal life which realism, however defined, must acknowledge. Certainly the novel of eighteenth and nineteenth centuries was not among them, with its common tendency to pass easily from speaking of realism to speaking of the 'characters of life' and so in some fashion to concerning itself with what makes people tick. Yet for all that it had, in the Jamesian view, landed up giving undue primacy to what things looked like rather than what they felt like. Its characteristic triumphs had often been, literally, with things rather than people: the landscapes of Sir Walter Scott or the crowded interiors of Dickens. And when it did approach people, it often did so through the objects associated with them: through their money, their possessions, the clothes they wore or the houses they lived in.

To James, then, the novel had run the risk of being external and hence of being, by his standards, superficial. The overstuffed plot which hurried the reader on from one stirring event to the next had cravenly surrendered itself to this fate. It had deserted the territory where the novel stood supreme in its ability, the territory where he sought to relocate it. This he called 'the drama of consciousness'. The memorable phrase described his own continual effort to capture the nuances of a passing moment, the impression that an event or a situation or an encounter made on one of its participants. And through his example, it stayed with novelists and critics for almost a century, seeming to come as close as any single phrase could to setting out what the whole effort of the novel was about.

The implications of the shift were immense. The novel, it appeared, could make do with less matter than it had previously supposed; indeed, it flourished on less matter. The large story, densely plotted, which a writer like Dickens had taken as a prerequisite turned out to be superfluous, even an impediment. The novel did not need to take a city, a war, an era or even a whole lifetime for its subject. All its external dimensions could be scaled down, deliberately pared to the minimum. Just a small group of people and a short period of time would be enough. In fact, such narrow boundaries helped the novel fulfil its destined task of getting inside to record the drama of consciousness. James Joyce's *Ulysses* (1922), Virginia Woolf's *Mrs Dalloway* (1925) and William Faulkner's *The Sound and the Fury* (1929) – to cite just three leading examples of modernist fiction – all in their different ways choose for their matter a handful of people on a single day. And 16 June 1904, the day when the action of *Ulysses* takes place, is notorious in the fictional calendar for being a day when nothing much happened.

Just how much did need to happen in a novel to make it work became a revealing point of contention between modernist novelists and an audience which came increasingly to find that 'serious' literature disappointed conventional expectations that 'popular' literature remained glad to fulfil. 'Yes – oh dear, yes – the novel tells a story', E. M. Forster conceded in

Aspects of the Novel (1927) with a theatrical sigh of sorrow, bullied into the admission by the average man on the golf course. The story, he was forced to admit, was not just 'the fundamental aspect' without which the novel could not exist but 'the highest factor common to all novels'. Yet, he added, 'I wish that it was not so, that it could be something different – melody, or perception of the truth, not this low atavistic form'.

It was not only the story that was disappearing, but the storyteller as well. In *Ulysses*, *The Sound and the Fury* and *Mrs Dalloway* – or at least for much of the time in these novels – the novelist is so determinedly concealed behind the characters as to appear, by the standards of the casual reader, to have deserted the narrative altogether. The result of the narrator's apparent absence was quite as disconcerting as the apparent lack of story, if not more so. All three books, in fact, use the technique known as 'stream of consciousness', though Joyce preferred to use a French label for it, *monologue intérieur*. Stream of consciousness adopts the perspective of a particular character and seeks to present it without, as it were, editorial tampering or mediation: preserving its original vocabulary and its sometimes fractured syntax, complete with the ellipses and loose ends of thought, the unsignalled shifts of attention and the lapses of concentration which mark the processes of consciousness in real life.

Virginia Woolf famously described the technique and its justification when, in her essay on 'Modern Fiction' (written in 1919 and collected in *The Common Reader* [1925]), she invited readers to compare the discrepancy between life as the novel had traditionally arranged it and life as it was actually experienced:

Examine for a moment an ordinary mind on an ordinary day. The mind receives a myriad impressions – trivial, fantastic, evanescent, or engraved with the sharpness of steel. From all sides they come, an incessant shower of innumerable atoms; and as they fall, as they shape themselves into the life of Monday or Tuesday, the accent falls differently from of old; the moment of importance came not here but there; so that if a writer were a free man and not a slave, if he could write what he chose, not what he must, if he could base his work upon his own feeling, and not upon convention, there would be no plot, no comedy, no tragedy, no love interest or catastrophe in the accepted style, and perhaps not a single button sewn on as the Bond Street tailors would have it. Life is not a series of gig lamps symmetrically arranged; but a luminous halo, a semi-transparent envelope surrounding us from the beginning of consciousness to the end. Is it not the task of the novelist to convey this varying, this unknown and uncircumscribed spirit, whatever complexity or aberration it may display, with as little mixture of the alien and external as possible?

By no means all the modernists, or even all the modernists who practised stream of consciousness, would have assented to everything in this argument. It is, for example, possible to value consciousness as highly as Virginia Woolf does and be as willing as she is to let the demands of representing it shape the novel without supposing, as she appears to, that consciousness is an inherently passive, almost helpless, process of reception. (Lawrence and Joyce would both have vigorously disputed her assumption, though without agreeing with each other.) Modernism and the post-Jamesian tradition was, after all, always a loose assortment of tendencies and never a commonly agreed dogma. But James himself would have found much to applaud in the passage from 'Modern Fiction', and his agreement would have begun with Woolf's call to the novelist to aim at absolute fidelity to life and her refusal to be enslaved by external restraints, however familiar convention might have made them and however dearly readers might still cherish them. He had, after all, taken exactly this stance himself.

Fundamental to his view of the novel was an acceptance that the 'drama of consciousness' could not simply be inserted in the existing design or method by way of substitute for those elements it rejected as superficial or unworthy. It demanded radical change, and nowhere did the change need to be more radical than in its redefinition of the storyteller. If the story was to deal properly with the internal, its teller had to inhabit a perspective which was relative where the stance of 'old-fashioned' tellers had usually been absolute. However much James might have admired the grasp of inner life displayed in *Tom Jones* or *Vanity Fair* or *Middlemarch*, he could not admire the way – the absolute way – in which it was grasped and displayed. In these novels the storytellers, as Thackeray put it, know everything. They know everything about the past and the future which lie either side of the action on which their stories concentrate. They know what all the characters are thinking and feeling, and why. And their moral authority is just as absolute as their literal authority. Frequently in the course of the tale they speak in their own voice, using the first person and confidently buttonholing the reader, to comment on the action, analyse it and judge it absolutely.

Real life simply does not work that way and so, if novels are to represent real life with any strict approach to fidelity, they cannot work that way either. To James the premise of traditional storytelling was every bit as unacceptably artificial as the traditional preference for conclusively happy endings or stirring events, and it was by definition even more deeply embedded in the fabric of the story. His own preferred method, governed as it was by a distaste for the 'terrible *fluidity* of self-revelation' and an inveterate suspicion of the first person in whatever guise it might surface in narrative, stopped well short of stream-of-consciousness. Instead, he took his cue from Flaubert's *Madame Bovary* (1857), confirming the status of that novel as the single most important example of a more demanding realism than Victorian writers in Britain had practised.

To borrow his own metaphor, James chose to make the story look out of just one of the many windows of 'the house of fiction'. In his mature work, at least, there is always a single observer, a single watcher at the window. These observers exist in the third person (always a 'he' or a 'she' rather than an 'I') but their perspective nevertheless dictates the narrative. The reader's knowledge is thus limited to what the observers see, hear, think, feel and believe. If the novelist knows more, he has hidden that knowledge as effectively as he has hidden his presence. Impersonal and objective, he has begun, at least, to aspire to the state which Stephen Dedalus memorably describes in Joyce's *A Portrait of the Artist as a Young Man* (1916): 'The artist, like the God of the creation, remains within or behind or beyond or above his hand-iwork, invisible, refined out of existence, indifferent, paring his fingernails'.

In practice, at any rate, the novelist has chosen not to tell. Indeed, as James insisted, it was not the business of the novel to tell but to show. Among the places he makes the point is the opening scene of *The Turn of the Screw* (1898), in which the country-house guests prepare to hear the story of the governess's encounter with the supernatural. 'The story will tell,' says the anonymous narrator confidently. 'Oh I can't wait for the story!' exclaims one of the other guests, speaking for the conventional reading public. But Douglas lays the governess's story before them with a warning and a rebuke: 'The story *won't* tell ... not in any literal vulgar way'. And, indeed, it does not tell in the way that conventional stories do. The whole question of whether the ghosts which the governess sees exist in sober fact or only in her imagination became, for many years, a matter for scholars to debate, returning in article after article to hunt for new clues which the text might have shown them without telling them.

The debate showed a great deal about the new climate which James had created for fiction. In his hands and those of the modernists who came after him, the novel no longer interpreted itself to the reader in the way previous novels had. This work was instead left to the reader by fiction that was, in its pursuit of its particular style of realism, growing 'inscrutable' – as James's contemporary Joseph Conrad liked to call his narrator, Marlow, and the tales he told. In Conrad's *Heart of Darkness* (1902) the tale and the teller come prefaced by the same sort of warning Douglas issues to his fellow-guests at the start of *The Turn of the Screw*. Marlow, we are told, is a seaman with a seaman's characteristic love of spinning yarns. Otherwise, he is an untypical seaman, for

to him the meaning of an episode was not inside like a kernel but outside, enveloping the tale which brought it out only as a glow brings out a haze, in the likeness of one of these misty halos that sometimes are made visible by the spectral illumination of moonshine.

To put it another way, the novel had become inconclusive, in the full sense of the word. James's objection to those last chapters which round out the elaborate narratives of his Victorian predecessors was not just a matter of disliking their vacuous happiness. He disliked the completeness with which they settled matters: marrying people off to each other, assigning prison sentences or fortunes in a spirit of final judgement, even peeking forward into the future to see how many children the hero and heroine had together. Even in *Washington Square* (1880), relatively conventional in its open debt to Jane Austen, he contrived to handle the matter differently by taking leave of his heroine in a single sentence:

Catherine, meanwhile, in the parlour, picking up her morsel of fancy-work, had seated herself with it again – for life, as it were.

She is, we gather, permanently consigned to spinsterhood and embroidery, but the point is made as if by a sudden freeze-frame in a film. This device, helping the novel move away from telling to showing, has appealed to later novelists working with the example of cinematic narrative directly to hand; the freeze-frame which ends David Lodge's *Changing Places* (1975), for example, is explicitly presented in the language of the screenplay.

James's decision to end a novel such as *The Ambassadors* (1903) in mid-dialogue has proved equally influential. There Strether, 'deterrent and conclusive' in his determination to return to the USA, has been talking with Maria Gostrey, who wishes he would remain in Europe with her:

She sighed it at last all comically, all tragically, away. 'I can't indeed resist you.'
'Then there we are!' said Strether.

Which, of course, leaves the reader wondering exactly where they are. So does the quarrel between Birkin and Ursula, abruptly broken off at the end of Lawrence's *Women in Love* (1920).

And beyond these endings, using dialogue to leave the fiction open rather than to close it, lie the yet more radical experiments of Joyce: the full stop missing from the end of Molly Bloom's monologue on the last page of *Ulysses*, and the incomplete fragment of a sentence which trips the reader up at the end of *Finnegans Wake* (1939). In fact, the fragment can be completed by going back to the sentence which began the book some seven hundred pages before. So *Finnegans Wake* is not so much inconclusive in the Jamesian sense of leaving the reader with work to do after the novelist has finished his, as never-ending. The implications of a never-ending book, a text that cannot be escaped, point – like so many aspects of Joyce's work – beyond realism and modernism to post-modernism.

I have dwelt so emphatically on James and the modernist generation, and will need to do so a while longer, because they set the seal on the view of fiction which held almost universal sway until recent decades. It was at once a theory of the novel, a historical interpretation of its origin, development and refinement to maturity, a series of prescriptions for reading and writing, and finally, of course, a canon of significant texts.

The prescriptions could be found in, for example, Percy Lubbock's *The Craft of Fiction* (1921), an organization of Jamesian commentary into something approaching dogma which held the field for some years. As for the canon, it was never more stringently defined than by F. R. Leavis in *The Great Tradition* (1948). He acknowledged Richardson and Austen but without discussing them in depth. The burden of his attention fell on George Eliot, James and Conrad; Lawrence was singled out from the modernist generation for treatment in a separate volume. Of Dickens's work only *Hard Times* was admitted to the canon, though Leavis later recanted and made Dickens the subject of an admiring full-length study. He treated Defoe, Fielding, Thackeray and Trollope with impatience and dismissed Sterne, the test case, in a characteristically savage footnote which spoke of his 'irresponsible (and nasty) trifling': the 'nasty' presumably referring to his badinage about sex and the 'irresponsible . . . trifling' to his refusal to live up to the demands of realism.

So narrow a definition of the canon – let alone the particular judgements it involved – was always contentious. Though it had considerable influence on the choice of set books for courses and exams, Leavis's Great Tradition never commanded anything like the widespread assent which some present commentators seem to imagine it once did. Yet even those critics who disagreed with Leavis were largely concerned to argue the case for specific writers whom he had slighted or for other traditions, admittedly less important but still not negligible. They did not necessarily dispute his underlying approach to fiction or his underlying belief that its natural issue was a coherently defined canon, since both assumptions were still a part of the prevailing orthodoxy. Leavis, it was generally felt, had simply drawn his battlelines with incautious and uncharitable tightness.

In fact, few critics drew their lines at all widely. Even a non-Leavisite and more generous canon was kept narrow by the reduction of all the large possibilities inherent in a phrase such as 'a long fictional narrative in prose' to novel-centred theory, and of novel-centred theory to a theory of realism, and of the theory of realism to its post-Jamesian rigour. I began this introduction by mentioning some of the works usually excluded from consideration for their lack of realism or 'novelistic' properties: *The Pilgrim's Progress* for its allegory and didacticism, *Gulliver's Travels* for its satire, and romances of whatever period for their love of dabbling in the marvellous and the impossible. Such examples by no means exhaust the list.

It included the results of the distinction between the 'serious' and the 'popular' which had helped to shape the novel from the nineteenth century onwards. 'Popular' categories such as 'science fiction' and 'detective fiction' were rigidly defined and labelled, as a means of holding them at bay. Science fiction might maintain some of the interests of the philosophic fable, and detective fiction might maintain the style of plotting which had animated the Victorian fiction, but these qualities did not earn them high esteem. With other categories of 'popular' literature, they were firmly relegated, in a hierarchical gesture, to a status irredeemably below the works from which the canon was made up. Collectively, they were sometimes known as 'genre' literature, a term which still has currency today. Implicitly, it seems to assert that the books commonly admitted to the canon – *Middlemarch*, or James's *The Portrait of a Lady* (1881), or Conrad's *Nostromo* (1904), or Woolf's *To the Lighthouse* (1927) – have no genre: they live purely by their own organic form, reflecting the very shapes of nature.

The American tradition was a different, and far more problematic, case. Early American novels, such as William Hill Brown's *The Power of Sympathy* (1789), could be regarded as provincial adjuncts to the English novel of the time: rather cruder, less sophisticated and, of course, following rather than setting taste. By the same token, the Leatherstocking Tales (of which the first, *The Pioneers*, had appeared in 1823) could be taken to identify James Fenimore Cooper as a sort of American Sir Walter Scott, deploying American Indians in a manner suggested by what Scott had done with his Highlanders. But Edgar Allan Poe, Nathaniel Hawthorne and Herman Melville – the generation whose work marked the so-called 'American Renaissance', or first great flowering of fiction in America – could not be digested so easily into established judgements. From Poe's *Tales of the Grotesque and Arabesque* (1840) to Melville's defiantly experimental *Moby-Dick* (1851) they refused the doctrines of realism being developed on the other side of the Atlantic.

Hawthorne's *The Scarlet Letter* (1850) is a good example of both this refusal and the deliberate fashion in which it was made, marking it as no mere provincial aberration but a fully fledged gesture of independence. The preface to the novel, which Hawthorne calls 'The Custom-House', gives a detailed account of his dreary round of work as a civil servant in Salem. Autobiography shades artfully into fiction with his supposed discovery of Hester Prynne's embroidered letter 'A', the starting-point and central emblem of the novel proper. His preoccupation with the 'A' thus leads him from present-day Salem into its past, from the mundane but all too real environment of the custom house into private speculation – from daylight into moonlight, as he puts it. The novelist has allowed himself to be led away from realism and in the direction of romance, to

a neutral territory, somewhere between the real world and fairy-land, where the Actual and the Imaginary may meet, and each imbue itself with the nature of the other. Ghosts might enter here without affrighting us. It would be too much in keeping with the scene to excite surprise, were we to look about us and discover a form, beloved, but gone hence, now sitting quietly in a streak of this magic moonshine, with an aspect that would make us doubt whether it had returned from afar, or had never once stirred from our fireside.

Hawthorne's tone may sound fey and self-indulgent, but we should never let his habit of self-deprecation make us underrate him. In fact, he was fully aware of that view of the novel which would have obliged him to take his life in the custom house itself as his subject:

The wiser effort would have been, to diffuse thought and imagination through the opaque substance of to-day, and thus to make it a bright transparency; to spiritualize the burden that began to weigh so heavily; to seek, resolutely, the true and indestructible value that lay hidden in the petty and wearisome incidents, and ordinary characters, with which I was now conversant. The fault was mine. The page of life that was spread out before me seemed dull and commonplace, only because I had not fathomed its deeper import. A better book than I shall ever write was there . . .

Modestly but firmly, he was turning his back on the European tradition of realism, or at least, as an American, putting a good deal of distance between it and himself. And he was speaking not just for himself but for a generation.

The arguments by which later critics and scholars, from both sides of the Atlantic, sought to explain the direction that the American novel had chosen never completely avoided condescension. It was not so much American art that was naive, it seemed, as America itself. Realism thrives on solid and developed social structures – all the questions of manners and morals which crowd Jane Austen's little bit (two inches wide) of ivory – and so it could hardly be expected to take root in a society barely settled, still inhabiting the very edge of the frontier. (No matter that Hawthorne himself had argued, by way of explaining his decision to set *The Marble Faun* [1860] in Italy, that it was easier to set romance amid the ruins and ivy of Europe than amid the 'commonplace prosperity' of his native land.) America would develop into realism in the course of its social development, when it achieved roughly the state English culture had achieved in giving birth to the novel in the eighteenth century.

The moment seemed to have arrived with William Dean Howells, James's contemporary and unexiled counterpart, and with American naturalists such as Frank Norris, Theodore Dreiser, Jack London and Stephen Crane, aspiring to a form of objective realism which owed a declared debt to developments in both Britain and France. As for the continuation and periodic re-emergence of the romance tradition in America (to give, for example, a coloration to Faulkner's work which distinguished it from the work of European modernists) it could be periodically noted but more often ignored. When they were not virtually forgotten – as Melville's *Moby-Dick* was for many years – the key works of the 'American Renaissance' could conveniently be relegated to the status of children's classics.

'Just childishness, on our part,' retorted D. H. Lawrence, noting the practice at the start of his *Studies in Classic American Literature* (1923). Yet it is worth noting how many English works could also suffer the same fate: not just books troublesome to the dominant critical assumptions, such as *The Pilgrim's Progress*, *Gulliver's Travels* and *Animal Farm*, but books with strong claims to belong inside the approved tradition, such as Defoe's *Robinson Crusoe*, Charlotte Brontë's *Jane Eyre* (1847) and the shorter works of Dickens. Virginia Woolf, almost casually, betrayed how common the practice was when she chose to phrase her admiration for *Middlemarch* by calling it – despite 'all its imperfections' – 'one of the few English novels written for grown-up people'.

The curious status thus conferred on Defoe, Charlotte Brontë, Dickens and the host of novelists unspecified by Virginia Woolf comes at first as something of a surprise. The novel had, after all, first achieved wide popularity and then formulated a theory of its own refinement; it had even come to influence, if not dominate, the other arts. By 1884 James had been able to speak of its powers as supreme: 'There is no impression of life, no manner of seeing it and feeling it, to which the plan of the novel may not offer a place'. Some forty years later D. H. Lawrence expressed a similar spirit of confidence and celebration in his own characteristic terms: 'being a novelist, I consider myself superior to the saint, the scientist, the philosopher, and the poet, who are all great masters of different bits of man alive, but never get the whole hog'. The novel, he added majestically, 'is the one bright book of life'.

The history of the novel and of novel criticism is full of such generous tributes. Yet it is also, though less obviously, punctuated by self-doubt and unease. The two stances were never more revealingly combined than by Lionel Trilling in *The Liberal Imagination* (1950):

For our time the most effective agent of the moral imagination has been the novel of the last two hundred years. It was never, either aesthetically or morally, a perfect form and its faults and failures can be quickly enumerated. But its greatness and its practical usefulness lay in its unremitting work of involving the reader himself in the moral life, inviting him to put his own motives under examination, suggesting that reality is not as his conventional education has led him to see it. It taught us, as no other genre ever did, the extent of human variety and the value of this variety. It was the literary form to which the emotions of understanding and forgiveness were indigenous, as if by the definition of the form itself.

Trilling was a subtle critic and an influential spokesman for the values nourished by James and the modernist generation, so this passage used often to be quoted by fellow critics, if only for its eloquence. But on those occasions it was customary to ignore the implications of the second sentence, which takes it for granted that the novel had never been 'aesthetically or morally, a perfect form' and that its faults and failures were so obvious they did not need to be specified.

So what was wrong with the novel? Part of the answer, of course, is apparent from what I have said so far. The evolutionary assumption that, from its point of origin in the eighteenth century, the novel needed both to be developed and refined implies it had a good deal of crudity about it to start with, if not for most of its short history. The Victorians remarked such crudity when they looked at the eighteenth century; in a different spirit James remarked it when he looked at the Victorians. For much of the twentieth century admirers and critics still assumed that there was a lot in Fielding or Dickens, even in *Middlemarch*, to apologize for or to pass over in the sort of near-silent embarrassment which Trilling betrays before getting down to his paean of praise.

Yet it is still striking to find him so ready to concede the imperfections of the novel in a general sense, almost indeed to suggest there is something inherently imperfect about it as a form. Two considerations hover somewhere behind his words, and both used to check the admiration even of the novel's greatest admirers. The first was a sense that realism always carried danger with it and that the novel, as the supreme expression of realism, was particularly vulnerable to the danger. The wonderful thing about the novel, said Lawrence, is that 'you know there is a water-closet on the premises'. Exactly. But not everybody likes to be reminded of the fact. The sheer power of the novel in capturing life, getting 'the whole hog', meant that it could all too easily capture what was crude, what was troubling, what was tasteless about life itself. The particular criteria for judging what comes under these headings might change dramatically from one era to the next – we smile at the Victorians recoiling from the frankness of *Tom Jones*, or at Virginia Woolf wrinkling her nose at some of what she found in *Ulysses* – but the underlying fear does not.

The second consideration which held sway over Trilling and his fellow critics bears more directly on the issues the rest of this introduction will broach. Most views of art which find meaning in the phrase 'perfect form', let alone prize what it embodies, believe poetry far more likely to answer their ideal than prose. The superior status of poetry has been an assumption embedded in our thinking about literature since the Greeks and if our thinking about the novel has at last reversed the judgement, then the change has occurred only in the very recent past.

Recent studies have been useful in reminding us that the rise of the novel did not successfully challenge the traditional view in the eighteenth century: orthodoxy assigned novels and novelists a more lowly position than Augustan poets and poetry enjoyed. Poets practised an art made respectable by ancient example, and they qualified for the aristocratic patronage on which a good deal of literary activity still depended. Novelists smelled of the modern printing house, and they struggled along with the other Grub Street hacks. The period when narrative became a dominant mode and the novel widened in popularity was also the Romantic era. And, as David Lodge pointed out in *Language of Fiction* (1966), the Romantics still regarded poetry as the highest form of literature: they wrote lyrics and dreamed of writing epics.

Coleridge's famous definitions of poetry as 'the most proper words in their proper places' and prose as 'proper words in their proper places' do, after all, contrive to suggest that prose is a comparatively rough and ready business. Even Thomas Hardy could accept the suggestion with embarrassing readiness when he expressed surprise on discovering that Joseph Warren Beach's study, *The Technique of Thomas Hardy* (1922), dealt only with his fiction: 'There isn't any technique about prose, is there? It just comes along of itself'.

Even in the wake of Henry James critics had not completely broken with these assumptions either. The era of Lionel Trilling was, after all, the era of the New Criticism – the most widely influential of the various sorts of formalism then current – and the New Criticism was far more at home talking about poetry than about prose. Locally, the methods of 'close reading' which it advocated excelled in analysing metaphor and the metaphoric language character-istic of poetry. When it turned to literary form, the New Criticism liked to contemplate texts almost as if they were sculptural objects, well-wrought urns seen in their totality, and experi-enced all at once, on the page open to the critic's gaze. Whatever the other merits of this approach, it will obviously get the reader much further with a sonnet or a lyric than with *Bleak House* or *Moby-Dick*.

So perhaps it was not so much a matter of the imperfection of the novel. Perhaps it was more a matter of the inadequacy of criticism, even after the efforts of Henry James and his followers. There was certainly a growing realization among critics that effectively they still possessed only a primitive vocabulary and barely any syntax for talking about fiction, or even prose in general. Though palpable, embarrassment at the laborious simplicity of what could be offered by way of generic definition ('a long fictional narrative in prose') was, if anything, less urgent than a sense that the prescribed ways for describing the operations of a given novel – in terms of 'plot', 'characters', 'theme' and so forth – looked woefully unsophisticated by comparison with what readers of poetry had at their disposal.

Filling such a gap has been in a very real sense the central effort of criticism in the last forty years or so, its energy at last moving decisively away from the consideration of poetry and its bias now making it reject approaches to literature which take poetry as their first or inher-ently most important, let alone their only, task. This, at any rate, has been the common ten-dency of Russian Formalism, structuralism, semiology, post-structuralism, deconstruction: all the various schools and styles of criticism which have, over the last forty years or so, looked either attractively fashionable or unappetizingly difficult in their reliance on theory (and, worse in the eyes of some British critics, their reliance on foreign theory). In the present con-text, their larger ideological agendas and their many points of disagreement with each other matter less than their common results in changing how we read novels and indeed, as part of the larger culture of post-modernism, changing how we write novels.

Where the older tradition proceeded from the Aristotelian concept of *mimesis*, or the ability of art to represent life and so be realistic, recent criticism has sought instead to construct a 'narratology', a poetics or science of narrative conceived as operating in its own terms. It has compared novels not to life but to other novels, and increasingly to other forms of fictional narrative, such as romance, allegory or satire, excluded from 'novel-centred theory'. Latterly, in a fruitful move depriving literature of the privileged but isolated position it used to be accorded, narratology has compared novels to all the other narratives which we encounter in our other reading and in our daily lives: to history books, reports of scientific experiments and newspaper reports, to jokes and gossip, lies and dreams.

The first significant blow was struck by Russian Formalists such as Vladimir Propp in the analysis of folk tales he carried out in the 1920s. It refined traditional but rather vague con-cepts of 'story' and 'plot' (on which my own discussion, for example, has so far relied) into a distinction between *fabula* and *sjužet*. The *fabula* is the chronological series of events which underlies the story; the *sjužet* is the particular sequence and shape into which the story arranges it. As such, the *sjužet* is local to the particular version or telling. The *fabula* is not, but is composed of common and finite elements of which it was the business of Formalism to pro-duce a taxonomy. This analysis helped to spur the structuralist effort to produce a grammar of narrative: a grammar in the sense that it took the theory of transformational grammar produced by linguistics as its model and assumed that narrative, too, had both a surface structure and a deep structure. Indeed, it was only in its surface structure that narrative was narrative as such, dealing with events related by time and causation. The deep structure was a matter of logical relations or, more usually, oppositions of meaning from whose friction the narrative was generated.

Some echo of these distinctions between *sjužet* and *fabula*, surface structure and deep structure, permeated most subsequent criticism, albeit in a bewildering variety of forms and under a bewildering variety of labels. Nowadays narratology commonly refers to them as 'narrative' (or 'text') and 'story' respectively. In a general sense, too, Russian Formalism and structuralism had effected a fundamental change in critical approach. The emphasis had shifted from looking at stories in terms of what happens in life – to determine what is 'realistic', what is 'plausible' and so forth – to looking at them in terms of what happens in other stories. In the process the carefully elaborated distinctions of novel-centred theory, marking the narrow boundaries of the territory on which the novel stood in splendidly achieved isolation, came to look altogether less tenable.

The question of exactly where life stood in relation to the newly enlarged territory of narrative was hotly debated under the first impact of these changes. The fashion in the first heady days of post-structuralism was, of course, to deny the relation altogether. Texts are not referential but self-referential: there is nothing outside their self-enclosed world of signs. Or, it was argued in Derridean fashion, texts promise referentiality but never achieve it: their meaning is endlessly deferred. Increasingly, however, the tendency has been to regard such questions as lying outside the province of narratology as such and, with some relief, to leave them suspended.

The tendency can perhaps best be seen in what has happened to the question of character in fiction. It had, obviously, played a central role in the tradition which had in large part come to celebrate realism as, in Wayne C. Booth's phrase, a 'realism of character'. Yet novelists themselves had worked with the slightly uneasy knowledge that, as Arnold Bennett said, 'you can't put the whole of a character into a book'. For its part, criticism had contributed little analysis to just how much character could be put into a book, and just how it could be put there. One of the very few attempts had been E. M. Forster's famous but avowedly crude distinction, in *Aspects of the Novel*, between 'flat' characters and 'round' characters: on the one hand, the caricatures in which Dickens excelled, vivid but limited in their repertoire of qualities, and on the other hand, the in-depth portraits created by Tolstoy and Proust, which can surprise the reader because they possess 'the incalculability of life'.

By interpreting narrative in terms of action, Russian Formalism and structuralism downgraded character to mere necessary agency or (in Jonathan Culler's phrase) the 'space in which forces and events meet rather than an individuated essence'. As structuralism shaded into post-structuralism Roland Barthes declared the character dead ('what can no longer be written is the Proper Name'); later semioticians, like Joel Weinsheimer in 1979, would treat characters as 'segments of a closed text'. In a slightly later work such as Shlomith Rimmon-Kenan's *Narrative Fiction: Contemporary Poetics* (1983) character returns, if only to play a fugitive and interrogative role. Yet in making exactly this point about Rimmon-Kenan, the influential narratologist Gérard Genette shows himself markedly reluctant to be drawn any further. The greatest concession narratology can make, he remarks in *Narrative Discourse Revisited* (1988; originally published in French in 1983), is to study not character but characterization, 'the technique of constituting characters with narrative texts'.

As these debates pursued their course, it had become apparent that Russian Formalism and structuralism did not fulfil the promise they had at first appeared to hold for students of narrative. The discovery of static opposition beneath narrative process was hardly welcome to those who sought an escape from the contemplation of static urns in which the New Criticism had dealt. Moreover, in their determination to identify what was common, and so fundamental, to separate narrative acts both Russian Formalism and structuralism tended to deal in what was inherently translatable: what could be transformed or transferred from one story to another, from one language to another, from one medium to another. The structures they uncovered stood too far removed from, and usually in too unspecific a relation to, the occasion of any particular telling in any particular text. As Rimmon-Kenan says, too many gaps remained between the different structural levels, and between those levels and linguistic structure.

Wayne C. Booth's *The Rhetoric of Fiction* (1961) opened an approach to specific narrative occasion and the linguistic structures it generated which was immediately more congenial and proved in the long term arguably more influential. At first blush it was a surprising achievement. Booth's own stance derived from the Chicago school of formalism, which had its affiliations with the New Criticism, and declared its origin even in the book's title. Booth read fiction as a rhetorical strategy, or series of rhetorical strategies, practised by the author on the reader. Exactly this sort of celebration of authorial dominance would soon become unfashionable. Booth's specific judgements were, moreover, coloured by hostility to recent developments such as the French *nouveau roman* (New Novel) by writers such as Alain Robbe-Grillet and Michel Butor, whereas the influential theories of Barthes had stemmed partly from the desire to defend just those developments and writers.

Booth's central purpose of rehabilitating the eighteenth-century novelists, notably Fielding, might have looked equally old-fashioned at the time, but in fact it soon turned out to be prophetic. *The Rhetoric of Fiction* was the first book to demonstrate that a return, in a new spirit of sympathy, to what the eighteenth century had achieved would become a crucial means of renewing the study of narrative. It demanded a confrontation with James and the modernist generation on two points which had grown into something like dogma: their dislike of intrusive narrative presences which disrupted what they took to be the proper purposes of the fiction, and their preference for discreet showing rather than overt telling. As I have shown, both views depended on the belief that, if narrators could not actually vanish altogether, they should at least try as hard as possible to do so and hence create the illusion of having pulled off the trick.

Booth takes it as axiomatic that narrators cannot vanish: 'though the author can to some extent choose his disguises, he can never choose to disappear'. In this assertion he creates what has itself become a new orthodoxy, if indeed one can speak of orthodoxy in describing the present disorderly and often discordant state of criticism. The very act of storytelling presupposes a teller; the very act of narrative presupposes a narrator. The proposition has sometimes been challenged (by, for example, Ann Banfield in *Unspeakable Sentences* [1982]) but the challenges have often produced rebuttals which in fact seek to broaden the terms of the original proposition. 'When I open a book,' says Genette in *Narrative Discourse Revisited*, 'whether it is a narrative or not, I do so to have the author *speak to me*. And since I am not yet either deaf or dumb, sometimes I even happen to answer him'. So it is not just all narratives in which the author speaks, but all books. By the same token, if there has to be an author who cannot avoid speaking, then there has to be a reader who cannot avoid answering, and not necessarily to assent. Increasingly, narratology has sought to explore this widened acknowledgement of the transactions taking place between authors and readers.

If the narrator is always present, however disguised, then it is the business of narratology to penetrate the disguise and make the identification. For a critic like Booth the task was to offer a taxonomy of the different identities narrators can possess and the disguises they can assume: a rhetoric of the strategies practised on the reader. The first necessary step was to distinguish between the narrator or storyteller – all narrators or storytellers, whether manifesting their presence openly in the first person, disguising themselves as one of the invented characters in the story or seeking invisibility behind some neutral façade – and the author whose name stands on the titlepage. The critic never encounters the author and cannot come to grips with him or her, only with the author-in-the-book.

This entity Booth labels the 'implied author'. He insisted on it in a spirit of formalist caution analogous to that which had already led critics of poetry to insist that the speaker of lyric verse was not the poet as such but a 'persona'. Discussion of the text was thus safely insulated from impertinent and extraneous information about the writer as a historical being and from *ex cathedra*, because extra-textual, statements by the writer about the intention or achievement of the text. In this respect Booth was simply applying a familiar approach more rigorously to fiction than critics had been accustomed to apply it. And, indeed, such caution and rigour could seem unnecessary in those cases where the author had already taken the trouble to adopt the mask of an invented character. No serious reader was ever likely to confuse Huck Finn with Mark Twain or Pip, in *Great Expectations*, with Charles Dickens.

So some critics otherwise influenced by Booth's approach have in the case of such novels regarded the 'implied author' as a redundancy. Genette, in particular, has been eager to shorten a chain of narrative transactions which already looked in danger of getting too long and too involved. But the concept of the implied author took on special relevance with the very texts Booth was most concerned to anatomize: the novels by Fielding, Thackeray or George Eliot where, as an older generation of critics had seen it, the author 'intruded' into an otherwise impersonal narrative to philosophize or moralize. The author at his or her desk is not lapsing into casual chatter and so jeopardizing a fiction which could and should proceed without such intervention. Instead, a shaping narrative presence, elsewhere implicit but no less present in the book, is choosing at these moments to manifest itself in a different form.

Booth himself regarded the implied author as an extension of the real author: borrowing a phrase which Edward Dowden had originally used in connection with George Eliot, he spoke of it as the author's 'second self'. Subsequent critics, working in the light of Barthes's suggestion that books write authors rather than authors writing books, have inclined to view the implied author as a construct of the text itself. The text is, after all, the implied author's only field of operation – the only evidence, indeed, that the reader has for the existence of the implied author. And, applying the same logic that leads from insisting on the universal presence of a speaker in narrative to insisting on the universal presence of a reader, critics have dwelt with increasing emphasis on a corresponding notion of an 'implied reader'. The capacity of texts to write authors means that they can write readers as well.

On the simplest level, those moments in Fielding, Thackeray and George Eliot when the implied author becomes manifest in a first person are likely to be moments when a reader is also implied. The proposition is not 'I' but 'you, dear reader' as well. Indeed the two are often linked together in a proposition, 'you and I', which Frank Kermode has seen as implying the 'acceptance of a contract': a common agreement on the value of the story, of the fiction, itself. And in a work like Sterne's *Tristram Shandy* (neglected by Booth but not by those who followed him) the reader makes regular appearances to quarrel, misunderstand or misread – answering back just as Genette has insisted readers are bound to do. Even in books that make a different and more conventional use of narrative than *Tristram Shandy*, the invented narrator is often matched by a corresponding invented narratee: the members of the audience who bring their particular expectations to the governess's story in James's *The Turn of the Screw* or the group of listeners on the yacht moored by the Thames who prepare themselves for another of Marlow's enigmatic and inconclusive tales in Conrad's *Heart of Darkness*.

In its way, Booth's taxonomy of 'dramatized narrators', as he called them, has proved as fertile for later criticism as his notion of the implied author. Effectively he classified them according to their relation, on the one hand, to the implied author and, on the other, to the action. In terms of the action they may be central characters, the heroes of their stories, such as Defoe's Moll Flanders, Sterne's Tristram Shandy, Charlotte Brontë's Jane Eyre, Dickens's David Copperfield, Mark Twain's Huck Finn, J. D. Salinger's Holden Caulfield in *The Catcher in the Rye* (1951) and all the others in the host of autobiographers who have made such regular appearances throughout the history of the novel. Or they may be observers, ranging from shadowy figures to substantially realized and significant witnesses such as Marlow in *Heart of Darkness*, Ishmael in *Moby-Dick* and Nick Carraway in F. Scott Fitzgerald's *The Great Gatsby* (1925).

All these witness-narrators, of course, are more than just witnesses. The narrative method gives them a status that can rival or overshadow the significance of the events and people they record in their testimony. *Heart of Darkness* is, in a real sense, as much 'about' Marlow, of whom we learn a great deal, as it is 'about' Mr Kurtz, of whom we and Marlow learn, on the face of it, disappointingly little. Elsewhere, the witness-narrator can prove vital to the conventions of a particular type of fiction. Ever since the example of Arthur Conan Doyle's Sherlock Holmes stories, detective fiction has relied on the advantages of using an 'idiot-friend' in the mould of Dr Watson as witness-narrator.

Booth himself went on to classify all the dramatized narrators he identified as either 'reliable' or 'unreliable', the criterion being their relation to the norms and values of the implied author. The distinction is sometimes subtle enough to lie at the very centre of the interpretative questions a text may pose. In *Heart of Darkness*, for example, Marlow and the implied author inhabit a stance which is, in a broad sense, compatible. But is it actually identical? Elsewhere the distinction is sharply drawn. Huck Finn clearly identifies himself as an unreliable narrator when he debates how to treat Nigger Jim, the escaped slave who joins him on the raft for the journey down the Mississippi. Conditioned by the Southern belief in slavery, Huck thinks himself 'wicked' for helping Jim's escape, whereas the implied author clearly sees his behaviour as natural and virtuous. By the same token, when Esther Summerson peppers her part of the narrative in *Bleak House* with continual protestations of her insignificance and ignorance, the reader receives them as 'unreliable'. Indeed, the reader takes them as signals that Esther will prove a major touchstone of the virtues otherwise so strikingly absent from the society portrayed in the book.

Booth's own analysis relied on a familiar notion of 'point of view', the perspective from which a given story is seen and told, which Gérard Genette proceeded to challenge and then refine in *Narrative Discourse* (1980; originally published in French in 1972). His argument raised the obvious point that the character who 'sees' the action in a story is not necessarily the person who tells the story. 'Point of view' thus blurs together the two separable processes of seeing and telling, which Genette proposed should in fact be distinguished by the terms 'focalization' and 'narration'. Other critics quickly appreciated and adopted them for their immediate utility in pinpointing a distinction crucial to the way a particular text may operate.* In *Great Expectations*, for example, there are two points of view, not one, and in a very real sense two Pips, not one. There is the Pip who focalizes the story, the child and then young man experiencing events in ignorance and misunderstanding. And there is the Pip who narrates the story, the older man aware of how events turned out and inclined to judge them and his youthful self in a very different light.

Genette's contribution had broader implications for narratology, now far removed from the early work of the Russian Formalists and structuralists in its willingness to attend to the local complexity which the narrative act may assume in a given instance. Take the case of Henry James and his decision, which I described earlier, to limit the narrative to the 'point of view' of a single observer but to stop short of using first-person narrative, let alone self-revelation of the sort which stream of consciousness would attempt. In Genette's terms the narrative result can now be described, more succinctly, by saying that in a novel such as *The Ambassadors* the focalization belongs to Strether but the narration belongs to the implied author.

What Maisie Knew (1897) is an even more pertinent example, for here the observer in question is not a richly reflective middle-aged gentleman like Strether – and Henry James – but a young girl. James himself commented in the preface on one crucial aspect of his preference for keeping focalization and narration separate:

Small children have many more perceptions than they have terms to translate them: their vision is at any moment much richer, their apprehension even constantly stronger, than their prompt, their at all producible vocabulary. Amusing therefore as it might at the first blush have seemed to restrict myself in this case to the terms as well as to the experience, it became at once plain that such an attempt would fail. Maisie's terms accordingly play their part – since her simpler conclusions quite depend on them; but our own commentary constantly attends and amplifies.

---

* In *Narratology* (first published 1977) Mieke Bal suggested that the concept of focalization itself still blurs two different strategies, and proposed a distinction between internal focalization (narrative focused through the consciousness of a character, as in James' fiction) and external focalization (narrative focused on the actions of a character without access to his thoughts and feelings, as in Hemingway's story 'The Killers' and the novels of Dashiell Hammett).

In other words, he could let the focalization, the experience of the story, belong to a child but insisted on reserving the narration, the terms of the story, to an adult level of discourse belonging to the implied author. The distinction between focalization and narration is plainly linguistic and of a much more complex order than the simple matter of whether Maisie is to be an 'I' or a 'she' in the novel.

In *A Portrait of the Artist as a Young Man* Joyce made a Jamesian decision to keep focalization and narration separate but a very unJamesian decision about the language of the narration. It bore immediate result in the novel's opening paragraphs:

Once upon a time and a very good time it was there was a moocow coming down along the road and this moocow that was coming down along the road met a nicens little boy named baby tuckoo . . . .
His father told him that story: his father looked at him through a glass: he had a hairy face.

The first paragraph, or so the reader realizes after a moment or two of being disconcerted, is not just the opening of the novel but also the opening of a story being told in appropriate baby talk to the infant hero, Stephen Dedalus, by his father. It disconcerts partly because it is shorn of the inverted commas, or quotation marks, which conventionally identify direct speech. Their omission is surely significant in a passage which, like the rest of the novel and indeed the rest of Joyce's work, raises the question of who is speaking in a particularly complex way. The second paragraph establishes that, though the focalization belongs to Stephen, the narration does not: Stephen is 'he' and not 'I'. Yet the language of the narration also in some obvious sense belongs to Stephen. It retains baby talk and baby syntax, speaking in abruptly simplified terms of Stephen's father as looking through a glass and having a hairy face rather than as wearing spectacles and having a moustache.

To describe such utterances critics and narratologists now commonly use the label 'free indirect discourse'. It is neither direct speech, which quotes its source in the language of the source, nor reported speech, which reports its source in the language of the reporter. Here in *A Portrait of the Artist* the free indirect discourse creates a form of linguistic middle ground between the narrator and a character. Actually, a good deal of what used in a loose fashion to be labelled 'stream of consciousness' inhabits this middle ground as well: in most of the chapters about Leopold Bloom in *Ulysses* and in the passages about Mrs Ramsay in *To the Lighthouse*, for instance, those characters are treated in the third person while allowing their language so to permeate the narrators' language as to create the illusion that their consciousness has in some way also become internal to it.

Free indirect discourse is also at work, though more discreetly, in traditional narrative. In describing his characters Dickens, for example, frequently borrows their characteristic words or turns of phrase without directly quoting them. Elsewhere, narrators in novels can borrow language not from the discourse of a particular character but identifiably from another source altogether. Fielding does this when he describes episodes in *Tom Jones* in the language of Homeric epic. So does Joyce at several points in *Ulysses*: in the 'Nausicaa' chapter when he describes Gertie MacDowell watching Bloom on the beach in the language of a romance in a women's magazine, and in the 'Oxen of the Sun' chapter when he describes the scene at the Holles Street hospital in a pastiche of prose style from Anglo-Saxon chronicles to the sermons of American evangelists.

Free indirect discourse, then, has a flexibility which makes it hard to say who is speaking, who is telling, and indeed simple-minded to expect an exact answer to the question. It challenges any monolithic idea of 'narrative voice', requiring us instead to speak of the voices which narrate, say, *Ulysses*. And may not accepting the plurality of narrative voice also oblige us to abandon any assumption that narrative establishes a single, authoritative norm? Such an assumption still seemed to be operating in James's own view of *What Maisie Knew*, in which the adult voice of the narrator presumably functions as a standard of measurement for the child's perception. Such an assumption was certainly still operating in Booth's account of the 'unreliable' narrator, whose unreliability could be determined and measured by reference to the norm which it was the business of the implied author to establish.

If recent narratology has been ready to challenge these assumptions, this is partly because deconstruction has taught critics to be sceptical of the belief that texts have stable and author-itative centres. It is also due in part to the Russian critic Mikhail Bakhtin (1895–1975), whose influence has belatedly made itself felt in the West through the work of critics such as Tzvetan Todorov and through studies such as David Lodge's *After Bakhtin: Essays on Fiction and Criticism* (1990).* Central to Bakhtin's approach is the belief that fiction is inherently mimetic. However, the mimesis he has in mind is not the Aristotelian representation of life but rather the mi-mesis to which Socrates referred in Plato's *Republic* in describing those occasions when the poet, rather than speaking in his own voice ('diegesis'), tries to convince us that somebody else is speaking. In this sense, drama is inherently mimetic. By any standard, fiction is also to some degree mimetic, if only in its use of dialogue supposedly uttered by the characters.

To Bakhtin, fiction – and, indeed, prose – are 'dialogic' in a more radical sense. They pro-ceed not by establishing and imposing a single voice but by exploiting a tension between voices: question and answer, statement and counter-statement, utterance and parody. Though written in the 1920s, his account comes as close as any single account could to describing the possibilities which narratology now seeks to explore:

The possibility of employing on the plane of a single work discourses of various types, with all their expressive capacities intact, without reducing them to a single common denominator – this is one of the most fundamental characteristics of prose. Herein lies the profound distinction between prose style and poetic style . . . For the prose artist the world is full of other people's words, among which he must ori-ent himself and whose speech characteristics he must be able to perceive with a very keen ear. He must introduce them into the plane of his own discourse, but in such a way that this plane is not destroyed. He works with a very rich verbal palette.

Bakhtin's account also indicates the possibilities which novelists themselves, in the culture of post-modernism, now seek to explore. Post-modernism can affront – indeed, can appear to make a point of affronting – conventional expectations of fiction as thoroughly as modernist experimentation once affronted E. M. Forster's man on the golf course. Yet, more thoroughly and with far more zest than Forster and most of the modernists, it has recovered and affirmed a belief in storytelling. Its belief, however, bears little relation to the old realist model which assumed that the value of stories lay in their direct representation of life: the word leading directly to the object, or at least bringing the picture of the object directly to the reader's mind. Post-modernism, rather, is preoccupied with the processes of storytelling itself and with the plurality of stories: the way any given story exists in relation to variants and alter-native versions of itself, to contradicting stories and counter-stories, and so to a world of stories which it is the business of fiction to embody but not necessarily to reconcile.

One obvious and tangible result of this approach is 'metafiction', or fiction which confesses and comments on its own fictionality, which eventually exploits its own fictionality. As such, it stands in sharp contrast to the Jamesian insistence that the novelist approach his subject (and his reader) as if he were a 'historian', rendering what is true, what is real, with the utmost fidelity of which he is capable. Metafiction takes its cue instead from a tradition stemming (at least) from *Tristram Shandy*, which starts from the postulate that all stories are tall stories and that no method of telling stands much chance of concealing quite how tall they are.

Many readers first became aware of metafiction in its contemporary, or post-modern, form with the success of John Fowles's *The French Lieutenant's Woman* (1969). Its elaborately researched and recreated Victorian setting seemed to promise the comforting solidity asso-ciated with Victorian novels themselves. Yet the narrator was willing, crucially, to admit: 'This story I am telling is all imagination. These characters I create never existed outside my own mind'. This acknowledgement made it possible for him to offer two different endings, one 'happy' and the other not, one to Victorian taste and the other challenging Victorian

---

* In this respect, it continued the valuable task his work has performed since *Language of Fiction* (1966), in mak-ing recent theory accessible and weighing the extent to which it can be reconciled with an older, broadly 'humanist', approach.

taste. Dickens had, in a sense, already perceived the same possibility when he came to end the story of Pip and Estella in *Great Expectations* and found it possible to conceive, and write, two different versions. Yet his definition of the novelist's function had required, as the contemporary novelist's does not, that he close the novel by lending his authority to one or the other.

If all stories are just stories and, as such, can never be permanently closed, then novelists are at liberty to take not 'life' or their own invention but a previous story, a previous text, as their subject. Indeed, they have particular reason to adopt this strategy since it makes the fictionality of what they are offering inherent in the very enterprise, rather than something to be conceded at some point in the telling. The extent to which novelists are now in the habit of continuing previous novels bears witness to how widely the assumptions of post-modernism have permeated recent writing, even writing not immediately or narrowly identified as post-modernist. The 1980s brought two significant continuations of Defoe's *Robinson Crusoe*, in Jane Gardam's *Crusoe's Daughter* (1985) and J. M. Coetzee's *Foe* (1986). So far the 1990s have seen, among other instances, the crime novelist Robert B. Parker continuing Raymond Chandler's *The Big Sleep* (1939) in *Perchance to Dream* (1991), Susan Hill continuing Daphne Du Maurier's *Rebecca* (1938) in *Mrs de Winter* (1993), Emma Tennant continuing Austen's *Pride and Prejudice* in *Pemberley* (1993) and *Emma* (1816) in *Emma in Love* (1996), and Elaine Feinstein continuing Lawrence's *Lady Chatterley's Lover* (1928) in *Lady Chatterley's Confession* (1995).

It is obviously no accident that the majority of these novelists, and the novelists they continue, should be women. Most of these recent books, in fact, owe a debt to the prescient example of Jean Rhys's *The Wide Sargasso Sea* (1966), not so much continuing Charlotte Brontë's *Jane Eyre* as filling in its *lacunae* by taking up directly the character of the first Mrs Rochester, the 'madwoman in the attic' whom feminist critics since Sandra Gilbert and Susan Gubar have also found a striking symbol with which to begin investigation of Victorian women's writing. Where past texts are female, their voice needs to be affirmed and engaged in dialogue. Where past texts are male, a female voice needs to be written into them or over them. So both Jane Gardam and J. M. Coetzee deal with female castaways Defoe neglected to invent.

In an important sense, post-modernism obviously makes the past itself a text. What, after all, is history but a story, or rather a world of stories? Its official texts, apparently monolithic in their authority, need to be placed in juxtaposition with its unofficial texts, unprinted or as yet unwritten, to emphasize the plurality that post-modernism seeks and values. In this spirit British writers have increasingly turned back to shaping events at the fringe of modern memory, like World War I, the focus of Pat Barker's *Regeneration* trilogy (1991–5). Americans have long since been in the habit of taking as their focus the Kennedy assassination, or, rather, have found in the Kennedy assassination the very starting-point of their own route into post-modernism. Don DeLillo's *Libra* (1988), for example, seeks to reconstitute the official reports, cover stories, lies, fantasies and conspiracy theories surrounding the events in Dallas as an archive in whose uncatalogued totality may somewhere reside fulfilment of the promise in the title: Libra, Lee Harvey Oswald's birth sign, the scales or balance.

Such approaches take on particular significance for the post-colonial writers from the Commonwealth whose work now makes up so large a part of our literature in English. They have particular need to re-read and re-write the official stories which Europe wrote on them, and to re-read and re-write the unofficial stories which in the process Europe sought to expunge. And with African, Indian, Aboriginal Australian or Maori New Zealanders, the awareness of 'different voices' which permeates all contemporary fiction takes on particular meaning as a matter, literally, of different languages: the adopted (or enforced) language of Britain, the Empire and the tradition of the novel, on the one hand, and, on the other, the original, indigenous language, sometimes half-forgotten and half-lost but at any rate previously unheard in the novel, which the new fiction must somehow seek to accommodate.

The implications of this struggle and the achievements which have emerged from it are too wide to be properly treated here. But for present purposes, it is significant to note how often the struggle has begun by taking at least one familiar figure as its necessary point of junction with and departure from the 'English novel'. It has started with Conrad and, above all, with

Heart of Darkness and *Nostromo*.* Conrad was himself a writer caught between languages and never so completely adopted by the English language as he sometimes liked to imagine. He directly addressed the issues of imperialism and did so, moreover, with his own profound sense of the hollowness of public and official rhetoric.

None of these qualities has made Conrad anything so simple as a model for or an influence on post-colonial literature, at least in the conventional meaning of these terms. Rather, these qualities have made Conrad the best place, almost the inevitable place, in previous traditions of fiction to start the quarrel: the place to start the business of re-reading and re-rewriting, writing back and writing over. Key texts which mark its various aspects and stages include: from Australia, Patrick White's *Voss* (1957), which adopts from *Heart of Darkness* the metaphorical implications of a journey into the interior of a continent; from Guyana, Wilson Harris's *Palace of the Peacock* (1960), yet more explicit in its reference to *Heart of Darkness*; and from Kenya, Ngugi wa Thiong'o's *A Grain of Wheat* (1967), confessedly Conradian in its address to political processes.

Implicitly *Heart of Darkness* also lies somewhere, as a fertile and troublesome text demanding an answer, in what remains the most famous African novel, Chinua Achebe's *Things Fall Apart* (1958). It tells of the collapse and defeat of tribal culture, in the person of Okonkwo, with the arrival of colonialism, in the person of the Commissioner. Thus, in a general sense, it tells a story similar to Marlow's story of colonialism and his own experience of Africa but from the opposed perspective. It looks and speaks from what Marlow could only perceive as a darkness which was also 'unspeakable'. At the end of *Things Fall Apart* the colonialist failure to see and to hear, while still believing something has been comprehensively understood, is captured when the Commissioner considers devoting 'not a whole chapter but a reasonable paragraph, at any rate' to Okonkwo's case in the book he plans to write, to be called *The Pacification of the Primitive Tribes of the Lower Niger*.

Yet Marlow's journey in *Heart of Darkness* also issues in texts – and even texts that have been written over – contained in the larger text of his own narrative. On his way to the station where Mr Kurtz lies dying he chances on a copy of *An Inquiry into Some Points of Seamanship*, already scribbled over in code by some previous owner who had cherished it. Marlow proceeds to cherish the book in his turn, for 'a singleness of intention, an honest concern for the right way of going to work' which are the very opposite of what he can see about the workings of imperialism around him. As for imperialism, it provides him with its text in the form of the report that Kurtz has been writing for the International Society for the Suppression of Savage Customs. Its central argument, on behalf of imperialism, is that 'By the simple exercise of our will we can exert a power for good practically unbounded'. Yet this text and its argument have also been written over, by the fever-ridden Kurtz voicing the other side of imperialism's dual nature in a chilling note: 'Exterminate all the brutes!'

I do not dwell in such detail on the texts, the different and discordant texts, which the larger text of *Heart of Darkness* contains just to show how infuriatingly suggestive Conrad can be for a post-colonial writer of today. I also do so to raise much larger points about post-modernism and narratology which should now be addressed directly. Both, to a degree, present themselves and are taken to be an abandonment and rejection of what went before: the working assumptions which supported fiction and the interpretation of fiction according to traditional theories of realism. Yet both have, and claim, a past. Both can discover unexpected points of affinity with a writer inside the older tradition, such as Conrad. And both can do more than that. They can help us look again at the older view of fiction which I began this introduction by summarizing. Then I treated the view with a certain implicit scepticism; now it can be directly re-read and re-written.

The older view took as its starting-point 'the rise of the novel' in the eighteenth century: a clearly defined form with a clearly defined character and a clearly defined goal emerging from

---

* *Nostromo* has also provided a point of departure for Latin American 'magic realism' as practised by Gabriel Garcia Márquez and others.

the mass of other literature at a clearly defined historical moment in clearly defined social circumstances. It presented literary history in terms of which Michel Foucault has taught us to be sceptical, terms which seek 'to discover already at work in each beginning, a principle of coherence and the line of future unity'. And if we look again at the texts produced by the first generation of eighteenth-century novelists without such preconceptions in mind, we find no such clear definition or common agreement. Instead we find stories and storytellers rejoicing in a pedigree as broad, as mixed and as bastard as anything post-modernism can offer.

In its narrative method as well as its subject Defoe's *Moll Flanders* proclaims its affinity with the criminal autobiographies, memoirs and confessions which had flourished since the Elizabethan era and would continue to flourish long after the eighteenth century. The epistolary method of Richardson's novels everywhere proclaims their affinity with letter-writing, one of the most common acts of storytelling which people undertake in any culture. In their different ways Fielding and Sterne proclaim their affinity with the philosophical essay: Fielding in the chapters introducing the various books into which he divides *Tom Jones*, Sterne in the digressions which mark his progress, or lack of it, in *Tristram Shandy*. In his capacity as 'Parson Yorick' Sterne proclaims his special affinity with the sermon. And, if only by the titles they select for their books, all these writers proclaim their affinity with the writing of 'histories'.

I describe them as 'proclaiming' these affinities because none of these writers makes any attempt to present his work under the label 'novel' as a separately conceived genre, or indeed under the label 'novel' at all. The passage quoted earlier (page 3) from Smollett's dedication to *Ferdinand Count Fathom* in which he speaks of the novel as 'a large diffused picture' marks, so far as scholarship can determine, the first occasion when any of the writers later called pioneers of the novel identified what they were writing as a novel. Smollett's book and dedication appeared in 1753, when Defoe, Richardson and Fielding had all done their work. Sterne, who had yet to publish *Tristram Shandy*, would come no closer to providing a generic label for what he was up to than to call it 'this rhapsodical work'.

Yet the term 'novel' was already available. It derived from the French *nouvelle*, cognate to the Italian *novella* and the Spanish *novela*; all derived from the Latin *novellus*, which could mean either 'news' or 'noteworthy saying'. *Nouvelle* had crossed the Channel in the late seventeenth century, acquiring with its anglicized spelling a shift of accent from the second to the first syllable. The related 'novelist' took on two meanings, of 'innovator' and 'journalist' (the latter in the general sense of one who carried or brought news, or journals, in whatever manner). As for 'novel', it was already being used in its later sense in 1692 by William Congreve to distinguish a type of fiction 'more familiar' than the romance, which dealt in exalted heroes, 'miraculous contingencies, and impossible performances' and 'lofty language'. Almost a century later, in 1785, Clara Reeve used the terms 'novel' and 'romance' to draw virtually the same distinction.

Their testimony shows that by no means everything the older school of commentators used to say about the history of the novel and the realist territory it marked out for itself can be discarded. Yet the usage of 'novel' and 'romance' between the time of Congreve and Reeve does little to support the distinction they drew. 'Novel' could be used for prose fiction shorter than the French romances of the time, which were often unendurably long; it thus carried some of the meaning which the English later attached to the Italian *novella*. Or it could be used for English rather than Continental fiction. Often 'novel' and 'romance' were used more or less indiscriminately, as Fielding did in *Tom Jones* when he referred to the 'swarm of foolish novels, and monstrous romances'. On this occasion he was concerned to distinguish *Tom Jones* from such lowly forms of life by calling it a 'history'. In the preface to *Joseph Andrews* (1742) he had already spoken of that book in terms of 'a comic romance' (though with the warning that the reader might well have 'a different idea of romance') and, as if to suggest a respectably antique precedent, 'a comic epic-poem in prose'.

Fielding was willing to regard himself as a 'novelist' in the sense of being an innovator: he spoke of his work as a 'hitherto unattempted species of writing', just as Richardson saw himself as attempting 'something that never yet had been done'. Yet neither laid claim to the available term 'novel', and indeed both were markedly reluctant to go beyond such vague and roundabout phrases in defining just what they were writing. Their reluctance suggests that they saw it as eclectic and heterogeneous, rather than easily capable of description. It also suggests that they proffered it to the public in a cautious, even tentative spirit.

Fielding spoke directly of his relations with his public in what we would call the introductory chapter to the first book of *Tom Jones*. He called it the 'bill of fare to the feast' and proceeded to elaborate the analogy between himself and an inn-keeper serving meals. An author like himself, he explains, is not a gentleman offering a private dinner to invited guests but 'one who keeps a public ordinary at which all persons are welcome for their money'. So the novelist, even when he did not yet dare to speak his name, was already in the marketplace offering his wares to a public which he had a special need to please:

Men who pay for what they eat will insist on gratifying their palates, however nice and even whimsical these may prove; and, if everything is not agreeable to their taste, will challenge a right to censure, to abuse, and to d – n their dinner without control.

Fielding, then, was aware of how popular fiction could be; indeed, he was aware of just how popular it should be if it fulfilled the goals of breadth and variety which were an essential part of his purpose. Yet this meant he also knew how vulnerable it was to censure and abuse. He had good reason to know. Literary historians used to speak in confident terms of the novel being welcomed, almost created, by a new middle-class public which found in it a congenial reflection of its own tastes and values. This is not how contemporaries commonly spoke of the matter. Who read novels? 'The giddy and licentious of both sexes,' said the journalist Owen Ruffhead; 'the young, the ignorant and the idle,' said Samuel Johnson. And what did reading novels do to them? It made them even worse, of course. Even before the novel attempted any definition of itself it was given a hostile definition by its critics, as a type of literature whose potent appeal could easily inflame and corrupt the most vulnerable.

Usually the most vulnerable were identified as young people, servants and women. These three classes feature prominently in virtually every account of the novel and its public which contemporaries proposed from the eighteenth century onwards. Novels, Sir Anthony Absolute remarked nervously in Sheridan's *The Rivals* (1775), passed from the circulating library into the hands of ladies' maids and then into the hands of their mistresses. Novels, said Napoleon in reproof of his marshals' reading habits, were fit only for chambermaids. Novels, said Trollope, were read by Prime Ministers but also (and presumably in much greater numbers) by scullery maids. If this novel is allowed to appear, said the prosecution counsel to the jury at the trial of Penguin Books for attempting to publish *Lady Chatterley's Lover* in 1960, it will be read by servants and children.

Such comments sometimes reflect the view that the novel was inherently light and frivolous, a mere time-waster. More often they underline a belief that the novel was not just powerful but always potentially subversive in its power. In times of special anxiety about the state of morals and society (which means most times from the eighteenth to the twentieth century) the belief could grow hysterical. Here, for example, is Hannah More writing in the 1790s:

Novels, which used to be dangerous in one respect, are now mischievous in a thousand. They are continually shifting their ground, and enlarging their sphere, and are daily becoming vehicles of wider mischief. Sometimes they concentrate their forces, and are at once employed to diffuse destructive politics, deplorable profligacy, and impudent infidelity.

Her accusations stand as the type of all those which have made the history of the novel recurrently a history of censorship, obscenity trials and *fatwas*.

For several generations most of what novelists said about their work was not intended so much to define it for theoretical purposes as to defend it for practical reasons. This is the spirit in which they first propounded the argument that fiction could be morally instructive or that there could be value in representing life as it was commonly lived. The suggestion that there could be value simply in amusing or entertaining readers, that fiction itself had inherent value, could come only later. In a famous passage in *Northanger Abbey* (1818) Jane Austen still found it necessary to complain that she and her tribe were 'an injured body':

Although our productions have afforded more extensive and unaffected pleasure than those of any other literary corporation in the world, no species of composition has been so much decried . . . There seems almost a general wish of decrying the capacity and undervaluing the labour of the novelist, and of slighting the performances which have only genius, wit, and taste to recommend them.

She then offered her own version of those imaginary dialogues with the reader which Sterne had loved to use as a way of making points about fiction:

'I am no novel reader – I seldom look into novels – It is really very well for a novel'. Such is the common cant. – 'And what are you reading, Miss – ?' 'Oh! it is only a novel!' replies the young lady; while she lays down her book with affected indifference, or momentary shame. – 'It is only Cecilia, or Camilla, or Belinda'; or, in short, only some work in which the greatest powers of the mind are displayed, in which the most thorough knowledge of human nature, the happiest delineation of its varieties, the liveliest effusions of wit and humour are conveyed to the world in the best chosen language.

Significantly, this despised world of writing and reading is composed entirely of women: the novels, with their eponymous heroines, which Austen lists are, respectively, *Cecilia* (1782) and *Camilla* (1796) by Fanny Burney and *Belinda* (1801) by Maria Edgeworth.

Jane Austen met criticism vigorously and on its own ground. For earlier novelists, innovators vulnerable to the charge of subversion, the best defence lay not just in vagueness but in misrepresentation. In *Oroonoko* (1688), for example, Aphra Behn claimed to have been 'an eye-witness to a great part' of the story and to have had the rest from 'the mouth of the chief actor in this history'. Defoe sought to blur any distinction between his work as a journalist and as novelist, creating what a modern critic, Leonard J. Davis in *Factual Fictions: The Origins of the English Novel* (1983), has called a 'news/novel discourse'. *A Journal of the Plague Year* (1722), ingeniously combining research and invention to reconstruct the impact of the Plague on seventeenth-century London, was advertised as 'Written by a citizen who continued all the while in London. Never made public before'. *Robinson Crusoe, Moll Flanders* and *The Memoirs of a Cavalier* (1724) were presented as real-life memoirs whose editors can vouch for their truth. In the preface to *Roxana* (1724) the 'editor' specifically

takes the liberty to say that this story differs from most of the modern performances of this kind, though some of them have met with a very good reception in the world: I say, it differs from them in this great and essential article, namely that the foundation of this is laid in truth of fact, and so the work is not a story but a history.

In the story itself the fictional heroine encounters a well-known contemporary of Defoe's, the economist Sir Robert Clayton. The Captain Carleton of Defoe's *The Memoirs of Captain Carleton* (1728) did exist but did not write his memoirs, despite the accompanying dedication to Carleton's real-life contemporary Spencer Compton, which boasted that fictitious and rhetorical flourishes formed no part of an old soldier's style.

So the first readers of Defoe's novels had no means of knowing, or being sure, that they were novels. Readers were liable to be hoaxed, as Dr Johnson apparently was by *The Memoirs of Captain Carleton*. Nor were Richardson's first readers expected to regard his decision to tell the story through an exchange of letters just as a literary device, in the way literary critics now do. Richardson himself objected to the preface his friend William Warburton supplied for *Clarissa* precisely because it spoke of the book as fiction and thus destroyed 'the air of genuineness' he wanted to maintain. And what were readers to make of *Gulliver's Travels*? Swift nowhere lent his name to it when it first appeared in 1726 as *Travels into Several Remote Nations of the World*. The titlepage identified the author as Lemuel Gulliver and the publisher's preliminary note to the reader spoke of Gulliver as an 'ancient and intimate friend', as well as a man whose reputation for telling the truth was proverbial among his neighbours.

In this case, at least, Swift was not so much laying claim to fact as making his readers ask themselves how many extravagant fictions they could swallow without their gorges rebelling. Writing and reading the 'news/novel discourse' quickly became a more sophisticated business. This could mean that the simple hoax as Defoe had practised it came to look faintly distasteful: *A Journal of the Plague Year* was, said Anna Laetitia Barbauld in 1810, 'an exercise in ingenuity not to be commended'. But it never entirely disappeared. Poe, who loved presenting the short story as a document rescued from oblivion or disaster ('Manuscript Found in a Bottle'), also managed to pass stories off on readers as genuine newspaper reports. Elsewhere presenting the novel as a real document became part of a game or joke with the reader, as it is at the beginning of Dickens's *Pickwick Papers*, fully entitled *The Posthumous Papers of the Pickwick Club, Containing a Faithful Record of the Perambulations, Perils, Travels, Adventures and Sporting Transactions of the Corresponding Members* when it first appeared in 1836–7. And Hawthorne's 'The Custom-House', proceeding from a true account of his mundane office work to a fictitious account of his discovery of the scarlet letter, invites the reader to contemplate not just the relations between 'novel' and 'romance' but also the extent to which 'romance' itself could still incorporate the facts of history.

Such devices have again grown familiar in the climate of post-modernism, which encourages Vladimir Nabokov to present *Lolita* (1955) as a psychiatrist's edition of Humbert Humbert's confession and *Pale Fire* (1962) as a scholarly edition of the work of a dead poet, and allows Kurt Vonnegut Jr to mix his own memories of the bombing of Dresden in World War II with extravagant science fiction in *Slaughterhouse-Five* (1969). Yet even before the advent of post-modernism, fiction had long been concerned to ingest the very texts it had begun by faking. Novels repeatedly present, or claim to reproduce, letters by their characters – like the one which announces Mr Collins's imminent arrival in *Pride and Prejudice* or the one Fanny Squeers uses to give her version of the hero's exit from Dotheboys Hall in Dickens's *Nicholas Nickleby* (1838–9). Novels frequently insert written confessions or memoirs, such as Miss Wade's remarkable 'History of a Self-Tormentor' in Dickens's *Little Dorrit* (1855–7), or diaries, such as Esther Summerson's in *Bleak House*.

Bleak House is a particularly relevant example since no Victorian novel, setting out to portray contemporary life, more determinedly portrays it as a mass of texts and documents. In a society where powerlessness continually threatens the characters, ultimate powerlessness is simply to be unable to read, to be illiterate like Jo the crossing sweeper:

It must be a strange state to be like Jo! To shuffle through the streets, unfamiliar with the shapes, and in utter darkness as to the meaning, of those mysterious symbols, so abundant over the shops, and at the corners of the streets, and on the doors, and in the windows! To see people read, and to see people write, and to see the postmen deliver letters, and not to have the least idea of all that language – to be, to every scrap of it, stone blind and dumb. It must be very puzzling to see the good company going to the churches on Sundays, with their books in their hands, and to think (for perhaps Jo *does* think at odd times) what does it all mean, and if it means anything to anybody, how comes it means nothing to me?

Chief among the texts which the novel has sought to ingest have been other novels. The process was clearly underway when Fielding presented *Joseph Andrews* as a dialogic answer to the questions raised by Richardson's *Pamela*, published only a couple of years before, in 1740–1. A century later Thackeray cut his teeth as a novelist in a manner equally recognizable to the post-modernist writer, by judging the ending of Scott's *Ivanhoe* (1819) unsatisfactory and embarking on his own continuation of it in *Rebecca and Rowena* (originally published in 1846, revised in 1850). Predictably his novella – part homage, part parody and part act of rebellion – reaches an ending which he finds unsatisfactory as well.

The same habit of reference stayed with Thackeray the mature novelist. When the narrator of *Vanity Fair* wishes to emphasize his commitment to domestic realism, he points out that though it might produce rather hum-drum effects some of the time it is nevertheless the result of deliberate choice: 'We might have treated this subject in the genteel, or in the romantic, or in the facetious manner'. Then he sketches all the alternative plots and novels that would issue. The characters could be lords and ladies; or they could be servants in a great house; or a burglar could break in and kidnap the heroine, not to release her until the third volume. 'But,' he concludes, 'my readers must hope for no such romance, only a homely story.'

The effect is at once to define *Vanity Fair* by rejecting other novels popular with Thackeray's readers and to give those novels a fugitive life inside *Vanity Fair* itself. Thackeray achieves it by precisely the means which a later realist like Henry James deplored: by 'intruding into the story' in the first person and by admitting that his story is only a fiction rather than a history. Yet James himself wanted to achieve a similar effect and found means which were consonant with his own aesthetic. In *Washington Square*, for example, he created what he liked to call a *ficelle*, a character whose function is to help the business of the plot or the business of making the plot intelligible to the reader. Here she is Mrs Penniman, Catherine Sloper's aunt and confidante in her disappointed love affair with Morris Townsend. Mrs Penniman 'wished the plot to thicken', but this does not mean that she assists it; instead she persists in misunderstanding it in the light of cheap popular novels of the same sort Thackeray had glanced at in *Vanity Fair*. Even as Morris's unsuitability grows manifest, she continues to hope that he will marry Catherine, preferably at a secret wedding: 'She had a vision of this ceremony being performed in some subterranean chapel; subterranean chapels in New York were not frequent, but Mrs Penniman's imagination was not chilled by trifles'.

James himself would presumably have said that Mrs Penniman's misreading is there to help the reader read *Washington Square* correctly. As novelists' quarrels with other novelists often do, it leads James to agree with those detractors of the novel who pointed to all the dangers of *Bovarysme*: of being misled, like Flaubert's heroine, into foolish fantasy and misguided action by the wrong reading. *Northanger Abbey* had already made the same point in showing how Gothic novels make Catherine Morland misread the plot of the novel she is actually in. *Ulysses* repeated it when Gertie MacDowell thinks she is in a woman's magazine story rather than *Ulysses*.

Yet in effect Mrs Penniman's presence also makes other novels present in *Washington Square*, makes other *Washington Squares* possible, even as it rejects them. So do the moments in *Vanity Fair*, *Northanger Abbey* and *Ulysses* I have just alluded to. Intertextuality does that, and it is definitely not the province of the post-modernists alone. It has identified the novel, however the term is defined or its history interpreted, as (in Leonard J. Davis's phrase) 'the ensemble of written texts that constitute the novel'. The fate of these other texts, fictional or factual, in any given text is perhaps nowhere more potently suggested than in *Nostromo*, where the pages of Conrad's supposed source of information about Costaguana, Don José Avallanos's *History of Fifty Years of Misrule*, are glimpsed floating separately across the waters of the harbour. The novel has always been, as Basil Creighton suggested in the 1920s, like Sin in Milton's *Paradise Lost*: 'continually giving birth to itself as the last outrage'.

Aaron's Rod A novel by D. H. LAWRENCE, first published in 1922. In his quest for emotional freedom and a fuller sense of being, the amateur flautist Aaron Sisson abandons his wife and children and his job in a Midlands colliery. First he joins the orchestra of a London opera house, then he goes to Italy and becomes the lover of the Marchesa del Torre. But he remains unable to liberate himself from the emotional bondage of conventional relationships. The novel includes a self-portrait of Lawrence (as Rawdon Lilly, a writer who tries to persuade Sisson to be his follower) and a portrait of NORMAN DOUGLAS (as James Argyle).

Abbey, Edward 1927–89 American. His work reflects his passion for the American West and his belief that it has been destroyed by corporations and industry. *The Monkey Wrench Gang* (1975) inspired a whole generation of environmental activism. Other novels include *The Brave Cowboy* (1956), *Fire on the Mountain* (1962), *Black Sun* (1971), *Good News* (1980), *Fool's Progress* (1988) and *Hayduke Lives!* (1990). Among his prolific non-fictional writing are *Desert Solitaire* (1968), *The Journey Home* (1977), *Abbey's Road* (1979), *One Life at a Time, Please* (1988) and *Confessions of a Barbarian* (1994), a posthumous compilation of his journals.

Abbot, The See SCOTT, SIR WALTER.

Abish, Walter 1931– American. His work is rich in linguistic and syntactical experiment. In *Alphabetical Africa* (1974), the words of each chapter are formed according to a scheme using the letters of the alphabet in ascending and descending order. *How German is It* (1980) offers a view of post-war Germany from the interior of consciousness. Other novels include *In the Future Perfect* (1977), *Ninety-Nine, The New Meaning* (1990) and *Eclipse Fever* (1993).

Abrahams, Peter 1919– South African. He has settled in Jamaica. Black deprivations under apartheid are vividly detailed in *Mine Boy* (1946) and *Path of Thunder* (1948) as well as in his account of a return visit, *Return to Goli* (1953), and an autobiography, *Tell Freedom* (1954). His understanding of Third World politics informs: *Wild Conquest* (1950), a historical novel; *A Wreath for Udomo* (1956), *A Night of Their Own* (1965) and *This Island Now* (1966), three remarkably prescient works; and *The View from Coyaba* (1985), an epic exploration of the black struggle against slavery and colonialism set in the Caribbean, Africa and North America.

Absalom, Absalom! A novel by WILLIAM FAULKNER, published in 1936. From their room at Harvard, Quentin Compson (see *THE SOUND AND THE FURY*) and Shreve McCannon reconstruct the story of Thomas Sutpen's failed attempt to found a dynasty in Jefferson, Mississippi. Sutpen manages to build a mansion but is finally defeated by the complex pattern of miscegenation embodied in his sons, Henry and Charles. Dividing its attention between Sutpen and Quentin's attempt to understand him, the novel is about the decay of the old South.

Absentee, The A novel by MARIA EDGEWORTH, published in the second series of *Tales of Fashionable Life* in 1812. It is set on a large landholding in Ireland, whose absentee landlord, Lord Clonbrony, is finally persuaded to return to his responsibilities by his son.

Achebe, Chinua 1930– Nigerian. His first novel, *THINGS FALL APART* (1958), has been recognized as an African classic. It was followed by *No Longer at Ease* (1960), *ARROW OF GOD* (1964; revised 1974), *A Man of the People* (1966) and *ANTHILLS OF THE SAVANNAH* (1987), about the failures of African politicians and intellectuals. He has also published *The Sacrificial Egg and Other Stories* (1962) and *Girls at War and Other Stories* (1972). *Chike and the River* (1966), *How the Leopard Got His Claws* (1972), *The Flute* and *The Drum* (1977) are children's books. His many other works, expressing his commitment to African literature and society, include: editions and co-editions of contemporary writing; *Morning Yet on Creation Day: Essays* (1975) and *Hopes and Impediments: Selected Essays, 1965–87* (1988); and *The Trouble with Nigeria*, a political statement written during the 1983 elections.

Acker, Kathy 1945–97 American. Her writing has often been compared to that of WILLIAM BURROUGHS in its use of surrealism, pornography, autobiography, and social commentary to portray a continuous battle between repressive political forces and liberatory language. Her novels, which often parody and 'plagiarize' classic works, include *Kathy Goes to Haiti* (1978), *Great Expectations* (1983), *Blood and Guts in High School* (1984), *Don Quixote, Which was a Dream* (1986), *Empire of the Senseless* (1988), *In Memoriam to Identity* (1990), *Hannibal Lecter, My Father* (1991), *My Mother, A Demonology* (1993) and *Pussy, King of the Pirates* (1996). *Portrait of an Eye* (1992) brings together *The Childlike Life of the Black Tarantula, I Dreamt I was a Maniac* and *The Adult Life of Toulouse Lautrec*, three early novels written under a pseudonym.

Ackroyd, Peter 1949– English. His lives of Ezra Pound (1980), T. S. Eliot (1984), DICKENS (1990) and William Blake (1995) have been acclaimed. Literary and biographical criticism also informs much of his fiction: *The Great Fire of London* (1982), about the filming of *LITTLE DORRIT; The*

Last Testament of Oscar Wilde (1983), a pastiche of OSCAR WILDE's final diary; *Hawksmoor* (1985; WHITBREAD AWARD), about the architect; and *Chatterton* (1987), about the boy-poet Thomas Chatterton; and *Milton in America* (1996), an 'alternative biography' in which the poet flees Restoration England for the New World. Other novels are *First Light* (1989), *English Music* (1992), *The House of Doctor Dee* (1993) and *Dan Leno and the Limehouse Golem* (1994).

Acton, Sir **Harold (Mario Mitchell)** 1904–94 English. He explored his own designation of himself as 'aesthete' in *Memoirs of an Aesthete* (1948) and *More Memoirs of an Aesthete* (1970). Part of the Oxford undergraduate group which included Brian Howard, HENRY GREEN, Sir John Betjeman and EVELYN WAUGH (who modelled Anthony Blanche in *BRIDESHEAD REVISITED* on him), he had published five books by the age of 24. His love for China and for Italy informs much of his work. A novel, *Peonies and Ponies* (1941), grew from his travels in China in the 1930s, as did translations from Chinese poetry and writings on Chinese art and culture. His Italian connections – Acton was born and later settled at the family villa near Florence – are evident in historical studies such as *The Last Medici* (1932) and *The Bourbons of Naples* (1957) and in much of his fiction. *Prince Isidore* (1950), an exhilaratingly mannered novel, charts the adventures of an aristocrat endowed with the Evil Eye. The short stories in *The Soul's Gymnasium* (1982) evoke the uneasy Golden Age of Anglo-American expatriates in Florence at the beginning of this century.

Adair, Gilbert 1944– English. He had already established himself as a film critic and cultural historian, and published two children's books, *Alice Through the Needle's Eye* (1984) and *Peter Pan and the Only Children* (1987), before he turned to adult fiction with *The Holy Innocents* (1988). *Love and Death on Long Island* (1990) prompted comparison with Thomas Mann and VLADIMIR NABOKOV, again evoked by *The Death of the Author* (1992), a satire on deconstruction and its derivatives. A similar concern informs the title essay of *The Postmodernist Always Rings Twice* (1992).

Adam Bede GEORGE ELIOT's first full-length novel, published in 1859.

Adam Bede, a carpenter in the Midland village of Hayslope, is in love with Hetty Sorrel, niece of the farmer Martin Poyser. The squire, Arthur Donnithorne, is attracted to Hetty and she is vain enough to dream of becoming his wife. Adam watches the flirtation with growing anxiety and tries unsuccessfully to intervene. Arthur abandons Hetty after seducing her. Adam earns the reward of his loyalty to Hetty when, heartbroken at Arthur's desertion, she agrees to marry him. But she finds herself pregnant and flies from home in a desperate search for her lover. Adam is supported in his grief by Dinah Morris, a young Methodist preacher, with whom his brother Seth is hopelessly in love. Unable to find Arthur, Hetty is arrested, charged with the murder of her child and convicted. Dinah becomes her comforter and the close of the novel describes how Hetty, with Dinah's help, faces her final ordeal. But she is reprieved and her sentence commuted to transportation. Adam later marries Dinah.

The novel was exceptionally well received by contemporary reviewers, who praised its evocation of English rural life and its character studies, particularly Martin's wife, Mrs Poyser.

Adams, Andy 1859–1935 American. He spent much of his life in the Texas cattle country and the mining centres of Colorado. He is best known for *The Log of a Cowboy* (1903), an authentic, unsentimental depiction of life on the open range. Other works include *The Outlet* (1905), *Cattle Brands* (1906), *Reed Anthony, Cowman* (1907), *Wells Brothers* (1911) and *The Ranch on the Beaver* (1927).

Adams, Arthur Henry 1872–1936 Born in New Zealand, he worked as a journalist there and in Australia. Novels and stories with an Australasian background include *Tussock Land* (1904), *The New Chum and Other Stories* (1909), *Galahad Jones* (1910), *The Australians* (1920) and *A Man's Life* (1929). His verse included a war poem, *My Friend, Remember* (1914). He also wrote *Three Plays for the Australian Stage* (1914) and light fiction under the pseudonyms of Henry James James and James James.

Adams, Douglas (Noël) 1952– English. *The Hitch-Hiker's Guide to the Galaxy* began as a BBC radio serial in 1978 before becoming a best-selling novel (1979). It was followed by *The Restaurant at the End of the Universe* (1980), *Life, the Universe and Everything* (1982), *So Long, and Thanks for All the Fish* (1984) and *Mostly Harmless* (1992). The series uses SCIENCE FICTION to satirize human delusions of significance. *Dirk Gently's Holistic Detective Agency* (1987) and *The Long Dark Tea-Time of the Soul* (1988) are absurdist DETECTIVE FICTION.

Adams, Richard (George) 1920– English. *WATERSHIP DOWN* (1972) – his first and most famous book, about the wanderings of a group of rabbits – was rejected by many publishers before appearing to acclaim from both children and adults. *Tales from Watership Down* (1996) returns to rabbit country. *Shardik* (1974), about a humanized bear, reflects his preoccupation with man's cruelty to beasts. He has also written humorous ballads for children but otherwise moved towards adult fiction with *The Plague Dogs* (1977) and *The Girl in a Swing* (1980), his first exclusively adult book. *Day Gone By* (1990) is his autobiography.

Ade, George 1866–1944 American. He made his mark with *Fables in Slang* (1899), *Forty Modern Fables* (1901), *People You Know* (1903) and *Hand-Made Fables* (1920), humorous stories peopled by everyday characters and rich in colloquial speech. His musical and dramatic comedies include *The Sultan of Sulu* (1903) and *The College Widow* (1904).

Advani, Rukun 1955– Indian. With its strong element of parody and pastiche, *Beethoven Among the Cows* (1994) is a rare example of Indian POST-MODERNISM. The title invokes respective icons of European and Indian cultures, and the clash between them provides the impetus of the novel.

Age of Innocence, The A novel by EDITH WHARTON, published in 1920 and awarded a PULITZER PRIZE. It is set mainly in New York during the 1870s. Newland Archer, a lawyer, falls in love with Ellen Olenska, the wife of a Polish count, but marries her cousin, May Welland. His continuing interest in Ellen prompts May to tell her that she is pregnant. Ellen leaves New York for Paris. Visiting the city 30 years later, the widowed Newland decides to preserve his idealized memories rather than call on her.

Agee, James 1909–55 American. He is perhaps best known for *Let Us Now Praise Famous Men* (with photographs by Walker Evans, 1941), describing the plight of three families in rural Alabama during the Depression. His novels, *The Morning Watch* (1951) and *A Death in the Family* (1957; PULITZER PRIZE), are partly autobiographical, the first dealing with religious piety and the second with the effects on a family of a father's early death. He also wrote filmscripts, including *The African Queen* (with John Huston, 1951), *The Bride Comes to Yellow Sky* (based on STEPHEN CRANE's short story, 1953) and *The Night of the Hunter* (1955). Agee's poems and short stories were collected and edited by Robert Fitzgerald (1968).

Agnes Grey A novel by ANNE BRONTË, published in 1847. It is based on her experiences as a governess. Agnes Grey, a rector's daughter employed by the Murray family, is badly treated and her loneliness is relieved only by the kindness of the curate, Weston, whom she eventually marries.

Aidoo, Ama Ata 1942– Ghanaian. After writing plays, including *The Dilemma of a Ghost* (1965), she made her fictional début with the 11 short stories in *No Sweetness Here* (1970), set in contemporary China. Her first novel, *Our Sister Killjoy* (1977), is about an African woman on a scholarship to Europe, while its successor, *Changes* (1991), is the story of a young Ghanaian whose husband, without warning, takes a second wife.

Aiken, Conrad (Potter) 1889–1973 American. His poetry and fiction both reflect his interest in psychology, and his reading of Freud, William James and French Symbolism, as well as of EDGAR ALLAN POE, his most obvious American antecedent. Volumes of poetry include: *Earth Triumphant, and Other Tales in Verse* (1914); *Turns and Movies* (1916); *The Jig of Forslin; A Symphony*

(1916); *Selected Poems* (1929); *And in the Human Heart* (1940), a sonnet sequence; *Collected Poems* (1929); and *Thee* (1967), a book-length poem. His five novels, often dealing with journeys of self-discovery, are *Blue Voyage* (1927), *Great Circle* (1933), *King Coffin* (1935), *A Heart for the Gods of Mexico* (1939) and *Conversation: or, Pilgrims' Progress* (1940). They were gathered in *The Collected Novels* (1964). His short stories include *Bring! Bring!* (1925), *Costumes by Eros* (1928) and *Among the Lost People* (1934).

Ainsworth, William Harrison 1805–82 English. *Rookwood* (1834), a novel romanticizing the 18th-century highwayman Dick Turpin, was a great commercial and popular success. *Jack Sheppard* (1839) features another notorious 18th-century criminal and so helped to fuel the controversy about the NEWGATE NOVEL. Other historical romances included: *The Tower of London* (1840), about the short reign of Lady Jane Grey; *Old St Paul's* (1841), which uses the Plague and Great Fire of London; *Windsor Castle* (1843), set in the reign of Henry VIII; and *The Lancashire Witches* (1849), set in Pendle Forest. (See also HISTORICAL FICTION.)

Alcott, Louisa May 1832–88 American. Daughter of the educationalist Bronson Alcott (1799–1888), she was only 16 when she finished her first book – later published as *Flower Fables* (1855) – and went on to produce nearly 300 titles in a variety of genres. She is best known for *LITTLE WOMEN*, which originally appeared in two parts, as *Little Women: or, Meg, Jo, Beth, and Amy* (1868) and *Good Wives* (1869). *Little Men: Life at Plumfield with Jo's Boys* (1871) and *Jo's Boys and How They Turned Out* (1886) are among Alcott's other wholesome domestic tales. *Work: A Study of Experience* (1873) is a feminist and autobiographical novel. When she became 'tired of providing moral pap for the young', Alcott wrote *A Modern Mephistopheles* (1877), in which an innocent young woman resists seduction by the diabolic genius with whom her poet-husband has made a Faustian pact; *Whisper in the Dark* (1889) has a similar theme.

Aldington, Richard 1892–1962 English. A member of the group which pioneered imagism, he published *Images 1910–1915* (1915) and *Collected Poems* (1928). He was married to the imagist poet Hilda Doolittle (H. D.) from 1913 to 1937. His novels include the savage *Death of a Hero* (1929), deriving from his experience of World War I, *The Colonel's Daughter* (1931), satirizing English village life, and *All Men are Enemies* (1933). He also wrote controversial biographies of D. H. LAWRENCE, in (*Portrait of a Genius, But . . .* , (1950) and T. E. Lawrence (1955). *Life for Life's Sake* (1941) is an autobiography. His correspondence with LAWRENCE DURRELL, *Literary Lifelines*, was published in 1981.

Aldiss, Brian W(ilson) 1925– English. Novels such as *Non-Stop* (1958) and *Greybeard* (1964) develop stock themes of SCIENCE FICTION. Other work pushes the conventions of the genre to new limits: *Hothouse* (1962) is a fantasia of the far future; *The Primal Urge* (1961) and *The Dark Light-Years* (1964) are satires; *Report on Probability A* (1968) is an anti-novel; and *Barefoot in the Head* (1969) is an extravaganza influenced by JAMES JOYCE. His most sustained exercise in invention is a trilogy, *Helliconia Spring* (1982), *Helliconia Summer* (1983) and *Helliconia Winter* (1985). Several short-story collections confirm his versatility. Non-fantastic fiction includes the Horatio Stubbs Trilogy, begun with *The Hand-Reared Boy* (1970) and the Squire Quartet, consisting of *Life in the West* (1980), *Forgotten Life* (1989), *Remembrance Day* (1993) and *Somewhere East of Life* (1994). He has also written a history of science fiction, *Billion-Year Spree* (1973; revised with David Wingrove as *Trillion-Year Spree*, 1986).

Aldrich, Thomas Bailey 1836–1907 American. His best-known work is *The Story of a Bad Boy* (1870), a novel based on his childhood. Other notable works are *Marjorie Daw and Other People* (1873), a collection of short stories, and *The Stillwater Tragedy* (1880), DETECTIVE FICTION. He was editor of *The Atlantic Monthly* in 1881–90.

Alexander, Lynne 1943– Born in the USA, she lives in Britain. Her small but distinguished body of fiction weaves together history, legend, lies and personal myths. It includes: *Safe Houses* (1985), told by two narrators who have never met but are both obsessed by what happened in wartime Budapest; *Resonating Bodies* (1988), a 'love-duet' whose experiment with musical form delighted critics as much as its story; *Taking Heart* (1991), in which a male cardiologist receives a woman's heart in a transplant operation; and *Adolf's Revenge* (1994), a modern fairy tale.

Alexander, Meena 1951– Though born in India, she spent part of her childhood in Sudan and has followed an academic career in the USA. Her verse includes *Stone Roots* (1980), *House of a Thousand Doors* (1988) and *The Storm: A Poem in Five Parts* (1989). Her novel *Nampally Road* (1991) describes the experiences of an educated woman returning to India after years in Britain. *Fault Lines* (1993) is an autobiography.

Alger, Horatio 1832–99 American. His adult novels were largely unsuccessful, in striking contrast to more than 100 novels he wrote for boys, most of them based on a rags-to-riches theme and the moral that a boy can rise from poverty to wealth if he has a good character. The most popular were *Ragged Dick* (1867), *Luck and Pluck* (1869) and *Tattered Tom* (1871). In the same vein as his fiction he wrote several biographies of famous self-made men, under such titles as *From Canal Boy to President* (1881), about Abraham Lincoln, and *From Farm Boy to Senator* (1882), about James Garfield.

Algerine Captive, The A novel by ROYALL TYLER, published in 1797. It makes a satiric commentary on American pretension and quackery through Underhill's narrative of his adventures. His experience of the South and of work as a doctor on board a slave ship prompts a sharp condemnation of slavery. Abandoned in Africa, he is himself made a slave by the Algerians but finally gains his freedom and returns to America.

Algren, Nelson 1909–81 American. He is best known for his novel about drug addiction, *The Man with the Golden Arm* (1949). Other books are *The Neon Wilderness* (1947), *Chicago: City on the Make* (1951), *A Walk on the Wild Side* (1956), *Who Lost an American?* (1963), *Notes from a Sea Diary: Hemingway All the Way* (1965), *The Last Carousel* (1973) and *The Devil's Stocking* (1983).

Ali, Ahmed 1910–94 Born in India, he moved to Pakistan after Partition. *Twilight in Delhi* (1940), written while he was still an Indian, is a magnificent historical novel about Muslim life in Delhi. *Ocean of Night* (1964), less well received, is set in Lucknow and depicts the decline of an aristocratic way of life. *Rats and Diplomats* (1985) is a novella, while *The Prison House* (1985) translates a selection of his Urdu stories.

Alice's Adventures in Wonderland A fantasy by LEWIS CARROLL, originally published as *Alice's Adventures Under Ground* (1865), with illustrations by Sir John Tenniel. Beginning famously as a story first told to children on a boating picnic in 1862, it is half dream, half nightmare and always diverting.

Plunging down a rabbit hole the seven-year-old Alice grows first too large and then shrinks too small. The Cheshire Cat, the Mad Hatter, the March Hare, the King and Queen of Hearts and other strange characters she meets involve her in logic-chopping, parody and punning. Favourite moments include the parodies 'You are Old, Father William' and 'Twinkle Twinkle Little Bat', the Lobster Quadrille, the Hatter's Tea Party and Alice's own understandable comment, 'Curiouser and curiouser'.

An immediate best-seller, the book had a lasting and revolutionary effect on children's literature by abandoning didacticism for good-humoured iconoclasm. THROUGH THE LOOKING-GLASS AND WHAT ALICE FOUND THERE (1871) is a sequel.

Alkali, Zaynab 1950– Nigerian. Born in Biu and educated at the University of Kanu, she is of special interest as one of the few English-language writers from northern Nigeria. *The Stillborn* (1984) and *The Virtuous Woman* (1985) are penetrating, but not uncompromising, studies of women in a patriarchal society.

Allan Quatermain A novel by HENRY RIDER HAGGARD, published in 1887. A sequel to *KING SOLOMON'S MINES*, it is more sombre in tone and more scholarly in its portrait of a 'primitive' people.

Curtis and Good return to Africa because they are disillusioned with 'civilization'; Quatermain joins their expedition because his life has become meaningless since the death of his only son. After various preliminary adventures, they reach the lost land of Zu-Vendis by a journey along an underground river. Zu-Vendis is ruled by two queens, the dark Sorais and her fair sister Nyleptha. Both fall in love with Curtis, who chooses Nyleptha. Sorais declares war but is defeated and kills herself. Curtis becomes king, but the price to be paid is the death of both Quatermain and the heroic 'primitive' Umslopogaas.

Allbeury, Ted See SPY FICTION.

Allen, (Charles) Grant (Blairfindie) 1848–99 English. His scientific books, influenced by Herbert Spencer, include *Physiological Aesthetics* (1877), *The Colour Sense* (1879), which won him high praise from the scientific community, *The Evolutionist at Large* (1881) and *The Evolution of the Idea of God* (1897). *The Woman Who Did* (1895) is the best-remembered of his nearly 30 novels. Its sensational story of a woman who lived unmarried with her lover but suffers the miseries of the outcast when he dies earned it a brief *succès de scandale*, though not the approval of feminists.

Allen, James Lane 1849–1925 American. His article, 'Realism and Romance' (1886), attacked claims for the primacy of REALISM as practised by WILLIAM DEAN HOWELLS and others, defending the merits of the older tradition of romance associated with NATHANIEL HAWTHORNE. Allen himself is best known for his romances set in the South, especially *A KENTUCKY CARDINAL* (1894) and its sequel, *Aftermath* (1895). Other works include *Summer in Arcady* (1896), *The Choir Invisible* (1897), *The Mettle of the Pasture* (1903), *The Bride of the Mistletoe* (1909), *The Kentucky Warbler* (1918) and a last collection of short stories, *The Landmark* (1925).

Allen, Walter (Ernest) 1911–95 English. He is best known for two popular studies, *The English Novel: A Short Critical History* (1954) and *Tradition and Dream* (1964; called *The Modern Novel in Britain and the United States* in the USA). Other critical works include *Writers on Writing* (1948; *The Writer on His Art* in the USA), *Reading a Novel* (1949), *The Novel Today* (1955) and studies of ARNOLD BENNETT (1948), JOYCE CARY (1953), DEFOE, FIELDING, SCOTT, DICKENS, STEVENSON and CONRAD jointly in *Six Great Novelists* (1955) and GEORGE ELIOT (1964). His early novels, *Innocence is Drowned* (1938), *Blind Man's Ditch* (1939) and *Living Space* (1940), are pictures of working-class life on the eve of World War II. Later fiction includes *The Black Country* (1946), *Rogue Elephant* (1946), *Dead Man Over All* (1950; *The Square Peg* in USA) and *All in a Lifetime* (1959; *Threescore and Ten* in USA).

Allfrey, Phyllis (Shand) 1915–86 Dominican. *The Orchid House* (1953) depicts the hot-house world of white Dominican society in the late colonial period; it has been seen as an influence on JEAN RHYS's *WIDE SARGASSO SEA*. Allfrey served as a minister in the short-lived West Indian Federal Government (1958–61) and wrote about the experience in an unpublished second novel, *In the Cabinet*.

Allingham, Margery (Louise) 1904–66 English. She made her reputation as a writer of DETECTIVE FICTION with Albert Campion, a light-hearted amateur detective modelled on DOROTHY L. SAYERS's Lord Peter Wimsey, who appeared in *The Crime at Black Dudley* (1929), *Mystery Mile* (1930), *Look to the Lady* (1931), *Police at the Funeral* (1931), *Sweet Danger* (1933), *Death of a Ghost* (1934), *Flowers for the Judge* (1936), *Dancers in Mourning* (1937), *The Case of the Late Pig* (1937) and *The Fashion in Shrouds* (1938). Her grasp of character and Dickensian eye for the oddities of London life are more strongly developed in post-war novels, particularly *The Tiger in the Smoke* (1952).

Alther, Lisa 1944– American. *Kinflicks* (1976) and *Original Sins* (1981) are set in the deep South but use the point of view of a protagonist who has left for the North. *Other Women* (1984), *Bedrock* (1990) and *Five Minutes in Heaven* (1995) have also been praised as substantial and witty additions to feminist literature.

Alton Locke: Tailor and Poet A novel by CHARLES KINGSLEY, published in 1850. It reflects the turbulence of the 1840s, expressing Kingsley's Christian Socialism and making a significant contribution to both the CONDITION OF ENGLAND NOVEL and the *ROMAN À THÈSE*.

As a tailor's apprentice, Alton Locke experiences the squalid conditions of sweated labour and takes readily to Chartism. His poetry brings him into contact with Eleanor Staunton, her cousin Lillian, and Saunders Mackaye, a Scottish bookseller loosely modelled on Thomas Carlyle. The Mackayes urge him to tone down his verse for publication, earning him the contempt of his Chartist comrades. Their taunts lead him to provoke a riot, and he is sentenced to three years' imprisonment. Lillian, with whom he has fallen in love, deserts him and it is Eleanor who nurses him when he catches typhus and helps convert him to Christian Socialism. He dies on his way to the USA.

Aluko, T(imothy) M(ofolorunso) 1918– Nigerian. His satirical fiction, in which the clash between old and new values generates comedy, includes: *One Man, One Wife* (1959), the first full-length novel in English to be published by a Nigerian publisher; *One Man, One Matchet* (1964); *Kinsman and Foreman* (1966); *Chief the Honourable Minister* (1970); *His Worshipful Majesty* (1973); and *Wrong Ones in the Dock* (1982).

Amadi, Elechi 1934– Nigerian. Although he is regarded as a leading African novelist, his reputation has tended to languish in the shade of CHINUA ACHEBE. His fiction includes a trilogy, *The Concubine* (1966), *The Great Ponds* (1969) and *The Slave* (1978), drawing on the traditional spiritual and mythic life of Eastern Nigeria, and *Estrangement* (1986), about the desolation and confusion following the Nigerian Civil War. *Sunset in Biafra* (1973) is an account of his own war experiences.

Amazing Marriage, The A novel by GEORGE MEREDITH, published in 1895. The rich and spoiled Lord Fleetwood reluctantly marries Carinthia Jane Kirby, daughter of a sea captain and a runaway countess, at the insistence of her uncle, Lord Levellier. When he abandons her, Carinthia takes shelter with Gower Woodseer, whose father is a minister to the poor in Whitechapel. Gower arranges a reconciliation but Carinthia resolves to go to Spain as an army nurse with her brother Chillon. Fleetwood becomes a monk.

Ambassadors, The A novel by HENRY JAMES, published in 1903.

Lambert Strether, a middle-aged widower, is sent to Paris by Mrs Newsome, a wealthy widow, to persuade her son Chad to return to his responsibilities as head of the family business in Massachusetts. His success as an ambassador will ensure his marriage to Mrs Newsome. He finds Chad sophisticated and refined by the influence of Madame de Vionnet. His letters to Mrs Newsome reveal declining enthusiasm for his embassy and she sends her daughter Sarah, with Sarah's husband and sister-in-law. They receive little help from Strether and their lack of success further estranges him from Mrs Newsome. In the ensuing action Strether makes two discoveries: that Chad's liaison with Madame de Vionnet is an intimate one, and that his sympathies rest with Chad. Content to observe life rather than participate in it, he eventually returns to Massachusetts.

Ambler, Eric 1909– English. Their fast-moving plots, carefully controlled suspense and skilful use of foreign locations have made his SPY FICTION and thrillers admired models for later writers. The best-known include *Epitaph for a Spy* (1938), *The Mask of Dimitrios* (1939; called *A Coffin for Dimitrios* in the USA), *Journey into Fear* (1940), *Judgment on Deltchev* (1951), *The Night-Comers* (1956), *Passage of Arms* (1959), *The Light of Day* (1962), *Dirty Story* (1967) and *Doctor Frigo* (1974). He has also written many screenplays, beginning with *The Way Ahead* (with Peter Ustinov; 1944). His teasing skirmishes with autobiography include *Here Lies Eric Ambler* (1981) and *The Story So Far: Memories and Other Fictions* (1993).

Amelia The last novel by HENRY FIELDING, published in 1751. Its intense depiction of evil and injustice has always made it less popular than his other work.

William Booth, an attractive but impetuous young army officer, runs away with the virtuous and beautiful Amelia against her mother's wishes. The couple fall foul of the predatory world of London. Unjustly imprisoned in Newgate, William is seduced by Miss Matthews. Amelia meanwhile resists the attentions of several men. She forgives William, but his gambling gets him imprisoned again. Their desperate suffering is ended by the discovery that Amelia, not her sister, is the rightful heiress to her family's property.

American, The A novel by HENRY JAMES, serialized in 1876–7 and published in volume form in 1877.

Christopher Newman, a wealthy American businessman, travels to Paris to find a wife. Mrs Tristram, an expatriate American, serves as his guide and confidante. His engagement to Claire de Cintré is ended by her aristocratic family, the Bellegardes. Newman introduces Valentin Bellegarde, Claire's brother, to Noémie Nioche, a copyist of paintings. Valentin fights a duel on her behalf and is killed. Before dying he sends Newman to Mrs Bread, the Dowager Marquise's maid, who reveals that the Marquise had caused her husband's death by withholding his medicine. Newman decides not to use this information to force the marriage. Claire becomes a nun.

American Senator, The A novel by ANTHONY TROLLOPE, serialized in 1876–7. Senator Gotobed comes to England to study English institutions. He stays in the town of Dillborough and visits Bragton Hall. His comments are outspoken and diverting, but some contemporary reviewers thought the novel spoiled by the addition of two love-affairs.

American Tragedy, An A novel by THEODORE DREISER, published in 1925. It is based on the Chester Gillette–Grace Brown murder case of 1906. Anxious to escape his family's dreary life, Clyde Griffiths gets a job in a factory belonging to his wealthy uncle, Samuel Griffiths. He falls in love with a rich girl, Sondra Finchley, but also seduces Roberta, a young factory worker. When she becomes pregnant and demands that he marry her, Clyde takes her to a lake resort and murders her. The rest of the novel traces the investigation of the case, describing Clyde's indictment, trial, conviction and execution in relentless detail.

Amis, Sir Kingsley 1922–96 English. During the 1940s and 1950s he was associated with the ANGRY YOUNG MEN generation and the poets of The Movement. His own poetry appeared in *Bright November* (1947), *A Frame of Mind* (1953), *A Case of Samples* (1956) and *Collected Poems 1944–1979* (1979). He achieved popular recognition with his first novel, *LUCKY JIM* (1954), showing a gift for comedy and mild satire continued in *That Uncertain Feeling* (1955), *I Like It Here*

(1958), and *Take a Girl Like You* (1960) and, with increasing vehemence, in *One Fat Englishman* (1963), *Ending Up* (1974) and *Jake's Thing* (1978). Other novels experiment with specific genres: the spy story in *The Anti-Death League* (1966) and *Colonel Sun* (1968); the ghost story in *The Green Man* (1969); DETECTIVE FICTION in *The Riverside Villas Murder* (1973); and SCIENCE FICTION and fantasy in *The Alteration* (1976). Later novels, such as *Stanley and the Women* (1984), *The Old Devils* (BOOKER PRIZE; 1986), *The Folks That Live on the Hill* (1990), *The Russian Girl* (1992) and *The Biographer's Moustache* (1995), sometimes turn to gloomy farce. *You Can't Do Both* (1994) is a *BILDUNGSROMAN* set in pre-war suburbia and Oxford. Non-fiction includes his vitriolic *Memoirs* (1991) and, distilling his preoccupation with the niceties of language and linguistic change, *The King's English: A Guide to Modern Usage* (1997).

Amis, Martin 1949– English. He is the son of KINGSLEY AMIS. *The Rachel Papers* (1973), *Dead Babies* (1975) and *Success* (1978) are ferociously witty, baleful satires of metropolitan torpor and cultural trendiness. His fiction has steadily grown more menacing and more experimental in: *Other People* (1981), a psychological thriller; *Money* (1984), a comedy set in high-life America; *LONDON FIELDS* (1989); *Time's Arrow* (1991), about the Nazi death camps; and *The Information* (1995). *Night Train* (1997) toys with the conventions of American hard-boiled DETECTIVE FICTION. *Einstein's Monsters* (1986) is a collection of short stories on the theme of nuclear destruction. *The Moronic Inferno* (1986) gathers non-fictional pieces about the USA.

Amory, Thomas *c.* 1691–1788 Irish. An acquaintance of Jonathan Swift, he wrote *The Memoirs of Several Ladies of Great Britain* (1755) and *The Life and Opinions of John Buncle, Esquire* (1756 and 1766). The first describes the adventures of Mrs Marinda Benlow, a bluestocking. The second, practically a sequel but purporting to be an autobiography, describes the travels and matrimonial adventures of its narrator.

Amours de Voyage A verse novel in five cantos by Arthur Hugh Clough (1819–61), published in 1858. It is narrated chiefly by Claude, a doubting intellectual, in letters from Rome, Florence, Bagni di Lucca and other towns visited by the middle-class English in the last century. The plot, which concerns Claude's tepid affair with Mary Trevellyn, is slight and the interest lies in Claude's reflections on art, ancient and modern Rome, patriotism, love, politics and Christian belief.

Anand, Mulk Raj 1905– Indian. His realistic novels, angry, satirical and generous, include: *UNTOUCHABLE* (1935), the trilogy headed by *The Village* (1939), *Across the Black Waters* (1940), *The Sword and the Sickle* (1942), *The Big Heart* (1945), *The Private Life of an Indian Prince* (1953); and *The Old Woman and the Cow* (1960; reissued as *Gauri*, 1976). A projected series of autobiographical novels, *The Seven Ages of Man*, has so far included *Seven Summers* (1951; revised as *Pilpali Sal*, 1985), *Morning Face* (1968; awarded a SAHITYA AKADEMI prize), *Confession of a Lover* (1976), *The Bubble* (1984) and the first section of a fifth, *Little Plays of Mahatma Gandhi* (1991). Anand has also published many short stories and *Conversations in Bloomsbury* (1981), recollections of T. S. Eliot, D. H. LAWRENCE and VIRGINIA WOOLF.

Anastasius See HOPE, THOMAS.

Anaya, Rudolfo 1937– American. A pioneering figure in Chicano literature, he is fascinated by Hispanic storytelling, folk tales, and mythology. His first novel, *Bless Me, Ultima* (1972), is a *BILDUNGSROMAN* of a young Chicano boy coming of age around World War II. Expanding the story into a loose trilogy, *Heart of Aztlan* (1976) follows a rural family's move from the country to the city and *Tortuga* (1979) examines the boy's recovery through therapy from paralysis. Other novels include *The Legend of La Llorona* (1984), *Albuquerque* (1992), *Zia Summer* (1995), *Jalamanta* (1996) and *Rio Grande Fall* (1996). Anaya has also written plays and edited volumes of Chicano stories.

Anderson, Barbara 1926– New Zealand. She is noted for her acute observation and sharp irreverent eye for absurdity. A collection of short stories, *I Think We Should Go into the Jungle* (1989), was followed by a novel, *Girls' High* (1991), about staff relationships in a school. Her relaxed interest in the world of upper middle-class Anglophile New Zealand is evident in *Portrait of the Artist's Wife* (1992), which won the GOODMAN FIELDER WATTIE BOOK AWARD, and *All the Nice Girls* (1993). *The House Guest* (1995) is about a young English academic whose investigations into the life of a dead poet get mixed up with his own present.

Anderson, Jessica 1925– Australian. She has published *An Ordinary Lunacy* (1963), *The Last Man's Head* (1970), *The Commandant* (1975), *Stories from the Warm Zone and Sydney Stories* (1987) and *Taking Shelter* (1990), but is best known for two novels, both winners of the MILES FRANKLIN AWARD: *Tirra Lirra by the River* (1978), an elderly woman's account of her constricting life, and *The Impersonators* (1980; called *The Only Daughter* in the USA), about a woman rediscovering her native Sydney. Her writing has a flair for the poetic and a laconic irony, reflecting her admiration for HENRY GREEN, EVELYN WAUGH and MURIEL SPARK. CHRISTINA STEAD is the most significant Australian influence on her work.

Anderson, Sherwood 1876–1941 American. *Windy McPherson's Son* (1916) was followed by *Marching Men* (1917), a novel about coal miners in Pennsylvania, and *Mid-American Chants* (1918), a volume of unrhymed verse. He achieved recognition with *WINESBURG, OHIO* (1919), interrelated stories of small-town life, and *Poor White* (1920), a novel exploring the effects of technological change on American culture. Later work includes short stories – *The Triumph of the Egg* (1921), *Horses and Men* (1923) and *Death in the Woods* (1933) – and the novels *Many Marriages* (1923), *Dark Laughter* (1925), *Tar: A Midwest Childhood* (1926) and *Beyond Desire* (1932). His autobiography, *A Story Teller's Story*, was published in 1924. A volume of *Letters* was issued in 1953, and a critical edition of his *Memoirs* in 1973. His minimalist prose style and bleak vision of life influenced such writers as ERNEST HEMINGWAY and WILLIAM FAULKNER.

Angel at My Table, An See *To the Is-Land*.

Angry Young Men A group of British writers of the late 1950s, characterized by what Kenneth Allsop defined in *The Angry Decade* (1958) as 'irreverence, stridency, impatience with tradition, vigour, vulgarity, sulky resentment against the cultivated'. Their stance arose from the sense of betrayal and futility which succeeded the exalted aspirations generated by post-war reforms. COLIN WILSON's study of alienation, *The Outsider* (1956), was judged by many an important manifesto. The seminal novels are JOHN WAIN's *Hurry on Down* (1953), KINGSLEY AMIS's *Lucky Jim* (1954), JOHN BRAINE's *Room at the Top* (1957) and ALAN SILLITOE's *Saturday Night and Sunday Morning* (1958). In the drama, the classic example is John Osborne's *Look Back in Anger* (1956), with a definitive anti-hero in Jimmy Porter.

Animal Farm A novel by GEORGE ORWELL, published in 1945. The satirical allegory or fable is directed primarily against Stalin's Russia. Led by the pigs, the animals on Mr Jones's farm expel their human masters and decide to run the farm on egalitarian principles. However, the pigs are corrupted by power and, under Napoleon (Stalin), a new tyranny is established. Snowball (Trotsky), an idealist, is driven out and Boxer, the noble carthorse, is sent to the knacker's yard. The final betrayal occurs when the pigs engineer a *rapprochement* with Mr Jones. Originally rejected for publication by T. S. Eliot, the book has remained very popular, especially with younger readers.

Anna of the Five Towns A novel by ARNOLD BENNETT, published in 1902. The harsh codes of her father, Ephraim Tellwright, and the economic realities of Bursley, a town in the Potteries, weigh heavily on the heroine. The news that she will inherit a fortune makes her attractive to a successful businessman, Henry Mynors, whom she eventually marries. In the process she is estranged from another suitor, Willie Price, an industrial tenant of her father, though she saves him from public disgrace when he and his father try to pay her father with a forged bill of credit. Ephraim disinherits her. Willie, learning that his father has embezzled £50 from the chapel building fund before committing suicide, commits suicide himself.

Annals of the Parish, The A novel by JOHN GALT, published in 1821. The Rev. Micah Balwhidder records life in his Lowland parish of Dalmailing, often in an unintentionally humorous way, over a period of 50 years (1760–1810).

Anne of Geierstein See SCOTT, SIR WALTER.

Anne of Green Gables A novel by L. M. MONTGOMERY, published in 1908. The 11-year-old Anne Shirley goes to help Matthew and Marilla Cuthbert, an elderly bachelor and his sister, on their farm on Prince Edward Island, and wins their hearts by her vulnerable but deeply affectionate character. The rest of the novel recounts the mini-adventures of an adolescent girl and her peer group, from attempts at amateur theatricals to first courtship.

Anstey, F. [Guthrie, Thomas Anstey] 1856–1934 English. He was diverted from the law by the success of *Vice Versa: or A Lesson to Fathers* (1882), the humorous story of a father and son who exchange ages and personalities. It was followed by *Tourmalin's Time Cheques* (1891), *The Brass Bottle* (1900), about an inefficient jinnee, and *In Brief Authority* (1915). He contributed regularly to *Punch* and joined the staff of the magazine in 1887.

Anthills of the Savannah A novel by CHINUA ACHEBE, published in 1987. Set in the imaginary West African country of Kangan (in effect Nigeria), it centres on three boyhood friends: Sam, the military leader; Ikem Osodi, a poet and newspaper editor; and Chris Oriko, a minister in Sam's administration. Achebe analyses the consequences of military rule in a country where constitutional processes have come to an impasse.

Anthony, Michael 1932– Trinidadian. His gentle, shrewdly observant talent is perhaps more recognized outside the Caribbean than within it. Four novels are concerned with childhood or adolescence: *The Games Were Coming* (1963), *The Year in San Fernando* (1965), *Green Days by the River* (1967) and *All That Glitters* (1981). *Streets of Conflict* (1976) is set in Rio de Janeiro in the late 1960s. He has also published a collection of short stories, *Cricket in the Road and Other Stories* (1973); a children's novel, *King of the Masquerade* (1974); and *The Bright Road to Eldorado* (1982). *Profile Trinidad* (1975) is a historical survey of the island's social and cultural life.

Anthony, Piers See SCIENCE FICTION.

Antiquary, The A novel by SIR WALTER SCOTT, published in 1816. When Isabella Wardour obeys her father, Sir Arthur, and rejects his suit, Major Neville calls himself William Lovel and follows her to Scotland. There he meets Jonathan Oldbuck, the eccentric antiquary of the title, and the king's bedesman, Edie Ochiltree. He saves Sir Arthur and Isabella from drowning and with Ochiltree's help exposes

Dousterswivel, a German scoundrel who has deceived Sir Arthur. Lovel proves to be the heir of Glenallan and all ends happily.

Anzaldúa, Gloria 1942– Chicana. Her writing reflects her concern with the lives of Chicana and lesbian women, as well as the geographical and social borders that separate people. It includes: *Borderlands/La Frontera: The New Mestiza* (1987); *La Prieta* (1995); and two collections, *The Bridge Called My Back: Writings by Radical Women of Color* (1981), co-edited with Cherríe Moraga and *Making Face, Making Soul = Haciendo caras: Creative and Critical Perspectives by Feminists of Color* (1990). She has also written for children.

Aquin, Hubert See FRENCH-CANADIAN NOVEL.

Arcadia, The A prose romance, interspersed with poems, by Sir Philip Sidney (1554–86), English courtier, poet and critic. Enormously popular, it appealed to the Renaissance love of pastoral but was also read as courtesy book, moral treatise, discussion of love and philosophy, and even rhetorical handbook. Sidney wrote the bulk of it in 1580 and dedicated it to his sister, the Countess of Pembroke; he never finished a later revision. As a result, the work exists in three different forms.

The unrevised *Old Arcadia*, circulated only in manuscript in the 16th century, was devised in five acts. Warned by an oracle of enigmatic disasters, Duke Basilius retires to Arcadia with his wife, Gynecia, and daughters, Philoclea and Pamela. Two princes, Pyrocles and Musidorus, arrive and fall in love with Philoclea and Pamela. A complex web of disguise and mistaken identity brings events to the brink of tragedy, narrowly averted at the end.

The second version, the *New Arcadia* (1590), perhaps published under the supervision of Sir Fulke Greville, presented the revised and greatly expanded text of the first three books. New subsidiary stories include that of the blind Paphlagonian king which Shakespeare borrowed for the Gloucester sub-plot in *King Lear*. *The Countess of Pembroke's Arcadia* (1593), perhaps published under the supervision of the Countess herself, is a hybrid version bringing together the first three revised books of the *New Arcadia* and the last two books of the unrevised *Old Arcadia*.

Archer, Jeffrey See GENRE FICTION.

Arden, John 1930– English. He established himself as the most allusive and socially conscious playwright of the post-war generation with work which includes: *Live Like Pigs* (1958), *Serjeant Musgrave's Dance* (1959), *The Workhouse Donkey* (1963), *Armstrong's Last Goodnight* (1964), *Left-Handed Liberty* (1965), *The Hero Rises Up* (1968) and his overtly political plays about Ireland, *The Ballygombeen Bequest* (1972), the six-part *The Non-Stop Connolly Show* (1975) and *Vandaleur's Folly* (1978). The essays in *To Present the Pretence* (1978) record his progress from liberal socialism to the

politics of revolution. His fiction – notably *Silence Among the Weapons* (1982), *Books of Bale* (1988) and *Jack Juggler and the Emperor's Whore* (1995) – shows the same combination of topical commitment with sense of history that informs his work for the stage.

Arlen, Michael [Kouyoumdjian, Dikran] 1895–1956 Born in Bulgaria of Armenian parents, he was educated in Britain but lived in the South of France after his marriage in 1928 and in New York after World War II. He achieved a brief popularity with his acerbic but stylish portrait of London life in collections of short stories such as *The Romantic Lady* (1921) and *These Charming People* (1923), and particularly in his best-selling novel *The Green Hat* (1924).

Armah, Ayi Kwei 1939– Ghanaian. His vivid, eloquent novels lament centuries of African suffering and cultural obliteration. THE BEAUTYFUL ONES ARE NOT YET BORN (1969), *Fragments* (1970) and *Why are We So Blest?* (1972) suggest almost total disillusionment with independent Africa. The need for a truly African cultural integrity is implicit in *Two Thousand Seasons* (1973), which rewrites the history of both Islamic and Christian assaults as simple epic, and *The Healers* (1978), about the crumbling 19th-century Ashanti empire.

Armstrong, Jeanette 1948– Canadian. Born on the Penticton Reservation in British Columbia, she is director of a Native education centre. She edited *Looking at the Words of Our People: An Anthology of First Nations Literature* (1993) and is the author of the novel *Slash* (1990), contemporary Native tales and children's books.

Arrow of God A novel by CHINUA ACHEBE, published in 1964 and revised in 1974. Like THINGS FALL APART, it deals with the impact of British colonialism on traditional Igbo life. Set in Eastern Nigeria during the entrenchment of colonial rule, it tells the tragic story of Ezeulu, Chief Priest of the god Ulu. His attempt to reconcile the demands of his god with his own quest for personal power brings calamity on himself, his family and his clan, and inadvertently fosters the hegemony of Christianity.

Arthur Mervyn A GOTHIC NOVEL by CHARLES BROCKDEN BROWN, published in two volumes in 1799 and 1800.

Dr Stevens, the narrator, cares for Arthur Mervyn, a farmboy who has come to Philadelphia and fallen ill during the plague year of 1793. Mervyn tells his story when suspicion arises that he is not the country innocent he appears. On first arriving in Philadelphia he had worked for Thomas Welbeck but discovered him to be a seducer, thief, forger and murderer. After Welbeck apparently died while trying to flee, Mervyn went to live on Mr Hadwin's farm, where he fell in love with his daughter Eliza. Later he discovered $20,000 of stolen money in a manuscript by Welbeck he had brought with him. When he encountered Welbeck, still alive, in Philadelphia, he burned the money before falling ill. Having dispelled the suspicions about his character, Mervyn returns to Eliza and finds that she has inherited the farm. He has a final confrontation with the now dying and repentant Welbeck. Meanwhile, new suspicions arise and Mervyn's explanations prove less satisfactory; indeed, the second part of the book casts doubt on the story he had originally told. At the end, when Eliza turns out not to have inherited the farm, he marries Mrs Fielding, a widow of means.

As for Me and My House A novel by SINCLAIR ROSS, published in 1941. A classic of Canadian Prairie fiction set in the Depression years, it tells the story of the newly appointed minister of the ironically named town of Horizon through the journal of his wife, Mrs Bentley. It paints a powerful portrait of the constrictions of small-town life and of artistic and spiritual failure, deriving much of its force from the ambiguities inherent in Mrs Bentley's narration.

As I Lay Dying A novel by WILLIAM FAULKNER, published in 1930. It treats the events surrounding the illness, death and burial of Addie Bundren, wife of Anse and mother of Cash, Darl, Jewel, Dewey Dell, and Vardaman. Anse is stubbornly insistent that her wish to be buried in her home town of Jefferson, Mississippi, should be respected, despite the accidents and setbacks which the family encounters on its 10-day journey with the coffin. Experimental in both subject and narrative structure, the novel is divided into 59 short interior monologues (see STREAM OF CONSCIOUSNESS) from the characters.

Ashford, Daisy 1881–1972 English. She dictated her first story at the age of four and gave up writing when she was 13. *The Young Visiters*, a long-forgotten, imperfectly spelled manuscript written when she was nine, was rediscovered and published with an introduction by J. M. BARRIE in 1919. A lively eye for detail and occasional understandable confusions combine to make the story – how Ethel Monticue is courted both by Bernard Clark, her favourite, and Mr Salteena – a classic of unconscious humour, never out of print since its first appearance. Other manuscripts written when Ashford was a child and since published are *Love and Marriage* (1965) and *The Hangman's Daughter* (1982).

Ashton-Warner, Sylvia 1908–84 New Zealand. She spent most of her career as a schoolteacher and did not publish her first novel, *Spinster* (1958), until she was nearly 50. It immediately made an impact in New Zealand as a ROMAN À CLEF and internationally for its STREAM OF CONSCIOUSNESS presentation of the teacher-protagonist's turbulent inner life. *Incense to Idols* (1960) and *Bell Call* (1965) use Romantic narrative modes which complement the challenge offered to conventional society and its notions of communication and education. *Teacher* (1963) and *Myself* (1967), supposedly the author's diary from the early 1940s, are presented in a documentary mode. *Greenstone* (1966), moving between fantasy and realism, draws heavily on Maori myth to make a plea for racial and cultural harmony. Ashton-Warner's other works include *Three* (1970) and *I Passed This Way* (1979).

Asimov, Isaac 1920–92 American. His pulp SCIENCE FICTION is among the most popular ever produced, especially those collected in the three-volume Foundation series (1942–50; in book form 1951–3) and the classic collection *I, Robot* (1950), which made famous the 'three laws of robotics'. This programmed ethical system was elaborated in *The Caves of Steel* (1954), *The Naked Sun* (1956) and *The Bicentennial Man and Other Stories* (1976). His other science fiction novels include *The Currents of Space* (1952), *The End of Eternity* (1955), *The Gods Themselves* (1972) and *Nemesis* (1989). In the years before his death he attempted to bind his two most famous series together into a single pattern of future history, as *Foundation's Edge* (1982), *The Robots of Dawn* (1983), *Robots and Empire* (1985), *Foundation and Earth* (1986) and *Prelude to Foundation* (1988).

Aspern Papers, The A story by HENRY JAMES, published in 1888. It was inspired by the rumours that Byron's mistress Claire Clairmont (1798–1879), who lived out her old age in Italy, preserved letters from the poet – though in fact Byron had carefully avoided writing to her.

The story is narrated by an American editor who travels to Venice in hopes of recovering letters written by Jeffrey Aspern, a Romantic poet of the early 19th century, to his mistress, 'Juliana'. He rents rooms from Juliana, now the aged Miss Bordereau, who lives with her niece, Tina, an unattractive spinster. After Miss Bordereau dies Tina says that she could give the letters only to 'a relative' of the family. The narrator balks at the veiled proposal and when they next meet Tina reveals that she has burned them.

Astley, Thea 1925– Australian. Her work frequently concentrates on outsiders and misfits, attacking the philistinism and hypocrisy of middle-class, small-town life, especially in Queensland. Novels include *Girl with a Monkey* (1958), *A Descant for Gossips* (1960), *The Well-Dressed Explorer* (1962), *The Slow Natives* (1965), *A Boat Load of Home Folk* (1968), *The Acolyte* (1972), *A Kindness Cup* (1974), *An Item from the Late News* (1982), *Beach-Masters* (1985), *It's Raining in Mango* (1987), *Reaching Tin River* (1990) and *Coda* (1994). *Hunting the Wild Pineapple* (1979) is a collection of related short stories; *Vanishing Points* (1992) links two novellas. *The Well-Dressed Explorer*, *The Slow Natives* and *The Acolyte* all won the MILES FRANKLIN AWARD.

Atwood, Margaret (Eleanor) 1939– Canadian.

She first attracted attention with poetry such as *The Circle Game* (1966), *The Animals in that Country* (1968) and *The Journals of Susanna Moodie* (1970), belonging to the mythopoeic tradition of Jay Macpherson. The novel *SURFACING* (1972) traverses similar terrain in relating its narrator-protagonist's quest for personal truth to a journey into the national past and ultimately prehistory, also a concern in a later novel, *Life Before Man* (1979). *Lady Oracle* (1976) is a social comedy in which the heroine once again 'escapes' from contemporary consumer society. *THE HANDMAID'S TALE* (1986) is a SCIENCE-FICTION allegory which comments on the rise of right-wing fundamentalism and new forms of patriarchy in North America in the 1980s. *Cat's Eye* (1989) is based on flashback, as the narrator, like earlier Atwood protagonists, reviews and reassesses her past. *The Robber Bride* (1993) examines the effect a latter-day Lady Macbeth has on three female contemporaries. *Alias Grace* (1996) is the story of a 19th-century maidservant convicted of murder. Atwood's other works include: novels, *The Edible Woman* (1969), *Bodily Harm* (1981); volumes of verse, *Procedures for Underground* (1970), *Power Politics* (1971), *Two-Headed Poems* (1978), *True Stories* (1981), *Interlunar* (1984), *Selected Poems: 1966–1984* (1990) and *Morning in the Burned House* (1995); and collections of short fiction, *Dancing Girls* (1977), *Bluebeard's Egg* (1983), *Wilderness Tips* (1991) and *Good Bones* (1992). *Survival: A Thematic Guide to Canadian Literature* (1972) is a work of archetypal criticism which shows the influence of Northrop Frye's *The Bush Garden*. *Second Words* (1982) is a collection of her shorter critical pieces. *Strange Things* (1995) discusses the 'imaginative mystique' of the North in Canadian literature. Atwood edited *The New Oxford Book of Canadian Verse in English* (1982).

Aubert de Gaspé, Philippe-Ignace-François and Philippe-Joseph See FRENCH-CANADIAN NOVEL.

Augie March, The Adventures of A novel by SAUL BELLOW, published in 1953. One of three sons born to a feeble-minded Jewish woman on Chicago's West Side, Augie does not finish college, becomes involved briefly in union organizing, travels to Mexico, returns to the USA and joins the navy, marries and, after leaving the service, goes to Europe to write his 'memoir'. In it he records his encounters with the people who have shaped (or tried to shape) his life: his Grandma Lausch; his employer William Einhorn; the wealthy Renlings, who want to adopt him; the tough waitress Mini Villar; the rich Thea Fenchel, who takes him to Mexico; the millionaire Robey, who hires him to help write a masterwork; Stella Chesney, the showgirl he marries; and the lunatic scientist Bateshaw, with whom he shares a lifeboat after their ship has been torpedoed.

Aurora Leigh A novel in verse by Elizabeth Barrett Browning (1806–61), published in 1856 (but postdated 1857). Her most sustained piece of work, it confronts many contemporary issues (the role of women, the plight of the poor and the efficacy of Utopian socialism) and embodies her 'highest convictions upon Life and Art'. The story traces Aurora's development as an artist in opposition to the active philanthropy of her cousin Romney. The resolution lies in the recognition by both cousins that each has placed too great an emphasis on limited aspects of man's character.

Austen, Jane 1775–1817 English. She was born at Steventon in Hampshire where her father, who was also her tutor, was rector. On his retirement in 1801 the family moved to Bath, a city that frequently appears in her fiction, but returned to Hampshire after his death in 1805. With her mother and sister, she lived first in Southampton and then in Chawton, near Alton, remaining there until she died. Her life was conspicuous for its lack of event – allowing biographers to make it a study in quiet contemplation or quiet frustration – and for the strength of her family ties, most importantly with her sister Cassandra. She died in Winchester at the age of 41 and is buried in the cathedral.

She began her literary career at the age of 15 with *Love and Friendship*, a burlesque of SAMUEL RICHARDSON; other pieces belonging to the 1790s caricature the excessive 'sensibility' fashionable in the 18th-century SENTIMENTAL NOVEL. Her eye for the ridiculous in contemporary taste also inspired *NORTHANGER ABBEY* (published posthumously in 1818 but probably her earliest extended work of fiction), which satirizes her heroine's penchant for the GOTHIC NOVEL, and *SENSE AND SENSIBILITY* (begun in 1797 but not published until 1811).

Begun in 1796 or 1797 and published after revision in 1813, *PRIDE AND PREJUDICE* has the same high spirits as its predecessors but, more clearly than they, marks out the territory, the subject and the mode of her mature work. It looks forward to her later novels: *MANSFIELD PARK* (begun 1811, published 1814), *EMMA* (begun 1814, published 1816) and *PERSUASION* (begun 1815, published posthumously in 1818). In these works she chose deliberately to portray small groups of people in a limited, perhaps confining, environment, and to mould the apparently trivial incidents of their lives into a poised comedy of manners. Her characters are middle-class and provincial; their most urgent preoccupation is with courtship and their largest ambition is marriage. The task she set herself required careful shaping of her material, delicate economy and precise deployment of irony to point the underlying moral commentary. She developed not by obvious enlargement of her powers but by the deepening subtlety and seriousness with which she worked inside the formal boundaries she had established.

Although her novels did not prove especially popular in her own day, *Emma* was reviewed favourably by SIR WALTER SCOTT and was dedicated to another admirer of her work, the Prince Regent. *Lady Susan*, an EPISTOLARY NOVEL, and *The Watsons* were not published until they appeared in the second edition of J. E. Austen Leigh's *Memoir of Jane Austen* (1871). The fragment of *SANDITON*, on which she was working in the last months of her life, was first published in 1925.

Auster, Paul 1947– American. His existentialist allegories, about men and women isolated in the concrete jungles of Manhattan or the labyrinths of memory, have been compared with the work of Kafka and EDGAR ALLAN POE. They include: *City of Glass* (1985), *Ghosts* (1986) and *The Locked Room* (1986), collected as *The New York Trilogy* (1990); *In the Country of Last Things* (1987); *Moon Palace* (1990); *The Music of Chance* (1990); *Leviathan* (1992); and *Mr Vertigo* (1994). He has also written the screenplays for two films based on his stories, *Smoke* (1995) and *Blue in the Face* (1996), and two collections of memoirs and essays, *The Invention of Solitude* (1982) and *The Art of Hunger* (1992), as well as poetry and translations from French literature.

Awakening, The A novel by KATE CHOPIN, published in 1899. Edna Pontellier, wife of a Creole speculator in Louisiana, is awakened by her flirtation with Robert Lebrun while spending the summer at Grand Isle. Questioning the roles of wife and mother she had previously fulfilled, she takes up painting, gains some financial independence and leaves the family home. After having an affair she again sees Lebrun, but the summons to help her friend Adele Ratignolle in childbirth provokes a crisis. In a last, desperate assertion of independence, she returns to Grand Isle and drowns herself.

Awkward Age, The A novel by HENRY JAMES, serialized in 1898–9 and published in volume form in 1899. It is written almost entirely in dialogue. Its heroine, Nanda Brookenham, is a 'knowing' young woman while her friend, Aggie, is a 'pure' young lady who has been strictly raised by her aunt, the Duchess. The action revolves around their relations with Mr Vanderbank and Mr Mitchett. Nanda loves Mr Vanderbank but, realizing that he does not return her feeling, graciously gives him up. Meanwhile, Mr Mitchett, who had hoped to marry Nanda, instead marries Aggie with the Duchess's encouragement. Nanda retires from the marriage market.

Awoonor, Kofi 1935– Ghanaian. Formerly known as George Awoonor Williams. he writes in both English and Ewe. His main reputation is as a poet who unites Ewe oral tradition with MODERNISM. In his allegorical novel, *This Earth, My Brother . . .* (1972), each chapter is accompanied by a kind of speculative commentary, a technique continued in the mythopoeic *Comes the Voyager At Last* (1992). Awoonor's survey of the history, culture and literature of Africa, *The Breast of the Earth* (1975), is regarded as seminal.

Ayala's Angel A novel by ANTHONY TROLLOPE, published in 1881. A playful, self-mocking book, it concerns two sisters, Ayala and Lucy Dormer. Romantic idealism leads Ayala to reject available suitors for an 'Angel of Light' of her imagination, though she finally discovers this angel in the ugly, fiery-complexioned soldier Jonathan Stubbs. The practical Lucy, despite living in luxury, remains true to the sculptor she loves and is enabled to marry him by the generosity of her uncle, Sir Thomas Tringle. His children, who fare less happily, are the subject of sub-plot.

Aylwin See WATTS-DUNTON, THEODORE.

Ayrshire Legatees, The A novel by JOHN GALT, published in 1820. It takes the form of letters from Dr Zachariah Pringle and his family in London to their friends in Scotland, describing their impressions of the capital and the events of 1820, when George IV succeeded George III.

Azadi A novel by CHAMAN NAHAL, published in 1975 and awarded a SAHITYA AKADEMI prize in 1977. Set during the Partition of India in 1947, it describes the flight of a Hindu grain merchant, Lala Kanshi Ram, and his family from Sialkot (now in Pakistan) to Delhi. The harrowing scenes of violence and terror are narrated partly by the merchant himself and partly by the young Arun, a Hindu in love with a Muslim girl.

B

Babbitt A novel by SINCLAIR LEWIS, published in 1922. It depicts the complacency and materialism of George F. Babbitt, a real-estate agent and representative middle-class family man from the city of Zenith in the American Midwest. He briefly rebels but soon finds the price of nonconformity too great and again resigns himself to the superficial values of his business culture.

Bacon, Sir Francis, 1st Viscount St Albans See *NEW ATLANTIS, THE.*

Bage, Robert 1728–1801 English. As well as running a paper-mill at Elford, near Tamworth, he produced six novels expressing radical views of politics and society: *Mount Henneth* (1781), *Barham Downs* (1784), *The Fair Syrian* (1787), *James Wallace* (1788), *Man As He Is* (1792) and *Hermsprong: or, Man As He is Not* (1796). In the last, Bage's most important work, Hermsprong claims to be an American Indian, and has fixed views on the importance of physical fitness, the corruption of the rich, and the necessity of female education and of equality. At the end he proves to be acceptable in polite society. SIR WALTER SCOTT deplored Bage's political and atheistic tendencies but commended his humour, very much in the vein of LAURENCE STERNE, and his command of dialogue. In his private life, he was, according to Scott, an impeccable exemplar of his beliefs.

Bagnold, Enid 1889–1981 English. Her first success was with a novel, *Serena Blandish* (1925), later dramatized by S. N. Behrman. She herself dramatized a more famous novel, *National Velvet* (1935), about a girl who wins the Grand National; it also became a popular film. *Lottie Dundas* was both a novel (1941) and a play (1943). *The Chalk Garden* (1955), a social comedy, was her last success in the theatre.

Bail, Murray 1941– Australian. Widely regarded as one of the most cosmopolitan of contemporary Australian writers, he frequently adopts a playful, Borgesian stance to take issue with the tradition of realism. His first collection, *Contemporary Portraits* (1975), was reissued as *The Drover's Wife and Other Stories* (1986) in tribute to the fame of its title-piece, ostensibly a response to Russell Drysdale's painting but implicity an ironic rebuttal of the classic story by HENRY LAWSON. His novels include *Homesickness* (1980), about tourism, and *Holden's Performance* (1987), a comic epic about the passage of an innocent through Australian society. Non-fictional works are *Longhand* (1989), a diary of his years in London, and a study of the artist Ian Fairweather (1981). He edited *The Faber Book of Contemporary Australian Short Stories* (1988).

Bailey, H. C. See DETECTIVE FICTION.

Bailey, Hilary 1936– English. She was already known for SCIENCE FICTION before turning to 'serious' fiction with studies of middle-class women in *Polly Put the Kettle On* (1975) and *Mrs Mulvaney* (1978). Subsequent novels adopt and challenge the work of earlier writers: PICARESQUE and DEFOE's *MOLL FLANDERS* in *All the Days of My Life* (1984), BUCHAN's adventure stories in *Hannie Richards, or, the Intrepid Adventures of a Restless Wife* (1985), MARY SHELLEY's *FRANKENSTEIN* in *Frankenstein's Bride* (1995), CHARLOTTE BRONTË's *JANE EYRE* in *Mrs Rochester* (1997) and HENRY JAMES's *THE TURN OF THE SCREW* in *Miles and Flora* (1997). *Cassandra* (1993) and *The Cry from Street to Street* (1994) give a voice to unheeded or unregarded women. *A Stranger to Herself* (1989) deals with the relations between biographers and their subjects.

Bailey, Paul 1937– English. *At the Jerusalem* (1967), the first of his austere and painstaking novels, poignantly depicts old age, a subject he returned to in *Old Soldiers* (1980). *Trespasses* (1971), *A Distant Likeness* (1973) and *Peter Smart's Confessions* (1977) share a preoccupation with madness and neurotic despair. *Gabriel's Lament* (1986), his most substantial work, is a study of bereavement which nevertheless presents a multiplicity of eccentric characters in the manner of DICKENS. *An English Madam* (1982) is an affectionate biography of the brothel-keeper Cynthia Payne and *An Immaculate Mistake* (1990) a wistful memoir of his early life.

Bainbridge, Beryl 1934– English. Works such as *The Dressmaker* (1973), *The Bottle Factory Outing* (1974), *Injury Time* (1977), *Mum and Mrs Armitage* (1985), *Filthy Lucre* (1986) and *An Awfully Big Adventure* (1989), are terse black comedies dealing in menace and grotesque violence. Several novels tackle historical subjects: Hitler's possible stay in Liverpool in *Young Adolf* (1978); a Victorian murder case in *Watson's Apology* (1984); Captain Scott's expedition in *The Birthday Boys* (1991); and the sinking of the Titanic in *Every Man for Himself* (1996; WHITBREAD AWARD). *Something Happened Yesterday* (1993) is a collection of journalism.

Baker, Nicholson 1957– American. *The Mezzanine* (1988), *Room Temperature* (1990) and *U and I* (1991), in which the 'U' is JOHN UPDIKE, are less conventional novels than fantastic speculations on reality and its minute interstices. *Vox* (1992) and *The Fermata* (1993) are explicit in their focus on the comic failures and confusions of human sexuality. *The Size of Thoughts: Essays and Other Lumber* (1996) is a miscellany of reflections that convey Baker's aesthetics and his fascination with minutiae.

Baldwin, James (Arthur) 1924–87 African-American. The promise of his first novel, *Go Tell It on the Mountain* (1953), reflecting his relations with his father, a Harlem preacher, was fulfilled in later work showing him to be a powerful enemy of racism. After *Giovanni's Room* (1956), set in Paris, where he lived, he returned to black America as a setting. *Another Country* (1962) takes place in Harlem. Other fiction includes *Going to Meet the Man* (1965), *Tell Me How Long the Train's Been Gone* (1968), *If Beale Street Could Talk* (1974) and *Just above My Head* (1979). His prolific essays appeared in *Notes of a Native Son* (1955), *Nobody Knows My Name: More Notes of a Native Son* (1961; as *No Name in the Streets* in Britain, 1972), *The Fire Next Time* (1963), *The Devil Finds Work* (1976), *The Evidence of Things Not Seen: An Essay* (1985) and *The Price of the Ticket: Collected Nonfiction, 1948–1985* (1986). His plays are: *Blues for Mr Charlie* (1964), *The Amen Corner* (1965), *One Day, When I was Lost* (1972) and *A Deed from the King of Spain* (produced 1974). *Jimmy's Blues* (1986) is a volume of poetry.

Ballantyne, R(obert) M(ichael) 1825–94 Scottish. His first adventure story for boys, *The Young Fur-Traders* (1856), was based on his experiences working for the Hudson's Bay Company. Many of the more than 80 books he went on to publish draw on firsthand knowledge in the same fashion: three weeks on Bell Rock led to *The Lighthouse* (1865) and a short spell as a London fireman to *Fighting the Flames* (1867). His most famous title, THE CORAL ISLAND (1858), describes how three young friends survive after being shipwrecked. A sequel, *The Gorilla Hunters* (1861), is disturbing in its enthusiasm for slaughtering wild animals. Such elements in Ballantyne's work, and his obtrusive piety, have guaranteed that his immense contemporary popularity should have faded.

Ballard, J(ames) G(raham) 1930– English. Novels such as *The Drowned World* (1962), *The Drought* (1965) and *The Crystal World* (1966), and the short stories in *The Four-Dimensional Nightmare* (1963) and *The Terminal Beach* (1964), are avant-garde SCIENCE FICTION, anticipating the more extreme experimentalism of *The Atrocity Exhibition* (1970), a collection of 'fragmented novels', and *Crash* (1973), belatedly made into an equally controversial film. Ballard's use of exotic and derelict landscapes to mirror the abnormal psychology of his characters continued in *Running Wild* (1988) and *Rushing to Paradise* (1994). However, he is now best known for the semi-autobiographical realism of *EMPIRE OF THE SUN* (1984), drawing on his boyhood experience of a Japanese internment camp in Shanghai during World War II, and its sequel, *The Kindness of Women* (1991), set in post-war Britain.

Banim, John 1798–1842 Irish. He collaborated with his elder brother MICHAEL BANIM on *Tales by the O'Hara Family* (1825–7). His tragedy *Damon and Pythias* was produced at Covent Garden in 1821, and his satirical essays, *Revelations of the Dead Alive*, appeared in 1824.

Banim, Michael 1796–1874 Irish. He collaborated with his younger brother JOHN BANIM in *Tales by the O'Hara Family* (1825–7). *The Croppy* (1828) is a novel set in the Irish rebellion of 1798; other fiction includes *Father Connell* (1842) and *The Town of the Cascades* (1864).

Banks, Iain (Menzies) 1954– Scottish. *The Wasp Factory* (1984) is a gruesome Gothic fantasy about a maladjusted adolescent who visits unspeakable horrors on his young relatives and the surrounding wildlife. Subsequent novels include colourful horror thrillers such as *Walking on Glass* (1985) and scientific fantasies (published as Iain M. Banks) such as *Consider Phlebas* (1987) and *The Player of Games* (1988). *Against a Dark Background* (1993), *Feersum Endjinn* (1994), *Whit* (1995), *Excursion* (1996) and *The Song of Stone* (1997), about an unnamed country ravaged by civil war, are equally diverse.

Banks, Russell 1940– American. His fiction portrays the working class and the disenfranchised in a society increasingly given over to materialism and consumerism. It includes: *Searching for Survivors* (1975); *Family Life* (1975); *Hamilton Stark* (1978); *The Book of Jamaica* (1980), based in part on his experience of the Caribbean; *Trailerpark* (1981), stories set in New England; *The Relation of My Imprisonment* (1983); *Continental Drift* (1985), about an out-of-work plumber's encounter with Haitian exiles; *Success Stories* (1986); *Affliction* (1989); *The Sweet Hereafter* (1991), about the effects of a school bus accident on a small town; and *Rule of the Bone* (1995).

Banville, John 1945– Irish. His novels are notable for their quizzical, burnished prose and their fabulous inhabitation of historical worlds. *Birchwood* (1974), a quirky variation on the Irish country-house narrative, has been followed by a loose tetralogy of novels essaying the fictional biography of pre-eminent scientific figures: *Doctor Copernicus* (1976), *Kepler* (1981), *The Newton Letter* (1982) and *Mefisto* (1987). *The Book of Evidence* (1989), a psychological thriller often acclaimed as his most substantial work, forms the first part of a thematic trilogy completed by *Ghosts* (1993) and *Athena* (1995). *The Untouchable* (1997) is about an art historian whose career recalls that of Anthony Blunt. *Long Lankin* (1970) is a collection of short stories.

Barchester Towers The second of ANTHONY TROLLOPE'S BARSETSHIRE NOVELS, published in 1857.

When the Bishop of Barchester dies the fall of the Conservative ministry means that he is succeeded not by his son, Archdeacon Grantly, but by the timeserving Dr Proudie, who arrives with his Low Church wife and evangelical chaplain Obadiah Slope. Battle is joined between them and Grantly's traditionalists. Mrs Proudie wants to appoint Quiverful to the wardenship of Hiram's Hospital but Slope, attracted to the newly widowed Eleanor Bold, supports the reappointment of her father Mr Harding. However, Slope becomes infatuated with the crippled Signora Neroni, daughter of Dr Vesey Stanhope, falls out with Mrs Proudie and is dismissed by the Bishop. Quiverful is appointed to the wardenship. Eleanor rejects both Slope and the charming wastrel Bertie Stanhope for the shy Francis Arabin, Dr Grantly's High Church champion, who becomes Dean of Barchester.

Barfoot, Joan 1946– Canadian. *Abra* (1978; reissued in Britain as *Gaining Ground*, 1980), *Dancing in the Dark* (1982), *Duet for Three* (1985) and *Family News* (1990) are women-centred fictions which present female protagonists isolated by choice, insanity or old age from defining social contexts.

Baring, Maurice 1874–1945 English. Closely associated with HILAIRE BELLOC and G. K. CHESTERTON, he published over 50 books. Of his fiction, the works most often remembered are: *Passing By* (1921), his first novel; *C* (1924), *Cat's Cradle* (1925) and *The Coat Without Seam* (1929), BILDUNGSROMANEN whose protagonists move among the cosmopolitan élite into which Baring himself had been born; and a novella, *The Lonely Lady of Dulwich* (1934). Two historical tales, *Robert Peckham* (1930) and *In My End is My Beginning* (1931), show the influence of Roman Catholicism, to which he became a convert. His plays include *The Black Prince* (1902) and *Diminutive Dramas* (1911). His experience as a diplomat and journalist in Moscow is reflected in several works on Russian literature, which helped to introduce the works of Chekhov. *The Puppet Show of Memory* (1922) is an autobiography.

Baring-Gould, Sabine 1834–1924 English. He was rector of Lewtrenchard in Devon for the last 40 years of his life. His first novel, *Through Fire and Flame* (1868), was based on his own marriage to a mill girl the previous year. It was followed by over 30 more, usually romantic in tone and melodramatic in plotting but with strongly realized rural settings, often in Devon. Contemporaries greatly admired *Mehalah* (1880), which takes place on the Essex salt marshes. Baring-Gould's non-fiction included several volumes of *The Lives of the Saints* (1872–7), a biography of the poet and clergyman R. S. Hawker (1876), and books about travel, folklore and West Country legend. 'Onward Christian Soldiers' is the most famous of his many hymns.

Barker, A(udrey) L(illian) 1918– English. She has been particularly admired for the short stories, seemingly disparate but thematically linked, in volumes such as *Innocents: Variations on a Theme* (1947), *Femina Real* (1971) and *Life Stories* (1981). *Innocents* was the first winner of the SOMERSET MAUGHAM AWARD. *Life Stories*

unsettlingly juxtaposes elements from her previous fiction with fragments of autobiography. Barker won a wider readership with her eighth novel, *The Gooseboy* (1987), showing her fascination and empathy with the young. She has continued to explore the serious games fiction can play in *The Woman Who Talked to Herself: An Articulated Novel* (1989), collapsing the boundaries between novel, fantasy and reality, and *Zeph* (1992), presenting the innermost thoughts of a young heroine bent on becoming 'the unintelligent woman's IRIS MURDOCH'.

Barker, Clive 1952– English. He has followed the graphic short horror stories collected in six volumes of *Books of Blood* (1984–5) with long novels which juxtapose horror and fantasy. They include *Weaveworld* (1987), *The Great and Secret Show* (1990), *Imajica* (1991) and *Everville* (1994). *The Thief of Always* (1992) is a fantasy for children. The most notable of his film scripts is for *Hellraiser* (1987), which he also directed.

Barker, Pat 1943– English. The linked stories of *Union Street* (1982) concentrate on working-class women, while *Blow Your House Down* (1984) depicts women in a northern town where a serial killer is at large. Masculinity gone bad also provides the theme of *The Man Who wasn't There* (1989). Barker's sense of history has informed *The Century's Daughter* (1986), surveying the 20th century through one woman's experience, and her most substantial achievement to date, the 'Regeneration' trilogy consisting of *Regeneration* (1991), *The Eye in the Door* (1993) and *The Ghost Road* (1995; BOOKER PRIZE). This account of World War I weaves together fictional characters and real-life figures such as the poets Siegfried Sassoon, Wilfred Owen and Robert Graves.

Barnaby Rudge A novel by CHARLES DICKENS, published in *MASTER HUMPHREY'S CLOCK* in 1841. It is set during the Gordon or 'No Popery' riots (1780), which provide the most vivid episodes in what is otherwise generally regarded as one of Dickens's least successful works. It is certainly less carefully conceived than *A TALE OF TWO CITIES*, his later venture into HISTORICAL FICTION.

Part of the plot derives from the unsolved murder of Reuben Haredale 20 years earlier. The villain is finally identified as his former steward, Mr Rudge. He is hanged and his son Barnaby, a half-crazed youth unwittingly drawn into the riots, only narrowly escapes the gallows. Another strand of the action concerns the hostility between Reuben's brother Geoffrey and the villainous Mr (later Sir John) Chester, who are nevertheless agreed in opposing a match between Chester's son Edward and Geoffrey's niece, Emma. Chester dies in a duel with Geoffrey. A rich cast of characters also includes: the beguiling Dolly Varden, her father Gabriel and suitor Joe Willet, and Joe's obstinate old father John; the ludicrous Simon Tappertit; and Dennis, the despicable hangman.

Barnes, Djuna 1892–1982 American. Her best-known work is the novel *Nightwood* (1936), about the relationships of a group of expatriates in Paris and Berlin. Other works include: *The Book of Repulsive Women* (1915), a collection of poems; *A Book* (1923), stories and plays, the stories revised and reissued as *A Night among the Horses* (1929) and later still as *Spillway* (1972); *Ryder* (1929), a satiric chronicle of family history; *Ladies' Almanack* (1929), a celebration of lesbian life and love; and *The Antiphon* (1958), a blank-verse tragedy about family history.

Barnes, Julian 1946– English. *Metroland* (1981) and *Before She Met Me* (1982) combine flamboyant wit with a psychological sensitivity recalling Flaubert, the oblique subject of *Flaubert's Parrot* (1984), a highly original mixture of biography, speculation and fantasy. *Staring at the Sun* (1986) and the more elegantly accomplished *A History of the World in 10½ Chapters* (1989) are comparably heterogeneous, ranging through history and diverse literary modes. *Talking It Over* (1991) returns to a realistic idiom, and *The Porcupine* (1992) is a novella about a political trial in a former Soviet satellite country. *Cross Channel* (1996) is a collection of short stories. As Dan Kavanagh, he has also written exuberantly low-life thrillers about Nick Duffy, an ex-policeman turned private eye.

Barnes, Linda See DETECTIVE FICTION.

Barren Ground A novel by ELLEN GLASGOW, published in 1925. Dorinda Oakley struggles with the unpropitious conditions of her life, working first in Nathan Pedlar's store and then in New York before returning to her native Virginia to restore the 'barren ground' of her father's farm. Her success is contrasted with the 'barren ground' of her marriage to Nathan Pedlar and her finally disillusioned love for Jason Greylock, whom she shelters out of kindness after her husband's death. She nurtures other people's children but has none of her own.

Barrie, Sir J(ames) M(atthew) 1860–1937 Scottish. He described the early encouragement he received from his mother in an admiring biography of her, *Margaret Ogilvy* (1896). His native Kirriemuir appears as 'Thrums' in a series of homely stories and novels which identified Barrie with the KAILYARD SCHOOL: *Auld Licht Idylls* (1888), *A Window in Thrums* (1889) and *The Little Minister* (1891). Subsequent work included *Sentimental Tommy* (1896) and *Tommy and Grizel* (1900). Theatrical recognition came with a dramatization of *The Little Minister* in 1897, *Quality Street* and *The Admirable Crichton* in 1902, and his overwhelming triumph, *Peter Pan*, in 1904. A story, *Peter Pan in Kensington*, appeared in 1906. It is unfortunate that Barrie has become so identified with Peter Pan. He was too ready to resort to cloying fantasy, as he did

again in plays such as *Dear Brutus* (1917) and *Mary Rose* (1920), but there is a shrewd feeling for the theatre in *What Every Woman Knows* (1908), the single completed act of *Shall We Join the Ladies?* (1921) and the excellent one-act comedy *The Twelve-Pound Look* (1910).

Barry Lyndon A novel by WILLIAM MAKEPEACE THACKERAY, serialized as *The Luck of Barry Lyndon* in 1844 and revised and reprinted as *The Memoirs of Barry Lyndon* in 1852. The boastful autobiography of an 18th-century Irish adventurer, it is a sustained exercise in the use of the unreliable narrator and makes a notable contribution to rogue literature (see PICARESQUE) – though, significantly, Thackeray thought it necessary to tone these aspects of the book down when he revised it.

Born Redmond Barry, the hero fights a duel, escapes to Dublin and changes his name to Barry Redmond. He serves as a soldier on both sides in the Seven Years War, eventually meeting his uncle, Cornelius Barry, who as the Chevalier de Balibari joins him in cardsharping. He marries the wealthy Countess of Lyndon, changes his name to Barry Lyndon and embarks on a career of cruelty and extravagance. With the death of his son Bryan in a riding accident, Barry's luck starts to run out, and after Lady Lyndon's death he ends his life in the Fleet prison, tended by his faithful old mother.

Barsetshire Novels, The A sequence of novels by ANTHONY TROLLOPE, set in the fictional West Country county of Barsetshire, or Barset, and particularly the cathedral city of Barchester, whose clergy are the main characters. It consists of *THE WARDEN* (1855), *BARCHESTER TOWERS* (1857), *DOCTOR THORNE* (1858), *FRAMLEY PARSONAGE* (1860–1), *THE SMALL HOUSE AT ALLINGTON* (1862–4) and *THE LAST CHRONICLE OF BARSET* (1866–7). Barchester itself owes something to both Winchester and Salisbury, but the terrain Trollope created bears none of the close resemblance to real geography that THOMAS HARDY's WESSEX does.

Barstow, Stan(ley) 1928– English. He probably remains best known for his first novel, *A Kind of Loving* (1960), an example of the northern working-class realism also developed by JOHN BRAINE and ALAN SILLITOE. Barstow has stayed largely faithful to northern subjects and settings in his stories and novels, which include two trilogies. One, retrospectively called *The Vic Brown Trilogy* (1981), grew from *A Kind of Loving* and was completed by *Watchers on the Shore* (1966) and *The Right True End* (1976); the second, about a family's fate during World War II, consists of *Just You Wait and See* (1986), *B-Movie* (1987) and *Give Us This Day* (1989). His adaptations include WINIFRED HOLTBY's *South Riding* for TV (1974) and Ibsen's *An Enemy of the People* for the stage (1978).

Barth, John (Simmons) 1930– American. *The*

Floating Opera (1956), about a nihilist contemplating suicide, is informed by the sense of the absurd which has coloured all his work. Other fiction, fluent in pastiche and helping to establish POST-MODERNISM by its narrative contingency, includes: *The End of the Road* (1958); *The Sot-Weed Factor* (1960), playing with American colonial history and the conventions of 18th-century fiction; *Giles Goat-Boy: or, The Revised New Syllabus* (1966), a gargantuan CAMPUS NOVEL; *Lost in the Funhouse* (1968); *Chimera* (1972); *LETTERS* (1979); *Sabbatical* (1982); *The Tidewater Tales* (1987); *The Last Voyage of Somebody the Sailor* (1991); and *Once Upon a Time: A Floating Opera* (1994).

Barthelme, Donald 1931–89 American. His novels, notably *Snow White* (1967) and *The Dead Father* (1975), are deliberately fragmented narratives made up of word games and allusions to literature and popular culture. His collections of stories – *Come Back, Dr Caligari* (1964), *Unspeakable Practices, Unnatural Acts* (1968), *City Life* (1970), *Guilty Pleasures* (1974) and *Amateurs* (1976) – also pursue a satiric commentary on contemporary American life and language.

Bartleby the Scrivener See PIAZZA TALES, THE.

Bartlett, Neil 1958– English. He had already established himself as an actor and playwright before publishing his first book, *Who Was That Man? A Present for Mr Oscar Wilde* (1988). It combines fiction and recollection to examine the continuing presence of OSCAR WILDE – as fact and as myth – in the lives of homosexual men. He has further explored gay themes in *Ready to Catch Him Should He Fall* (1990) and *Mr Clive and Mr Page* (1996), linking the Chicago of the 1880s and the death of Rock Hudson from AIDS in 1985.

Bates, H(erbert) E(rnest) 1905–74 English. His work is often set in the countryside of his native Midlands. *The Woman Who Had Imagination* (1934), *My Uncle Silas* (1939), *Colonel Julian* (1951), *The Daffodil Sky* (1955) and *The Enchantress* (1961) are among his outstanding collections of stories. Wartime experience in the RAF prompted his best-known novel, *Fair Stood the Wind for France* (1944), about a bomber crew shot down in occupied France. *The Darling Buds of May* (1958), *A Breath of French Air* (1959), *Hark, Hark, the Lark* (originally called *When the Green Woods Laugh*, 1960), *Oh! To Be in England* (1963) and *A Little of What You Fancy* (1970) are a popular series of novels about the hedonistic Larkin family and their Edenic life in Kent.

Battle of Life, The A Christmas story by CHARLES DICKENS, published in 1846 and collected in *CHRISTMAS BOOKS* (1852). It follows the fortunes of Dr Anthony Jeddler, who regards the world as 'a gigantic practical joke', and his daughters, Grace and Marion. Into the girls' lives come Alfred Heathfield, an honest young medical student, and Michael Warden, a wastrel who

reforms. Lesser figures – the lawyer Snitchey, the sour Benjamin Britain ('Little Britain') and the worthy Clemency Newcombe – round off a brisk, expressive tale.

Baumgartner's Bombay A novel by ANITA DESAI, published in 1988. The hero is a German Jew who flees Nazi persecution in the 1930s and arrives in India, where, after six years' internment as an enemy alien, he tries to build a new life. He remains marginal, however, living largely for his collection of stray cats. Ironically, he meets his nemesis attempting to help a young drop-out, Kurt, his compatriot and thus a product of the very culture which had persecuted him.

Bawden, Nina 1925– English. Novels for children such as *The Witch's Daughter* (1966), the highly successful *Carrie's War* (1973) and *Keeping Henry* (1988) show good-humoured understanding of the child's point of view. Her adult fiction provides a consistently incisive analysis of life among the upper middle classes. *The Birds in the Trees* (1969) is about a tormented adolescent; *Anna Apparent* (1972) and *Familiar Passions* (1979) explore illegitimacy and adoption. *Circles of Deceit* (1987) was shortlisted for the BOOKER PRIZE. *In My Own Time* (1994) is her autobiography.

Baynton, Barbara 1857–1929 Australian. Although she also published a novel, *Human Toll* (1907), her reputation rests on the stories in *Bush Studies* (1902). While not without humour, they present the bush as a harsh, inimical environment, in contrast to the robust nationalism of A. B. PATERSON and even the equivocal attitudes which characterize many of HENRY LAWSON's stories. Stories such as 'Squeaker's Mate' and 'The Chosen Vessel' vividly dramatize the plight of bush women, frequently regarding them as victims of both malevolent nature and male brutality.

Beardsley, Aubrey (Vincent) 1872–98 English. His sensuous black-and-white drawings created a visual style for the 1890s. Art editor of *The Yellow Book* in 1894–5, he illustrated OSCAR WILDE's *Salome*, Alexander Pope's *The Rape of the Lock* and Ben Jonson's *Volpone*. A censored version of his erotic novel, *The Story of Venus and Tannhauser*, originally appeared in *The Yellow Book* as *Under the Hill*; it was privately printed in an unexpurgated edition in 1907.

Beats, The A group of American poets and novelists centred in San Francisco and New York City in the latter half of the 1950s. The term 'beat', first used in JOHN CLELLON HOLMES's novel, *Go* (1952), has been variously interpreted as meaning 'beaten down' and 'beatific'. The Beats despised middle-class values, commercialism and conformity, and sought visionary states through religious meditation, sex, jazz and drugs. The group included JACK KEROUAC, WILLIAM S. BURROUGHS, Allen Ginsberg,

Gregory Corso, Gary Snyder and Lawrence Ferlinghetti.

Beattie, Ann 1947– American. Often associated with the 'minimalist' school of RAYMOND CARVER and others, she depicts the domestic lives and psychological complexities of contemporary Americans in spare detail and with subtle touches of black humour. Collections of stories include *Distortions* (1976), *Secrets and Surprises* (1978), *The Burning House* (1982), *Where You'll Find Me* (1986) and *What Was Mine* (1991). *Chilly Scenes of Winter* (1976), *Falling in Place* (1980), *Love Always* (1985), *Picturing Will* (1989), *Another You* (1995) and *My Life, Starring Dara Falcon* (1997) are novels. She has also written a study of the artist Alex Katz (1987).

Beauchamp's Career A novel by GEORGE MEREDITH, serialized in 1874–5 and published in volume form in 1876. It portrays the political life, tracing Nevil Beauchamp's career from his early commission in the navy through his attempt to stand for Parliament after the Crimean War. At first torn between a married Frenchwoman, Renée de Croisnel, and Cecilia Halkett, he marries the ward of his Radical friend Dr Shrapnel. He drowns trying to rescue a child from the sea.

Beautyful Ones are Not Yet Born, The A novel by AYI KWEI ARMAH, published in 1969. The title is taken from a slogan on a Ghanaian bus. A bitter indictment of Nkrumah's post-colonial betrayal of Ghana's independence, the novel is set in Accra, where physical filth adumbrates the moral corruption of the ruling class. The anonymous hero, the Man, is a modern urbanized African whose integrity is scorned by his family and his wife's relations.

Beckett, Samuel (Barclay) 1906–89 Irish. As a young man he left Dublin for Paris, where he became JAMES JOYCE's associate and assistant. He usually wrote in French and translated himself into English. Early work, including the novel *Murphy* (1938), made little impact on its first publication and his fame (which won him the Nobel Prize for Literature in 1969) rests almost entirely on his writings after 1950.

Beckett's major novels, the French 'trilogy' *Molloy* (1951; translated 1955), *Malone meurt* (1951; *Malone Dies*, 1956) and *L'Innommable* (1953; *The Unnameable*, 1958) and the English *Watt* (1953), exist in and through their narrators: social misfits, old and ill, embarked on a quest for the explanation of 'I'. The difficult *Comment c'est* (*How It Is*, 1961) is insistently aural, while the short prose fictions that followed replace the puzzled subjectivity of the novels with a bleak objectivity which still finds room for unexpectedly spry humour. They include: *Stories and Texts for Nothing* (1967); *Mercier and Camier* (1974); the trilogy (later published as *Nohow On*, 1989) formed by *Company* (1980), *Ill Seen Ill Said* (1981) and *Worstward Ho* (1983); and *Stirrings Still* (1988), a meditation on ageing.

Beckett is probably more widely known for his plays, above all for *Waiting for Godot* (produced in French in 1953, in English in 1955), which identified him as a leading exponent of the Theatre of the Absurd. Three full-length works, *Godot*, *Endgame* (produced in French in 1957, in English in 1958) and *Happy Days* (1961) are all concerned with human suffering, survival and immobility. The shorter, but still substantial, *Krapp's Last Tape* (1958) and *Play* (1963) seek to identify moments in the characters' past when something actually happened, as does the radio play *All That Fall* (1957). In the fragmentary *Breath* (1970) the image is all we have. The mysterious *Come and Go* (1966), a 'dramaticule', does not allow the audience to hear the whispers that may explain the patterned movements of its three female characters. In *Not I* (1972) and *Footfalls* (1976) stage lighting dictates what the audience sees (a mouth and feet respectively) as the spoken words reverberate.

Beckford, William 1759–1844 English. A compulsive builder and collector, he reconstructed his Wiltshire mansion as an elaborate Gothic fantasy, Fonthill Abbey, substantially complete in 1809 but abandoned after the fall of its immense tower in 1825. His travel book *Dreams, Waking Thoughts and Incidents* (1783) was revised and reissued as the first volume of *Italy, with Sketches of Spain and Portugal* (1834). Beckford's fantastic story *VATHEK* was written in French and published in an English translation in 1786. Two pseudonymous burlesques, *Modern Novel Writing: or, the Elegant Enthusiast* (1796) and *Azemia* (1797), were followed by another travel book, *Recollections of an Excursion to the Monasteries of Alcobaça and Batalha* (1835).

Bede, Cuthbert [Bradley, Edward] 1827–89 English. His comic account of undergraduate life, *The Adventures of Mr Verdant Green, an Oxford Freshman* (1853–6), enjoyed great popularity in its day. Bradley had not attended Oxford, however: he was among the early graduates from University College, Durham.

Bedford, Sybille 1911– The child of an aristocratic German father and an Anglo-Jewish mother, she spent much of her youth on the Continent. Her reputation rests on a handful of books – *A Legacy* (1956), *A Favourite of the Gods* (1962), *A Compass Error* (1968) and *Jigsaw* (1989), part fiction and part autobiography – which evoke, in sombre and menacing fashion, the Kaiser's Germany and the inter-war years as lived by the European aristocracy. Her non-fiction, frequently preoccupied with crime, justice and punishment, includes: *The Best We Can Do* (1958), about the trial of Dr John Bodkin Adams; *The Faces of Justice* (1961), about judicial procedure; and *As It Was* (1990). She also wrote ALDOUS HUXLEY's official biography (1973–4).

Beeding, Francis See SPY FICTION.

Beerbohm, Sir **(Henry) Max(imilian)** 1872–1956

English. A precociously poised figure in the decadent literary world of the 1890s, he began by publishing caricatures in *The Strand Magazine* and essays in *The Yellow Book*, the latter facetiously gathered as *The Works of Max Beerbohm* (1896). He succeeded GEORGE BERNARD SHAW as dramatic critic of *The Saturday Review* in 1898. Three works best epitomize his sunny and gentle wit: *ZULEIKA DOBSON* (1911), his only novel; *A Christmas Garland* (1912), containing parodies of HENRY JAMES, JOSEPH CONRAD, H. G. WELLS and ARNOLD BENNETT, among others; and *Seven Men* (1919), which includes a spoof of Decadent poetry in 'Enoch Soames' and of portentous historical drama in 'Savonarola Brown'. *The Poets' Corner* (1904), a collection of cartoons, wryly comments on major writers. In later years Beerbohm became a noted broadcaster.

Behn, Aphra 1640–89 English. Probably the first Englishwoman to see herself as a professional writer, she led an adventurous life, although our knowledge of its details is unreliable. A childhood in the West Indies apparently suggested the setting for her best prose romance, *OROONOKO*, published *c.* 1678 and included in *Three Histories* (1688). Imprisoned for debt in the late 1660s, she turned to writing plays after her release. Her early work was in what contemporaries took to be the style of Beaumont and Fletcher. Even the more distinguished comedies – *The Town Fop* (1676), *The Rover* (1677), *Sir Patient Fancy* (1678), *The Second Part of the Rover* (1681) and *The Lucky Chance* (1686) – are derivative, while a political piece *The City Heiress* (1682) borrows from Thomas Middleton's *A Mad World, My Masters*. The farce *The Emperor of the Moon* (1687), based on the Italian *commedia dell'arte*, helped make popular the harlequinade, forerunner of the English pantomime.

Belchamber See STURGIS, HOWARD.

Bell, Currer, Ellis and Acton Pseudonyms of CHARLOTTE, EMILY and ANNE BRONTË.

Bell, Neil See SCIENCE FICTION.

Bellamy, Edward 1850–98 American. He was working as a journalist when he wrote *LOOKING BACKWARD: 2000–1887* (1888), an immensely popular Utopian romance. In *The New Nation*, a journal he founded in 1891, and in *Equality* (1897), a sequel to *Looking Backward*, he developed and disseminated his political ideas – notably a government programme of strict state capitalism, resulting in non-revolutionary socialist reform. Bellamy clubs and a Nationalist party were founded in support. Earlier, less political writings include *The Duke of Stockbridge* (1879), about Shay's Rebellion, and *Dr Heidenhoff's Process* (1880) and *Miss Ludington's Sister* (1884), novels dealing with psychic phenomena in the tradition of NATHANIEL HAWTHORNE. *The Blind Man's World and Other Stories* (1898) was published just before his death.

Belloc, (Joseph) Hilaire (Pierre René) 1870–1953 Born in France of a French father and English mother, he became a British citizen in 1902. His close friendship with G. K. CHESTERTON was based on common beliefs and interests; their anti-Imperial, pro-Boer stance made GEORGE BERNARD SHAW nickname them the 'Chesterbelloc'. As well as a serious advocate of his beliefs, Belloc was also an industrious hack whose writing covered many genres. His poetry, in particular the darkly comic verses for children in *The Bad Child's Book of Beasts* (1896) and *Cautionary Tales* (1907), has found a permanent niche. His travel books, particularly *The Path to Rome* (1902), *The Old Road* (1904), *The Pyrenees* (1909) and *The Cruise of the Nona* (1925), deserve to be better remembered. His fiction is slight and his interest in the form almost non-existent. *Emmanel Burden, Merchant* (1904), *Mr Clutterbuck's Election* (1908) and *A Change in the Cabinet* (1909) are hasty satires directed at the machinations of international financiers and of politicians. *The Girondin* (1911) is set during the French Revolution. *The Green Overcoat* (1912) is a fable. Belloc also recorded his disillusionment with party politics in *The Party System* (with Cecil Chesterton, 1911) and *The Servile State* (1912), as well as publishing collections of essays and some lively and partisan works of history.

Bellow, Saul 1915– American. *Dangling Man* (1944) and *The Victim* (1947) were followed by the exuberant PICARESQUE of *THE ADVENTURES OF AUGIE MARCH* (1953), *Seize the Day* (1956) and *Henderson the Rain King* (1959), about a middle-aged American's travails in Africa. *HERZOG* (1964) and *Humboldt's Gift* (1975; PULITZER PRIZE), his most widely admired novels, best exemplify his reputation for interpreting the struggles of contemporary city dwellers to define their roles and responsibilities. His other fiction includes the novels *Mr Sammler's Planet* (1970), *The Dean's December* (1982), *More Die of Heartbreak* (1987) and *The Bellarosa Connection* (1989), the novellas *A Theft* (1989) and *The Actual* (1997), and several collections of shorter work: *Mosby's Memoirs and Other Stories* (1968), *Him with His Foot in His Mouth and Other Short Stories* (1984) and *Something to Remember Me By* (1993). He has also written essays, plays and non-fiction which includes *The Future of the Moor* (1970), *To Jerusalem and Back: A Personal Account* (1976) and *It All Adds Up: From the Dim Past to the Uncertain Future* (1994). He received the Nobel Prize for Literature in 1976.

Beloved A novel by TONI MORRISON, published in 1987 and awarded a PULITZER PRIZE. The story is told in a series of flashbacks and reminiscences about a slave woman, Sethe, who escapes with her husband and three children from a Kentucky plantation. After her husband deserts her, she sends the children ahead to Ohio and gives birth to another along her journey.

Eighteen years later another former slave from her plantation, Paul D, arrives at her home as well as a malevolent apparition which Sethe believes to be her dead daughter. By turns DETECTIVE FICTION, ghost story and family narrative, the novel examines the legacy of slavery in the consciousness of those who survived it.

Belton Estate, The A novel by ANTHONY TROLLOPE, serialized in 1865-6 and published in volume form in 1866. Although not rated highly by Trollope himself, it is of some interest for its characteristically sympathetic exploration of the plight of the single, dependent woman. Clara Amedroz, daughter of the squire of Belton Castle, at first refuses her cousin Will Belton, heir to the estate, but eventually accepts him after becoming disillusioned with the lukewarm Captain Aylmer.

Ben-Hur: A Tale of the Christ A historical novel by LEW WALLACE, published in 1880. After years of unmerited suffering as a galley slave, Judah Ben-Hur returns to Judaea, a free man and Roman officer. At the chariot races in Caesarea he defeats Messala, who had made false accusations against him. He rescues his mother and sister, now lepers, and with them witnesses the Crucifixion. Ben-Hur recognizes Christ as a man who had shown him compassion while he was a slave. Christ's passing cures the lepers. Ben-Hur and his family become Christians.

Benchley, Peter See GENRE FICTION.

Benchley, Robert (Charles) 1889-1945 American. Theatre critic for The New Yorker in 1929-40, he also wrote humorous sketches about the daily lives of ordinary people. They were collected in Of All Things (1921), Love Conquers All (1922), Pluck and Luck (1925), The Early Worm (1927), 20,000 Leagues Under The Sea: or, David Copperfield (1928), The Treasurer's Report (1930), My Ten Years in a Quandary (1936), After 1903 What? (1938), Inside Benchley (1942) and Benchley Beside Himself (1943). He frequently appeared in films and on the radio.

Benét, Stephen Vincent 1898-1943 American. He is best known for John Brown's Body (1928; PULITZER PRIZE), a collection of verse about the Civil War. Western Star (1943) deals with American roots in 17th-century European migrations. His career as a novelist started with a college story, The Beginning of Wisdom (1921), and continued with Young People's Pride (1922), Jean Huguenot (1923), Spanish Bayonet (1926) and James Shore's Daughter (1934). These books were less well regarded than the short stories found in, for example, Thirteen O'Clock (1937) and Tales Before Midnight (1939); the former collection includes the popular 'The Devil and Daniel Webster', which was made into an opera and a film. His radio scripts were collected in We Stand United (1945).

Benito Cereno See PIAZZA TALES, THE.

Bennett, (Enoch) Arnold 1867-1931 English. Deeply influenced by French REALISM, and to a lesser extent by NATURALISM, he found his most congenial subject in his native Potteries (or Five Towns), in novels such as ANNA OF THE FIVE TOWNS (1902) and the two works widely regarded as his greatest achievement, THE OLD WIVES' TALE (1908) and CLAYHANGER (1910), as well as the stories in Tales of the Five Towns (1905) and The Grim Smile of the Five Towns (1907). The fortunes of the Clayhanger family are followed further in Hilda Lessways (1911), These Twain (1916) and The Roll Call (1918). His preoccupation with the rich and the worldly is apparent in lesser novels such as The Grand Babylon Hotel (1902), The Card (1911), Mr Prohack (1922), Lord Raingo (1926) and Imperial Palace (1930). RICEYMAN STEPS (1923; JAMES TAIT BLACK MEMORIAL PRIZE), in which he again considered the lives of ordinary and undistinguished people, greatly enhanced his reputation.

Milestones (with Edward Knoblock, 1912) was the most successful of his plays. Also a busy working journalist for much of his career, he contributed an influential series on 'Books and Persons' to Lord Beaverbrook's Evening Standard from 1926 until his death. His three-volume Journal (1932-3), inspired by the example of the Goncourt brothers, was begun in 1896.

Benson, E(dward) F(rederic) 1867-1940 English. He wrote some 93 books, the most popular being his comic novels about Dodo (Dodo, Dodo the Second and Dodo Wonder, 1914-21) and Lucia, starting with Queen Lucia (1920) and Lucia in London (1927). He also published five volumes of personal and family reminiscences (1911-40). His elder brother was A. C. Benson, a prolific writer remembered for contributing the words of 'Land of Hope and Glory' to Elgar's music.

Bentley, E(dmund) C(lerihew) 1875-1956 English. He earned a minor place in literary history by inventing the comic verse form known as the clerihew, after the middle name he used as the pseudonym for his first collection, Biography for Beginners (1905). Trent's Last Case (1903) was meant as an exposure of DETECTIVE FICTION but was quickly hailed as a classic of the genre. Bentley revived his artist-detective in Trent's Own Case (with H. Warner Allen; 1936) and a collection of short stories, Trent Intervenes (1938). Elephant's Work: An Enigma (1950) is a thriller. More enduring than these works is 'Greedy Night' (1939), a wickedly accurate parody of DOROTHY L. SAYERS.

Bentley, Phyllis 1894-1977 English. Born and brought up in the West Riding of Yorkshire, she drew on her mother's family recollections for her best-known novel, Inheritance (1932), which chronicles the lives of families involved in the textile industry. Her other work includes The World's Bane (1918), a volume of four allegorical stories influenced by OLIVE SCHREINER, Cat-in-the-Manger (1918), The Spinner of the Years (1928),

The Partnership (1928) and several studies of the BRONTË sisters.

Beresford, J. D. See SCIENCE FICTION.

Berger, John 1926– English. His preoccupation with the nature and possibilities of individual freedom is expressed in several novels: *A Painter of Our Time* (1958), about an artist's career; *Corker's Freedom* (1964), about the hero's attempt to break free of suburbia; and *G* (1972; BOOKER PRIZE), which mixes narrative, reflection, political treatise and historical reconstruction in pursuing the fortunes of its ambiguous central figure. *Into Their Labours*, a trilogy consisting of *Pig Earth* (1979), *Once in Europa* (1989) and *Lilac and Flag* (1991), is about modern peasant life in the French Jura; it combines fiction, poetry and reportage. *To the Wedding* appeared in 1995. His interest in photography has led to collaborations with Jean Mohr in *A Fortunate Man* (1967) and *Another Way of Telling* (1982). Art criticism, influenced by Marxism, includes *Permanent Red* (1960), *Ways of Seeing* (1972), *The White Bird* (1985) and *Keeping a Rendezvous* (1991).

Berger, Thomas (Louis) 1924– American. His fiction examines the disjunction between appearance and essence; his characters search for immutable truth and a secure place in the world. The Reinhart tetralogy – *Crazy in Berlin* (1958), *Reinhart in Love* (1962), *Vital Parts* (1970), and *Reinhart's Women* (1981) – is a tour of post-World War II American culture. Berger reinvents classic fictional forms in *Little Big Man* (1964), his most famous book, and *Regiment of Women* (1973), *Arthur Rex* (1978) and *Orrie's Story* (1990). *Who is Teddy Villanova?* (1977) and its sequel, *Nowhere* (1985), *Neighbors* (1980), *The Feud* (1983) and *The Houseguest* (1988) are comedies. Other novels include *Killing Time* (1967), *Sneaky People* (1975), *Being Invisible* (1987), *Changing the Past* (1989), *Meeting Evil* (1992), *Robert Crews* (1994) and *Suspects* (1996).

Bernières, Louis de See DE BERNIÈRES, LOUIS.

Berridge, Elizabeth 1921– English. Critics have praised her work for its poised style, its uncomfortably acute observation tempered by compassion and its undertow of wit and laughter. Her short stories have been gathered in *Selected Stories* (1947) and *Family Matters* (1980). Her fiction stretches from *House of Defence* (1945) to *People at Play* (1982). Particularly notable are *Upon Several Occasions* (1953), about village life during wartime, and three novels dealing with the struggles of their heroines, *Rose Under Glass* (1961), *Across the Common* (1964) and *Sing Me Who You Are* (1967).

Bertrams, The A novel by ANTHONY TROLLOPE, published in 1859. Although Trollope considered the plot 'more than ordinarily bad', the novel is redeemed by his unconventional handling of the hero and heroine, George Bertram and Caroline Waddington, as disenchantment overtakes their initial high hopes. They meet and fall in love in the Holy Land but break off their engagement after it has dragged on for three years. Her marriage to Sir Henry Harcourt, the Solicitor-General, fails and he commits suicide. In due course Caroline and George are reconciled and marry.

Besant, Sir Walter 1836–1901 English. His early novels, of which *Ready Money Mortiboy* (1872) and *The Golden Butterfly* (1876) were the most popular, were collaborations with James Rice. His own later HISTORICAL FICTION was less widely read than two realistic works, *All Sorts and Conditions of Men* (1882) and *Children of Gibeon* (1886), which exposed conditions in the East End of London. His Royal Institution lecture of 1884 on the status of the novel provoked HENRY JAMES's famous reply, 'The Art of Fiction'. In 1890 he completed *Blind Love*, the novel WILKIE COLLINS had left incomplete when he died. Besant also planned and inaugurated a great 10-volume topographical survey of London, which appeared after his death under the names of other editors (1902–12).

Bester, Alfred See SCIENCE FICTION.

Betrothed, The See SCOTT, SIR WALTER.

Between the Acts VIRGINIA WOOLF's last novel, published posthumously in 1941.

Pointz Hall, an English country house owned by the ageing Bartholomew Oliver and his widowed sister, Lucy Swithin, is also home to their nephew, Giles Oliver, a stockbroker, and his wife, Isa, whose poetic inner thoughts are rendered in STREAM OF CONSCIOUSNESS and correspond to the metaphorical impulse which underlies the main action. This centres on the performance of a village pageant during a June afternoon in 1939 in the grounds of Pointz Hall. It is directed by Miss La Trobe, a lesbian artist whose creative aspirations are continually thwarted by reality. The pageant itself, a fragmentary re-enactment of English history, occupies the bulk of the novel. The intention is apparently to celebrate the lasting values in English country life and to indict the present for its shallow pretensions. The imminent threat of annihilation in World War II is a recurrent background theme.

Bhattacharya, Bhabani 1906–88 Indian. A trained historian who began his literary career writing children's stories in Bengali and translating RABINDRANATH TAGORE, he won international acclaim with *So Many Hungers* (1947), a novel set during the 1943 Bengal famine. Four of five subsequent novels, including *He Who Rides a Tiger* (1954) and *Shadow from Ladakh* (1966; awarded a SAHITYA AKADEMI prize in 1967), deal with the problems of the emerging Indian nation.

Bible in Spain, The GEORGE BORROW's colourful narrative of his travels through Portugal and Spain, published in 1843. Ostensibly an account of his five years' service (1835–40) as an agent of the British and Foreign Bible Society, it describes adventures in remote regions, encounters with gypsies and bandits and frequent confrontations with authority. The reader has no means of distinguishing between fact and fiction. The book was a best-seller on both sides of the Atlantic and was never out of print during the 19th century.

Bierce, Ambrose (Gwinnett) 1842–c.1914 American. As a journalist in San Francisco he contributed to the *Overland Monthly* and became an influential member of the Western literary circle which originally included BRET HARTE, MARK TWAIN and Joaquin Miller. A prolific writer, he is chiefly remembered for *IN THE MIDST OF LIFE* (1891; originally entitled *Tales of Soldiers and Civilians*), a volume of short stories drawn largely from his own disillusioning experiences during the Civil War. *The Cynic's Word Book* (1906) is a volume of ironic definitions. A solitary and discontented man, Bierce disappeared in Mexico during its Civil War; it is not known exactly when or how he died.

Big Money, The See *USA*.

Bildungsroman A 'novel of development', tracing the protagonist's growth, usually from birth or early childhood, into adulthood and maturity. The prototype is Goethe's *Wilhelm Meister's Apprenticeship* (1795–6), translated into English by Thomas Carlyle in 1824. Goethe's novel expressed the interest in childhood which characterized Romanticism, and the particular value which Romantics had attached to childhood since Jean-Jacques Rousseau. Later *Bildungsromanen* would show the impact of subsequent theories of childhood, notably those of Freud and modern psychology. Even an incomplete list of major examples in English fiction suggests how important a part the form has played: DICKENS's *DAVID COPPERFIELD* and *GREAT EXPECTATIONS*, THACKERAY's *PENDENNIS*, SAMUEL BUTLER's *THE WAY OF ALL FLESH*, D. H. LAWRENCE's *SONS AND LOVERS*, JOYCE's *PORTRAIT OF THE ARTIST AS A YOUNG MAN* and E. M. FORSTER's *THE LONGEST JOURNEY*. Most of these works contain a strong element of autobiography and several focus on the development of the artistic sensibility: Joyce's title, with or without a change of gender, could still do duty for many contemporary novels, particularly first novels. American fiction, from MARK TWAIN's *HUCKLEBERRY FINN* to J. D. SALINGER's *THE CATCHER IN THE RYE*, has often avoided the full-scale *Bildungsroman* to concentrate instead on a particular rite of passage or initiation in the hero's youth.

Billy Biswas, The Strange Case of A novel by ARUN JOSHI, published in 1971. Increasingly alienated from his Indian upper-middle-class environment and dimly aware of powerful forces inside him, Billy deserts an anthropological expedition to join a primitive tribe. The efforts of his family and his friend Romi to find him end ironically when he is accidentally shot by the police.

Billy Budd, Sailor A short novel by HERMAN MELVILLE, begun in 1886 and left in a semi-final draft at his death in 1891. It was first published in 1924. It is set aboard HMS *Bellipotent* in 1797, following the naval mutinies during the war between England and France. Billy Budd, the 'Handsome Sailor', is impressed from a merchantman and quickly becomes a favourite of the crew. But he also arouses the hostility of the brutal master-at-arms, John Claggart, who falsely accuses him of being involved in a mutinous plot. Unable to answer the charge because of a chronic stammer, Billy strikes Claggart and kills him. Captain Vere, though sympathizing with the agonized Billy, calls a drumhead court and in effect instructs it to find him guilty of a capital crime. Billy is hanged from the yard-arm after crying out, 'God bless Captain Vere!'

Binding Vine, The A novel by SHASHI DESHPANDE, published in 1992. It begins with the discovery by the protagonist, Urmila, of diaries and poetry left by her mother-in-law, Mira, at her death some thirty years before. They hint at harrowing experiences of marital rape. The hospital where Urmila works admits a destitute young woman with severe injuries, the result of a far more brutal rape. The two events complement the theme of male brutality which runs through the book.

Bingham, John See SPY FICTION.

Bird, Robert (Montgomery) 1806–54 American novelist. *Nick of the Woods: or, The Jibbenainosay* (1837) is a novel about a bloodthirsty Quaker and ignoble Indians, set at the end of the American Revolution. Other novels include *Calavar: or, the Knight of the Conquest* (1834) and its sequel, *The Infidel: or, The Fall of Mexico* (1835), *The Hawks of Hawk-Hollow* (1835), about a well-to-do Pennsylvania family's fatal lack of patriotism, and *Sheppard Lee* (1836), a satire on contemporary society informed by Bird's Whig politics. His work for the stage includes historical dramas and romantic plays about Philadelphia life.

Birdsell, Sandra 1942– Canadian. Her first volume of stories, *Night Travellers* (1982), a linked sequence set in a small Manitoba town and concentrating on a particular family, is reminiscent of ALICE MUNRO's *LIVES OF GIRLS AND WOMEN*. *Ladies of the House* (1984) includes stories set in both rural environments and Winnipeg. The two collections have been published together as *The Agassiz Stories* (1987). In her novels, *The Missing Child* (1987) and *The Chrome Suite* (1992), dangerous undercurrents lurk beneath the apparently calm surface of small-town life.

Birmingham, George A. [Hannay, James Owen] 1865–1950 Irish. Originally a Church of Ireland clergyman, he settled in England in 1924. Early novels such as *Hyacinth* (1906) and *The Bad Times* (1908) are serious, compassionate explorations of recent Irish history. The more light-hearted *Spanish Gold* (1908) won him a large popular audience, but he unintentionally offended Roman Catholic and extreme nationalist sensibilities with *The Seething Pot* (1905), *Red Hand of Ulster* (1912) and a stage comedy, *General John Regan* (1913). His later books are chiefly well-observed light comedies of Irish (and English) life.

Bissoondath, Neil 1955– A nephew of V. S. NAIPAUL, he left his native Trinidad for Canada in 1973. He has published two volumes of short stories, *Digging Up the Mountains* (1985) and *On the Eve of Uncertain Tomorrows* (1990), and the novels, *A Casual Brutality* (1988) and *The Innocence of Age* (1992). His fiction revolves around three pivotal points: India, the fictional Caribbean island of Casaquemada and Canada. They are as much psychic possibilities for his characters as physical locations, though Bissoondath is a master of realized social detail. *Selling Illusions* (1994) is a controversial critique of Canadian multicultural policy.

Black, William 1841–98 Scottish. He is best remembered for his novels with a Scottish setting, such as *A Daughter of Heth* (1871), *A Princess of Thule* (1874) and *Macleod of Dare* (1878). *The Strange Adventures of a Phaeton* (1872) combines elements of fiction, romance, guidebook and natural description. Black contributed a study of OLIVER GOLDSMITH (1878) to the English Men of Letters series.

Black Arrow, The A novel by ROBERT LOUIS STEVENSON, serialized in 1883 and published in book form in 1888. Stevenson himself ridiculed it as a pseudo-historic pot-boiler.

It is set in late 15th-century England, during the final stages of the Wars of the Roses. The diffuse plot has three main strands: the first concerns the conflict between Yorkists and Lancastrians, the second the Brotherhood of the Black Arrow, an outlaw band led by 'John Amend-All' (Ellis Duckworth), and the third Richard Shelton, Joanna Sedley, and their relations with his deceitful uncle and guardian, Sir Daniel Brackley. The book ends with Dick and Joanna's marriage and his retreat into private life, abandoning the 'heroism' which the novel has exposed as self-seeking and treacherous.

Black Beauty A novel for children by ANNA SEWELL, published in 1877. It charts the decline and fall of a well-bred horse brought low by neglectful grooms and overwork in the cab trade. He also suffers sadly from the hated 'bearing rein', a harness designed to keep a horse's head up; the novel's protest helped to end this practice. Black Beauty himself is finally saved from the knacker's yard to enjoy an honourable retirement. Less fortunate is his high-spirited friend in harness, Ginger, who dies ignobly in the streets of London.

Black Dwarf, The See SCOTT, SIR WALTER.

Blackmore, R(ichard) D(oddridge) 1825–1900 English. Called to the Bar in 1852, he preferred instead to divide his time between writing and market gardening. His earliest published works were poems and translations but he gained his first real success, and lasting fame, with *LORNA DOONE* (1869), HISTORICAL FICTION set on Exmoor. Other books, all overshadowed by the popularity of *Lorna Doone*, include *Clara Vaughan* (1864), *Alice Lorraine* (1875), *Cripps the Carrier* (1877), *Christowell: A Dartmoor Tale* (1881) and *Springhaven: A Tale of the Great War* (1887), set in southern England during the Napoleonic era.

Blackwood, (Lady) Caroline (Maureen) 1931–96 English. Her fiction plays on the macabre, the exotic and often the cruel and terrifying. *The Stepdaughter* (1976), an EPISTOLARY NOVEL, was followed by: *Great Granny Webster* (1977), about the clash between ancestral splendour and present need; *The Fate of Mary Rose* (1981), about the effect of a child's murder on a village community; and *Corrigan* (1984), about seemingly unforgiveable deception. Of her non-fiction, *On the Perimeter* (1984) deals with her visits to Greenham Common and *In the Pink* (1987) takes swipes at both fox-hunters and hunt saboteurs. *The Last of the Duchess* (1995), her biography of Wallis Simpson, was sadly mutilated by the lawyers.

Blais, Marie-Claire See FRENCH-CANADIAN NOVEL.

Blaise, Clark 1940– Of Canadian parentage, he was born in the USA and lived in Canada for many years. His short-story collections, *A North American Education* (1973) and *Tribal Justice* (1974), and his novels, *Lunar Attractions* (1979) and *Lusts* (1983), focus on the often victimized outsider, the isolated individual struggling to find a place in an increasingly bizarre contemporary society. *Resident Alien* (1986) combines autobiographical essays and autobiographical fiction. He has collaborated with his wife, the novelist Bharati Mukherjee, on *Days and Nights in Calcutta* (1977), an account of a stay in India, as well as publishing a further short-story collection, *Man and His World* (1992) and a 'post-modern autobiography', *I Had a Father* (1993).

Blake, Nicholas See DAY-LEWIS, C.

Blatty, William Peter See GENRE FICTION.

Bleak House A novel by CHARLES DICKENS, published in monthly parts in 1852–3 and in volume form in 1853.

An indictment of the Court of Chancery and its endless bungling of the case of Jarndyce v. Jarndyce gives the novel its scope and meaning. In one main plot Esther Summerson (who narrates much of the story) becomes protégée of John Jarndyce, also guardian of two wards of Chancery, Ada Clare and Richard Carstone. Ada and Richard marry but he dies worn out after enmeshing himself in the Jarndyce lawsuit. Another plot concerns Sir Leicester Dedlock and his proud wife, whose guilty past – an affair with Captain Hawdon which produced Esther – is unravelled by the calculating lawyer Tulkinghorn. Before he can expose her, Tulkinghorn is murdered by her waiting woman Mademoiselle Hortense, who is brought to book by Inspector Bucket. Lady Dedlock dies at the graveyard where the Captain lies. Esther eventually marries the surgeon Allan Woodcourt.

Other characters who contribute to the complex portrait of society include: the selfish Harold Skimpole (modelled on Leigh Hunt) and the boisterous Boythorn (modelled on Walter Savage Landor); Krook, who dies by 'Spontaneous Combustion'; Gridley and Miss Flite, ruined by Chancery; Mrs Jellyby, exponent of 'Telescopic Philanthropy'; the greasy Mr Chadband; the grasping Smallweeds; and the lawyers Conversation Kenge and Mr Vholes. The brutish life and death of Jo the crossing-sweeper is central to the moral design of the novel.

Blessington, Marguerite, Countess of 1789–1849 English. One of the most colourful figures of the Regency, she was a literary hostess, the companion of Count d'Orsay and the friend of Byron, whom she remembered in her *Journal of Conversations with Lord Byron* (1832). She published it because of her pressing need for money after the Earl of Blessington's death in 1829, and continued to support herself by contributions to periodicals, annuals and magazines, and by travel books such as *The Idler in Italy* (1839) and *The Idler in France* (1841). She also turned to fiction, usually preferring the SILVER-FORK NOVEL or the tale of Irish life; examples include *Grace Cassidy* (1833), *The Confessions of an Elderly Gentleman* (1836), *The Victims of Society* (1837), *The Governess* (1839), *The Lottery of Life* (1842), *Strathern* (1845) and *Country Quarters* (1850).

Blish, James See SCIENCE FICTION.

Blithedale Romance, The A novel by NATHANIEL HAWTHORNE, published in 1852. It is partly based on his observation of the Transcendentalist experiment at Brook Farm and of the writer Margaret Fuller (1810–50), whom he portrays as Zenobia.

The narrator, Miles Coverdale, goes to the Utopian community of Blithedale, where he meets Zenobia, Hollingsworth and Priscilla. Zenobia, an exotic feminist, loves the egotistic Hollingsworth, who wants to make Blithedale an institution for criminal reform. Priscilla has escaped from the control of the evil Westervelt. Fearing competition for Hollingsworth from Priscilla, Zenobia delivers her back to Westervelt, but Hollingsworth intervenes to save the girl. It emerges that she is Zenobia's half-sister and will receive the inheritance Zenobia thought was hers. Hollingsworth has chosen her because he needs the money to realize his plans. Zenobia drowns herself. Hollingsworth and Priscilla marry but he is a broken man. Coverdale lapses back into a lonely bachelor's life, explaining that all along he has been in love with Priscilla.

Blixen, Karen See DINESEN, ISAK.

Bloomsbury Group, The The name given to a group of British writers, artists and intellectuals who began meeting in about 1905 at the Bloomsbury house of the Stephen sisters, Vanessa Bell and VIRGINIA WOOLF. It grew to include Clive Bell, DAVID GARNETT, Duncan Grant, Maynard Keynes, Desmond MacCarthy, Adrian and Thoby Stephen, Lytton Strachey, Saxon Sydney-Turner, LEONARD WOOLF and, peripherally, E. M. FORSTER. Strachey's death in 1932 and Virginia Woolf's suicide in 1941 can both be seen as ends of an era.

Although its members denied being a group in any formal sense, they were united in an abiding belief in the importance of the arts. Their philosophy can perhaps best be summarized in G. E. Moore's statement that 'one's prime objects in life were love, the creation and enjoyment of aesthetic experience and the pursuit of knowledge'. They were sceptical and tolerant, reacting against the artistic and social restraints of Victorian society. Through writing (biography, novels, art criticism, economics, political theory), painting (in the works of Vanessa Bell and Duncan Grant), publishing and support of new developments in the arts, they exercised a considerable influence on the *avant-garde* of the early 20th century.

Blyton, Enid (Mary) 1897–1968 English. She was a prodigiously energetic children's writer. Her 'Famous Five' adventures, appearing from 1942, feature a gang of well-born, privately educated children who solve various mysteries during their largely unsupervised vacations. Little Noddy and Big Ears, introduced after the war, are humanized toys enjoying mild adventures in a bland, domestic setting. Critics have questioned the effect of Blyton's limited literary style on young children and pointed to her racist and snobbish attitudes, but without destroying her popularity, which continues even today.

Boldrewood, Rolf [Browne, Thomas Alexander] 1826–1915 Australian. His family emigrated from London to Sydney in 1830. His best-known novel, *Robbery under Arms* (serial, 1881; volume, 1888), is a racy tale, with authentic scenes and dialogue, about an infamous bush-ranger, Captain Starlight. It soon established itself as a classic adventure story. Of some 17 other novels the most popular were *The Miner's Right* (1890), *A Colonial Reformer* (1890) and *The Squatter's Dream* (1890), first published in 1878 as *Ups and Downs of Australian Life*.

Bone People, The A novel by KERI HULME, published in 1984. After winning the NEW ZEALAND BOOK AWARD in 1984 and then the BOOKER PRIZE in 1985 it became internationally the best-known New Zealand novel. It centres on the white foundling Simon, his adoptive Maori father Joe, and their friend Kerewin. The style combines the mandarin with the colloquial, and the story juxtaposes myth with harrowingly realistic violence. A theme of wounding and healing holds together the personal relationships and also suggests the possibility of national reconciliation.

Some commentators have found the range of reference, from Maori mythology to J. R. R. TOLKIEN and Sufi, too rich or just confusing. Others applaud the use of Maori spirituality as a controlling motif and hail the book as an instance of 'the Empire writing back', reinventing English literature and transforming its language to assert an indigenous cultural identity.

Bonfire of the Vanities, The A novel by TOM WOLFE, heavily revised after its serialization in *Rolling Stone* magazine in 1984–5 and published between hard covers in 1987. It describes the fall – and eventually redemption – of Sherman McCoy, WASP, Wall Street bond salesman and, as he believes, 'master of the universe'. His ordeal starts when he and his mistress Maria Ruskin accidentally take a wrong turn into the blighted landscape of the Bronx. A traffic accident exposes McCoy to the New York criminal justice system and the media, destroying the certainties of his life. The moral stance underlying Wolfe's satire of the fragmentation of urban society in the USA is indicated by the title, which refers to the symbolic annual purge of vice and corruption organized by Savonarola in late 15th-century Florence.

Bontemps, Arna (Wendell) 1902–73 African-American. *Black Thunder* (1936) and *Drums at Dusk* (1939) are novels about slave revolts in Virginia and in Haiti. *God Sends Sunday* (1931) was dramatized by Countee Cullen as *St Louis Woman* (1946). The children's books he wrote with JACK CONROY include *Sam Patch* (1951). His non-fiction includes *They Seek a City* (with Conroy; 1945), *The Story of the Negro* (1948) and *100 Years of Negro Freedom* (1961).

Booker Prize An annual award open to new novels by British and Commonwealth writers, inaugurated in 1969 and now the most widely known literary prize in Britain. It is administered by the Book Trust (formerly the National Book League) and sponsored by the multinational conglomerate Booker McConnell. Winners have been: P. H. NEWBY, *Something to Answer For* (1969); BERNICE RUBENS, *The Elected Member* (1970); V. S. NAIPAUL, *In a Free State* (1971); JOHN BERGER, *G* (1972); J. G. FARRELL, *The Siege of Krishnapur* (1973); NADINE GORDIMER, *THE CONSERVATIONIST* with STANLEY MIDDLETON,

Holiday (1974); RUTH PRAWER JHABVALA, *Heat and Dust* (1975); DAVID STOREY, *Saville* (1976); PAUL SCOTT, *Staying On* (1977); IRIS MURDOCH, *The Sea, The Sea* (1978); PENELOPE FITZGERALD, *Offshore* (1979); WILLIAM GOLDING, *Rites of Passage* (1980); SALMAN RUSHDIE, *MIDNIGHT'S CHILDREN* (1981); THOMAS KENEALLY, *SCHINDLER'S ARK* (1982); J. M. COETZEE, *LIFE AND TIMES OF MICHAEL K* (1983); ANITA BROOKNER, *Hôtel du Lac* (1984); KERI HULME, *THE BONE PEOPLE* (1985); KINGSLEY AMIS, *The Old Devils* (1986); PENELOPE LIVELY, *Moon Tiger* (1987); PETER CAREY, *OSCAR AND LUCINDA* (1988); KAZUO ISHIGURO, *The Remains of the Day* (1989); A. S. BYATT, *Possession* (1990); BEN OKRI, *The Famished Road* (1991); BARRY UNSWORTH, *Sacred Hunger* with MICHAEL ONDAATJE, *THE ENGLISH PATIENT* (1992); RODDY DOYLE, *Paddy Clarke Ha Ha Ha* (1993); JAMES KELMAN, *How Late It Was, How Late* (1994); PAT BARKER, *The Ghost Road* (1995); GRAHAM SWIFT, *Last Orders* (1996); and Arundhati Roy, *The God of Small Things* (1997). In 1993 *Midnight's Children* was voted the 'Booker of Bookers'.

Borrow, George (Henry) 1803–81 English. The son of a recruiting officer in the militia, he spent most of his childhood moving around Britain and had only three or four years of formal schooling. Nevertheless, he acquired an intimate knowledge of gypsy life and fluency in at least 12 languages, including Latin, Greek, French, Welsh, Irish, Italian, German, Danish and Dutch; he later added Portuguese, Russian, Arabic and Spanish. In 1824–32 he divided his life between Norwich and London, where he tried to establish himself as a writer with a translation of *Faustus: His Life, Death, and Descent into Hell* (1825), hackwork such as a six-volume edition of *The Newgate Calendar* (1826), and *Romantic Ballads, Translated from the Danish* (1826). His linguistic proficiency commended him to the British and Foreign Bible Society, for which he worked in St Petersburg (1833–5) and in Portugal and Spain (1835–40), where he supervised the printing and distribution of the New Testament in Spanish and Basque. His experiences gave imaginative substance to the two books which made him famous: *The Zincali* (1841) and *THE BIBLE IN SPAIN* (1843).

After his marriage in 1840 Borrow lived on his wife's estate at Oulton, Norfolk, albeit with long periods in Yarmouth (1853–60) and London (1860–?70). During this period he wrote the three works on which his reputation chiefly depends: *LAVENGRO* (1851), *THE ROMANY RYE* (1857) and *Wild Wales* (1857). Though he declined to provide the literal autobiography he at one time promised, these works, especially the first two, for many years enjoyed the status of established classics, simultaneously delighting and puzzling the reader with a racy, convincing, but impenetrable amalgam of fact and fiction. He spent his later years in further forays into translation (a second edition of his *Gypsy Luke*) and philology (*Romano Lavo-Lil*), at the same time consolidating his reputation as a traveller by walking tours through Norfolk, Wales, Ireland and Scotland.

Bosman, Herman Charles 1905–51 South African. His reputation rests especially on *Mafeking Road* (1947), *Unto Dust* (1963), *Jurie Steyn's Post Office* (1971) and *A Bekkersdal Marathon* (1971), collections of stories about rural Afrikaner life, told with sardonic detachment, shrewd observation and folk comedy. Bosman spent several years in prison for killing his stepbrother; *Cold Stone Jug* (1949) recounts his experience with humour and pathos. *A Cask of Jerepigo* (1957) gathers essays and sketches. *Jacaranda in the Night* (1947) and *Willemsdorp* (1977) are novels. *Collected Works* (2 vols) appeared in 1981.

Bostonians, The A novel by HENRY JAMES, serialized in 1885–6 and published in volume form in 1886. A satirical study of the movement for female emancipation in New England, it recounts the story of Basil Ransom, a young Southern lawyer who comes to Boston on business. He meets his cousins, the widowed Mrs Luna, who falls in love with him, and the feminist Olive Chancellor. At a suffragette meeting both Olive and Basil are struck by a beautiful young speaker, Verena Tarrant. Olive sets out to make her a leader of the feminist cause, pleading with her to forswear the thought of marriage, but Basil falls in love with her. Forced to choose between Olive and Basil, Verena finally accepts Basil's proposal.

Bowen, Elizabeth (Dorothea Cole) 1899–1973 Born in Dublin, she lived in Ireland, France, Italy and London. Volumes of stories, notable for their subtle use of language, include *Encounters* (1923), *Ann Lee's* (1926), *Joining Charles* (1929), *The Cat Jumps* (1934), *Look at All Those Roses* (1941) and *The Demon Lover* (1945). Her *Collected Stories*, introduced by ANGUS WILSON, appeared in 1980. Early novels included *The Hotel* (1927), *The Last September* (1929), *Friends and Relations* (1931) and *The House in Paris* (1935). Best known, however, are THE DEATH OF THE HEART (1938), a sensitive study of the adolescent Portia Quayne, and *The Heat of the Day* (1949), a tragic love-story set in war-time London. Later novels were *A World of Love* (1955) and *Eva Trout* (1969). Her writing follows HENRY JAMES in its attention to style and its subtle delineation of character (especially female character) and setting. Her impressionistic descriptions of the landscape, both urban and rural, and its seasonal changes add a highly effective dimension to her work. She also wrote *Seven Winters* (1942), a partial autobiography, and *Bowen's Court* (1942), a history of the family seat in Dublin which she inherited.

Bowering, George 1935– Canadian. His early

poetry, strongly influenced by the Black Mountain school, includes *Points on the Grid* (1964), *Baseball* (1967), *Rocky Mountain Foot* (1968) and *The Gangs of Kosmos* (1969). Later works include *In the Flesh* (1974) and *Another Mount* (1979) and several book-length poems: *George, Vancouver* (1970) and *Autobiology* (1972), collected in *The Catch* (1976) and *West Window* (1982). His most acclaimed novel, *Burning Water* (1980), is a deconstructionist account of Vancouver's search for the Northwest Passage. *Caprice* (1987) and *Harry's Fragments* (1990) adopt a playful stance towards narrative conventions. *Shoot!* (1994) is about a gang of outlaws which operated in the interior of British Columbia in the late 19th century. *Flycatcher* (1974), *Protective Footwear* (1978), *A Place to Die* (1983) and *The Rain Barrel* (1994) are collections of short stories. His critical books include *A Way with Words* (1982) and *Imaginary Hand* (1988).

Bowles, Paul 1910– American. While living in Paris he wrote music and music criticism before publishing his first novel, *The Sheltering Sky* (1949). *The Delicate Prey* (1950; called *A Little Stone* in Britain), *Let It Come Down* (1952) and *The Spider's House* (1955) further explore the lives of spiritually weary Westerners in the Orient. Resident in Tangier since 1952, he has tape-recorded and translated several original accounts of indigenous life. His short stories are found in *Pages from Cold Point and Other Stories* (1968), *Collected Stories* (1979), *Midnight Mass* (1985), *Call at Corazón* (1988) and *A Thousand Days for Mokhtar* (1989). Other work includes travel sketches, poetry, letters and autobiography in *Without Stopping* (1972) and two volumes of journals, *Two Years beside the Strait* (1990) and *Days: A Tangier Journal, 1987–89* (1991).

Box, Edgar See VIDAL, GORE.

Boyd, Martin (A'Beckett) 1893–1969 Australian. Born in Lucerne (Switzerland) and brought up in Melbourne, Boyd divided his time between Australia and Europe. *The Montforts* (1928), one of the early novels he published under the pseudonym of Martin Mills, is a dense but elegant and ironic family chronicle of Anglo-Australian life. Its preoccupations recur in much of his best work, which includes *Lucinda Brayford* (1946), *Such Pleasure* (1949), *The Cardboard Crown* (1952), *A Difficult Young Man* (1955), *Outbreak of Love* (1957) and *When Blackbirds Sing* (1962).

Boyd, William 1952– English. A fluent and good-humoured writer, he has used Africa, his childhood home, as the setting for several works. *A Good Man in Africa* (1981), a winner of both the WHITBREAD AWARD for First Novel and a SOMERSET MAUGHAM AWARD, chronicles the misadventures of the lecherous Morgan Leafy. *An Ice-Cream War* (1982) deals with an obscure African interstice of World War I, while *Brazzaville Beach* (1990) tells a sober tale of a female animal behaviourist observing chimpanzees. Leafy reappears in a collection of short stories, *On the Yankee Station* (1981). *Stars and Bars* (1984) is a more predictable comedy about an Englishman in the USA. *The New Confessions* (1987), his most substantial book, is an energetic fictive history of the 20th century. Recent work has included *The Blue Afternoon* (1993), a novel, and *The Destiny of Natalie X and Other Stories* (1995).

Boyle, Kay 1903–93 American. Resident in Europe for many years, she was a foreign correspondent for *The New Yorker* in 1946–54. Her fiction often deals with young and unworldly Americans abroad. It includes *Year before Last* (1932), *My Next Bride* (1934), *Monday Night* (1938), *The Crazy Hunter: Three Short Novels* (1940), *Avalanche* (1944) and *A Frenchman Must Die* (1946). Collections of short stories include *Short Stories* (1929), *Wedding Day and Other Stories* (1930), *The First Lover and Other Stories* (1936), *The White Horse of Vienna and Other Stories* (1936) and *Thirty Stories* (1946).

Boyle, T(homas) Coraghessan 1948– American. *Water Music* (1981) and *Budding Prospects: A Pastoral* (1984) introduced readers to the love of bizarre incident and outlandish humour which identify his fiction with POST-MODERNISM. In *World's End* (1987), his greatest critical and popular success, the lessons of history are unlearned and repeated over ten generations in the Hudson River Valley. Subsequent novels are *East is East* (1990), a Japanese man's attempts to locate his American father, *The Road to Wellville* (1993), about the Kellogg cereal founder, and *The Tortilla Curtain* (1996), about illegal Mexican immigrants in California. His short fiction has been gathered in *The Descent of Man* (1979), *Greasy Lake and Other Stories* (1985) and *If the River Was Whiskey* (1990).

Boz The early pseudonym of CHARLES DICKENS.

Bracebridge Hall: or, The Humorists: A Medley A book of 49 tales and sketches by WASHINGTON IRVING, published in 1822 under the pseudonym, Geoffrey Crayon, Gent., which he had also used for its predecessor, *THE SKETCH BOOK*. Though the collection uses English, French and Spanish settings, the best-remembered tales, 'Dolph Heylinger' and 'The Storm-Ship', are set in America.

Bracewell, Michael 1958– English. He began with a novella, *The Crypto-Amnesia Club* (1988), about an institution bearing a suspicious resemblance to the Groucho Club. The dreams, absurdities and underlying despair of many of its characters, and of the London they inhabit, recur in subsequent work: *Divine Concepts of Physical Beauty* (1989), about the web of love and desire enmeshing a man and three women; *Conclave* (1992), an almost indecently prompt indictment of the 1980s and one of its fallen idols; and *Saint Rachel* (1995), a bleak but compassionate portrait of London's drug culture.

Brackenridge, Hugh Henry 1748–1816 American. Born in Scotland, he was taken to Pennsylvania by his family when he was five. At Princeton University he collaborated with the poet Philip Freneau on *Father Bembo's Pilgrimage to Mecca* (1770), a prose satire on American manners, and a patriotic poem, *The Rising Glory of America* (1772), which he followed with several patriotic works during the Revolutionary War. A distinguished lawyer who ended his career on the Pennsylvania Supreme Court, he acted as a mediator during the Whiskey Rebellion provoked by Alexander Hamilton's excise tax on liquor, describing it in *Incidents of the Insurrection in the Western Parts of Pennsylvania, in the Year 1794* (1795). As founder of *The Pittsburgh Gazette* (1786), the first Western newspaper, he frequently contributed satires on Eastern and Western manners and on Federalist and Republican politics. His literary reputation rests on MODERN CHIVALRY, a seven-volume satirical novel he published in instalments between 1792 and 1815.

Bradbury, Malcolm (Stanley) 1932– English. *Eating People is Wrong* (1959) and *Stepping Westward* (1965) follow the example of the CAMPUS NOVEL set by *LUCKY JIM*. *The History Man* (1975), with its bitter portrait of a sociology lecturer, was hailed as the definitive fictional response to 1960s culture. *Rates of Exchange* (1982) continues the preoccupation with academic life, though its whimsical self-consciousness anticipates *Cuts* (1987), a novella, and *Dr Criminale* (1992), a novel. In 1970–95 Bradbury was professor of American Studies at the University of East Anglia, where with ANGUS WILSON he presided over Britain's only notable university course in creative writing. His academic publications include: *Possibilities* (1973), a collection of essays on contemporary fiction; *The Modern American Novel* (1983); and *Dangerous Pilgrimages: Trans-Atlantic Mythologies* (1995), a study of Anglo-American literary and historical relations.

Bradbury, Ray (Douglas) 1920– American. His early work was mainly SCIENCE FICTION. He made his reputation with *The Martian Chronicles* (1950; called *The Silver Locusts* in Britain), about the conquest and colonization of Mars. *Fahrenheit 451* (1953) is set in a future when the written word is forbidden. Among his other works are *Something Wicked This Way Comes* (1962), a novel, and many short-story collections: *The Illustrated Man* (1951), *The Golden Apples of the Sun* (1953), *The October Sky* (1955), *A Medicine for Melancholy* (1959; called *The Day It Rained Forever* in Britain), *The Machineries of Joy* (1964), *I Sing the Body Electric!* (1969), *The Last Circus and the Electrocution* (1980) and *A Memory of Murder* (1984). His poetry is collected in *The Complete Poems of Ray Bradbury* (1982). *Death is a Lonely Business* (1985), *A Graveyard for Lunatics* (1990) and *Green Shadows, White Whale* (1992) are non-fantastic novels.

Braddon, Mary Elizabeth 1835–1915 English. She lived with John Maxwell, a magazine publisher, for 14 years before the death of his wife allowed them to marry. LADY AUDLEY'S SECRET (1862), her first published work, became the most popular SENSATION NOVEL of the day. Its success overshadowed the rest of a long and hard-working career in which she produced some 80 novels. Some were in the same vein as *Lady Audley's Secret*: *Aurora Floyd* (1863), *John Marchmont's Legacy* (1863), *Henry Dunbar: The Story of an Outcast* (1864), *Sir Jasper's Tenant* (1865), *Birds of Prey* (1867) and *Charlotte's Inheritance* (1868). Others demonstrate a greater range and seriousness: *The Doctor's Wife* (1864) adapts Flaubert's *Madame Bovary*; *The Lady's Mile* (1866) and *The Lovels of Arden* (1871) are novels of society; *Vixen* (1871) is a satire; *Ishmael* (1884) is a historical romance; and *Dead Love Has Chains* (1907) is a tragedy.

Bradford, Barbara Taylor See GENRE FICTION.

Brady, Joan 1939– Born in the USA, she lives in Britain. Since *The Impostor* (1979), her first novel, she has published: *Theory of War* (1993; WHITBREAD AWARD), her most ambitious work, based on the life of her paternal grandfather, sold into slavery at the age of four; *Death Comes for Peter Pan* (1995), about a mortal illness and its impact on the dying man's wife; and a novella, *God on a Harley: A Spiritual Fable* (1996). Her autobiography, *The Unmaking of a Dancer* (1982), was revised as *Prologue: An Unconventional Life* (1994).

Bragg, Melvyn 1939– English. The principal achievement of his broadcasting career has been the creation of a distinguished television arts programme, *The South Bank Show*. As a novelist, he is unashamedly provincial, usually returning to his native Cumbria for the settings of works which range from *The Hired Man* (1969), sober and emotionally exact, to the breathless *A Time to Dance* (1990). *The Silken Net* (1974) is a sensitive study of a woman's inter-war life and *The Maid of Buttermere* (1987) an ingenious treatment of an episode from Lake District history. *Credo* (1996) explores the formative tensions of Celtic Christianity.

Braine, John 1922–86 English. He is best known for his first novel, *Room at the Top* (1957), a classic product of the ANGRY YOUNG MEN generation. Set against a sharp picture of Northern life, the unscrupulous and opportunistic hero, Joe Lampton, chooses wealth and success rather than true love. A sequel, *Life at the Top*, appeared in 1962. None of Braine's other novels attracted comparable attention.

Brautigan, Richard 1935–84 American. A leading exponent of radical values in the 1960s, he is usually remembered for *Trout Fishing in America* (1967), a best-selling novel about an unfulfilled search for a morning of good fishing in a crystal-clear stream. His many other novels include *A Confederate General from Big Sur* (1964) and *In*

Watermelon Sugar (1968), about a commune. His best-known collection of poetry is *The Pill versus the Springhill Mine Disaster* (1968).

Brave New World A novel by ALDOUS HUXLEY, published in 1932. The title is taken from Miranda's words in *The Tempest*: 'O brave new world/ That has such people in't!' The story presents a scathing criticism of the myth of social salvation through technological expertise.

In the year 632 After Ford (i.e. the 26th century) the world has attained a kind of scientific Utopia in which biological engineering fits different categories of workers – Alphas, Betas, Gammas, etc. – to their stations in life, and universal happiness is preserved by psychotropic drugs. The Savage, raised in a reservation of American Indian primitives, comes into this world as a stranger, takes up the arguments introduced by the disaffected intellectuals Bernard Marx and Helmholtz Watson, and finally kills himself in disgust.

Brayfield, Celia See GENRE FICTION.

Brazil, Angela 1868–1947 English. In more than 50 novels for children, from *The Fortunes of Philippa* (1906) to *The School on the Loch* (1946), she made the girls' boarding-school into an idealized world, emphasizing hearty games-playing and the strong emotions that often spring up between pupils. She sometimes earned the disapproval of teachers and parents for her use of schoolgirl slang.

Breytenbach, Breyten 1939– South African. He has lived in Paris most of his adult life, as voluntary expatriate and enforced exile, though he served seven years in a South African prison after illegally re-entering the country in 1975. He writes in English, Afrikaans and French. *Memory of Snow and of Dust* (1989), a novel which won a CNA LITERARY AWARD, examines the themes of exile, love and death which predominate in all his work. *Mouroir: Mirror Notes to a Novel* (1984) was written in prison. Three autobiographies, *A Season in Paradise* (1973), *True Confessions of an Albino Terrorist* (1984) and *Return to Paradise* (1993), dissect his love-hate relationship with his country as a dissident Afrikaner.

Bride of Lammermoor, The A novel by SIR WALTER SCOTT, published in 1818 in the third series of *Tales of My Landlord*. It tells the story of the Master of Ravenswood's unhappy and eventually tragic love for Lucy Ashton, opposed by her mother, the imperious and deceitful Lady Ashton. Donizetti used the story as the basis for his opera, *Lucia di Lammermoor* (1835).

Brideshead Revisited: The Sacred and Profane Memories of Captain Charles Ryder A novel by EVELYN WAUGH, published in 1945. It broke with the satirical mode of his earlier works.

Billeted at Brideshead during the war, Ryder recalls his past experiences there as a guest of the Marchmains, a great Roman Catholic family, whom he met through his dazzling young Oxford friend, Sebastian Flyte. Sebastian sinks into alcoholism, and after the death of his mother, Lady Marchmain, becomes a menial in an African monastery. Ryder's feelings centre on Julia but she marries a non-Catholic, a vulgar politician, and then after her divorce is prompted to return to the faith by her father's deathbed reconciliation with Catholicism. Ryder's doubts about his own faith are resolved by her renunciation of him, and his agnosticism withers.

Brighton Rock A novel by GRAHAM GREENE, published in 1938.

Pinkie ('The Boy'), a 17-year-old Brighton gang leader hell-bent on establishing himself, kills Fred Hale, a journalist who indirectly caused the death of the gang's former leader. Realizing that Rose, an innocent young waitress, unknowingly holds evidence against him, Pinkie dates her and then reluctantly agrees to marriage, to prevent her testifying against him. The middle-aged Ida Arnold, a brief but loyal acquaintance of Hale's, fails to persuade Rose to abandon Pinkie. He panics and arranges a fake suicide pact. Rose's conscience stops her going through with it, and Ida arrives with a policeman; blinded by the vitriol he always carries, Pinkie falls to his death over a cliff.

Though Greene called the novel an 'entertainment' (in the US edition), it is profoundly influenced by his Catholicism. The tensions between Pinkie (a nominal Catholic, still superstitious), the saintly Rose and the fun-loving, secular Ida Arnold create an ambiguous moral drama foreshadowing his later novels.

Brink, André 1935– South African. An Afrikaans writer concerned with Afrikaner history and morality, he has also written in English, especially after *Kennis van die aand* (1973) was banned. He translated it as *Looking on Darkness* (1974) and has since published his novels in both languages. Works published in English include: *The Ambassador* (1964); *An Instant in the Wind* (1976); *Rumours of Rain* (1978); *A DRY WHITE SEASON* (1979); *A Chain of Voices* (1982); *The Wall of the Plague* (1984); *States of Emergency* (1988); *An Act of Terror* (1991); *On the Contrary* (1993); *The First Life of Adamastor* (1993; as *Cape of Storms: The First Life of Adamastor* in the USA); and *Imaginings of Sand* (1996). *Rumours of Rain*, *A Chain of Voices* and two of his works in Afrikaans have won the CNA LITERARY AWARD. Brink has also written short stories and plays in Afrikaans, children's books, travel books, academic criticism and many translations into Afrikaans. A selection of his essays appeared as *Mapmakers: Writing in a State of Siege* (1983).

Brodber, Erna 1942– Jamaican. *Jane and Louisa Will Soon Come Home* (1980), written in a distinctively original poetic prose, shows how the folk traditions of Jamaica have been undervalued and how negative stereotyping has stultified the emotional and intellectual development of black women. *Myal* (1988) takes the Afro-Caribbean religious cult of Myalism (formerly criminalized by the colonial authorities) as its central metaphor for black Jamaican spiritual survival. *Louisiana* (1994) is about an African-American anthropologist achieving self-discovery through spiritual communication with the dead woman who had previously been her main informant. In her role as professional sociologist Brodber has also published *A Study of Yards in the City of Kingston* (1975) and *Perceptions of Caribbean Women* (1982).

Brodkey, Harold 1930–96 American. He is known for the improvisational quality and emotional depth of his style. His short stories are gathered in *First Love and Other Sorrows* (1957), *Stories in an Almost Classical Mode* (1988), and *The World is the Home of Love and Death* (1997). *The Runaway Soul* (1991) and *Profane Friendship* (1994) are novels. *This Wild Darkness: The Story of My Death* (1996) is about his experience suffering from AIDS.

Bromfield, Louis 1896–1956 American. His work often reflects a profound distrust of industrialism and materialism, which he saw as dehumanizing factors in 20th-century American life. His novels include *The Green Bay Tree* (1924), *Possession* (1925), *Early Autumn* (1926; PULITZER PRIZE), *The Farm* (1933), *The Rains Came* (1937), *Night in Bombay* (1940), *Wild is the River* (1941), *Mrs Parkinson* (1943) and *Pleasant Valley* (1945). He also published collections of short stories, including *Awake and Rehearse* (1929), *It Takes All Kinds* (1939) and *The World We Live In* (1944), and such plays as *The House of Women* (1927) and *De Luxe* (1935).

Brontë, CHARLOTTE 1816–55; BRONTË, EMILY (JANE) 1818–48; BRONTË, ANNE 1820–49 English. They were daughters of Patrick Brontë, a Church of England clergyman born in Ireland, and his Cornish wife, Maria Branwell. The couple's other children were Maria (1813–25), Elizabeth (1815–25), born at Hartshead near Dewsbury in Yorkshire, and Patrick Branwell (1817–48), born, like the novelists, at Thornton near Bradford. In 1820, the year before his wife's death, Mr Brontë took up the living of Haworth, a weaving village a few miles north-west of Thornton. The Haworth parsonage and its surrounding moorland became, as it always remained, the centre of his children's lives. All the girls save Anne attended the Clergy Daughters' School run by the Reverend William Carus Wilson at Cowan Bridge. Its harsh regime contributed to the early deaths of Maria and Elizabeth. In 1831–2 Charlotte was sent to Miss Wooler's school at Roe Head, near Dewsbury, where she met her lifelong friends Mary Taylor and Ellen Nussey. During her subsequent time as governess there (1835–8), Emily and Anne were also pupils.

Their real education, however, was at the

Haworth parsonage, where they read the Bible, Homer, Virgil, Shakespeare, Milton, Byron, SIR WALTER SCOTT, Aesop and *The Arabian Nights' Entertainments*, as well as illustrated keepsakes and periodicals. Around a set of wooden soldiers they wove tales and legends associated with remote Africa, where they situated an imaginary Glass Town. Later came narratives about the kingdom of Angria recorded by Charlotte and Branwell in minute notebooks; Emily and Anne created the Gondal saga. The strength of the children's attachment to each other and to the Haworth parsonage is shown by the desultory and usually unhappy nature of their forays into the world beyond. Branwell's plan to study painting at the Royal Academy lasted only a few days, and he went on to fail both as a portrait painter and as a railway clerk. His sisters worked as governesses. Anne's longest stint (1840–5) was with the Robinson family at Thorp Green Hall, near York; she left when Branwell, who held a tutorial post in the same household, became involved with its mistress. The most important sojourn away from home for any of the family was Charlotte's time at the *pensionnat* run by M. Constantin Heger and his wife in Brussels (1840–4). For much of her stay she was anxious, melancholy and hostile to the atmosphere around her, and her position was not improved by her growing attachment to M. Heger, who broke off the correspondence she attempted after her return to England.

A joint publication, *Poems by Currer, Ellis and Acton Bell* (1846), passed unnoticed by the reading public. Charlotte's first novel, THE PROFESSOR, which drew heavily on her experiences in Brussels, was rejected and did not appear until in 1857. But the encouragement she received from George Smith emboldened her to complete and submit *JANE EYRE*. It appeared in 1847, two months before Emily Brontë's *WUTHERING HEIGHTS* and Anne Brontë's *AGNES GREY*. Anne's second novel, *THE TENANT OF WILDFELL HALL*, appeared in 1848. The public interest aroused by these works, particularly *Jane Eyre*, was made the more piquant by the sisters' continued use of their apparently male pseudonyms, Currer, Ellis and Acton Bell. By this time, however, the family was involved in private sorrow. Branwell's alcoholism contributed to his early death in September 1848. He was followed by Emily, who died of tuberculosis in December, and by Anne, who died calmly and resignedly at Scarborough in July 1849.

Charlotte survived to cope with a father now sorely tried and going blind. She published *SHIRLEY* (1849) and *VILLETTE* (1853), again drawing on her life in Brussels. She began to move in literary society, meeting WILLIAM MAKEPEACE THACKERAY, G. H. Lewes, and becoming friendly with HARRIET MARTINEAU and, particularly, ELIZABETH GASKELL, her future biographer. In

June 1854 she married her father's curate, Arthur Bell Nicholls; the couple lived together with Mr Brontë at the parsonage. She died the following March, apparently from the complications of a chill caught during early pregnancy. Her father survived until 1861 and her husband until 1906.

Brooke, Henry 1703–83 Irish. He is remembered today for his popular SENTIMENTAL NOVEL, *THE FOOL OF QUALITY* (1766–72). A second novel, *Juliet Grenville* (1774), was soon forgotten. His poetry includes: *Design and Beauty: An Epistle* (1734); the ambitious *Universal Beauty* (1734–6), on the perfection of design in the universe; and a translation of Books I and II of Tasso's *Gerusalemme Liberata* (1738). His tragedy, *Gustavus Vasa* (1739; called *The Patriot* for its Dublin production, 1744) was banned because Sir Robert Walpole fancied a likeness to himself in the villain of the piece.

Brooke-Rose, Christine 1926– English. Born in Geneva, she teaches in Paris. A European intellectual influenced by the French *avant-garde* of the 1950s, she moved from the satire of early work such as *The Languages of Love* (1957) to a concern with the nature of words and their meanings in *Such* (1966), *Between* (1968), *Thru* (1975), *Amalgamemnon* (1984), *Xorander* (1986), *Verbivore* (1990) and *Textermination* (1991). *Remake* (1996) is an autobiographical novel of broad sweep. Her criticism includes *A Grammar of Metaphor* (1958), *A ZBC of Ezra Pound* (1971), *A Rhetoric of the Unreal: Studies in Narrative and Structure, Especially the Fantastic* (1981) and *Stories, Theories and Things* (1991).

Brookner, Anita 1928– English. Her wry, delicate stories of single women and their failure to secure lasting relationships have been compared to the novels of BARBARA PYM and ELIZABETH TAYLOR. *Hôtel du Lac* (1984), which won the BOOKER PRIZE, remains the best known; others are *A Start in Life* (1981), *Providence* (1982), *Look at Me* (1983), *A Misalliance* (1986), *A Friend from England* (1987), *Lewis Percy* (1989), *A Closed Eye* (1991), *Incidents in the Rue Laugier* (1995), *Altered States* (1996) and *Visitors* (1997). *Family and Friends* (1985) differs in attempting a concentrated family saga. *Soundings* (1997) brings together pieces on art and literature.

Brophy, Brigid (Antonia) 1929–95 English. A lively writer with the disciplined mind of a classical scholar, she used the term 'baroque' for her technique of presenting contrasted forces and unexpected views. Her novels include *Hackenfeller's Ape* (1954), *Flesh* (1963), *The Snowball* (1964) and *Palace without Chairs* (1978). The interest in sexual ambiguity and homosexuality which informs her work is particularly evident in *The Finishing Touch* (1963) and *In Transit* (1970), and in critical biographies of AUBREY BEARDSLEY (1969) and RONALD FIRBANK (*Prancing Novelist*, 1973). Her criticism included a study of Mozart

(1964), and two collections of miscellaneous pieces, *Baroque 'n' Roll* (1987) and *Reads* (1989). With MAUREEN DUFFY, she was a leading campaigner for the Public Lending Right, which grants authors the equivalent of royalties on books borrowed from libraries.

Broughton, Rhoda 1840–1920 English. She made her reputation with *Not Wisely, But Too Well* and *Cometh Up As a Flower*, both published in 1867, considered audacious for their treatment of love. Subsequent novels, which include *Red as a Rose Is She* (1870), *Good-bye Sweetheart!* (1872), *Nancy* (1873), *Joan* (1876), *Second Thoughts* (1880) and *Belinda* (1883) were more restrained, but she maintained her popularity, having (said OSCAR WILDE) 'that one touch of vulgarity that makes the whole kin'. She herself said of her career that she began as Zola and ended as CHARLOTTE M. YONGE.

Brown, Charles Brockden 1771–1810 He is often considered America's first professional author. He briefly practised law in his native Philadelphia before moving to New York in 1796 and devoting himself to writing. *Alcuin: A Dialogue* (1798) was a treatise on the rights of women, influenced by WILLIAM GODWIN. Brown went on to produce four novels which translate the GOTHIC NOVEL into an American idiom: *WIELAND* (1798), *ARTHUR MERVYN* (1799–1800), *Ormond* (1799) and *Edgar Huntly* (1799). Although widely read in America and England, they were not commercially successful. Two more novels sold well, while lacking the artistic innovation of their predecessors: *Clara Howard* (1801; called *Philip Stanley* in England) and *Jane Talbot* (1801). *Memoirs of Carwin*, a sequel to *Wieland*, was serialized in Brown's newly founded and highly successful *The Literary Magazine and American Register* in 1803–5, but remained unfinished at his death in 1810.

Brown, George Mackay 1921–96 Scottish. Growing out of his life in the Orkney Islands, his poems were influenced by the 13th-century Icelandic *Orkneyinga Saga*, the work of Gerard Manley Hopkins and EDWIN MUIR, and the symbolic structures of Roman Catholicism. Early volumes, such as *The Storm* (1954), *Loaves and Fishes* (1959) and *The Year of the Whale* (1965), were followed by *Fishermen with Ploughs* (1971), *Winterfold* (1976), *Voyages* (1983), *Andrina* (1983) and several limited editions. His novels include: *Greenvoe* (1972); *Magnus* (1973), a lyrical account of the Orkney saint's martyrdom; *Time in a Red Coat* (1984); and *Beside the Ocean of Time* (1994), nominated for the BOOKER PRIZE. Short stories include *A Calendar of Love* (1967), *The Golden Bird: Two Orkney Stories* (1987) and *The Masked Fisherman and Other Stories* (1989). For many years Mackay Brown collaborated with the composer Peter Maxwell Davies, an adoptive Orcadian.

Brown, Rita Mae 1944– American. *Rubyfruit Jungle* (1973), about a young girl growing up 'different' in America, put her at the forefront of the feminist and gay rights movements. Other novels include *In Her Day* (1976), *Six of One* (1978), *Southern Discomfort* (1982), *Sudden Death* (1983), *High Hearts* (1986), *Bingo* (1988), *Venus Envy* (1993), *Dolley: A Novel of Dolley Madison in Love and War* (1994) and *Riding Shotgun* (1996). She has also written a series of mysteries set in small towns, including *Wish You Were Here* (1990), *Rest in Pieces* (1992), *Murder at Monticello* (1994) and *Pay Dirt* (1995).

Brown, William Hill 1765–93 American. His first book, *THE POWER OF SYMPATHY* (1789), is generally considered to be the first American novel. Before his early death at the age of 28, he contributed poetry and literary and political essays to Boston magazines. Posthumously published works include a tragedy, *West Point Preserved: or, the Treason of Arnold* (1797), and a second novel, *Ira and Isabella: or, The Natural Children* (1807), with a plot similar to that of *The Power of Sympathy* except for its happy ending.

Browning, Elizabeth Barrett See *AURORA LEIGH*.

Brownson, Orestes (Augustus) 1803–76 American. Although associated with Transcendentalism and the Brook Farm experiment, his own activities were often more radical. *New Views of Christianity, Society and the Church* (1836) attacked organized Christianity. *Charles Elwood: or, The Infidel Converted* (1840) is a semi-autobiographical novel about a man's conversion to Unitarianism. *The Meditational Life of Jesus* (1842) outlines his Roman Catholic tendencies. *The Spirit Rapper: An Autobiography* (1854) is less an autobiography than a novel about the Satanic influences evident in contemporary spiritualism. *The Convert: or, Leaves from My Experiences* (1857) is an account of his religious growth.

Brunner, John See SCIENCE FICTION.

Buchan, John 1875–1940 Scottish. He is most famous for his five Richard Hannay novels – particularly the first, *The Thirty-Nine Steps* (1915) – which made a decisive contribution to SPY FICTION. His 100 books include nearly 30 novels and seven collections of short stories. Many are still widely praised and read, both HISTORICAL FICTION such as *Salute to Adventurers* (1915), *Midwinter* (1923), *Witch Wood* (1927) and *The Blanket of the Dark* (1931), and contemporary tales such as the charming *Huntingtower* (1922) or *Castle Gay* (1930) and the profounder Sir Edward Leithen novels, especially Buchan's last, *Sick Heart River* (1941). His 24-volume *Nelson's History of the War* (1915–19) has a global view free from jingoism. He wrote biographies of Montrose (1913, 1928), SIR WALTER SCOTT (1932), Oliver Cromwell (1934) and Augustus (1937). As Lord Tweedsmuir he became Governor General of Canada, where he lent his support – but, controversially, did not fund – the establishment of the GOVERNOR GENERAL'S AWARDS.

Buchanan, Robert (Williams) 1841–1901 Scottish. Several strands are detectable in his varied output of poetry: an attraction to mean streets and squalid city lives in *London Poems* (1866); an interest in his Scottish roots in *Idyls and Legends of Inverburn* (1865), *Ballad Stories of the Affections* (1866) and *North Coast and Other Poems* (1867); a penchant for epic in *The Book of Orm* (1870), *Balder the Beautiful* (1877) and *The City of Dream* (1888); and a fascination with the USA in *Saint Abe and His Seven Wives* (1872) and *White Rose and the Red* (1873). He also wrote plays, including *Sophia* (an adaptation of *Tom Jones*; 1886), and a good many novels, including *The Shadow of the Sword* (1876), *God and the Man* (1881), *Foxglove Manor* (1885) and *Effie Hetherington* (1886). The literary histories usually remember him for 'The Fleshly School of Poetry', a scurrilous attack on the Pre-Raphaelites which developed from a magazine article into a pseudonymous pamphlet (1872). Dante Gabriel Rossetti, the chief target, replied in 'The Stealthy School of Criticism' and Swinburne in *Under the Microscope* (1872).

Buck, Pearl S(ydenstricker) 1892–1973 American. A prolific writer who produced over 100 titles – novels, collections of stories, plays, screenplays, verse, children's books and non-fiction – she won the Nobel Prize for Literature in 1938. Many of her novels are set in China, where she spent much of her life. *The Good Earth* (1931), awarded a PULITZER PRIZE and probably her best-known novel, is the story of a peasant's relationship with the soil. It opens a trilogy continued in *Sons* (1932) and *A House Divided* (1935), and collectively called *The House of Earth*. Other novels about China include *East Wind, West Wind* (1930), *The Mother* (1934), *This Proud Heart* (1938), *Dragon Seed* (1941) and *Kinfolk* (1949). Her biographies of her parents, *The Exile* (1936) and *Fighting Angel: Portrait of a Soul* (1936), are considered classics.

Buckler, Ernest (Redmond) 1908–84 Canadian. His best-known work, *The Mountain and the Valley* (1952), is a classic novel of life in maritime Canada. Other works include *The Cruelest Month* (1963), *Ox Bells and Fireflies: A Memoir* (1968) and *Whirligig: Selected Prose and Verse* (1977). Some of his engaging short stories were collected in *The Rebellion of Young David and Other Stories* (1975).

Bukowski, Charles 1920–94 American. His screenplay for the film *Barfly* (1987) introduced to a wider audience an angry, irreverent outsider descended from the BEATS. His novels include *Post Office* (1971), *Factotum* (1975), *Women* (1978), *Ham on Rye* (1982) and *Pulp* (1994). Collections of verse include *Drowning in Flame: Selected Poems 1955–1973* (1974), *Love is a Dog from Hell: Poems 1974–1977* (1977), *War All the Time: Poems 1981–1984* (1984), *Roominghouse Madrigals: Early Selected Poems 1946–1966* (1988), *Septuagenarian Stew: Stories and Poems* (1990) and *The Last Night of the Earth* (1992). *Run With the Hunted* (1993), edited by John Martin, brings together poems, stories and novels.

Bulwer Lytton, Edward (George Earle Lytton), 1st Baron Lytton 1803–73 English. Few writers are known by such a variety of names. He began as plain Edward Bulwer, though often calling himself Edward Lytton Bulwer. After being knighted in 1837 he expanded his name to Sir Edward (Lytton) Bulwer Lytton. Raised to the peerage in 1866, he was known thereafter as Lord Lytton. He is sometimes confused with his son, EDWARD ROBERT BULWER LYTTON.

One of the most accomplished authors of his day, he is marked above all by the versatility of his talents. His two dozen novels, written over an active career of 45 years, tackle almost every genre popular with contemporaries. They include: HISTORICAL FICTION, notably *THE LAST DAYS OF POMPEII* (1834), *RIENZI* (1835), *THE LAST OF THE BARONS* (1843) and *Harold* (1848); tales of magic, spiritualism and SCIENCE FICTION such as *ZANONI* (1842), *A Strange Story* (1862) and *THE COMING RACE* (1871); SILVER-FORK NOVELS of high society such as *PELHAM* (1828); light novels of middle-class domestic life such as *The Caxtons* (1849), *My Novel* (1853) and *What Will He Do with It?* (1858); NEWGATE NOVELS such as *Paul Clifford* (1830) and *EUGENE ARAM* (1832); and philosophical novels about gifted young men seeking the meaning of life, such as *Godolphin* (1833), *Ernest Maltravers* (1837) and *Alice* (1838). He also published 10 plays, including *The Lady of Lyons* (1838), *Richelieu* (1839) and *Money* (1840), as well as short stories, poetry, translations and a pioneering study, *England and the English* (1833). That he is now forgotten would have surprised contemporaries, many of whom regarded him as England's leading man of letters.

Bunyan, John See *HOLY WAR, THE*; *LIFE AND DEATH OF MR BADMAN, THE*; and *PILGRIM'S PROGRESS, THE*.

Burgess, Anthony [Wilson, John Anthony Burgess] 1917–93 English. His experience as an educational officer in the Colonial Service is reflected in *Time for a Tiger* (1956), *The Enemy in the Blanket* (1958) and *Beds in the East* (1959), published together as *The Malayan Trilogy* (1972; reissued as *The Long Day Wanes*, 1982). *A CLOCKWORK ORANGE* (1962), a dystopian novel, achieved cult popularity after the controversial film version by Stanley Kubrick (1972). Its verbal inventiveness and social satire, though not its bleakness, are typical of the many works which followed. They include *The Wanting Seed* (1962), *Nothing Like the Sun* (about Shakespeare, 1964), *Napoleon Symphony* (1974), *ABBA ABBA* (1977) and a comic sequence, *Inside Mr Enderby* (1963), *Enderby Outside* (1968), *The Clockwork Testament* (1974) and *Enderby's Dark Lady* (1984). Notably ambitious are *Earthly Powers* (1980) and *The Kingdom of the Wicked* (1985), about early Christianity. Posthumously published fiction includes *A Dead Man in Deptford* (1993), about Christopher Marlowe, and *Byrne* (1995), a PICARESQUE verse-novel revisiting characteristic themes. Among his many other writings are: *Here Comes Everybody* (1965) and *Joysprick* (1973), studies of JAMES JOYCE; *Urgent Copy* (1968) and *Homage to Qwertyuiop* (1987), culled from reviews and essays; and *Mozart and the Wolf Gang* (1991), a playful meditation on the composer. *Little Wilson and Big God* (1987) and *You've Had Your Time* (1990), are teeming volumes of autobiography.

Burke, James Lee 1936– American. He began by publishing 'mainstream' novels set in various parts of the South: *Half of Paradise* (1965), *To the Bright and Shining Land* (1970), *Lay Down My Sword and Shield* (1971) and *Two for Texas* (1983). The portrait of a Korean war veteran and country musician in crisis in *The Lost Get-Back Boogie*, published after some years' delay in 1986, directly prefigured the novels with which Burke made his name. Featuring Dave Robicheaux, Vietnam veteran and recovering alcoholic, they marry the conventions of hard-boiled DETECTIVE FICTION with those of Southern Gothic. Robicheaux quits his job with the New Orleans police at the end of the first, *The Neon Rain* (1987), allowing Burke to explore Louisiana's Cajun country in a series which has included *Heaven's Prisoners* (1988), *Black Cherry Blues* (1989), *A Morning for Flamingos* (1990), *A Stained White Radiance* (1992), *In the Electric Mist with Confederate Dead* (1993), *Dixie City Jam* (1994) and *Burning Angel* (1995) and *Cadillac Jukebox* (1996).

Burnett, Frances (Eliza) Hodgson 1849–1924 American. She was born in Manchester and moved to Tennessee in 1865. Although she became popular with her first book, a sentimental novel entitled *That Lass o'Lowrie's* (1877), she is remembered for her children's books: *Little Lord Fauntleroy* (1886), *The Little Princess* (1905) and *The Secret Garden* (1911). In *Little Lord Fauntleroy* the title character is Cedric Erroll, curly-haired and velvet-suited, affectionate and loved by all, who comes to England from New York to win the heart of his estranged grandfather, the Earl of Dorincourt. In *The Secret Garden* the orphaned Mary and her cousin Colin achieve happiness reviving an abandoned garden. Other works include *Editha's Burglar* (1888), *The White People* (1917), a novel about the supernatural, and *The One I Knew Best of All* (1893), an autobiography. She was also instrumental in establishing the legal precedent which gave American authors control over the publication of their work in Britain.

Burney, Fanny [Frances] 1752–1840 English. The daughter of the musician Dr Charles Burney, she enjoyed from early youth the entrée to literary society, notably Samuel Johnson's circle. After uncongenial service as Second Keeper of the Robes to Queen Charlotte in 1786–91, she married a French refugee officer, General Alexandre Gabriel Jean-Baptiste d'Arblay, in 1793 and lived in France with him in 1802–12. She spent her time in Bath and, after her husband's death, in London, devoting much of her later life to editing *The Memoirs of Dr Burney* (1832).

As a novelist, she inherited the form from SAMUEL RICHARDSON and HENRY FIELDING and handled it in a way that would prove useful to JANE AUSTEN. Her strength lay in comedy, particularly the comedy of domestic life, developed around innocent heroines as they enter a sophisticated social world. Her first novel, *EVELINA: or, The History of a Young Lady's Entrance into the World* (1778), made her famous while her second, *CECILIA: or, Memoirs of an Heiress* (1782), and third, *CAMILLA: or, A Picture of Youth* (1796), confirmed her reputation. *The Wanderer* (1814) proved unsuccessful. Of her eight plays only one, *Edwy and Elgiva*, was produced during her lifetime. Her diaries are not the least of her literary achievements. The *Early Diary 1768–78* (1889) gives firsthand accounts of Johnson and David Garrick, and the *Diary and Letters 1778–1840* (1842–6) includes the years at court.

Burroughs, Edgar Rice 1875–1950 American. He began writing for pulp magazines in 1912, when he published the first of many SCIENCE-FICTION fantasies (reprinted as *A Princess of Mars*, 1917) and the first of many novels about Tarzan, an English aristocrat raised by apes in the African jungle. His extravagant and exotic adventure stories deteriorated after 1925, but his early books have an escapist verve which overrides their essential silliness.

Burroughs, William S(eward) 1914–97 American. Associated with the BEATS, he spent much of his life in Paris and Tangier. He achieved immediate notoriety with two books drawing on his experience of heroin addiction: *Junkie: Confessions of an Unredeemed Drug Addict* (published under the pseudonym of William Lee; 1953) and *The Naked Lunch* (1959), banned for obscenity. Later books, progressively less noticed as his cult reputation waned, included *The Soft Machine* (1961), *The Ticket That Exploded* (1962), *Nova Express* (1964), *The Wild Boys: A Book of the Dead* (1971), *Exterminator!* (1973), *Cities of the Red Night* (1981), *The Place of Dead Roads* (1984) and *Queer* (1986). He also produced filmscripts, recordings, and essays.

Bury, Lady Charlotte See SILVER-FORK NOVEL.

Butler, Robert Olen 1945– American. He won recognition for his stories of Vietnamese immigrants in Louisiana, *A Good Scent from a Strange Mountain* (1992; PULITZER PRIZE). Other work includes: *The Alleys of Eden* (1981), set in Vietnam; *Sun Dogs* (1982); *Countrymen of Bones* (1983), set in the wastes of the Los Alamos nuclear testing site; *On Distant Ground* (1985), containing stories about the war in Vietnam; *Wabash* (1987); *The*

Deuce (1989); *The Whisper* (1994); and *Tabloid Dreams: Stories* (1996).

Butler, Samuel 1835–1902 English. His unhappy childhood in a strictly religious household is described in his semi-autobiographical novel THE WAY OF ALL FLESH (1903). He rejected his father's wish that he take holy orders and emigrated to New Zealand, where he became a successful sheep-farmer. His first publications were *A First Year in Canterbury Settlement* (1863) and an anonymous pamphlet, *The Evidence for the Resurrection of Jesus Christ as Given by the Four Evangelists Critically Examined* (1865), which became the core of *Fair Haven* (1873), a satire so veiled that some orthodox readers missed the joke. Returning home in 1865, he embarked on a career as a painter, exhibiting at the Royal Academy. *EREWHON* (1872) is a satirical novel, to which he later added a sequel, *Erewhon Revisited* (1901). On a visit to Canada in 1874–5 he found the material for the satirical poem 'A Psalm of Montreal' (1878) and started *Life and Habit* (1877), the first of a series of works, which included *Evolution Old and New* (1879), *Unconscious Memory* (1880) and *Luck or Cunning* (1886), pursuing his critical debate with Darwin's theory of natural selection.

Butler's eclectic interests and unfocused talent, best displayed in the *Notebooks* (1912), later surfaced in art criticism, to which he contributed *Alps and Sanctuaries* (1881) and *Ex Voto* (1888), and music. In collaboration with H. Festing Jones, he composed Handelian pieces and a comic oratorio, *Narcissus* (1888). Two further areas of study produced *The Authoress of the 'Odyssey'* (1897), arguing that Homer was a woman, and *Shakespeare's Sonnets Reconsidered* (1899).

Byatt, A(ntonia) S(usan) 1936– English. *Possession* (1990), which won the BOOKER PRIZE, uses a biographical investigation of an imaginary 19th-century poet to explore the process of literary interpretation. Its predecessors are *Shadow of a Sun* (1964) and *The Game* (1967), and a trilogy tracing English life from the mid-1950s, *The Virgin in the Garden* (1978), *Still-Life* (1985) and *Babel Tower* (1996). *Sugar* (1987) and *The Matisse Stories* (1993) are collections of short stories, *Angels and Insects* (1992) consists of two novellas on Victorian themes, and *The Djinn in the Nightingale's Eye* (1994) contributes to the feminist fairy tale. She has also published a monograph on IRIS MURDOCH (1965), a critical study of Wordsworth and Coleridge (1970) and *Passions of the Mind* (1991), a collection of essays. *Imaginary Characters: Six Conversations about Women Writers* (1995), with the psychologist Ignês Sodré, includes discussions of JANE AUSTEN, ANNE BRONTË, GEORGE ELIOT and WILLA CATHER. Byatt's sister is MARGARET DRABBLE.

C

Cabell, James Branch 1879–1958 American. He is best known for creating a mythical French province, Poictesme, whose 'history' from 1234 to 1750 he chronicled in a cycle of 18 novels commenting obliquely on American life. It began with *The Soul of Melicent* (1913) and ended with *Straws and Prayer-Books* (1924). One volume, *JURGEN: A Comedy of Justice* (1919), was suppressed on the grounds of obscenity from 1920 to 1922. The case stirred public curiosity, and Cabell enjoyed a large popular following in the 1920s.

Cable, George Washington 1844–1925 American. Born in New Orleans, he became one of the leading local-colour writers of the 'New South', producing 18 volumes of fiction between 1879 and 1918. The best of them are generally considered to be the collection of short stories entitled *OLD CREOLE DAYS* (1879) and the novels *THE GRANDISSIMES* (1880) and *MADAME DELPHINE* (1881). He also wrote a history, *The Creoles of Louisiana* (1884), and *The Silent South* (1885), a treatise advocating reforms for improving the lives of blacks. Because of the offence these books caused to some of his Southern neighbours he moved to Northampton, Massachusetts, in 1885. Several novels – *Dr Sevier* (1884), *Bonaventure* (1888), *John March, Southerner* (1894) and *Bylow Hill* (1902) – treat the collision between Northern and Southern manners and morals.

Cahan, Abraham 1860–1951 American. The realistic presentation of Jewish immigrants in his first novel, *Yekl: A Tale of the New York Ghetto* (1896), became the hallmark of his work. *The Imported Bridegroom and Other Stories of the New York Ghetto* (1898) further established him as a leading Jewish-American writer, a position exemplified by his best-known work, *The Rise of David Levinsky* (1917), about a rich but dissatisfied garment manufacturer.

Cain, James M(allahan) 1892–1977 American. His work combined NATURALISM in the tradition of FRANK NORRIS and THEODORE DREISER with features of the hard-boiled school of DETECTIVE FICTION. In both his best-known novels, *The Postman Always Rings Twice* (1934) and *Double Indemnity* (1936), an unmarried man and a married woman plot her husband's murder for money. Cain's other novels include *Serenade* (1937), *Career in C Major* (1938), *The Embezzler* (1940), *Mildred Pierce* (1941), *Love's Lovely Counterfeit* (1942), *The Butterfly* (1947) and *The Root of His Evil* (1951). *Past All Dishonor* (1946) and *Mignon* (1962) are set in the period following the Civil War.

Caine, Sir (Thomas Henry) Hall 1853–1931 English. He became a trusted friend of Dante Gabriel Rossetti and was with him at his death in 1882. *Recollections of Rossetti* was published the same year. Caine's melodramatic novels, popular in their day but soon forgotten, include *The Shadow of a Crime* (1885), *The Deemster* (1887), *The Bondman* (1890), *The Scapegoat* (1891), *The Manxman* (1894), *The Prodigal Son* (1904) and *The Woman Thou Gavest Me* (1913).

Caldwell, Erskine 1903–87 American. He is best known for his portrayal of poor whites and blacks in the rural deep South in novels such as *Tobacco Road* (1932; dramatized by Jack Kirkland in 1933), *God's Little Acre* (1933), *Journeyman* (1935), *Trouble in July* (1940), *A House in the Uplands* (1946), and *Jenny by Nature* (1961). Collections of stories include *American Earth* (1930), *Jackpot* (1940) and *The Courting of Susie Brown* (1952). *You Have Seen Their Faces* (1937) is a documentary study of Southern sharecroppers.

Caleb Williams, The Adventures of: or, Things as They Are A novel by WILLIAM GODWIN, first published in 1794. As the subtitle indicates, he intended the book as a radical critique of an unjust social system, but he went beyond his polemical purpose by effective use of conventions borrowed from the GOTHIC NOVEL.

Caleb, who tells the story, rises from humble origins to become secretary to the polished and accomplished local squire, Falkland. Disturbed by his master's fits of melancholy, he enquires into Falkland's past and discovers that he has murdered a boorish neighbour, Tyrrel. Falkland falsely accuses Caleb of theft, has him imprisoned and, when he escapes, relentlessly hunts him down. Caleb at last confronts Falkland and forces him into public confession. He collapses and dies, leaving Caleb feeling not triumphant but guilty at what he has done.

Calisher, Hortense 1911– American. Her wide-ranging work includes studies of family relationships and racial conflict. *The Collected Stories of Hortense Calisher* (1975) gathers together many previous volumes of shorter work. *False Entry* (1962) began her equally prolific output of novels, which has included *Textures of Life* (1963), *Journal from Ellipsia* (1965), *The Railway Police and the Last Trolley Ride* (1966), *The New Yorkers* (1969) *Queenie* (1971), *The Bobby-Soxer* (1986), *Age* (1987) and *In the Palace of the Movie King* (1993). Her non-fiction includes a memoir, *Kissing Cousins* (1988), and *In the Slammer with Carol Smith* (1993).

Call of the Wild, The A novel by JACK LONDON, published in 1903. The 'hero' is Buck, a dog kidnapped and sold into service in the Klondike, where he suffers brutal mistreatment until he is rescued by a kind gold prospector, John Thornton. Buck's fierce loyalty to Thornton cannot prevent the man eventually being killed in an Indian raid. Masterless, but now at home in the Alaskan wilds, the dog abandons human civilization to become the leader of a wolf pack.

Callaghan, Morley (Edward) 1903–90 Canadian. ERNEST HEMINGWAY encouraged him to publish his first novel, *Strange Fugitive* (1928). Other titles include *They Shall Inherit the Earth* (1935), *More Joy in Heaven* (1937), *The Loved and the Lost* (1951), *The Many-Coloured Coat* (1960), *Close to the Sun Again* (1975) and *A Wild Old Man on the Road* (1988). His distinctively spare prose is displayed to greatest advantage in the collections of short stories, *A Native Argosy* (1929), *No Man's Meat* (1931), *Now That April's Here* (1936) and *Morley Callaghan's Stories* (1959).

Cambridge, Ada 1844–1926 She emigrated from Britain to Australia in 1870. A prolific writer, she produced many romantic stories and novels, first serialized in Australian newspapers or magazines such as the *Australasian*, *Age* and *Sydney Mail*. *My Guardian* was the first of her novels to be republished in Britain, in 1878, and *The Making of Rachel Howe* the last, in 1914. The most substantial are probably *A Marked Man* (1890; serialized in Australia as *A Black Sheep*, 1888–9), *The Three Miss Kings* (1891; serialized in 1883), *Not All in Vain* (1892; serialized in 1890–1) and *Fidelis* (1895). They touch on the same questions of religious doubt and social conscience broached in a controversial volume of poetry, *Unspoken Thoughts* (1887), which Cambridge later withdrew. *Thirty Years in Australia* (1903) and *The Retrospect* (1912) are volumes of reminiscence. Interest in colonial women's writing has brought some of her work back into print and made her the subject of two biographies, by Audrey Tate and by Margaret Bradstock and Louise Wakeling (both 1991).

Camilla: *or, A Picture of Youth* FANNY BURNEY'S third novel, published in 1796. It involves a large cast of diverse characters but concentrates on Camilla Tyrold, daughter of a respectable but modestly placed rector, her sisters Eugenia and Lavinia, her brother Lionel, cousins Indiana and Clermont Lynmere, and her eligible suitor Edgar Mandlebert. With an eye to the market, Burney introduced tender sentiment, dramatic incident and Gothic colour, but without deflecting attention from 'the human heart in its feelings and changes'.

Campbell, Alistair 1925– New Zealand. A latter-day Romantic and one of his country's finest lyric poets, he has shown a strong empathy for nature since his first volume, *Mine Eyes Dazzle* (1950). He has been deeply influenced by Maori oral culture, and he also draws on the legends of his native Cook Islands. *Island to Island* (1984) is an autobiography of his early years. *The Frigate Bird* (1989), the first novel in a projected trilogy, has a Cook Island writer as its narrator; it has been followed by *Sidewinder* (1991).

campus novel *(or university novel)* A type of novel dealing with academic life, fashionable since the 1950s. It differs from novels dealing with student life and its aftermath, such as MARY MCCARTHY'S *The Group* (1963), in its preoccupation with the personal and professional lives of teachers and with the university as a structure. The term 'campus novel' can be defended against 'university novel' on the grounds that even non-American writers have often found the American campus their best subject.

The tone, generally comic and often satiric, was set by KINGSLEY AMIS'S *LUCKY JIM* (1954) and VLADIMIR NABOKOV'S, *Pnin* (1957). Both novels expose the mysteries and absurdities of academic life by using an innocent and naïve protagonist. The device was used again by JOHN BARTH, who raised the campus novel to cosmic proportions in *Giles Goat-Boy* (1966), as well as MALCOLM BRADBURY in *Eating People is Wrong* (1959) and *Stepping Westward* (1965) and DAVID LODGE in *Changing Places* (1975). Other writers, such as TOM SHARPE in *Porterhouse Blue* (1974) and *Wilt* (1976) and Howard Jacobson (1942–) in *Coming from Behind* (1983), have broadened the comic tone. Bradbury's *The History Man* (1975), Lodge's *Small World* (1983) and JANE SMILEY'S *Moo* (1995) have adopted the knowing, but not forgiving, stance of insiders – as befits an era when novelists themselves are as likely to be established academics as temporary writers-in-residence.

Can You Forgive Her? The first of ANTHONY TROLLOPE'S PALLISER NOVELS, serialized in 1864–5. It deals with three related love-triangles, in each of which a woman hesitates between a suitable and an unsuitable lover.

In the main plot, Alice Vavasor breaks off her engagement to an honourable country gentleman, John Grey, for a reckless politician, George Vavasor, her cousin. Grey regains Alice after Vavasor flees to America, a ruined man. The second plot concerns Alice's cousin and friend, Lady Glencora, who has made a prudent marriage to Plantagenet Palliser, a rising Liberal politician, despite her continuing attraction to the charming wastrel Burgo Fitzgerald. Realizing that his devotion to politics has made married life dull for her, Palliser refuses the coveted post of Chancellor of the Exchequer to take her on an extended European holiday. The novel ends with the birth of their son, Lord Silverbridge, thus ensuring a succession to the Omnium title, and with Mr Grey's election to the Palliser pocket borough of Silverbridge, thereby satisfying Alice's political interests. In a third, comic plot Alice's aunt, a wealthy widow, chooses a dashing suitor in preference to a solid one.

Cantwell, Robert 1908–78 American. A proletarian writer, he described life in a lumber mill in his first novel, *Laugh and Lie Down* (1931). His second, *The Land of Plenty* (1934), about factory life, is widely considered one of the finest left-wing novels which the USA has yet prompted. In addition to a few uncollected short stories, Cantwell also wrote biography and criticism.

Capote, Truman 1924–84 American. His novels include: *Other Voices, Other Rooms* (1948), a study of youthful innocence in a decadent world; *The Glass Harp* (1951); and *Breakfast at Tiffany's* (1958), a comedy of life in New York. His stories appeared in *A Tree of Night and Other Stories* (1949) and *A Christmas Memory* (1966). He is best remembered, however, for *In Cold Blood* (1966), which combines the methods of journalism and fiction to investigate the apparently motiveless murder of a Kansas family by two youths. *Local Color* (1950), *Selected Writings* (1963), *The Dogs Bark* (1973) and *Music for Chameleons* (1981) are collections of journalism. *Answered Prayers*, a final, incomplete novel on which Capote had made desultory progress for many years, appeared to general disappointment in 1986.

Captain Singleton, The Life, Adventures and Piracies of the Famous A novel by DANIEL DEFOE, published in 1720. It is a narrative of romantic adventure, culled from Defoe's wide reading, and told in the first person. As a child Singleton is kidnapped and sent to sea. Put ashore off Madagascar after an unsuccessful mutiny, he crosses Africa, acquiring a fortune in gold on the way. He squanders it recklessly in England and turns to piracy, from which he acquires a second fortune. At the end of the novel he is back in England, married to the sister of his virtuous shipmate William Walters. Because of his upbringing, Singleton himself is a man without 'sense of virtue or religion'.

Carey, Peter 1943– Australian. His fantasies have a concrete particularity rare in POST-MODERNISM. *Exotic Pleasures* (1980) brings together the short stories in *The Fat Man in History* (1974) and *War Crimes* (1979) which first won him prominence. Of his novels, *Bliss* (1981; MILES FRANKLIN AWARD) is a sardonic black comedy and *Illywhacker* (1985) the story of a 139-year-old confidence trickster looking back on his life. *OSCAR AND LUCINDA* (1988) won the BOOKER PRIZE as well as the Miles Franklin Award. *The Tax Inspector* (1991) is set during the audit of Catchprice Motors in the Sydney of the 1990s. *The Unusual Life of Tristan Smith* (1995) satirizes Australia's subservience to American cultural imperialism. *Jack Maggs* (1997) takes DICKENS's *GREAT EXPECTATIONS* as its point of departure.

Carleton, William 1794–1869 Irish. His sketches of the Irish scene were collected as *Traits and Stories of the Irish Peasantry* (first series, 1832; second series, 1833) and *Tales of Ireland* (1834). *Fardorougha the Miser* (1839) is the best-known of his novels, which also include *The Misfortunes of Barry Branagan* (1841), *Valentine McClutchy* (1845) and *The Evil Eye* (1860).

Carr, Emily 1871–1945 Canadian. *The Book of Small* (1942) and the first part of her posthumously published 'autobiography', *Growing Pains* (1946), give vivid, though partly fictionalized, accounts of her early years. She went on to become Canada's best-known woman painter, taking her subjects mainly from the culture of the Western Canadian Indians. She supported herself by a variety of means, including running a boarding house in Victoria, an experience described in *The House of All Sorts* (1944). She had turned to writing only when bedridden in later life, beginning with *Klee Wyck* (1941), short stories about the Indians of British Columbia. She occupies a particular place in Canadian literature as a fond chronicler of late 19th-century and early 20th-century life, as well as for the close affinity she demonstrates for Indian peoples.

Carr, J(ames) (Joseph) L(loyd) 1912–94 English. *A Month in the Country* (1980), his best-known novel, is an intricately symbolic love story involving a World War I veteran. His fiction is notable for its discreet articulation of Englishness, often found in sports like cricket (*A Season in Sinji*, 1967) or football (in *How Steeple Sinderby Wanderers Won the FA Cup*, 1975). Other novels include *The Battle of Pollocks Crossing* (1985), *What Hetty Did* (1988) and *Harpole and Foxberrow, Publishers* (1992). *Carr's Dictionary of Extraordinary Cricketers* (1977), one of the tiny pamphlets he published himself, won a deserved reputation.

Carr, John Dickson 1906–77 An American, he spent much of his working life in Britain. His prolific output of DETECTIVE FICTION displays a fascination with the locked-room puzzle and the macabre, both derived from EDGAR ALLAN POE, together with a love of farce and an interest in historical settings. Four early books feature a French detective, Henri Bencolin; the best is the last, called *The Corpse in the Waxworks* in the USA and *The Waxworks Murder* in Britain (1932). *Hag's Nook* (1933) introduced Dr Gideon Fell, modelled on G. K. CHESTERTON, at his best in *The Three Coffins* (called *The Hollow Man* in Britain; 1935) and *The Crooked Hinge* (1938). Carr also used the pseudonym of Carter Dickson to write about Sir Henry Merrivale, notably in *The Plague Court Murders* (1934), the first of the series, and *The Judas Window* (1938).

Carrier, Roch 1937– French-Canadian. Born in Québec, he writes in Québécois French (see FRENCH-CANADIAN NOVEL). His work combines fantasy, dreamlike reverie, gentle satire, folklore and poignant insight. His first book of short stories, *Jolis deuils* (1964), won the Prix de la Province du Québec. His 'sombre trilogy' began with *La Guerre, Yes Sir!* (1968; translated under the same title, 1970), his most famous work, about the Québécois French during World War II, and continued with *Floralie, où es-tu?* (1969; translated as *Floralie, Where are You?*, 1971) and *Il* *est par là, le soleil* (1970; translated as *Is It the Sun, Philibert?*, 1972). Subsequent novels include the ambitious *De l'amour dans le feraille* (1984). A volume of stories, *Les Enfants du bonhomme dans la lune* (1979), was translated the same year as *The Hockey Sweater and Other Stories*.

Carroll, Lewis [Dodgson, Charles Lutwidge] 1832–98 English. He studied mathematics at Christ Church, Oxford, obtaining a university post but lecturing and teaching with difficulty because of his habitual shyness and bad stammer. For the same reasons he preached only occasionally after his ordination in 1861. He produced mathematical textbooks and some occasional comic writing. Both he and his friends were surprised by the immediate success of his masterpiece, *Alice's Adventures under Ground* (now usually known as *ALICE'S ADVENTURES IN WONDERLAND*; 1865), a book which revolutionized children's literature by putting previous literary pieties aside and opening the door to entertainment for its own sake. At this stage in his life he also took great interest in photography and in the company of young children, particularly girls. Later successes were equally original, notably *THROUGH THE LOOKING-GLASS AND WHAT ALICE FOUND THERE* (1871) and a long nonsense poem, *The Hunting of the Snark* (1876). After these Dodgson's genius faded, although his fame continued to grow. Today, while his life has become a quarry for psychological speculation, his best works remain as fresh and ultimately elusive as they have always been.

Carter, Angela 1940–92 English. Her fiction, often classified as MAGIC REALISM, mounts a witty, resourceful attack on received notions of 'reality' by using extravagant fantasy, a baroque multiplicity of characters who change role, status and even sex, and pastiches of genres from SCIENCE FICTION to PICARESQUE. Outstanding novels include *The Magic Toyshop* (1967), which won the JOHN LLEWELLYN RHYS PRIZE, *Heroes and Villains* (1969), *Nights at the Circus* (1984) and *WISE CHILDREN* (1991). *Bloody Chamber* (1979) is a collection of stories retelling classic fairy tales, a recurrent preoccupation which also led Carter to edit the two-volume *Virago Book of Fairy Tales* (1990 and 1992). Non-fiction includes: *The Sadeian Woman* (1979), a major feminist essay; *Nothing Sacred* (1982); and two posthumous collections, *Expletives Deleted* (1992) and *Shaking a Leg* (1997). Other posthumous collections are: *American Ghosts and Old World Wonders* (1993), short stories and meditations; *Burning Your Boats: The Complete Short Stories* (1995); and *The Curious Room: Collected Dramatic Works* (1996).

Cartland, Barbara See GENRE FICTION.

Carver, Raymond 1939–88 American. His short stories depict the apparently contingent lives of its small-town protagonists in unadorned prose. They are collected in *Will You Please be Quiet,*

Please? (1976), *What We Talk about When We Talk about Love* (1981), *Cathedral* (1983) and *Fires: Essays, Stories, Poems* (1983). His poetry appeared in *Near Klamath* (1968), *Winter Insomnia* (1970), *At Night the Salmon Move* (1976), *Where Water Comes Together with Other Water* (1985) and *Ultramarine* (1986).

Cary, (Arthur) Joyce (Lunel) 1888–1957 English. His first four novels – *Aissa Saved* (1932), *An American Visitor* (1933), *The African Witch* (1936) and *Mister Johnson* (1939) – derive from his experience in the Nigerian colonial service and deal with the confrontation between African tribal culture and British administration. *Castle Corner* (1938) is the only completed volume of a planned trilogy about the decline of the British Empire, and *Charley is My Darling* (1940) and *House of Children* (1941) are about childhood. His best-known works are two trilogies: *Herself Surprised* (1941), *To be a Pilgrim* (1942) and *The Horse's Mouth* (1944), about the world of art; and *Prisoner of Grace* (1952), *Except the Lord* (1953) and *Not Honour More* (1955), about politics. In both trilogies the story is told through first-person narratives by each of the three main characters. The narrative by the amoral artist Gully Jimson in *The Horse's Mouth* holds a particular appeal. Cary also published poetry and works on aesthetics and politics.

Castle Dangerous See SCOTT, SIR WALTER.

Castle of Otranto, The: *A Gothic Story* A novel by HORACE WALPOLE, published in 1764. He originally presented it as a translation from an imaginary Italian original but later acknowledged his authorship. The circumstances suggest that the tale was playfully conceived, though it proved influential in establishing the fashion for the GOTHIC NOVEL.

Set in the 13th century, the story concerns Manfred, who holds the princedom of Otranto only because his grandfather had poisoned the rightful prince, Alfonso. A prophecy has foretold that the usurpers would remain in power as long as they had male issue to continue their line and the castle remained large enough to hold the lawful ruler. Manfred's plan to marry his only son, Conrad, to Isabella is frustrated by Conrad's mysterious death and his subsequent plan to marry Isabella himself is thwarted by her escape with Theodore. Finally the ghost of Alfonso, grown too enormous to be contained by the castle, overthrows it and rises from the ruins. Manfred confesses the usurpation by his family, and the ghost proclaims Theodore the lawful prince. Theodore and Isabella marry.

Castle Rackrent A novel by MARIA EDGEWORTH, published in 1801. Thady Quirk, steward to the Rackrents, tells the story of the family's path to ruin, beginning three generations before with the hard-drinking Sir Patrick. Like *THE ABSENTEE*, the book criticizes 18th-century Irish landlords, vividly depicting the results of their profligacy and corruption.

Castle Richmond A novel by ANTHONY TROLLOPE, published in 1860. Set in 1846–7, it is of interest for its portrayal of the Irish Famine and for the character of Lady Desmond, hopelessly in love with a younger man, Owen Fitzgerald, who wants to marry her daughter Clara.

Castro, Brian 1950– Australian. *Birds of Passage* (1983), his first novel, juxtaposes the experiences of a Chinese on the Australian goldfields in the mid-19th century with those of his descendant in the present. Subsequent novels – *Pomeroy* (1990), *Double-Wolf* (1991), *After China* (1992) and *Drift* (1994) – experiment with fictional techniques to explore a diversity of cultural exchanges and conflicts. They have won him a reputation as an exponent of POST-MODERNISM.

Catch-22 A novel by JOSEPH HELLER, published in 1961. It established itself as a cult classic, and in coining the phrase 'Catch-22' made a permanent addition to the language.

Captain John Yossarian, an American airman, is determined to survive World War II. His attempt to get a medical discharge and so avoid further combat is thwarted by the rule – 'Catch-22' – which ordains that anyone rational enough to want to be grounded cannot be insane and is therefore capable of returning to flight duty. The non-chronological narrative technique emphasizes the displacements that war, and the absurd hierarchies of military life, produce. Heller is also concerned to indict a post-war culture dominated by personal competition and commercial ethics.

Catcher in the Rye, The A novel by J. D. SALINGER, published in 1951. It has attained canonical status as a tale of growing-up in post-war America.

The 16-year-old Holden Caulfield narrates his own story of rebellion against the banality and 'phoniness' of middle-class values. Expelled from private school, he goes by himself to New York City, where he has an unsuccessful encounter with a prostitute, a meeting with an old girlfriend, Sally Hayes, and an unsettling reunion with his former schoolteacher, Mr Antolini, who makes homosexual advances to him. Planning to 'go West' but wanting to say goodbye to his sister Phoebe, he is overwhelmed by his love for her and decides to stay. He then suffers a nervous breakdown, and tells his story as he is recovering.

Cather, Willa (Siebert) 1873–1947 American. Born in rural Virginia and brought up in Nebraska, she worked as a journalist and teacher in Pittsburgh before joining the staff of *McClure's Magazine* in New York. An early volume of poetry and a collection of short stories were followed by more stories in magazines and her first novel, *Alexander's Bridge* (1912). Her most important novels are commonly considered to be *O PIONEERS!* (1913) and *MY ÀNTONIA* (1918), both set in rural Nebraska, and *DEATH COMES FOR THE ARCHBISHOP* (1927). Others include: *The Song of the Lark* (1915); *One of Ours* (1922), her first popular success, which won a PULITZER PRIZE; *A Lost Lady* (1923), about the moral decline of a woman from a small Nebraska town; *The Professor's House* (1925), set in a small Midwestern college and in New Mexico in the post-war years; *My Mortal Enemy* (1926); *Shadows on the Rock* (1931); *Lucy Gayheart* (1935); and *Sapphira and the Slave* (1940), her only novel set in Virginia. The three tales that make up *Obscure Destinies* (1932) take place in the Midwest. *Not Under Forty* (1936; later retitled *Literary Encounters*) is a volume of critical essays.

Catherine: *A Story, by Ikey Solomons, Esq., Junior* A short novel by WILLIAM MAKEPEACE THACKERAY, serialized in 1839–40. Based on the career of Catherine Hayes, executed in 1726 for murdering her husband, it is a deliberately sordid tale written in reaction against the sentimental view of criminals offered by the NEWGATE NOVEL.

Catriona See KIDNAPPED.

Cecilia: *or, Memoirs of an Heiress* FANNY BURNEY's second novel, published in 1782. The story concerns the fortunes of Cecilia Beverley, victimized by her three unscrupulous guardians, Harrel, Briggs and the Hon. Compton Delvile. Driven by ill usage to insanity and the point of death, she eventually finds a modicum of happiness with her lover Mortimer Delvile. The novel was highly successful, confirming the reputation Burney had won for herself with *EVELINA*.

Celebrated Jumping Frog of Calaveras County, The A collection of stories by MARK TWAIN, published in 1867. The title sketch, which had first appeared in 1865, was based on an old Californian folk tale. Dan'l Webster, the champion jumping frog, is beaten in a contest when his gullet is filled with quail shot to weigh him down.

Chance A novel by JOSEPH CONRAD, published in 1913.

Marlow is the chief of several narrators who tell the story of Flora de Barral. Her self-confidence is undermined by an uncaring governess and her father's financial ruin and imprisonment. Her marriage to Captain Roderick Anthony is blighted by doubts about her own worth and remains unconsummated. After her father's release from prison all three live on board Anthony's ship, *Ferndale*. But de Barral, regarding his daughter's marriage as a betrayal, tries to poison Anthony and takes his own life when discovered by Powell, the second mate. Though she is unaware of these facts, her father's death helps Flora communicate with Anthony. When Anthony dies in an accident several years later, there is some prospect of a romance between Powell and Flora.

Chandler, Raymond (Thornton) 1888–1959 American. Born in Chicago and brought up in England, he worked as a journalist and businessman before starting to write DETECTIVE FICTION at the age of 45. His stories, regularly published in *Black Mask*, the most influential of the 'pulp' mystery magazines, are collected in *Trouble is My Business* (1950), *Killer in the Rain* (1964) and *The Smell of Fear* (1965). His most famous character, the disillusioned but chivalric detective Philip Marlowe, appeared in a series of novels: *The Big Sleep* (1939), *Farewell, My Lovely* (1940), *The High Window* (1942), *The Lady in the Lake* (1943), *The Little Sister* (1949), *The Long Goodbye* (1953) and *Playback* (1958). Chandler discusses his work in *The Simple Art of Murder* (1950) and the posthumous *Raymond Chandler Speaking* (1962).

Charlotte Temple: *A Tale of Truth* A novel by SUSANNA ROWSON, published in England in 1791 and in America in 1794. Modelled on SAMUEL RICHARDSON'S *CLARISSA*, it sold poorly in England but was a great success in the USA. The story, a highly moral warning against the dangers of seduction, describes how Charlotte elopes from school to New York with Montraville. He soon deserts her for an heiress, Julia Franklin, and she eventually dies after giving birth to his illegitimate child, Lucy. Charlotte's father adopts Lucy. *Charlotte's Daughter: or, The Three Orphans* (1828) is a belated sequel.

Charyn, Jerome 1925– American. He began with comic but rather conventional novels, such as *Once Upon a Droshky* (1964), *On the Darkening Green* (1965) and *Going to Jerusalem* (1967), before adopting more experimental structures and plots in *Eisenhower, My Eisenhower* (1972), *The Tar Baby* (1972), *The Franklin Scare* (1977) and *The Catfish Man: A Conjured Life* (1980). *Blue Eyes* (1975), *The Education of Patrick Silver* (1976), *Marilyn the Wild* (1976), *Secret Isaac* (1978), *The Good Policeman* (1990) and *Little Angel Street* (1994) form a series about a New York detective and a family of criminals.

Chatterjee, Upamanyu 1959– Indian. Born in the state of Bihar, he is culturally a Bengali. *English, August* (1988) is a humorous, and clearly in part autobiographical, account of a trainee in the élite Indian Administration Service posted to an obscure city in southern India. *THE LAST BURDEN* (1993) examines the complex relations in an Indian extended family.

Chatwin, Bruce 1940–89 English. His *sui generis* works frequently challenge the boundaries between travel writing, autobiography, history and fiction. *In Patagonia* (1977) alternates between minute esoterica and vast imaginative leaps. *The Songlines* (1987) develops a partly fictionalized investigation of nomadism into speculation on the origins of human civiliza-tion. *The Viceroy of Ouidah* (1980) is a predominantly historical monograph about the African slave kingdom of Dahomey. *On the Black Hill* (1982; WHITBREAD AWARD for First Novel) is in pastoral mode and *Utz* (1988) is a brief, lapidary novel about a collector of Dresden china. *What am I Doing Here* (1989) consists of posthumously gathered shorter pieces.

Chaudhuri, Nirad C(handra) 1897– Indian. His literary career began late, with *The Autobiography of an Unknown Indian* (1951), described by V. S. NAIPAUL as 'the one great book to come out of the Anglo-Indian encounter', and continued with a massive sequel, *Thy Hand, Great Anarch!* (1987), as well as a short travel book, *A Passage to England* (1960). Although he has never published fiction, Chaudhuri remains one of India's most controversial prose writers.

Cheever, John 1912–82 American. Much of his work deals humorously and compassionately with the spiritually and emotionally impoverished life in materially affluent communities. His novels include *The Wapshot Chronicle* (1957), *The Wapshot Scandal* (1964), *Bullet Park* (1969), *Falconer* (1977) and *Oh, What a Paradise It Seems* (1982). His short stories, many of which appeared originally in *The New Yorker* and *The New Republic*, were published in various volumes and gathered in *The Stories of John Cheever* (1978; PULITZER PRIZE). His posthumously published letters (edited by Benjamin Cheever; 1988) and journals (1991) reveal a tormented private life apparently at odds with the often urbane character of his fiction.

Chen, Willi 1934– Trinidadian, of Chinese descent. *King of the Carnival* (1988), his first collection of short stories, is set mainly in rural Trinidadian East Indian communities and draws on folk traditions. The stories are notable for their wit and comic compassion. Chen's plays include *Freedom Road* (1985), *Tainted Blood* (1987) and *Stickman* (1993). He is also a painter and sculptor.

Cheney-Choker, Syl 1945– Sierra Leonean. Initially known for three collections of poetry, he has also published *The Last Harmattan of Alusine Dunbar* (1990), an expansive novel drawing on the conventions of MAGIC REALISM. It won the COMMONWEALTH WRITERS PRIZE (Africa section) in 1991.

Chesney, Sir George Tomkyns 1830–95 English. *The Battle of Dorking*, a fictional account of an enemy attack on England, was published by *Blackwood's Magazine* in 1871 and frequently reprinted (see SCIENCE FICTION and SPY FICTION). Other novels were *The Dilemma* (1876), set at the time of the Indian mutiny, *The New Ordeal* (1879), *The Private Secretary* (1881) and *The Lesters* (1893).

Chesnutt, Charles W(addell) 1858–1932 African-American. His first two collections of stories, *The Conjure Woman* and *The Wife of His Youth and Other Stories of the Color Line* (both 1899), display a fluent, urbane style aimed at a popular readership in which he nevertheless achieved a probing exploration of racial themes and a realistic view of slavery and Reconstruction. Later work concentrated on the problems of racial and class identity in a changing society. Chesnutt wrote three novels, *The House behind the Cedars* (1900), *The Marrow of Tradition* (1901) and *The Colonel's Dream* (1906), as well as essays and reviews.

Chesterton, G(ilbert) K(eith) 1874–1936 English. He was closely identified with his friend HILAIRE BELLOC in temperament and belief: a dislike of imperialism, particularly during the Boer War; an opposition to modern industrialism and centralized power; and a love of celebrating the 'Englishness' of England. The last is a common theme in his verse, gathered in *Collected Poems* (1933). His novels, *The Napoleon of Notting Hill* (1904) and *The Man Who was Thursday: A Nightmare* (1908), are exuberant political fantasies which celebrate the romance of an earlier preindustrial world. *The Innocence of Father Brown* (1911) started an enduringly popular series of DETECTIVE FICTION about an unassuming Catholic priest whose gift for solving complex mysteries springs largely from his insight into evil. Chesterton himself became a Roman Catholic in 1922.

Of his literary criticism, Chesterton's book on DICKENS (1906) is particularly memorable; he also published studies of Robert Browning (1903), GEORGE BERNARD SHAW and William Blake (both 1910), and Chaucer (1932). Works on social, political and religious subjects include *Heretics* (1905), *Orthodoxy* (1909), *St Francis of Assisi* (1923) and *St Thomas Aquinas* (1933). Collections of his essays appeared as *All Things Considered* (1908), *A Miscellany of Men* (1912), *The Uses of Diversity* (1920), and *As I was Saying* (1936).

Child, Lydia M(aria) 1802–80 American. A leading Abolitionist, she wrote an 'Appeal in Favor of that Class of Americans Called Africans' (1833) and letters to the governor of Virginia published as *Correspondence* (1860). Novels include *Hobomok* (1824), about the Indians of colonial Massachusetts, *The Rebels: or, Boston before the Revolution* (1825), and *Philothea* (1836), set in classical Greece.

Child of the Jago, A A novel by ARTHUR MORRISON, published in 1896. 'The Jago' is Morrison's name for 'The Nichol' in London's Bethnal Green, where Dick ('Dicky') Perrott spends his childhood. A boy with good intentions, he is constantly frustrated by his environment. His father is hanged for murder and Dicky himself is killed in a street fight at the age of 17. Morrison's terse, straightforward style owes something to GEORGE MOORE and NATURALISM.

Childers, (Robert) Erskine 1870–1922 Anglo-Irish. A supporter of Irish Home Rule, he was executed for his role in the Irish Republican Army after the establishment of the Irish Free State. His political pamphlets are forgotten but his one novel, *The Riddle of the Sands* (1903), is not. Slow but cunningly paced SPY FICTION, packed with yachting lore and warnings of Germany's military ambitions, it remains notable for its two well-contrasted heroes, Carruthers and Davies.

Children of the New Forest, The See MARRYAT, CAPTAIN FREDERICK.

Chimes, The The second of CHARLES DICKENS's Christmas stories, published in 1844 and collected in *CHRISTMAS BOOKS* (1852). Mesmerized by chiming bells and influenced by spirits, the simple, good-hearted Toby ('Trotty') Veck witnesses the hardships of his daughter Meg, the falsely accused Will Fern and the orphaned Lilian. They are maltreated or condescended to by Sir Joseph Bowley, Alderman Cute, Mr Filer and others. A final burst of goodwill effects a happy ending.

Chin, Frank 1940– Asian-American. His work portrays the contradictions inherent in the social lives and customs of the Chinese communities in the USA. It includes *The Chinaman Pacific and Frisco R.R. Co.* (1988), a collection of stories, and *Donald Duk* (1991) and *Gunga Din Highway* (1994), both novels. *The Chickencoop Chinaman* and *The Year of the Dragon*, published together in 1981, are plays.

Chinodya, Shimmer 1957– Zimbabwean. He has published *Dew in the Morning* (1982), *Farai's Girls* (1984) and *Harvest of Thorns* (1989), a complex and compelling account of Benjamin Tichafa's rite of passage, or 'harvest of thorns', as he grows to maturity against the background of Rhodesia in the 1970s.

Chopin, Kate 1851–1904 American. Born in St Louis, Missouri, she moved to New Orleans following her marriage and devoted herself to writing after the death of her mother and husband. *At Fault* (1890), a novel showing Maupassant's influence, was followed by two collections of short stories set among Creoles and Acadians in Louisiana, *Bayou Folk* (1894) and *A Night in Acadie* (1897). Her best-known work, *THE AWAKENING* (1899), provoked hostile criticism by its sympathetic portrayal of a woman who rejects the constraints of marriage and motherhood.

Christie, Dame Agatha (Mary Clarissa) 1890–1976 English. Her DETECTIVE FICTION began with *The Mysterious Affair at Styles* (1920), introducing the Belgian private detective Hercule Poirot whose career extended through many books to *Curtain* (1975). *The Murder at the Vicarage* (1930) introduced the shrewd, gentle Miss Marple, whose career rivalled Poirot's in length and popularity, ending with *Sleeping Murder* (1976). Classic books – *The Murder of Roger Ackroyd* (1926), *Peril at End House* (1932), *Lord Edgeware Dies* (1933), *Murder on the Orient Express*

(1934), *Why Didn't They Ask Evans?* (1934), *The ABC Murders* (1936) and *Ten Little Niggers* (1939; since usually retitled *Ten Little Indians*) – are perfunctory in setting and characterization, concentrating almost exclusively on the tantalizing ingenuity of plot for which her name has become a by-word. Of the several short stories Christie adapted for the stage, *The Mousetrap* (1952) and *Witness for the Prosecution* (1953) were prodigiously successful. She also wrote light romantic novels as Mary Westmacott.

Christmas Books A collection of Christmas stories by CHARLES DICKENS, published together for the first time in 1852: *A CHRISTMAS CAROL* (1843), *THE CHIMES* (1844), *THE CRICKET ON THE HEARTH* (1845), *THE BATTLE OF LIFE* (1846) and *THE HAUNTED MAN AND THE GHOST'S BARGAIN* (1848).

Christmas Carol, A A novella by CHARLES DICKENS, published in 1843. The first and most popular of his Christmas stories, it was gathered with its successors in *CHRISTMAS BOOKS* (1852).

On Christmas Eve the miserly Ebenezer Scrooge is visited by the shade of his dead partner, Jacob Marley, and then by The Ghost of Christmas Past, The Ghost of Christmas Present, and The Ghost of Christmas Yet to Come. They show him the scenes of his youth, the family life of his loyal clerk, Bob Cratchit, whose household includes the sadly crippled Tiny Tim, and an ominous future. Chastened, he resolves to lead a better life, sending a turkey to the Cratchits, visiting his honest nephew, donating to charity and raising Bob's salary.

Chronicles of the Canongate The inclusive title given by SIR WALTER SCOTT to stories presented as the recollections of Mrs Bethune, Baliol of the Canongate in Edinburgh. They are written down by her friend Mr Chrystal Croftangry, whose own remarkable story serves as an introduction. The first series, consisting of *The Highland Widow*, *The Two Drovers* and *The Surgeon's Daughter*, was published in 1827 and the second, *St Valentine's Day: or, The Fair Maid of Perth*, in 1828. The fair maid is Catharine Glover, who lives during the reign of Robert III in the 14th century. Henry Smith, an armourer, loves her and defeats the evil designs of the worthless Duke of Rothsay, the king's son, and his friend, Sir John Ramorny. The gentle Catharine eventually accepts Henry after he sickens of combat.

Cisneros, Sandra 1954– Chicana. As well as publishing several volumes of poetry – *Bad Boys* (1980), *The Rodrigo Poems* (1985), *My Wicked, Wicked Ways* (1987) and *Loose Women* (1995) – she attracted attention with her first novel, *The House on Mango Street* (1986), a loosely tied collection of vignettes about a girl coming of age in the Hispanic section of Chicago. *Woman of Hollering Creek and Other Stories* (1991) marked her as an important voice in Hispanic literature.

Clarissa: or, The History of a Young Lady A novel by SAMUEL RICHARDSON, the first two volumes published in 1747, the last five in 1748. An EPISTOLARY NOVEL, like its predecessor *PAMELA*, it consists of a four-way correspondence between the principal characters: Clarissa Harlowe's to her friend Miss Howe and Robert Lovelace's letters to his friend John Belford predominate.

Clarissa is a well-bred young lady attracted to the dashing Lovelace, an unscrupulous man of whom her parents strongly disapprove. In deference to their wishes, Clarissa resists his advances, but also refuses to marry the man they have selected instead, the detestable Mr Solmes. Confined to her room (for the first 500 pages of the plot) she secretly corresponds with Lovelace, and runs away with him, only to discover his real nature. He instals her under the watchful eye of Mrs Sinclair, a bawd, and woos her ardently. When his subtlety gives way to impatience he drugs and then rapes her. Denounced by her family, she rejects Lovelace totally, ignores the pleas of his family and friends to accept his proposal of marriage, and retires into solitude. She dies of shame and grief, and Lovelace is killed in a duel with her cousin. Belford, the libertine correspondent, turns over a new leaf, becomes Clarissa's executor, and edits her letters.

Though the action of the novel encompasses less than a year, the intense degree of characterization is extraordinarily sustained, buoyed up by Richardson's careful unification of the narrative elements. *Clarissa* is widely regarded as his masterpiece, and, running to over a million words, is the longest novel in the English language.

Clarke, Arthur C(harles) 1917– English, resident in Sri Lanka. His early SCIENCE FICTION, *Childhood's End* (1953) and *The City and the Stars* (1956), showed the influence of OLAF STAPLEDON but most of his novels aim at technological realism. They include *Rendezvous with Rama* (1973), *Imperial Earth* (1975), *The Fountains of Paradise* (1979), *The Songs at Distant Earth* (1986) and *The Hammer of God* (1993). Clarke worked closely with Stanley Kubrick on the film *2001: A Space Odyssey* (1968), carrying the story forward in *2010: Odyssey Two* (1982) and *2061: Odyssey Three* (1988). *Cradle* (1988) and three further novels in the *Rama* sequence were written with Gentry Lee.

Clarke, Austin 1934– Barbadian/Canadian. His fiction blends humour and anger in its criticism of colonial Barbados and contemporary Canada. The trilogy formed by *The Meeting Point* (1967), *Storm of Fortune* (1973) and *The Bigger Light* (1975) is his major work to date. Other novels include *Survivors of the Crossing* (1964), *Among Thistles and Thorns* (1965), *The Prime Minister* (1977), *Proud Empires* (1988). *When He Was Free and Young and He Used to Wear Silks* (1971), *When Women Rule* (1985) and *Nine Men Who Laughed* (1986) are collections of stories. *Growing Up Stupid under the Union Jack* (1980) and *Colonial Innocency* (1982) are memoirs.

Clarke, Marcus 1846–81 Australian. Born in London, he emigrated to Victoria in 1863 and worked as a journalist, publishing his first novel, *Long Odds* (1869), in his own magazine, *The Colonial Monthly*. His best-known work, HIS NATURAL LIFE (serialized in 1870–2, revised for book publication in 1874), presented a vivid picture of the penal settlement in Tasmania. Other works included collections of short stories – *Old Tales of a Young Country* (1871) and *The Man with the Oblong Box* (1878) – and a pantomime, *Twinkle, Twinkle Little Star* (1873).

Claverings, The A novel by ANTHONY TROLLOPE, serialized in 1866–7. Harry Clavering, a schoolmaster resolved to become an engineer, is jilted by Julia Brabazon in favour of Lord Ongar. He falls in love with Florence Burton, the daughter of a partner in his firm, but is again drawn into contact with Julia, now widowed, to protect her from the sinister Count Pateroff and his scheming sister Sophie Gordeloup. Harry is drawn into a second proposal before he realizes that Florence will be a better wife. Julia surrenders her claim and Harry finds himself heir to the Clavering estate.

Clayhanger A novel by ARNOLD BENNETT, published in 1910. The first of a trilogy, it was followed by *Hilda Lessways* (1911) and *These Twain* (1916). A fourth novel, *The Roll Call* (1918), is loosely connected with the series.

It follows 20 years in the life of Edwin Clayhanger, from the day he leaves school, concentrating on his struggle with his dominating father, Darius, and his dream of escaping the Potteries town of Bursley. Edwin falls in love with Hilda Lessways, whom he meets through the cultivated Orgreaves family, but she mysteriously disappears and he hears of her subsequent marriage. Years later, after his father's death, Edwin traces Hilda and her son to a Brighton boarding house and learns of her ruin at the hands of the bigamous George Cannon. The novel ends with their plan to marry.

Cleland, John 1709–89 English. He is best known for *Memoirs of a Woman of Pleasure* (1748–9), usually called *Fanny Hill*, long suppressed as obscene, though it was one of the most popular novels of the 18th century. He also wrote *Memoirs of a Coxcomb: or, The History of Sir William Delamere* (1751) and *The Surprises of Love* (1764) as well as plays and philological studies.

Cliff-Dwellers, The A novel by HENRY BLAKE FULLER, published in 1893. One of the earliest American novels to have the monstrous and impersonal city as its setting, it satirizes greed and social striving in Chicago. The 'cliff-dwellers' are the inhabitants of a skyscraper called the Clifton Building. They include:

Arthur Ingles, the rich owner; Erasmus Brainard, an antisocial banker; Eugene H. McDowell, a crooked real-estate agent; George Ogden, an ambitious clerk who works in Brainard's bank; and the various women who contribute to their fortunes and misfortunes.

Clive, Caroline 1801–73 English. Under the pseudonym V she published *IX Poems* (1840), well received and followed by several other volumes. Her most popular work was a SENSATION NOVEL, *Paul Ferroll* (1855), whose wealthy and cultured hero is forced to confess to the murder of his wife many years after the event. A sequel, *Why Paul Ferroll Killed His Wife* (1860), describes the provocation that drove him to the crime.

Clockwork Orange, A A satirical dystopian novel by ANTHONY BURGESS, published in 1962. Its central achievement is the inventively futuristic street-slang, incorporating many Russian words, in which Alex tells the story. The leader of a violent teenage gang, he is made the subject of an experiment in behavioural engineering. While his emotional responses are stimulated by classical music, electric shocks condition him to be sickened by violence. Robbed of the ability to make moral choices, he becomes a victim of violence himself, until the political tide turns and he is cynically 'rehabilitated'.

The novel achieved a new notoriety when Stanley Kubrick withdrew his film version (1971) following charges that it had inspired 'copycat' violence.

Cloete, Stuart 1897–1976 South African. Born in Paris, he was educated in England. A prolific author of non-fiction, adventure novels and short stories, he is at his best in a sequence of realistic, unsentimental novels covering 19th-century Afrikaner history: *Turning Wheels* (1937), *The Curve and the Tusk* (1953) and *The Abductors* (1970). *A Victorian Son* (1971) and *The Gambler* (1973) are autobiographies.

Cloister and the Hearth, The: *A Tale of the Middle Ages* A novel by CHARLES READE, published in 1861. Set in the 15th century, it concerns Gerard, a Dutch mercer's son, who loves Margaret, the daughter of a poor scholar, Peter Brandt. Both the burgomaster and Gerard's family oppose the marriage and contrive to have Gerard imprisoned. He escapes and wanders through Europe, the incidents of his exile enlivened by atmospheric scenes in taverns, stews, castles and monasteries. In Italy a false report of Margaret's death drives him into a Dominican monastery. Returning to Holland, he discovers Margaret; she has borne him a son who will grow up to be Erasmus. No longer able to marry, he spends the rest of his life at Gouda near his family. (See also HISTORICAL FICTION.)

Clough, Arthur Hugh See *AMOURS DE VOYAGE*.

CNA Literary Award A South African award sponsored since 1961 by the Central New Agency, a chain of booksellers. Until 1995 it was restricted to fiction, short fiction, poetry, drama, biography, history or travel in two sections: English and Afrikaans. Since then it has been open to works in any of South Africa's 11 official languages, which compete for prizes in three categories: creative literature, non-fiction and children's literature.

Twenty-five novels in English have won the award. NADINE GORDIMER won four times, with THE CONSERVATIONIST (1974), Burger's Daughter (1979), July's People (1981) and My Son's Story (1990). J. M. COETZEE won three times, with In the Heart of the Country (1977), Waiting for the Barbarians (1980) and LIFE AND TIMES OF MICHAEL K (1983). ANDRÉ BRINK won twice, with Rumours of Rain (1978) and A Chain of Voices (1982), as well as winning twice in the Afrikaans section. BREYTEN BREYTENBACH also won in the English section, with Memory of Snow and of Dust (1989), and the Afrikaans section. Other notable winners have been: Siegfried Stander, with The Desert Place (1961) and The Horse Thief (1968); MARY RENAULT, with The Bull from the Sea (1962); LAURENS VAN DER POST, with The Seed and the Sower (1963) and The Hunter and the Whale (1967); Jack Cope, with The Rain-Maker (1971); Sheila Fugard, with The Castaways (1972); and CHRISTOPHER HOPE, with White Boy Running (1988). ALAN PATON won the award twice, for his biographies Hofmeyr (1964) and Apartheid and the Archbishop (1973).

In 1991 the award Best Book Design which had been instituted in 1986 was replaced by the Debut Award, intended to encourage new writers. Winning novels have included David Lambkin's Plain of Darkness (1993) and Isaac Mogotsi's The Alexandra Tales (1994).

Cockton, Henry 1807–53 English. He achieved temporary success with broadly comic novels in the manner of the early DICKENS, notably The Life and Adventures of Valentine Vox the Ventriloquist (1840).

Cody, Liza See DETECTIVE FICTION.

Coetzee, J(ohn) M(ichael) 1940– South African. Although he takes his themes from his political environment, his writing draws attention to the nature of language and fiction. His work includes: Dusklands (1974), consisting of two novellas; In the Heart of the Country (1977; as From the Heart of the Country in the USA), about an Afrikaner spinster isolated on her farm; Waiting for the Barbarians (1980), an allegorical exploration of power-sickness and justice; LIFE AND TIMES OF MICHAEL K (1983); Foe (1986), the multi-layered tale of a woman castaway excluded from DEFOE's ROBINSON CRUSOE; Age of Iron (1990), about a woman dying from cancer who is cared for by an alcoholic vagrant; and The Master of St Petersburg (1994), a rearrangement of part of Dostoyevsky's life and an investigation into the boundaries between fact and fiction. In the Heart of the Country, Waiting for the Barbarians and Life and Times of Michael K all won the CNA LITERARY AWARD, and Life and Times of Michael K also received the BOOKER PRIZE. Coetzee's criticism includes White Writing (1988) and Giving Offense: Essays on Censorship (1996).

Cohen, Leonard 1934– Canadian. Internationally known as a singer and composer, he has also published fiction and poetry. His poetry includes The Spice-Box of Earth (1961), Flowers for Hitler (1964), Selected Poems (1968), The Energy of Slaves (1972), Death of a Lady's Man (1978) and Book of Mercy (1984). Like his songs, it explores contemporary mythologies but frequently uses traditional forms. His novels include The Favourite Game (1963) and Beautiful Losers (1968), a counter-cultural religious epic which has attained classic status. Among his record albums are Songs of Leonard Cohen (1967), Songs of Love and Hate (1971), New Skins for the Old Ceremony (1974), The Best of Leonard Cohen (1975) and Death of a Lady's Man (1977). Stranger Music (1993) is a selection of his poems and songs.

Cohen, Matt 1942– Canadian. After two experimental novels, Korsoniloff (1969) and Johnny Crackle Sings (1971), he turned to realism with his four 'Salem' novels, The Disinherited (1974), The Colours of War (1977), The Sweet Second Summer of Kitty Malone (1979) and Flowers of Darkness (1981). Other novels are: Wooden Hunters (1975); The Spanish Doctor (1984), an epic work about the Jewish diaspora in medieval Europe; Emotional Arithmetic (1990), about a woman scarred by her internment by the Nazis in World War II. He has also published several short-story collections: Columbus and the Fat Lady (1972), Night Flights (1978), Café le Dog (1983), Living on Water (1988) and Lives of the Mind Slaves (1994).

Cold Comfort Farm The first and most famous novel by Stella Gibbons (1902–89), published in 1932. It uses the visit paid by the heroine, Flora Poste, to the appalling and grotesque Starkadder family as an excuse for parody of the rural fiction made popular by THOMAS HARDY, D. H. LAWRENCE and, in a debased form, writers like MARY WEBB, whose Precious Bane had been a best-seller in the previous decade. Like many first-rate parodies, it remains funny even for those without a detailed knowledge of the texts it refers to.

Colegate, Isobel 1931– English. Her work scrutinizes the contending claims to power of various social groups: landed aristocrats in her first novel, The Blackmailer (1958), or more sympathetically viewed in her best-known novel, The Shooting Party (1980); nouveaux riches in A Man of Power (1960); and the Victorian bourgeoisie in The Summer of the Royal Visit (1991). In Orlando King (1968), Orlando at the Brazen Threshold (1971) and Agatha (1973), brought together as The Orlando Trilogy (1984), politicians, entrepreneurs, manufacturers, aristocrats, visionaries and traitors jockey for position from the Depression to the 1950s. Related concerns inform

Deceits of Time (1988), about a woman writing the biography of a minor cabinet minister.

Coleridge, Mary Elizabeth 1861–1907 English. A descendant of Samuel Taylor Coleridge, she published her first volumes of poetry, *Fancy's Following* (1896) and *Fancy's Guerdon* (1897), under the pseudonym Anodos. Her first novel, *The Seven Sleepers of Ephesus* (1893), drew praise from ROBERT LOUIS STEVENSON; its dream-like atmosphere was typical of her work. Later titles include a historical romance, *The King with Two Faces* (1897), as well as *The Fiery Dawn* (1901) and, usually the most highly regarded, *The Lady on the Drawing Room Floor* (1906). *Poems Old and New* (1907) and *Gathered Leaves* (1910) appeared posthumously.

Collins, Jackie See GENRE FICTION.

Collins, Merle 1950– Grenadian. Born in Aruba, she worked for Maurice Bishop's People's Revolutionary Government before moving to London and then to the USA. She is best known for her novel *Angel* (1987), which links personal and political themes as a young Grenadian woman comes of age during the country's revolution. She has published a second novel, *The Colour of Forgetting* (1995), and a collection of stories, *Rain Darling* (1990). *Because the Dawn Breaks* (1985) and *Rotten Pomerack* (1987) are volumes of poetry. With Rhonda Cobham, Collins edited *Watchers and Seekers: Writing by Black Women in Britain* (1987).

Collins, Tom See FURPHY, JOSEPH.

Collins, (William) Wilkie 1824–89 English. Son of the landscape painter William Collins, he was named after his father's friend Sir David Wilkie. He began by writing a memoir of his father (1848); *Antonina; or, The Fall of Rome* (1850), HISTORICAL FICTION in the manner of BULWER LYTTON; and the charming *Rambles beyond Railways* (1851), about Cornwall. He first met DICKENS in 1851, joining him in amateur theatricals and contributing to his magazine *Household Words*. They collaborated on, among other pieces, *The Lazy Tour of Two Idle Apprentices* (1857) and two melodramas, *The Lighthouse* (1855) and *The Frozen Deep* (1857).

A succession of short stories and several novels, *Basil: A Story of Modern Life* (1852), *Hide and Seek* (1854) and *The Dead Secret* (1857), were the prelude to his work of the 1860s, when Collins emerged as the most skilful writer of SENSATION NOVELS with THE WOMAN IN WHITE (1860), *No Name* (1862), *Armadale* (1866) and THE MOONSTONE (1868). Collins's subsequent determination to tackle social issues and commit himself to the ROMAN À THÈSE disconcerted his audience; increasingly, it also dispersed his narrative powers. He attacked athleticism in *Man and Wife* (1870), attitudes to fallen women in *The New Magdalen* (1873), the Jesuits in *The Black Robe* (1881) and vivisection in *Heart and Science* (1883). *The Evil Genius* (1886) dealt with adultery and

divorce, *The Legacy of Cain* (1889) with heredity and environment. Collins returned to mystery and suspense, with varying success, in *Poor Miss Finch* (1872), *The Law and the Lady* (1875), *My Lady's Money* (1878) and *I Say No* (1884). *Blind Love* (1890) was completed by WALTER BESANT.

Colonel Jack A novel by DANIEL DEFOE, published in 1722 under the title of *The History and Remarkable Life of the Truly Honourable Colonel Jacque, Commonly Called Colonel Jack*. Like CAPTAIN SINGLETON, it is a romantic adventure told in the first person. Abandoned by his parents, 'Colonel Jack' falls into bad company, becomes a pickpocket, and reaches early manhood living on his wits. He enlists as a soldier but soon deserts. Next he is abducted and shipped to Virginia, where he is sold as a slave to a planter. Promoted to overseer and then freed, he succeeds as a planter himself. By the end of the tale he is back in England, prosperous and mellow.

Coming Race, The A novel by EDWARD BULWER LYTTON, published in 1871. At the centre of the earth an American mining engineer encounters people who derive unbounded powers from a mysterious kinetic energy called 'Vril'. The book is in part a satire on Darwinian evolutionary theory and on the emancipation of women. For a time the word 'Vril' became associated with any strength-giving elixir: hence Bo(vine)vril.

Commonwealth Writers Prize An annual prize for new novels by Commonwealth writers, inaugurated in 1987 and sponsored by the Commonwealth foundation. Less well-known than the BOOKER PRIZE, which selects its winners from a similar range of Commonwealth fiction, it is generally considered more open to non-British Commonwealth fiction. Each of four regions (Africa; Canada and the Caribbean; Eurasia; and Southeast Asia and the South Pacific) selects a best book and a best first book, which then compete for the final awards in each category, judged by a pan-Commonwealth panel. The awards ceremony rotates round the Commonwealth and has taken place in Britain, Australia, Canada, Singapore and Zimbabwe. Winners of the best-book prize have been: OLIVE SENIOR (Jamaica), *Summer Lightning* in 1987; FESTUS IYAYI (Nigeria), *Heroes* in 1988; JANET FRAME (New Zealand), *The Carpathians* in 1989; MORDECAI RICHLER (Canada), *SOLOMON GURSKY WAS HERE* in 1990; DAVID MALOUF (Australia), *The Great World* in 1991; ROHINTON MISTRY (Canada), *SUCH A LONG JOURNEY* in 1992; Alex Miller (Australia), *The Ancestor Game* in 1993; VIKRAM SETH (India), *A SUITABLE BOY* in 1994; LOUIS DE BERNIÈRES (Britain), *Captain Corelli's Mandolin* in 1995; ROHINTON MISTRY (Canada), *A Fine Balance* in 1996; and EARL LOVELACE (Trinidad), *Salt* in 1997.

Compton-Burnett, Dame Ivy 1884–1969 English. Her first novel, *Dolores* (1911) was a pale imitation of GEORGE ELIOT, and it was not until *Pastors* *and Masters* (1925) that her distinct and highly individual style emerged. From the late 1920s until her death she produced a new novel almost every two years: *Brothers and Sisters* (1929), *Men and Wives* (1931), *More Women than Men* (1933), *A House and Its Head* (1935), *Daughters and Sons* (1941), *A Family and a Fortune* (1939), *Parents and Children* (1941), and so on, a total of over 20 novels. *Mother and Son* (1955) won the James Tait Black Memorial Prize. As their titles suggest, the novels are preoccupied with domestic scenes and family strife; their central theme is the abuse of power. The plots are realized almost exclusively through dialogue, dispensing with conventional authorial comment.

Comyns, Barbara (Irene Veronica) 1909– English. Much of her work is preoccupied with childhood as a place of seeming sanctuary shot through with the fear, or sometimes fact, of violence and mortality. It includes: the eccentrically spelled and punctuated *Sisters By a River* (1947); *Our Spoons Came from Woolworths* (1950); *Who was Changed and Who was Dead* (1955); *The Vet's Daughter* (1959), her best-known work, adapted by Sandy Wilson as a musical, *The Clapham Wonder* (1978); *The Skin Chairs* (1962); *The Juniper Tree* (1985), based on one of Grimms' fairy tales; and *The House of Dolls* (1989), an unnervingly jolly account of a household of elderly prostitutes.

Conan, Laure See FRENCH-CANADIAN NOVEL.

Condition of England novel A type of novel reflecting concern about the 'Condition of England' in the 19th century, particularly in the 1840s. The concern was largely stimulated by Thomas Carlyle's message in *Chartism* (1839) and *Past and Present* (1843) that *laissez-faire* policies, combined with neglect of the industrial poor, were driving the ranks of society further apart and could easily lead to revolution. Recurrent preoccupations of the Condition of England novel are: the use of power, mechanical and social; the sense of a breach between man and man and the importance of healing it; the need for education; and the fear of revolution. Examples include: DISRAELI's *CONINGSBY* (1844) and *SYBIL* (1845); CHARLES KINGSLEY's *YEAST* (1848) and *ALTON LOCKE* (1850); GASKELL's *MARY BARTON* (1848) and *NORTH AND SOUTH* (1855); CHARLOTTE BRONTË's *SHIRLEY* (1849); DICKENS's *HARD TIMES* (1854); and DINAH MULOCK's *JOHN HALIFAX, GENTLEMAN* (1857).

Similar concerns sometimes prompted later writers to revive the Condition of England novel, at least in its broadest impulse, as ANTHONY TROLLOPE did in *THE WAY WE LIVE NOW* (1875) – whose title might serve as an alternative label for the form – and H. G. WELLS did in *TONO-BUNGAY* (1909). The Thatcherism of the 1980s and early 1990s prompted a new clutch of Condition of England novels, ranging from DAVID LODGE's *Nice Work* (1988) to DAVID

DABYDEEN's *Disappearance* (1993). TOM WOLFE's *THE BONFIRE OF THE VANITIES* (1987) could be read as their counterpart in the USA. See also *ROMAN À THÈSE*.

Condon, Matthew 1962– Australian. The distinct culture, past and present, of his native Brisbane provides the setting for the reminiscent *Motorcycle Café* (1988), the satiric *Usher* (1991) and the comic and discontinuous *A Night at the Pink Poodle* (1996).

Condon, Richard See SPY FICTION.

Confidence-Man, The: His Masquerade A novel by HERMAN MELVILLE, published in 1857, the last to appear during his lifetime. It takes place on the Mississippi river steamer *Fidèle*. Many of the characters are different manifestations of the confidence-man, who appears successively as a deaf mute, herb doctor, salesman of phoney stock, beggar, collector for charity and, for the second half of the novel, as Frank Goodman, who engages in philosophical conversations with other passengers. The book ends with a discussion about the status of the apocryphal scriptures, fusing the book's thematic concern with trust with the literary issue of narrative as a bearer of meaning.

Coningsby: or, The New Generation A novel by BENJAMIN DISRAELI, published in 1844. A *ROMAN À THÈSE*, it addresses the problem of leadership for England under a regenerated, idealistic Conservative Party. The answer, for Disraeli, lies in the symbolic marriage of his hero, the aristocratic Harry Coningsby, with a daughter of the 'millocracy', Edith Millbank. Edith's father originally opposes the match but later consents. The true hero, however, is the aloof Sidonia, fiercely proud of his Jewishness, who combines wealth, wisdom and cosmopolitan culture. While Coningsby and his brother-in-law, Oswald Millbank, go into Parliament, Sidonia reverts to the faith of his fathers, thus cutting him off from his place as a natural leader in England, and guards the purity of his race by not marrying.

Connecticut Yankee in King Arthur's Court, A A satirical fantasy by MARK TWAIN, published in 1889. Hank Morgan, chief superintendent at the Colt arms factory, awakes to find himself in Camelot. Originally conceived as a comic experiment in anachronistic contrast, the novel gradually develops into a darker, more violent story. Hank's introduction of 19th-century 'enlightenment', with its ideology of progress and its powerful gadgets, leads to civil war in Arthur's England, and to an apocalyptic last battle in which both sides are destroyed by advanced technology.

Connell, Evan (Shelby), Jr 1924– American novelist. He is best known for *Mrs Bridge* (1959) and *Mr Bridge* (1969). *Mrs Bridge* examines the life of India Bridge, a wealthy woman consumed by materialism and social pretension; *Mr Bridge*

is told from the viewpoint of her husband Walter, a self-satisfied lawyer. Other novels include *The Patriot* (1960), *The Diary of a Rapist* (1966), *The Connoisseur* (1974) and *The Alchymist's Journal* (1991). His stories are collected in *The Anatomy Lesson and Other Stories* (1957) and *At the Crossroads* (1965). He has also published verse, essays and *Son of the Morning Star* (1984), about General Custer.

Connolly, Cyril (Vernon) 1903–74 English. His reputation for intellectual precocity set him a target of promise that his output consistently failed to fulfil. His single novel is *The Rock Pool* (1936), set in the South of France. Other books include the partly autobiographical *Enemies of Promise* (1938) and *The Unquiet Grave* (1944), nostalgic-hedonist maxims by 'Palinurus'. Connolly founded and edited the influential *Horizon* (1939–50) and became principal book reviewer for *The Sunday Times*.

Conrad, Joseph [Korzeniowski, Jozef Teodor Konrad] 1857–1924 He was born in Podolia in the Ukraine, the child of Polish parents opposed to the Tsarist domination of their country. His father's involvement in political conspiracy resulted in exile to Volgoda, north-west of Moscow, where Conrad's mother died when he was seven. His father died in Poland four years later and Conrad was guided through youth by his uncle Tadeusz. In 1874 he went to Marseilles and began a 20-year career as a sailor. After a reckless and improvident period, which involved gun-running for the Carlists in Spain and culminated in a suicide attempt in 1878, Conrad made steady progress. Serving on English ships, he passed his second mate's examination in 1880 and his first mate's examination in 1884. He became a naturalized British subject in 1886, and received his master's certificate from the Board of Trade.

He abandoned the sea in 1894 and married Jessie George in 1896, settling permanently in England and embarking on a second career as a writer. He was, he said, adopted by the genius of the English language. *Almayer's Folly's* (1895) and *An Outcast of the Islands* (1896) mark his literary apprenticeship. *THE NIGGER OF THE 'NARCISSUS'* (1897), recalling a voyage from Bombay to Dunkirk in 1884, ushered in his mature period. It was followed by *LORD JIM* (1900); *HEART OF DARKNESS* (published with *Youth*, 1902), using his experiences as a river captain in the Congo; and *Typhoon* (1903). While declaring their debt to a long tradition of maritime adventure which he had first encountered when he read MARRYAT as a child, Conrad's 'sea novels' frequently hinge on a decisively testing moment or experience which exposes the individual's fallibility. *NOSTROMO* (1904), *THE SECRET AGENT* (1907) and *UNDER WESTERN EYES* (1911) increasingly connect such private failures with the public world of politics and political ideologies,

presented in an unblinkingly sceptical fashion.

These works earned Conrad little money or popularity, but brought him the respect of leading contemporaries such as ARNOLD BENNETT, JOHN GALSWORTHY and FORD MADOX FORD, with whom he wrote *The Inheritors* (1901) and *Romance* (1903), as well as his fellow expatriates in Sussex and Kent, STEPHEN CRANE and HENRY JAMES. Wider public recognition came with *CHANCE* (1913) and *VICTORY* (1915). *The Shadow Line* (1917), *The Arrow of Gold* (1919), *The Rescue* (1920) and *The Rover* (1923) were among his later works. *The Mirror of the Sea* (1906) and *A Personal Record* (1912) are reminiscences.

Conran, Shirley See GENRE FICTION.

Conroy, Jack 1899–1980 American. His novel *The Disinherited* (1933) is a classic of proletarian literature, exploring working-class life in the Depression with unsentimental directness. Other works include *A World to Win* (1935), *Anyplace but Here* (with ARNA BONTEMPS; 1966) and children's books with Arna Bontemps. Conroy also founded *The Anvil* and *The New Anvil*, left-wing magazines which published work by writers such as RICHARD WRIGHT, ERSKINE CALDWELL, Frank Yerby, JAMES T. FARRELL, MICHAEL GOLD, LANGSTON HUGHES and MERIDEL LE SUEUR, and published *Writers in Revolt: The Anvil Anthology* (with Curt Johnson, 1973).

Conservationist, The A novel by NADINE GORDIMER, published in 1974. It won a CNA LITERARY AWARD in South Africa and the BOOKER PRIZE in Britain. The title is ironic since Mehring, a wealthy white businessman, misuses natural resources and tries to preserve his own way of life against a changing society. The novel depicts his growing self-removal from meaningful human contact, leading to paranoia, mental breakdown and, finally, his own destruction.

Contarini Fleming: A Psychological Romance A novel by BENJAMIN DISRAELI, published in 1832. It purports to be the autobiography of Contarini Fleming, son of a Venetian noblewoman and an aristocratic English politician. After a failed marriage to his cousin, Alceste, and a prolonged tour of Europe and the East, he settles in Rome, devoting himself to art.

Cook, Robin (Robert William Arthur) 1931–94 English. He began with darkly comic novels about a decadent upper class, notably *The Crust on Its Uppers* (1962) and *Bombe Surprise* (1963). After a period of silence, during which he moved on the fringes of the underworld, he re-emerged with a series of 'Factory' novels featuring an unnamed Detective Sergeant: it includes *He Died with His Eyes Open* (1984), *The Devil's Home On Leave* (1985), *How the Dead Live* (1986) and *I was Dora Suarez* (1990). This extravagant and horrifying DETECTIVE FICTION, descended from EDGAR ALLAN POE via CORNELL WOOLRICH and JIM THOMPSON, appeared in

Britain under the pseudonym of Derek Raymond. In France, where Cook then lived, the novels became cult classics. *The Hidden Files* (1992) is an autobiography.

Cooke, John (Esten) 1830–86 American. He wrote novels about the Civil War and HISTORICAL FICTION about colonial Virginia in the manner of JAMES FENIMORE COOPER: *Leather Stocking and Silk* (1854), *The Virginia Comedians* (1854), *Henry St John, Gentleman* (1859), *Her Majesty the Queen* (about the Cavaliers; 1872), *Canolles* (about Virginia during the Revolution; 1877) and *My Lady Pokahontas* (1885). He wrote a life of Stonewall Jackson (1863) while fighting for the Confederates in the Civil War and a life of Robert E. Lee (1871).

Cookson, Catherine See GENRE FICTION.

Coolidge, Susan [Woolsey, Sarah Chauncy] 1845–1905 American. She became popular with several generations of young readers for the heroine introduced in her second book, *What Katy Did* (1872), the tall, rebellious daughter of a small-town family very much like its creator's own. Katy's adventures in succeeding books cover her schooldays, foreign travel and engagement.

Cooper, James Fenimore 1789–1851 American. His first novel was *Precaution* (1820), a study of manners in the tradition of JANE AUSTEN. *THE SPY* (1821), set during the American Revolution, and *The Pilot* (1823), a tale of the sea, were more characteristic of the vein of romance he would develop. *The Pioneers* (1823) began the LEATHERSTOCKING TALES, the series of novels for which he is chiefly remembered; subsequent volumes were *The Last of the Mohicans* (1826), *The Prairie* (1827), *The Pathfinder* (1840) and *The Deerslayer* (1841). *Lionel Lincoln* (1825) is a story of Boston during the Revolution.

Cooper soon established a reputation as one of America's leading authors. The long stay in Europe which he began in 1826 made him one of the first American writers to become widely popular outside his own country, hailed as an American counterpart of SIR WALTER SCOTT. While in Europe he wrote: *The Red Rover* (1827), a sea story; *The Wept of Wishton-Wish* (1829), a novel of early American frontier life; *The Water Witch* (1830), another sea story; *Notions of America* (1828), an essay partly inspired by his friend the Marquis de Lafayette; and a trilogy of HISTORICAL FICTION, *The Bravo* (1831), *The Heidenmauer* (1832) and *The Headsman* (1833). After his return to the USA he damaged his popularity by the conservative views advanced in non-fictional works such as *The Monikins* (1835) and *The American Democrat* (1838) and dramatized in the novels *Homeward Bound* (1838) and *Home as Found* (1838). The 21 books he produced during the last decade of his life include two more sea novels, *Afloat and Ashore* and *Miles Wallingford*, and a historical trilogy about a New York family, known

as the *Littlepage Manuscripts* and consisting of *Satanstoe* (1845), *The Chainbearer* (1845) and *The Redskins* (1846).

Cooper, William [Huff, Harry Summerfield] 1910– English. His most important novel is *Scenes from Provincial Life* (1950), a seminal influence on JOHN BRAINE and the generation of ANGRY YOUNG MEN. *Scenes from Married Life* (1961), *Scenes from Metropolitan Life* (1982) and *Scenes from Later Life* (1983) are sequels. An autobiography, *From Early Life*, appeared in 1990.

Coover, Robert (Lowell) 1932– American. His novels and stories include *The Origin of the Brunists* (1966), *The Universal Baseball Association, Inc., J. Henry Waugh, Prop.* (1968), *Pricksongs and Descants* (1969), *The Public Burning* (1977), *Spanking the Maid* (1981), *Gerald's Party* (1986), *A Night at the Movies, or, You Must Remember This* (1987), *Whatever Happened to Gloomy Gus and the Chicago Bears* (1988). Representative of POST-MODERNISM, they explore the fabulistic, multiple possibilities of contemporary life and the ways in which we perceive reality as a palimpsest of overlapping narratives.

Coppard, A(lfred) E(dgar) 1878–1957 English. His first volume of poetry, *Hips and Haws*, appeared in 1922. He is chiefly remembered for the collections of short stories which began with *Adam and Eve and Pinch Me* (1921) and included *The Black Dog and Other Stories* (1923), *Fishmonger's Fiddle: Tales* (1925) and *The Field of Mustard* (1926). They contain tales as diverse as the rich and mysterious 'Dusky Ruth' and 'The Presser', about a 10-year-old boy apprenticed to a Whitechapel tailor, but above all Coppard's work conveys the flavour of the English countryside.

Coral Island, The An adventure story by R. M. BALLANTYNE, published in 1858. Three youths, Ralph, Jack and Peterkin, are wrecked on a desert island. They survive in true *ROBINSON CRUSOE* fashion, encounter cannibals and a shark, and finally return to civilization none the worse for their ordeal. WILLIAM GOLDING'S *LORD OF THE FLIES* is a pessimistic reworking of a similar situation.

Corelli, Marie 1855–1924 English. Her father was the minor poet and man of letters Charles Mackay. She achieved extraordinary popularity with wildly over-written romantic novels, of which *Barabbas* (1893) and *The Sorrows of Satan* (1895) were perhaps the most famous. Others include *Vendetta* (1886), *Thelma* (1887), *Ardath* (1889), *The Soul of Lilith* (1892), *The Mighty Atom* (1896), *The Master Christian* (1900) and *Temporal Power* (1902). A habit of creating exotic legends about her own life and an unfailing talent for publicity helped to keep her in the public eye.

Corkery, Daniel 1878–1964 Irish. Professor of English at University College, Cork, from 1931 to 1947, he was mentor to younger writers such as FRANK O'CONNOR and SEAN O'FAOLAIN as well as a critic whose work made a most sustained attempt to formulate a nationalist version of the Irish literary tradition. His own best stories can be found in the collections *A Munster Twilight* (1916), *The Stormy Hills* (1929) and, to a lesser extent, in *Earth out of Earth* (1939). He also published a number of plays, of which those in *The Yellow Bittern and Other Plays* (1920) are the most notable.

Cornish Trilogy, The A trilogy by ROBERTSON DAVIES, consisting of *The Rebel Angels* (1981), *What's Bred in the Bone* (1985) and *The Lyre of Orpheus* (1988). This intricately plotted, unchronological series centres on the life and legacy of Francis Cornish, a painter and collector whose own story occupies the second book. The other two volumes deal with manoeuvrings among his executors and the trustees of the Cornish Foundation. The numerous characters are mostly connected with the University of St John and the Holy Ghost ('Spook'), and Davies' habitual use of an eclectic range of arcane knowledge – here picture restoration, opera, Arthurian legend and alchemy – breathes a largeness of vision into the potentially claustrophobic world of the campus novel.

Corris, Peter See DETECTIVE FICTION.

Corvo, Baron See ROLFE, FREDERICK WILLIAM.

Count Robert of Paris See SCOTT, SIR WALTER.

Country of the Pointed Firs, The A novel by SARAH ORNE JEWETT, published in 1896. The unnamed female narrator takes a summer vacation in the imaginary town of Dunnet Landing in rural Maine, where the townspeople, at first somewhat distant, gradually include her in their daily lives. The novel reveals the dramatic depth and intensity in the life of an apparently placid community, concentrating on women and on ageing.

Couvreur, Jessie 1848–97 Anglo-Australian. She used the pseudonym of Tasma. The novel *Uncle Piper of Piper's Hill* (1889) and *A Sydney Sovereign and Other Tales* (1890), her best-known works set in Australia, were written while she was Brussels correspondent for the London *Times*. Patricia Clarke's biography, *Tasma*, appeared in 1994.

Coventry, Francis d.?1759 English. His prose tale, *The History of Pompey the Little* (1751), gives a lapdog's observation of life as he is passed from one owner to another.

Cowan, Peter 1914– Australian. Associated with MODERNISM in the early 1940s, he became identified as a regional writer after he moved to Western Australia in 1964. He is chiefly known for his short stories, published in *Drift* (1944), *The Unploughed Land* (1958), *The Empty Street* (1965), *The Tins* (1973), *New Country* (1976), *Mobiles* (1979) and *Voices* (1988). *A Window in Mrs X's Place* (1986) draws on earlier collections. *Summer* (1964), *Seed* (1966), *The Colour of the Sky* (1986) and *The Hills of Apollo Bay* (1989) are novels.

Cozzens, James Gould 1903–78 American. His novels explore the social order of American life and its potential for stability and hierarchy, by portraying professional men caught in moral and cultural dilemmas. *The Last Adam* (1933) is about the medical profession, *Men and Brethren* (1936) is about the ministry, and *The Just and the Unjust* (1942) and *By Love Possessed* (1957), his most controversial novel, are about the law. *Guard of Honor* (1948; PULITZER PRIZE) is an ambitious novel set during World War II. His last publications were the children's stories in *Children and Others* (1964) and a novel, *Morning, Noon and Night* (1968).

Craik, Dinah Maria See MULOCK, DINAH MARIA.

Crane, Stephen 1871–1900 American. He worked as a journalist while writing his first novel, eventually published as *MAGGIE* (1893). It was not widely noticed but *THE RED BADGE OF COURAGE* (1895) achieved critical and popular success. A collection of short stories, *The Little Regiment* (1896) again dealt with the Civil War, while another novel, *George's Mother* (1896), turned to working-class life in New York. *The Third Violet* (1897) is a short novel about a young artist. *The Monster* (1898) is a volume of short stories. The novel *Active Service* (1899) derived from his experience of the Graeco-Turkish War. *The Black Rider* (1895) and *War is Kind* (1900) are collections of poetry. Until his health betrayed him Crane continued to work as a journalist, travelling to the Southwest, Mexico, Cuba and Greece. His experience after a shipwreck on his Cuban trip formed the basis for one of his most famous stories, the title piece of *The Open Boat and Other Stories* (1898). After settling in England he met JOSEPH CONRAD and HENRY JAMES, two of his most distinguished admirers. Posthumous publications include the sketches and stories from his life as a correspondent in *Wounds in the Rain* (1900); and *Whilomville Stories* (1900), about a childhood in a small town in New York state.

Cranford A novel by ELIZABETH GASKELL, serialized in DICKENS's magazine *Household Words* in 1851–3. Set in the early 19th century, it describes the warm-hearted Miss Matilda (Miss Matty) Jenkyns and her little circle of genteel spinsters and widows. A tenuous narrative takes Miss Matty from quiet satisfaction to adversity resolved by the reappearance of a long-lost brother. This is less important than the series of vignettes which gently reveal Miss Matty's essential virtue and the small foibles of the other characters: the pompous Mrs Jamieson and her awesome butler, Mulliner; the genial, straightforward Captain Brown, killed while looking up too late from reading; Miss Deborah Jenkyns, Miss Matty's elder sister and an ardent Johnsonian; and Martha, the cumbersome but loyal housemaid.

Crawford, Francis Marion 1854–1909 American. The nephew of Julia Ward Howe (the poet remembered for 'The Battle Hymn of the Republic'), he had a cosmopolitan upbringing and travelled widely, becoming an accomplished linguist. *Mr Isaacs: A Tale of Modern India* (1882) was the first of almost 50 successful romances, historical novels and tales of adventure. They include *A Tale of a Lonely Parish* (1886), *Don Orsini* (1891), *Corleone: A Tale of Sicily* (1896), *Via Crucis* (1898), *In the Palace of the King: A Love Story of Old Madrid* (1900) and *The White Sister* (1909). *The Novel: What It Is* (1893) identified his purpose as being simply to entertain. Many of his novels were adapted for the stage, and the play *Francesca da Rimini* (1902) was written for Sarah Bernhardt.

Creasey, John See DETECTIVE FICTION.

Crews, Harry (Eugene) 1935– American. An interest in violence and the grotesque identifies him with the tradition of Southern Gothic. His many novels include *The Gospel Singer* (1968), *Naked in Garden Hills* (1969), *This Thing Don't Lead to Heaven* (1970), *Karate is a Thing of the Spirit* (1971), *Car* (1972), *The Hawk is Dying* (1973), *The Gypsy's Curse* (1974), *A Feast of Snakes* (1976), *The Enthusiast* (1981), *All We Need of Hell* (1987), *The Knockout Artist* (1988), *Body: A Tragicomedy* (1990), *Scar Lover* (1992) and *The Mulching of America* (1995). *Classic Crews* (1993) collects a number of his works. *A Childhood: The Biography of a Place* (1978) is more restrained than his fiction.

Cricket on the Hearth, The A Christmas story by CHARLES DICKENS, published in 1845 and collected in *CHRISTMAS BOOKS* (1852). After he introduces an elderly stranger into his house, John Peerybingle becomes jealous of his younger wife Dot but is prevented from wreaking vengeance by the 'Cricket on the Hearth in Faery shape'. Meanwhile, the villainous Tackleton woos Dot's friend, May Fielding, but is forestalled by the stranger, really her fiancé, the young Edward Plummer. Another narrative strand concerns Edward's blind sister Bertha and their father, the simple Caleb, who works for Tackleton. The story ends with reconciliation and rejoicing, in which even Tackleton joins.

crime and mystery fiction See DETECTIVE FICTION.

Crispin, Edmund See DETECTIVE FICTION.

Crock of Gold, The A prose fantasy by JAMES STEPHENS, published in 1912. It blends Irish faery and folk idioms with legend in a meandering tale which depends for its elusive charm on inconsequential asides and false trails. The Two Philosophers live in the centre of a pine wood called Coilla Doraca and are married to the Grey Woman of Dun Gortin and the Thin Woman of Inis Magrath. Other characters arrive and vanish at will, among them the Philosophers' children Seumas Beg and Brigid Beg, the farmer Meehawl MacMurrachu and his daughter Caitlin, who follows Pan and marries the god Angus Og.

Crockett, S. R. See KAILYARD SCHOOL.

Crofts, Freeman Wills 1879–1957 English. His DETECTIVE FICTION reflects his background as a railway engineer in its immaculately detailed construction and its fondness for mysteries which hinge on timetable alibis. After distinguished early novels which included *The Cask* (1920) and *The Pit-Prop Syndicate* (1922), Crofts introduced his most enduring hero in *Inspector French's Greatest Case* (1925). The Scotland Yard detective made his last appearance in *Anything to Declare?* (1957).

Crompton, Richmal [Lamburn, Richmal Crompton] 1890–1969 English. The mischievous small boy called William, his irritable father, long-suffering mother and permanently suspicious older brother and sister were introduced in short stories for magazines, first collected in *Just William* (1922). At first, the 'William' stories were also aimed at a grown-up audience, allowing his creator to enjoy the mayhem he brings to his family and its suburban environs without adding any admonitory note. More 'William' books followed in quick succession after the success of *Just William*, outshining Richmal Crompton's modestly successful adult fiction. By the time of her death more than 8 million copies had been sold, and William had also been featured on radio, film and television.

Cronin, A(rchibald) J(oseph) 1896–1981 Scottish. After the success of *Hatter's Castle* (1931) he abandoned medicine for popular novels drawing on his Scottish childhood and experience of the Welsh coal-mining valleys. Like *Hatter's Castle*, many became successful films: *The Stars Look Down* (1935) in 1939, *The Keys of the Kingdom* (1942) in 1944 and *The Green Years* (1944) in 1946. *Jupiter Laughs* (1940) is a play, and *Adventures in Two Worlds* (1952) an autobiography. Later works included *The Judas Tree* (1961) and *A Pocketful of Rye* (1969). He also wrote the series *Dr Finlay's Casebook* for radio and television.

Cross, Amanda See DETECTIVE FICTION.

Crossing the River A novel by CARYL PHILLIPS, published in 1993. It tells four separate stories ranging over a period of 250 years, each about an aspect of the African diaspora. The narratives complement one another and are framed by short opening and closing sections, in which the main characters are linked, unifying the book into more than a collection of stories. The final section suggests a liberation from the seemingly self-perpetuating legacy of bitterness created by the slave trade.

Crotchet Castle A novel by THOMAS LOVE PEACOCK, published in 1831. As in *NIGHTMARE ABBEY* and *GRYLL GRANGE*, the plot is minimal and subordinate to a conversation about conservatism and progress which serves as a vehicle for Peacock's highly individual brand of satire. The chief participant is the Rev. Dr Folliott, gourmet, classicist and Tory, who disputes with other characters, notably Mr Skionar, a transcendental philosopher resembling Samuel Taylor Coleridge, Mr MacQuedy, a Scottish political economist, and Mr Chainmail, in love with the Middle Ages.

Crowe, Catherine 1800–76 English. Her novels include *Susan Hopley* (1841) and *Lilly Dawson* (1847), but her most popular work was a collection of stories on ghostly and supernatural themes, *The Night Side of Nature* (1848).

Cunningham, E. V. See FAST, HOWARD.

D

Dabydeen, David 1956– Guyanese/British. He first attracted attention when he won the Commonwealth Poetry Prize for *Slave Song* (1984), which makes violent use of a form of Caribbean Creole. Subsequent collections of verse are *Coolie Odyssey* (1988) and *Turner* (1994). He has moved from poetry to fiction with *The Intended* (1991) and *Disappearance* (1993), a CONDITION OF ENGLAND NOVEL in which a young West Indian engineer is appointed to help shore up a cliff-top village. *The Counting House* (1996) is a historical novel about a young couple who leave India to become indentured labourers on a plantation in Guyana. Dabydeen's non-fiction includes *Hogarth's Blacks* (1985), a study of 'images of blacks in eighteenth-century art', and *The Black Presence in English Literature* (1985).

D'Aguiar, Fred 1960– Guyanese/British. Many of the poems in *Mama Dot* (l985) and *Airy Hall* (1989) deal with the Guyana of his youth; his most vivid creation is the title-character of *Mama Dot*, an archetypal grandmother-figure. His first novel, *The Longest Journey* (1994), is a vivid and complex account of slavery on a Virginian plantation, reminiscent of CARYL PHILLIPS's *Cambridge* and the work of TONI MORRISON. *Dear Future* (1996), set in London and a fictionalized Guyana, combines political satire with poetic accounts of growing up in both environments. D'Aguiar has also written plays, *High Life* (1986) and *A Jamaican Airman Sees His Death* (1989), and edited the Black British section of *The New British Poetry* (1988).

Dahlberg, Edward 1900–77 American. *Bottom Dogs* (1929) is a semi-autobiographical novel about a childhood in slums and orphanages. A man of wide-ranging interests, Dahlberg went on to publish: *From Flushing to Calvary* (1932), about the slums of New York; *Those Who Perish* (1934), about the effects of Nazism on American Jews; studies of myth in *The Sorrows of Priapus* (1957) and *The Carnal Myth* (1968); essays on literature and society in *Do These Bones Live?* (1941), *The Flea of Sodom* (1950), *Truth is More Sacred* (1961) and *Alms for Oblivion* (1964); poetry; correspondence; and a richly eloquent autobiography, *Because I was Flesh* (1964).

Daisy Chain, The A novel by CHARLOTTE M. YONGE, published in 1856. The story concerns the large family (the 'Daisy Chain' of the title) of Dr May, tragically widowed in the early chapters. His ugly but warm-hearted daughter, Ethel, with her untidiness, her clumsiness and her marked capacity for scholarship, is the most memorable character.

Daisy Miller A short novel by HENRY JAMES, published in 1879. Daisy tours Europe with her mother and brother. The expatriate American community interprets her lack of concern for social convention as immodesty, though one of its number, Frederick Winterbourne, is also charmed by her innocence. In Rome Daisy takes up with Giovanelli, a young Italian without social position, and visits the Coliseum with him at night. On meeting them, Winterbourne berates her. She returns to her hotel, contracts malaria and dies after a week.

D'Alpuget, Blanche 1944– Australian. Her novels include: *Monkeys in the Dark* (1980) and *Turtle Beach* (1981), dramatizing Australian relationships with the Far East; *Winter in Jerusalem* (1986), about a young woman's attempt to understand the place where she was born; and *White Eye* (1991). She has also written biographies of Sir Richard Kirby (1977) and Bob Hawke (1982).

Damnation of Theron Ware, The See THERON WARE, THE DAMNATION OF.

Dance to the Music of Time, A A sequence of 12 novels by ANTHONY POWELL, consisting of *A Question of Upbringing* (1951), *A Buyer's Market* (1952), *The Acceptance World* (1955), *At Lady Molly's* (1957), *Casanova's Chinese Restaurant* (1960), *The Kindly Ones* (1962), *The Valley of Bones* (1964), *The Soldier's Art* (1966), *The Military Philosophers* (1968), *Books do Furnish a Room* (1971), *Temporary Kings* (1973) and *Hearing Secret Harmonies* (1975). The sequence is a ROMAN FLEUVE, constituting a history of 20th-century English life among artists and fashionable society as observed by the narrator, Nicholas Jenkins. His own life takes place 'off stage', but he is constantly present as the selective recorder of the temporal flow of events, eventually formalizing them into the pattern of a dance like the painting by Poussin from which the sequence takes its title. Among the most memorable characters is the power-hungry Kenneth Widmerpool.

Dane, Clemence [Ashton, Winifred] 1888–1965 English. Her first and second novels, *Regiment of Women* (1917) and *Legend* (1919), were widely acclaimed, but she turned her attention to drama before returning to fiction with *Broome Stages* (1931), *The Moon is Feminine* (1938) and *He Brings Great News* (1944). Her first play, *A Bill of Divorcement* (1921), is about a woman who divorces her husband on grounds of insanity. Its success was never quite repeated by *Will Shakespeare* (1921), *Granite* (1926) and *Wild Decembers* (1932), about the BRONTË sisters. *Enter Sir John* (1928), *Printer's Devil* (1930; called *Author Unknown* in the USA) and *Re-Enter Sir John* (1932), all written in collaboration with Helen Simpson, are

DETECTIVE FICTION featuring the actor-manager Sir John Saumarez.

Dangarembga, Tsitsi 1959– Zimbabwean. She has published a play, *She No Longer Weeps* (1987). Her novel *Nervous Conditions* (1988) is a BILDUNGSROMAN whose heroine is caught between African and British cultural models.

Dangor, Achmat 1948– South African. He abandoned Afrikaans, his first language, in solidarity with the 1976 rebellion against the use of Afrikaans in schools and now writes only in English. *Waiting for Leila* (1981), which had won the Mofolo-Plomer Prize for unpublished fiction in 1979, consists of the title novella and five short stories. *The Z-Town Trilogy* (1990), three novellas linked by the background of the Z-Town township, deals with the state of emergency and its destructive effect on the Meraai family. Dangor has also published a play, *Majiet* (1988), and poetry, in *Bulldozer* (1983) and *Private Voices* (1992).

Daniel Deronda GEORGE ELIOT's last novel, published in 1876. It is principally concerned with the destinies of Daniel Deronda, the adopted child of an English aristocrat, and Gwendolen Harleth, the spoiled and selfish elder daughter of a widow. In order to avoid penury as her family approaches destitution, Gwendolen agrees to marry Henleigh Grandcourt, fully aware that he has children by his mistress. The marriage proves unhappy and Gwendolen finds herself drawn to Deronda for spiritual guidance. Deronda, who has rescued the Jewish girl, Mirah Lepidoth, from suicide, gradually discovers a dense Jewish world through Mirah and her brother, Mordecai. He eventually learns that he too is a Jew and the novel ends with his determination to seek for his ancient racial and religious roots in Palestine.

Although the novel has seemed awkward and unbalanced to some critics, it has also been acknowledged to be George Eliot's most ambitious work, combining scholarship and a challenging shape which contrasts the lax, aristocratic mores of her English characters with the fervour and moral intensity of her Jewish ones.

Dark, Eleanor 1901–85 Australian. Her novels frequently explore the results of catastrophes and experiment with time. They include *Slow Dawning* (1932), *Prelude to Christopher* (1933), *Sun Across the Sky* (1937), *Waterway* (1938), *Return to Coolami* (1935) and *The Little Company* (1945). *The Timeless Land* (1941), *Storm of Time* (1948) and *No Barrier* (1953), a trilogy covering the first 25 years of the Sydney settlement, have been recognized as masterpieces of carefully researched HISTORICAL FICTION.

Davenport, Guy 1927– American. His short stories are marked by poetic language, literary and historical allusions, and a keen eye for detail. Collections include *Tatlin!* (1974), *Da Vinci's Bicycle: Ten Stories by Guy Davenport* (1979),

Eclogues: Eight Stories by Guy Davenport (1981), *Trois Caprices* (1982), *Apples and Pears and Other Stories* (1984), *The Bicycle Rider* (1985), *The Jules Verne Steam Balloon* (1987), *The Drummer of the Eleventh North Devonshire Fusiliers* (1990) and *A Table of Green Fields* (1993). He has also published translations, poems, and essays on art and literature.

David Copperfield A novel by CHARLES DICKENS, published in monthly parts in 1849–50 and in volume form in 1850 as *The Personal History, Experience and Observations of David Copperfield the Younger, of Blunderstone Rookery, Which He Never Meant to be Published On Any Account*.

David traces his childhood and youth, marred by his widowed mother's remarriage to Mr Murdstone and death, and by his experience working in a London factory (an incident modelled on Dickens's own boyhood suffering). Escaping from London, he takes refuge at Dover with his aunt, Betsey Trotwood, and, after a period of conventional schooling and a brief legal career, becomes a novelist. His marriage to Dora Spenlow proves unhappy but David is nonetheless devastated by her early death. His friendship for James Steerforth is equally disturbed by Steerforth's elopement with Emily, the niece of the Yarmouth fisherman, Mr Peggotty. He finally finds happiness with the faithful Agnes Wickfield, whom he has known since childhood and whose own future had seemed to be threatened by the wiles of her father's sometime clerk, Uriah Heep. The improvidence and verbal extravagance of Wilkins Micawber, with whom David lodges during his unhappy London days, is to some extent modelled on that of Dickens's own father.

David Simple, The Adventures of: *Containing an Account of His Travels through the Cities of London and Westminster in the Search of a Real Friend.* A novel by SARAH FIELDING, first published in 1744. Learning that his younger brother has tried to rob him of his inheritance, David sets out on a journey to rediscover honest friendship. Encounters with Mr Orgueil and his insolent wife, Mr Spatter and Mr Varnish nearly drive him to despair. Then he makes friends with three fellow victims of injustice, Cynthia, Camilla and Camilla's brother Valentine. David falls in love with Camilla, Valentine with Cynthia. The two couples settle down in a happy community established by David's generosity.

Davies, Robertson 1913–95 Canadian. He achieved distinction in several fields during a long and varied career. As editor of *The Peterborough Examiner*, a paper previously owned by his father, he contributed articles under the pseudonym of Samuel Marchbanks, collected as *The Diary of Samuel Marchbanks* (1947), *The Table Talk of Samuel Marchbanks* (1949) and *Marchbanks' Almanack* (1967). His commitment to the theatre made him a successful stage director, taking an important part in the Ontario Stratford

Shakespeare Festival. His plays include *Fortune, My Foe* (1949), *A Jig for the Gypsy* (1954) and *Hunting Stuart and Other Plays* (1972). He made his major reputation as a novelist, even though he was 38 before he published *Tempest-Tost* (1951). Together with *Leaven of Malice* (1954) and *A Mixture of Frailties* (1958), it makes up *The Salterton Trilogy*, the first of three major trilogies. The second is THE DEPTFORD TRILOGY: *Fifth Business* (1970), *The Manticore* (1972) and *World of Wonders* (1975). THE CORNISH TRILOGY consists of *The Rebel Angels* (1981), *What's Bred in the Bone* (1985) and *The Lyre of Orpheus* (1988). *Murther and Walking Spirits* (1991) makes thoughtful, witty use of the supernatural and *The Cunning Man* (1994) of diagnostic medicine, seen as a rival to religion. Strongly influenced by his interest in Jungian archetypes, his fiction is about myth, magic and miracles, contrasting the limited perspectives offered by provincial Canada with the psychic fulfilment to be discovered through encounters with the 'world of wonders'.

Davin, Dan(iel) 1913–90 New Zealand. He went to Oxford as a Rhodes Scholar in 1936 and returned there after World War II to work for Oxford University Press. He established his reputation as a leading New Zealand writer with a series of realistic novels: *Cliffs of Fall* (1945); *For the Rest of Our Lives* (1947), about his war experiences; *Roads from Home* (1949); and *The Sullen Bell* (1956), about New Zealanders in post-war London. *The Gorse Blooms Pale* (1947) is a volume of short stories. Later work, sometimes judged not to fulfil his early promise, included: *Not Here, Not Now* (1970) and *Brides of Price* (1972), both novels; *Breathing Spaces* (1975), short stories; and *Closing Times* (1975), a volume of memoirs.

Daviot, Gordon See MACKINTOSH, ELIZABETH.

Davis, Rebecca (Blane) Harding 1831–1910 American. Much of her fiction is set in her native Philadelphia, including her best-known story, 'Life in the Iron Mills' (1861), about the tragic life of Hugh Wolfe, a furnace-tender in a mill. One of the earliest exponents of American REALISM, she portrayed the bleak lives of industrial workers in *Margaret Howth* (1862) and of blacks in *Waiting for the Verdict* (1868). *John Andross* (1874) is a tale about political corruption.

Davis, Richard Harding 1864–1916 American. The son of REBECCA HARDING DAVIS, he became one of the most prolific and popular writers of his day. His travels and work as a war correspondent provided the material for a succession of books, in addition to seven novels, over 80 short stories and 25 plays – successful in their day, though quickly forgotten. His novels include *Soldiers of Fortune* (1897), *The Bar Sinister* (1903) and *Vera the Medium* (1908); *Ranson's Folly* (1902) and *Miss Civilization* (1905) were among his most popular plays.

Davison, Frank Dalby 1893–1970 Australian. He won a reputation as a sensitive writer in the 'bush' tradition with *Man-Shy* (1931), the story of wild red heifer, and *Dusty* (1946), the story of a half-dingo, half-kelpie, together with the short-story collections *The Woman and the Mill* (1940) and *The Road to Yesterday* (1964). However, *The White Thorntree* (1968), his last work, is about sexuality in suburbia.

Dawson, Jennifer 1929– English. She won immediate recognition with her first novel, *The Ha-Ha* (1961), which won the JAMES TAIT BLACK MEMORIAL PRIZE. Its preoccupation with the benefits as well as the terrors of madness has been continued in different registers by *Fowler's Snare* (1962), *The Cold Country* (1965) and *The Upstairs People* (1988), her first novel since *Strawberry Boy* (1976). *Judasland* (1989), set in an Oxford library, echoes the world created by BARBARA PYM in which 'excellent women' minister to self-absorbed men.

Day, Clarence (Shepard) 1874–1935 American. A regular contributor to *The New Yorker*, he is best known for humorous autobiographical writings about upper-class life in 19th-century New York. They include *God and My Father* (1932), *Life with Father* (1935), *Life with Mother* (1937) and *Father and I* (1940). *Life with Father* was dramatized by Howard Lindsay and Russel Crouse in 1939 and became a long-running success.

Day, Thomas 1748–89 English. An early and eccentric disciple of Rousseau, particularly in educational matters, he published the influential *History of Sandford and Merton* (three parts; 1783, 1786 and 1789). Totally didactic in purpose, it follows the contrasting fortunes of Tommy Merton, the idle son of a rich gentleman, and Harry Sandford, the industrious son of a hardworking farmer. Day also wrote another moral tale, *The History of Little Jack* (1788), about a child suckled by goats and raised by a God-fearing old man before returning to civilization to make his fortune.

Day-Lewis, C(ecil) 1904–72 English. He was the only poet in W. H. Auden's circle at Oxford to become an active Communist. His politics clash with a tendency to Romanticism in *The Magnetic Mountain* (1933), *A Time to Dance* (1935) and *Overtures to a Death* (1938), which contains his best political poems, 'Newsreel' and 'The Bombers'. After World War II conflict was replaced by dry formalism, and his respectability was confirmed by his appointment as Poet Laureate in 1968. *The Poems of C. Day-Lewis 1925–1972* appeared in 1977. Under the pseudonym of Nicholas Blake he wrote DETECTIVE FICTION in some 20 novels, beginning with *A Question of Proof* (1935) and ending with *The Morning After Death* (1966); their hero, Nigel Strangeways, was originally modelled on Auden.

De Bernières, Louis 1954– English. A trilogy, *The War of Don Emmanuel's Nether Parts* (1990), *Señor*

Viva and the Coca Lord (1991) and *The Troublesome Offspring of Cardinal Guzman* (1992), is set in a fictional South American country. Indebted to the MAGIC REALISM of Gabriel Garcia Márquez, it describes governmental collusion with drug barons, police corruption and press censorship, as well as the gallant battle waged against them by the citizens, including Señor Viva. *Captain Corelli's Mandolin* (1994) reached a wider audience. Set on the Greek island of Cephallonia during the Italian occupation in World War II, it both studies the relations between invaders and invaded and celebrates Greece's capacity to defeat conquerors by the sheer power of its own history and culture.

De Boissière, Ralph 1907– Trinidadian, of French Creole descent. In Trinidad he was involved in both trade union activity and the influential Beacon Group, which helped to promote a sense of local cultural identity. His novels were published in Australia after he emigrated there in 1948. The best is *Crown Jewel* (1952), set in Trinidad on the eve of World War II, a long-neglected work successfully republished in 1981. Later novels are *Rum and Coca-Cola* (1956), a sequel to *Crown Jewel*, and *No Saddles for Kangaroos* (1964).

De Forest, John W(illiam) 1826–1906 American. His *History of the Indians of Connecticut* (1851) was marked by the same objectivity which characterized his fiction. *MISS RAVENEL'S CONVERSION FROM SECESSION TO LOYALTY* (1867), a romance set during the Civil War and Reconstruction, includes grimly realistic battle scenes which anticipate those of STEPHEN CRANE. Later novels include *Kate Beaumont* (1872), about South Carolina plantation society, and *Honest John Vane* (1875), a satire of political corruption. De Forest's Civil War memoirs, *A Volunteer's Adventures*, appeared posthumously in 1946, and *A Union Officer in the Reconstruction* in 1948.

de la Roche, Mazo 1879–1961 Canadian. Her childhood on a farm in Ontario provided the background and setting for her popular and optimistic regional idylls. Success came with *Jalna* (1927), set in an old house of that name, and its sequel, *The Whiteoaks of Jalna* (1929). Another 14 novels were eventually added to the series. She also wrote children's books, one-act plays, historical studies and an autobiography, *Ringing the Changes* (1957).

De Lisser, H(erbert) G(eorge) 1878–1944 Jamaican. He edited *The Daily Gleaner*, Jamaica's leading newspaper, and played a prominent part in public life. Also the most popular Jamaican novelist of his day, he mainly wrote historical romances: the best-known, *The White Witch of Rosehall* (1929), was based on Annie Palmer, a 19th-century white Creole plantation owner. Only occasionally, as in his most highly regarded novel, *Jane's Career* (1914), or *Susan*

Proudleigh (1915) and *Under the Sun* (1937), did he write about contemporary society. Other novels include *Triumphant Squalitone* (1917), *Revenge* (1919), *Psyche* (1952) and *Morgan's Daughter* (1953).

de Morgan, William (Frend) 1839–1917 English. A friend and colleague of William Morris in the Arts and Crafts Movement, he made stained glass and decorative tiles. Only in retirement did he turn to writing, achieving considerable success with *Joseph Vance* (1906) and eight more novels, the last two completed by his wife, which cast a Dickensian eye over the London of his youth.

De Vries, Peter 1910–93 American. A staff member of *The New Yorker* for many years, he published 24 novels. The most popular are typified by worldly satire of suburban mores and sexual intrigue. Significant titles include: *The Tunnel of Love* (1955), *The Mackerel Plaza* (1958), a popular favourite; *The Blood of the Lamb* (1962), valued for its tragi-comedy; *Madder Music* (1978); and *Slouching Towards Kalamazoo* (1983). De Vries also published two collections of stories, *No, But I Saw the Movie* (1952) and *Without a Stitch in Time: A Selection of the Best Humorous Short Pieces* (1972).

Death Comes for the Archbishop A novel by WILLA CATHER, published in 1927. Bishop Jean Latour arrives in the New Mexico territory shortly after its annexation by the USA and establishes a new diocese with his vicar, Father Joseph Vaillant. Together they overcome the persistence with which the Navajo and Hopi Indians cling to their ancient beliefs, and succeed in building a cathedral at Santa Fe. Latour is made an archbishop and the novel closes with his death. The story is based on the careers of two 19th-century French missionaries, Jean-Baptiste Lamy and Joseph Machebeuf.

Death of the Heart, The A novel by ELIZABETH BOWEN, published in 1938. A sensitive study of adolescence, it shows the influence of HENRY JAMES, particularly *WHAT MAISIE KNEW*, but does not suffer by the comparison. The central character is Portia Quayne, an innocent and emotionally vulnerable girl in the care of her half-brother Thomas and his wife Anna. Her love for Eddie, an admirer of Anna, leads to suffering and disillusionment.

Decline and Fall EVELYN WAUGH's first novel, published in 1928. Its title ironically echoes Edward Gibbon's *The History of the Decline and Fall of the Roman Empire* (1776–88).

Sent down from Oxford through no fault of his own, Paul Pennyfeather teaches at Llanabba Castle, a Welsh boarding school hopelessly administered by a staff which includes Mr Prendergast, a former clergyman, and Captain Grimes, a one-legged drunkard and bigamist. He is taken up by the sophisticated Margot Beste-Chetwynde, mother of one of his pupils. They become engaged but he is arrested for having unwittingly involved himself in her activities in the white-slave trade. In prison he meets Captain Grimes, a fellow prisoner, and Prendergast, now the prison chaplain. Margot engineers his escape and transports him to her villa in Corfu. He returns to Oxford as his own very distant cousin.

Deeping, (George) Warwick 1877–1950 English. A prolific writer, he produced 70 novels and five volumes of short stories, which attempt to keep alive the idea and spirit of Edwardian Britain. Deeping's experiences in the Royal Army Medical Corps during World War I were the inspiration for his most famous work, *Sorrell and Son* (1925), the moving story of Captain Sorrell trying to make a life for his son Kit.

Deerslayer, The See LEATHERSTOCKING TALES, THE.

Defoe, Daniel 1660–1731 English. Born Daniel Foe, he attended the Stoke Newington Academy for Dissenters and remained a Presbyterian throughout his life. In youth he went into trade (business projects never ceased to fascinate him), travelled widely in Europe until his marriage in 1683, took part in Monmouth's rebellion in 1685 and joined William III's army in 1688 – the first of several changes of allegiance that earned him a mercenary reputation. His first writing, the *Essay on Projects* (1697), was on economics but his first literary success was *The True-Born Englishman* (1701), a satiric poem championing the cause of the foreign-born monarch. Afterwards he abandoned satire to cultivate his skills in stylistic impersonation and irony. A pamphlet, *The Shortest Way with the Dissenters* (1702), mimicked the extreme attitudes of High Anglican Tories by advocating the extermination of Dissenters. Neither party was amused. Defoe was fined, imprisoned and pilloried – experiences prompting a mock ode, *Hymn to the Pillory* (1703) – but became a popular hero.

In 1704 Robert Harley, Earl of Oxford, helped Defoe to publish his first issue of *The Review*, a thrice-weekly newspaper which survived until 1713. Defoe contributed articles on topics ranging from the commercial to the moral, pioneering examples of the literary essay which was emerging as one of the distinctive genres of the period. Harley also employed him as an undercover field-agent, a clandestine occupation suiting his personality. His own political beliefs remained resolute, however, irrespective of changes in party policies. A committed anti-Jacobite, he published *Reasons against the Succession of the House of Hanover* (1712), another satire misunderstood by the authorities and leading to a second term of imprisonment. He went on to edit *Mercator*, a trade journal, and supported free trade in *A General History of Trade* (1714). After the death of Queen Anne and the accession of the Hanoverians he became agent to Lord Townshend, the Whig Secretary of State,

and may have operated in a double capacity as informer, reporter and monitor of events.

By 1720 Defoe had abandoned political controversy. He wrote instead a conduct book, *The Family Instructor* (1715–18), and several histories, *The History of the Wars of His Present Majesty Charles XII King of Sweden* (1715), *Memoirs of the Church of Scotland* (1717) and *The Life and Death of Count Puktil* (1717). His earliest venture into fiction had been *A True Relation of the Apparition of One Mrs Veal* (1706), an embroidered account of a current ghost story, but in his 60th year Defoe seems to have discovered a new well of talent for narrative. During the next five years he produced a flow of novels, beginning with ROBINSON CRUSOE and *The Farther Adventures of Robinson Crusoe* (1719), followed shortly by *The Serious Reflections . . . of Robinson Crusoe*, CAPTAIN SINGLETON (1720), MOLL FLANDERS, *A JOURNAL OF THE PLAGUE YEAR* and COLONEL JACK (1722), MEMOIRS OF A CAVALIER and ROXANA (1724). As if these were not enough, he also produced: *The Great Law of Subordination Considered* (1724), an examination of the treatment of servants; *A Tour Thro the Whole Island of Great Britain* (3 vols, 1724–7), an outstanding guide book; *The Complete English Tradesman* (1726), which identifies the new respectability of the merchant classes; and *Augusta Triumphans* (1728), an optimistic Utopian project.

It has proved difficult to establish the full extent of his output but, with over 500 verified publications to his name, Defoe is the most prolific author in the language. His enduring reputation rests on his novels, the form in which he was one of the great innovators. Concerned with social man rather than individual psychology, his fiction reveals a swashbuckling love of travel, adventure and piracy that subsequently became the stock material of the genre. As an essayist he was recognizably unlike most of his important contemporaries in the Augustan Age, street-wise where they tended to be aesthetic, and a master of the plain style rather than the politely allusive mode cultivated by Jonathan Swift and Alexander Pope.

Deighton, Len [Leonard] (Cyril) 1929– English. He came to the fore with SPY FICTION such as *The Ipcress File* (1962), *Funeral in Berlin* (1964) and *Billion-Dollar Brain* (1966), featuring an unnamed secret agent whom the film versions called Harry Palmer. Their laconic style and apparent authenticity sharply distinguished the books from IAN FLEMING's James Bond novels. Deighton's subsequent output has alternated between exhaustively researched, bulky novels about World War II air combat, such as *Bomber* (1970) and *Goodbye Mickey Mouse* (1982), and more spy novels. These have included three trilogies concentrating on the intelligence career of Bernie Samson: *Berlin Game* (1983), *Mexico Set* (1984) and *London Match* (1985); *Spy*

Hook (1988), *Spy Line* (1989) and *Spy Sinker* (1990); and *Faith*(1994), *Hope* (1995) and *Charity* (1996).

Delafield, E. M. [Dashwood (*née* De La Pasture), Edmée Elizabeth Monica] 1890–1943 English. She wrote mildly satirical novels about the day-to-day upheavals of provincial life. *Messalina of the Suburbs* (1923) was based upon a famous murder case. The success of *The Diary of a Provincial Lady* (1930) launched a series which provided the basis for popular films. Delafield's other works included: *Faster! Faster!* (1936) and *Nothing is Safe* (1937); three plays, *To See Ourselves* (1930), *The Glass Wall* (1933) and *The Mulberry Bush* (1935); and a study of the BRONTË sisters (1938).

Delany, Samuel R(ay) 1942– African-American. His early SCIENCE FICTION – the novels *Babel-17* (1966), *The Einstein Intersection* (1967) and *Nova* (1968), and the short stories in *Driftglass* (1971) and *Distant Stars* (1981) – display a vivid romanticism. He broke new ground with a counter-cultural epic, *Dhalgren* (1975), and the 'ambiguous heterotopia' of *Triton* (1976). Critical writings, including *The Jewel-Hinged Jaw* (1977), *The American Shore* (1978) and *Starboard Wine* (1984), show his interest in the language of science fiction. Explorations in semiotics and post-structuralism have influenced the fantasy series which includes *Tales of Nevèrÿon* (1979), *Neveryóna* (1983), *Flight from Nevèrÿon* (1985) and *The Bridge of Lost Desire* (1987). An autobiography, *The Motion of Light in Water* (1988), documents the homosexual subculture of New York in the early 1960s.

DeLillo, Don 1936– American. Widely recognized as leading examples of American POST-MODERNISM, his novels are highly self-aware evocations of a contemporary society which defines itself through the pseudo-religious rituals of its subcultures. They include *Americana* (1971), *End Zone* (1973), *Great Jones Street* (1974), *Ratner's Star* (1976), *Players* (1977), *Running Dog* (1979), *The Names* (1983), *White Noise* (1986), *LIBRA* (1988) and *Underworld* (1997). The handling of the relations between literature and terrorism in *Mao II* (1991) was inspired by the *fatwa* against SALMAN RUSHDIE.

Dell, Floyd 1887–1969 American. A radical journalist, he edited *The Masses* (1914–17) and *The Liberator* (1918–24). *Moon-Calf* (1920), its sequel *The Briary-Bush* (1921), *Janet March* (1923) and *Runaway* (1925) are about the disillusionment of the post-war generation and the turmoil of the Jazz Age. Other novels include *An Old Man's Folly* (1926), about pacificists in World War I, and *An Unmarried Father* (1927), a comedy which Dell and Thomas Mitchell dramatized as *Little Accident* (1928). Non-fiction includes a study of UPTON SINCLAIR (1927) and *Love in the Machine Age* (1930). *Homecoming* (1933) is his autobiography.

Deloney, Thomas ?1543–1600 English. A silk-weaver by trade, he began by writing ballads and broadsides. *Canaan's Calamity* is an attempt at a poem of greater length and sustained construction. His prose fiction draws on such popular works as jest-books, the chronicles of Edward Hall and Holinshed and Foxe's *Acts and Monuments*, with occasional excursions into fashionable EUPHUISM and romance, to describe and glorify the English artisan. *Thomas of Reading* (licensed 1602) depicts the clothier's craft, *Jack of Newbury* (licensed 1597, first extant edition 1619) that of the weaver, and *The Gentle Craft* (licensed 1597, first extant edition 1637) shoemakers. The last contains his finest creation, Long Meg of Westminster and also the story of Simon Eyre, a shoemaker who became Lord Mayor of London, which served as the source for Dekker's *The Shoemaker's Holiday*. Despite being dismissed by better-educated contemporaries and neglected by critics, Deloney has good claim to have formed the English 'novel'.

***Demos*: A Story of English Socialism** A novel by GEORGE GISSING, published in 1886. It is in fact an attack on the validity of socialism, portraying working-class agitators like Richard Mutimer and Daniel Dabbs as short-sighted, self-deceived, self-serving and ultimately corrupt. The story hinges on the establishment by Mutimer of an ironworks in an unspoiled valley, a model community in the tradition of Robert Owen. It is finally closed, through a complex plot involving the loss and rediscovery of a will, and the money reverts to the rightful, aristocratic owner.

Denis Duval An unfinished novel by WILLIAM MAKEPEACE THACKERAY, published in *The Cornhill Magazine* in 1864, the year after his death. The setting is Rye in the late 18th century, and the book would have attempted the sort of full-scale HISTORICAL FICTION he had handled so successfully in *HENRY ESMOND*. In the fragment which Thackeray lived to write Denis Duval describes his involvement with smugglers and his love for Agnes de Saverne.

Deptford Trilogy, The A trilogy of novels by ROBERTSON DAVIES, consisting of *Fifth Business* (1970), *The Manticore* (1972) and *World of Wonders* (1975). Events in the fictional village of Deptford, Ontario, link the lives of the three central characters from childhood onwards: Dunstan Ramsey, narrator of the first volume and the central arbitrating consciousness of the sequence; Percy 'Boy' Staunton, whose flamboyant career ends in his mysterious death; and Paul Dempster, son of the disgraced wife of the Baptist minister, who transforms himself into the master-magician Magnus Eisengrim. All three volumes focus on metamorphoses of identity, on characters who are 'born again', whether through the agency of myth, magic, theatre or Jungian psychology.

Desai, Anita 1937– Indian. With a Bengali

father and German mother, she admits to a certain ambivalence about Indian life. Her novels include *Cry, the Peacock* (1963), *Voices in the City* (1965), *Bye-Bye, Blackbird* (1971), *Where Shall We Go This Summer?* (1975), *Fire on the Mountain* (1977; awarded a SAHITYA AKADEMI prize), *Clear Light of Day* (1980), *In Custody* (1984) and *BAUMGARTNER'S BOMBAY* (1988). As well as a collection of stories, *Games at Twilight* (1978), she has also published several books for children.

Desai, Boman 1950– Indian. He was educated in the USA, his interests moving from architecture through philosophy to psychology (the subject of his first degree) and, eventually, English. *The Memory of Elephants* (1988), revolving round the invention of a 'memoscan', is a rare example of Indian SCIENCE FICTION.

Desani, G(ovindas) V(ishnoodas) 1909– Indian. He ranks among the most important 20th-century Indian writers in English on the strength of one novel, *All About H. Hatterr* (1948), an eccentric and comic book about an Anglo-Indian in search of wisdom which combines linguistic dexterity and philosophical curiosity. Its admirers have included T. S. Eliot, ANTHONY BURGESS and SALMAN RUSHDIE.

Deshpande, Shashi 1938– Indian. Although she dislikes the label of 'feminist writer', she concentrates on the problems faced by Indian women in *The Dark Holds No Terrors* (1980), *If I Die Today* (1981), *Come Up and Be Dead* (1982), *Roots and Shadows* (1983), *That Long Silence* (1988) – a winner of the SAHITYA AKADEMI award – and *THE BINDING VINE* (1992). She is also a prolific writer of short stories.

Desperate Remedies The first published novel by THOMAS HARDY, appearing in 1871. Having failed to find a publisher for *The Poor Man and the Lady*, he deliberately adopted the popular formulas of the SENSATION NOVEL.

Set mainly in Dorset, the complicated narrative of intrigue, violence and deception follows the welfare of Cytherea Graye, forced to become lady's maid and later companion to the imperious Miss Aldclyffe, mistress of Knapwater House. Cytherea is in love with Edward Springrove, a fledgling architect, but Miss Aldclyffe hopes she will marry her illegitimate son, Aeneas Manston. Manston's villainy fuels most of the interest and much of the plot. He is finally brought to book for murdering his first wife, Eunice, and hangs himself in his cell. Miss Aldclyffe dies and Cytherea and Springrove are reunited.

detective fiction A sub-genre of fiction which presents a mysterious event or crime, usually but not necessarily murder, at first concealing the solution from the reader but finally revealing it through the successful investigations of a detective. Some commentators prefer to call it 'mystery fiction' or 'crime and mystery fiction'. W. H. Auden summarized a typical plot: 'a murder occurs; many are suspected; all but one suspect, who is the murderer, are eliminated; the murderer is arrested or dies'.

Historians of the form have tried to trace its origin to the puzzle tales of the Enlightenment (Voltaire's *Zadig*) or even to the Bible (Daniel, Susanna and the elders), but there is a general agreement that its real history starts in the 19th century. EDGAR ALLAN POE brought all the basic ingredients together in his 'tales of ratiocination' of the 1840s. His detective, the brilliant and eccentric Dupin, is accompanied by an obligingly imperceptive friend who narrates the story; he confronts mystery with a coherent, though not exclusively scientific, methodology of detection; and he produces the solution with a triumphant flourish that surprises and satisfies the reader. Without providing either a murder or an infallible detective, WILKIE COLLINS showed in *THE MOONSTONE* (1868) how the formula could be expanded to fit the requirements of the full-length novel. In his SHERLOCK HOLMES STORIES, begun in the late 1880s, ARTHUR CONAN DOYLE masterfully orchestrated the hints Poe had sketched out.

The success of Sherlock Holmes bred imitation ranging from distinguished contributions like G. K. CHESTERTON's Father Brown stories and E. C. BENTLEY's *Trent's Last Case* (1913) to forgotten works like ARTHUR MORRISON's Martin Hewitt stories, WILLIAM HOPE HODGSON's Carnacki stories and M. P. SHIEL's tales of Prince Zaleski. It also bred new awareness of the form, distinguishing detective fiction from all the other types of popular fiction which dabble in crime and mystery. According to Monsignor Ronald Knox (1888–1957) and his followers in the Detection Club, it should be concerned with puzzles rather than crime as such, and should elaborate its puzzles in strict obedience to the rules of logic and fair play. From such prescriptions arose the so-called Golden Age of the detective novel in the 1920s and 1930s. Writers became known for their expert refinements of the puzzle: R. AUSTIN FREEMAN (1862–1943) for scientific expertise; FREEMAN WILLS CROFTS (1879–1957) for juggling with timetables and alibis; JOHN DICKSON CARR (who also wrote as Carter Dickson; 1905–77) for variations on the locked-room mystery; and, most famous of all, AGATHA CHRISTIE for her ingenuity in making the least likely suspect turn out to be the murderer.

Setting and characterization inevitably took second place, but they, too, followed well-worn paths. Detectives tended to be gentlemen amateurs rather than policemen or private enquiry agents. H. C. Bailey (1878–1961) was perhaps the first, in his Reggie Fortune stories, to make his gentleman amateur a facetious dandy. Fortune was soon joined by a lengthening list of detectives who owed as much to SAKI and P. G. WODE-

HOUSE as to Conan Doyle: Lord Peter Wimsey (DOROTHY L. SAYERS), Albert Campion (MARGERY ALLINGHAM) and even Nigel Strangeways (Nicholas Blake, the pseudonym of C. DAY-LEWIS). Settings were equally genteel, with country houses and Oxbridge colleges among the favourites, and the work of Michael Innes (J. I. M. STEWART) offering perhaps the best representative selection.

Detective stories in this classic mould were not confined to Britain, as the popularity of S. S. VAN DINE, ELLERY QUEEN and REX STOUT in America showed. Nor did they entirely disappear after the 1930s. Christie, Allingham, Blake, Innes and NGAIO MARSH all continued their careers after the war, with some adjustment to the change in public taste, joined by Edmund Crispin (Robert Bruce Montgomery, 1921–78) and Michael Gilbert (1912–). Contemporaries like P. D. JAMES and Colin Dexter (1930–) in Britain and EMMA LATHEN in America can still follow the classic formula. But it came increasingly under challenge from writers who, whatever else they may not have shared, were agreed in finding it restrictive and in wishing to break down the barriers that separated detective fiction from other popular forms like the thriller, adventure story, chase novel and spy story, or from the concerns of serious literature.

By far the most significant challenge came from America, where DASHIELL HAMMETT, RAYMOND CHANDLER and other contributors to 'pulp' magazines such as *Black Mask* pioneered 'hard-boiled' detective fiction. Its aims were succinctly indicated by Chandler when he praised Hammett for putting murder back in the hands of people who commit it with real weapons for real reasons, not just to provide the reader with a puzzle. Hard-boiled detective fiction replaced genteel amateurs with tough, down-at-heel private eyes, privileged or genteel settings with a sleazy urban milieu of vice and hoodlums, and puzzle-plots with stories that moved quickly from violent action to violent action.

The example of Hammett and Chandler quickly came to dominate the American approach as thoroughly as the example of Conan Doyle once had in Britain. The tradition, first maintained in the Lew Archer novels of ROSS MACDONALD, has continued, though with modifications, in the novels of ROBERT B. PARKER, LOREN D. ESTLEMAN, ANDREW VACHSS, JAMES LEE BURKE and WALTER MOSLEY. The possibilities of vernacular speech which Hammett and Chandler first broached have been explored by writers as diverse as JAMES ELLROY, CARL HIAASEN, ELMORE LEONARD and George V. Higgins (1939–), notably in *The Friends of Eddie Coyle* (1972). Quintessentially American though it might seem, and stubbornly incapable of taking root in Britain, hard-boiled fiction could be transplanted to France or Australia, where Peter Corris (1942–) has set his Cliff Hardy novels.

Several subsequent tendencies, all with international ramifications, are worth noting. The first is the 'crime novel', so called because an interest in the criminal and criminal psychology can replace the intricate technical puzzle, and even overshadow the element of mystery. Pioneered by Anthony Berkeley Cox (who also wrote as Anthony Berkeley; 1893–1971), writing as Francis Iles in the 1930s, it has since attracted distinguished adherents in the American PATRICIA HIGHSMITH, JULIAN SYMONS and RUTH RENDELL, particularly in the novels she has published as Barbara Vine. The second is the 'police novel', determined to make good the genre's earlier neglect of the police. It can concentrate on police procedure, as John Creasey (1908–73), using the pseudonym of J. J. Marric, did in his novels about Gideon of Scotland Yard and the American Ed McBain (EVAN HUNTER) has done in his 87th Precinct novels. Later writers – such as Reginald Hill (who also writes as Patrick Ruell; 1936–) in Britain and James McClure (1939–) in South Africa – have approached the form less rigidly, while NICOLAS FREELING has located the police novel in a preoccupation with place and character which deliberately recalls its great French precedent in Simenon's Maigret novels.

In the 1980s and 1990s the most interesting development has come from the impact of feminism on hard-boiled detective fiction, a form which at first sight appears as quintessentially male as it is quintessentially American. Therein lies the challenge which SARA PARETSKY has taken up in her V. I. Warshawski novels, closely followed in their popularity by the work of other American writers such as Sue Grafton (1940–), Karen Kijewski (19??–) and Linda Barnes (1949–), and in Britain by Liza Cody (1944–) and Val McDermid (19??–). These female PI novels bend and subvert the conventions they inherit from Hammett and Chandler but never entirely reject them, in proof of the detective novel's continuing ability to adapt and survive.

The use of pseudonyms by crime and mystery writers remains common, as befits a form which deals with people's masks rather than their real faces. Mainstream novelists and writers otherwise known for 'serious' work who have published in this fashion include JULIAN BARNES (as Dan Kavanagh), HOWARD FAST (as E. V. Cunningham), JAMES HILTON (as Glen Trevor), PAMELA HANSFORD JOHNSON (as Nap Lombard), GORE VIDAL (as Edgar Box) and the literary critic Carolyn Heilbrun (1926–), adopting the name Amanda Cross for her long-running series about Kate Fansler.

Dexter, Colin See DETECTIVE FICTION.

Diana of the Crossways A novel by GEORGE MEREDITH, published in 1885. Diana Warwick is accused of adultery by her husband, a government official of limited sensibilities, and, though an action for divorce fails, they agree to live apart. Diana has an affair with a rising young politician, Percy Dacier, and marries an old admirer, Thomas Redworth, after her husband's death. The nervous, impulsive and inconsistent heroine is said to have been modelled on THE HON. MRS CAROLINE NORTON.

Diary of a Nobody, The A comic novel of late-Victorian manners by GEORGE AND WEEDON GROSSMITH, published in 1892. The humour derives from the accident-prone Charles Pooter's unconsciousness of how ridiculous he makes himself by his petty snobberies, and from his invariably unsuccessful wrangles with his rebellious son Lupin. Nevertheless, a character of respectability and even integrity emerges, so that the reader rejoices in the eventual rise in the fortunes of Pooter and his faithful, though frequently irritated, wife Carrie.

Dibdin, Michael 1947– English. He began his career in DETECTIVE FICTION with a pastiche, or ironic deconstruction, of the SHERLOCK HOLMES STORIES in *The Last Sherlock Holmes Story* (1978). Since then he has kept up a reputation for diversity with books such as: *A Rich Full Death* (1986), a Victorian pastiche in which Robert Browning appears; *The Tryst* (1989), probing the psychology of crime; and *Dark Spectre* (1995), grappling rather uncertainly with American culture. He is best known, however, for creating Aurelio Zen, the Italian policeman who has appeared in *Ratking* (1988), *Vendetta* (1990), *Cabal* (1992), *Dead Lagoon* (1994) and *Così fan Tutti* (1996).

Dick, Kay 1915– English. She has produced a small but distinguished body of fiction. Between 1949 and 1962 she published five novels, including *Young Man* (1951), a lively picture of the wartime book-trade, and *Sunday* (1962), drawing on her own family's unhappily tangled affairs. A long silence was broken with *They: A Sequence of Unease* (1977), a dystopian tale of a future Britain where totalitarianism prevails. *The Shelf* (1984) takes the form of a letter in which Cassie, an uneasily bisexual woman, struggles to recall a past affair. Dick has also written *Ivy and Stevie* (1971), recollections of IVY COMPTON-BURNETT and STEVIE SMITH, and *Friends and Friendship* (1974).

Dick, Philip K(endred) 1928–82 American. He began his career as a writer of SCIENCE FICTION with paperback novels written for money. *The World Jones Made* (1956) and *Eye in the Sky* (1957) are striking among them. His mature work often studies the gradual mechanization of the environment and deals with false realities created by hallucinogenic drugs or schizophrenic delusion. It includes *The Man in the High Castle* (1962), *Martian Time-Slip* (1964), *Now Wait for Last Year* (1966), *Do Androids Dream of Electric Sheep?* (1969), *Flow My Tears, the Policeman Said* (1974) and *A Scanner Darkly* (1977). Dick turned with

deepening interest to metaphysics and hypothetical theology in *Valis* (1981) and *The Divine Invasion* (1981). Non-science fiction work, including *Confessions of a Crap Artist* (1975) and *The Transmigration of Timothy Archer* (1982), shows his concern for the plight of the meek.

Dickens, Charles (John Huffam) 1812–70 English. Born at Portsmouth, the son of John Dickens, a clerk in the Navy Office, and his wife Elizabeth, he had an unsettled childhood in London, Chatham and London again. After the family's second move to London his parents slid into financial difficulties which resulted in John Dickens's imprisonment for debt in the Marshalsea. Two days after his 12th birthday Dickens was put to work in Warren's blacking factory, a humiliating experience which he nursed in memory until the end of his life. On his release John Dickens sent his son to Wellington House Academy, where he remained until early 1827. He then became office boy in a firm of attorneys, rising swiftly to work as reporter in Doctors' Commons. Characteristically alert to self-advancement, he went on to work for his uncle's Hansard-style *Mirror of Parliament* and for *The True Sun* before becoming parliamentary journalist for *The Morning Chronicle* in 1833. Deeply wounded by his unsuccessful courtship of Maria Beadnell, Dickens finally married Catherine Hogarth in April 1836.

By this time he was more than a mere reporter. *Sketches by Boz* (1836–7) gathered his early work into a book anticipating his novels in its fascination with the variety of London life. The month of his marriage saw the unpromising start of THE PICKWICK PAPERS (1836–7). The introduction of Sam Weller in its fourth number made Dickens famous. With success assured, he worked and lived with even greater intensity than before. Overlapping with the serialization of *Pickwick Papers* came first OLIVER TWIST (1837–9) and then NICHOLAS NICKLEBY (1838–9). As *Nicholas Nickleby* came to its conclusion he conceived MASTER HUMPHREY'S CLOCK, a weekly miscellany whose failure forced him to expand a story originally designed for the miscellany into a full-length serial, THE OLD CURIOSITY SHOP (1840–1); this he quickly followed with BARNABY RUDGE (1841). Always prickly with publishers, he quarrelled with John Macrone and friction with RICHARD BENTLEY caused him to resign the editorship of BENTLEY'S MISCELLANY in 1839. He enlarged his family, rescued his parents from financial difficulties, met his future biographer John Forster and widened his circle of friends beyond journalism.

Dickens made his first visit to America in 1842, though the criticisms expressed in *American Notes* (1842) and his next novel, MARTIN CHUZZLEWIT (1843–4), caused lasting resentment among his American audience. In 1843 he produced his first and most famous Christmas story, *A CHRISTMAS CAROL*. In the spring of the next year he went to live in Genoa, returning to England in 1845 and publishing *Pictures from Italy*. In the mid-1840s, too, Dickens produced *THE CHIMES*, *THE CRICKET ON THE HEARTH*, *THE BATTLE OF LIFE* and *THE HAUNTED MAN*, republished together with *A Christmas Carol* as *Christmas Books* (1852). As a journalist, he edited the newly founded *Daily News* for a mere 17 numbers in 1846 before a disagreement with the publishers caused him to withdraw. In 1850 he founded his own magazine, *Household Words*, succeeded by *All the Year Round* in 1859. More important was the publication of *DOMBEY AND SON* (1846–8), the novel which ushered in the mature period of his art, followed in the next decade by *DAVID COPPERFIELD* (1849–50), *BLEAK HOUSE* (1852–3), *HARD TIMES* (1854), *LITTLE DORRIT* (1855–7) and *A TALE OF TWO CITIES* (1859). Where his early work had overflowed with improvisatory energy, the novels of the 1850s and beyond are more tightly controlled. No less wide-ranging in their subjects, they are unified by theme, image and symbol as much as by their complex and ramifying plots.

Outside literature, Dickens's energy continued unabated. He indulged his love of travel and of amateur theatricals, acting in *The Frozen Deep* (written in collaboration with his friend WILKIE COLLINS) and other pieces. He also concerned himself with capital punishment, the reform of prostitutes and model flats in Bethnal Green among other issues. By the late 1850s he had been captivated by the young actress Ellen Ternan; his marriage came to a publicly acrimonious end in 1858. The same year saw the first of his public readings from his work, successfully repeated throughout England and on a second visit to the United States in 1867, before the strain forced him to give them up. It is ironic that the 1860s should also have produced some of his best work: *GREAT EXPECTATIONS* (1860–1), *OUR MUTUAL FRIEND* (1864–5) and the tantalizingly incomplete *MYSTERY OF EDWIN DROOD*, halted in its serialization by his death.

It is hard to accept that in the space of 58 years Dickens should have written even as much as the foregoing, though his canon also includes: pamphlets such as the anti-Sabbatarian *Sunday under Three Heads* (1836); *A Child's History of England* (1851–3); short stories such as 'To be Read at Dusk' (1852), 'Hunted Down' (1859), 'A Holiday Romance' (1868) and 'George Silverman's Explanation' (1868); pieces for *Household Words* and *All the Year Round*, some of them gathered in *The Uncommercial Traveller* (1860; enlarged in 1865 and 1875); several comic plays; and speeches and letters which have occupied the attention of modern editors. So prolific is his output and so frenzied his life, it seems miraculous he lived as long as he did.

Dickens, Monica (Enid) 1915–92 English. She was the grand-daughter of CHARLES DICKENS. The most famous of her novels is *The Happy Prisoner* (1946), one of several inspired by her wartime nursing career. Her five volumes of autobiography include the highly successful sequence *One Pair of Hands* (1939), *One Pair of Feet* (1942) and *My Turn to Make the Tea* (1951).

Dickson, Carter See CARR, JOHN DICKSON.

Didion, Joan 1934– American. She is perhaps best known for her essays, prime examples of the New Journalism which coolly explore the spookier fringes of American society and politics: *Slouching toward Bethlehem* (1969), *The White Album* (1979), *Salvador* (1983), *Miami* (1988) and *Sentimental Journeys* (1993). Three novels – *Run, River* (1964), *Play It As It Lays* (1971) and *Democracy* (1984) – chronicle exhausted marriages and peripatetic lives on the edge of violence. *A Book of Common Prayer* (1977), set in a fictional South American republic, and *The Last Thing He Wanted* (1996), set on an unnamed Caribbean island, deal with politics impinging on individual lives.

Dillard, Annie 1945– American. Winner of the 1975 PULITZER PRIZE for her reflections on living in and with nature, *Pilgrim at Tinker Creek* (1974), Dillard's precise, detailed writing frequently crosses the boundaries between non-fiction and fiction to meditate on interactions between human life and the natural world. Her work includes two poetry collections, *Tickets for a Prayer Wheel* (1974), and *Found Poems* (1995); two collections of essays on nature and nature writing, *Holy the Firm* (1977), *Teaching a Stone to Talk* (1982); *Living By Fiction* (1982), a gathering of essays on contemporary writers and writing; *An American Childhood* (1987) and *The Writing Life* (1989), autobiographical reflections on growing up and living as a writer in the USA; and *The Living* (1992), a historical fiction.

Dinesen, Isak [Blixen (*née* Dinesen), Karen Christentze] 1885–1962 Danish-born, she wrote in English, rewriting her work for Danish publication. She went to East Africa in 1913 to marry her cousin, Baron Blor von Blixen-Finecke, and farmed coffee outside Nairobi. After the failure of the marriage and the farm she returned to Denmark in 1937. *Seven Gothic Tales* (1934) is a collection of sometimes portentous neo-Gothic stories. *Out of Africa* (1937), drawing on her own experiences, is remarkable for its clarity and intellectual breadth; *Shadows on the Grass* (1960) continued the same theme. Other collections, *Winter's Tales* (1942), *Last Tales* (1957) and *Anecdotes of Destiny* (1958), deal with provincial as well as sophisticated situations and the insoluble difficulty of reconciling art and nature.

Disch, Thomas M(ichael) 1940– American. His characteristic mode of SCIENCE FICTION is satirical black comedy. His novels include: an apocalyptic novel, *The Genocides* (1965); *Camp*

Concentration (1968); *Black Alice* (as 'Thom Demijohn', with John Sladek; 1968); *Clara Reeve* (as 'Leonie Hargrave'; 1975), a pastiche GOTHIC NOVEL; *On Wings of Song* (1979); and *Neighbouring Lives* (with Charles Naylor; 1981), about the world of Victorian letters. *The Businessman: A Tale of Terror* (1984), *The M. D.: A Horror Story* (1990) and *The Priest: A Gothic Romance* (1995) embed sharp social criticism in neo-Gothic tales of cruelty and madness. Among his short stories are *Under Compulsion* (1968; also known as *Fun with Your New Head*), *334* (1972), *Getting into Death* (1973), *Fundamental Disch* (1980) and *The Man Who Had No Idea* (1982). His poetry includes *The Right Way to Figure Plumbing* (1971), *Burn This* (1982) and *Here I am, There You are, Where were We?* (1984).

Diski, Jenny 1947– English. Her work has provoked controversy but also flattering comparison with MURIEL SPARK and ANGELA CARTER. Her first novel, *Nothing Natural* (1986), an exploration of female sado-masochism, has been followed by: *Rainforest* (1987), concerned with the limitations of scientific enquiry and 'trained observation', a recurrent theme in her work; *Like Mother* (1988), in which a literally brainless child narrates her mother's life story; and *Monkey's Uncle* (1994), penetrating the world of female madness. Her preoccupation with the teasing and sometimes arbitrary distinctions between fantasy and reality informs the stories gathered in *The Vanishing Princess* (1995) as well as another novel, *The Dream Mistress* (1996). *Skating to Antarctica* (1997) is a memoir.

Disraeli, Benjamin, 1st Earl of Beaconsfield 1804–81 English. The eldest son of the man of letters Isaac d'Israeli, he was baptized at the age of 13, despite his Jewish descent. After losing money on the Stock Exchange and in trying to found a newspaper, *The Representative*, he published his first novel, *VIVIAN GREY* (1826), which gave the youthful hero his own wit and arrogance. It was followed by a satirical work, *The Voyage of Captain Popanilla* (1827) and another society novel, *The Young Duke* (1831). A tour of Spain, Greece, Albania and Egypt left its mark on his writing, including his next novels, *CONTARINI FLEMING* (1832) and *Alroy* (1833). Despite his increasing involvement in politics, he continued to publish throughout the 1830s: a light-hearted satire of contemporary politics, *The Infernal Marriage* (1834), and two more novels, *HENRIETTA TEMPLE* (1837) and *Venetia* (1837), a fictionalized account of events in the lives of Shelley and Byron. In 1837 he succeeded in becoming Conservative MP for Maidstone, marrying the widow of the previous member two years later. During his early years in the Commons Disraeli showed his concern for the condition of the working class and associated himself with other reforming Tories in the 'Young England' group. The same attitudes underlie the ROMAN À THESE trilogy for which he is best known: *CONINGSBY: or, The New Generation* (1844), *SYBIL: or, the Two Nations* (1845) and *TANCRED: or, The New Crusade* (1847).

Disraeli first achieved political office in Lord Derby's Conservative administration of 1852. He was twice Prime Minister, in 1868 and in 1874–80. In 1876 he took the title Earl of Beaconsfield, one he had invented for a character in his first novel. His success in politics overshadowed, but did not end, his writing career. *LOTHAIR* (1870) is about religious conflict, *ENDYMION* (1880) about politics. He also left a fragment of an unfinished novel, *Falconet*.

Diviners, The A novel by MARGARET LAURENCE, published in 1974. It is the last, longest and most ambitious book in her 'Manawaka' sequence. The narrator, Morag Gunn, is a novelist who reviews her life through flashbacks which enable her to formulate a revisionist view of Western Canadian history, women's roles and the position of minorities within Canada, as well as investigating her personal past and the relationships between different generations. The novel uses a range of narrative modes to highlight the problem of giving a definitive account of the past.

Dixon, Stephen 1936– American. His many short stories and several novels depict the daily lives of city dwellers, often through abrasive, comic monologues and dialogues. Among his story collections are *Work* (1977), *Fourteen Stories* (1980), *Movies* (1983), *Love and Will* (1989), *All Gone* (1990) and *Long Made Stories* (1994). His novels include *Quite Contrary: The Mary and Newt Story* (1979), *Fall & Rise* (1984), *Garbage* (1988), *Frog* (1991), *Interstate* (1995) and *Gould: A Novel in Two Novels* (1997).

Dr Jekyll and Mr Hyde, The Strange Case of A novel by ROBERT LOUIS STEVENSON, published in 1886. Apart from *TREASURE ISLAND*, it is probably his best-known work.

The mystery is gradually revealed to the reader through the narratives of Mr Enfield, Mr Utterson, Dr Lanyon and Jekyll's butler, Poole. Seeking to separate the good and evil aspects of his nature, the doctor secretly develops a drug which frees his evil propensities into the repulsive form of Mr Hyde. It grows harder and harder for Jekyll to return to his own personality. With his supply of the drug exhausted and Hyde wanted for murder, Jekyll kills himself. The body discovered in his sanctum is that of Hyde, but the confession Jekyll leaves behind establishes the common identity of the two men. The story has attracted much commentary, being read as a version of the Scottish Arminianism of JAMES HOGG's *PRIVATE MEMOIRS AND CONFESSIONS OF A JUSTIFIED SINNER*, a variant of the *Doppelgänger* myth, and a pre-Freudian study of ego and libido.

Doctor Thorne The third of ANTHONY TROLLOPE's

BARSETSHIRE NOVELS, published in 1858. Trollope's best-selling work in his own lifetime, it extends the range of the sequence to take in the life of county society.

The unmarried Dr Thorne, a country practitioner, lives in Greshamsbury with Mary, illegitimate child of his brother Henry. The plot deals with her love for Frank Gresham, son of the local squire's family, and the obstacles posed by the Greshams and their aristocratic relatives, the De Courcys. The death of Sir Roger Scatcherd, brother of Mary's mother, and Scatcherd's son Louis brings Mary a fortune which enables her to marry Frank. A subsidiary plot deals with the relations between Frank's sister and a social-climbing lawyer, and his eventual marriage to her treacherous De Courcy cousin.

Dr Wortle's School A novel by ANTHONY TROLLOPE, serialized in 1880 and published in volume form in 1881.

Dr Jeffrey Wortle, a high-spirited and worldly clergyman, runs a successful private school to which he appoints Mr Peacocke as an assistant master and Peacocke's beautiful American wife as matron. It emerges that the couple had married in the mistaken belief that her first husband was dead. Dr Wortle's courage in standing by his conviction of the Peacockes' integrity against pressure from his bishop, the press and the malevolent gossip of an ex-parent is rewarded when Peacocke goes to America and returns with proof that the first husband has subsequently died. The couple are married again in London. Conventional love interest is provided by a romance between the doctor's daughter Mary and one of his former pupils, Lord Carstairs.

Doctorow, E(dgar) L(awrence) 1931– American. *Welcome to Hard Times* (1960; called *Bad Man from Bodie* in Britain) was followed by *The Book of Daniel* (1971), about the espionage trial of Julius and Ethel Rosenberg and its aftermath. He remains best known for *RAGTIME* (1975), which exemplifies his technique of mixing fictional characters with historical figures. Other novels are *Big as Life* (1966), *Loon Lake* (1980), *World's Fair* (1985), *Billy Bathgate* (1989), about the New York gangland of the 1930s, and *Waterworks* (1994). *Lives of the Poet, Six Stories and a Novella* (1984) addresses the position of the writer, and *Jack London, Hemingway and the Constitution* (1993) is a collection of essays.

Dodgson, Charles Lutwidge See CARROLL, LEWIS.

Dodsworth A novel by SINCLAIR LEWIS, published in 1929. Sam Dodsworth, a retired car manufacturer from the Midwest, travels to Europe with his wife Fran. She becomes impatient with his supposed gaucheness and flirts with other men. They separate and she plans to marry Kurt von Obersdorf, an Austrian aristocrat. When her hopes are disappointed, Sam takes her back, despite his growing friendship with Edith Cortright, an American living in Italy. Soon, however, Fran's shallowness makes him realize his feelings for Edith. He divorces Fran and joins Edith in Europe.

Dombey and Son A novel by CHARLES DICKENS, published in monthly parts in 1846–8 and in volume form in 1848, as *Dealings with the Firm of Dombey and Son, Retail, Wholesale and for Exportation*. It is commonly taken to herald the start of Dickens's maturity, for its careful planning marks a break from the high-spirited improvisation which often sustains his early fiction.

The stern, unbending Mr Dombey, preoccupied with his desire for a son and heir to the firm, ignores and resents his daughter Florence. Mrs Dombey dies at the beginning of the book in giving birth to a son, Paul, but he proves weak and dies in the fifth number (chapter 16). The bereavement further alienates Florence from her father. Dombey's second marriage, to Edith Grainger, proves loveless and childless. She finally runs away with Dombey's business manager, Carker, though she soon abandons him and he dies in a railway accident. Dombey's ensuing mental and physical decline parallels his business difficulties. Only as a ruined man can he at last respond to Florence's love. The novel contrasts the cold unhappiness of the Dombey household with the cheerful homes of the Toodle family and of Sol Gills and his nephew Walter Gay, Florence's future husband.

Dominic, R. B. See LATHEN, EMMA.

Donleavy, J(ames) P(atrick) 1926– Born of Irish parents in New York, he settled in Ireland. He remains best known for a determinedly Rabelaisian novel of Dublin literary life, *The Ginger Man*; it was first published in Paris in 1955, then in a revised edition in New York in 1958 and in an unexpurgated edition in New York in 1965, since when it has never been out of print. Other novels include *A Singular Man* (1961). His autobiography, *The History of the Ginger Man*, appeared in 1994.

Donoghue, Emma 1969– Irish. Her first novel, *Stir-fry* (1994), tells the now-familiar lesbian coming-out story in the less familiar context of contemporary Dublin. She deepened her lesbian theme with *Hood* (1995), in which a woman's death in a car crash prompts others to examine their loss. *Kissing the Witch* (1997) reworks old fairy tales and offers new ones. A historical study, *Passions Between Women: British Lesbian Culture, 1668–1801*, appeared in 1993 and an anthology, *What Sapphoe Would Have Said: Four Centuries of Love Poems Between Women*, in 1997.

Dos Passos, John (Roderigo) 1896–1970 American. His early works include a collection of essays, a volume of poems and two novels, *One Man's Initiation: 1917* (1920) and *Three Soldiers* (1921), deriving from his experiences as an ambulance driver in France and Italy during World War I. He came to prominence with MANHATTAN TRANSFER (1925), a novel whose aim of providing a 'collective' portrait of New York embodied his left-wing views. A similar purpose underlay his most important work, *USA*, a trilogy consisting of *The 42nd Parallel* (1930), *1919* (1932) and *The Big Money* (1936), which together seek to provide a portrait of American life in the first decades of the century. *The Moon is a Gong* (1926; later renamed *The Garbage Man*), *Airways, Inc.* (1928) and *Fortune Heights* (1934) are plays stemming from his involvement with experimental theatre. His disillusionment with communism is made clear in *The Adventures of a Young Man* (1939), the first volume of another trilogy, *District of Columbia*, completed by *Number One* (1943), about the dangers of demagogy, and *The Grand Design* (1949), about the threat of bureaucracy. Later novels include *Chosen Country* (1951) and *Midcentury* (1961). Dos Passos's many works of non-fiction include a biography of Thomas Jefferson (1954). *The Fourteenth Chronicle* (1973) contains selections from his letters and diaries.

Double Hook, The A novel by SHEILA WATSON, published in 1959. Described as the first 'truly modern Canadian novel', it uses an elliptical and imagistic style, drawing on both Christian and Native Canadian myth, and is influenced by British and American MODERNISM, particularly WYNDHAM LEWIS and GERTRUDE STEIN. The probing examination of epistemological questions depicts the attempt of a small community in the Cariboo region of British Columbia to find redemption.

Douglas, George [Brown, George Douglas] 1869–1902 Scottish. He earned his living contributing short stories and boys' stories to magazines but is remembered for his realistic story of Scottish life, THE HOUSE WITH GREEN SHUTTERS (1901).

Douglas, (George) Norman 1868–1952 English. He achieved his first and only popular success with *SOUTH WIND* (1917), a novel whose frank discussion of moral and sexual questions caused considerable debate. *Siren Land* (1911), *Fountains in the Sand* (about Tunisia, 1912) and *Old Calabria* (1915) are travel books reflecting Douglas's wide-ranging interests as biologist, geologist, art lover, archaeologist and classicist. *They Went* (1920) and *In the Beginning* (1927) are fantasies about early mankind, and *Looking Back* (1933) is a fragmentary autobiography.

Doyle, Sir Arthur Conan 1859–1930 English. He had abandoned his family's Roman Catholicism by the time he completed his medical studies at Edinburgh. *The Stark Munro Letters* (1894) reflects his experiences as a general practitioner. Other early fiction includes *The Firm of Girdlestone* (1890), a SENSATION NOVEL. With his SHERLOCK HOLMES STORIES he turned to DETECTIVE FICTION.

The saga began with two novels, *A Study in Scarlet* (1887) and *The Sign of Four* (1890), though its popularity dated from the short stories in *The Strand Magazine*, collected as *The Adventures of Sherlock Holmes* (1892) and *The Memoirs of Sherlock Holmes* (1894). Doyle's attempt to kill off his creation was unsuccessful and Holmes reappeared in two novels, *The Hound of the Baskervilles* (1902) and *The Valley of Fear* (1915), and several collections of short stories, *The Return of Sherlock Holmes* (1905), *His Last Bow* (1917) and *The Case-Book of Sherlock Holmes* (1927).

To Doyle's own annoyance, the popularity of Sherlock Holmes overshadowed the other fruits of his versatile and hardworking career. His HISTORICAL FICTION comprises *Micah Clarke* (1889), *The White Company* (1891), *Rodney Stone* (1896), *The Exploits of Brigadier Gerard* (1896), *Uncle Bernac* (1897), *The Adventures of Gerard* (1903) and *Sir Nigel* (1906). *The Tragedy of the 'Korosko'* (1898) is an adventure story. Doyle's SCIENCE FICTION is found in his Professor Challenger stories, *The Lost World* (1912), *The Poison Belt* (1913) and *The Land of Mist* (1926). The last of them reflects the belief in spiritualism which preoccupied much of his later life.

Doyle, Roddy 1958– Irish. North Dublin is the setting for his fiction, which has been highly praised for its picaresque evocation of Irish working-class life, largely through pithy, colloquial dialogue. *The Commitments* (1988), about an Irish soul band's bid for stardom, *The Snapper* (1990) and *The Van* (1991) form a trilogy dealing with the Rabbitte family. Subsequent novels include *Paddy Clarke Ha Ha Ha* (1993), which won the BOOKER PRIZE, and *The Woman Who Walked into Doors* (1996), about a woman's struggle with domestic violence and alcoholism.

Drabble, Margaret 1939– English. Often preoccupied with the individual's struggle against a conventional or repressive background, her fiction has grown steadily broader in its consideration of the contemporary social climate. It includes: *A Summer Birdcage* (1963); *The Garrick Year* (1964); *The Millstone* (1965); *Jerusalem the Golden* (1967); *The Waterfall* (1969); *The Ice Age* (1977); a trilogy following the friendship of three women, *The Radiant Way* (1987), *A Natural Curiosity* (1989) and *The Gates of Ivory* (1991); and *The Witch of Exmoor* (1996). In the course of a prolific career which has included public work for literary causes, she has also written a biography of ANGUS WILSON (1995) and studies of Wordsworth (1966), ARNOLD BENNETT (1974) and the relationship between writers and landscape in *A Writer's Britain* (1979), as well as editing *The Oxford Companion to English Literature* (1984). Her sister is A. S. BYATT and her husband the biographer Michael Holroyd.

Dracula A novel by BRAM STOKER, published in 1897. Presented in diaries, letters and news items, its story of a bloodsucking vampire who preys on the living but can be repelled by garlic and crucifixes, is both absurd and powerful. Like MARY SHELLEY's *FRANKENSTEIN*, it has become modern myth – the subject of many film versions, imitations and parodies.

Jonathan Harker, a London solicitor, falls victim to Count Dracula in his Transylvanian castle. The Count then travels to England, arriving at Whitby, where the story is taken up in accounts by Harker's fiancée Mina Murray, her friend Lucy Westenra and Dr John Seward. Van Helsing, a Dutch doctor and expert in vampirism, leads the fight against Dracula. When Lucy becomes his victim a stake is driven through her heart so that she can rest in peace. Dracula turns his attention to Mina, but is pursued to Transylvania and vanquished.

Dream of John Ball, A A prose tale by the artisan, poet and socialist William Morris (1834–96), serialized in 1886-7 and published in book form in 1888. The dream takes Morris back to the Peasants' Revolt of 1381 and an encounter with the dissenting priest John Ball. As Morris describes the Industrial Revolution and 19th-century society, Ball realizes he is himself dreaming of the future course of history and still unfulfilled ideals. *A Dream of John Ball* is the forerunner of Morris's greatest socialist work, *NEWS FROM NOWHERE*. For Morris, see also *THE WELL AT THE WORLD'S END*.

Dreiser, Theodore (Herman Albert) 1871–1945 American. Born in Terre Haute, Indiana, he worked as a journalist in New York. *SISTER CARRIE* (1900) and *JENNIE GERHARDT* (1911) were attacked for their candid and uncompromising NATURALISM. *The Financier* (1912) and *The Titan* (1914) were the first two volumes of Dreiser's *Cowperwood* trilogy, based on the life of the business magnate, Charles T. Yerkes; it was completed by *The Stoic*, posthumously published in 1947. *The Genius* (1915) is a partly autobiographical novel examining the artistic temperament. Dreiser at last earned popular acclaim with *AN AMERICAN TRAGEDY* (1925), based on the Chester Gillette–Grace Brown murder case of 1906. *The Bulwark* appeared posthumously in 1946.

Dreiser Looks at Russia (1928) describes a visit to the Soviet Union, while *Tragic America* (1931) and *America is Worth Saving* (1941) express his belief in socialism. Dreiser also published plays, verse, short stories, essays and an autobiography.

Drewe, Robert (Duncan) 1943– Australian. His experience in journalism gives his fiction a straightforward, visual style and the habitual stance of an outside observer. The stories in *The Body Surfers* (1983), his best-known work, first identified Australian culture as drawn from the beach rather than the bush. His novels include: *The Savage Crows* (1976), contrasting a contemporary journalist with a 19th-century 'protector' of Aborigines; *A Cry in the Jungle* (1979), about an Australian 'expert' let loose in Asia; *Fortune* (1986), a 'faction' based on his experience of America; and *Our Sunshine* (1991). *The Bay of Contented Men* (1989) is a further collection of stories.

Dry White Season, A A novel by ANDRÉ BRINK, published in 1979. It was banned before publication date in 1978 but unbanned in 1979. Like many of his novels, it charts the distancing of an ordinary Afrikaner from his community. Ben du Toit is drawn into a struggle with the security police when he investigates the death in detention of Gordon Ngubane, a black employee at his school. He eventually becomes dislocated from his society, family, friends, colleagues and church, and seeks understanding in a romance with an English journalist. *A Dry White Season* was filmed in 1989.

du Fresne, Yvonne 1929– New Zealand. Two collections of stories, *Farvel* (1982) and *The Growing of Astrid Westergaard* (1985), and her first novel, *The Book of Ester* (1982), draw on her own mixed cultural background as a French Huguenot who grew up in a Danish community in the Manawatu region. Later work includes *Frederique* (1987), a novel, and *The Bear from the North: Tales of a New Zealand Childhood* (1989).

Du Maurier, Dame Daphne 1907–89 English. Daughter of the actor Sir Gerald Du Maurier and granddaughter of GEORGE DU MAURIER, she spent most of her adult life in Cornwall, whose wild weather and scenery contribute the setting and atmosphere for her tense romances. The most famous are *Jamaica Inn* (1936), *Rebecca* (1938) and *My Cousin Rachel* (1951). Her short story, 'The Birds', was filmed by Hitchcock (1963) and 'Don't Look Now' by Roeg (1973). Her memoirs appeared in *Vanishing Cornwall* (1967).

Du Maurier, George (Louis Palmella Busson) 1834–96 English. He regularly contributed drawings to *Punch*. Apart from *TRILBY* (1894), he wrote *Peter Ibbetson* (1891), *The Martian* (1897) and humorous verse. He was father of the actor Gerald Du Maurier and grandfather of DAPHNE DU MAURIER.

Du Plessis, Ménan 1952– South African. *A State of Fear* (1983), winner of the OLIVE SCHREINER PRIZE and the Sanlam Literary Award for Fiction, and *Longlive!* (1989), adopt the perspective of the marginalized. They deal with the struggle against alienation, the difficulties of changing allegiances and the awareness of what it means to be South African in a transforming society. Intense descriptions of the landscape (Cape Town) are closely entwined with the emotional response of her characters.

Dubliners A volume of short stories by JAMES JOYCE, published in 1914 after delays caused by the printer's objections to a passage in 'Two Gallants'. The stories present Dublin in four aspects – childhood, adolescence, maturity and public life – and Joyce claimed to have written them in a style of 'scrupulous meanness'. The last, 'The Dead', is commonly considered the volume's masterpiece.

Duckworth, Marilyn 1935– New Zealand. *A Gap in the Spectrum* (1959) and *A Barbarous Tongue* (1963) are concerned with individual identity and language. In turning from experiment towards realism, *Over the Fence is Out* (1969) anticipates the novels which followed, after a long silence, in the second phase of her career. These include *Disorderly Conduct* (1984; winner of the NEW ZEALAND BOOK AWARD), set against the divisive South African rugby tour in 1981, and *Married Alive* (1985). Exploration of contemporary New Zealand life continues in: *Unlawful Entry* (1992), about coping in family relationships; *Seeing Red* (1993), set in Wellington; and *Fooling* (1994), a novella about a woman's search for identity, or at least truth. *Leather Wings* (1995) reveals a dark side of suburbia. She has also published stories, *Explosions on the Sun* (1989), and poetry.

Ducornet, Rikki 1943– American. Interested in the power of language to construct reality, she writes 'historiographic metafiction' combining the fantastic and the surreal with actual history. Novels include: *Entering the Fire* (1987); *The Cult of Seizure* (1989); *The Fountains of Neptune* (1992); *The Jade Cabinet* (1994), about Lewis Carroll; *Phospher in Dreamland* (1995); and *The Stain* (1995). Her stories are collected in *The Complete Butcher's Tales* 1994.

Duff, Alan 1950– New Zealand. His first novel, *Once Were Warriors* (1990), was a winner of the GOODMAN FIELDER WATTIE BOOK AWARD, an immediate best-seller and the basis for a film (1994) directed by Lee Tamahori. Whether it is an uncompromising portrayal of urban Maori life or an exaggeration pandering to the fears of a white audience continues to be debated. *One Night Out Stealing* (1991) and *State Ward* (1994) deal with urban deprivation, crime and the neglect of children. *What Becomes of the Broken Hearted?* (1996) won the Montana New Zealand Book Award (see NEW ZEALAND BOOK AWARD). *Maori: The Crisis and the Challenge* (1993) is a highly polemical series of essays.

Duffy, Maureen (Patricia) 1933– English. Intensely literary yet capable of simplicity and directness, her wide-ranging novels include: *That's How It Was* (1962), about an illegitimate child's relationship with her mother; *The Paradox Players* (1967), about a bitter winter on a Thames houseboat; *The Microcosm* (1966), a study of lesbianism which became her best-known work; *Gorsaga* (1981), SCIENCE FICTION which explores the concerns about animal rights addressed in her study, *Men and Beasts* (1984); *Change* (1987), about young people in wartime Britain; *Illuminations* (1991); and *Occam's Razor* (1993). Several novels feature ungendered characters, and *Love Child* (1971) conceals the sex of

both the narrator and the narrator's rival in love. Duffy has also published *Collected Poems* (1985), a study of APHRA BEHN, *The Passionate Shepherdess* (1977), and a biography of Henry Purcell (1994). With BRIGID BROPHY, she was a leading campaigner for the Public Lending Right, which grants authors the equivalent of royalties on books borrowed from libraries.

Duke's Children, The The sixth and last of ANTHONY TROLLOPE'S PALLISER NOVELS, serialized in 1879–80 and published in volume form in 1880.

The Duke of Omnium (Plantagenet Palliser) is widowed and no longer Prime Minister. His eldest son, Lord Silverbridge, finds a gambling partner in the disreputable Major Tifto, stands for Parliament as a Conservative rather than a Liberal and further disappoints his father by falling in love with the beautiful and wealthy American girl, Isabel Boncassen. The duke's daughter, Lady Mary Palliser, also disappoints him by falling in love with Frank Tregear, a promising man without wealth or social rank. Gradually Isabel's charm and Silverbridge's determination win the duke over. He surrenders gracefully and the novel ends with both his children marrying. This closing harmony is shadowed by the loneliness of Lady Mabel Grex, who loses both the man she loves, Tregear, and the man who could have given her wealth and social position, Silverbridge. Isabel Boncassen anticipates HENRY JAMES's American girl, Isabel Archer, in *THE PORTRAIT OF A LADY* (1881).

Dunbar, Paul (Laurence) 1872–1906 American. The son of former slaves, he wrote four novels – *The Uncalled* (1898), *The Love of Landry* (1900), *The Fanatics* (1901) and *The Sport of the Gods* (1902) – but was known in his day primarily as a writer of dialect verse. It appeared in *Oak and Ivy* (1893), *Majors and Minors* (1895), *Lyrics of Lowly Life* (1896), *Lyrics of the Hearthside* (1899), *Lyrics of Love and Laughter* (1903) and *Lyrics of Sunshine and Shadow* (1905). WILLIAM DEAN HOWELLS contributed a preface to the third volume. Dunbar has been severely criticized for his sentimental depiction of black life in the South, though some of his work reveals a concern with the troubled social climate of his times.

Duncan, Sara Jeanette 1861–1922 Canadian. She was married to Everard Charles Cotes, a British journalist in India, the setting for some of her novels. Of more than 20 titles, the most notable are *A Social Departure: or, How Orthodocia and I Went Round the World by Ourselves* (1890), *An American Girl in London* (1891), *The Imperialist* (1904), set in the small Canadian town of 'Elgin', and *Cousin Cinderella: A Canadian Girl in London* (1908).

Dunmore, Helen 1952– English. Her fiction combines disturbing matter with lyrically sensuous prose. *Zennor in Darkness* (1993) creatres the distrust and terror engulfing a

Cornish village, whose inhabitants include D. H. LAWRENCE and his wife Frieda, during World War I. Subsequent work includes: *Burning Bright* (1994), about the links between love and violence; *A Spell of Winter* (1995), which won the ORANGE PRIZE, about a painful journey towards recovery and renewal; and *Talking to the Dead* (1996), taking up characteristic themes of the dangerous intensity of family relations and the threat posed by the imperfectly suppressed past. *Love of Fat Men* (1997) contains short stories.

Dunn, Nell 1936– English. She made her name with *Up the Junction* (1963), stories about young South London women whose factory life is punctuated only by the Saturday-night delights of the bars and cafés of Clapham. It won the JOHN LLEWELLYN RHYS PRIZE. *Poor Cow* (1967), her first novel, followed its spirited heroine, Joy, and her resourceful response to the challenges of poverty. *My Silver Shoes* (1996) is a belated sequel. Critics have consistently admired Dunn's formal skill, economical dialogue and concisely poetic prose. She has also published interviews with working women in *Talking to Women* (1965) and *Grandmothers* (1991).

Durrell, Lawrence (George) 1912–90 English. He was elder brother of the traveller and naturalist Gerald Durrell (1925–95), and a friend of HENRY MILLER and ANAÏS NIN in Paris. The Eastern Mediterranean, where he spent much of his life, is the subject or setting of his best-known work, notably his books on Greece, *Prospero's Cell* (1945) and *Bitter Lemons* (1957), and the four novels forming the *Alexandria Quartet*: *Justine* (1957), *Balthazar* (1958), *Mountolive* (1958) and *Clea* (1960). Subsequent fiction includes *Tunc* (1968), *Nunquam* (1970) and the posthumously collected *Avignon Quintet* (1992): *Monsieur* (1974), *Livia* (1978), *Constance* (1982), *Sebastian* (1983) and *Quinx* (1985). His poetry, which began precociously with *Quaint Fragment: Poems Written between the Ages of Sixteen and Nineteen* (1931), includes *Collected Poems* (1960), *The Ikons* (1966) and *Vega and Other Poems* (1973).

E

East Lynne A novel by MRS HENRY WOOD, published in 1861. Immensely popular in its day, it was also dramatized with great success. Lady Isobel Vane deserts her husband, Archibald Carlyle, for Sir Francis Levison but returns, unrecognizably disfigured by a train crash, to work as governess to her own children. She asks for Carlyle's forgiveness on her deathbed, a scene which provides a richly melodramatic climax to the book.

Edgell, Zee 1940– Belizean. *Beka Lamb* (1982), the first Belizean novel to find an international audience, deals with the heroine's transition from unreflective child to responsible young woman. The connection made between her growing pains and the forces of social change links it with work by ERNA BRODBER, MERLE COLLINS and JAMAICA KINCAID. *In Times Like These* (1991) also entwines personal and public crises in its account of a Belizean woman's return to her country as Independence approaches.

Edgeworth, Maria 1767–1849 Anglo-Irish. Her father, the eccentric Richard Lovell Edgeworth, was a wealthy landowner in Ireland and a powerful influence on his daughter's interests and literary career. She collaborated with him on *Practical Education* (1798), adapting and modifying Rousseau's theories, and completed the second volume of his *Memoirs* in 1820. Her first work, *Letters to Literary Ladies* (1795), was a defence of female education. *The Parent's Assistant* (1796–1800) is a collection of stories for children, to which she later added a volume of *Little Plays*. CASTLE RACKRENT (1800), THE ABSENTEE (in the second series of *Tales of Fashionable Life*, 1812) and *Ormond* (1817) are novels of Irish life, which won the admiration of SIR WALTER SCOTT and influenced his 'Waverley' novels. *Belinda* (1801), *Leonora* (1806), *Patronage* (1814) and *Helen* (1834) deal with English society.

Edson, J. T. See GENRE FICTION.

Edwin Drood, The Mystery of CHARLES DICKENS's last novel, left half-finished at his death in 1870. Like WILKIE COLLINS's THE MOONSTONE, published only two years before, it uses features of the SENSATION NOVEL to pioneer the conventions of DETECTIVE FICTION.

In the cathedral city of Cloisterham, John Jasper leads a double life as choirmaster and opium addict. The story centres on the disappearance of his nephew Edwin Drood shortly after the young man has broken off his engagement to Rosa Bud, whom Jasper loves. Most attempts to complete the narrative presume that Jasper has murdered Drood, though some scholars have suggested that Drood is in fact alive and would have returned to accuse Jasper

of attempted murder. Other matters are less clear, notably the role to be played by Neville and Helena Landless, the twins who come to live with Mr Crisparkle, canon at the cathedral, and the true identity of Dick Datchery, the detective who arrives in Cloisterham as Dickens's fragment breaks off.

Egan, Pierce, the elder 1772–1849 English. He became known for his sports reports in the newspapers and *Boxiana: or, Sketches of Modern Pugilism* (1818–24) but is remembered for LIFE IN LONDON (1820–1), a comic portrait of Regency manners. Egan's weekly newspaper, *Life in London and Sporting Guide*, later merged into *Bell's Life in London*, first appeared in 1824.

Egan, Pierce, the younger 1814–80 English. The son of PIERCE EGAN THE ELDER, he was a pioneer of cheap literature. His HISTORICAL FICTION includes *Wat Tyler* (1841) and *Paul Jones* (1842).

Eggleston, Edward 1837–1902 American. The older brother of GEORGE EGGLESTON, he abandoned the Methodist ministry at the age of 37 to found a Church of Christian Endeavour in Brooklyn, New York, and later to write. His first success, and still his best-known novel, was *The Hoosier Schoolmaster* (1871), a realistic if pious portrait of rural Indiana. His next novels were: *The End of the World* (1872), set in Indiana; *The Mystery of Metropolisville* (1873), set in Minnesota; *The Circuit Rider* (1874), set in Ohio; and *Roxy* (1878), set in Indiana. After turning his attention to history and biography, he published three more novels: *The Hoosier Schoolboy* (1883), a boy's view of the life described in *The Hoosier Schoolmaster*; *The Graysons: A Story of Illinois* (1888), about Abraham Lincoln; and *The Faith Doctor* (1891), a satire of Christian Science.

Eggleston, George Cary 1839–1911 American. The younger brother of EDWARD EGGLESTON, he taught in Indiana and practised law before editing the New York *Evening Post* and working on the *New York World*. He also wrote books for boys and several novels set in the South, including *A Man of Honour* (1873), *Dorothy South* (1902), *The Master of Warlock* (1903) and *Evelyn Byrd* (1904). With Dorothy Marbourg he co-wrote the novel *Juggernaut* (1891), set in Indiana. *A Rebel's Recollections* (1874) is based on his experiences during the Civil War.

Egoist, The A novel by GEORGE MEREDITH, published in 1879. The central character of this elegant comedy is Sir Willoughby Patterne, rich, selfish and conceited. He is loved by Laetitia Dale but proposes to Constantia Durham, who learns in time what sort of man he is and elopes with an officer of Hussars. Sir Willoughby then turns his attention to Clara Middleton and enlists her epicurean father Dr Middleton on his side. She remains equivocal and he proposes to Laetitia, but is overheard and exposed by the boy Crossjay. Clara has in any case fallen in love with Vernon Whitford, a handsome scholar. Stripped of his pretensions, Sir Willoughby finally persuades Laetitia to marry him.

The character of Dr Middleton is modelled on THOMAS LOVE PEACOCK, Meredith's father-in-law, and that of Vernon on Sir Leslie Stephen (for whom, see VIRGINIA WOOLF), who also served as the original for Knight in THOMAS HARDY's *A PAIR OF BLUE EYES*. ROBERT LOUIS STEVENSON thought he recognized himself in Sir Willoughby, but Meredith insisted he was all of us.

The Egoist was also the name of the journal originally founded by Dora Marsden and REBECCA WEST as *The New Freewoman* in 1913. It published JAMES JOYCE's *A PORTRAIT OF THE ARTIST AS A YOUNG MAN* during the editorship of Harriet Shaw Weaver. Her Egoist Press was responsible for the first book publication of *ULYSSES*.

Ekwensi, Cyprian 1921– Nigerian. A popular and prolific writer, he dramatizes the attitudes of ordinary people buffeted by historical change. His many works include *People of the City* (1954), *JAGUA NANA* and *Burning Grass* (both in 1962), *Beautiful Feathers* (1963), *Iska* (1966), *Survive the Peace* (1976) and *For a Roll of Parchment* (1976), set in London. More recent works are the historical study, *Divided We Stand* (1980), and the political allegory, *King For Ever!* (1992). He has also written short stories and children's literature.

Eldershaw, M. Barnard [Eldershaw, Flora Sydney Patricia (1897–1956) and Barnard, Marjorie Faith (1897–1987)] Australian. Their best-known novels, *A House is Built* (1929) and *Green Memory* (1931), are set in 19th-century Australia. They also wrote short stories, histories and literary criticism. Barnard published a seminal biography of MILES FRANKLIN (1967) and a collection of stories, *The Persimmon Tree* (1943), frequently anthologized.

Eldred-Grigg, Stevan 1952– New Zealand. *Oracles and Miracles* (1987), a winner of the GOODMAN FIELDER WATTIE BOOK AWARD, is HISTORICAL FICTION celebrating the culture of working-class women in Christchurch in the 1930s and 1940s. It begins a trilogy completed in *The Shining City* (1991), dealing with the next generation, and *Mum* (1995), which opens in 1975. *Gardens of Fire* (1993), another historical novel, deals with the plight of working girls in a fire at a Christchurch department store. *My History, I Think* (1994) is a reflective commentary blurring the distinctions between autobiography and fiction. *A Southern Gentry* (1980) and *New Zealand Working People* (1990) are about New Zealand history.

Eliot, George [Evans, Mary Anne (Marian)] 1819–80 English. Born at Arbury, Warwickshire, the daughter of a land agent, she attended schools in Nuneaton and Coventry, where she went to live with her father on his retirement in 1841. Having already read widely in theology, the Romantic poets and German literature, she was drawn to an intellectual circle that included Charles Bray and Charles Hennell, whose influences directed her towards free-thinking in religious opinion. In 1842 she refused to attend church with her father and in 1846 she completed a translation of Strauss's *Leben Jesu*, a central document of the Higher Criticism. In London she was closely associated with John Chapman, proprietor of *The Westminster Review*, of which she was assistant editor in 1852–4. Her next publication of consequence was a translation of Feuerbach's *Essence of Christianity* (1854). By this time she had met George Henry Lewes, with whom she went to live in 1853. Their union, happy despite Lewes's irregular marital situation, lasted until his death in 1878.

George Eliot's interest in writing fiction went back to her schooldays in the early 1830s but she did not make her début until the serialization of 'The Sad Fortunes of the Reverend Amos Barton', 'Mr Gilfil's Love-Story' and 'Janet's Repentance' in 1857. These tales were collected, and well received, as *SCENES OF CLERICAL LIFE* (1858). They were followed by *ADAM BEDE* (1859), *THE MILL ON THE FLOSS* (1860) and *SILAS MARNER* (1861). After a brief Florentine visit George Eliot deserted her native literary landscapes to publish *ROMOLA* in *The Cornhill Magazine* in 1862–3. Next came *FELIX HOLT THE RADICAL* (1866) in some respects anticipating *MIDDLEMARCH*, published in independent parts in 1871–2, and *DANIEL DERONDA*, which appeared in the same way in 1874–6. Her last work was *The Impressions of Theophrastus Such* (1879), a series of essays linked by a narrator. George Eliot also wrote some novellas and a surprising amount of poetry, including *The Spanish Gypsy* (1868), the product of a trip to Spain in 1867, and *The Legend of Jubal and Other Poems* (1874). In addition, she was one of the finest letter-writers in the language.

After the death of Lewes, she married John Walter Cross, many years her junior, in the spring of 1880. She died in December of the same year. Cross's biography was published in 1885.

Elkin, Stanley (Lawrence) 1930–95 American. Preoccupied with alienation, evil and mortality yet still predominantly comic, his work presents salesmen, con artists, thieves, politicians and artists in extreme or absurd situations. Novels include *Boswell* (1964), *A Bad Man* (1967), *The Dick Gibson Show* (1971), *The Franchiser* (1976), *The Living End* (1979), *George Mills* (1982), *The Magic Kingdom* (1985), *The Rabbi of Lud* (1987), *The*

MacGuffin (1991) and *Mrs Ted Bliss* (1995). *Cries and Kibitzers, Kibitzers and Criers* (1966) and *Searches and Seizures* (1973; published in Britain as both *Eligible Men*, 1974, and *Alex and the Gypsy*, 1977) and *Van Gogh's Room at Arles* (1993) contain short stories and novellas. *Stanley Elkin's Greatest Hits* (1980) is an omnibus collection of his stories. *Pieces of Soap* (1992) is a collection of his non-fiction.

Elliott, Janice 1931– English. Since *Cave With Echoes* (1962) her work has explored the darker aspect of human bonds and the fate of people caught in events too large to understand or control. It includes: *State of Peace* (1971), *Private Life* (1972) and *Heaven on Earth* (1975), a 'CONDITION OF ENGLAND' trilogy; *Secret Places* (1981) and *Dr Gruber's Daughter* (1986), both about Nazism; *The Italian Lesson* (1985), about Anglo-Italian encounters; *The Sadness of Witches* (1987); *Life on the Nile* (1989), about relations with Egypt; *Necessary Rites* (1990), about the power of neglected emotions to wreak revenge; *City of Gates* (1992), about pilgrims to Jerusalem; and *Figures in the Sand* (1994), set in Syria under the Roman Empire, which has been compared to WILLIAM GOLDING's LORD OF THE FLIES. *The Noise from the Zoo* (1991) is a collection of stories. She has also written for children.

Ellis, Alice Thomas [Haycraft, Anna] 1932– English. *The Sin Eater* (1977) established her characteristic fictional components of neurotic religion, chintzy eccentricity and suddenly graceful insight. It has been followed by *The 27th Kingdom* (1982), often considered her most successful novel, *The Other Side of the Fire* (1983), *The Fly in the Ointment* (1989) and the trilogy consisting of *The Clothes in the Wardrobe* (1988), *The Skeleton in the Cupboard* (1988) and *The Inn at the End of the World* (1990). Two studies written with the psychiatrist Tom Pitt-Aikens, *Secrets of Strangers* (1986) and *Loss of Good Authority* (1989), express her preoccupation with juvenile delinquency. *A Welsh Childhood* (1990) is autobiographical.

Ellison, Harlan See SCIENCE FICTION.

Ellison, Ralph (Waldo) 1914–94 African-American. His reputation as the most important literary heir to RICHARD WRIGHT – matched only by that of JAMES BALDWIN – depends on his novel *INVISIBLE MAN* (1952), which weathered critical controversy to hold its place as a central text of the 20th-century Afro-American experience. Parts of an incomplete second novel, including a section entitled 'And Hickman Arrives', have appeared in print. 'Flying Home' and 'King of the Bingo Game' are widely anthologized stories. *Shadow and Act* (1964) and *Going to the Territory* (1986) collect some of his many essays on black music, literature and American culture. Interviews can be found in *Conversations with Ralph Waldo Ellison* (1995), edited by Harryemma Amritjit Singh.

Ellroy, James 1948– American. His first novel, *Brown's Requiem* (1981), and a trilogy about the Los Angeles policeman Lloyd Hopkins, *Blood on the Moon* (1984), *Because the Night* (1985) and *Suicide Kill* (1986), are bleak and violent but conventional DETECTIVE FICTION in the contemporary American manner. His 'LA Quartet', composed of *The Black Dahlia* (1987), *The Big Nowhere* (1989), *LA Confidential* (1990) and *White Jazz* (1992), is a more ambitious saga of corrupt police in the 1950s, dramatizing an era which is both his own traumatic childhood and the heyday of a society headed, quite explicitly by the end of *American Tabloid* (1995), towards the Kennedy assassination.

Elsie Venner: A Romance of Destiny A novel by OLIVER WENDELL HOLMES, serialized as *The Professor's Story* in 1860–1 and published in volume form in 1861. A fable designed to test the doctrine of original sin, it tells the story of Elsie Venner, whose mother is bitten by a rattlesnake three weeks before giving birth. Elsie exhibits snake-like qualities which she loses only as she dies.

Emecheta, Buchi 1944– Nigerian. She moved to Britain in 1962, an experience reflected in *In the Ditch* (1972) and *Second-Class Citizen* (1974), published together as *Adah's Story* (1983). Her championship of women's rights gives compassion and anger to her other novels, mostly set in West Africa: *The Bride Price* (1976), *The Slave Girl* (1977), *THE JOYS OF MOTHERHOOD* (1979), *Destination Biafra* (1982), *Naira Power* (1982), *Double Yoke* (1982), *The Rape of Shavi* (1983), *A Kind of Marriage* (1986), *The Family* (1990, also called *Gwendolen*) and *Kehinde* (1994).

Emma A novel by JANE AUSTEN, written in 1814–15 and published in 1816.

It follows Emma Woodhouse's slow, painful progress toward maturity. Left alone with her hypochondriacal father when her governess, Miss Taylor, marries a neighbour, Mr Weston, Emma makes a protégée of Harriet Smith, an illegitimate girl of no social status, and sets about arranging her life. She makes sure that Harriet rejects a proposal from a young farmer, Robert Martin. Emma's brother-in-law, George Knightley of Donwell Abbey, frowns on this manipulation but, undeterred, she tries to marry Harriet to Mr Elton, a young clergyman. Elton, however, despises Harriet and has set his sights on Emma herself. For her part, Emma half fancies herself in love with Mr Weston's son by his first marriage, Frank Churchill. Harriet, meanwhile, has become interested in Knightley's unaffected warmth and intelligence. Emma, reassuring Harriet after Elton's departure, is now considering Frank Churchill for her. Without giving the thought expression, she has always regarded Knightley as hers and the realization that Harriet might supplant her in Knightley's affections, together with the discovery that Frank Churchill is engaged to Jane Fairfax, forces her to examine her own conduct and resolve to behave better. Knightley proposes to her while Harriet, left to decide for herself, marries Robert Martin.

Empire of the Sun A novel by J. G. BALLARD, published in 1984. The story is loosely based on Ballard's own experiences as a teenager, when Shanghai fell to the invading Japanese and its inhabitants were interned for the duration of World War II. After the city is annexed, the schoolboy Jim spends several weeks living rough among the grandiose homes of the British and French Concessions before being captured and sent to the Lunghua prison camp. He takes a jaundiced view of the British internees, finding more congenial company among the American prisoners of war, but is fascinated by the Japanese guards. This fragile but stable society is returned to chaos by the atom bomb, which ushers in a new era of dangerous freedom.

Endymion BENJAMIN DISRAELI's last novel, published in 1880. It describes the rise to eminence of Endymion and Myra Pitt Ferrars, twin children of a promising politician who dies penniless. Myra's husband, the Foreign Secretary Lord Roehampton, is able to help Endymion. Roehampton is modelled on Palmerston and St Barbe on WILLIAM MAKEPEACE THACKERAY.

Engel, Marian 1933–85 Canadian. Most of her novels focus on the roles of women in contemporary consumer society. Her best-known work, *Bear* (1976), is a female quest novel which has affinities with MARGARET ATWOOD's SURFACING. Other novels include: *The Honeymoon Festival* (1970), a study of motherhood; *Monodromos* (1973; reissued as *One-Way Street*, 1974), a tragicomic account of a Canadian woman's life on a Greek island; and *The Glassy Sea* (1978), in which the protagonist joins an Anglican order of nuns. She also published two short-story collections, *Inside the Easter Egg* (1975) and *The Tattooed Woman* (1985).

English Patient, The A novel by MICHAEL ONDAATJE, published in 1992 and joint winner of that year's BOOKER PRIZE. Anthony Minghella's film version (1997) made it a popular as well as a critical success. The story centres on four displaced people who come together in a semi-ruined Tuscan villa at the end of World War II: Hana, a young Canadian nurse; Caravaggio, a thief who previously appeared in Ondaatje's *In the Skin of a Lion*; Kip, a Sikh bomb disposal expert; and the mysterious 'English patient', a silent, bedridden casualty of a plane crash, who is revealed to have been a desert explorer and probably to be Hungarian rather than English. Written in charged poetic prose, the novel is an allegory about the ruins of 20th-century European civilization, the demise of Empire and the problematic nature of national categories.

Entail, The A novel by JOHN GALT, published in 1823. Claud Walkinshaw, a packman, is obsessed with recovering the estates which formerly belonged to his family and can achieve this only by disinheriting his eldest son in favour of his second, an idiot. The story follows the disastrous recoil on the Walkinshaw children and grandchildren.

Envoy from Mirror City, The See TO THE IS-LAND.

epistolary novel A novel in which the story is told through letters between the characters. The form was made fashionable in the 18th century by SAMUEL RICHARDSON in *PAMELA* (1740–1) and *CLARISSA* (1747–8). Both books, but particularly *Pamela*, signal a connection between the newly emerging genre of the novel and two types of book already familiar: the instruction manual in letter-writing and the conduct book which inculcates its lessons through a fictional correspondence. And both novels exploit the breathless immediacy which can result from handing the narrative over to participants who write as events unfold and without knowing where they will eventually lead.

SMOLLETT's *EXPEDITION OF HUMPHRY CLINKER* (1771) and FANNY BURNEY's *EVELINA* (1778) – and, for that matter, Rousseau's *La Nouvelle Héloïse* (1761) and Laclos' *Les Liaisons dangereuses* (1782) – show that the epistolary novel remained popular throughout the century. It had already migrated to America, where WILLIAM HILL BROWN's *THE POWER OF SYMPATHY* (1789) would also later be claimed as the first American novel. Subsequently it was used less often, though writers showed themselves aware of the advantages of interjecting a letter into an ordinary narrative: allowing a character to condemn themselves out of their own mouth (as Mr Collins does in JANE AUSTEN's *PRIDE AND PREJUDICE* and Fanny Squeers does in DICKENS's *NICHOLAS NICKLEBY*) or offering sudden revelation of a character who has previously been viewed only through the eyes of others (as D. H. LAWRENCE does at the end of *The Virgin and the Gipsy*). In *THE WOMAN IN WHITE* (1860), *THE MOONSTONE* (1868) and his other works WILKIE COLLINS developed a variant of the epistolary novel in which the story is told, not through letters, but through retrospective memoirs by the various characters. A recent work such as JOHN BARTH's *LETTERS* (1979) shows the potentialities that POST-MODERNISM can still discover in the epistolary novel.

Erdrich, (Karen) Louise 1954– Native American. A member of the Turtle Mountain Band of Chippewa, she secured her reputation with a series of novels, combining social realism with dreamlike sequences, about the Chippewa community in North Dakota: *Love Medicine* (1984; new and expanded version, 1993), *The Beet Queen* (1986), *Tracks* (1988) and *The Bingo Palace* (1994). She has also published poetry and children's stories, and co-written *Crown of Columbus* (1991) with Michael Dorris.

Erewhon A satirical novel by SAMUEL BUTLER, published in 1872. Erewhon (an anagram of 'nowhere') is discovered by Higgs, the narrator, on the far side of a chain of unexplored mountains. His description embodies Butler's attack on the stagnation and hypocrisy of England, and particularly on attitudes to crime, religion and child-rearing. Higgs escapes in a balloon, accompanied by the girl with whom he has fallen in love. In a belated sequel, *Erewhon Revisited* (1901), he returns 20 years later to discover that his ascent in the balloon has inspired a religion, Sunchildism.

Essop, Ahmed 1931– South African. Born in India, he went to South Africa in 1934. His fiction, remarkable in its range and variety of tones, is located almost entirely in Johannesburg, usually the Indian areas of Fordsburg, Vrededorp and Lenasia. His stories are found in *The Hajji and Other Stories* (1978), winner of the OLIVE SCHREINER PRIZE, and *Noorjehan and Other Stories* (1990). *The Visitation* (1980) is a dark comedy about the inevitable downfall of a greedy merchant, Emil Sufi. *The Emperor* (1984) recounts the rise and fall of the headmaster of a South African Indian school.

Esther Waters A novel by GEORGE MOORE, first published in 1894. Strongly influenced by French literature and particularly by Zola's NATURALISM, it was his first great success and is still regarded as his most important work.

Esther Waters, a member of the strict religious sect of Plymouth Brethren, goes into service at Woodview, the home of the Barfields. When William Latch, the footman, seduces and deserts her, she is dismissed and only Mrs Barfield – a fellow member of the Brethren – tries to be kind. Esther endures a bitter, humiliating struggle to bring up her son. William Latch returns and she marries him for their son's sake. He makes a good husband and father, but his life as a Soho publican and bookmaker ruins his health and his death leaves his family penniless. Esther returns to Woodview, where Mrs Barfield now lives alone, and at last finds peace.

Estleman, Loren D. 1952– American. After a false start in DETECTIVE FICTION writing fashionable pastiches of the SHERLOCK HOLMES STORIES in the 1970s, he made his mark with hard-boiled novels in the tradition of RAYMOND CHANDLER. *Motor City Blue* (1980) introduced Amos Walker, a Detroit private investigator who has featured in a long-running series which includes *Angel Eyes* (1981), *The Midnight Man* (1982), *The Glass Highway* (1983), *Sugartown* (1984), *Every Brilliant Eye* (1986), *Lady Yesterday* (1987), *Downriver* (1988), *Silent Thunder* (1989), *Sweet Women Lie* (1990). *Kill Zone* (1984) began another series, about a professional hitman, Peter Macklin. *Whiskey River*

(1990) and *Edsel* (1995) explore the past of Detroit, which Estleman has called 'a reformed prostitute of a town'.

Ethan Frome A novel by EDITH WHARTON, published in 1911. Ethan Frome and his slatternly wife Zeena (Zenobia) are joined by her cousin, Mattie Silver, on their poor farm in western Massachusetts. Ethan and Mattie are attracted to each other, and Zeena drives her off the farm. As he takes Mattie to the railroad station, Ethan tries to kill them both in an accident. They survive and spend the rest of their lives as invalids under Zeena's care.

Eugene Aram A novel by EDWARD BULWER LYTTON, published in 1832. A NEWGATE NOVEL based on a real crime, it tells how Aram, a scholar, is denounced and arrested on his wedding day for a murder to which he had been an accomplice some 14 years earlier. The portrait of the high-minded, guilt-ridden murderer was condemned in some quarters as immoral, but the book confirmed Bulwer's standing as England's most popular novelist.

Euphues: or, The Anatomy of Wit A prose romance by John Lyly (?1554–1606), probably first published in 1578. With its equally popular sequel, *Euphues and His England* (1580), it gave its name to the style known as EUPHUISM. Lyly probably found the word 'euphues', Greek for 'well-endowed', in Roger Ascham's *The Schoolmaster* (1570).

The Anatomy of Wit takes its slight plot from Boccaccio, as well as the parable of the Prodigal Son. Euphues leaves his native Athens to visit Naples, where he pledges friendship with Philautus. Rivalry over Lucilla causes the friends to reproach each other but they are reconciled when she transfers her affections to Curio. These events are only the skeleton of a book fleshed out with discourses on wit, religion and education, as well as love, friendship and the possible conflicts between them, all expressed in elaborate rhetorical artifices. *Euphues and His England* chronicles the friends' visit to England and Philautus' love-affairs there. Euphues ends the story by entering a Greek monastery, while Philautus gets married.

Lyly's fellow-playwright and pamphleteer Robert Greene (*c.* 1558–92) attempted a continuation in *Euphues, His Censure of Philautus* (1587).

euphuism A prose style fashionable in the late 16th century. It takes its name from Lyly's *EUPHUES*, where it first appears in full flower, though there are earlier hints of it in Sir Thomas North's *Dial of Princes* (1557) and George Pettie's *Petite Palace of Pettie His Pleasure* (1576?). Its characteristic quality is an obvious and exaggerated artifice, which exploits the figures and 'flowers' of rhetoric, and a fondness for *sententiae* (moral maxims), allusions to myth and history, and what Sir Philip Sidney calls 'strange similes'. Lyly has an especial liking for balanced antitheses, often reinforced by alliteration: 'Here may you see, gentlemen, the falsehood in fellowship, the fraud in friendship, the painted sheath with the leaden dagger, the fair words that make fools vain.'

Europeans, The A novel by HENRY JAMES, published in 1878. Felix Young, an artist, and his sister Eugenia, the estranged wife of a German nobleman, arrive in Massachusetts to visit their relatives, the Wentworths. Mr Wentworth's daughter Gertrude falls in love with Felix, despite her understanding with the Unitarian minister, Mr Brand; his son Clifford Wentworth becomes infatuated with Eugenia, who is looking for a wealthy husband. Matters are further complicated by Robert Acton, who is drawn to Eugenia, and Lizzie Acton, drawn to Clifford. In the end Felix marries Gertrude, Clifford marries Lizzie and Mr Brand marries Gertrude's sister Charlotte. Robert Acton does not marry Eugenia, who returns to Europe alone.

Eustace Diamonds, The The third of ANTHONY TROLLOPE'S PALLISER NOVELS, serialized in 1871–3 and published in volume form in 1873. One of Trollope's darker novels, it is a study in moral duplicity with a plot that owes something to WILKIE COLLINS'S *THE MOONSTONE*.

When she is widowed, the beautiful Lizzie Eustace claims the Eustace family diamonds but is opposed by the family lawyer, Mr Camperdown. She turns for help first to Lord Fawn, a dull but ambitious politician to whom she becomes engaged, and then to her cousin Frank Greystock. She claims the diamonds have been stolen but her dishonesty becomes apparent when they are really stolen. Lord Fawn breaks his engagement and she loses the disillusioned Frank, who finally marries Lucy Morris. Rejected even by the Byronic Lord George Carruthers, Lizzie ends by marrying the shady Mr Emilius, a converted Jew turned fashionable preacher.

Evan Harrington A novel by GEORGE MEREDITH, published in 1861. Evan is the son of Melchisedec ('the Great Mel') Harrington, an exquisitely mannered tailor. The plot centres on Evan's determination to clear his father's debts and the efforts of his sisters, who have all married well, to secure his marriage to the eligible Rose Jocelyn of Beckley Court. He finally gains both Rose and a diplomatic post in Naples. Though too long to sustain its attenuated narrative, the book is notable for its crispness of language, comedy, analysis of snobbery and the lively characterization of lesser figures like Jack Raikes, George Uploft and Mr Parsley, as well as Evan's sister Louisa, the wily Countess.

Evelina: or, A Young Lady's Entrance into the World An EPISTOLARY NOVEL by FANNY BURNEY, published anonymously in 1778.

In seven months (and three volumes) the young Evelina undergoes her education in self-knowledge, prudence and discretion under the tutelage of her guardian Villars, the sensible Lady Howard and the judicious Lord Orville, whom she eventually marries. The vivid portraits of her undesirable relatives, Sir John Belmont, Mme Duval and the Branghtons, typify the book's accomplished and witty style.

Burney's first novel, *Evelina* rapidly became a fashionable success and attracted the admiration of Edmund Burke, Joshua Reynolds and Samuel Johnson, who said that it gave the impression of 'long experience and deep and intimate knowledge of the world'.

Executioner's Song, The A novel by NORMAN MAILER, published in 1979 and awarded the PULITZER PRIZE. It documents the life and death of Gary Gilmore, whose execution for murder at the Utah State Penitentiary in 1977 was the first execution to have taken place in the USA for over a decade. Drawn from hundreds of interviews and sources, Mailer's book presents itself as a 'true life history' of Gilmore's criminality and his complex relations with various relatives, friends, and lovers, in which the author is merely a data processor. In fact, *The Executioner's Song* is both a compelling narrative and a vehicle for Mailer to express his views on crime, punishment and the symptomatic status of the criminal in America.

Expedition of Humphry Clinker, The See *HUMPHRY CLINKER, THE EXPEDITION OF*.

Eyeless in Gaza A novel by ALDOUS HUXLEY, published in 1936. The title and epigraph are from Milton's description of the hero's fate in *Samson Agonistes*: 'Eyeless in Gaza at the mill with slaves'.

Largely autobiographical, it uses flashbacks covering the years 1902–35 to chart the career of Anthony Beavis and friends, including Brian Foxe (a sensitive and intellectual schoolfriend who later commits suicide), Hugh Ledwidge and his wife Helen (who becomes Beavis's lover) and Mark Staithes (who turns to Marxism). The main purpose is to reveal Beavis's increasing sense of the futility and meaninglessness of his life – and by extension, of contemporary Western society. Finally an anthropologist, James Miller, introduces him to mysticism and pacifism.

F

Fair, A. A. See GARDNER, ERLE STANLEY.

Fair Maid of Perth, The See CHRONICLES OF THE CANONGATE.

Fairbairns, Zoë 1948– English. After a precocious false start as an undergraduate, she retreated into almost a decade's silence, broken with a collection of stories, *Tales I Tell My Mother* (1978), by members of her women's writing group, which included SARA MAITLAND and MICHÈLE ROBERTS. *Benefits* (1979) is an angry dystopia prompted by Thatcherism. Other works embody her feminism and socialism in popular forms: the family saga in *Stand We At Last* (1983) and *Daddy's Girls* (1991), DETECTIVE FICTION in *Here Today* (1984), and women's romance in *Closing* (1987).

Fairly Good Time, A A novel by MAVIS GALLANT, published in 1970. Set in Paris, it is primarily about a young Canadian widow, Shirley Norrington. The characters perceive the world 'through a glass darkly'. Experience for them is fleeting, fragmentary, misunderstood or imperfectly remembered – hence less satisfying than the stories which they edit for themselves, freed from temporal, spatial or logical limitations. Gallant's style mixes narrative with reverie and imagined events to create fertile complexities.

Falkner, J(ohn) Meade 1858–1932 English. His first novel, *The Lost Stradivarius* (1895), was soon eclipsed by *Moonfleet* (1898), a children's adventure story about 18th-century smuggling, obviously indebted to ROBERT LOUIS STEVENSON's *TREASURE ISLAND*. Nothing Falkner wrote afterwards had the same power.

Famished Road, The A novel by BEN OKRI, published in 1991. Its most original aspect is the use of Azaro, an *abiku* or spirit child, to chronicle an unspecified but unmistakable Nigeria in pre-independence years. The *abiku* is complemented by shifting images of the road, which provides a (somewhat ambivalent) metaphorical base. The central device is finally applied directly to Azaro's (and Okri's) Nigeria, itself an *abiku* country in that it is never born but struggles abortively between each fresh attempt. *The Famished Road* won the BOOKER PRIZE.

Fanny Hill [The Memoirs of a Woman of Pleasure] See CLELAND, JOHN.

Far from the Madding Crowd A novel by THOMAS HARDY, published in 1874. The first of his books to achieve popular success, it was also the first to use the name WESSEX for its fictional territory. The title is taken from Gray's *Elegy Written in a Country Churchyard*.

The capricious but strong-minded Bathsheba Everdene is wooed by three men: the loyal Gabriel Oak, who becomes her shepherd and then bailiff after his own farm fails; the braggart Sergeant Troy, who has already abandoned the pregnant Fanny Robin; and a neighbouring farmer, Boldwood. She marries Troy, but he deserts her and is thought drowned. She then yields to Boldwood's frenetic attentions, but Troy reappears at their engagement party. Boldwood shoots him and then unsuccessfully turns the gun on himself; his death sentence is later commuted to life imprisonment. Soon afterwards Oak, her first suitor, who has been overseeing the farms of Bathsheba and Boldwood, again proposes and is accepted.

Farah, Nuruddin 1945– Somali. He has written in Somali as well as English, following the creation of a written form of the Somali language in the early 1970s. *From a Crooked Rib* (1970), about a Somali girl's resistance to the traditional life she is expected to lead in a nomadic community, has been hailed as one of the best portrayals of a woman in African fiction. It has been followed by novels presenting Somali society as a corrupt and repressive patriarchal tyranny: *A Naked Needle* (1976); *Sweet and Sour Milk* (1979), *SARDINES* (1981), and *Close Sesame* (1983), which form a trilogy entitled *Variations on the Theme of an African Dictatorship*; and *Maps* (1984).

Farewell to Arms, A A novel by ERNEST HEMINGWAY, published in 1929. Set mainly in war-torn Italy in 1917–18, it is about the love-affair between Frederic Henry, an American ambulance driver for the Italian army, and Catherine Barkley, a young English nurse. Eventually, Frederic deserts and flees to neutral Switzerland with Catherine. He is left desolate when their son is stillborn and Catherine dies soon afterwards.

Farmer, Beverley 1941– Australian. Her work handles potentially feminist material with a compassion that is both sensitive and detached. In *Alone* (1980) the protagonist retreats into unsatisfying lesbianism. Two collections of stories, *Milk* (1983) and *Hometime* (1985), draw on Farmer's marriage to a Greek and her experience of life in a Greek village; a novel, *The House in the Light* (1995), returns to this setting. *A Body of Water* (1990) is a writer's diary, placing newly written stories in the matrix of reading, thought and observation from which they emerged. *The Seal Woman* (1992) is about a woman's recovery from pain and loss.

Farnol, (John) Jeffery 1878–1952 English. *The Broad Highway* (1910) was the first of his romantic cloak-and-dagger novels, often set in the Georgian or Regency period. He is probably best remembered for *The Amateur Gentleman* (1913).

Other works include *Our Admirable Betty* (1918), *The Crooked Furrow* (1939), *The Happy Harvest* (1939) and *The Glad Summer* (1951).

Farrar, Frederick William 1831–1905 English. A headmaster of Marlborough (1871–6) influenced by Thomas Arnold's example at Rugby, and finally Dean of Canterbury, he published many sermons and theological writings, including *The Life of Christ* (1874). He was chiefly famous, however, for heavily moralistic children's stories: *Eric: or, Little by Little* (1858), *Julian Home: A Tale of College Life* (1859) and *St Winifred's: or, The World of School* (1862).

Farrell, J(ames) G(ordon) 1935–79 English. His second novel, *The Lung* (1965), drew on his experience as a polio victim. The 'Empire trilogy', his major achievement, is HISTORICAL FICTION dramatizing episodes from the imperial past: the Irish civil disturbances during the 1920s in *Troubles* (1969), the Indian Mutiny in *The Siege of Krishnapur* (1973; BOOKER PRIZE) and the fall of Singapore in *The Singapore Grip* (1978). It combines scrupulous research with a multiplicity of characters and quirky comedy. A novel about British India, *The Hill Station* (1981), was unfinished at his death.

Farrell, James T(homas) 1904–79 American. He supported the Communist Party from 1932 to 1935 but was one of the first American intellectuals to break with it over the totalitarian character of Stalin's regime. He is best known for *The Studs Lonigan Trilogy*, consisting of *Young Lonigan: A Boyhood in Chicago Streets* (1932), *The Young Manhood of Studs Lonigan* (1934) and *Judgment Day* (1935). Set on the South Side of Chicago and charting the short, violent and dissolute life of its protagonist, it is a powerful indictment of the American Dream. Other series of novels in Farrell's prolific output include: *A World I Never Made* (1936), *No Star is Lost* (1938), *Father and Son* (1940), *My Days of Anger* (1943) and *The Face of Time* (1953), contrasting the middle-class O'Flahertys and the working-class O'Neills; and *Bernard Clare* (1946), *The Road Between* (1949) and *Yet Other Waters* (1952), chronicling the difficulties faced by radical literary intellectuals after World War II.

Farrell, M. J. See KEANE, MOLLY.

Fast, Howard 1914– American. He became known with novels such as *Conceived in Liberty* (1939), *The Unvanquished* (1942), *Citizen Tom Paine* (1943), *The Proud and the Free* (1950) and *April Morning* (1961), often set during the American Revolution and reflecting his left-wing politics. Other works dealing with remote or recent American history include *The Last Frontier* (1941), *Freedom Road* (1944), *The American* (1946) and *Clarkton* (1947). Novels about the ancient world include *My Glorious Brother* (1948), *Moses, Prince of Egypt* (1958) and *Agrippa's Daughter* (1964); *Spartacus* (1951) served as the basis for Stanley Kubrick's film. More recent novels include a trilogy consisting of *The Immigrants* (1977), *Second Generation* (1978) and *The Establishment* (1979), *The Legacy* (1981), *Max* (1982), *The Outsider* (1984), *The Dinner Party* (1987) and *The Bridge Builder* (1995). He has also written DETECTIVE FICTION under the pseudonym of E. V. Cunningham. *The Naked God* (1957), a work of non-fiction, describes his disenchantment with the Communist Party during the Stalinist era.

Faulkner, William (Cuthbert) 1897–1962 American. His work combines a commitment to MODERNISM, notably in the use of STREAM OF CONSCIOUSNESS, and to his native South, the fictional Yoknapatawpha county (based on his native Mississippi) serving as a recurrent location.

Soldiers' Pay (1926) centres on the return of a disabled soldier from World War I. *Mosquitoes* (1927) is about artists and intellectuals in New Orleans. *Sartoris* (1929; reissued under its original title as *Flags in the Dust*, 1973) was his first novel to be set in Yoknapatawpha. His most productive period began with THE SOUND AND THE FURY (1929), about another Yoknapatawpha family, and AS I LAY DYING (1930). *Sanctuary* (1931) was aimed at a popular audience. *LIGHT IN AUGUST* (1932), though set in Yoknapatawpha county, differs from his other early novels in not concentrating on a single family. *Pylon* (1935) is about aviation. *ABSALOM, ABSALOM!* (1936) concerns the frustrated attempts of Thomas Sutpen to found a Southern dynasty in 19th-century Mississippi. Following *The Unvanquished* (1938), *The Wild Palms* (1939) and *The Hamlet* (1940) – the first of three novels about the Snopes family – came *Go Down Moses* (1942), composed of several interrelated stories about Southern blacks; one of them, 'The Bear', is among his most frequently reprinted pieces. *Intruder in the Dust* (1948) tells the story of Lucas Beauchamp, a black man unjustly accused of murder. *Requiem for a Nun* (1951), a sequel to *Sanctuary*, offers a less brutal treatment of sexual themes than its horrifying predecessor.

A more optimistic tone emerges in *A Fable* (1954), an allegory of Jesus in a World War I setting which won Faulkner a belated PULITZER PRIZE. *The Town* (1957) and *The Mansion* (1959) complete the Snopes family trilogy. *The Reivers* (1962) is a mildly comic portrait of several characters from earlier books. Other works include: *Knight's Gambit* (1949), a collection of DETECTIVE FICTION; *Collected Stories* (1950) and *Uncollected Stories of William Faulkner* (1979); *Mayday* (1976), stories about a medieval knight; and *Vision in Spring* (1984), poems originally written for his wife. His Hollywood screen credits include work on Howard Hawks's versions of ERNEST HEMINGWAY's *To Have and Have Not* (1945) and RAYMOND CHANDLER's *The Big Sleep* (1946). Faulkner received the Nobel Prize for literature in 1950.

Fauset, Jessie R(edmon) 1882–1961 African-American. As editor of W. E. B. Du Bois's magazine *Crisis* she published many writers of the HARLEM RENAISSANCE. Her four novels, *There is Confusion* (1924), *Plum Bun* (1929), *The Chinaberry Tree* (1931) and *Comedy: American Style* (1934), depict the experience of black women.

Federman, Raymond 1928– American. Influenced by SAMUEL BECKETT (of whom he has published a study) and the 'metafiction' movement of the 1960s, Federman has coined such terms as 'surfiction' and 'critifiction' to describe his work. It combines surrealism, philosophy, experimental writing and literary theory. Many of his books originally appeared in French or German, or in bilingual editions. *Double or Nothing* (1971), *Take It or Leave It* (1976), *The Voice in the Closet* (1979), *The Twofold Vibration* (1982), *Smiles on Washington Square* (1985) and *To Whom It May Concern* (1990), are novels. Prose and poetry collections include *Me Too* (1975) and *Playtexts* (1989).

Feinstein, Elaine 1930– English. *The Circle* (1970), about a woman's attempt to reconcile the needs for independence and marriage, and *The Amberstone Exit* (1972), in which dreams, images and memories pass through the mind of a woman about to give birth, have been followed by *The Survivors* (1982), an epic incorporating part of her own history into the story of two Jewish emigré families, *The Border* (1984), *Mother's Girl* (1988), *All You Need* (1989), *Loving Brecht* (1992) and *Dreamers* (1994), set in Vienna's Jewish community in 1848. Volumes of poetry include *The Celebrants and Other Poems* (1973), *Some Unease and Angels* (1977), *Feast of Eurydice* (1980) and *City Music* (1989). She has also published translations of Marina Tsvetayeva, Margaret Aliger, Yunna Moritz and Bella Akhmadulina, a biography of Tsvetayeva (1987) and a study of D. H. LAWRENCE (1993). *Lady Chatterley's Confession* (1995) reworks and continues *LADY CHATTERLEY'S LOVER*.

Felicia's Journey A novel by WILLIAM TREVOR, published in 1994. It won the WHITBREAD AWARD as Book of the Year. Felicia, a young woman from a small Irish town, searches desperately for her cruelly absent lover, Johnny Lysaght. Her journey takes her through the Midlands, a landscape of literal and spiritual desolation. Johnny remains elusive but Felicia finds, or is found by, the all-too-solicitous Mr Hilditch. What at first appears to be an accomplished but conventional psychological thriller is in fact shaped by Trevor's characteristic themes: the scars people carry from childhood into adulthood; the tangled roots of love and hate; the contiguity of good and evil; and the unexpected workings of grace.

Felix Holt, the Radical A novel by GEORGE ELIOT, published in 1866.

The respectably educated Felix Holt returns to his native village and maintains his mother. He burns to participate in politics so that he may improve the lot of his fellow artisans. Contrasted with Felix Holt is the intelligent, economically secure Harold Transome, who intends to enter Parliament as a Liberal, contrary to his family's traditional Toryism. He is opposed to the electioneering practices of the time and his growing disdain for his agent, the dishonest lawyer Jermyn, forms an important narrative line. Much of the action centres upon the hustings and the drunken behaviour of the mob, whose violent activities Felix tries unsuccessfully to quell. His efforts earn him a prison sentence for alleged manslaughter. Both Felix and Transome vie for the hand of Esther, supposed daughter of the quixotic Dissenting minister, Rufus Lyon. She has a legitimate claim to the Transome estates but resigns it shortly before marrying Felix. The story is enhanced by character studies of Harold Transome's mother and the corrupt political agent Johnson, as well as Mr Christian, Sir Maximus Debarry and the loyal servant Denner.

Fellowship of the Ring, The See LORD OF THE RINGS, THE.

Female Quixote, The See LENNOX, CHARLOTTE.

Ferber, Edna 1885–1968 American. *Dawn O'Hara* (1911) launched her career producing best-selling and, at the time, critically acclaimed fiction which has since been largely forgotten. *Show Boat* (1925) formed the basis of a musical by Oscar Hammerstein and Jerome Kern (1927), and *Giant* (1952) was made into a film (1956) with James Dean. Ferber sometimes created independent-minded heroines, such as the farmer's widow Selina De Jong in *So Big* (1924; PULITZER PRIZE) or the divorcee Emma McChesney, who appears in the stories gathered in *Roast Beef Medium* (1913), *Personality Plus* (1914) and *Emma McChesney and Company* (1915). Otherwise, she turned her attention to the history of various regions, frequently to celebrate American values: she set *Cimarron* (1930), her best book, in Oklahoma, *American Beauty* (1931) in Connecticut, *Come and Get It* (1935) in Wisconsin and Michigan, and *Great Son* (1945) in Seattle and the Klondike. She also wrote several plays in collaboration with George S. Kaufman.

Ferdinand Count Fathom, The Adventures of A novel by TOBIAS SMOLLETT, published in 1753. Though among his weaker works, it is notable for moving away from the PICARESQUE and anticipating features of the GOTHIC NOVEL. An amoral, self-seeking villain, Ferdinand adopts the title of Count Fathom and is received into the family of a benevolent German nobleman, Count de Melville, which he proceeds to plunder. His wickedness is eventually revealed but forgiven, and he reforms.

Fernando, Lloyd 1926– Malaysian. Born in Ceylon (now Sri Lanka), he graduated from the University of Malaya (then in Singapore), but has subsequently lived in Malaysia. His pioneering novel, *Scorpion Orchid* (1976), has a major character from each of Malaysia's four largest ethnic communities. He has also edited important anthologies of Malaysian short stories.

Ferrier, Susan (Edmonstone) 1782–1854 Scottish. She knew the literary society of Edinburgh through her father's friends and was warmly esteemed by SIR WALTER SCOTT. *MARRIAGE* (1818), *THE INHERITANCE* (1824) and *Destiny* (1831), her three novels of Scottish life, mix comedy resembling JANE AUSTEN'S with explicit didacticism.

Fielding, Henry 1707–54 English. Born in Somerset, of aristocratic descent, he studied law in London during the late 1720s and briefly attended Leyden University. But his first ambition was the theatre, and between 1728 and 1737 he produced some 25 plays, ranging in form from the ballad opera to conventional comedy. An early success, *Tom Thumb: A Tragedy* (1730; revised as *The Tragedy of Tragedies*, 1731), is a burlesque of heroic drama, set in an absurd court of King Arthur. Its attack on Sir Robert Walpole's Whig administration was continued in *The Historical Register for the Year 1736*, a satire produced in 1737, the year when the authorities imposed stage censorship by introducing the Licensing Act.

Aged 30 and with a wife to support (he had married Charlotte Cradock in 1734), Fielding was effectively barred from writing for the theatre. He resumed his legal studies – eventually being called to the Bar in 1740 – and threw himself into political journalism as vigorous in its satire as his plays had been. Adept at parody too, he responded to the success of SAMUEL RICHARDSON's *PAMELA* (1740) with *An Apology for the Life of Mrs Shamela Andrews* (1741), a skilful squib which makes the innocent virtue of Richardson's heroine appear scheming. His first – and funniest – novel, *JOSEPH ANDREWS* (1742), followed up the idea by making Pamela's brother the central character. Its shapely narrative follows the mishaps of the innocent Joseph and his equally innocent companion, Parson Adams, as they travel through the predatory world of Georgian England. The third volume of Fielding's *Miscellanies* (1743) presented *THE LIFE OF JONATHAN WILD THE GREAT*, a finely ironic fable inspired by the famous contemporary thief and thief-taker, pretending to equate goodness with greatness. The *Miscellanies* also contained *A Journey from this World to the Next*, a spirited satire in the Lucianic mould which describes the progress of the soul. Some time after the death of his beloved Charlotte in 1744 and his marriage to her former maid, Mary Daniel, Fielding began work on what is probably his greatest achievement, *THE HISTORY OF TOM JONES, A FOUNDLING* (1749). Ambitious in scope and scrupulous in design, it presents a refreshingly un-idealized hero and a narrator who is virtually a character in his own right. His last novel, *AMELIA* (1751), is less exuberant, reflecting his own grim experience of social hardships in the metropolis.

In 1748 Fielding had been appointed a Justice of the Peace for Westminster and for Middlesex. His concern at social abuses and judicial corruption is reflected in *A Charge Delivered to the Grand Jury* (1749), *An Enquiry into the Causes of the Late Increase of Robbers* (1751), *Examples of the Interposition of Providence in the Detection and Punishment of Murder* (1752) and *A Proposal for Making an Effectual Provision for the Poor* (1753). As a magistrate, Fielding was both dedicated and effective: together with his blind half-brother, John, he was responsible for Britain's first organized detective police force, the Bow Street Runners. A return to journalism as editor of *The Covent Garden Journal* in 1752 brought him into conflict with TOBIAS SMOLLETT. Fielding was already badly ill, with asthma and gout, when he set sail in 1754 for Lisbon, where he died. *The Journal of a Voyage to Lisbon* (1755) is sharply observed but unavoidably depressing.

Despite the legends of his rakish life-style, Fielding also had a deserved reputation for generosity of spirit and natural sympathy for his fellow man. As a novelist, he was a committed critic of society's corruptions and hypocrisy and a strong believer in benevolence or 'good nature'. In formal terms, he drew eclectically on various traditions – classical epic prose romances, the European PICARESQUE, and the learned fooling of the Scriblerian satirists – while also managing to create a new degree of psychological realism and a linear narrative strength.

Fielding, Sarah 1710–68 English. HENRY FIELDING's sister, she scored a considerable success with *THE ADVENTURES OF DAVID SIMPLE* (1744). *Familiar Letters between the Principal Characters in David Simple* and a second edition of *The Adventures* appeared in 1747, both with prefaces by her brother. *The Governess: or, The Little Female Academy* (1749) preceded *David Simple: Volume the Last* (1753). Other works were *The Cry: A New Dramatic Fable* (with Jane Collier; 1754), *The Lives of Cleopatra and Octavia* (1757), *The History of the Countess of Dellwyn* (1759) and *The History of Ophelia* (1760). She also translated Xenophon's *Memorabilia* and *Apologia* (1762).

Fiesta See *SUN ALSO RISES, THE*.

Fifth Business See *DEPTFORD TRILOGY, THE*.

Figes, Eva 1932– Born in Berlin, she left Germany for Britain with her family in 1939. A lyrical writer who has been compared to VIRGINIA WOOLF in her preoccupation with the inner self, she has published *Equinox* (1966), *Winter Journey* (1968), *Nelly's Version* (1977), *Light* (1983), *The Seven Ages* (1986), *Ghosts* (1988) and *The Tree of Knowledge* (1990). She has also written several radio plays and translated works by Martin Walser, Bernhard Grzimek and George Sand.

Findley, Timothy 1930– Canadian. He is best known for *The Wars* (1977), the story of a young Canadian officer in World War I. Other novels include: *The Last of the Crazy People* (1967), a study of a decaying southern Ontario family; *The Butterfly Plague* (1969), about a Hollywood family; *Famous Last Words* (1981), the fictional story of Ezra Pound's Hugh Selwyn Mauberley; and *Not Wanted on the Voyage* (1984), a highly imaginative account of the Great Flood; *The Headhunter* (1994); and *The Piano Man's Daughter* (1995). *Dinner along the Amazon* (1984) and *Stones* (1988) are collections of short stories. *Inside Memory* (1990) contains short pieces about Findley's careers as actor, novelist and activist on cultural issues. With his collaborator William Whitehead he has won several awards for television scripts.

Finnegans Wake A novel by JAMES JOYCE, published in 1939. He began it in 1922 and published individual sections as *Work in Progress* during the 17 years of its composition. Joyce's last work, it embodies his most extreme experiments with language and narrative. Puns, verbal compounds and foreign words are combined with allusions from every conceivable source to create an obscure and densely structured text. Its aim is to relate the minimal central story to a historical, psychological, religious and artistic cosmology, a procedure which has been likened to that of scholasticism and medieval allegory.

On a literal level, the novel presents the dreams and nightmares of Humphrey Chimpden Earwicker (a Dublin inn-keeper) and his family (wife Anna, their sons Shem and Shaun, and daughter Isabel) as they lie asleep throughout one night. This, however, provides only a rationale for what is really a novel without narrative or plot, in which human experience is ultimately viewed as fragmentary and human identity as multiple. The major characters mutate and proliferate. The initials of Earwicker's name develop into Haveth Childers Everywhere, Howth Castle and Environs and even Here Comes Everybody. Anna becomes Anna Livia Plurabelle, with implicit references both to river (the Liffey) and mountain (Alp). Shem and Shaun are the type of the warring twins whose previous embodiments are found throughout history (in, for example, Wellington and Napoleon).

Major sources of influence have been identified in Freud's dream psychology, Vico's ideas of cyclical repetition, and Bruno's theory of the complementary but conflicting nature of opposites. The title is itself a compound of Finn MaCool, the Irish folk-hero who is supposed to return to life at some future date to become the saviour of Ireland, and Tim Finnegan, the hero of a music-hall ballad, who sprang to life in the middle of his own wake.

Firbank, (Arthur Annesley) Ronald 1886–1926 English. Eccentric and delicate in health, he was wealthy enough to indulge his own way of life and develop his own distinctive style of fiction: witty, sinister and meticulously, even artificially, written. He is best known for *Vainglory* (1915), *Inclinations* (1916), *Caprice* (1917), *Valmouth: A Romantic Novel* (1919), the short story *Santal* (1921), *The Flower beneath the Foot* (1923), *Prancing Nigger* (1924) and *Concerning the Eccentricities of Cardinal Pirelli* (1926). A play, *The Princess Zoubaroff: A Comedy* (1920), was not produced during his lifetime, and several short poems were published posthumously. His friend OSBERT SITWELL describes him in *Noble Essences* (1950).

Fitzgerald, F(rancis) Scott (Key) 1896–1940 American. He established himself as a leading spokesman of 'The Jazz Age' (his own phrase) with the critical and financial success of his early works: *This Side of Paradise* (1920), a loosely autobiographical novel; *Flappers and Philosophers* (1920), a collection of stories; *The Beautiful and Damned* (1922), a disappointing second novel; and *Tales of the Jazz Age* (1922), which includes 'The Diamond as Big as the Ritz'. THE GREAT GATSBY (1925), which many consider his masterpiece, was followed by *All the Sad Young Men* (1926), a third collection of stories.

During these years he and his wife Zelda travelled back and forth between America and Europe, becoming friends with ERNEST HEMINGWAY and GERTRUDE STEIN in Paris. Their boisterous, decadent existence was undermined by alcoholism and a series of nervous breakdowns which periodically hospitalized Zelda from 1930 until her death in 1948. TENDER IS THE NIGHT (1934), his fourth novel, reflected a new and subdued mood of self-revaluation, continued, after another collection of stories, *Taps at Reveille* (1935), in a series of confessional essays 'The Crack-Up', 'Pasting It Together' and 'Handle with Care'. These were eventually included in *The Crack-Up* (1945), a selection of Fitzgerald's essays, notes and letters edited by his friend EDMUND WILSON. From 1927 onwards Fitzgerald worked sporadically and unsuccessfully in Hollywood, completing only one screenplay, *Three Comrades* (1938), and still suffering from his drinking problem. He returned to fiction in his last months, producing the pieces gathered as *The Pat Hobby Stories* (1962) and starting a novel about a Hollywood producer, *The Last Tycoon*, published in its unfinished state in 1941.

Fitzgerald, Penelope 1916– English. Her witty, economical fiction includes: *The Golden Child* (1977); *The Bookshop* (1978); *Offshore* (1979; BOOKER PRIZE); *Human Voices* (1980), set in Broadcasting House during World War II; *At*

Freddie's (1982), an exploration of child sexuality, set in an acting school; *Innocence* (1986); *The Beginning of Spring* (1988), about an English-run printworks in Moscow in 1913 and *The Gate of Angels* (1990), both shortlisted for the Booker Prize; and *The Blue Flower* (1995; National Book Critics Circle prize), about the German poet Novalis. She has also written biographies of Edward Burne-Jones (1975) and Charlotte Mew (1984), and a portrait of her father Edmund Knox and his brothers (1977).

Fleming, Ian (Lancaster) 1908–64 English. *Casino Royale* (1952) was the first of 13 novels whose knowing, exotic detail and racy adventure made their hero, James Bond, one of the most popular secret agents in the history of SPY FICTION. After Fleming's death KINGSLEY AMIS (in *Colonel Sun*, 1968) and John Gardner continued Bond's career in pastiche thrillers. Film adaptations have starred, successively, Sean Connery, George Lazenby, Roger Moore, Timothy Dalton and Pierce Brosnan. By increasingly relying on hi-tech gadgetry and special effects, they have removed their hero from the essentially old-school world of adventure, the world of JOHN BUCHAN, E. Phillips Oppenheim and Sapper, which he originally inhabited.

Fool of Quality, The A SENTIMENTAL NOVEL by HENRY BROOKE, published in 1766–72. The title-character is Henry, son of the Earl of Moreland, rejected by his parents because he seems dull and unintelligent in comparison with his brother. He grows into a young man of strength, beauty and virtue who spends his time helping the unfortunate. On this slender framework Brooke hangs a number of discourses on various aspects of the human condition and, in the latter part, on Christian mysticism.

For the Term of His Natural Life See *HIS NATURAL LIFE*.

Ford, Ford Madox [Hueffer, Ford Hermann] 1873–1939 English. The grandson of the painter Ford Madox Brown and the nephew of William Michael Rossetti, he changed his name from Hueffer in 1919. In the course of a turbulent life, punctuated by various romantic liaisons, he lived in France and the USA as well as Britain. At several points he exerted a powerful and benign influence on contemporary writers. During his brief editorship of *The English Review*, founded in 1908, he managed to sponsor Ezra Pound, D. H. LAWRENCE and WYNDHAM LEWIS as well as publishing work by HENRY JAMES, THOMAS HARDY, ARNOLD BENNETT, JOHN GALSWORTHY and Yeats. *The Transatlantic Review*, which he founded in Paris in 1924 with ERNEST HEMINGWAY as his deputy editor, included Pound, JAMES JOYCE, GERTRUDE STEIN, e e cummings and JEAN RHYS among contributors. He also gave support to many of the younger American Southern Agrarians such as Allen Tate, CAROLINE GORDON, KATHERINE ANNE PORTER and Robert Lowell. Ford collaborated with JOSEPH CONRAD on two novels, *The Inheritors* (1901) and *Romance* (1903). His own novels include: a trilogy of HISTORICAL FICTION, *The Fifth Queen* (1906–8); *A Call* (1910); *THE GOOD SOLDIER* (1915); and a tetralogy, *PARADE'S END* (1924–8). *It Was the Nightingale* (1933), about his years in Paris, is one of many works of personal recollection. His last work, *The March of Literature* (1939), is a monumental survey of ancient literature and Mediterranean culture.

Ford, Richard 1944– American. Although his career began with the downbeat stories collected in *Rock Springs* (1988), his novels seek wider contexts. *A Piece of My Heart* (1976) is a Californian tale of brittle love and violence. *The Ultimate Good Luck* (1981) follows a Vietnam veteran to Mexico. His most acclaimed work, *The Sportswriter* (1986), is an urbane account of a novelist who turns sportswriter; *Independence Day* (1995), which won a PULITZER PRIZE, is a sequel in which the protagonist, Frank Bascombe, is now a failed husband and father struggling with mid-life confusion. *Wildlife* (1990), about an adolescent boy watching his parents' marriage unravel, is infused with a characteristic tone of hopeful melancholy.

Forester, C(ecil) S(cott) 1899–1966 English. He was best known for his popular 'Hornblower' series, starting with *The Happy Return* (1937), which, in the dozen novels that followed, charted the hero's rise from midshipman to admiral during the Napoleonic Wars. Other novels include: *Brown on Resolution* (1929); *Death to the French* (1932) and *The Gun* (1933), both set during the Peninsula War; *The African Queen* (1935), which became a famous film in 1952; and *The General* (1936), reworking his favourite theme of individual fortitude in war. *Payment Deferred* (1926) and *Plain Murder* (1930) are DETECTIVE FICTION.

Forster, E(dward) M(organ) 1879–1970 English. Born in London, he was educated at Tonbridge School, which he hated, and King's College, Cambridge, where he was elected to the Apostles and met future members of the BLOOMSBURY GROUP. He returned to King's on a three-year fellowship in the 1920s and as a permanent honorary fellow after his mother's death in 1945.

Although *WHERE ANGELS FEAR TO TREAD* (1905), *THE LONGEST JOURNEY* (1907) and *A ROOM WITH A VIEW* (1908) were widely noticed, it was *HOWARDS END* (1910) that fully established his reputation. However, *The Celestial Omnibus* (1911), a relatively minor volume of short stories, was followed by more than a decade of silence, during which he wrote *MAURICE*, about a successful homosexual relationship, not published until 1971. During World War I he served in the International Red Cross in Alexandria. *Alexandria: A History and a Guide* (1922; revised

1938) was followed by *Pharos and Pharillon* (1923), a collection of Alexandrian essays which included translations of poems by his friend C. P. Cavafy. A second visit to India in 1921–2 as secretary and companion to the Maharajah of Dewas Senior prompted him to complete *A PASSAGE TO INDIA* (1924), his most acclaimed novel but also his last. Thereafter he published: *Aspects of the Novel* (1927), a shrewd piece of criticism based on his Clark lectures; *The Eternal Moment* (1928), a volume of pre-war short stories about the supernatural; two volumes of essays, *Abinger Harvest* (1936) and *Two Cheers for Democracy* (1951), whose mildness of tone does not conceal the commitment to tolerance and individual liberty which characterized his thinking; and *The Hill of Devi* (1953), about his second visit to India. He also wrote, with Eric Crozier, the libretto for Benjamin Britten's *Billy Budd* (1949). *The Life to Come* (1972), a collection of earlier short stories which, like *Maurice*, treated the homosexual theme, also had to await posthumous publication.

Forster, Margaret 1938– English. Her tough-minded but compassionate fiction often concentrates on women's lives or the female perspective. Memorable protagonists include the heroines of: *Georgy Girl* (1965), which first made her reputation; *The Travels of Maudie Tipstaff* (1967); *Miss Owen-Owen is at Home* (1969); *The Seduction of Mrs Pendlebury* (1974); *Mother Can You Hear Me?* (1979); and *Lady's Maid* (1990), treating Elizabeth Barrett Browning from her maid's point of view. *Have the Men Had Enough?* (1989) deals with the care of the elderly, and *The Battle for Christabel* (1991) with an orphaned child. Male vulnerability is at the centre of the fictional *William Makepeace Thackeray: Memoirs of a Victorian Gentleman* (1978). She has also written biographies of Elizabeth Barrett Browning (1988) and DAPHNE DU MAURIER (1993), and *Significant Sisters: Grassroots of Active Feminism, 1839–1939* (1984).

Forsyte Saga, The A sequence of novels by JOHN GALSWORTHY, comprising *The Man of Property* (1906), *In Chancery* (1920) and *To Let* (1921; with two interludes, 'Indian Summer of a Forsyte', 1918, and *Awakening*, 1920), published together in 1922.

It follows three generations of the Forsyte family, from the 1880s to the early 1920s. Soames Forsyte, a successful solicitor, builds a house at Robin Hill. His wife Irene deserts him for the architect, Bosinney, but returns after Bosinney dies in a street accident. *In Chancery* describes how she deserts Soames and marries his cousin, Jolyon. They have a son, Jon. The embittered Soames marries Annette Lamotte, who gives birth to Fleur. In *To Let* the young Jon and Fleur fall in love but, learning of the family past, he leaves her and goes to America, where Irene joins him after Jolyon's death. Fleur

throws herself at an admirer, Michael Mont. Soames learns that Annette has been unfaithful. Robin Hill is left empty and Timothy Forsyte, last of the old generation, dies at the age of 100.

Forsyth, Frederick See GENRE FICTION.

Fortunes of Nigel, The A novel by SIR WALTER SCOTT, published in 1822. It is set in the reign of James I. Impoverished by his father's loan to the king, Nigel Oliphaunt, Lord Glenvarloch, comes to London to recover the debt but is opposed by Prince Charles, the Duke of Buckingham and their favourite, Lord Dalgarno. Margaret Ramsay, a London clockmaker's daughter, succeeds in saving him from their schemes and in securing reparation for Dalgarno's wronged wife, Lady Hermione. Nigel marries Margaret and returns to Scotland. Dalgarno pursues him but is killed by robbers on the way.

42nd Parallel, The See USA.

Foster, David (Manning) 1944– Australian. His novels can intimidate by their complexity and their vehement satire, as also by the diversity of their settings: Australian small-town life, the USA, 19th-century Scotland, the worlds of 14th-century alchemy, 18th-century comedy and a heavy metal rock band on tour. They include *The Pure Land* (1974), *Moonlite* (1981), *Plumbum* (1983), *Dog Rock* (1985), *The Adventures of Christian Rosy Cross* (1986), *Testostero* (1987), *The Pale Blue Crotchet Coathanger* (1988), *Mates of Mars* (1991) and *The House within the Grove* (1996), which won the MILES FRANKLIN AWARD). Foster has also published: a SCIENCE-FICTION novel, *The Empathy Experiment* (with D. K. Lyall; 1977); a collection of stories, *Escape to Reality* (1977); two collections of novellas, *North South West* (1973) and *Hitting the Wall* (1989); and poetry.

Fowles, John (Robert) 1926– English. Superficially diverse in both subject and manner, his fiction is preoccupied with the possibilities of genuinely free action. *The Collector* (1963) is a psychological thriller; *The Magus* (1966, revised 1977) is a long, compulsive masquerade of sexual enticement on a Greek island; and *THE FRENCH LIEUTENANT'S WOMAN* (1969), still his best-known work, is a pastiche of Victorian fiction undercut by 20th-century literary and social insight. Its heroine, the governess Sarah Woodruff, is one version of the inscrutable woman who appears throughout his work, notably in the title novella of *The Ebony Tower* (1974), a collection of shorter fiction. Later works include: *Daniel Martin* (1977), a dense, realistic BILDUNGSROMAN; *Mantissa* (1983), a sexual *jeu d'e-sprit* and satire of structuralism; and *A Maggot* (1985), an 18th-century murder mystery. Of his non-fiction, *The Aristos* (1964, revised 1980) is a 'self-portrait in ideas' and *The Tree* (1979) an autobiographical essay attesting to his interest in the natural world.

Frame, Janet 1924– New Zealand. Misdiagnosed schizophrenic, she spent most of her time between 1947 and 1955 in psychiatric hospitals. She was saved by her writing: her first collection of stories, *The Lagoon* (1951), won the Hubert Church award shortly before she was due to have a leucotomy. After her release she lived in Ibiza, Andorra, Britain and the USA before returning to New Zealand. Her works include: *Owls Do Cry* (1957), in which the protagonist has her imagination cut away by a leucotomy; *Faces in the Water* (1961), fictionalizing her experience of psychiatric hospitals; *The Edge of the Alphabet* (1962); *Scented Gardens for the Blind* (1963); *The Adaptable Man* (1965); *Intensive Care* (1970), an ambitious future-fiction; *Daughter Buffalo* (1972; winner of the GOODMAN FIELDER WATTIE BOOK AWARD) and *Living in the Maniototo* (1979; winner of the NEW ZEALAND BOOK AWARD), complex metafictional experiments set in North America; and *The Carpathians* (1988), which won the New Zealand Book Award and the COMMONWEALTH WRITERS PRIZE. Two themes dominate her work: the clash of inner and outer worlds, often expressed through the figure of the misfit (epileptic, mental patient, artist); and the complexity of language, crucial to identity but also perilously unstable. Generally recognized as her country's finest novelist, she reached a wider audience with *TO THE IS-LAND* (1982), *An Angel at my Table* (1984) and *The Envoy from Mirror City* (1985), autobiographical works which uncover the sources of her writing. She has also published several volumes of short stories, a collection of poetry, *The Pocket Mirror* (1967), and a children's book.

Frame, Ronald 1953– Scottish. He is particularly known for the short stories gathered in *Watching Mrs Gordon* (1985), *A Long Weekend with Marcel Proust* (1986) and *A Woman of Judah* (1988). His novels include: *A Winter Journey* (1984); *Sandmouth People* (1988), set in a seaside resort in the 1950s; *Penelope's Hat* (1989), the unreliable 'biography' of a novelist; *Bluette* (1990), the story of a woman who lives different lives; *Underwood and After* (1991); and *Walking with My Mistress in Deauville* (1992).

Framley Parsonage The fourth of ANTHONY TROLLOPE'S BARSETSHIRE NOVELS, serialized in 1860–1. It features familiar Barsetshire characters – the Grantlys and their daughter Griselda (who marries Lord Dumbello), Bishop and Mrs Proudie, and the Rev. Josiah Crawley – but concentrates on the fortunes of Mark Robarts. Given the living of Framley by the widowed Lady Lufton through his friendship with her son, Lord Ludovic Lufton, he becomes involved with the spendthrift Mr Sowerby and the disreputable Duke of Omnium. Ludovic helps to rescue him from these unsuitable acquaintances and, overcoming his mother's opposition, marries Mark's sister Lucy. The rich Miss Dunstable, whom Sowerby had hoped to marry, marries Dr Thorne.

Francis, Dick (Richard) [Stanley] 1920– . English. His career as a National Hunt jockey – described in an autobiography, *Sport of Queens* (1957) – gave a fine authenticity to his evocation of the racing world in early thrillers such as *Dead Cert* (1962), *Nerve* (1964), *For Kicks* (1965), *Odds Against* (1965), *Flying Finish* (1966), *Blood Sport* (1967), *Forfeit* (1968), *Enquiry* (1969), *Rat Race* (1970) and *Bone-crack* (1971). Later books, from the period of *Reflex* (1980) and *Banker* (1982) onwards, have used less vividly realized settings, created by elaborate research, just as they have turned away from violence to develop an increasingly moral tone. The annual Dick Francis remains a fixture on the international best-seller lists.

Frank, Waldo (David) 1889–1967 American. *City Block* (1922), *Holiday* (1923), *The Death and Birth of David Markand* (1934) and *The Bridegroom Cometh* (Britain, 1938; USA, 1939) are novels advocating social and political reform. *Chalk Face* (1924) is a horror novel, and *New Year's Eve* (1929) a play influenced by expressionism. Frank also wrote a good deal of historical and social criticism.

Frankau, Pamela 1908–67 English. The daughter of one best-selling novelist, Gilbert Frankau (1884–1952) and the grand-daughter of another, Frank Danby (the pseudonym of Julia Frankau, 1864–1916), she was a prolific and popular writer. *The Willow Cabin* (1949), her most successful novel, explores love and loss; special gifts render the protagonist, like the hero of *The Winged Horse* (1953), an outsider. Frankau's skill at handling family tensions is evident in *Sing for Your Supper* (1963), set among a pierrot troupe in a seaside town in the 1920s. It forms the first volume of a trilogy, *Clothes of a King's Son*, continued in *Slaves of the Lamp* (1965), set in London in the late 1930s, and *Over the Mountains* (1967), her last completed work, set in Europe during wartime.

Frankenstein*: or, *The Modern Prometheus A GOTHIC NOVEL by MARY SHELLEY, published in 1818. Frankenstein, a student of natural philosophy in Geneva, builds a creature in the semblance of a man and gives it life. Possessed of unnatural strength, it inspires horror but is miserably eager to be loved. It pursues Frankenstein to Chamonix, where he agrees to make a mate. When he changes his mind, the creature kills Frankenstein's bride on their wedding night. Frankenstein's father dies of grief, and the scientist's mind gives way. Eventually he recovers and sets out to destroy his creation. After a chase across the world, the two confront each other in the Arctic wastes. Frankenstein dies and the creature disappears into the frozen wilderness, hoping for annihilation.

Franklin, (Stella Maria Sarah) Miles 1879–1954 Australian. *My Brilliant Career* (1901), dubbed 'the very first Australian novel', and its sequel

My Career Goes Bung (1946) describe the adventures and misadventures of Sybylla Melvyn, who aspires to the cultivated life of a writer but is hampered by the backwardness of bush society. The author denied that Sybylla, with her determined independence, fiery self-confidence and inopportune blundering, was a self-portrait. Other novels include *Some Everyday Folk – and Dawn* (1909), *Old Blastus of Bandicoot* (1931), *Bring the Monkey* (1933) and *All That Swagger* (1936). A bequest from her estate founded the MILES FRANKLIN AWARD, a prize for fiction.

Fraser, George MacDonald 1925– Scottish. *Flashman* (1969) began his popular series of novels tracing the disreputable career of Flashman, the bully from THOMAS HUGHES's *TOM BROWN'S SCHOOLDAYS*, through the major historical events of the 19th century. *The General Danced at Dawn* (1970), *McAuslan in the Rough* (1974) and *The Sheikh and the Dustbin* (1988) are collections of stories about life in a modern Highland regiment. *The Candlemass Road* (1993) is a novel of Border history and *Black Ajax* (1997) the story of the black prizefighter Tom Molyneux. Also a respected historian, Fraser has published *The Steel Bonnets: The Story of the Anglo-Scottish Border Reivers* (1971) and an account of the Burma Campaign (1992).

Frayn, Michael 1933– English. He is best known for his stage and television comedies, which include *Alphabetical Order* (1975), *Donkeys' Years* (1976), and *Noises Off* (1982). He has also translated and adapted work by Chekhov and Tolstoy. His novels include *The Tin Men* (1965), which won the SOMERSET MAUGHAM AWARD, and *The Russian Interpreter* (1966), which won the HAWTHORNDEN AWARD. A philosopher by academic training, he has increasingly used his comic and satiric skills to dissect public and private morality, as in the novel, *Now You Know* (1992), about the fruits and perils of 'open government'.

Frederic, Harold 1856–98 American. *Seth's Brother's Wife* (1886) portrays life on an American farm and examines the worlds of politics and journalism. *The Lawton Girl* (1890) and *The Return of the O'Mahoney* (1892) extended his reputation as a local colourist. *In the Valley* (1890) deals with the American Revolution, *The Copperhead* (1893) and *Marsena and Other Stories* (1894) with the Civil War. His best-known novel, *THE DAMNATION OF THERON WARE* (1896), depicts the religious and psychological decline of a Methodist minister. His last three novels – *March Hares* (1896), and the posthumously published *Gloria Mundi* (1898) and *The Market Place* (1899) – are HISTORICAL FICTION set in England.

Freeling, Nicolas 1927– English. His immersion in European culture gives his DETECTIVE FICTION its characteristic locations, richly reflective style and increasing indifference to generic labels. *Love in Amsterdam* (1962) began a series featuring the Dutch detective Van der Valk, who quickly outgrew the model of Simenon's Maigret. *A Long Silence* (1972; *Auprès de Ma Blonde* in the USA) killed off Van der Valk, though he has been revived in *Sand Castles* (1989). *A Dressing of Diamonds* (1974) introduced Henri Castang, a French policeman who has regularly appeared in subsequent novels, sometimes joined by Van der Valk's widow Arlette, herself the central character of *The Widow* (1979).

Freeman, Mary (Eleanor) Wilkins 1852–1930 American. Her first collections, *A Humble Romance and Other Stories* (1887) and *A New England Nun and Other Stories* (1891), focus on women in small New England villages who are forced to defend their values against the community. *Pembroke* (1894), one of her more successful novels, is a study of New England character and life. Other works include *Giles Corey, Yeoman: A Play* (1893), *Madelon* (a novel, 1896), *Silence and Other Stories* (1898), *The Heart's Highway: A Romance of Virginia* (1900) and *The Fair Lavinia and Others* (1907).

Freeman, R(ichard) Austin 1862–1943 English. His DETECTIVE FICTION featured Dr Thorndyke, a medical jurist, introduced in a novel, *The Red Thumb Mark* (1907), but seen to greatest advantage in collections of short stories such as *The Singing Bone* (1912). Freeman's stories are notable for their precise attention to scientific detail and for their use of the so-called 'inverted tale'. This formula reverses the normal procedure of detective fiction by revealing the criminal's identity in an elaborate description of the crime at the start of the story; the puzzle thus becomes, not who done it, but how the detective will succeed in catching the criminal out.

Freemantle, Brian See SPY FICTION.

French, Marilyn 929– American. Her first novel, *The Women's Room* (1977), was hailed as a pioneering feminist text for its angry study of the continuing subjection of women. Further novels are *The Bleeding Heart* (1981), *Her Mother's Daughter* (1987), *Our Father* (1994) and *My Summer with George* (1996). She has also published *Beyond Power: On Women, Men and Morals* (1985), *The War against Women* (1992) and studies of JOYCE's *ULYSSES* (1976) and Shakespeare (1981).

French-Canadian novel The logbooks of Jacques Cartier (1491–1557) about his mission to the New World have been considered the 'genesis of Canada'. The 'relation of the voyage', tracing the origins of places and peoples, became a distinct genre and later provided a point of reference for the French-speaking communities of Canada in maintaining oral traditions and in developing a distinctive form of fiction.

In Québec (Quebec) the first French-Canadian novel – *L'Influence d'un livre* by Philippe-Ignace-François Aubert de Gaspé (1814–41), written with the help of his father, Philippe-Joseph (1786–1871) – did not appear until 1837. The attempt to provide a literary tradition, largely with HISTORICAL FICTION influenced by SIR WALTER SCOTT, soon met with an entrenched opposition to the 'immorality' of literature. Polemicists such as Etienne Parent and authorities such as the Abbé Henri-Raymond Casgrain (1831–1904) assured the death of books which were not patriotic, morally edifying or in conformity with the received opinion of the Roman Catholic Church. The ban remained in general force until the 1960s. Among notable exceptions were the work of Patrice Lacombe (1807–63), who wrote the first *roman paysan, La Terre paternelle* (1847), which set the standard for over a century; Laure Conan (pseudonym of Marie-Louise-Félicité Angers, 1845–1924), Québec's first woman novelist; Ringuet (Philippe Panneton, 1865–1960), who wrote *Trente Arpents* (1938; translated as *Thirty Acres,* 1940); and Marie-Claire Blais (1939–).

With the 'quiet revolution' in the 1960s against the restraints imposed by the Church came an intensified interest in a sense of place. *Québécois* replaced 'French-Canadian' as a designation and *joual,* the Franco-English street patois of Montréal, became a recognized language. The literature that resulted generally reflects a growing feeling of disenchantment and hopelessness of living in a relegated society – moods epitomized in the suicide of the writer Hubert Aquin (1929–77) out of despair at the prospects for an independent Québec. A singular luminary in this bleak landscape is ROCH CARRIER, whose irrepressible characters are witty, resourceful and full of integrity.

Acadie (Acadia), derived from the Arcadia of ancient Greece, is the name given in the 16th century to the French-Canadian settlements in Nova Scotia, New Brunswick and Prince Edward Island. The myth of an Edenic paradise on earth was largely created by Marc Lescarbot (*c.* 1570–1642), a Parisian who fled 'corrupt European society' for the New World, in his *Histoire de la Nouvelle-France* (1609). An oral tradition of allegories, myths, animal fables, children's stories and fantasy echoed the idealization for a century and a half. It was shattered by the British defeat of French colonists and the deportation of Acadians in 1755–62 to, among other places, Louisiana, where their name became corrupted to 'Cajun'. The upheaval left, in scattered chronicles and folk tales, the memory of a glorious past and the belief that Acadian survival would be assured by loyalty to language and cultural heritage. No major Acadian novels appeared until the work of ANTONINE MAILLET, most notably *Pélagie-la-Charrette* (1979), which takes up the theme of Acadian dispersal, survival and return. The new feeling of equality which Maillet's work has helped to foster in 'a minority within a minority' opens up the possibility of relegating Aacadian suffering to the past.

See also HÉBERT, ANN and TREMBLAY, MICHEL.

French Lieutenant's Woman, The A novel by JOHN FOWLES, published in 1969. At Lyme Regis on the Dorset coast Charles Smithson, a young Victorian palaeontologist, is beguiled and eventually infatuated by Sarah Woodruff, an enigmatic governess ostracized for her reported liaison with a French sailor. But on the single occasion when the affair is consummated he discovers Sarah to be a virgin. Charles's engagement to Ernestina Freeman is broken off, and the novel supplies alternative endings: both a lasting reunion with Sarah and a bleak realization that they are irrevocably separated.

Fuller, Henry Blake 1857–1929 American. He was born in Chicago and lived there all his life except for a two-year tour of Europe. His best-known novel is probably THE CLIFF-DWELLERS (1893), satirizing the social ambitions of people living in a skyscraper. WITH THE PROCESSION (1895) also deals with social climbers. *Bertram Cope's Year* (1919) takes up the topic of homosexuality. All three novels are striking examples of American REALISM. In addition to other novels and short stories, Fuller also wrote plays.

Fuller, Roy (Broadbent) 1912–91 English. Influenced by W. H. Auden, the early work in *Poems* (1939), *The Middle of a War* (1942), *A Lost Season* (1944) and *Epitaphs and Occasions* (1949) is leftwing in sympathy and concerned with man as a social animal. His many subsequent volumes, culminating in *New and Collected Poems* (1985) and *Consolations* (1987), are more interested in outlining individual psychologies. He developed into a master technician, urbane, detached and ironic. His novels, more than an interesting sideline, include *Image of a Society* (1956), *The Ruined Boys* (1959), *The Father's Comedy* (1961), *The Perfect Fool* (1963), the excellent *My Child My Sister* (1965) and *Stares* (1990). He made a distinctive contribution to DETECTIVE FICTION in *With My Little Eye* (1948), *The Second Curtain* (1953) and *Fantasy and Fugue* (1954). His lectures as professor of poetry at Oxford in 1968–73 appeared in *Owl and Artificers* (1971) and *Professors and Gods* (1974). *Spanner and Pen* (1991) is an autobiography.

Furphy, Joseph 1843–1912 Australian. He described his work as being of 'Temper democratic; bias offensively Australian'. *Such is Life: Being Certain Extracts from the Life of Tom Collins* (1903) is a PICARESQUE novel with no formal plot and many digressions, which one critic has described as 'a primary document for any student of Australian attitudes'. The rich material trimmed from the unwieldy manuscript of *Such is Life* created two more books, published after Furphy's death: *Rigby's Romance* (1946) and *The Buln-Buln and the Brolga* (1948).

G

Gaddis, William 1922– American. *The Recognitions* (1955) focuses on a group of artists and poets in Greenwich Village during the late 1940s and early 1950s. *JR* (1975), written entirely in dialogue, takes place mostly at a school on Long Island. *Carpenter's Gothic* (1985) examines the impact of the Vietnam war. *A Frolic of His Own* (1994) is a biting satire of the legal profession, depicted as self-serving and destructive; once again the interplay of a host of voices is central.

Gaines, Ernest J(ames) 1933– African-American. *Catherine Carmier* (1964) describes the difficulties encountered by a black college graduate on returning home to Louisiana. *Of Love and Dust* (1967) is set on a Louisiana plantation in the 1940s. *Bloodline* (1968) is a collection of stories. His best-known novel, *The Autobiography of Miss Jane Pitman* (1971), presents the recollections of a 110-year-old black woman whose experiences range from slavery to the civil rights movement of the 1960s. Gaines's concern with the effects of racism is further revealed in *My Father's House* (1978), about the conflict between a black preacher and his more radical son. *A Lesson Before Dying* (1993) is about a black man who witnesses an armed robbery and is arrested, tried and sentenced to death. Interviews can be found in *Porch Talk with Ernest J. Gaines: Conversations on the Writer's Craft* (1990).

Gale, Zona 1874–1938 American. She rose to prominence as a writer in the 'local colour' vein with *Romance Island* (1906), a novel, and *Friendship Village* (1908), a collection of stories. Her sentimental tendencies gave way to sterner realism in *Birth* (1918), *Miss Lulu Bett* (1920), her best-known novel, and *Faint Perfume* (1923). Her stage adaptation of *Miss Lulu Bett* won a PULITZER PRIZE in 1922. Later novels, such as *Preface to a Life* (1926) and *Borgia* (1929), reflect her interest in Eastern mysticism. *Papa La Fleur* (1933), *Light Woman* (1937) and the posthumously published *Magna* (1939) share a concern with the gap between the pre-war and post-war generations. Some of her best stories are collected in *Yellow Gentians and Blue* (1927) and *Bridal Pond* (1930).

Galford, Ellen 1947– Born in the USA, she has been resident in Scotland since 1971. She is preoccupied with the relations between history, feminism, myth and, often, religion. *Moll Cutpurse: Her True History* (1984) deals with Mary Frith, mythologized as 'The Roaring Girl' by Thomas Middleton and Thomas Dekker. *The Fires of Bride* (1986) is set mainly on an imaginary Scottish island. *Queendom Come* (1990) is an exuberant dystopia. In *The Dyke and the Dybbuk* (1993) a Jewish taxi-driver attracts the attention of an 18th-century dybbuk.

Gallant [née Young], Mavis 1922– Canadian. An expatriate writing, with a mercilessly detached awareness, about isolation and displacement in Paris, Montreal or in post-war Germany, she has won recognition in Britain and the USA as well as Canada. Collections of stories include *The Other Paris* (1956), *My Heart is Broken* (1964; as *An Unmarried Man's Summer* in Britain), *The Pegnitz Junction* (1973), *The End of the World and Other Stories* (1974), *From the Fifteenth District* (1979), *Home Truths* (1981), *Overhead in a Balloon* (1985), *In Transit* (1988), *Across the Bridge* (1993) and *The Muslim Wife* (1995). She has also written two novels, *Green Water, Green Sky* (1959) and *A FAIRLY GOOD TIME* (1970), and a play, *What is to be Done?* (1983).

Galloway, Janice 1956– Scottish. *The Trick is To Keep Breathing* (1990), her first novel, portrays a woman suffering from schizophrenia. *Foreign Parts* (1994) explores the mixed blessings of female friendship and the disappointments of heterosexuality. Brutality is the keynote of many of the stories gathered in *Blood* (1991) and *Where You Find It* (1996).

Galsworthy, John 1867–1933 English. As a novelist he is best known for THE FORSYTE SAGA, published complete in 1922, a family history and chronicle of the prosperous classes. It was begun in *The Man of Property* (1906), his first success, and continued by *In Chancery* (1920) and *To Let* (1921, with two interludes, 'Indian Summer of a Forsyte', 1918, and *Awakening*, 1920). A second Forsyte chronicle, *A Modern Comedy* (1929), included *The White Monkey* (1924), *The Silver Spoon* (1926), *Swan Song* (1928) and two interludes, 'A Silent Wooing' and 'Passers By'. Other work included a trilogy, *End of the Chapter* (1925), on the family history of the Charwells, relatives of the Forsytes.

Many of his 31 full-length plays and several successful one-acters, show him less comfortable with his own privileged background and comment on social injustice. *The Silver Box* (1906) introduced his favourite device of parallel and contrasted families, one rich and the other poor. *Justice* (1910) led to reform of solitary confinement in prisons. *Strife* (1909) is about the effects of a strike, and *The Skin Game* (1920) about privilege and social snobbery. *Collected Plays* appeared in 1929 and *Collected Poems* in 1934.

Galsworthy received the Nobel Prize for Literature in 1932.

Galt, John 1779–1839 Scottish. He is best remembered for his ironic, richly observant novels about Lowland Scots life. They include THE

Ayrshire Legatees (1820), *The Annals of the Parish* (1821), *The Provost* (1822), and *The Entail* (1823). *Voyages and Travels in the Years 1809, 1810 and 1811* (1812) describes his Continental wanderings, which included a visit to Greece and Turkey in the company of Byron, of whom he later wrote a biography (1830).

García, Cristina 1958– Cuban-American. Her novels, set in both Cuba and the USA, deal with families riven by political disagreement and the experience of exile following Castro's revolution of 1959. *Dreaming in Cuban* (1992) deals with Celia, a Castro supporter, and her estranged daughters, Felicia, who supports the Cuban *santería* cult, and Lourdes, who lives in New York and has a turbulent relationship with her own punk-artist daughter, Pilar. *The Agüero Sisters* (1997) also deals with the Cuban diaspora, but concentrates on Constancia and Reiba, half-sisters who meet in Miami after thirty years apart. García's use of MAGIC REALISM is balanced by her insistence on the mundane.

Gardam, Jane 1928– English. Her ability to recreate the confusions of adolescence caused early works such as *A Few Fair Days* (1971), *A Long Way from Verona* (1971), *After the Funeral* (1973) and *Bilgewater* (1977) to be classified as juvenile fiction. The success of another study of adolescence, *God on the Rocks* (1978), helped to rectify the misunderstanding. The adventures of the child-heroine in *Crusoe's Daughter* (1985) are indebted to Shakespeare, VIRGINIA WOOLF and DEFOE'S *ROBINSON CRUSOE*. *The Queen of the Tambourine* (1991; WHITBREAD AWARD) traces a suburban woman's descent into manic delusion. *Faith Fox* (1996) returns to the theme of the child as focus of other people's dreams and conflicts. Gardam's stories include *Black Faces, White Faces* (1975), *The Sidmouth Letters* (1980), *The Pangs of Love* (1983), *Showing the Flag* (1989), *Trio* (1993) and *Going into a Dark House and Other Stories* (1994). Her work specifically for children includes *The Hollow Land* (1981).

Gardner, Erle Stanley 1889–1970 American. Trained as a lawyer, he began contributing DETECTIVE FICTION under a wide variety of pseudonyms to 'pulp' magazines such as *Black Mask* in the 1920s. He became one of the most productive as well as popular detective novelists of all time. His best-known work is the series of 82 novels, starting with *The Case of the Velvet Claws* (1933) and finishing with *The Case of the Postponed Murder* (1973), which chronicle the cases of the defence attorney Perry Mason, together with his secretary Della Street and the private investigator Paul Drake. The hero's transition from hard-boiled hero to a model of liberal values was completed by the TV series begun in 1957, starring Raymond Burr. Gardner stayed closer to his hard-boiled origins in 29 novels about Bertha Cool and Donald Lam, originally published under the pseudonym of A. A.

Fair; the first was *The Bigger They Come* (1939; called *Lam to the Slaughter* in the UK). He also wrote nine novels about a District Attorney, Doug Selby, starting with *The DA Calls It Murder* (1937).

Gardner, John 1933–82 American. His most highly praised book, *Grendel* (1971), retells *Beowulf* from the monster's point of view and focuses on the potential meaninglessness of life, a theme also examined in *The Sunlight Dialogues* (1972). His other novels include: *The Wreckage of Agathon* (1970), set in Sparta; *Nickel Mountain* (1973), about a middle-aged motel proprietor's struggle against loneliness and the fear of death; *October Light* (1976), about ageing; *Freddy's Book* (1980); and *Mickelsson's Ghosts* (1982). Collections of stories include *The King's Indian Stories and Tales* (1974) and *The Art of Living and Other Stories* (1981). Gardner also wrote: an epic poem, *Jason and Medea* (1973); three libretti, *William Wilson*, *Frankenstein* and *Rumpelstiltskin* (collected in *Three Libretti*, 1979); *Poems* (1978); and *The Forms of Fiction* (1962), *On Moral Fiction* (1978) and *The Art of Fiction: Notes on Craft for Young Writers* (1984).

Garland, (Hannibal) Hamlin 1860–1940 American. He is chiefly remembered for MAIN-TRAVELLED ROADS (1891), stories and sketches about the Midwest. Two further collections, *Prairie Folks* (1892) and *Wayside Courtships* (1897), were combined as *Other Main-Travelled Roads* (1910). His writing often tended towards propaganda, especially in his novels. *Jason Edwards, An Average Man* (1892) is a plea for Henry George's Single Tax Theory, while *A Spoil of Office* (1892) campaigns for the Populist Party. Less political novels include two books about life in Dakota farm country, *A Little Norsk* (1892) and *Rose of Dutcher's Coolly* (1895). *The Captain of the Gray-Horse Troop* (1902) and *Cavanagh, Forest Ranger* (1910) are novels about the Far West. *A Son of the Middle Border* (1917) and *A Daughter of the Middle Border* (1921) are autobiographical narratives. His essays on his theory of realistic fiction, which he called 'veritism', appeared as *Crumbling Idols* (1894).

Garner, Helen 1942– Australian. She achieved overnight fame with her first novel, *Monkey Grip* (1977), written in the fragmentary post-modernist manner which typifies all her work. It was filmed in 1981. She has secured her reputation in subsequent works chronicling contemporary Australian life-styles at home and abroad. They include: *Honour and Other People's Children* (1980), two novellas; *The Children's Bach* (1984), a novel; *Postcards from Surfers* (1985), a collection of short stories; and *Cosmo Cosmolino* (1992), a novel. *The First Stone* (1995), an account of a real-life court case about sexual harassment, stirred controversy in feminist circles.

Garner, Hugh 1913–79 Canadian. Born in Batley, Yorkshire, he was taken to Toronto in 1919.

Storm Below (1949) was based on his wartime experience in the navy. *Cabbagetown*, written earlier, appeared in a butchered version in 1950 and a complete version in 1968. His finest novel, it gives a vivid account of the working-class district where he grew up. Other works include *The Silence on the Shore* (1962), *A Nice Place to Visit* (1970), *The Intruders* (1976) and three detective novels. His short stories are collected in *The Yellow Sweater* (1952), *Hugh Garner's Best Stories* (1963), *Men and Women* (1966), *Violation of the Virgins* (1971) and *Hugh Garner Omnibus* (1978). *One Damn Thing after Another* (1973) is his autobiography.

Garnett, David 1892–1981 English. The grandson of RICHARD GARNETT and the son of Constance and Edward Garnett, he was associated with the BLOOMSBURY GROUP. His first novel, *Lady into Fox* (1922), is a fantasy about a young wife, Sylvia Tebrick, who is changed into a vixen. It won both the HAWTHORNDEN PRIZE and the JAMES TAIT BLACK MEMORIAL PRIZE. *A Man in the Zoo* (1924) and *The Grasshoppers Come* (1931) were not as successful and Garnett abandoned fantasy. *A Rabbit in the Air* (1932) drew on his early attempts to become an aviator. *Aspects of Love* (1955) is a delicate and bizarre love story. Later works include *A Shot in the Dark* (1958) and *A Net for Venus* (1962). His non-fiction included editions of the letters of T. E. Lawrence (1938), the novels of THOMAS LOVE PEACOCK (1924–34) and his own correspondence with T. H. WHITE (1968). *The Golden Echo* (1953), *The Flowers of the Forest* (1955) and *The Familiar Faces* (1962) comprise his autobiography.

Garnett, Eve 1900–91 English. She is remembered for *The Family from One End Street* (1937), about the Ruggles family, one of the first 20th-century children's books to discuss the realities of domestic poverty. Two sequels produced some years later were less successful.

Garnett, Richard 1835–1906 English. He is chiefly remembered for his collection of short stories, *The Twilight of the Gods* (1888), many of which had originally appeared in *The Yellow Book*. A prodigious memory and a career working for the British Museum Library (as Superintendent of the Reading Room in 1875–84) gave him an encyclopaedic knowledge of the classics and international literature. He published short biographies of Milton, Carlyle and Emerson, edited *Relics of Shelley* (1862) and wrote a *History of Italian Literature* (1897). His son and grandson, Edward Garnett (1868–1937) and DAVID GARNETT, both became writers.

Gaskell, Elizabeth (Cleghorn) 1810–65 English. After a peripatetic youth she married William Gaskell, a Unitarian parson and professor of English history and literature at Manchester New College, in 1832. Her response to life in Manchester dominates her first novel, *MARY BARTON* (1848), a tale of industrial strife and

unrest. It earned her the friendship and respect of DICKENS, who encouraged her to continue contributing to his magazine *Household Words*. *CRANFORD*, which appeared in its pages in 1851–3, is a gentle tale about a spinster and her circle. *RUTH* (1853) boldly takes an unmarried mother's problems as its subject. *NORTH AND SOUTH* (1855) is another industrial story. An eight-year interval in novel-writing closed with *SYLVIA'S LOVERS* (1863). *WIVES AND DAUGHTERS*, not quite finished before her death and posthumously published in 1866, stands in striking contrast to her early work by allying itself with the tradition and style of JANE AUSTEN. Mrs Gaskell also wrote longer short stories bordering on the novella, collected in volumes such as *Life in Manchester* (1848), *Lizzie Leigh and Other Tales* (1855), *Round the Sofa* (1859) and *Cousin Phillis and Other Tales* (1865).

Given her close friendship with CHARLOTTE BRONTË, whom she first met in 1850, it was not surprising that she should have undertaken a biography after Charlotte's early death in 1855. *The Life of Charlotte Brontë* (1857) ran into difficulties because of its account of the Brontë children at the Clergy Daughters' School at Cowan Bridge and, in particular, its indiscreet allusions to Branwell's relations with Mrs Edmund Robinson. These resulted in threats of legal action and, ultimately, the withdrawal of questionable passages.

In a century rich in women writers Mrs Gaskell stands to the forefront in her sympathy for the deprived, her evocations of nature, her gentle humour and her narrative pace. Of note is her exceptionally direct development from loosely structured melodramatic writing to the urbanity and balanced form of her later work, particularly *Wives and Daughters*.

Gass, William H(oward) 1924– American. He experiments with language and the depiction of inner states in the novel *Omensetter's Luck* (1966), *In the Heart of the Heart of the Country and Other Stories* (1968), and the novella *Willie Masters' Lonesome Wife* (1971). *The Tunnel* (1995), a novel on which Gass worked for more than 30 years, reflects on constructions of history from the inside and the outside. His non-fiction includes *Fiction and the Figures of Life* (1970), *On Being Blue: A Philosophical Inquiry* (1975), *The World Within the Word* (1978), *Habitations of the Word: Essays* (1985) and *Finding a Form* (1996).

Gee, Maggie (Mary) 1948– English. Her first novel, *Dying, in Other Words* (1981), is her most experimental and her second, *The Burning Book* (1983), about nuclear annihilation, her most substantial. Since *Light Years* (1985), an unsuccessful venture into whimsical comedy, she has produced a psychological thriller in *Grace* (1988), a chronicle of sexual ardour in *Where are the Snows* (1991), and *Lost Children* (1995).

Gee, Maurice 1931– New Zealand. He secured his reputation with *Plumb* (1978), which broke with the realism of his earlier work. It became the first volume of a trilogy, completed by *Meg* (1981) and *Sole Survivor* (1983), chronicling three generations of a family during this century and exploring the effects of New Zealand's Puritan inheritance on individual and social relations. *Plumb* won both the NEW ZEALAND BOOK AWARD and the GOODMAN FIELDER WATTIE BOOK AWARD; *Meg* received the Goodman Fielder Wattie. Later novels include *Prowlers* (1987), *The Burning Boy* (1990), another winner of the New Zealand Book Award and *Going West* (1993), another winner of the Goodman Fielder Wattie. *Crime Story* (1994) extends his range with a view of social problems among the newly rich and newly poor in suburban Wellington. His fine stories for children include *Under the Mountain* (1979), *The Fire-Raiser* (1986) and *The Fat Man* (1994).

genre fiction Fiction written to prototypical formulations of plot and subject. SIR WALTER SCOTT's HISTORICAL FICTION, WILKIE COLLINS's DETECTIVE FICTION, ALDOUS HUXLEY's SCIENCE FICTION and GRAHAM GREENE's SPY FICTION all show that generic conformity does not prevent original and distinguished writing. But overwhelmingly genre fiction is prompted more by a sense of audience and market, and the commercial advantage in satisfying it, than by any attempt at self-expression. It is often published to visually recognizable, economically efficient specifications. Victor Gollancz gave all his crime and science fiction titles yellow jackets, and the romances issued by Mills and Boon are condensed or expanded at editorial stage to a uniform length.

As with detective and science fiction, popular fiction's other principal genres offer therapeutic and consolatory characteristics for the reader. The thriller is written to excite and enthral through the diversion of a fast-moving adventure plot, perhaps comprehending political or financial intrigue, violence, military engagements, extended chase sequences and a cast of colourful villains pitted against the hero. Early exponents include ROBERT LOUIS STEVENSON, with *KIDNAPPED* (1886). EDGAR WALLACE was perhaps the first author to make both a fortune and a huge reputation catering to the popular demand for thrillers. Since the heyday of E. Phillips Oppenheim (1866–1946) in the 1920s, writers have commonly exploited the advantages of rich characters (whose consumer tastes can be detailed in the brand names) and exotic locations (starting with the Côte d'Azur but soon ranging ever further afield). The complexity of modern current affairs, coupled with residual historical fears, offer contemporary thrillers an enormous range of contexts: Islamic fundamentalism, drugs cartels, environmental polluters and so forth. Notable writers, whose work traces the changing patterns of attention and anxiety for the last 40 years or so, are Alistair Maclean (1922–87), Robert Ludlum (1927–), Frederick Forsyth (1938–) and Jeffrey Archer (1940–).

Similarly, genre fiction can both arouse and allay common social fears of disaster. Air crashes, ocean liner sinkings, financial crises and medical experimentation are all employed to tense effect, especially by spin-off feature films. Steven Spielberg's film of *Jaws* (1974) by Peter Benchley (1940–) was a particularly lucrative instance. In order to authenticate their potentially overheated plot, thrillers have increasingly affected an authority of saturated learning, as in *Hotel* (1965) and *Airport* (1968) by Arthur Hailey (1920–). Know-how about computers or genetic engineering swells the pages of many current best-sellers.

Genre fiction is rarely subversive or radical. Indeed, its popular appeal depends on literary and political conservatism. Detective novels affirm that crimes will be solved and murderers punished, Cold War thrillers that the West will always outwit Communism, romances that the protagonists will always find true love. Occasionally the necessary accommodation to changing social trends can significantly transform a genre, particularly in its customarily stereotyped sexual politics. Romance has proved less adaptable. Aimed at a female audience, it has exhibited at most a decline in chastity and an increase in materialism in developing from the bloodless, virginal tales of Barbara Cartland (1901–) and Mills and Boons novels to the 'bodice-ripper' or historical romance of Susan Howatch (1940–), inspired belatedly by the example of *GONE WITH THE WIND*, and the equally lengthy sagas of Shirley Conran (1932–) and Celia Brayfield (1945–). It has varied its appeal by offering either an aspirational glimpse of top people's high living, as in the novels of Jackie Collins (who does not make her date of birth public) or Barbara Taylor Bradford (1933–), or a consolatory empathy with working-class community, as in the tales of North Tyneside by Catherine Cookson (1906–).

The most geographically specific genre of all, the Western, may have died out altogether, or at least transmuted its essential appeal into other genres. The classic fables of OWEN WISTER, ZANE GREY, Louis L'Amour (1908–88) and J. T. Edson (1928–) owed much of their success to Hollywood directors like John Ford. As Hollywood has moved on, so the Western's myths of the frontier spirit can be seen surviving in many science fiction and disaster narratives. The horror novel, inherently devoted to effect, has also continued to survive by linking itself to the feature-film business. Early post-war writers such as Dennis Wheatley (1897–1977) established an adequate market for their tales of diabolic possession, but film adaptations of *The Exorcist* (1970) by William Peter Blatty (1928–) and the novels of Stephen King (1947–) and Dean R. Koontz (1945–) offer a more graphic medium for horror's visceral stock-in-trade.

Gerhardie, William 1895–1977 He was born into a family of English merchants in St Petersburg. While still at Oxford he published his first novel, *Futility* (1922), and a study of Chekhov (1923), a central influence on his own fiction. Extravagantly plotted, his novels disconcertingly juxtapose the absurd and the profound, the comic and the tragic. *Futility*, *The Polyglots* (1925) and their successors, notably *Pending Heaven* (1930), *Resurrection* (1934) and *Of Mortal Love* (1936), enjoyed brief critical success. Gerhardie published no more books after 1940 and the major novel on which he was rumoured to be working during the years of his obscurity never materialized. He changed the spelling of his name from 'Gerhardi' in old age.

Ghose, Zulfikar 1935– Indian/Pakistani. His verse includes *The Loss of India* (1964), *Jets from Orange* (1967) and *The Violent West* (1972). The stories in *Statement against Corpses* (1964), with B. S. JOHNSON, and the novels *Contradictions* (1966) and *The Murder of Aziz Khan* (1967) seek a 'still point' between Western rationality and Eastern 'nothingness'. Two critical works, *Hamlet, Prufrock, and Language* (1978) and *The Fiction of Reality* (1984), point to the nature of his sophisticated and challenging novels since 1972: a trilogy, THE INCREDIBLE BRAZILIAN, consisting of *The Incredible Brazilian: The Native* (1972), *The Beautiful Empire* (1975), and *A Different World* (1978); *Crump's Terms* (1975); *Hulme's Investigations into the Bogart Script* (1981); *A New History of Torments* (1982); *Don Bueno* (1983); and *Figures of Enchantment* (1986). *Confessions of a Native-Alien* (1965) is an autobiography.

Ghosh, Amitav 1956– Indian. An anthropologist by training, he has a professional interest in the subjects of exile and diaspora which inform his fiction. *The Circle of Reason* (1986) is a sprawling novel, moving from rural Bengal through India to the Middle East and Algeria. THE SHADOW LINES (1988; awarded a SAHITYA AKADEMI prize) transcends conventional portrayals of East-West relations to become a meditation on borders, physical and psychological. *In an Antique Land* (1993), set in Egypt past and present, draws on the author's ethnographical fieldwork and historical studies. The futuristic *The Calcutta Chromosome: A Novel of Fevers, Delirium and Discovery* (1996) introduces elements of SCIENCE FICTION and the political thriller.

Gibbon, Lewis Grassic [Mitchell, James Leslie] 1901–35 Scottish. Mitchell used the pseudonym of Lewis Grassic Gibbon for his specifically Scottish undertakings, most notably *A Scots Quair*, a trilogy of novels set in his native Howe of Mearns: *Sunset Song* (1932), *Cloud Howe* (1933) and *Grey Granite* (1934). He collaborated with Hugh MacDiarmid on *Scottish Scene: or, The Intelligent Man's Guide to Albyn* (1934), an important contribution to the Scottish renaissance. Under his own name he published seven English novels, many short stories and works of history, archaeology and anthropology.

Gibbons, Stella See COLD COMFORT FARM.

Gibson, William 1948– American. Most of his SCIENCE FICTION – including the novels *Neuromancer* (1984), *Count Zero* (1985), *Mona Lisa Overdrive* (1988), *Idoru* (1996) and the short stories collected in *Burning Chrome* (1986) – is typical of so-called 'Cyberpunk' fiction, which deals with the intimate interaction of people and electronic machinery in an overpopulated, decadent near future. *Virtual Light* (1993) is a 'technothriller'. *The Difference Engine* (with Bruce Sterling; 1990) is an alternative history novel in which Victorian England undergoes a technological revolution thanks to Charles Babbage's mechanical computer.

Gilbert, Michael See DETECTIVE FICTION.

Gilchrist, Ellen 1935– American. Usually set in the South, her fiction maps the spoiled, anchorless lives of its upper classes. *In the Land of Dreamy Dreams* (1981), *Victory over Japan* (1984), *Drunk with Love* (1986), *Light Can Be Both Wave and Particle* (1989), *The Age of Miracles* (1995) and *Courts of Love* (1996) are volumes of stories. *The Annunciation* (1983), *The Anna Papers* (1988), *Net of Jewels* (1992), *Starcarbon: A Meditation on Love* (1994) and *Sarah Conley* (1997) are novels, while *I Cannot Get You Close Enough* (1990) contains three novellas.

Gilded Age, The: *A Tale of Today* A satirical novel by MARK TWAIN and CHARLES DUDLEY WARNER, published in 1873 and dramatized by Twain and G. S. Densmore the following year. Set in Missouri, New York and Washington, DC, the story tells of unscrupulous people, their personal relationships and their financial enterprises, by way of commenting on the greed, exploitation and economic speculation during the period of post-Civil War Reconstruction. The book gave a name to the era.

Gilman, Charlotte Perkins 1860–1935 American. *This Our World* (1893) is a collection of poems about 19th-century womanhood and *Women and Economics* (1898) an indictment of patriarchal culture. Other reforming works, including *Concerning Children* (1900) and *The Home: Its Work and Influence* (1903), discuss the detrimental effects that restrictions on women have on the family. *The Yellow Wallpaper* (1899) is a semi-autobiographical treatment of a woman writer's breakdown. Two novels, *What Diana Did* (1910) and *The Crux* (1911), originally published in her journal, *The Forerunner*, developed her ideas about sexual relations and oppression in modern society. Her autobiography appeared in 1935.

Gissing, George (Robert) 1857–1903 English. After being expelled from Owens College (later the University of Manchester) for stealing, he spent a month in prison, wandered for a year in America and then settled in London, where he survived by private coaching. He married two working-class girls in succession. Consciousness of his humble origins made him proud and lonely; his only close friend in the literary world was H. G. WELLS.

Hardworking, prolific and obsessed with his vocation, he became respected as an exponent of NATURALISM in the French manner, usually taking poverty and failure as his subjects. His first novel, WORKERS IN THE DAWN (1880), was followed by *The Unclassed* (1884), *Eve's Ransom* (1885), *Isabel Clarendon* and *Demos* (both 1886), *Thyrza* (1887), *A Life's Morning* (1888), *The Nether World* (1889), *The Emancipated* (1890), NEW GRUB STREET (his best-known novel, 1891), *Born in Exile* (1892), *Denzil Quarrier* (1892), THE ODD WOMEN (1893), *Sleeping Fires* (1895), *The Whirlpool* (1897), *Human Odds and Ends* (short stories, 1897), *The Town Traveller* and a critical study of DICKENS (both 1898), *The Crown of Life* (1899), *Our Friend the Charlatan* (1901) and *By the Ionian Sea* (impressions of Italy, 1900), THE PRIVATE PAPERS OF HENRY RYECROFT (1903) is semi-autobiographical. After his death came a historical romance of 6th-century Italy, *Veranilda* (1904), *Will Warburton* (1905), *The House of Cobwebs* (short stories, 1906), *The Sins of the Fathers* (1924), *The Immortal Dickens* (1925), *A Victim of Circumstances* (1927), *Brownie* (1931), *Notes on Social Democracy* (1968), *George Gissing's Commonplace Book* (edited by J. Korg; 1962) and *The Diary of George Gissing, Novelist* (edited by P. Coustillas; 1978). In recent years he has received increasing critical attention.

Glaister, Lesley 1956– English. She established a reputation for 'female Gothic' with *Honour Thy Father* (1990) and *Trick or Treat* (1991). *Digging to Australia* (1992) depicts a child menaced by an adult world bound up in the past, *Limestone and Clay* (1993) explores the fantasy world of a childless couple, while *Partial Eclipse* (1994) mingles the past of two women separated by more than a century. In *Easy Peasy* (1997) the suicide of the heroine's father prompts a reappraisal of her childhood and his suffering as a POW in Japanese hands.

Glasgow, Ellen 1874–1945 American. She is best remembered for BARREN GROUND (1925) and VEIN OF IRON (1935). The old agrarian South is the subject of HISTORICAL FICTION beginning with *The Voice of the People* (1900) and including *The Battle-Ground* (1902), *The Deliverance* (1904), *The Wheel of Life* (1906), *The Ancient Law* (1908), *The Romance of a Plain Man* (1909) and *The Miller of Old Church* (1911). *Virginia* (1913) and *Life and Gabriella* (1916) examine the position of women in the modernization of the Old South. Other novels include *The Builders* (1919), *One Man in His*

Time (1922), *The Romantic Comedians* (1926), *They Stooped to Folly* (1929), *The Sheltered Life* (1932) and *In This Our Life* (1941; PULITZER PRIZE), about the decay of an aristocratic Virginia family. Her short stories are found in *The Shadowy Third* (1923) and *Collected Stories* (1963), and the prefatory essays to her novels in *A Certain Measure* (1943). *The Woman Within* (1954) is autobiographical.

Glaspell, Susan 1882–1948 American. With her husband, George Cram Cook, she was a founder of the Provincetown Players, responsible for producing the early work of Eugene O'Neill. Her plays include one-act pieces, such as *Trifles* (1916), as well as full-length works, such as *Inheritors* (1921), *The Verge* (1921), about a woman simultaneously on the verge of madness and true discovery, and *Alison's House* (1930; PULITZER PRIZE), about Emily Dickinson. Her novels are unimpressive but the short stories collected in *Lifted Masks* (1912) and *A Jury of Her Peers* (1927) display the intensity of her quest for social justice. *The Road to the Temple* (1927) is an evocative account of her life with Cook.

Gloag, John See SCIENCE FICTION.

Glyn, Elinor 1864–1943 English. Her 21 romantic novels were popular and controversial for their treatment of sex, particularly women's sexual feelings. *Three Weeks* (1907), the best known because of erotic scenes played out on a tiger-skin, describes the sensual awakening of Paul, a young English nobleman, in his affair with a Slavonic beauty of noble rank. The ending punishes the lovers.

Go-Between, The A novel by L. P. HARTLEY, published in 1953. In old age Leo Colston recalls the summer of 1900, when he stayed with a schoolfriend, Marcus Maudsley, at a Norfolk country house. He became a go-between, innocently carrying messages for a local farmer, Ted Burgess, and Marcus's older sister Marian, who were conducting a secret affair despite Marian's engagement to an amiable but unimaginative young viscount, Hugh Trimingham. In the process Leo slowly became aware of adult sexuality, a discovery rendered dramatic and shameful when Marian's mother, suspicious of her daughter's behaviour, forced him to betray the guilty couple and to surprise them making love. Subsequently Burgess killed himself and Marian married Trimingham, while Leo grew into a damaged and repressed adult. In the epilogue he visits Marian 50 years later and agrees to contact her grandson to explain what really happened.

Godden, (Margaret) Rumer 1907– English. She was born and spent much of her life in India. Beginning as an adult author, she won acclaim with a series of successful novels including *Black Narcissus* (1939), *Breakfast with the Nickolides* (1942) and *The Greengage Summer* (1958), a story of first love set in France and now also considered a children's book. Her books written expressly for children include *The Dolls' House* (1947) and *The Mousewife* (1951), based on a note in Dorothy Wordsworth's diary. Other successful books, suitable for both old and young readers, include *The Diddakoi* (1972) and *Peacock Spring* (1978), another tale of disappointed love, set in India.

Godwin, William 1756–1836 English. He began by becoming a Dissenting minister but his reading of Rousseau, d'Holbach and Helvetius undermined his faith and he embraced atheism in 1783. The French Revolution stirred his interest in political philosophy and emancipatory politics. *Enquiry concerning Political Justice* (1793), his response to the debates and polemics of the time, was an immediate success and included the young Wordsworth, Southey and Coleridge among its admirers. The inner social and psychological drama masked by its elaborate philosophical method is impressively externalized in his novel, *Caleb Williams* (1794). Godwin was the anarchist of the Age of Reason. Nothing if not consistent in his rationalistic individualism, he opposed both all existing institutions and all organized resistance to them. He never revised his model of reason, and jealously defended his system against the slightest imputation of activism. Although this position alienated him from radical groups like the London Corresponding Society, it did not prevent him becoming the scapegoat of the loyalist reaction orchestrated by Pitt. By the time he published *The Enquirer* (1797) he had been thoroughly and systematically defamed. It was a blow from which he never recovered intellectually and which permanently soured his personal relations.

His wife, Mary Wollstonecraft, died a few days after the birth of their daughter, the future Mary Shelley, in 1797. He wrote her biography, *Memoirs of the Author of the Vindication of the Rights of Woman* (1798), edited her posthumous works and portrayed her in his novel *St Leon* (1799). His subsequent remarriage to Mrs Clairmont was largely an alliance of convenience. In 1814 Shelley eloped with Mary and Claire Clairmont, eventually marrying Mary in 1816. Godwin's adroit manipulation of the poet's generosity helped to alleviate his financial problems. During the last two decades of his life he repudiated many of the more radical aspects of *Political Justice* – in, for example, *Thoughts on Man* (1831) – and in the late 1820s he spoke out against the increasingly powerful movement for reform. The only significant work of this period was *Of Population* (1820), an answer to Malthus's *Essay on the Principle of Population*. His substantial output also includes a life of Chaucer (1803–4) and the novels *Fleetwood* (1805), *Mandeville* (1817), *Cloudesly* (1830) and *Deloraine* (1833).

Golden Bowl, The A novel by Henry James, published in 1904.

Maggie is the daughter of Adam Verver, an American millionaire and art collector living in Europe. Her friend Fanny Assingham finds her an Italian prince, Amerigo. Charlotte Stant, prevented from marrying Amerigo by their lack of money, wants to buy a gilded crystal bowl as a present for Amerigo but he declines the gift because it is flawed. Adam Verver marries Charlotte, but Charlotte and Amerigo have not forgotten their feelings for each other and meet in secret. Maggie buys a bowl for her father's birthday but learns from the dealer that it is the same one Amerigo and Charlotte had rejected. Maggie makes clear to Fanny that she knows the whole truth about Charlotte and Amerigo, and smashes the bowl. Amerigo stops seeing Charlotte; Adam gives no hint to her that he knows of her liaison; Maggie conducts herself with unruffled serenity. Charlotte is left wondering at her lover's withdrawal and Adam finally resolves the situation by returning to America with her.

Golding, Sir **William (Gerald)** 1911–93 English. Much of his writing explores moral dilemmas at the centre of human existence, and he often places his characters in extreme situations to suggest a 'mythological' dimension to their lives. Preoccupied with evil and original sin, he treated these subjects in a way that transcends the boundaries of orthodox Christianity.

He achieved success with his first novel, *Lord of the Flies* (1954), now regarded as a modern classic. It was followed by: *The Inheritors* (1955), about primeval man; *Pincher Martin* (1956), in which a drowning man is tormented by his past life; *Free Fall* (1959); *The Spire* (1964), a densely symbolic account of the building of Salisbury Cathedral spire; *The Pyramid* (1967); *The Scorpion God* (1971); *Darkness Visible* (1979); and *The Paper Men* (1984), an uncharacteristically comic account of a famous author plagued by an American academic. *The Ends of the Earth* (1991) is historical fiction, bringing together a trilogy of powerful novels reflecting his abiding fascination with the sea: *Rites of Passage* (1980), which won the Booker Prize, *Close Quarters* (1987) and *Fire Down Below* (1989). *The Double Tongue* appeared posthumously in 1995. Other works include a play, *The Brass Butterfly* (1958), and collections of essays, *The Hot Gates* (1965) and *A Moving Target* (1982). He was awarded the Nobel Prize for Literature in 1983.

Goldsmith, Oliver See *Vicar of Wakefield, The*.

Goldsworthy, Peter 1950– Australian. He adopts a stance of cool detachment, and often takes his subjects from his work as a doctor, in the stories gathered in *Archipelagoes* (1982), *Zooing* (1986), *Bleak Rooms* (1988) and *Little Deaths* (1993). His novels are: *Maestro* (1989), about the influence of an Austrian refugee from the

Holocaust over his Australian protégé in music; *Honk If You are Jesus* (1992) and *Wish: A Biologically Engineered Love Story* (1995). The first of his books of poetry, *Reading from Ecclesiastes* (1982), won the Commonwealth Poetry Prize.

Gone with the Wind The only novel by the American writer Margaret Mitchell (1900–49), published in 1936 and awarded a PULITZER PRIZE. An immediate best-seller, it has sold more than 25 million copies, been translated into 27 languages and inspired an enduringly popular film (1939) starring Vivien Leigh and Clark Gable. Set largely on a Georgia plantation, Tara, the story follows the fortunes of a wilful Southern belle, Scarlett O'Hara, against the backdrop of the Civil War, the defeat of the South and reconstruction.

Gonzalez, N(estor) V(icente) M(adali) 1915– Filipino. Brought up in a Visayan-speaking family, he has published several volumes of short stories as well as novels: *The Winds of April* (1941), *A Season of Grace* (1954) and *The Bamboo Dancers* (1959). Common to all his fiction is a sympathy for marginalized, rural Philippine society facing urban or foreign encroachment.

Good Soldier, The: *A Tale of Passion* A novel by FORD MADOX FORD, published in 1915. The narrator, John Dowell, controls the reader's view of what he calls 'the saddest story', an account of his entangled relations with his wife Florence, their friend Edward Ashburnham (the good soldier) and his Irish-Catholic wife Leonora, and Nancy Rufford, ward of Edward and Leonora. The story moves towards a dénouement at once melodramatic and formally ordered.

Goodman, Paul 1911–72 American. His many non-fictional works include: *Utopian Essays and Proposals* (1962), on political theory; *Gestalt Therapy* (1951), on psychology; *Communitas* (with his brother Percival; 1947), on city planning; *Compulsory Mis-Education* (1964); *Growing Up Absurd* (1960), an influential study of youth and delinquency. His novels include *The Empire City* (1959), set in New York from 1930 to 1950, and the autobiographical *Making Do* (1963). He also wrote for *Partisan Review* and *The New Republic*. *Five Years: Thoughts during a Useless Time* (1966) is autobiographical. *Collected Poems* appeared in 1974.

Goodman Fielder Wattie Book Award An annual award for three works of New Zealand fiction or non-fiction. It was inaugurated in 1968 and taken over by Montana in 1994; the Montana Book Award was in turn amalgamated with the NEW ZEALAND BOOK AWARD in 1996 to form the Montana New Zealand Book Award. Goodman Fielder Wattie encouraged the recognition of Maori culture and Maori writers, particularly WITI IHIMAERA, though it passed over *THE BONE PEOPLE* and gave only belated acknowledgement to KERI HULME.

Winners for fiction were: C. K. STEAD, *Smith's Dream* (1972); MAURICE SHADBOLT, *Strangers and Journeys* (1973); JANET FRAME, *Daughter Buffalo* (1973); Witi Ihimaera, *Pounamu, Pounamu* (1973); Witi Ihimaera, *Tangi* (1974); Noel Hilliard, *Maori Woman* (1975); M. K. Joseph, *A Soldier's Tale* (1976); VINCENT O'SULLIVAN, *The Boy, the Bridge, the River* (1978); MAURICE GEE, *Plumb* (1979); ALBERT WENDT, *Leaves of the Banyan Tree* (1980); Maurice Shadbolt, *The Lovelock Version* (1981); Sue McCauley, *Other Halves* (1982); Witi Ihimaera, *The Matriarch* (1986); PATRICIA GRACE, *Potiki* (1986); Keri Hulme, *Te Kaihau: The Windeater* (1986); Maurice Shadbolt, *Season of the Jew* (1987); STEVEN ELDRED-GRIGG, *Oracles and Miracles* (1988); ALAN DUFF, *Once were Warriors* (1991); BARBARA ANDERSON, *Portrait of the Artist's Wife* (1992); and Maurice Gee, *Going West* (1993). Winners after the prize became the Montana Book award were: Vincent O'Sullivan, *Let the River Stand* (1994) and Witi Ihimaera, *Bulibasha* (1995).

Gooneratne, Yasmine 1935– Sri Lankan. She was a prolific poet before emigrating to Australia in 1972. After a period of relatively little creative writing but substantial critical work (including studies of JANE AUSTEN, Alexander Pope and RUTH PRAWER JHABVALA), she has published novels: *A Change of Skies* (1991), about South Asian immigrants in Australia, and *The Pleasures of Conquest* (1995), a sophisticated post-colonial fable set in a thinly disguised Sri Lanka.

Goonewardene, James 1921– Sri Lankan. His novels give satirical, and often disturbing, portraits of modern Sri Lankan life. They range in subject from the clash between urban and rural values in *A Quiet Place* (1968) and *Call of the Kirala* (1971) to the 1971 insurgency in *An Asian Gambit* (1985) and recent ultra-nationalist tendencies in *One Mad Bid for Freedom* (1990). The protagonist of *The Tribal Hangover* (1995) is an adopted Sri Lankan child in Australia.

Gordimer, Nadine 1923– South African. Instants, symptoms and symbols of the South African malaise are captured by the short stories in volumes beginning with *Face to Face* (1949) and including, in her later career, *Livingstone's Companions* (1972), *Selected Stories* (1975), *Some Monday for Sure* (1976), *A Soldier's Embrace: Stories* (1980), *Something Out There* (1984), *Jump and Other Stories* (1991), *Crimes of Conscience* (1991) and *Why Haven't You Written? Selected Stories 1952–1972* (1992). Early novels – *The Lying Days* (1953), *A World of Strangers* (1958), *Occasion for Loving* (1963) and *The Late Bourgeois World* (1966) – chart the fluctuations of hope and disillusion in her view of South Africa.

A Guest of Honour (1971) and *THE CONSERVATIONIST* (1974) announce the maturity of her fiction, successfully integrating the personal with the political. Later novels have included: *Burger's Daughter* (1979), a response to events in Soweto in 1976; *July's People* (1981), about a family caught in the upheaval of two orders; *A Sport of Nature* (1987), about a young white woman developing political maturity; *My Son's Story* (1990), about a young Coloured man trying to come to terms with his heritage; and *None To Accompany Me* (1994), about a white lawyer's struggle to incorporate her past into her present. *The Conservationist*, *Burger's Daughter*, *July's People* and *My Son's Story* all won the CNA LITERARY AWARD. *The Black Interpreters* (1973), *The Essential Gesture: Writing, Politics and Places* (1988) and *Writing and Being* (1995) are collections of essays.

She received the Nobel Prize for Literature in 1991.

Gordon, Caroline 1895–1981 American. Born in Kentucky, she treated the history of the South in novels such as *Penhally* (1931), *Aleck Maury Sportsman* (1934) and *None Shall Look Back* (1937). Her short story 'Old Red', awarded the O. Henry Prize in 1934, reappeared in *The Forest of the South* (1945), *Old Red and Other Stories* (1963) and *The Collected Stories of Caroline Gordon* (1981).

Gordon, Mary (Catherine) 1949– American. Her themes are sacrifice and love. Her first three novels – *Final Payments* (1978), *The Company of Women* (1981), *Men and Angels* (1985) – explore the demands of Roman Catholicism. *The Other Side* (1989) examines five generations of an immigrant family. Other works include a collection of stories, *Temporary Shelter* (1987), *The Rest of Life: Three Novellas* (1993), *Good Boys and Dead Girls: And Other Essays* (1992) and *The Shadow Man: A Daughter's Search for her Father* (1996).

Gore, Mrs Catherine Grace 1799–1861 English. Of the 70 assorted works she produced in under 40 years, the best-known were SILVER-FORK NOVELS of fashionable life and high society. They include *Manners of the Day* (1830), *Mrs Armytage: or, Female Domination* (1836), *Cecil: or, The Adventures of a Coxcomb* (1841) and *The Banker's Wife* (1843).

Gothic novel A type of romance popular in the late 18th and early 19th centuries. 'Gothic' had come to mean 'wild', 'barbarous' and 'crude', qualities which writers cultivated in reaction against the neoclassicism of earlier 18th-century culture. Gothic novels were usually set in the past (most often the Middle Ages) and in foreign countries (particularly the Catholic countries of southern Europe). Monasteries, castles, dungeons and mountainous landscapes were made settings for plots which hinged on suspense or mystery and flirted with the fantastic or supernatural. HORACE WALPOLE's *THE CASTLE OF OTRANTO* (1764), the first Gothic novel proper, influenced the work of ANN RADCLIFFE, WILLIAM BECKFORD, M. G. LEWIS and CHARLES MATURIN. The wider ramifications of the taste for Gothic fiction continued in some Romantic poetry, MARY SHELLEY's *FRANKENSTEIN* and the novels of the BRONTË sisters. The novels of

CHARLES BROCKDEN BROWN and the tales of EDGAR ALLAN POE show the taste for Gothic rooting itself in American culture, where it continued to flourish in a long tradition stretching beyond the work of NATHANIEL HAWTHORNE to the 'Southern Gothic' of 20th-century writers such as WILLIAM FAULKNER.

Gould, Nathaniel ['Nat'] 1857–1919 English. His first novel, *The Double Event* (1891), written while he was working in Australia, combined his knowledge of the country with his love of racing. Later sporting novels include *Banker and Broker* (1893), *The Famous Match* (1898) and *Left in the Lurch* (in *Nat Gould's Annual*, 1903).

Governor General's Awards Canada's most prestigious literary prizes, awarded annually and including a category for fiction. They were inaugurated in 1936, when JOHN BUCHAN agreed to lend his title but, controversially, did not make any funds available. The Canadian Authors Association acted as judges until 1944, when an independent board was established; the Canada Council took over in 1959.

Virtually all Canada's major writers of fiction for the last half century have won Governor General's Awards for their novels or short stories. They include HUGH MACLENNAN, Gabrielle Roy, MORLEY CALLAGHAN, ADELE WISEMAN, HUGH GARNER, MARGARET LAURENCE, ALICE MUNRO, MORDECAI RICHLER, ROBERT KROETSCH, ROBERTSON DAVIES, RUBY WIEBE, MARIAN ENGEL, TIMOTHY FINDLEY, JACK HODGINS, GEORGE BOWERING, MAVIS GALLANT, GUY VANDERHAEGHE, MARGARET ATWOOD, NINO RICCI, MICHAEL ONDAATJE, ROHINTON MISTRY and CAROL SHIELDS.

Grace, Patricia 1937– New Zealand. Her writing explores the opposition of Maori and Pakeha (European) worlds from a point of view within contemporary Maori culture. *Waiariki* (1975) was the first collection of stories by a Maori woman writer. Since then she has published three further collections, *The Dream Sleepers* (1980), *Electric City* (1987) and *The Sky People and Other Stories* (1993), showing a progressive darkening of tone. *Selected Stories* appeared in 1991. Her novels are *Mutuwhenua: The Moon Sleeps* (1978), *Potiki* (1986; winner of the NEW ZEALAND BOOK AWARD and the GOODMAN FIELDER WATTIE BOOK AWARD) and *Cousins* (1992), incorporating the life stories of three women in a family saga covering half a century.

Grafton, Sue See DETECTIVE FICTION.

Grahame, Kenneth 1859–1932 English. His book of essays, *The Golden Age* (1895), and its sequel, *Dream Days* (1898), paint a convincingly unsentimental picture of childhood. After his marriage in 1899 Grahame took to telling stories to his young son Alastair, continued in a series of letters. These formed the basis for *THE WIND IN THE WILLOWS* (1908), which – after several rejections by publishers – came out to scant critical acclaim. Its fame quickly grew and the addition of illustrations by E. H. Shepard and Arthur Rackham helped it to classic status. Grahame wrote nothing else of substance, becoming something of a recluse after his son's suicide at the age of 19.

Grain of Wheat, A A novel by NGUGI WA THIONG'O, published in 1967. Set chiefly in the days just before Kenyan Independence, it traces the experiences of several characters – including Mugo, Gikonyo, Karanja and Mumbi – in the freedom struggle and especially their relationship to Kihika, a martyr of the revolution hanged by the colonial authorities. JOSEPH CONRAD's influence, acknowledged by Ngugi, is apparent both in the preoccupation with personal and political betrayal and in the chronological shifts of the narrative.

Grandissimes, The: A Story of Creole Life A novel by GEORGE WASHINGTON CABLE, published in 1880, and set in New Orleans in the early 19th century. Two aristocratic families, the Grandissimes and the De Grapions, are locked in a feud. Honoré Grandissime falls in love with Clotilde, daughter of the widowed Aurora and last of the De Grapions. On his deathbed Honoré's uncle Agricola, who had killed Aurora's father Dr Nancanou in a duel, clears away objections to the marriage by revealing that he had promised Dr Nancanou 20 years earlier to allow it. Agricola himself now approves because it will continue the French Creole aristocracy to which the families belong.

Grapes of Wrath, The A novel by JOHN STEINBECK, published in 1939 and awarded a PULITZER PRIZE. Forced to leave their Oklahoma farm, the Joads drive to California, which they imagine to be a land of plenty. The grandparents die on the journey and in California the Joads suffer the hard life of migrant fruit-pickers. Tom Joad joins Jim Casy, a minister turned labour organizer, and, when Casy is killed, himself kills a man in revenge. Ma Joad finally decides that Tom must leave for the good of the family. In a controversial end to the novel, Rose of Sharon, the eldest daughter, who has just given birth to a stillborn child, nurses a starving man with her own milk.

Graves, Richard 1715–1804 English. He is best remembered for THE SPIRITUAL QUIXOTE: or, The Summer's Ramble of Mr Geoffry Wildgoose: A Comic Romance (1773), a satire of Methodism. Other novels, interesting for their portrayal of social conditions, are Columella: or, The Distressed Anchoret (1779), Eugenius: or, Anecdotes of the Golden Vale (1785) and Plexippus: or, The Aspiring Plebeian (1790). The rector of Claverton, near Bath, and a popular figure in local society, he was a friend of the poet William Shenstone, whom he portrayed in Columella and made the subject of Recollections (1788).

Graves, Robert (von Ranke) 1895–1985 English.

His early poems were dominated by his experiences in World War I. Subsequent work, gathered successively in Poems 1914–26 (1927), Poems 1926–30 (1931), Poems 1938–45 (1946) and two editions of Collected Poems (1938 and 1975), records the development of a highly individual style, always returning to classical literature and mythology for inspiration. His poetry went hand in hand with a mass of other work. A controversial memoir, Goodbye to All That (1929), ends with his departure from England. Critical books include A Survey of Modernist Poetry (with Laura Riding; 1928), attacking both popular attitudes to poetry and MODERNISM in its more fashionable forms. The White Goddess (1948) elaborates his mythology of poetic inspiration in erudite, passionate, sometimes baffling terms. His interest in myth and classical culture also prompted, among many other books, the two most famous of his 13 novels, I, Claudius (1934) and Claudius the God (1934), and a minor classic in The Greek Myths (1955). The Anger of Achilles: Homer's Iliad (1957) is among his translations from the classics.

Gravity's Rainbow A novel by THOMAS PYNCHON, published in 1973 and awarded a PULITZER PRIZE. A long and extremely dense work set in the wasted landscape of World War II's European theatre, it involves more than 400 characters and concerns itself with the constructions of self and history in the face of modern technology and in the aftermath of nuclear destruction. Its immense array of allusions, suggesting the extent to which it charts Western fears and fantasies, ranges from classical music theory to film and comic-strip characters. The literary figures evoked include WILLIAM FAULKNER, Emily Dickinson, Rilke, Borges and JAMES JOYCE, to whose ULYSSES the novel has often been compared.

Gray, Alasdair 1934– Scottish. He is the most prominent member of a new wave in Scottish writing. Glasgow, his home city, provides the location for Lanark (1981) and 1982, Janine (1984), huge, sprawling PICARESQUE narratives indebted to LAURENCE STERNE and JAMES JOYCE. His early shorter fiction is collected in Unlikely Stories, Mostly (1983); subsequent volumes include Ten Tales Tall and True (1993) and Mavis Beltrage (1995). Among his other works are: The Fall of Kelvin Walker (1985); McGrotty and Ludmilla (1990), a short political satire issued by his own publishing imprint, the Dog and Bone Press; Something Leather (1990); Poor Things (1992; WHITBREAD AWARD); and A History Maker (1994). He addressed the question of Scottish sovereignty in Independence: Why Scots Should Rule Scotland (1992).

Gray, Stephen 1941– South African. His verse collections are It's About Time (1974), Hottentot Venus and Other Poems (1979), Love Poems, Hate Poems: From Notebooks (1974–1981) (1982), Apollo

Café and Other Poems (1990) and *Season of Violence* (1992), with *Selected Poems, 1962–1992* (1994). His novels are *Local Colour* (1975), *Visible People* (1977), *Caltrop's Desire* (1980), *John Ross: The True Story* (1987), *Time of Our Darkness* (1988), *Born of Man* (1989) and *Drakenstein* (1994). Gray draws on South African history to illustrate how present difficulties are rooted in the past. His novels are satirical; recurring themes include the complexities of homosexual relationships, relationships across the colour bar, and the interaction of people in a politically restrictive society. *War Child* (1991) is semi-autobiographical. Short stories and other pieces are collected in *Human Interest* (1993); *Accident of Birth* (1993) is his autobiography.

Great Expectations A novel by CHARLES DICKENS, serialized in his magazine *All the Year Round* in 1860–1 and published in volume form in 1861. Despite its melodramatic plotting and its gallery of comic characters, it is a work of sober and sustained purpose.

Philip Pirrip (Pip) describes the three stages of his 'great expectations'. He spends an orphaned childhood on the Kentish marshes with his harsh sister and her kindly blacksmith husband, Joe Gargery. When young, he helps an escaped convict, Abel Magwitch, who is soon recaptured. Later he is summoned to Satis House, where Miss Havisham has lived in seclusion since being jilted by her fiancé, and becomes devoted to her ward, the coldhearted Estella. The lawyer Jaggers arrives with news that Pip has been awarded a generous allowance, which he mistakenly assumes to come from Miss Havisham. In London he lives with Herbert Pocket and falls into extravagant ways in the attempt to become a gentleman. Magwitch reappears and announces that he is Pip's benefactor. Pip's attempt to get him safely out of the country fails and Magwitch dies in prison. Estella, dramatically revealed as Magwitch's daughter, marries an upper-class lout, Bentley Drummle, who mistreats her before his early death. Pip, learning both loyalty and humility from his experiences, meets Estella again some years later. In the original ending the two remain separate, but Dickens altered it to provide a conventionally happy ending.

Great Gatsby, The A novel by F. SCOTT FITZGERALD, published in 1925.

The narrator, Nick Carraway, is fascinated by Jay Gatsby, his neighbour in West Egg, Long Island, who makes his mansion the scene of extravagant nightly parties. Many of those who attend are uninvited and none seem to know the truth about Gatsby's past or the source of his wealth. Nick learns that Gatsby is obsessed with winning back Daisy, whom he had loved before she married the rich but boring Tom Buchanan. The tensions in the group of charac-

ters reach a climax when Daisy, driving Gatsby's car, accidentally runs over Tom's mistress Myrtle Wilson. Tom tells Myrtle's husband that Gatsby was the driver, and Wilson kills Gatsby before committing suicide. Nick is left to piece together Gatsby's past and to arrange the funeral, which hardly anyone attends.

Great Hoggarty Diamond, The A story by WILLIAM MAKEPEACE THACKERAY, published in 1841. The gift of the Diamond from his aunt involves Samuel Titmarsh with swindlers, shady dealings and misfortunes, from which his wife rescues him.

Great Indian Novel, The A novel by SHASHI THAROOR, published in 1989. Its title and inspiration come from the Indian epic of the *Mahabharata* (in Sanskrit, 'Great India'). The outline of the epic's dynastic feud between Kauravas and Pandavas, ending with the apocalyptic battle of Kurukshetra, is altered remarkably little to provide a political allegory of modern India from the Independence movement to the rule of Indira Gandhi.

Green, Henry [Yorke, Henry Vincent] 1905–73 English. While still at Oxford he attracted attention with his first novel, *Blindness* (1926). His work is distinguished by elegant impressionist prose, oblique dialogue, rapid cutting from scene to scene, and a vein of poetry most strongly evident in his second novel, *Living* (1929). This is set in the sort of engineering works he knew well from his own work as foundryman, engineer and managing director of his family's company in Birmingham. *Party Going* (1939) portrays an upper-class group with wealth but without responsibility. Other works include: *Caught* (1943), about the Auxiliary Fire Service in World War II; *Loving* (1945), set in a remote castle in Ireland; *Back* (1946); *Concluding* (1948); *Nothing* (1950); and *Doting* (1952). Green also wrote *Pack My Bag: A Self Portrait* (1940).

Green Carnation, The See HICHENS, ROBERT.

Green Mansions: *A Romance of the Tropical Forest* A novel by W. H. HUDSON, published in 1904. Abel Guevez de Argensola (Mr Abel), a political refugee, settles in the Venezuelan jungle (the 'green mansions') with the Indian tribe of his friend Runi. He falls in love with Rima, a girl whose spirit has strong affinities with that of the forest itself, and sets out with her grandfather, Nuflo, to try to locate Rima's mother. They return to discover that the Indians have destroyed Rima's hut and burnt her to death. Abel revenges himself by attacking the Indians' village and slaying Runi. He returns to civilization with Rima's ashes. The Hudson Memorial in Hyde Park features a sculpture of Rima by Sir Jacob Epstein, commissioned in 1925.

Greene, (Henry) Graham 1904–91 English. His preoccupation with pursuit, guilt, treachery and failure is already apparent in his first novel, *The Man Within* (1929). Popular success, however, did not come until he adopted the conventions of SPY FICTION in *Stamboul Train* (1932; called *Orient Express* in the USA), the first of the novels which he termed 'entertainments'. These continued with *It's a Battlefield* (1934), *England Made Me* (1935), *A Gun for Sale* (1936; called *This Gun for Hire* in the USA), *The Confidential Agent* (1939), *Loser Takes All* (1955) and *Our Man in Havana* (1958). A convert to Catholicism in 1926, he tackled explicitly Catholic themes in *BRIGHTON ROCK* (1938), *THE POWER AND THE GLORY* (1940), *THE HEART OF THE MATTER* (1948), *The End of the Affair* (1951) and *THE QUIET AMERICAN* (1955). Four more novels deal with the committed and the uncommitted in a political context: *A Burnt-Out Case* (1961), set in the Belgian Congo; *The Comedians* (1966), in Haiti; *The Honorary Consul* (1973), in Argentina; and *The Human Factor* (1978), in the underworld of spies. Later novels include *Doctor Fischer of Geneva* (1980) and *The Captain and the Enemy* (1989). *Travels with My Aunt* (1969) and *Monsignor Quixote* (1982) are ventures into comedy. His short stories appeared in *The Basement Room and Other Stories* (1935), *Nineteen Stories* (1947), *Twenty-One Stories* (1954), *May We Borrow Your Husband?* (1967) and *The Last Word* (1990).

Two travel books – *Journey without Maps* (1936), about Liberia, and *The Lawless Roads* (1939), about the visit to Mexico which also prompted *The Power and the Glory* – stand out from the mass of his other work. Particularly memorable, too, is the screenplay for Carol Reed's *The Third Man* (1949). *A Sort of Life* (1971) and *Ways of Escape* (1980) are autobiographical.

Greene, Robert See *EUPHUES*.

Greenwood, Walter 1903–74 English. His first novel and only commercial success was *Love on the Dole* (1933), about the misfortunes of a Lancashire family, the Hardcastles, during the Depression. It was dramatized (1934) and filmed (1941). *There was a Time* (1967) is his autobiography.

Grenville, Kate (Catherine Elizabeth) 1950– Australian. *Bearded Ladies* (1984), a collection of stories, and *Lilian's Story* (1985), a novel, explore how women have been disadvantaged and manipulated. *Dreamhouse* (1986) uses the structure of a thriller to reveal a woman's misery in a one-sided relationship. *Joan Makes History* (1988) offers a feminist revision of Australian history. *Dark Places* (1994) retells the story of the abused Lilian in the earlier novel from her father's point of view.

Grey, (Pearl) Zane 1872–1939 American. In 60 books, which sold over 15 million copies in his lifetime, he developed the Western novel in the tradition of OWEN WISTER. *Riders of the Purple Sage* (1912), *To the Last Man* (1922), *Nevada* (1928), *Wild Horse Mesa* (1928) and *Code of the West* (1934) present the West as a moral landscape which destroys or redeems characters according to their response to its violent code. Over 100 films were based on his stories.

Griffin, Gerald 1803–40 Irish. The fame of his 'true-life' crime novel, *The Collegians* (1829), was eclipsed by Dion Boucicault, who dramatized it as *The Colleen Bawn* (1860). In it, a husband plots to kill his wife so that he can marry an heiress, but is frustrated by a comic vagabond. The story also inspired an opera, *The Lily of Killarney* (1863), by Julius Benedict.

Grossmith, George 1847–1912 and GROSSMITH, WEEDON 1854–1919 English. They were joint authors of a comic masterpiece, *THE DIARY OF A NOBODY* (1892), which Weedon also illustrated. George started his career as a police court reporter for *The Times*, Weedon as an artist. Both later became actors, George creating many of the most famous baritone *buffo* roles in Gilbert and Sullivan's Savoy Operas. Weedon also wrote a novel, *A Woman with a History* (1896), and several plays, of which the most successful was *The Night of the Party* (1901). George published two volumes of memoirs, *Reminiscences of a Clown* (1888) and *Piano and I* (1910).

Group of Noble Dames, A Ten short stories by THOMAS HARDY, collected in 1891. Largely romantic and melodramatic, they are derived from Dorset local history and set in various mansions and castles. Hardy rewrote and bowdlerized a good deal in gathering them together, without making them more than minor work.

Grove, Frederick Philip 1871–1948 Canadian. Born in Russia and brought up in Europe, he eventually became a teacher in Manitoba. Written despite considerable hardship, *Over Prairie Trails* (1922), *The Turn of the Year* (1923) and the powerful and controversial *Settlers of the Marsh* (1925) established him as Canada's first accomplished exponent of realism. His later works were *A Search for America* (1927), *Our Daily Bread* (1928), *It Needs to be Said* (a volume of essays; 1929), *The Yoke of Life* (1930), *Fruits of the Earth* (1933), *Two Generations* (1939), *The Master of the Mill* (1944) and *Consider Her Ways* (1946). *In Search of Myself* (1946) is an autobiography. 'Felix Powell's Career' and 'The Seasons', which he thought his best work, remained unfinished at his death.

Gryll Grange THOMAS LOVE PEACOCK's last novel, published in 1860–1. The setting is a house party held at the edge of the New Forest. The host, Mr Gryll, personifies the England of the immediate rosy past, as it exists in the minds of those who dislike the present. Taking part in the conversations which make up much of the book are: Dr Opimian, an amiable clergyman; Mr Falconer, a romantic without delusions about reforming mankind; and Miss Ilex, an old maid of real charm.

Guide, The A novel by R. K. NARAYAN, published in 1958 and awarded a SAHITYA AKADEMI prize in

1960. Released after two years in prison, Raju shelters in a deserted shrine and is adopted as a *swami* by a nearby village. His confession of his dubious past fails to shake the villagers' faith, and he is soon obliged to satisfy their spiritual and material needs. By the end, his spurious teachings have further rebounded on him when he is committed to a twelve-day fast in an attempt to bring rain.

Gulliver's Travels A prose satire by Jonathan Swift (1667–1745), poet, pamphleteer and satirist. It was published in 1726 as *Travels into Several Remote Nations of the World, in Four Parts, by Lemuel Gulliver*.

In Book I Lemuel Gulliver, the ship's surgeon who narrates the story, is shipwrecked on the island of Lilliput, where he is taken prisoner by the population, who are only six inches tall. The Emperor and his court offer a physical counterpart to the small-minded attitudes underlying human behaviour, for they are suspicious, deceitful and petty. There are specific satires on contemporary topics such as religious disputes (which end an egg should be opened) and in-fighting at court (rope-dancing). In Book II Gulliver finds himself stranded in Brobdingnag, a kingdom where the gigantic inhabitants are twelve times taller than himself. His own attitudes and pomposity are exposed when, after a series of undignified adventures, he boasts to the King about the marvels of European civilization, such as gunpowder and the judicial system.

Book III, the last to be written, is less unified and has always held least appeal. Gulliver visits Laputa, a flying island where the nobles quite literally have their heads in the clouds. So immersed are they in impractical theories of knowledge that nothing works properly. He visits nearby Lagado and its Academy (a satire on the Royal Society), full of 'projectors' working on outlandish scientific schemes such as breeding sheep with no wool and extracting sunbeams from cucumbers. Gulliver visits Glubbdubrib, the Island of Sorcerers, where famous historical figures are summoned from the past, and meets the terrifying race of immortals, the Struldbruggs, whose fate is to become increasingly decrepit. Book IV is perhaps the most intellectual in concept, describing the country of the Houyhnhnms, coldly rational horse-like creatures who govern their nature dispassionately, and keep in subservience the filthy brutes called Yahoos, in whom Gulliver finds an unwelcome resemblance to himself. The two races represent the extremes of human potential, bestial physicality and remote rationality. Gulliver returns home thoroughly imbalanced, and passes most of his time in the stable, preferring the company of his horse to that of his family.

Gulliver's Travels is a seriously reductive work,

a satire on pride and folly. Gulliver himself is a human ambassador: gullible, snobbish and servile, holding ridiculous yet common opinions. The book is also lastingly funny, the hero's antics arising entertainingly from the bizarre proportions of his various surroundings. This element of the fantastic has maintained the book's appeal for children in many languages.

Gunn, Mrs Aeneas 1870–1961 Australian. Out of her brief exposure to the outback in the Northern Territory she created two popular books, *The Little Black Princess* (1905) and *We of the Never Never* (1908), presenting an idealized picture of Aboriginal life and of relations between the white farmers and the native population.

Gunn, Neil M(iller) 1891–1973 Scottish. A friend of Hugh MacDiarmid, he was a socialist involved in the politics of nationalism. Like many of his novels, *Morning Tide* (1930) and *Highland River* (1937) are set in his native Highlands. *Sun Circle* (1933) deals with the Viking invasion, *Butcher's Broom* (1934) with the Highland Clearances, and *The Silver Darlings* (1941), widely considered his best novel, with the aftermath of the Clearances. After the pastoral idyll of *Young Art and Old Hector* (1942) he responded to the dangers of fascism with *The Green Isle of the Great Deep* (1944), in which Art and Hector find their way to a dystopian world. His later fiction culminates in a more 'metaphysical' vision of existence in *The Well at the World's End* (1951). He also produced essays, short stories, travel writings and an autobiography, *The Atom of Delight* (1956).

Gunny Sack, The A novel by MOYEZ G. VASSANJI, published in 1989. In this chronicle of Indian life in East Africa over four generations, the 'gunny sack' is both a metaphor for the creative imagination and literally the sack of memorabilia bequeathed to the narrator by his great-aunt. Each of the novel's three sections centres on a powerful woman: the great-aunt herself (brought from India for an arranged marriage), the narrator's mother and his great love, the politically active Aminta.

Gurnah, Abdulrazak 1948– Tanzanian. He is now based in Britain. *Paradise* (1994), his finest novel, describes the life of the young Yusif, working off his father's debt with an Arab merchant at the beginning of the century in what is now Tanzania. Gurnah's other novels are *Memory of Departure* (1987), *Pilgrim's Way* (1988), *Dottie* (1990) and *Admiring Silence* (1996), about the chaos of the colonial past and post-colonial present in Zanzibar.

Guy Livingstone A novel by GEORGE ALFRED LAWRENCE, published in 1857. Guy is a true patrician hero, with the virtues and failings of his class: pride, courage, sportsmanship and love of fighting. He protects a weaker boy (the narrator) at school, beats a professional boxer and excels at hunting. He is estranged from his fiancée Constance through the machinations of

Flora; the couple are reconciled only on Constance's deathbed. He dies after a fall in the hunting field.

Guy Mannering A novel by SIR WALTER SCOTT, published in 1815. It is set in the 18th century. The title notwithstanding, it tells the story of Harry Bertram, dispossessed of his estate of Ellangowan by the lawyer Glossin. Serving with the army in India, he falls in love with Julia, the daughter of his colonel, Guy Mannering. A mis- understanding between the two men leads to a duel in which Harry is left for dead. On his journey to Ellangowan he meets the Lowland farmer Dandy Dinmont and the gypsy Meg Merrilies, who help frustrate Glossin's murderous schemes. The novel ends happily with Harry regaining his inheritance and Guy Mannering's good opinion, thus leaving the way clear for his marriage to Julia.

H

Hadrian the Seventh See ROLFE, FREDERICK WILLIAM.

Haggard, Sir Henry Rider 1856-1925 English. Born into the Norfolk squirearchy, he joined the colonial service as personal aide to Sir Henry Bulwer, the designated Lieutenant-Governor of Natal. His two periods of residence in South Africa (1875-9 and 1880-1) convinced him of British imperial responsibility. He was distracted from his study of the law by the runaway success of KING SOLOMON'S MINES (1885), *ALLAN QUATERMAIN* (1887) and *SHE: A History of Adventure* (1887). They established him as co-founder, with ROBERT LOUIS STEVENSON, of a new 'school of romance' which was praised as a healthy antidote to analytic fiction and NATURALISM. Haggard's fascination with Zulu culture continued in *Nada the Lily* (1892) and a trilogy, *Marie* (1912), *Child of Storm* (1913) and *Finished* (1917). By no means simply paternalist or racist, his versions of the 'primitive' draw on a considerable knowledge of history, tradition and mythographic theory, probably encouraged by his friendship with Andrew Lang, with whom he collaborated in *The World's Desire* (1890).

Apart from his African romances, his best works are *Eric Brighteyes* (1891), a recreation of the spirit of the Icelandic sagas, and *Montezuma's Daughter* (1893), a version of Cortes's conquest of Mexico. Haggard's experience farming his wife's Norfolk estate prompted *A Farmer's Year* (1899) and, more importantly, *Rural England* (1902), a survey of agricultural decline which brought him into contact with THOMAS HARDY.

Hailey, Arthur See GENRE FICTION.

Hajji Baba of Ispahan, The Adventures of See MORIER, JAMES JUSTINIAN.

Hale, Sarah 1788-1879 American. She edited *The Ladies' Magazine* in 1828-37 and *Godey's Lady's Book* for the next 40 years. Her massive *Women's Record* (1853; expanded 1855 and 1870) details the achievements of over 1500 women. By no means a radical feminist, she was a forceful advocate of education for women, as well as of child welfare. Her novel *Northwood: A Tale of New England* (1827) attacked slavery. Her short stories were collected in *Sketches of American Character* (1829).

Haley, Russell 1934- New Zealand. After publishing two volumes of poetry he turned to fiction with a collection of stories, *The Sauna Bath Mysteries* (1978), which was one of the earliest examples of POST-MODERNISM in New Zealand writing. He has continued in this mode in *Real Illusions* (1985) and *The Transfer Station* (1989), with nine linked stories reflecting on the meaning of death, and in two novels, *The Settlement* (1986) and *Beside Myself* (1990).

Haliburton, Thomas Chandler 1796-1865 Canadian. His 'Sam Slick' papers, observations by a shrewd itinerant clockmaker, were collected as *The Clockmaker: or, the Sayings and Doings of Samuel Slick* (1837) and *The Attaché: or, Sam Slick in England* (1843-4). They influenced the American homespun philosophy and frontier humour practised by Josh Billings, ARTEMUS WARD and MARK TWAIN. Among other titles are *The Letter Bag of the Great Western: or, Life in a Steamer* (1840) and *The Old Judge: or, Life in a Colony* (1849).

Hall [née Fielding], Anna Maria 1800-81 Irish. Her most successful works were delicate and humorous portraits of Irish life, among them *Sketches of Irish Character* (1829), *Lights and Shadows of Irish Life* (1838), *Marian* (1839) and *The White Boy* (1845).

Hall, (Marguerite) Radclyffe 1886-1943 English. She is chiefly known for her novel, *The Well of Loneliness* (1928), a sympathetic study of lesbianism which was successfully prosecuted for obscenity. It has since been frequently reprinted. Later works include *The Master of the House* (1932), *The Sixth Beatitude* (1936) and a volume of short stories, *Miss Ogilvie Finds Herself* (1934).

Hall, Rodney 1935- Australian. His novels include: *The Ship on the Coin* (1972), satirizing the American way of life; *A Place Among the People* (1975) and *Just Relations* (1982), satirizing small-town Australia; *Kisses of the Enemy* (1987), about a future Australia dominated by America; and *Captivity Captive* (1988), *The Second Bridegroom* (1991) and *The Grisly Wife* (1993), a trilogy spanning the first century of settlement in north-eastern Australia. *Just Relations* and *The Grisly Wife* both won the MILES FRANKLIN AWARD. Since *Penniless Till Doomsday* (1962), his poetry has included *Selected Poems* (1975), *Black Bagatelles* (1978) and *The Most Beautiful World* (1981).

Halper, Albert 1904-84 American. His fiction takes working-class life as its subject, and adopts an increasingly radical stance. It includes: *Union Square* (1933); *On the Shore* (1934); *The Foundry* (1934), about electrotype workers in Chicago just before the 1929 crash; *The Chute* (1937), about workers in a mail-order house; *Sons of the Fathers* (1940), about a Jewish immigrant; *The Little People* (1942), short stories; *Only an Inch from Glory* (1943); *The Golden Watch* (1953), *Atlantic Avenue* (1956), about Brooklyn and the New York waterfront; and *The Fourth Horseman of Miami Beach* (1966). *Goodbye, Union Square* (1970) is Halper's memoir of the 1930s.

Hamilton, Cicely See SCIENCE FICTION.

Hamilton, Mary Agnes [née Adamson] 1884–1962 English. Her abundant writings, which include studies of the ancient world, historical figures and Labour politicians, reveal her keen sense of the significance and workings of gender in private and political life. The same approach to militarism, nationalism, employment legislation, women's education and family life underpins much of her fiction: *Dead Yesterdays* (1916), for example, explores men and women's different attitudes to war, whose destructive aftermath informs *Special Providence* (1930). She was Labour MP for Blackburn in 1929–31 and a Governor of the BBC in 1933–7. Her remarkably active life is recorded in *Remembering My Good Friends* (1944) and *Up-hill All the Way* (1953).

Hamilton, (Anthony Walter) Patrick 1904–62 English. His particular gift was for portraying the seedier Bohemian quarters of London, where lonely and desperate lives are lived out in boarding-houses and pubs. This vision, influenced both by GEORGE GISSING and Marxism, grows increasingly bleak in a succession of novels: *Craven House* (1926); *Twenty Thousand Streets Under the Sky* (1935), a trilogy consisting of *The Midnight Bell* (1929), *The Siege of Pleasure* (1932) and *The Plains of Cement* (1934); and his two masterpieces, *Hangover Square* (1941) and *The Slaves of Solitude* (1947). At the end of a career curtailed by heavy drinking, he also produced three novels about an amoral villain, Ernest Ralph Gorse, modelled on the murderer Neville Heath: *The West Pier* (1951), *Mr Stimpson and Mr Gorse* (1953) and *Unknown Assailant* (1955). Though he is now most admired for his fiction, Hamilton also wrote plays, including *Rope* (1929), based on the Leopold and Loeb murder case in the USA, and *Gaslight* (1939), a pastiche of Victorian melodrama. Both were successfully filmed, *Gaslight* in a British version in 1940 and George Cukor's American version in 1944, and *Rope* by Alfred Hitchcock in 1948.

Hamilton, Thomas 1789–1842 Scottish. The younger brother of the philosopher Sir William Hamilton (1788–1856), he wrote *Cyril Thornton* (1827), a popular novel about university and military life.

Hamilton-Paterson, James 1941– English. He had already published poetry, travel writing and works of history and natural history before turning to fiction displaying an attractive blend of humour, erudition and scepticism. *Gerontius* (1989; WHITBREAD AWARD for First Novel), was based on a little-known journey to the Amazon by the composer Elgar in 1923. It has been followed by: *The Bell-Boy* (1990); *Griefwork* (1993), in which the curator of a palm house in a botanical garden struggles to preserve his vulnerable exotic plants; and *Ghosts of Manila* (1994), reflecting his intimate knowledge of the Philippines.

The View from the Dog (1986) and *The Music* (1995) are volumes of short stories.

Hammett, (Samuel) Dashiell 1894–1961 American. His experience working as an investigator for the Pinkerton Agency in San Francisco served him well when he turned to writing DETECTIVE FICTION. The short stories published in *Black Mask*, the most influential of the 'pulp' mystery magazines, were later collected in *The Adventures of Sam Spade* (1944), *The Creeping Siamese and Other Stories* (1950) and *The Continental Op* (1974). His novels are *Red Harvest* (1929), *The Dain Curse* (1929), *The Maltese Falcon* (1930), *The Glass Key* (1931), *The Thin Man* (1934) and an unfinished autobiographical novel, *Tulip*, included in a selection from his work, *The Big Knockover* (1966), by his longtime companion Lilian Hellman. This handful of work, essentially complete when he was 40, helped to transform detective fiction by establishing a 'hard-boiled' style in defiance of the genteel English approach: tough characters, violent action and fast-moving plots, described in unadorned prose.

Hammick, Georgina 1939– English. She published poetry before coming comparatively late to fiction with *People for Lunch* (1987) and *Spoilt* (1992), collections of stories which maintain a tense balance between comedy and menace. In her first novel, *The Arizona Game* (1996), the adult narrator tries to make sense of a fractured childhood. *The Virago Book of Love and Loss* (1992) presents a personal selection of other women writers' stories.

Hanagan, Eva Helen (Ross) 1923– Scottish. Women and girls inhabiting apparently serene landscapes but facing difficult challenges are at the heart of her tightly constructed and lucid novels. They include *In Thrall* (1977), *Playmates* (1978), *The Upas Tree* (1979), *Holding On* (1980) and *A Knock at the Door* (1982), about the effects of ill-informed intervention on the life of a Holocaust survivor. A long silence was broken with *Alice* (1996), in which a woman grapples with a disturbing mystery surrounding her dead aunt.

Hand of Ethelberta, The: A Comedy in Chapters A novel by THOMAS HARDY, published in 1876. His only venture into social comedy, it is among the least read of his works. Despite being a butler's daughter, Ethelberta Chickerel marries the son and heir of Sir Ralph and Lady Petherwin. When he dies on the honeymoon, she turns to making her living as a 'Professed Story-Teller'. Three suitors pay her court: the painter Eustace Lovell, Alfred Neigh and the elderly Lord Mountclere, whom she marries. An earlier suitor, the organist Christopher Julian, marries her sister Picotee.

Handful of Dust, A A novel by EVELYN WAUGH, published in 1934. Tony Last is the proud owner of a Victorian gothic country house, Hetton. His wife, Lady Brenda, becomes infatuated with a young socialite, John Beaver, and deserts Tony after their son, John Andrew, is killed in a hunting accident. Refusing to grant her a divorce, Tony departs for an extended trip to Brazil and accompanies a casual acquaintance, Dr Messinger, on a disastrous journey up the Amazon. He is rescued from near-death by a mad recluse, Mr Todd, who forces him to become his 'companion' and spend his life reading aloud the works of Dickens. In England Tony is reported dead and Brenda marries a politician, Jock Grant-Menzies. In an 'Alternative Ending' Tony returns to be greeted by a repentant Brenda.

Handley Cross A novel by R. S. SURTEES, first published in book form in 1843; an expanded version (1854) was illustrated by John Leech. It continues the adventures of John Jorrocks, the sporting grocer who appeared in *JORROCKS'S JAUNTS AND JOLLITIES* (1838) and returns in *HILLINGDON HALL* (1845). Here his position as master of the Handley Cross foxhounds provides the excuse for hunting scenes which Surtees describes with his usual dash and authenticity. Jorrocks's public lectures on hunting, though delivered in the broadest cockney, are replete with technical knowledge and common sense.

Handmaid's Tale, The A novel by MARGARET ATWOOD, published in 1986. Offred, the narrator, is a handmaid in the household of a Commander of the late 20th-century theocratic state of Gilead, which reduces women's lives to utilitarian functions and assigns handmaids the role of bearing children for a society brought to the brink of extinction by pollution. Offred eventually escapes to an indeterminate future, and the novel ends with an academic paper produced 200 years later, which discusses her story in a chillingly detached manner. The particular form of patriarchal authoritarianism attacked is the right-wing evangelism of the USA in the 1980s, but this classic of dystopian fiction can be read as a feminist counterpart of ALDOUS HUXLEY's *BRAVE NEW WORLD* or GEORGE ORWELL's *NINETEEN EIGHTY-FOUR*.

Handy Andy: *A Tale of Irish Life* A comic novel by SAMUEL LOVER, published in 1842. It tells of Andy Rooney, the hopelessly inefficient servant of Squire Egan, who proves to be the heir of Lord Scatterbrain.

Hannay, James 1827–73 English. After being dismissed from the navy, he contributed to *Punch*, edited the Edinburgh *Evening Courant* and published two novels of naval life, *Singleton Fontenoy* (1850) and *Eustace Conyers* (1855).

Hannay, James Owen See BIRMINGHAM, GEORGE A.

Hanrahan, Barbara 1939–91 Australian. Her paintings hang in the National Gallery of Australia. As a writer, she remains best known for *The Scent of Eucalyptus* (1973), an autobiographical first novel giving an evocative account of an adolescent girl's growth. *Sea-Green* (1974) is another highly personal work and *Kewpie Doll* (1984) an equally poetic sequel to *The Scent of Eucalyptus*. Other novels in her short but prolific career include a group set in the 19th and early 20th centuries: *The Albatross Muff* (1977), *Where the Queens All Strayed* (1978), *The Peach Groves* (1979), *The Frangipani Gardens* (1980) and *Dove* (1982).

Hard Times: *For These Times* A novel by CHARLES DICKENS, serialized in his magazine *Household Words* in 1854. It contrasts Fact, Dickens's name for the coldness and lovelessness he associated with Utilitarianism, and Fancy, which represents the warmth of the imagination.

The fable traces the life of the warm-hearted Sissy Jupe, a circus child deserted by her father and adopted into the household of the fact-ridden Thomas Gradgrind, whose children Tom and Louisa are reared in ignorance of love and affection. Louisa is driven to a miserable marriage with the boastful, wealthy Josiah Bounderby and then almost to an affair with the dandified James Harthouse. Tom descends to thieving and is saved only through Sissy and the circus folk. Of comparable significance is the story of Stephen Blackpool, the honest worker in Bounderby's mill, driven out of the community and suspected in his absence of Tom Gradgrind's crime. He is exonerated only after death.

Hardy, Frank 1917–94 Australian. He achieved notoriety when his muck-raking first novel, *Power Without Glory* (1950), became the subject of a criminal libel suit. *The Hardy Way* (1961) gives his version of these events. Other novels include *The Four-Legged Lottery* (1958), *The Outcasts of Foolgarah* (1971) and the more experimental *But the Dead are Many* (1975), *Who Shot George Kirkland?* (1980) and *The Obsession of Oscar Oswald* (1983). However, Hardy's reputation after *Power Without Glory* depended less on his novels than on his collections of short stories in the 'folk yarn' tradition.

Hardy, Thomas 1840–1928 English. The son of a builder and master mason, he was born in Higher Bockhampton, near Dorchester, a town which remained the centre of his life and became the centre of his fictional WESSEX. A precocious child, he was given a thorough education at the village school and in Dorchester but still remained close to rural culture, playing beside his father in the village band. While apprenticed to the local architect John Hicks in 1856–62 he became a friend of the poet William Barnes, who helped complete his classical education, and the brilliant but unstable Horace Moule, who later committed suicide. During these years he was first exposed to the unsettling influence of Darwin's *Origin of Species* (1859) and the controversial theology of *Essays* *and Reviews* (1860). After a five-year stint (1862–7) working for the architect Arthur Blomfield in London he returned, his health undermined, to Hicks's office and soon afterwards began the lost and partly cannibalized novel, *The Poor Man and the Lady*. GEORGE MEREDITH, then a reader for Chapman and Hall, saw merit in it but advised against publication. While working for the firm of Crickmay in Weymouth, Hardy began a more acceptable novel, DESPERATE REMEDIES (1871). In the same year he met Emma Lavinia Gifford while surveying the church at St Junot in Cornwall. They were married in 1874.

Desperate Remedies launched Hardy on a hard-working career as a novelist, with UNDER THE GREENWOOD TREE (1872), A PAIR OF BLUE EYES (1873) and his first real success, FAR FROM THE MADDING CROWD (1874). During the years when Hardy and his wife led a wandering existence in London, Swanage, Sturminster Newton, London again and then Wimborne he wrote THE HAND OF ETHELBERTA (1876), THE RETURN OF THE NATIVE (1878), THE TRUMPET-MAJOR (1880), A LAODICEAN (1881) and TWO ON A TOWER (1882). THE MAYOR OF CASTERBRIDGE (1886) followed his return to Dorchester. Max Gate, the house he built for himself, remained home for the rest of his life, though he continued to spend a few months in London each year for 'the season'. *Wessex Tales* (1888), A GROUP OF NOBLE DAMES (1891), *Life's Little Ironies* (1894), and a later volume, *A Changed Man and Other Tales* (1913), are short stories. The major novels continued with THE WOODLANDERS (1887), TESS OF THE D'URBERVILLES (1891), THE WELL-BELOVED (1897, but written several years earlier) and JUDE THE OBSCURE (1895).

The increasing pessimism and the handling of sexual relations in *Tess* and *Jude* provoked a storm of controversy which encouraged Hardy to give up novels and return to poetry, which he had always regarded as his first calling. The volumes he published in the last 30 years of his life began with *Wessex Poems and Other Verses* (1898) and *Poems of the Past and Present* (1902). His epic verse-drama, *The Dynasts* (1903–8), was followed by *Time's Laughingstocks and Other Verses* (1909), *Satires of Circumstance, Lyrics and Reveries* (1914), a collection of particular interest for the elegiac 'Poems of 1912–13', written out of remorse and expiatory sadness at the sudden death of Emma Hardy in 1912. The poetry continued with *Moments of Vision and Miscellaneous Verses* (1917), *Late Lyrics and Earlier* (1922), *Human Shows, Far Phantasies, Songs and Trifles* (1925) and the posthumous *Winter Words in Various Moods and Metres* (1928). *The Famous Tragedy of the Queen of Cornwall* (1923) is a verse-drama about Tristram and Iseult.

Increasingly the mantle of the Grand Old Man of English Letters tightened across Hardy's shoulders as distinctions and accolades – the Order of Merit and various honorary degrees – came to him. He continued to live simply in the melancholy twilight of Max Gate, and in 1914 married Florence Emily Dugdale (1879–1937). With her he destroyed many letters, notes and writings of a personal nature, received the inevitable admirers and receded into old age until death came peacefully. *The Early Life of Thomas Hardy, 1840–1891* (1928) and *The Later Years of Thomas Hardy, 1892–1928* (1930), two sometimes misleading volumes which Hardy himself had compiled in his last years, were published under his wife's name.

Harland, Henry 1861–1905 American. Under the pseudonym of Sidney Luska he wrote several realistic novels about Jewish immigrants in New York: *As It was Written: A Jewish Musician's Story* (1885), *Mrs Peixada* (1886), *The Yoke of the Thorah* (1887) and *My Uncle Florimund* (1888). Migrating to Paris in 1889 and to London the following year, he dropped the pseudonym for his later short stories and novels, of which the most successful were *The Cardinal's Snuff Box* (1900) and *My Friend Prospero* (1904). He is best remembered as the first editor of *The Yellow Book*.

Harlem Renaissance A term (like the 'Black Renaissance' or 'New Negro') for the period of cultural activity by black American artists in the 1920s and 1930s. In his introduction to the anthology *The New Negro* (1925), which served as a manifesto, Alain Locke noted a new spirit of 'group expression and self-determination' among black writers, in contrast to the solitary efforts of earlier figures. The Renaissance was also marked by its emphasis on the African heritage of American blacks. Leading writers associated with it include CLAUDE MCKAY, JEAN TOOMER, LANGSTON HUGHES, ZORA NEALE HURSTON, JESSIE R. FAUSET, ARNA BONTEMPS, Countee Cullen and Sterling A. Brown.

Harraden, Beatrice 1864–1936 English. *Ships That Pass in the Night* (1893), set in the Kurhaus at Petershof, a winter resort for consumptive patients, reflects many of her feminist beliefs. *In Varying Moods* (1894) was a collection of short stories written in Sussex, Cannes and Menton. Other titles include *Hilda Strafford* (1897), *The Fowler* (1899), *Katharine Frensham* (1903), *Interplay* (1908), *Youth Calling* (1924) and *Search Will Find It Out* (1928).

Harris, Frank (James Thomas) 1856–1931 Born in Ireland, he lived in the USA before making his career in London. His notoriety as a braggart and liar was epitomized in *My Life and Loves* (1922–7), highly unreliable memoirs of his early life as a precocious intellectual and sexual buccaneer. In the course of his prolific career, largely as journalist and literary editor, he also found time to write plays, popular studies of Shakespeare and untrustworthy biographies of OSCAR WILDE (1916) and GEORGE BERNARD SHAW (1931). Of his fiction, the stories in *Elder Conklin*

(1894) and his novel *The Bomb* (1908) reflect his youthful experiences in the USA. The highly praised title-story of *Montes the Matador* (1900) shows his fascination with Spain. *Great Days* (1914) is a historical novel about the French Revolution. Several of the stories in *Unpath'd Waters* (1913), like his last novel, *Pantopia* (1930), embody his thinking about religion.

Harris, George Washington 1814–69 American. A Tennessee River steamboat captain before he turned to writing, he is best known for *Sut Lovingood: Yarns Spun by a 'Nat'ral Born Durn'd Fool'* (1867), a collection of tall tales and sketches full of Southwestern frontier dialect and humour.

Harris, Joel Chandler 1848–1908 American. He is best known as the creator of the black story-teller, Uncle Remus, and the humanized animals, Br'er Rabbit, Br'er Fox and Br'er Wolf. *Uncle Remus: His Songs and Sayings* (1881) was followed by several other collections: *Nights with Uncle Remus* (1883), *Uncle Remus and His Friends* (1892), *Mr Rabbit at Home* (1895), *The Tar Baby and Other Short Rhymes of Uncle Remus* (1904) and *Uncle Remus and Br'er Rabbit* (1906). They offer traditional black folk-wisdom in what MARK TWAIN considered a flawless duplication of Southern black speech. *On the Plantation* (1892) recounts the childhood experiences in Georgia that inspired much of his work.

Harris, Robert See SCIENCE FICTION and SPY FICTION.

Harris, (Theodore) Wilson 1921– Guyanese. He published two volumes of verse, *Fetish* (1951) and *Eternity to Season* (1954), before moving to London in 1959. He is known particularly for *PALACE OF THE PEACOCK* (1960), later grouped with *The Far Journey of Oudin* (1961), *The Whole Armour* (1962) and *The Secret Ladder* (1963) as *The Guyana Quartet* (1985). Other 'Guyanese' novels, fusing a poetic imagination, wide reading and a passionate response to landscape, include *Heartland* (1964), *The Eye of the Scarecrow* (1965), *The Waiting Room* (1967), *Tumatumari* (1968) and *Ascent to Omai* (1970). Since his volumes of salvaged or imagined pre-Columbian legends, *The Sleepers of Roraima* (1970) and *The Age of the Rainmakers* (1971), he has written novels set in Scotland, South America, Mexico and London: *Black Marsden* (1972), *Companions of the Day and Night* (1975), *Da Silva da Silva's Cultivated Wilderness* with *Genesis of the Clowns* (1977), *The Tree of the Sun* (1978), *The Angel at the Gate* (1982) and his *Carnival* trilogy, *Carnival* (1985), *The Infinite Rehearsal* (1987) and *The Four Banks of the River of Space* (1990). *Resurrection at Sorrow Hill* (1993), an account of a journey up-river into the Guyanese heartland, returns to the physical and psychic terrain of *Palace of the Peacock*. *Jonestown* (1996), another exploration of shifting psychic identities, takes the 1978 People's Temple massacre as its point of departure. Critical writings include *Tradition, the Writer and Society* (1967), *Explora-*

tions (1981), *The Womb of Space: The Cross-Cultural Imagination* (1983) and *The Radical Imagination* (1992).

Harrison, Jim (James Thomas) 1937– American. Preoccupied with natural life, he began as a poet before publishing three novels: *Wolf: A False Memoir* (1971), *A Good Day to Die* (1973) and *Farmer* (1975). The three novellas in *Legends of the Fall* (1979) express his characteristic concern with nature and the environment and the personal search for stability and redemption. Subsequent novels include *Warlock* (1981), *Sundog: The Story of an American Foreman* (1984) and *Dalva* (1988). *The Woman Lit by Fireflies* (1990) and *Julip* (1994) contain novellas and *Just Before Dark* (1991) is a collection of stories.

Harrower, Elizabeth 1928– Australian. Most of her fiction deals with struggles in personal relationships and with conflicting moral issues. *Down in the City* (1957) and *The Long Prospect* (1958) appeared while she was living in Britain. *The Catherine Wheel* (1960), published after her return to Australia, describes the experiences of a young Australian woman in London. The title of *The Watch Tower* (1966) refers to an elegant house in a Sydney suburb which proves an emotional and intellectual prison for the heroine and her sister.

Harry Richmond, The Adventures of A novel by GEORGE MEREDITH, published in 1871. Richmond Roy elopes with the daughter of a wealthy squire, Beltham, who bears him a son, Harry, before his irresponsibility drives her to an early grave. When Roy gets himself accepted at the courts of petty German princes, Harry falls in love with Princess Ottilia and resolves to overcome all obstacles to the impossible marriage. However, Beltham's plans for him are finally realized: he settles in England and marries Janet Ilchester.

Harte, (Francis) Bret(t) 1836–1902 American. He went to California at the age of 18, working as prospector, teacher, Wells Fargo expressman, secretary of the US Mint in San Francisco and journalist. In 1868 he helped to establish *Overland Monthly*, which he edited for its first two-and-a-half years. His own contributions included the stories gathered in *THE LUCK OF ROARING CAMP AND OTHER SKETCHES* (1870). After returning East, he served as US consul in Germany and then in Glasgow, spending his last years in London. His stories are collected in *Mrs Skaggs's Husbands* (1873), *Tales of the Argonauts* (1875), *An Heiress of Red Dog, and Other Sketches* (1878), *A Sappho of Green Springs, and Other Stories* (1891) and *Colonel Starbottle's Client, and Some Other People* (1892). He also published poetry, comic ballads and parodies; several novels, including *Gabriel Conroy* (1876) and *Jeff Briggs's Love Story* (1880); and two plays, *Two Men of Sandy Bar* (1876) and *Ah Sin* (1877), the latter in collaboration with MARK TWAIN.

Hartley, L(eslie) P(oles) 1895–1972 English. He established himself as a leading writer of short stories with many collections, including *Night Fears* (1924), *The Killing Bottle* (1932), *The Travelling Grave* (1951), *The White Wand* (1954) and *Two for the River* (1961). His first novel, *Simonetta Perkins* (1925), was set in Venice, where he spent much of his life. *The Shrimp and the Anemone* (1944), *The Sixth Heaven* (1946) and *Eustace and Hilda* (1947) are a trilogy, indebted to HENRY JAMES and Freud, following the lives of a brother and sister from childhood. Childhood is also a central pre-occupation of *THE GO-BETWEEN* (1953), his best-known novel. Other novels include *A Perfect Woman* (1955), *The Hireling* (1957), *Facial Justice* (1960), *The Brickfield* (1964) and its sequel *The Betrayal* (1966), *Poor Clare* (1968) and *The Love Adept* (1969).

Harvey, Caroline See TROLLOPE, JOANNA.

Hasluck, Nicholas (Paul) 1942– Australian. His first novels, *Quarantine* (1978) and *The Blue Guitar* (1980), were about moral pressures in, respectively, a Middle Eastern quarantine station and the world of pop music. They were followed by: *The Hand That Feeds You* (1982), about corruption in a future Republican Australia; *The Bellarmine Jug* (1984), his best-known novel, about the efforts of a 20th-century historian to track down a document about a 17th-century massacre; *Truant State* (1987), about financial chicanery in Western Australia at the time of secession; *The Country without Music* (1990), about the corrupting effect of an imperialist Australia on imaginary French colonies; and *The Blosseville File* (1992), a discontinuous narrative satirizing contemporary Perth society. *The Hat on the Letter O and Other Stories* (1978) demonstrates the variety of forms in which he works. The poetry in *Anchor and Other Poems* (1976) and *On the Edge* (with William Grono; 1980) is more conservative. He has also published essays, in *Offcuts from a Legal Literary Life* (1993), and a collection of legal stories, *A Grain of Truth* (1994).

Haunted Man and the Ghost's Bargain, The A Christmas story by CHARLES DICKENS, published in 1848 and collected in *CHRISTMAS BOOKS* (1852). An evil phantom visits the sadly reflective Mr Redlaw and makes a compact with him to obliterate the sorrows, wrongs and troubles he has known. In return, Redlaw agrees to transmit this oblivion to others but his influence is baleful upon everyone he encounters. Ultimately, through the goodness embodied in William Swidger's wife Milly, the unhappy man's bargain is terminated.

Hau'ofa, Epeli 1939– Tongan. One of the most distinctive voices in South Pacific literature, he is unusual in his comic treatment of post-colonial themes. The stories in *Tales of the Tikongs* (1983) draw on the Tongan oral tradition of the tall tale to create a fictional world in which contemporary South Pacific society is gently ridiculed. His novel *Kisses in the Nederends* (1987) is a *tour de force* of comic-grotesque realism in which the central character searches for a cure to his ulcerated anus through all the region's problem-solving agencies. Hau'ofa has also written poetry and works of social anthropology.

Hawkes, John (Clendennin Burne) Jr 1925– American. Highly regarded for its experimentation with style, his work examines identity and desire in the post-existentialist age. *The Cannibal* (1949), set in post-war Germany, has been followed by novels using nightmarish surrealism to explore landscapes replete with violence and eroticism: *The Beetle Leg* (1951), *The Goose on the Grave: Two Short Novels* (contains *The Owl*; 1954), *The Lime Twig* (1961), *Second Skin* (1964), *Lunar Landscapes: Stories and Short Novels 1949–63* (1969), *Death, Sleep and the Traveler* (1974), *Travesty* (1976), *The Passion Artist* (1979), *Virginie: Her Two Lives* (1981), *Adventures in the Alaskan Skin Trade* (1985), *Whistlejacket* (1989), *Sweet William: A Memoir of Old Horse* (1993), and *The Frog* (1996). *Humors of Blood and Skin: A John Hawkes Reader* (1984) has an introduction by WILLIAM GASS.

Hawkins, Sir Anthony Hope See HOPE, ANTHONY.

Hawthornden Prize An annual prize for 'the best work of imaginative literature' by a British writer. First awarded in 1919, it has honoured poetry, drama, biography and history as well as fiction. Prize-winning fiction from its early years includes DAVID GARNETT's *Lady into Fox* (1922), HENRY WILLIAMSON's *Tarka the Otter* (1927), Siegfried Sassoon's fictionalized autobiography, *Memoirs of a Fox-Hunting Man* (1928), GRAHAM GREENE's *THE POWER AND THE GLORY* (1940) and *England is My Village* (1941) by John Llewellyn Rhys, whose widow founded the JOHN LLEWELLYN RHYS PRIZE in his memory. Post-war winners include ALAN SILLITOE's *The Loneliness of the Long-Distance Runner* (1959), MICHAEL FRAYN's *The Russian Interpreter* (1966), DAVID LODGE's *Changing Places* (1975), ROBERT NYE's *Falstaff* (1976) and TIMOTHY MO's *Sour Sweet* (1982).

Hawthorne, Nathaniel 1804–64 American. Born in Salem, Massachusetts, into a prominent family whose ancestors were among the earliest settlers of the colony, he was brought up in seclusion by his widowed mother. When he was 11 they moved to Maine, where he attended Bowdoin College. In 1825 he returned to Salem, producing a weak first novel, *Fanshawe* (1828), and the historical and allegorical stories later collected in *Twice-Told Tales* (1837; expanded 1842), exploring the impact of Puritanism on the guilty conscience of New England. He then worked as editor and hack writer for the publisher Samuel Goodrich, and as surveyor for the Boston Custom House, and involved himself in the Brook Farm experiment, before moving with his wife Sophia Peabody to Concord in 1842. Here he wrote *Mosses from an Old Manse* (1846), which contains the story 'Young Goodman Brown'. After serving as customs surveyor at Salem in 1846–9 he finally produced his first significant novel, THE SCARLET LETTER (1850). It was rapidly followed by: THE HOUSE OF THE SEVEN GABLES (1851); The Snow Image and Other Tales (1851), which includes such stories as 'Ethan Brand' and 'My Kinsman Major Molineux'; A Wonder Book (1852), which retells Greek myths for children; THE BLITHEDALE ROMANCE (1852); and Tanglewood Tales (1853).

Hawthorne never equalled such productivity again. In 1853 he was appointed US consul at Liverpool, living in England for four years and in Italy for two. On his return to the USA he published his final novel, THE MARBLE FAUN (1860), and Our Old Home (1863), a book of essays on England. Four unfinished novels eventually appeared as Septimius Felton: or, the Elixir of Life (1872), The Dolliver Romance (1876), Dr Grimshawe's Secret (1882) and The Ancestral Footstep (1883). His wife edited his notebooks as Passages from the American Notebooks (1868), Passages from the English Notebooks (1870) and Passages from the French and Italian Notebooks (1871).

Hay, Ian [Beith, John Hay, Major-General] 1876–1952 English. His light-hearted novels about life in boys' boarding-schools include A Man's Made (1909), A Safety Match (1911), The Middle Watch (1930) and The Housemaster (1936). As well as adapting his own work for the stage, he dramatized stories by his friend P. G. WODE-HOUSE.

Haywood, Eliza c. 1693–1756 English. In a career spanning nearly 40 years she wrote a few unsuccessful plays and collaborated with William Hatchett on Tom Thumb the Great (1733), a comic opera adapted from HENRY FIELDING's Tragedy of Tragedies, edited The Female Spectator, a monthly collection of essays, in 1744–6, and produced many novels. These include: The Life of Mr Duncan Campbell (1720), written in collaboration with DEFOE; Memoirs of a Certain Island Adjacent to Utopia (1725), a ROMAN À CLEF; and The History of Jemmy and Jenny Jessamy (1753), praised in SIR WALTER SCOTT's OLD MORTALITY. Though she consistently asserted her moral purpose, Alexander Pope condemned her as 'the libellous Novelist' and Jonathan Swift as a 'stupid, infamous, scribbling woman'.

Hazard of New Fortunes, A A novel by WILLIAM DEAN HOWELLS, published in 1890. The title refers to Basil March's decision to move his family from Boston to New York and work for Every Other Week, a new magazine financed by Jacob Dryfoos. Dryfoos's son Conrad also works for the magazine, though he really wants to become a minister. He loves Margaret Vance, a young society woman he has met through his charitable work. When Dryfoos learns that Lindau, whom March has hired, is a socialist, he demands that he be sacked. March refuses but Lindau resigns in outrage at having been employed by a strike-breaking capitalist. Conrad is killed by a stray police bullet during a streetcar-workers' strike and Lindau dies later from his injuries. Disheartened, Jacob sells the magazine and takes his family to Europe. Margaret Vance becomes an Episcopalian nun.

Hazzard, Shirley 1931– Australian. For many years employed by the United Nations, she lives in Manhattan but pays frequent visits to Italy, the setting of The Evening of the Holiday (1966) and The Bay of Noon (1970), two early but formally assured works in the tradition of Flaubert and HENRY JAMES. She first achieved recognition for the short stories in Cliffs of Fall (1963). People in Glass Houses (1967), a series of interconnected satirical portraits of people working for a dehumanizing institution, confirmed her stature. Her reputation further increased with The Transit of Venus (1980), an account of the odyssey of two sisters in Australia and England.

He Knew He was Right A novel by ANTHONY TROLLOPE, serialized in 1868–9 and published in volume form in 1869.

Louis Trevelyan marries Emily Rowley but the couple separate because of his unreasonable jealousy of Colonel Osborne. Sure that he is right in his suspicions, Trevelyan hires a private detective to watch Emily and abducts their young son with his help. They go to Italy where Trevelyan declines into complete mental and physical breakdown; Emily persuades him to return to England, where he dies. In one of several sub-plots Emily's sister Nora falls in love with Trevelyan's friend Hugh Stanbury, choosing him in preference to a wealthy aristocratic suitor, Mr Glascock. The novel's interest in the question of women's independence is reflected in the hostile portrait of an American feminist, Wallachia Petrie.

Head, Bessie 1937–86 South African. When Rain Clouds Gather (1968), Maru (1971) and A QUESTION OF POWER (1974) examine lonely people in corporate environments, probing connections between personal morality and political integrity. The Collector of Treasures (1977) retells village tales, Serowe: Village of the Rain Wind (1981) recreates the history of the Bamangwato capital in Botswana from oral tradition, and A Bewitched Crossroad (1984) is a novel about peace and security under the benevolent Bamangwato king, Khama III (1875–1923). Posthumous publications include A Woman Alone: Autobiographical Writings (1990), A Gesture of Belonging: Letters from Bessie Head, 1965–79 (1990) and Tales of Tenderness and Power (1990).

Head, Richard ?1637–?1686 English. He worked first as a bookseller and then as a poorly paid publisher's hack. His most famous work is a licentious PICARESQUE novel, The English Rogue: Described in the Life of Meriton Latroon, A Witty Extravagant (1665), much of it autobiographical. His many other productions include an eccentric comedy of Irish life, *Hic et ubique: or, The Humours of Dublin* (1663).

Headlong Hall THOMAS LOVE PEACOCK's first novel, published in 1816. Like most of his fiction, it is an amiably satiric commentary on both trends in contemporary thought and the quirks of his friends among the Romantics.

The guests debating civilization and progress over Christmas at Squire Headlong's Welsh country house include: Mr Foster, the perfectibilian, who rehearses the rational optimism of Condorcet and WILLIAM GODWIN; Mr Escot, the deteriorationist, a blend of Rousseau, Malthus and the notes to Shelley's *Queen Mab*; Mr Jenkison, the status quo-ite; and the gourmandizing Rev. Doctor Gaster. They are joined by Dr Cranium, the phrenologist, and his daughter Cephalis; Mr Milestone, the landscape gardener; Mr Panscope, the polymath; and assorted musicians, poets and marriageable daughters. In a finely worked comic episode Mr Milestone's criticism of the unimproved gardens causes his host to blow away an offending rock with near-fatal consequences for two guests. The Squire again proves true to his name at the end, when he arranges no fewer than four marriages, including his own.

Heard, Gerald See SCIENCE FICTION.

Hearn, (Patricio) Lafcadio (Tessima Carlos) 1850–1904 Born in Greece of Irish-Greek parentage, and educated in France and England, he emigrated in 1869 to the USA, where his writings included colourful descriptions of Creole life in New Orleans. *Gombo Zhebes* (1885) is a collection of proverbs in French from Louisiana and the West Indies, and *Chita* (1889) a novel set on the Gulf Coast of Louisiana. *Two Years in the French West Indies* (1890) is about his experience of Martinique. In 1890 he went to Japan, becoming a Japanese citizen, adopting the name Yakimo Koizumi and writing *Gleanings in Buddha-Fields* (1897), *In Ghostly Japan* (1899), *A Japanese Miscellany* (1901) and *Japan: An Attempt at Interpretation* (1904).

Hearne, John 1926–94 Jamaican. Articulate, middle-class characters respond generously to calls on their humanity, but with disastrous personal consequences, in *Voices under the Window* (1955), *Stranger at the Gate* (1956) and *The Autumn Equinox* (1959). The latter two novels and *The Faces of Love* (1957) and *Land of the Living* (1961) are about the fictional Caribbean island of Cayuna. *The Sure Salvation* (1981), his finest novel, is set on a slave ship. As John Morris, Hearne wrote thrillers with Morris Cargill.

Heart of Darkness A story by JOSEPH CONRAD, published in the same volume as *Youth* in 1902. It is told mainly by Marlow to his friends on a yacht in the Thames estuary.

Years earlier he had been hired by a European trading company to replace a steamship captain on a great African river (plainly the Congo, though it is unnamed). The Westerners he meets at the trading post and the Central Station are interested only in extracting ivory and do not notice the suffering of the native workers. Marlow is sent upriver to rescue Kurtz, an agent, now seriously ill, whose commercial success is matched by his reputation for idealism. Expecting to meet an apostle of Western civilization, he finds a man who has made himself the natives' god. His depravity is signalled by the human heads which decorate the posts outside his hut. His deathbed cry – 'The horror! The horror!' – intimates a kind of desperate but incommunicable self-knowledge.

Heart of Midlothian, The A novel by SIR WALTER SCOTT, published in 1818 as the second series of *Tales of My Landlord*. The heart of Midlothian is the Tolbooth prison in Edinburgh, focal point of the Porteous Riots of 1736.

Effie Deans, imprisoned in the Tolbooth on a charge of child murder, is sentenced to death when her half-sister Jeanie refuses to lie on her behalf. But Jeanie walks to London and secures a royal pardon for Effie. Robertson, one of the rioters, is revealed as George Staunton, a wild son of good family and the father of Effie's son. He persuades Effie to marry him and, as Lady Staunton, she learns that her son is still alive, left with a band of robbers after being stolen by the crazed Madge Wildfire. Staunton is unwittingly killed by his own son when he tries to rescue him.

Modern readers and critics have usually agreed that *Heart of Midlothian* is the finest of Scott's novels and that Jeanie Deans is his best-realized character. The book is notable, too, for the lyric, 'Proud Maisie', sung by the dying Madge Wildfire.

Heart of the Matter, The A novel by GRAHAM GREENE, published in 1948.

It takes place in West Africa, a harsh physical and moral wilderness, during World War II. Scobie, the deputy commissioner of police, becomes the victim of his compassion for others: first for his unstable wife, Louise, then for a young widow, Helen, with whom he has an affair. He falls into debt, and inadvertently causes the death of his servant Ali. Resolving to commit suicide, a mortal sin in terms of his Catholic creed, he tries to conceal this from his wife by fabricating his diary. His fate is observed throughout by a young intelligence agent, Wilson, who is in love with Louise but acts in his official capacity to uncover Scobie's posthumous deceit.

Heat and Dust A novel by RUTH PRAWER JHABVALA, published in 1975. The unnamed narrator comes to India to learn more about her grandfather's first wife, Olivia, who had left her Anglo-Indian husband to live with a local Nawab. Her account shifts between the past (embodied in surviving letters) and the present (her own journal), with an increasing sense of *déjà vu*.

Heath, Roy (Aubrey Kelvin) 1926– Guyanese, resident in London. Calling himself 'a chronicler of Guyanese life in this century', he has written about slum poverty in *A Man Come Home* (1974), psychotic behaviour in *The Murderer* (1978), middle-class respectability in the trilogy, *From the Heat of the Day* (1979), *One Generation* (1981) and *Genetha* (1981), rural destitution in *Kwaku* (1982), the clash between the values of 'civilization' and the hinterland in *Orealla* (1984). His narrative technique successfully blends social realism with the Amerindian, African and Indian folk legend and myth in Guyanese popular beliefs.

Hébert, Anne 1916– French-Canadian. She was born in Québec and writes in Québécois French (see FRENCH-CANADIAN NOVEL). She accommodates herself to personal tragedy, the French-Canadian sense of exile, and the restrictions imposed by family and the Roman Catholic Church with a series of protracted, solipsistic and confessional internal monologues which contain recurring symbols, flashback and STREAM OF CONSCIOUSNESS. The title-story of *Le Torrent* (1950; translated as *The Torrent*, 1967) and the novel *Kamouraska* (1970; translated, 1974) are among her most notable works. *Kamouraska*, about a murder in 19th-century Québec, began a historical cycle continued in *Les Enfants du sabbat* (1975; translated as *Children of the Black Sabbath*, 1978), *Héloïse* (1980; translated 1982) and *Les Fous de Bassan* (1983; translated as *In the Shadow of the Wind*, 1986).

Heilbrun, Carolyn See DETECTIVE FICTION.

Heinlein, Robert A(nson) 1907–88 American. His understanding of technology and enthusiasm for the conquest of space made him an outstanding pulp writer of SCIENCE FICTION, and one of the first such authors to break into more respectable markets. *The Past through Tomorrow* (1967) gathered the short stories which form a coherent future history, featuring as an 'alternate world' in some of his subsequent work. Novels include a political fantasy, *Double Star* (1956), a future war story, *Starship Troopers* (1959), and, in abrupt change of direction, *Stranger in a Strange Land* (1961), about a messianic hero. *The Cat Who Walked through Walls* (1985) and its sequel *To Sail beyond the Sunset* (1987) are typical examples of his later work.

Heir of Redclyffe, The A novel by CHARLOTTE M. YONGE, published in 1853. Sir Guy Morville secretly pays the debts of his reprobate uncle and cannot explain his supposed extravagance. His malicious cousin Philip accuses him of gambling, which prompts Guy's guardian to banish him from his house and his daughter Amy, whom Guy loves. Guy is later rehabilitated and married to Amy. In Italy they encounter Philip dangerously ill with fever. Guy nurses him back to health but dies from the fever himself. Philip becomes the heir of Redclyffe. The book was immensely successful, passing through 17 editions in 15 years.

Heller, Joseph 1923– American. He is still best known for his anti-war satire, *CATCH-22* (1961). A play, *We Bombed in New Haven* (1968), again drew on his military experience. His subsequent novels are *Something Happened* (1974), *Good as Gold* (1979), *God Knows* (1984), *Picture This* (1988) and *Closing Time* (1994), a belated sequel to *Catch-22*. His experience as a victim of Guillain-Barré syndrome, a debilitating virus, is described in *No Laughing Matter* (with Speed Vogel; 1986). Interviews can be found in *Conversations with Joseph Heller* (1993), edited by Adam J. Sorkin.

Helps, Sir Arthur 1813–75 English. A friend of Queen Victoria, he edited *Speeches and Addresses of the Prince Consort* (1862) and Victoria's *Leaves from the Journal of Our Life in the Highlands* (1868). He also published: three novels, including the popular *Realmah* (1868), a fantastic tale including lightly disguised portraits of contemporary politicians; a book of aphorisms, *Thoughts in the Cloister and the Crowd* (1835); three plays; essays and dialogues; biographies of Columbus and Cortes; and a history of the Spanish conquest of America (1855–61).

Helwig, David 1938– Canadian. The early poems in *Figures in a Landscape* (1967) deal mainly with everyday subjects, but subsequent work has tended towards the sinister and violent. It includes *The Sign of the Gunman* (1969), *The Best Name of Silence* (1972), *Atlantic Crossings* (1974), *A Book of the Hours* (1979) and *Talking Prophet Blues* (1989). *The Glass Knight* (1976), *Jennifer* (1979), *It is Always Summer* (1982) and *A Sound like Laughter* (1983) form a tetralogy of novels set in Kingston. Other novels are *The Day before Tomorrow* (1971), *A Postcard from Rome* (1988), *Old Wars* (1989) and *Of Desire* (1990). *The Streets of Summer* (1969) is a collection of short stories. He has also edited *A Book about Billie* (1972), from interviews with a habitual criminal.

Hemingway, Ernest (Miller) 1898–1961 American. In an adventurous life, lived increasingly in the public eye, he moved from his native Illinois to Kansas, Chicago, Toronto, Europe and, finally, Cuba. His years in Paris, where he was part of the circle including Ezra Pound, GERTRUDE STEIN and FORD MADOX FORD, were his most creative period. It produced two significant collections of stories, *IN OUR TIME* (1925; expanded 1930), partly looking backward to his childhood in the Great Lakes, and *Men without Women* (1927), as well as two significant novels, *THE SUN ALSO RISES* (1926; called *Fiesta* in Britain), and *A FAREWELL TO ARMS* (1929). Their laconic, disillusioned stance captured the mood of the 'lost generation' who had survived World War I, and their spare style helped to refresh

20th-century prose. *Death in the Afternoon* (1932), a study of bullfighting, was followed by: *Winner Take Nothing* (1933), a collection of stories; *Green Hills of Africa* (1935), about big-game hunting; *To Have and Have Not* (1937), a short novel about smuggling in the Key West–Havana region; and *The Fifth Column and the First Forty-Nine Stories* (1938), in which the title-piece is a play about the Spanish Civil War and the stories include 'The Snows of Kilimanjaro'. The Spanish Civil War also provided the subject of *For Whom the Bell Tolls* (1940), an ambitious novel whose title – borrowed from John Donne – implies that the loss of freedom anywhere diminishes it everywhere.

Across the River and into the Trees (1950), his first novel in a decade, was poorly received but *The Old Man and the Sea* (1952), a parable of inner strength and courage, won Hemingway a belated PULITZER PRIZE and helped to earn him the Nobel Prize for Literature in 1954. Consciousness of his literary decline, as well as ill health, contributed to his suicide. Posthumous publications include: a memoir of his years in Paris, *A Moveable Feast* (1964); two novels, *Islands in the Stream* (1970) and *The Garden of Eden* (1986); and *The Dangerous Summer* (1985), about a trip to Spain in 1959.

Henrietta Temple A novel by BENJAMIN DISRAELI, published in 1837. It follows the tangled love affairs of the poor but noble Ferdinand Armine, who proposes to his wealthy cousin, Katherine Grandison, but also becomes engaged to the penniless Henrietta Temple. When his treachery is exposed Henrietta deserts him and agrees to marry Lord Montfort. Katherine, meanwhile, forgives Ferdinand and, with the help of Count Mirabel, disentangles the situation. She marries Lord Montfort and Henrietta, who inherits a fortune, helps Ferdinand.

Henry, O. [Porter, William Sidney] 1862–1910 American. He was a popular and prolific writer of stories characterized by a twist of plot which turns on an ironic or coincidental circumstance and by a surprise ending. They were collected in *Cabbages and Kings* (1904), *The Four Million* (1906), *Heart of the West* (1907), *The Trimmed Lamp* (1907), *The Gentle Grafter* (1908), *The Voice of the City* (1908), *Options* (1909), *Roads of Destiny* (1909), *Whirligigs* (1910), *Strictly Business* (1910) and four posthumous volumes, *Sixes and Sevens* (1911), *Rolling Stones* (1912), *Waifs and Strays* (1917) and *Postscripts* (1923).

His name is remembered in the O. Henry Awards, founded in 1919 and given to the best short stories of each year, gathered in an annual volume, *Prize Stories: The O. Henry Awards*.

Henry Esmond, The History of A novel by WILLIAM MAKEPEACE THACKERAY, published in 1852. Set in the reign of Queen Anne, it is generally considered the finest Victorian example of HISTORICAL FICTION.

Henry Esmond tells the story of his life, though predominantly in the third person. Believing he is the illegitimate son of the 3rd Viscount Castlewood, he spends a lonely childhood in Jacobite circles, lightened when his cousin Francis Esmond inherits the title and comes to live at Castlewood with his young wife Rachel and their two children, Frank and Beatrix. He returns from Cambridge to find the dissolute Lord Mohun a regular guest, gambling with Lord Castlewood and pursuing his wife. The two lords fight a duel in London and Castlewood is killed, leaving a confession which reveals Henry to be the true heir of Castlewood. He burns the document. Imprisoned and rejected by Rachel for his part in the duel, he goes abroad to fight in the War of the Spanish Succession. On visits home he is reconciled with Rachel and falls in love with the proud and beautiful Beatrix. She becomes engaged to the Duke of Hamilton, who fights a duel with Lord Mohun. Both men die. In a last effort to please Beatrix, Henry joins in a plot to restore James Edward Stuart, the Old Pretender, to the throne but it fails because of the Prince's reckless pursuit of Beatrix to Castlewood. Disillusioned with power and worldliness, Esmond marries Rachel and retires with her to a life of domestic tranquillity in Virginia. THE VIRGINIANS continues the story of the Esmond family.

Henty, G(eorge) A(lfred) 1832–1902 English. His experience as a war correspondent in the Crimean War and other conflicts served him well when he started writing adventure stories for boys. Henty produced about 80 novels (sometimes at the rate of three a year), usually concentrating on action-packed episodes from British history. Typical titles include *Under Drake's Flag* (1883), *The Lion of the North* (1885) and his last book, *With the Allies in Pekin* (1904).

Herbert, A(lan) P(atrick) 1890–1971 English. His experiences in World War I resulted in two volumes of poetry (1916 and 1918) and a novel, *The Secret Battle* (1919). He joined the staff of *Punch* in 1924. His mock law reports were collected as *Misleading Cases in the Common Law* (1929). *Holy Deadlock* (1934), a novel, exposed the need for reform of the divorce law, one of several campaigns he undertook as Independent MP for Oxford University (1935–50). The battle over his Marriage Bill was related in *The Ayes Have It* (1937). *Independent Member* (1950) described his years in Parliament. His most popular novel, *The Water Gipsies* (1930), reflected his long-standing love for the English waterways. He also wrote libretti for several successful musicals, including *Riverside Nights* (1926), *Tantivy Towers* (1930) and *Bless the Bride* (1947). *APH: His Life and Times*, his autobiography, appeared in 1970.

Herbert, Frank 1920–86 American. A writer of SCIENCE FICTION, he caught the mood of the day with the intense ecological mysticism of his epic novel *Dune* (1965), describing the advent of a messiah-figure in a desert world. Five sequels were added. *The Green Brain* (1966) and *Hellstrom's Hive* (1973) developed his interest in ecology. His fascination with religion continued in *The God Makers* (1972) as well as *The Jesus Incident* (1979), *The Lazarus Effect* (1983) and *The Ascension Factor* (1988), the sequels which he and Bill Ransom added to his solo novel *Destination: Void* (1966).

Herbert, (Alfred Francis) Xavier 1901–84 Australian. His best-known work is *Capricornia* (1938), a sprawling chronicle of Aborigines and white men set in the Northern outback. Other novels are *Seven Emus* (1958) and *Soldiers' Women* (1960). In *Poor Fellow My Country* (1975), which won the MILES FRANKLIN AWARD, he returned to the outback with a saga notable for passages dealing with Aboriginal life. He is also the author of short stories, in *Larger Than Life* (1963), and an autobiography, *Disturbing Element* (1963).

Herbst, Josephine (Frey) 1897–1969 American. Like many of her generation, she aligned herself with the political left. *Pity is Not Enough* (1933), *The Executioner Waits* (1934) and *Rope of Gold* (1939) form a trilogy about the decay of capitalism and the failure of a revolutionary movement to bring about the new Communist social order it seeks. Other novels include *Nothing is Sacred* (1928), *Money for Love* (1929), *Satan's Sergeants* (1941) and *Somewhere the Tempest Fell* (1947).

Hermsprong See BAGE, ROBERT.

Herr, Michael 1940– American. His best-known book, *Dispatches* (1978), is a vivid and shocking account of the Vietnam War which influenced a whole generation of Hollywood films about Vietnam, notably Coppola's *Apocalypse Now* (1979), for which he wrote the narration, and Stanley Kubrick's *Full Metal Jacket* (1987), which he co-wrote with Kubrick and Gustave Hasford. *Walter Winchell* (1991) is a novel in the form of a screenplay.

Herrick, Robert 1868–1938 American. Many of his novels depict men who find that worldly success leaves them unfulfilled, though Van Harrington, the hero of his best-known novel, *Memoirs of an American Citizen* (1905), makes a fortune and wins a seat in the Senate without experiencing regret. *The Man Who Wins* (1897), his first novel, and *Web of Life* (1900) are about doctors, and *The Common Lot* (1904) is about an architect; *The Real World* (1901; republished as *Jock O'Dreams*, 1908), *A Life for a Life* (1910) and *Waste* (1924) tell the stories of business executives. Herrick also published short stories and *Sometime* (1933), a satirical Utopian novel.

Hersey, John (Richard) 1914–73 American. A war reporter whose *Hiroshima* (1946) described the fate of six survivors of the A-Bomb attack in 1945, Hersey often tackled subjects of similar magnitude and adopted a similar approach in his fiction. *A Bell for Adano* (1944; PULITZER PRIZE)

deals with the American liberation of Sicily in 1943 and *The Wall* (1950) with the Jews of the Warsaw ghetto in 1939–43. Less ambitiously, but with greater depth of meaning, *The War Lover* (1959) studies an American bomber crew based in Britain. Other novels include *The Child Buyer* (1960), denouncing the American educational system, and *White Lotus* (1965), a parable of race relations.

Herzog A novel by SAUL BELLOW, published in 1964. Moses Herzog, a 47-year-old scholar, undergoes an emotional, intellectual and moral crisis. From his summer home in the Berkshire Mountains he writes letters, in his head or on paper, to friends, relatives, his psychiatrist, politicians, philosophers (such as Heidegger and Nietzsche), the public and even God. Flashbacks provide the reader with information about Herzog's relations with his family, his two ex-wives (Daisy and Madeleine), his Japanese mistress Sono, and his current lover, Ramona. A trip to Chicago, to avenge himself on Madeleine and her lover, Valentine Gersbach, ends in humiliation. At the end, he rejects his brother's suggestion that he go into a mental hospital, plans for the future and feels relative peace.

Hewett, Dorothy (Coade) 1923– Australian. For many years a member of the Communist Party, she drew on her experience of factory work in her novel, *Bobbin' Up* (1959). Her second novel, *The Toucher*, appeared in 1993. In the interval she concentrated on the theatre, producing mainly expressionistic works which feature music and poetry. They include *This Old Man Comes Rolling Home* (1967), *The Chapel Perilous* (1971), *Bon Bons and Roses for Dolly* (1972), *The Tatty Hollow Story* (1974), *Pandora's Cross* (1978), *The Man from Muckinupin* (1979) and *The Fields of Heaven* (1982). *Collected Poems* appeared in 1991. Structural weaknesses in most of her writing are overridden by a powerful Rabelaisian personality which is fully revealed in *Wild Card: An Autobiography* (1990).

Hewlett, Maurice (Henry) 1861–1923 English. *The Forest Lovers* (1898), a medieval romance which became an immediate success, was followed by *Richard Yea and Nay* (1900) and *The Queen's Quair* (1904). A trilogy of modern life, *Halfway House* (1908), *Open Country* (1909) and *Rest Harrow* (1910), centres on John Maxwell Senhouse, a gentle itinerant scholar. *The Song of the Plow* (1916) is a poem considering the agricultural labourer's lot.

Heyer, Georgette See HISTORICAL FICTION.

Hiaasen, Carl 1953– American. He turned from journalism to fiction with thrillers written in collaboration with William Montalbano: *Trap Line* (1981), *Powder Burn* (1982) and *Death in China* (1984). His solo work has increasingly shed its link with DETECTIVE FICTION in favour of outrageous comedy. The real subject of *Tourist Sea-*

son (1986), *Double Whammy* (1988), *Skin Tight* (1989), *Native Tongue* (1991), *Strip Tease* (1993) and *Stormy Weather* (1995) is the tackiness and sleaze of Hiaasen's native Florida, which he regards with simultaneous fascination and disgust. The recurrent appearances of Clinton Tyree ('Skink'), former governor of the state turned wild man of the swamps, signal Hiaasen's preoccupation with damage to the environment.

Hichens, Robert (Smythe) 1864–1950 English. None of the 66 books he went on to publish made as great an impact as his first novel, *The Green Carnation* (1894). An amiable ROMAN À CLEF, in which OSCAR WILDE appears as Esmé Amarinth and Lord Alfred Douglas as Lord Reginald Hastings, it first appeared anonymously. Some readers mistakenly attributed it to the poet Alfred Austin, MARIE CORELLI or Wilde himself, though Wilde and Douglas suspected ADA LEVERSON of being the author. The slight plot, which has Lord Reggie toying with the idea of marriage to Lady Locke but offering a green carnation to her son, is less memorable than the cunning parody of Wilde's style.

Higgins, George V. See DETECTIVE FICTION.

High Wind in Jamaica, A See HUGHES, RICHARD.

Highland Widow, The See CHRONICLES OF THE CANONGATE.

Highsmith, Patricia 1921–95 American. Born in Texas and brought up in New York, she lived alternately in the USA and Europe. The ingenious symmetry of her first novel, *Strangers on a Train* (1950), encouraged reviewers to label her work DETECTIVE FICTION, which did not help it find its best audience. Her real preoccupation is with guilt, unease and the refuges offered by obsession and fantasy. The last theme marks *The Cry of the Owl* (1962), *The Glass Cell* (1964), *The Story-Teller* (1965; as *A Suspension of Mercy* in the UK), *The Tremor of Forgery* (1969) and, outstanding among her later work, *Edith's Diary* (1977). Her unjudging authorial stance generates irony and black comedy in several collections of short stories and the novels about the likeable psychopath Tom Ripley: *The Talented Mr Ripley* (1955), *Ripley under Ground* (1970), *Ripley's Game* (1974), *The Boy Who Followed Ripley* (1980) and *Ripley under Water* (1991).

Highwater, Jamake 1952– Native American. Descended from the Blackfeet and Cherokee tribes, he is probably best known for his cycle tracing the adventures of Sitko Ghost Horse as he searches for his place in the world: *Legend Days* (1984), *The Ceremony of Innocence* (1985), *Eyes of Darkness* (1985), *I Wear the Morning Star* (1986) and *Kill Hole* (1992). His other novels includes *Anpao: An American Indian Odyssey* (1977), *Journey to the Sky: A Novel about the True Adventures of Two Men in Search of the Lost Maya Kingdom* (1978), *The Sun. He Dies: A Novel about the End of the Aztec World* (1980) and *Dark Legend* (1994). He has also published a volume of poetry, *Moonsong Lullaby*

(1981), and many studies of Native American culture and folklore.

Hijuelos, Oscar 1951– Cuban-American. His first novel, *Our House in the Last World* (1983), records the fortunes of the Santinio family in New York after the death of its patriarch. *The Mambo Kings Play Songs of Love* (1989), winner of a PULITZER PRIZE and his most accomplished work, traces the fortunes of two brothers, Cesar and Nestor Castillo, who ride the 1950s mambo craze to instant fame but fall quickly into obscurity. Its experimentation with point of view was continued in *The Fourteen Sisters of Emilio Montez O'Brien* (1993), about several generations of women in a Cuban-Irish family in Pennsylvania. *Mr Ives' Christmas* (1995), in which the protagonist faces the season fraught with memories of his most hopeful and most discouraging experiences, is a work of abundant humanity.

Hill, Reginald See DETECTIVE FICTION.

Hill, Susan 1942– English. Her work treats loneliness with psychological precision and narrative composure: *In the Springtime of the Year* (1974) explores a woman's bereavement; *A Change for the Better* (1969) depicts a group of damaged, isolated people; and *I'm the King of the Castle* (1970), winner of a SOMERSET MAUGHAM AWARD and still probably her best-known book, exposes the brutality latent in childhood innocence. Several years' self-imposed literary silence were broken by: *The Woman in Black* (1983) and *The Mist in the Mirror* (1992), both pseudo-Victorian ghost stories; *Air and Angels* (1991); and *Mrs de Winter* (1993), a continuation of DAPHNE DU MAURIER's *Rebecca*.

Hillingdon Hall A novel by R. S. SURTEES, published in volume form in 1845. The third in the Jorrocks trilogy begun with *JORROCKS'S JAUNTS AND JOLLITIES* and *HANDLEY CROSS*, it deals with his life in retirement. He becomes a JP and we leave him when he has just been elected to Parliament; the appalling Mrs Jorrocks is *grande dame* of the village.

Hilton, James 1900–54 English. He made his name with *Goodbye, Mr Chips* (1934), a sentimental tale about an English public school master, and *Lost Horizon* (1933), which described 'Shangri-La', an imaginary land where the inhabitants are liberated from the stresses of normal life. The name has since been used for any idyllic retreat from the world. Using the pseudonym of Glen Trevor, Hilton also contributed to DETECTIVE FICTION with *Murder at School* (1931), republished under his own name as *Was It Murder?*.

Himes, Chester (Bomar) 1909–84 African-American. He began writing while serving a sentence in the Ohio State Penitentiary. His early work includes: *If He Hollers Let Him Go* (1945), about racial conflict in Los Angeles defence plants during World War II; *Lonely Crusade* (1947), about racial discrimination and violence in the wartime labour unions of California; and *Cast the First Stone* (1952), based on his prison experiences. Himes found his true metier with richly detailed, extravagantly plotted DETECTIVE FICTION, set in Harlem and usually following the exploits of two policemen, Coffin Ed Johnson and Grave Digger Jones. Written while he was living in France, they won him a substantial reputation there before being noticed in his home country. The first, *For Love of Imabelle* (1957), later retitled *A Rage in Harlem*, originally appeared as *La Reine des pommes*; its successors include *The Real Cool Killers* (1959), *All Shot Up* (1960), *Cotton Comes to Harlem* (1965), *The Heat's On* (1966), *Blind Man with a Pistol* (1969).

His Natural Life A novel by MARCUS CLARKE, serialized in 1870–2 and revised and shortened in 1874. A longer title, *For the Term of His Natural Life*, was first used in 1885, four years after Clarke's death.

In the original version Rufus Dawes is wrongly convicted of murder and transported to the Norfolk Island settlement in Australia. His cousin Maurice Frere, the sadistic commandant, marries and destroys Dora, whom Dawes has loved since she was a child. After 30 years of suffering Dawes clears his name and is reunited with his wife. Dorcas, the child of Dora and Frere, marries his upright nephew Arthur Devine. The revised version shortens the prologue explaining Dawes's sentence, changes Dora's name to Sylvia, and ends as Dawes dies reunited with her while escaping from Norfolk Island.

historical fiction Fiction set in a period of the past, whether recent or distant, realized with some degree of attention to the atmosphere and details which differentiate it from the present. Customarily, though not invariably, historical novels mingle real events (such as a war or revolution) and real public figures (a king or queen, a political or military leader) with fictional characters and events. Often they narrate incidents in the life of a protagonist which involve him or her, however peripherally, with history in the making.

For most practical purposes the history of the form begins in the early 19th century with SIR WALTER SCOTT. It is true that, before him, novelists who did not choose to aim at fidelity to contemporary life had already begun to abandon the deliberately unspecific settings – unspecific in place as well as time – which the romance and the fable had preferred. DANIEL DEFOE's *A JOURNAL OF THE PLAGUE YEAR* (1722) is a striking early instance of a novel which mingles documentary fact with invention to recreate a historical event which had taken place some 60 years earlier. And in the case of a minor but popular novelist like JANE PORTER, who wrote about William Wallace and Robert Bruce in *The Scottish Chiefs* (1810), Scott could find a pertinent model.

Yet nothing matches his 'Waverley' novels in the magnitude of their achievement or their influence. Books like *WAVERLEY* (1814), *ROB ROY* (1817) and *IVANHOE* (1819), made available to future novelists large reaches of Scottish history, particularly the period surrounding the Jacobite rebellions, as well as medieval English history. In doing so, they also made history itself available.

Scott approached the past with a scholar's respect for accuracy and an antiquarian's love of picturesque detail. He set a standard for subsequent historical novelists, who have accepted that they need to come to their subject equipped with a good deal of solid information. He was also fertile in showing how historical fact might be integrated with invention. His custom of relegating major historical figures to brief, though crucial, walk-on appearances, for example, and his custom of making major historical events function as rites of passage or moments of self-discovery in the lives of his protagonists would grow into durable conventions.

Such tributes to the resources of his craft, however, frequently overlook the seriousness of his underlying purpose. That lay in seeing the past not just as linked to the present by the feelings common to people of whatever time and place, which is how preceding generations had viewed it. To him the past was also different, shaped by its own specific circumstances, customs, beliefs, dilemmas and passions. To convey its remoteness as well as its familiarity, to see its relation to the present in terms of change as well as continuity: that effort, already central to the agenda of Romanticism, would remain central to endeavour in virtually all the arts and the academic disciplines throughout the 19th century. Scott's example guaranteed that historical fiction would play a major part in the inquiry.

The names of EDWARD BULWER LYTTON, CHARLES KINGSLEY and CHARLES READE head the list of 19th-century writers who regularly wrote historical novels, or contributed memorable examples, but they fall a long way short of completing it. Indeed, the list of those who did not attempt historical fiction would be a good deal shorter, and it would not include any of the century's acknowledged major writers. WILLIAM MAKEPEACE THACKERAY published *THE HISTORY OF HENRY ESMOND* (1852), set during the reign of Queen Anne, and DICKENS *A TALE OF TWO CITIES* (1859), set during the French Revolution. GEORGE ELIOT published *ROMOLA* (1863), set in Renaissance Florence, and THOMAS HARDY *THE TRUMPET-MAJOR* (1880), set during the Napoleonic Wars. The periods which they and other Victorians chose to write about indicate the particular contemporary issues for which they wished to find comparison and contrast: the Roman Empire for the birth of Christianity or the rise and fall of empire, the Reformation and Elizabethan England for the rise of Protestantism and the British nation state, the 18th century for society before the Industrial Revolution, the French Revolution for social unrest, and so forth.

All the novels listed above are among their creator's most carefully meditated, as well as their most carefully researched, work. Yet none (unless it be Thackeray's *Henry Esmond*) is among their best. The sheer weight of their purpose – let alone the accumulated information they feel obliged to offer the reader – leaves them worthy but lifeless. That is always the risk with full-dress historical fiction. Victorian novelists were usually at their most creative when writing what could be called quasi-historical fiction. These were novels set not in a remote past which had to be researched, but in a more recent past which could be captured largely through recollection, since it lay somewhere in the writer's childhood or only just beyond. When Hardy set the opening of *THE MAYOR OF CASTERBRIDGE* (1886) 'before the nineteenth century had reached one-third of its span' he was following a common practice, usually so discreetly carried out that later readers would often fail to notice that what they were being offered was a kind of historical fiction. Yet this is the perspective from which history is contemplated, in terms of what has survived and what has changed, in Thackeray's *VANITY FAIR* (1848), Dickens's *LITTLE DORRIT* (1857) and *GREAT EXPECTATIONS* (1861) and George Eliot's *MIDDLEMARCH* (1871–2).

As the quasi-historical novel proved the subtler instrument for rendering the processes of history, the full-dress historical novel increasingly shed its earnest purpose and became more and more a matter of dress. Period details and stirring historic events were exploited simply to provide a colourful backdrop for an undemanding tale of love or adventure. During the High Victorian era itself this approach was already being adopted in, for example, the work of WILLIAM HARRISON AINSWORTH and G. P. R. JAMES, CAPTAIN FREDERICK MARRYAT'S *The Children of the New Forest* (1847), R. D. BLACKMORE'S *LORNA DOONE* (1869) and ROBERT LOUIS STEVENSON'S *THE BLACK ARROW* (1883). It dominated work by the next generation of historical novelists: SIR ARTHUR CONAN DOYLE, BARONESS ORCZY, STANLEY WEYMAN, JOHN BUCHAN and A. E. W. MASON. A similar pattern can be found in the USA, where historical fiction had begun in Scott's shadow with the work of JAMES FENIMORE COOPER and achieved its own national identity in NATHANIEL HAWTHORNE'S *THE SCARLET LETTER* (1850), before it surrendered to the picturesque charms of the ante-bellum South in the tradition culminating in Margaret Mitchell's *GONE WITH THE WIND* (1936).

Historical fiction had shrunk into the 'historical romance', to be classified with DETECTIVE FICTION and SCIENCE FICTION as GENRE FICTION: books with popular appeal, often a mass market, but lying outside what critics agreed to regard as the mainstream of serious literature. And there for much of the 20th century historical fiction has remained. Serious attempts in the Victorian manner continued to be made, of course, but they usually served only to enforce the lesson their Victorian predecessors had already taught. EVELYN WAUGH's *Helena* (1950), set in Rome under Constantine's rule, is a sadly typical case, standing in the same relation to the rest of Waugh's *oeuvre* as *Romola* does to the rest of George Eliot's. Successes were few and localized. They came largely from scholars (usually classicists), such as ROBERT GRAVES and MARY RENAULT, or from children's writers, such as ROSEMARY SUTCLIFF, HENRY TREECE and GEOFFREY TREASE, who could use the unobserved freedom of their ghettoes to produce books of surprising worth. Yet such examples were by no means enough to challenge the dominance of popular romance, in the hands of writers such as Georgette Heyer (1902–74), or the prevailing view that the historical novel had in general exhausted whatever energy it might once have possessed.

At least, that was the case until some few decades ago. Since then this confident dismissal has been challenged by novelists themselves and novelists, moreover, of no single school or identifiable persuasion – not even loose allegiance to the conventions established by Scott. The list of recent or contemporary British writers who have turned to historical fiction includes figures as diverse as: J. G. FARRELL in his 'Empire' trilogy; WILLIAM GOLDING in the trilogy begun in *Rites of Passage* (1980), about 18th-century seafaring; CHARLES PALLISER in *The Quincunx: The Inheritance of John Huffam* (1989), about Victorian England; PAT BARKER in her 'Regeneration' trilogy (1991–5), about World War I; HILARY MANTEL in *A Place of Greater Safety* (1992), about the French Revolution; and BARRY UNSWORTH, in *Sacred Hunger* (1992), about the 18th-century slave trade. The list could easily be lengthened. In the USA it is somewhat shorter, though no less diverse. It includes: JOHN BARTH, for *The Sot-Weed Factor* (1960), about colonial America; E. L. DOCTOROW, for *RAGTIME* (1975), about America in the era of J. P. Morgan and Harry Houdini; LARRY MCMURTRY, for *Lonesome Dove* (1986), about the pioneer days of the West; JANE SMILEY, for *The Greenlanders* (1988), returning to the world of the Viking sagas; and CHARLES RICHARD JOHNSON for *The Middle Passage* (1990), about the slave trade.

On the face of it, this revival is particularly surprising, since it occurred at just the time when academic historians had finally turned their backs on the storytelling confidence which had supported predecessors from Gibbon to Macaulay and even A. J. P. Taylor. Some had begun explicitly to challenge the idea that history itself is, after all, a story. Yet their shift in thinking has links with critical theories of literature which have challenged the notion that texts are ever stable or final. Historical document and invented story may thus meet as equals in a fertile middle ground, to be treated by the contemporary novelist in a fashion every bit as learned as the Victorian novelist did but with a playful freedom alien to the Victorian inquiry.

The goal of contemporary inquiry, when it is not simply the playfulness itself, has usually been revision: rewriting officially received history, writing new stories into history. Such revision has, of course, a crucial role to play in literature which seeks to find words for those minorities who have not previously been given words in the printed texts of history. Feminist novelists most often take fairy tales and biblical legends as the texts most ripe for revision, but they also borrow a hint from VIRGINIA WOOLF's ORLANDO (1928) and turn to history and hence, in some fashion, the historical novel – as SUSAN SWAN has done in *The Biggest Modern Woman of the World* (1983), ELLEN GALFORD in *Moll Cutpurse: Her True History* (1984) and JEANETTE WINTERSON in *The Passion* (1987).

The case of post-colonial literature is perhaps more clear-cut, for how else could it begin but by creating historical fiction of its own? This was what PATRICK WHITE memorably did for modern Australian literature in *Voss* (1957). Revisiting the imperial past in *THINGS FALL APART* (1958), CHINUA ACHEBE made a territory already familiar, from Victorian histories and historical novels, into something new and rich in a potential which African literature is still far from exhausting. And that achievement is, after all, not so very remote from what Scott achieved when, at the end of a century which had threatened to end Scottish history and extinguish Scottish identity, he made Scottish history and Scottish identity the very heart of his work.

Hoban, Russell (Conwell) 1925– Born in the USA, he settled in Britain in 1960. For many years an illustrator, he became a writer for children before turning to adult fiction as well. *The Mouse and His Child* (1969) is regarded as a modern children's classic. Many of his lively picture-books have been illustrated by Quentin Blake. His novels include: *Turtle Diary* (1975); *Riddley Walker* (1980), ostensibly a scenario of a Britain reverted to primitivism after a late 20th-century holocaust; *Pilgermann* (1983), continuing his metaphysical and mystical fabulation; *The Medusa Frequency* (1987); and *Fremder* and *The Trokeville Way* (both 1996).

Hobbes, John Oliver [Craigie (née Richards), Pearl Mary Teresa] 1867–1906 Born in Boston, she finally settled in Britain and turned to writing after the failure of her marriage. Three witty and epigrammatic novels – *Some Emotions and a Moral* (1891), *The Sinner's Comedy* (1891) and *A Study in Temptations* (1893) – caused a considerable stir. Her conversion to Catholicism left its mark on subsequent work, such as *School for Saints* (1897) and *Robert Orange* (1899); *School for Saints* contained a portrait of BENJAMIN DISRAELI, whose fiction she greatly admired. *The Ambassador* (1898) was her most successful play. She also published essays on GEORGE ELIOT (1901) and George Sand (1902).

Hodgins, Jack 1938– Canadian. His fiction combines a strong regional flavour (much of it is set on his native Vancouver Island) and a post-modernist approach that has affinities with MAGIC REALISM. Novels include *The Invention of the World* (1977), *The Resurrection of Joseph Bourne* (1979), *The Honorary Patron* (1987) and *Innocent Cities* (1990). *Spit Delaney's Island* (1976) and *The Barclay Family Theatre* (1981) are volumes of short stories. He has also written a children's book, *Left Behind in Squabble Bay* (1988), and an Australian travel journal, *Over Forty in Broken Hill* (1992).

Hodgson, William Hope 1877–1918 English. He used his youthful experience of the sea in short stories for magazines, many of them horror stories featuring monstrous life-forms. Two novels, *The Boats of the 'Glen Carrig'* (1907) and *The Ghost Pirates* (1909), are in the same vein, while the stories in *Carnacki, The Ghost Finder* (1910) ingeniously combine the supernatural with DETECTIVE FICTION. *The House on the Borderland* (1908) is a visionary allegory extending over vast reaches of time and space and *The Night Land* (1912) is a bizarre far-future fantasy. The cosmic perspective of his more ambitious work is a remarkable, if eccentric, product of the age which also produced H. G. WELLS's *THE TIME MACHINE*. Hodgson was killed in World War I.

Hogan, Desmond 1951– Irish. He made his reputation with *The Ikon Maker* (Dublin 1976, London 1979) and *The Leaves on Grey* (1980), explorations of male adolescents wrestling with their often homosexual emotions. He has developed a lyrical and passionate romanticism in *A Curious Street* (1984), in which interlinking stories carry the book from 17th-century Europe to contemporary Belfast, and *A Farewell to Prague* (1995), in which an Irishman journeys through Europe and the USA. He has also published short stories, including *The Diamonds at the Bottom of the Sea* (1979), which won the JOHN LLEWELLYN RHYS PRIZE, *Children of Lir: Short Stories from Ireland* (1981), *The Mourning Thief and Other Stories* (1987) and *Lebanon Lodge* (1988).

Hogg, James 1770–1835 Scottish. The son of a poor farmer at Ettrick Forest in Selkirkshire, he worked as a shepherd and sheep-farmer before moving to Edinburgh and establishing his reputation as a poet with *The Queen's Wake* (1813). *The Jacobite Relics of Scotland* (1819) includes some of his best lyric poetry. He joined the editorial board of *Blackwood's Edinburgh Magazine*, in whose pages he was known as the 'Ettrick Shepherd', and enjoyed the friendship of Byron, Southey, SIR WALTER SCOTT (of whom he published a memoir in 1834) and Wordsworth, who mourned him in a fine elegy, 'Extempore Effusion upon the Death of James Hogg'. Nowadays he is usually remembered for his novel THE PRIVATE MEMOIRS AND CONFESSIONS OF A JUSTIFIED SINNER (1824), for long neglected but gradually recognized as a masterpiece. Other novels are *The Three Perils of Man* (1822) and its weaker sequel, *The Three Perils of Women* (1823).

Holcroft, Thomas 1745–1809 English. His *Memoirs* (edited by William Hazlitt; 1816) describe his early struggles as pedlar, Newmarket stable-boy, tutor and strolling actor. His acting experiences furnished material for his first novel, *Alwyn: or, The Gentleman Comedian* (1780). *Anna St Ives* (1792) and *Hugh Trevor* (1794), reflect his friendship with Tom Paine and WILLIAM GODWIN. Though acquitted of high treason in 1794, he remained under suspicion as a free-thinker for the rest of his life. Holcroft's dramatic writing began with a comedy, *Duplicity* (1781), and continued with an adaptation of Beaumarchais's *The Marriage of Figaro* as *The Follies of a Day* (1784), *The School for Arrogance* (1791), the outstandingly successful *The Road to Ruin* (1792) and *Love's Frailties* (1794). *A Tale of Mystery* (1802), adapted from Pixérécourt's *Coelina*, was the first English play to be called a 'melodrama'.

Hole in the Wall, The A novel by ARTHUR MORRISON, published in 1902. The Hole in the Wall is a seedy pub in London's East End where Stephen Kemp lives with his grandfather, Captain Nat Kemp. The plot centres on the struggle for illegal insurance money, which Stephen innocently acquires and his grandfather first wishes to keep and then to surrender. His plan fails and The Hole in the Wall is burned down. He rebuilds the public house, but with another name, and turns to legitimate business. Stephen goes to school at last.

Holme, Constance 1881–1955 English. She was born at Milnthorpe on Morecambe Bay, where many of her novels are set. They include *The Lonely Plough* (1914), *The Splendid Faring* (1916), *The Old Road from Spain* (1916), *Beautiful End* (1918), *The Trumpet in the Dust* (1921), *The Things Which Belong* (1925) and *He-Who-Came* (1930).

Holmes, John Clellon 1926–88 American. He recorded the lifestyle of the BEATS in his first novel, *Go* (1952; as *The Beat Boys* in Britain), as well as *Nothing More to Declare* (1967), a collection of essays, and a memoir of JACK KEROUAC (1980). *The Horn* (1958) describes the jazz scene. He published two collections of poems, *The Bowling*

Green Poems (1977) and *Death Drag: Selected Poems* (1979).

Holmes, Oliver Wendell 1809–94 American. He was Parkman Professor of Anatomy and Physiology at Harvard in 1847–82. A popular teacher and entertaining after-dinner speaker, he achieved considerable success with *The Autocrat of the Breakfast Table* (1858), a collection of humorous essays, poems and occasional pieces originally published in *The Atlantic Monthly*, which he had co-founded with James Russell Lowell in 1857. Later collections include *The Professor at the Breakfast Table* (1860), *The Poet at the Breakfast Table* (1872) and *Over the Teacups* (1891). Holmes also wrote three novels exploring the biological and psychological factors determining human behaviour: *ELSIE VENNER* (1861), *The Guardian Angel* (1867) and *A Mortal Antipathy* (1885).

Holtby, Winifred 1898–1935 English. Her pithy style is best savoured in her last novel, *South Riding* (1936), whose heroine, Sarah Burton, is a strong-willed headmistress. Most notable among her earlier works are: *The Crowded Street* (1924); *The Land of Green Ginger* (1927); *Poor Caroline* (1931), an indictment of moribund charities; and *Mandoa! Mandoa!* (1933), satirizing the effects of European civilization on Africa. Other works include a study of VIRGINIA WOOLF (1932) and two volumes of short stories, *Truth is Not Sober* (1934) and *Pavements at Anderby* (1937). Her life and achievement are commemorated in Vera Brittain's *Testament of Friendship* (1940).

Holy War, The: *Made by Shaddai upon Diabolus* The last major work of the Nonconformist preacher and writer John Bunyan (1628–88), published in 1682. A complex religious allegory, it links the conversion of the individual soul to the early history of the world, events in recent and contemporary history, and the forthcoming millennium. The City of Mansoul (man's soul), built by King Shaddai, is alternately conquered by Diabolus and recaptured by Emmanuel. For Bunyan, see also THE LIFE AND DEATH OF MR BADMAN and THE PILGRIM'S PROGRESS.

Hood, Hugh 1928– Canadian. He is essentially a novelist of ideas and his intellectual Catholicism frequently manifests itself in the form of religious allegory. Artists are the central figures in several early novels: *White Figure, White Ground* (1964), *The Camera Always Lies* (1967) and *A Game of Touch* (1970). *You Can't Get There From Here* (1972) is a political novel. *The Swing in the Garden* (1975), *A New Athens* (1977), *Reservoir Ravine* (1979), *Black and White Keys* (1982), *The Scenic Art* (1984), *The Motor Boys in Ottawa* (1986), *Tony's Book* (1988), *Property and Value* (1990) and *Be Sure to Close Your Eyes* (1993) belong to an ambitious projected sequence of 12 novels, entitled *The New Age/Le Nouveau Siècle*. His volumes of short stories include *Flying in a Red Kite* (1962),

Around the Mountain (1967), *The Fruit Man, the Meat Man and the Manager* (1971), *Dark Glasses* (1976), *None Genuine without This Signature* (1980), *August Nights* (1985) and *You'll Catch Your Death* (1992). He has also published *The Governor's Bridge* (1973), a volume of essays.

Hook, Theodore Edward 1788–1841 English. Editor of the Tory *John Bull*, he moved in the fashionable society he described in SILVER-FORK NOVELS such as *Maxwell* (1830), *Gilbert Gurney* (1836) and *Jack Brag* (1837). He was the model for Mr Wagg in THACKERAY's *PENDENNIS*.

Hope, Anthony [Hawkins, Sir Anthony Hope] 1863–1933 English. He achieved success in 1894 with *The Dolly Dialogues*, a series of witty sketches of the London season, and a romance, THE PRISONER OF ZENDA, which earned high praise from ROBERT LOUIS STEVENSON and Andrew Lang. A sequel, *Rupert of Hentzau* (1898), proved equally popular. Other novels include *Tristram of Blent* (1901), *Sophy of Kravonia* (1906) and *Lucinda* (1920). His reminiscences appeared as *Memories and Notes* (1927).

Hope, Christopher (David Tully) 1944– Born in South Africa, he has been based in London since 1975. *Cape Drives* (1974), his first volume of poems published in Britain, has been followed by *In the Country of the Black Pig* (1981) and *Englishmen* (1985), subsequently dramatized by the BBC. His main output has been fiction. His first novel, *A Separate Development* (1980), written in his robust satirical style, has been followed by *Kruger's Alp* (1984; WHITBREAD AWARD), *The Hottentot Room* (1986), the novella *Black Swan* (1987), *My Chocolate Redeemer* (1989), *Serenity House* (1992) and *Darkest England* (1986). His early stories, *Private Parts* (1981), have been reissued with additions as *Learning to Fly* (1990). *The Love Songs of Nathan J. Swirsky* (1993), linked sketches about Johannesburg in the 1950s, contains material broadcast on the BBC. A play, *Ducktails*, televised in 1977, deals with his youth in Pretoria, as does his semi-autobiographical *White Boy Running* (1988), winner of a CNA LITERARY AWARD. His journalism includes *Moscow! Moscow!* (1990).

Hope, Thomas ?1770–1831 English. A wealthy collector who patronized major contemporary artists, he also wrote on ancient costume and on taste and design. His most important work, however, was *Anastasius: or, Memoirs of a Greek* (1819), a lively PICARESQUE novel which drew on his knowledge of the Near East. Published anonymously, it was once attributed to Byron.

Hopley, George See WOOLRICH, CORNELL.

Horler, Sydney See SPY FICTION.

Hornung, E(rnest) W(illiam) 1866–1921 English. The brother-in-law of ARTHUR CONAN DOYLE, he created A. J. Raffles, the gentleman-burglar whose exploits are related by his faithful friend Bunny in several collections of short stories, *The Amateur Cracksman* (1899), *The Black Mask* (1901)

and *A Thief in the Night* (1905), and a novel, *Mr Justice Raffles* (1909). Raffles was also popular on the stage and in the cinema, where he was portrayed by John Barrymore, Ronald Colman and David Niven, among others. The setting of other books, notably *Stingaree* (1905), reflects the time Hornung spent in Australia as a young man.

Horse's Mouth, The A novel by JOYCE CARY published in 1944, the culminating volume of a trilogy begun with *Herself Surprised* (1941) and *To Be a Pilgrim* (1942). Perhaps the best known of Cary's works, it traces the last stages in the career of Gulley Jimson, an amoral and egocentric artist endowed with a powerful genius and a grandiose conception of the artist's role which coincides uneasily with the values of modern society.

Horse-Shoe Robinson: *A Tale of the Tory Ascendancy* A novel by JOHN PENDLETON KENNEDY, published in 1835 and set in Virginia and the Carolinas during the last months of the Revolutionary War. The characters include Mildred Lindsay, who secretly marries Arthur Butler, a Revolutionary patriot; Tyrrel, the British spy Mildred's father wants her to marry; and Horse-Shoe Robinson, a blacksmith who comes to Mildred's aid when the British capture Arthur. Tyrrel is eventually hanged.

Hosain, Attia 1913– Indian. Born and raised in an orthodox Muslim family in Lucknow, she emigrated to Britain in 1947. The pieces in her collection *Phoenix Fled and Other Stories* (1953) are set in pre-Independence India. Her single novel, the autobiographical *Sunlight on a Broken Column* (1961), is a remarkable evocation of Muslim (and Indian) life in the 1930s.

Hospital, Janette Turner 1942– Australian, resident in North America. Her novels, variously set in India, Australia and North America, include *The Ivory Swing* (1982), *The Tiger in the Tiger Pit* (1983), *Borderline* (1985) and *The Last Magician* (1992). *Collected Stories: 1970–1995* appeared in 1995. A complex, post-modernist writer, she deals with nomads, whom she describes as 'characters who cross borders, who straddle cultures and countries, who live with a constant sense of dislocation'. She also publishes DETECTIVE FICTION under the pseudonym of Alex Juniper.

Hound of the Baskervilles, The See SHERLOCK HOLMES STORIES.

House at Pooh Corner, The See MILNE, A. A.

A House for Mr Biswas A novel by V. S. NAIPAUL, published in 1961 and set in Trinidad's East Indian community. Mohun Biswas's life centres on his quest to own a home of his own, and his fortunes are closely related to the various houses in which he lives, alternating between reliance on his in-laws, the Tulsis, and attempts to assert his independence. He finally acquires his own, jerry-built house shortly before his death. Generally regarded as Naipaul's masterpiece, the novel is notable for its richly comic portraiture and its sympathetic rendition of Mr Biswas.

House of Mirth, The A novel by EDITH WHARTON published in 1905. Set in New York society during the first years of the 20th century, it records the disastrous social career of Lily Bart, a penniless orphan related to some of the city's prominent families. Having failed to secure a rich husband, she is unjustly accused of having an affair with another woman's husband, disinherited by her wealthy aunt and forced to take a job as a milliner. The novel ends with her death from an overdose of a sedative.

House of the Seven Gables, The A novel by NATHANIEL HAWTHORNE, published in 1851. It is set in the mid-19th century.

Generations earlier, 'Wizard' Maule cursed Colonel Pyncheon before being hanged for witchcraft. His death allowed Pyncheon to take possession of a disputed plot of land and build the House of the Seven Gables. The current owner is the hypocritical Judge Pyncheon, who lets his poor cousin Hepzibah and her debilitated brother Clifford live there. Clifford has just been released from 30 years' wrongful imprisonment, to which the judge sentenced him for murdering their rich uncle. Clifford and Hepzibah are joined by Phoebe, a young cousin from the country, and Holgrave, a daguerreotypist. The Judge's sudden death ends his persecution of Clifford, and leaves him and Hepzibah wealthy. Holgrave reveals that he is the last descendant of 'Wizard' Maule and explains how both the 'murdered' uncle and the Judge were victims of the Maule curse, not of human wrongdoing. The curse will be lifted by his marriage to Phoebe.

House with the Green Shutters, The A novel by GEORGE DOUGLAS, published in 1901. A sharp and unsentimental study of small-town life in Scotland, it centres on John Gourlay, an arrogant and mean-spirited businessman who is finally killed by his own son.

Household, Geoffrey (Edward West) 1900–88 English. He achieved fame with his second novel, *Rogue Male* (1939), combining elements of SPY FICTION and the adventure story. Its hero tries but fails to assassinate a foreign dictator (presumably Hitler) and is himself hunted by an enemy agent. Most of the 20 novels that followed explore the psychology of the chase, notably *Watcher in the Shadows* (1960), *Dance of the Dwarfs* (1968) and the belated sequel *Rogue Justice* (1982).

Hove, Chenjerai 1956– Zimbabwean. He has published three collections of poetry and *Matende Mashama* (1981), a collection of stories. His first novel, *Masimbo Evanhu* (1986), in Shona, was followed by two novels in English: *Bones* (1989), winner of a NOMA AWARD and widely acclaimed for its evocation of peasant life, and

Shadows (1991), about inter-generational conflict and the clash between urban and rural values.

Howard, Edward See *RATTLIN THE REEFER*.

Howard, Elizabeth Jane 1923– English. Her first novel, *The Beautiful Visit* (1950), is a *BILDUNGSROMAN* about an adolescent girl during World War I. *The Sea Change* (1959) draws on her experience of acting. Recurrent themes include the poignancies and cruelties of marriage, in *The Long View* (1956), *Something in Disguise* (1969) and *Odd Girl Out* (1972), and the power of the past, in *After Julius* (1965). *The Light Years* (1990), *Marking Time* (1991) and *Confusion* (1993) have begun a projected tetralogy, 'The Cazalet Chronicles', tracing a family through the middle years of the 20th century. Elizabeth Jane Howard has been married to the naturalist Peter Scott and KINGSLEY AMIS.

Howard, Maureen 1930– American. Often likened to JAMES JOYCE, she is known for novels filled with detail and stories in which contemporary lives intersect with history and ancestry. Her novels include *Not a Word about Nightingales* (1962), *Before My Time* (1974), *Facts of Life* (1978), *Grace Abounding* (1982), *Expensive Habits* (1986), and *Natural History* (1992), about the inhabitants of a fictionalized Bridgeport, Connecticut, comparable to Joyce's Dublin.

Howards End A novel by E. M. FORSTER, published in 1910. 'Only connect', its epigraph, expresses Forster's lifelong belief in salvation through fraternal sympathy.

The story centres on the cultured Schlegel sisters, Margaret and Helen, and the materialistic Wilcox family, which consists of Henry, his sons Charles and Paul, his daughter Evie and the dying Mrs Wilcox. She leaves Margaret her house, Howards End, in a note which the surviving Wilcoxes destroy. Margaret and Henry become engaged. Helen arrives angrily at the Wilcoxes' second home at Oniton with Leonard Bast, a young clerk whom she and Margaret have tried to help but whom Henry has treated with indifference. Bast's wife Jacky and Henry Wilcox recognize each other as ex-lovers. Margaret forgives his past adultery and they marry. Helen is pregnant by Leonard. Charles thrashes him to death for what he takes to be callous seduction and goes to prison. The sisters are reunited at Howards End.

Howatch, Susan See GENRE FICTION.

Howe, E(dgar) W(atson) 1853–1937 American. He owned and edited the *Daily Globe of Atchison* in Kansas (1877–1911), and *E. W. Howe's Monthly* (1911–37). Despite its melodramatic plot, his novel *THE STORY OF A COUNTRY TOWN* (1883) drew high praise when it first appeared and is recognized as a landmark of American REALISM.

Howells, William Dean 1837–1920 American. He was born and brought up in Ohio, where he began his career as a journalist. His work as US consul in Venice in 1861–5 provided the basis for two travel books, *Venetian Life* (1866) and *Italian Journeys* (1867). On his return to the USA he settled in Boston and worked as assistant editor and then editor-in-chief of *The Atlantic Monthly*, among other prestigious journalistic posts.

The first of his 40 or so novels were *Their Wedding Journey* (1872) and *A Chance Acquaintance* (1873), drawing on his travel experiences. *A Foregone Conclusion* (1874) and *The Lady of the Aroostook* (1879) deal with the contrast between Americans and Europeans. Thereafter Howells moved away from the comedy of manners to tackle larger social issues, in works such as *The Undiscovered Country* (1880), a novel about spiritualism and the Shakers, *A Modern Instance* (1882), *A Woman's Reason* (1883) and *The Rise of Silas Lapham* (1885). *Indian Summer* (1886) is a delicately handled story of romance in middle age. *A Hazard of New Fortunes* (1890), written after he had moved to New York, announced a stronger political awareness while affirming his commitment to realism.

His later fiction includes: *The Quality of Mercy* (1892), about embezzlement; *An Imperative Duty* (1892), which has a black heroine; *The World of Chance* (1893), examining the lack of causality in human affairs; and *A Traveller from Altruria* (1894), a Utopian novel. Among his critical works are *Criticism and Fiction* (1891) and *Life and Literature: Studies* (1902). *Literary Friends and Acquaintance: A Personal Retrospect of American Authorship* (1900) and *My Mark Twain: Reminiscences and Criticism* (1910) document his wide-ranging friendships in the literary world. His achievements in journalism and fiction earned him the title of the 'dean of American letters'.

Huckleberry Finn, The Adventures of A novel by MARK TWAIN, published in 1884. A sequel to *THE ADVENTURES OF TOM SAWYER*, it achieves a moral dimension lacking in its predecessor by its satire and its treatment of slavery.

Huck narrates the story. He has been adopted by Widow Douglas and her sister Miss Watson but his blackguard father returns and kidnaps him. He frees himself by making it appear as if he has been murdered and meets Jim, Miss Watson's goodhearted slave, who has decided to run away. Together they travel down the Mississippi on a raft, undergoing a series of encounters with feuding clans, murderers, lawless 'aristocrats' and mobs, all of which they survive by luck, wit and determination. A dense fog causes them to miss Cairo, where Jim planned to leave the Mississippi and travel up the Ohio River to freedom. Finally, in Arkansas, Jim is captured and sold to a farmer and his wife, who by coincidence are Tom Sawyer's Uncle Silas and Aunt Sally Phelps. Tom himself arrives and

involves Huck in an absurdly romantic plan to rescue Jim, even though he knows that Miss Watson's death has left Jim a free man. The arrival of Tom's Aunt Polly sets matters straight. At the end Huck decides to 'light out' for the territories rather than face life with Aunt Sally, who plans to 'sivilize' him.

Hudson, W(illiam) H(enry) 1841–1922 Born to American parents in Argentina, he emigrated to Britain in 1869. *The Purple Land That England Lost* (1885), a series of stories set in South America, later became famous. Other stories and two novels, *A Crystal Age* (1887) and *Fan* (1892), followed but most of his writing during the 1890s was the work of a naturalist with an attractive, clear-cut style. *The Naturalist in La Plata* (1892), *Birds in a Village* and *Idle Days in Patagonia* (both 1893), *British Birds* (1895), *Birds in London* (1898), *Nature in Downland* (1900) and *Birds and Man* (1901) earned some acclaim but his first real success came with a romance, *GREEN MANSIONS* (1904). Hudson published 12 more books, of which *A Shepherd's Life* (1910) and the autobiographical *Far Away and Long Ago* (1918) established his place in literature.

Hueffer, Ford Madox See FORD, FORD MADOX.

Hughes, Glyn 1935– English. He published three volumes of poetry before turning to fiction dealing with history, particularly the history of his adoptive Yorkshire: *Where I Used To Play on the Green* (1982), about an 18th-century evangelical preacher; *The Hawthorn Goddess* (1984); *The Rape of the Rose* (1987); *The Antique Collector* (1990), in which a drag-artist embarks on his memoirs in the momentous year of 1915; and *Brontë* (1996), about the BRONTË family.

Hughes, Langston 1902–67 African-American. He emerged as a leading figure of the HARLEM RENAISSANCE with poetry, *The Weary Blues* (1926) and *Fine Clothes to the Jew* (1927), and a novel, *Not Without Laughter* (1930). *The Ways of White Folks* (1934) is a collection of satiric short stories; two later collections, *Laughing To Keep from Crying* (1952) and *Something in Common* (1963), again highlight the absurdities of racial prejudice. Later poetry includes *Shakespeare in Harlem* (1942), *Fields of Wonder* (1947), *Montage of a Dream Deferred* (1951), and *Ask Your Mama* (1961). Hughes also produced: plays, collected in *Five Plays* (1963); two autobiographies, *The Big Sea* (1940) and *I Wonder as I Wander* (1956); another novel, *Tambourines to Glory* (1958); books, essays and articles on society, history and music; collections of black folklore, poetry and stories; and *Simple Speaks His Mind* (1950), *Simple Takes a Wife* (1953), *Simple Stakes a Claim* (1957) and *Simple's Uncle* (1965), in which a seemingly slow-witted black outsmarts his antagonists.

Hughes, Richard (Arthur Warren) 1900–76 English. He is chiefly remembered for *A High Wind in Jamaica* (1929; as *The Innocent Voyage* in the USA), an unsentimental and disturbing novel about seven English schoolchildren kidnapped by Captain Jonsen and his crew of pirates during a voyage to England. *In Hazard: A Sea Story* (1938) tells of men at sea whose lives are threatened first by a hurricane and then by fears of a mutiny. Hughes later broke a long silence with two novels launching an ambitious multi-volume sequence, *The Human Predicament*, which was to include historical as well as fictional characters. It was never completed. *The Fox in the Attic* (1961) opens in Wales at the end of World War I. *The Wooden Shepherdess* (1973) met with little critical enthusiasm. Hughes's plays include *The Sister's Tragedy* (1922) and *A Comedy of Good and Evil* (1924).

Hughes, Thomas 1822–96 English. While studying for the Bar he became a supporter of Christian Socialism. He helped to found the Working Men's College in London and acted as its principal in 1872–83. His most famous work, TOM BROWN'S SCHOOLDAYS (1857), is a lightly fictionalized account of Rugby, his old school, under the headmastership of Thomas Arnold. Hughes did not repeat the success in *Tom Brown at Oxford* (1861) or an intervening novel, *The Scouring of the White Horse* (1861), a slight compilation of legends connected with the countryside round Uffington, his birthplace. In later years, when he was a Liberal MP and a circuit judge in Chester, he wrote admiring biographies, *Alfred the Great* (1869) and *David Livingstone* (1889), a book on his religious views (*The Manliness of Christ*; 1879), and the touching *Memoir of a Brother* (1873) in tribute to George Hughes.

Hulme, Keri 1947– New Zealand. She published stories and poems in magazines and a volume of poetry, *The Silences Between (Moeraki Conversations)* (1982), before becoming internationally famous with THE BONE PEOPLE (1984), a novel which won the NEW ZEALAND BOOK AWARD and the BOOKER PRIZE. She has also published a collection of stories, *Te Kaihau: The Windeater* (1986; winner of the GOODMAN FIELDER WATTIE BOOK AWARD) and two volumes of poetry, *Lost Possessions* (1985) and *Strands* (1992).

Hume, Fergus (Wright) 1859–1932 Born in Britain, he emigrated first to New Zealand and then Australia. He achieved local success in Melbourne with his first novel, *The Mystery of a Hansom Cab* (1886), DETECTIVE FICTION modelled on the work of Emile Gaboriau. It became an international best-seller after it was issued in Britain the following year, eventually selling some half a million copies in his lifetime. None of the 140 detective and mystery novels that followed equalled its popularity.

Humphry Clinker, The Expedition of An EPISTOLARY NOVEL by TOBIAS SMOLLETT, published in 1771.

Matthew Bramble, a cranky but kind-hearted Welsh squire, travels through England and Scotland with his family: his unpleasant,

husband-hunting sister Tabitha; his amiable nephew Jerry; his teenage niece, Lydia; and Tabitha's maid, Winifred Jenkins. Humphry Clinker, an ostler, becomes their resourceful and devoted servant. The family's travels take them to Bristol, Bath, Harrogate, York, Scarborough and Durham, where they are joined by Lieutenant Obadiah Lismahago, an impecunious Scots soldier. Humphry, a Methodist, converts Tabitha, who succeeds in marrying Lismahago. Lydia falls in love with a handsome young actor who proves to be of good family. Winifred and Humphry fall in love, and he turns out to be Matthew Bramble's long-lost son. These adventures allow Smollett to comment on contemporary life and manners, especially in the spa towns and resorts, more gently than in earlier work. *Humphry Clinker* has often been considered his finest novel.

Hunt, Violet 1866–1942 English. The daughter of the painter Alfred William Hunt, she wrote several novels – *The Maiden's Progress: A Novel in Dialogue* (1894), *Unkist, Unkind* (1897) and *The Tiger Skin* (1924) – and interesting if unreliable reminiscences of the Pre-Raphaelites in *Those Flurried Years* (1926) and *The Wife of Rossetti* (1932).

Hunter, Evan [Lombino, Evan] 1926– American. The best-known novel he has published under his own name is still probably *The Blackboard Jungle* (1954), about an urban high school. Other novels written as Evan Hunter generally deal with social problems, including *Second Ending* (1956), *Mothers and Daughters* (1961), *Sons* (1969) and *Love, Dad* (1981). He has also produced plays and screenplays. As Ed McBain he also writes DETECTIVE FICTION: a popular and long-running series about Steve Carella and the police of the 87th Precinct, introduced in *Cop Hater* (1965), and a series about the Florida lawyer Matthew Hope. He has also written as Hunt Collins and Richard Marsten.

Hurston, Zora Neale 1903–60 African-American. *Mules and Men* (1935) and *Tell My Horse* (1938) gather black traditions of the American South and the Caribbean. Her best-known novel, THEIR EYES WERE WATCHING GOD (1937), portrays the life of an independent black woman. Another novel, *Moses: Man of the Mountain* (1939), examines Moses as he appears in the Old Testament and black myth. *Dust Tracks on a Road* (1942) is an autobiography. *I Love Myself When I am Laughing* (1979) is a collection edited by ALICE WALKER and *Spunk* (1984) is a collection of short stories.

Hutchinson, R(ay) C(oryton) 1907–75 English. *The Unforgotten Prisoner* (1933) deals with poverty and distress in post-war Germany, *Testament* (1938) with the Russian Revolution, and *A Child Possessed* (1964) with the love of a French *routier* for his idiot child. His finest work grappled with grand themes, often of tragedy in foreign countries he did not know well. It attracted a small but loyal readership.

Huxley, Aldous (Leonard) 1894–1963 English. He was the grandson of the scientist T. H. Huxley, the nephew of MRS HUMPHRY WARD and the younger brother of Sir Julian Huxley. In youth he wrote journalism, poetry and a collection of short stories, *Limbo* (1920), but made his name as a witty and satirical commentator on his contemporaries with *Crome Yellow* (1921), a combination of ROMAN À CLEF and ROMAN À THÈSE in the tradition of THOMAS LOVE PEACOCK. It was followed by *Antic Hay* (1923), *Those Barren Leaves* (1925) and *Point Counter Point* (1928), which contains portraits of D. H. LAWRENCE and John Middleton Murry.

BRAVE NEW WORLD (1932), his most succinct *roman à these*, turned its attention to the threat posed by scientific totalitarianism. Subsequent novels, equally marked by Swiftian despair and disgust, include *EYELESS IN GAZA* (1936) and, after Huxley moved to California in 1937, *Time Must Have a Stop* (1944), *Ape and Essence* (1948) and *The Genius and the Goddess* (1955). *Island* (1962), about a Utopian community, reflects his search for an extension of awareness. This quest, begun with *The Perennial Philosophy* (1946), led to the experiments with mescalin described in *The Doors of Perception* (1954) and *Heaven and Hell* (1956).

Huxley's other works include *The Devils of Loudon* (1952), a study of demonic possession during the reign of Louis XIII (dramatized by John Whiting as *The Devils* in 1961), and many essays (in *Collected Essays*, 1959). He also wrote two travel books (*Jesting Pilate*, 1926; and *Beyond the Mexique Bay*, 1943) and edited *The Letters of D. H. Lawrence* (1932). Huxley's short stories, which many class with his best work, were reprinted in *Collected Short Stories* (1957).

Hyde, Robin [Wilkinson, Iris Guiver] 1906–39 New Zealand. Her fiction includes *Passport to Hell* (1936), an account of the early life of Douglas Stark, a World War I bomber pilot, and its sequel, *Nor the Years Condemn* (1938), which give a vivid picture of New Zealand life in the opening years of this century. The interaction between private and public history is also the theme of her two best works, *Check to Your King* (1936), a fictionalized biography of Charles, Baron de Thierry, who attempted to establish a Utopian community for English settlers and Maoris in early 19th-century New Zealand, and the autobiographical *The Godwits Fly* (1938). *Persephone in Winter* (1937) is the most substantial volume of verse she published in her lifetime, but her best-known poetry is found in the posthumous *Houses by the Sea* (1952), a sequence recreating the natural and social environment of her youth.

Hypatia: *or, New Foes with an Old Face* A historical novel by CHARLES KINGSLEY, serialized in 1852–3 and published in volume form in 1853. (See also HISTORICAL FICTION.)

The setting is Alexandria in the 5th century AD, a city governed ineffectually by the pagan prefect, Orestes, and threatened by the barbarian tribes advancing from the heart of Europe. Philammon, a young monk from the desert, is repelled by the fanaticism of the Christian church, led by the patriarch Cyril, and drawn to the beautiful Hypatia, who teaches neo-Platonic philosophy. He witnesses a Christian mob cutting Hypatia to pieces and returns, disillusioned, to the desert.

I

Ihimaera, Witi 1944– New Zealand. The first significant Maori writer in English, he published *Pounamu, Pounamu* (1972), a collection of short stories, and two novels, *Tangi* (1973) and *Whanau* (1974), defending what is most valuable in traditional Maori culture. The stories in *The New Net Goes Fishing* (1977) deal with the city. Later works include *The Matriarch* (1986), an ambitious attempt at a modern epic, *The Whale Rider* (1987) and *Dear Miss Mansfield* (1989), which rewrites stories by KATHERINE MANSFIELD. He has widened his range with *Nights in the Gardens of Spain* (1994), which celebrates gay life-styles and shows the influence of Hollywood movies. *Bulibasha* (1994) is a novel based on the rivalry of two Maori families in the first half of the 20th century. *Pounamu, Pounamu, Tangi* and *The Matriarch* all won the GOODMAN FIELDER WATTIE BOOK AWARD, and *Bulibasha* won the Goodman Fielder Wattie Book Award after it became the Montana Book Award. Ihimaera has also co-edited *Into the World of Light: An Anthology of Maori Writing* (1982), edited the first in a series of contemporary Maori writing, *Te Ao Morama* (1993), and written opera libretti.

Iles, Francis See DETECTIVE FICTION.

Imlay, Gilbert 1754–1828 American. He lived in London during the 1790s, publishing *A Topographical Description of the Western Territory of North America* (1792) and *The Emigrants* (1793), an EPISTOLARY NOVEL about the frontier area of Pennsylvania. In France he frequented the radical circles of Joel Barlow and Thomas Paine and lived for a time with MARY WOLLSTONECRAFT, who bore him a daughter.

In a Glass Darkly A book of short stories by SHERIDAN LE FANU, published in 1872. It is presented as a collection of cases investigated by Dr Martin Hesselius, who explores the supernatural in terms of psychopathology. 'Green Tea', 'The Watcher', 'The Room in the Dragon Volant' and 'Carmilla', about vampirism, have become classics of occult literature.

In Chancery See FORSYTE SAGA, THE.

In Our Time A collection of short stories by ERNEST HEMINGWAY, published in 1925 and expanded in 1930. Nick Adams, the hero of several stories, is a young boy in 'Indian Camp' and an adult, psychologically shattered by World War I, in 'Big Two-Hearted River'. Other stories include 'The Three-Day Blow', 'Mr and Mrs Elliot' (apparently a caricature of T. S. Eliot and his wife), 'Cross-Country Snow' and 'My Old Man'. 'On the Quai at Smyrna' was added to the 1930 edition.

In the Castle of My Skin A novel by GEORGE LAMMING, published in 1953. The finest of a group of novels about Caribbean boyhood which appeared in the 1950s and 1960s, it is about a boy growing up and losing his innocence. His story is complemented by that of a village losing the sense of security it has hitherto enjoyed in the quasi-feudal world of late colonial Barbados. The novel uses an innovative technique, moving between first- and third-person narrative and dramatic dialogues rooted in the conventions of oral storytelling.

In the Midst of Life A collection of stories by AMBROSE BIERCE, published in 1891 as *Tales of Soldiers and Civilians* and retitled in Britain and in the 1898 US edition. More than half the stories derive from his experience as a soldier in the Civil War. Violence and the macabre predominate. The best-known stories include: 'The Middle Toe of the Right Foot', about a murderer haunted to death by his victim; 'A Horseman in the Sky', about a Union soldier forced by circumstances to kill his own father; and 'An Occurrence at Owl Creek Bridge', presenting the fantasy which a man being hanged experiences in his last seconds of life.

Inchbald, Elizabeth 1753–1821 English. She ran away from home in 1772, defying a speech impediment to become an actress but devoting herself to writing after 1789. She is best remembered for a novel, *A SIMPLE STORY* (1791). Her first play, *A Mogul Tale* (1784), exploiting the craze for hot-air balloons, was followed by comedies, notably *I'll Tell You What* (1785), *The Child of Nature* (1788) and *Lovers' Vows* (1798), an adaptation of Kotzebue which plays a memorable role in JANE AUSTEN's *MANSFIELD PARK*. She also edited three multi-volume collections, *The British Theatre* (1808), *Farces* (1809) and *The Modern Theatre* (1809).

Incredible Brazilian, The A trilogy of novels by ZULFIKAR GHOSE, consisting of *The Incredible Brazilian: The Native* (1972), *The Beautiful Empire* (1975), and *A Different World* (1978). It chronicles four centuries of Brazilian colonial history through the reincarnations of its protagonist, Gregório Peixota da Silva Xavier. The trilogy is written according to the conventions of contemporary PICARESQUE, combining the realistic and the fabulous.

Indian Summer A novel by WILLIAM DEAN HOWELLS, published in 1886. In Florence a middle-aged American newspaper publisher, Theodore Colville, encounters a friend from his childhood, Evalina Bowen, now widowed. Her young friend Imogene Graham is attracted to Colville and her feelings are strengthened when she learns of his suffering in an unhappy youthful romance. Eventually, however, she falls truly in love with a young clergyman, Morton, leaving the way clear for Colville and Evalina, who have secretly loved one another almost from the beginning, to marry.

Inheritance, The A novel by SUSAN FERRIER, published in 1824. The Earl of Rossville repudiates his son when he marries beneath him, but after the son's death acknowledges his daughter-in-law and makes his grand-daughter, Gertrude, heiress presumptive. She falls in love with the profligate Colonel Delmour and becomes engaged to him after the Earl's death. He abandons her when she turns out to be an adopted child and hence not an heiress. Her cousin, the faithful Edward Lyndsay, eventually wins her.

Innes, Michael See STEWART, J. I. M.

Innocent Voyage, The See HUGHES, RICHARD.

Interpreters, The A novel by WOLE SOYINKA, published in 1965. It is a dense compound of existentialist novel and trenchant satire. Several young Western-educated intellectuals – the civil servant Egbo, the engineer Sekoni, the journalist Sagoe, the artist Kola, the university lecturer Bandele – face difficult moral choices as they attempt to find meaning for their lives. The background against which they must make their choices provides ample opportunity for a scathing indictment of Nigeria's post-independence black élite.

Invisible Man A novel by RALPH ELLISON, published in 1952. Set in the 1930s, it details the often incoherent experiences of its nameless black narrator as a bright high-school student in the South, a disoriented college student who is eventually expelled from his Southern 'negro' college, a factory worker in New York and a rising figure in left-wing politics. He eventually realizes that his black skin makes him 'invisible' to white eyes and retreats to an underground sewer, where he lives while writing his book.

The novel's exploration of identity and alienation alludes to Dostoyevsky and Sartre as well as HERMAN MELVILLE's 'Benito Cereno', in THE PIAZZA TALES, and RICHARD WRIGHT's NATIVE SON. Ellison's title lends itself to confusion with The Invisible Man (1897) by H. G. WELLS.

Ireland, David 1927– Australian. He wrote plays and verse before turning to fiction. Using discontinuous narrative, surrealism and a range of metafictive techniques, it is frequently highly political and frequently concerned with gender stereotypes and subcultures. His novels include: The Chantic Bird (1968), the confession of a youthful outsider which has been compared to J. D. SALINGER's THE CATCHER IN THE RYE; The Unknown Industrial Prisoner (1971), about the pressures of working for a multinational oil company; The Flesheaters (1972), adapted from his best-known play, Image in the Clay (1964); The Unknown Industrial Prisoner (1971), which, like The Glass Canoe (1976) and A Woman of the Future

(1979), won the MILES FRANKLIN AWARD; Burn (1974); City of Women (1981); Archimedes and the Seagle (1984); and Bloodfather (1988), which has been called Joycean in its range of characters and structural invention.

Irish, William See WOOLRICH, CORNELL.

Iron Heel, The A novel by JACK LONDON, published in 1908. A socialist vision of the future, it is presented as a manuscript written by Avis Cunningham Everhard in 1912–32 about the fight against the Oligarchy, the Iron Heel of the title, a proto-fascist conglomeration of major trusts and their private militias. A socialist revolution is crushed and the manuscript breaks off on the eve of a second uprising, with Avis's husband Ernest already dead and Avis apparently about to be executed. Iron Heel's eventual defeat is recorded by the editor, Anthony Meredith, writing 700 years later in the 4th century of the Brotherhood of Man. The novel proved controversial and was banned in several parts of America.

Irving, John 1942– American. Setting Free the Bears (1969), The Water-Method Man (1972) and The 158-Pound Marriage (1974) attracted little attention but he made his name with The World According to Garp (1978), a long, energetic BILDUNGSROMAN. It has been followed by The Hotel New Hampshire (1981) and, moving away from the comic exuberance and surreal invention of his earlier fiction, The Cider House Rules (1985), A Prayer for Owen Meany (1989) and A Son of the Circus (1994). Trying to Save Piggy Sneed (1996) is a memoir.

Irving, Washington 1783–1859 American. His early humorous works include The Letters of Jonathan Oldstyle, Gent. (1803), Salmagundi (with William Irving and James Kirke Paulding; 1807–8) and the highly successful History of New York (1809), a burlesque. The last was written under the pseudonym of Dietrich Knickerbocker, a name adopted by the Knickerbocker Group, of which he was a leading member.

His arrival in England in 1815 began a 17-year stay in Europe, during which he formed friendships with several writers (notably SIR WALTER SCOTT) and himself became the first American writer to enjoy an international reputation. His success was largely due to THE SKETCH BOOK OF GEOFFREY CRAYON, GENT. (1820), a collection of tales and sketches which included 'Rip Van Winkle' and 'The Legend of Sleepy Hollow', and BRACEBRIDGE HALL (1822). Tales of a Traveller (1824) was less well received. His stay in Spain as diplomatic attaché to the American embassy in Madrid inspired several historical works: Life and Voyages of Columbus (1828), Conquest of Granada (1829), Voyages and Discoveries of the Companions of Columbus (1831) and The Alhambra (1832).

The Crayon Miscellany (1835), published after

his return to America, combines memories of Europe in 'Abbotsford and Newstead Abbey' and 'Legends of the Conquest of Spain' with impressions of America in 'A Tour of the Prairies'. Later books include *Astoria* (1836), an ill-judged book about the Astor fur-trade empire, *Adventures of Captain Bonneville, USA* (1837), *Mahomet and his Successors* (1850), *Wolfert's Roost* (1855) and a life of George Washington (1855–9).

Isherwood, Christopher (William Bradshaw) 1904–86 British. He is best remembered for *Mr Norris Changes Trains* (1935) and *Goodbye to Berlin* (1939), episodic, semi-autobiographical works about the Bohemian society of Berlin, where he lived in 1929–33. The latter contains 'Sally Bowles', a sketch about a cabaret artiste, later dramatized by John van Druten as *I am a Camera* (1951) and turned into a musical, *Cabaret* (1968). Isherwood collaborated with W. H. Auden on three plays, *The Dog beneath the Skin* (1935), *The Ascent of F6* (1936) and *On the Frontier* (1939), and an account of their visit to China, *Journey to a War* (1938). After emigrating to the USA in 1939 he wrote screenplays, took an increasing interest in Indian philosophy and religion, and published several novels: *Prater Violet* (1945), *The World in the Evening* (1954), *Down There on a Visit* (1962) and *A Single Man* (1964). His autobiography, *Christopher and His Kind* (1972), gives a frank account of his homosexuality.

Ishiguro, Kazuo 1954– Born in Nagasaki, he came to Britain as a student. A graduate of MALCOLM BRADBURY's creative writing course at the University of East Anglia, he began with two novels on Japanese themes, *A Pale View of Hills* (1981) and *An Artist of the Floating World* (1986; WHITBREAD AWARD). *The Remains of the Day* (1990), which won the BOOKER PRIZE, is a deadpan first-person account of an ageing butler's motoring tour of England in the 1950s, using minute ironies to reveal a familiar English ferment of emotional starvation. He abandoned elegantly compact proportions in *The Unconsoled* (1995), a moral quest set somewhere in central Europe.

Israel Potter: His Fifty Years of Exile A novel by HERMAN MELVILLE, serialized in 1854–5 and published separately in 1855. Loosely based on an anonymous tract, *Life and Remarkable Adventures of Israel R. Potter* (1824), it follows its hero's adventures during the Revolutionary War. He enlists in the Revolutionary army, is captured by the British, escapes, meets George III, takes messages to Benjamin Franklin and serves under John Paul Jones. He finally settles in London and is prevented by poverty from revisiting Boston until he is in his 80s.

Ivanhoe SIR WALTER SCOTT's most popular novel, and the first of his works to be set in England, published in 1819. The period is the reign of Richard I.

Wilfred of Ivanhoe loves Rowena, but his father Cedric plans to marry her to Athelstane of Coningsburgh. Ivanhoe serves with Richard in the crusades. Returning after his imprisonment in Austria to confront his usurping brother John, Richard appears at the tournament at Ashby-de-la-Zouch, where he helps Ivanhoe defeat the knights of John's party, among them the Templar, Sir Brian de Bois-Guilbert. Bois-Guilbert falls in love with Rebecca, a beautiful and courageous Jewess, who loves Ivanhoe. Rebecca, her father Isaac, Rowena, Cedric and the wounded Ivanhoe are taken captive by the Norman barons and imprisoned in Torquilstone Castle. The King and a Saxon force, with the help of Locksley (Robin Hood) and his band of outlaws, take the castle and release the prisoners except Rebecca, who is carried off by Bois-Guilbert. Though his designs are frustrated, Rebecca is further imperilled by a trial for witchcraft at which Ivanhoe appears as her champion and Bois-Guilbert as her reluctant accuser. Bois-Guilbert falls dead, a victim of his conflicting emotions. Seeing Ivanhoe's love for Rowena, Rebecca leaves England with her father.

Iyayi, Festus 1947– Nigerian. Representative of the new generation of Nigerian novelists which has turned away from anti-colonial and often village-based themes, he has presented the poverty, corruption and alienation of city life in *Violence* (1979), *The Contract* (1982) and *Heroes* (1986), about the Nigerian Civil War. *Heroes* was awarded the COMMONWEALTH WRITERS PRIZE.

Jackson, Helen (Maria) Hunt 1830–85 American. Her poetry is collected in *Verses by H. H.* (1870) and *Sonnets and Lyrics* (1886). Concern for the American Indians prompted her to write *A Century of Dishonor* (1881), a historical study, and *Ramona* (1884), a novel. Other works include children's books, a travel book and magazine articles, some written under the pseudonym Saxe Holm. Her novel *Mercy Philbrick's Choice* (1876) is probably a fictionalized portrait of her friend Emily Dickinson.

Jackson, Shirley 1919–65 American. Her best-known story, 'The Lottery' (1948), and her second novel, *The Hangsaman* (1951), typify her interest in the dark side of human nature. She also produced humorous stories and articles, some collected in *Life among the Savages* (1953) and *Raising Demons* (1957). Other works include *The Bird's Nest* (1954), *Witchcraft of Salem Village* (1956), *The Bad Children* (1959), *The Sundial* (1958), *The Haunting of Hill House* (1959), *Special Delivery* (1960), *We Have Always Lived in the Castle* (1962), *Nine Magic Wishes* (1963) and two collections edited by her husband, *The Magic of Shirley Jackson* (1966) and *Come Along with Me* (1968).

Jacob, Naomi 1884–1964 English. In all, she produced almost 80 books. Her best-known work is *The Gollantz Saga*, a seven-volume sequence of novels celebrating European Jewry. Beginning with *Young Emmanuel* (1932), based on her father's own history, it includes the enormously successful *Four Generations* (1934), and *Private Gollantz* (1943). The history of her Yorkshire mother's farming family provided material for many popular regional novels, such as *They Left the Land* (1940). An 11-volume autobiography begins with *Me: A Chronicle about Other People* (1933) and ends with *Me – and the Stage* (1964).

Jacob's Room A novel by VIRGINIA WOOLF, published in 1922. It is an episodic tale evoking the inner life of Jacob Flanders (based on Woolf's brother Thoby), and his social milieu during the first decade and a half of the 20th century. At the beginning, Jacob is discovered wandering on a Cornish beach away from his recently widowed mother. The novel ends during World War I, when Jacob has been killed and two friends are visiting his room in Bloomsbury to dispose of his possessions.

Jacobs, W(illiam) W(ymark) 1863–1943. English. He wrote some 20 volumes of humorous stories about barge crews, night-watchmen and other coastal workers. The first was *Many Cargoes* (1896); others are *The Skipper's Wooing* (1897), *Light Freights* (1901) and *Sea Whispers* (1926). He also wrote tales of horror, the best known being 'The Monkey's Paw'.

Jacobson, Dan 1929– South African. He settled in Britain in 1958. His fiction, often concerned with uncontrolled states of mind in varying relationships with personal or political power, has developed from naturalism to the play on narration and fictionality first evident in *The Rape of Tamar* (1970). Other novels include: *The Trap* (1955); *A Dance in the Sun* (1956); *The Price of Diamonds* (1957); *Evidence of Love* (1960); *The Beginners* (1966); *The Wonder-Worker* (1973); *The Confessions of Joseph Baisz* (1977); *Her Story* (1987), set in the future; *Hidden in the Heart* (1991); and *The God-Fearer* (1992). Judaism is an important theme. His volumes of short stories include *Beggar My Neighbour* (1964). *Time and Time Again* (1985) is an autobiography, while *The Electronic Elephant* (1995) blends travel with autobiography.

Jacobson, Howard See CAMPUS NOVEL.

Jaeger, Muriel See SCIENCE FICTION.

Jagua Nana A novel by CYPRIAN EKWENSI, published in 1961. Jagua Nana is an experienced Lagos 'high-lifer' who hopes to finance her young lover's legal studies in England, so that he can provide for her declining years. Freddie never goes to England, however, but seduces and marries Nancy Oll, the 19-year-old daughter of Jagua's great professional rival. Jagua nevertheless acquires a fortune from embezzled political funds, spending much of it on worthy causes. She then uses the remainder to establish herself as a 'merchant princess' in the market town of Onitsha.

James, G(eorge) P(ayne) R(ainsford) 1799–1860 English. He wrote over 100 popular historical novels (see also HISTORICAL FICTION). They include *Richelieu* (1829), *The Huguenot* (1838), *The Man-at-Arms* (1840), *Arabella Stuart* (1844), *The Cavalier* (1859) and *The Man in Black* (1860). His style was parodied by WILLIAM MAKEPEACE THACKERAY in *PUNCH'S PRIZE NOVELISTS*.

James, Henry 1843–1916 American. The brother of the philosopher and psychologist William James (1842–1910) and the diarist Alice James (1848–92), he was born in New York and attended schools in Boulogne, Paris, Geneva, Bonn and Newport, Rhode Island. After a brief spell at Harvard Law School he concentrated on writing, encouraged by Charles Eliot Norton and WILLIAM DEAN HOWELLS, publishing reviews and essays in *The North American Review* and *The Atlantic Monthly*. His first novel, *Watch and Ward*, was serialized in the latter journal in 1871. *A Passionate Pilgrim and Other Tales* (1875) and *Transatlantic Sketches* (1875) reflect his experiences of Europe on extended visits in 1869 and 1872–4. After spending 1875 in Paris he settled in

England in 1876, making London his base for over 20 years before moving to Lamb House in Rye, Sussex. He became a British subject in 1915.

Deeply influenced by Continental literature (he had met Turgenev, Daudet, Flaubert, the Goncourts and Zola in Paris), James took the American experience of Europe as the theme of his first important works: RODERICK HUDSON (1876), THE AMERICAN (1877), THE EUROPEANS (1878), DAISY MILLER (1879), An International Episode (1879) and, his masterpiece of this period, THE PORTRAIT OF A LADY (1881). WASHINGTON SQUARE (1880) and THE BOSTONIANS (1886) use an American setting, and THE PRINCESS CASAMASSIMA (1886) studies the political underworld of London, while THE ASPERN PAPERS (1888) returns to his 'international theme'. In addition to short stories, essays and travel writings, he also published significant critical studies of French poets and novelists (1878), of HAWTHORNE (1879) and of 'The Art of Fiction' (1884).

James continued to publish short stories: The Lesson of the Master (1892), which includes 'The Pupil', 'The Solution' and 'Sir Edmund Orme', The Real Thing and Other Tales (1893), Terminations (1895), which includes 'The Altar of the Dead', and Embarrassments (1896), which includes 'The Figure in the Carpet'. But he spent much of the early 1890s in a fruitless preoccupation with drama, culminating in the failure of Guy Domville (1895). The novels which followed – notably THE SPOILS OF POYNTON (1897), WHAT MAISIE KNEW (1897), THE AWKWARD AGE (1899) and THE SACRED FOUNT (1901) – abandon his 'international theme', though it returns in his last three major works: THE WINGS OF THE DOVE (1902), THE AMBASSADORS (1903) and THE GOLDEN BOWL (1904). THE TURN OF THE SCREW (1898) is his most famous venture into the uncanny.

James revised his novels for the New York Edition (1907–9) and contributed 18 new prefaces which form a major statement of his approach to fiction. The American Scene (1907) records his impressions of his native country after long absence. His last completed novel was The Outcry (1911); The Ivory Tower and The Sense of the Past were left unfinished.

James, M(ontague) R(hodes) 1862–1936 English. In the course of his distinguished career he became Provost of King's College, Cambridge (1905) and Provost of Eton (1918), serving also as director of the Fitzwilliam Museum (1893–1908) and Vice-Chancellor of the University of Cambridge (1913–15). His broad interests embraced biblical studies, palaeography and medieval art and literature. Beyond the scholarly world he is best remembered for Ghost Stories of an Antiquary (1904), More Ghost Stories of an Antiquary (1911), A Thin Ghost, and Others (1919), The Five Jars (1922) and A Warning to the Curious, and Other Ghost Stories (1925). The first

volume contained the much-anthologized 'Oh, Whistle and I'll Come to You, My Lad'. Collected Ghost Stories appeared in 1931.

James P.D. [White, Phyllis Dorothy], Baroness James of Holland Park 1920– English. Her experience working for the National Health Service and the Home Office is clearly reflected in the settings of her DETECTIVE FICTION. It features two recurrent detectives: the policeman Adam Dalgliesh (Cover Her Face, 1962; A Mind to Murder, 1963; Unnatural Causes, 1967; Shroud for a Nightingale, 1971; The Black Tower, 1975; Death of an Expert Witness, 1977; A Taste for Death, 1986; Devices and Desires, 1989; A Certain Justice, 1997) and the private detective Cordelia Gray (An Unsuitable Job for a Woman, 1972; The Skull beneath the Skin, 1982). By comparison with the classic efficiency of her early work, Innocent Blood (1980) and Original Sin (1994) mark a dissatisfaction with the conventional boundaries of detective fiction. The Children of Men (1992) ventures into SCIENCE FICTION.

James Tait Black Memorial Prize An annual prize for the best biography and the best work of fiction published in Britain. Founded in memory of a partner in the publishing house of A & C Black, it is now administered by the English faculty of the University of Edinburgh. Since HUGH WALPOLE's The Secret City became the first winner of the fiction category in 1919, the prize has often proved a reliable guide to works destined to endure. Winners in the early 1920s, for example, included D. H. LAWRENCE's The Lost Girl, DAVID GARNETT's Lady into Fox, ARNOLD BENNETT's RICEYMAN STEPS, E. M. FORSTER's A PASSAGE TO INDIA and LIAM O'FLAHERTY's The Informer. The awards to MARY LAVIN's Tales from Bective Bridge (1942) and JENNIFER DAWSON's The Ha-Ha (1961) recognized these authors at the start of their careers. Recent winners include: Jenny Joseph's Persephone (1986), JAMES KELMAN's A Disaffection (1989), IAIN SINCLAIR's Downriver (1991), Allan Hollinghurst's The Folding Star (1994), Christopher Priest's Prestige (1995), and Alice Thompson's Justine (1996) and GRAHAM SWIFT's Last Orders (1996).

Jameson, (Margaret) Storm 1891–1986 English. Her many novels include sagas depicting English life between the wars, notably two trilogies about a family of Yorkshire shipbuilders: The Triumph of Time, comprising The Lovely Ship (1927), The Voyage Home (1930) and A Richer Dust (1931), and The Mirror in Darkness, comprising Company Parade (1934), Love in Winter (1935) and None Turn Back (1936). She also wrote poetry, essays, criticism, biography and several substantial volumes of autobiography, including Journey from the North (1969).

Jane Eyre A novel by CHARLOTTE BRONTË, published in 1847.

Jane is an orphan whose independent spirit does not fit the household of her unpleasant aunt, Mrs Reed, and cousins. As pupil and then teacher at Lowood Institution she suffers appalling physical conditions but learns self-control from her friend Helen Burns, who dies of consumption. She leaves Lowood to become governess at Thornfield Hall. Its master, Edward Rochester, is attracted by her wit and self-possession, and proposes marriage. Their wedding is interrupted by the revelation that Rochester is already married and that his wife, now mad, is secretly confined at the Hall. Jane leaves and is finally taken in by a clergyman, St John Rivers, and his sisters Diana and Mary. They turn out to be her cousins and Jane to be heir to a fortune, which she shares with them. The dedicated but narrow-minded St John proposes that she accompany him to India as his wife. She almost consents but Rochester's voice calls to her out of the air. Returning to Thornfield, she discovers that a fire has destroyed it and the first Mrs Rochester, leaving Rochester himself maimed and blind. At last they can marry.

Contemporary praise for *Jane Eyre* was mixed with criticism of its harsh portrait of Lowood and its Evangelical headmaster, Brocklehurst, and a more general unease about the book's morality. While observing the conventional code of female behaviour, Jane's actions still make a powerful statement of women's claim to independence.

Janet's Repentance See SCENES OF CLERICAL LIFE.

Jefferies, (John) Richard 1848–87 English. He is mostly remembered for novels and essays celebrating the countryside of southern England. He established himself in the public view during the early 1870s with articles on wild life for *The Pall Mall Gazette* and a long letter to *The Times* on the plight of the agricultural labourer in Wiltshire, his native county.

His fiction began with melodramatic and for the most part unsuccessful works: *The Scarlet Shawl* (1874), *Restless Human Hearts* (1875) and *The World's End* (1877). More convincing are his last novel, *Amaryllis at the Fair* (1887), with its portrait of his father in the character Iden, and, among earlier works, the autobiographical *Bevis, the Story of a Boy* (1882) and his actual autobiography, *The Story of My Heart* (1883). Books of essays reflecting his close engagement with rural England include *The Amateur Poacher* (1879), *The Gamekeeper at Home* (1880), *Hodge and His Masters* (1880), *Greene Ferne Farm* (1880), *The Open Air* (1885) and the posthumous *Field and Hedgerow* (1889). Present but not precisely visible in these works is the thoroughgoing distaste for 19th-century industrialism implicit in *After London* (1885), a novel presenting a vision of future disaster which forces people to trust in their knowledge of the earth, animals and plants for survival.

Jenkins, (John) Robin 1912– Scottish. One of the most prolific post-war Scottish writers, he has often been neglected, perhaps because of his distance from both the Scottish renaissance and MODERNISM. His novels, often autobiographical in origin, include *Happy for the Child* (1953), *The Cone-Gatherers* (1955), *Guests of War* (1956), *The Changeling* (1958), *A Would-be Saint* (1978) and a comic masterpiece, *Fergus Lamont* (1979). Spells of teaching abroad prompted *Dust on the Paw* (1961), *The Sardana Dancers* (1964), *The Holy Tree* (1969) and *A Figure of Fun* (1974). More recent work includes *Poverty Castle* (1991), *Willie Hogg* (1993), *The Thistle and the Grail* (1994) and *Leila* (1996), which returns to Fifeshire. *A Far Cry from Bowmore* (1973) and *Ludderston Tales* (1997) are collections of short stories..

Jennie Gerhardt A novel by THEODORE DREISER, published in 1911. Jennie, pretty but poor, is forced to leave home when she becomes pregnant by Senator George Brander. She works as a maid for the Bracebridges and meets Lester Kane, who persuades her to live with him. His wealthy family disapproves and his father makes his inheritance conditional on his abandoning Jennie. He eventually marries Letty Pace Gerald, a widowed socialite. Jennie's daughter, Vesta, dies and she adopts two orphans. The dying Lester summons her to express his regret at leaving her. She attends his funeral, masked behind a veil.

Jerome, Jerome K(lapka) 1859–1927 English. *On Stage and Off* (1885) and *Idle Thoughts of an Idle Fellow* (1886) were lighthearted essays which set the tone for his most enduring work, *Three Men in a Boat* (1889), about an accident-prone rowing holiday on the Thames. *Three Men on the Bummel* (1900) took the same characters on a tour of Germany. He founded *The Idler*, a humorous periodical, in 1892, and wrote many plays, the most successful being *The Passing of the Third Floor Back* (1907). His own favourite work was *Paul Kelver* (1902), an autobiographical novel.

Jewett, Sarah Orne 1849–1909 American. Her fiction was shaped by youthful observation of the decaying farms and fishing towns of Maine and by the example of HARRIET BEECHER STOWE's stories of New England. *Deephaven* (1877), a collection of stories, takes its name from a harbour town based on York, near her home town of South Berwick. It was followed by two novels, *A Country Doctor* (1884) and *A Marsh Island* (1885), and further collections of stories: *A White Heron* (1886), *The King of Folly Island* (1888), *A Native of Winby* (1893) and *The Life of Nancy* (1895). THE COUNTRY OF THE POINTED FIRS (1896), set in the imaginary town of Dunnet Landing, gained a lasting place in American literature. Later work included two books for children; a historical romance, *The Tory Lover* (1901); and the posthumous *Verses* (1916).

Jewsbury, Geraldine (Endsor) 1812–80 English. The friend of Thomas and Jane Carlyle, she produced *Zoe: The History of Two Lives* (1845), *The Half-Sisters* (1848) and *Marian Withers* (1851), unjustly neglected novels treating contemporary social and political issues and, particularly, showing her interest in the role of women. *Constance Herbert* (1855), *The Sorrows of Gentility* (1856) and *Right or Wrong* (1859) are weaker. *The History of an Adopted Child* (1853) and *Angelo: or, The Pine Forest in the Alps* (1856) were written for children.

Jhabvala, Ruth Prawer 1927– Indian. The child of Polish parents, she was educated in Britain and migrated to India after her marriage, experiencing joint family life as a satirically minded outsider. She skilfully exploits this duality in her early novels: *To Whom She Will* (1955), *The Nature of Passion* (1956), *Esmond in India* (1958) and *The Householder* (1960). Harsher in tone are *Get Ready for Battle* (1962), *A Backward Place* (1965), *A New Dominion* (1972; as *The Travelers* in the USA) and *HEAT AND DUST* (1975). *In Search of Love and Beauty* (1983) and *Three Continents* (1987) have American backgrounds. *Like Birds, Like Fishes* (1963), *A Stronger Climate* (1968), *An Experience of India* (1971) and *How I Became a Holy Mother* (1976) are collections of stories. Part of the Merchant-Ivory film-making team, she has written the scripts for *Shakespeare Wallah* (1965) and *Autobiography of a Princess* (1975), as well as adapting HENRY JAMES's *THE EUROPEANS* (1979) and *THE BOSTONIANS* (1984) and E.M. FORSTER's *A ROOM WITH A VIEW* (1986) and *HOWARDS END* (1992).

John Halifax, Gentleman A novel by DINAH MULOCK, published in 1856. It is a CONDITION OF ENGLAND NOVEL, set in Tewkesbury (called Norton Bury). The hero is a poor, friendless orphan sustained by a proud consciousness of independence and integrity. The tanner Abel Fletcher gives him work and Abel's son Phineas befriends him. Through industry and perseverance he eventually succeeds in the world and marries Ursula March, becoming a 'gentleman' by merit rather than birth.

John Inglesant A novel by JOSEPH HENRY SHORTHOUSE, privately printed in 1880 and published in 1881. It is set in the early 17th century. Influenced by Nicholas Ferrar's religious community at Little Gidding, Inglesant works for the Royalists in the Civil War. After Charles I's execution he goes to Rome, where he witnesses the intrigues attending the election of Innocent X's successor and meets Molinos, the Spanish mystic who propounded the doctrine of Quietism. The climax of the story comes when Inglesant finds his brother's murderer in his power but renounces vengeance.

John Llewellyn Rhys Prize An annual prize for the best work of fiction or non-fiction by a British or Commonwealth writer aged under 35. First awarded in 1942, it was founded by the widow of John Llewellyn Rhys, the short-story writer killed in World War II, and because of current sponsorship is now technically known as the *Mail on Sunday*/John Llewellyn Rhys Prize. Winning works of fiction and their dates of publication (one year before the award) have included: V. S. NAIPAUL's *The Mystic Masseur* (1957), NELL DUNN's *Up the Junction* (1963), ANGELA CARTER's *The Magic Toyshop* (1967), A. N. WILSON's *The Sweets of Pimlico* (1977), DESMOND HOGAN's collection of stories, *The Diamonds at the Bottom of the Sea* (1979), Lisa St Aubin de Terán's *The Slow Train to Milan* (1983), TIM PARKS's *Loving Roger* (1986), JEANETTE WINTERSON's *The Passion* (1987), Matthew Kneale's *Sweet Thames* (1992), Jonathan Coe's *What A Carve Up!* (1994) and Nicola Barker's collection of stories, *Heading Inland* (1996).

Johns, W(illiam) E(arle) 1893–1968 English. An ex-RAF officer and pilot in the Royal Flying Corps during World War I, he introduced his most famous hero, Biggles (Captain James Bigglesworth), in short stories published in the magazine *Popular Flying*, he founded in 1932. Along with his companions Ginger, Algy and Bertie, Biggles provided young readers with an idealized image of toughness, honesty and stoicism in over 70 novels. Johns also created a slightly less popular commando hero, Gimlet, and a female Biggles, Worrals of the WAAF.

Johnson, B(rian) S(tanley) 1933–73 English. *Travelling People* (1963), *Albert Angelo* (1964), *Trawl* (1966; SOMERSET MAUGHAM AWARD), *The Unfortunates* (1969), *Christie Malry's Own Double Entry* (1973) and *See the Old Lady Decently* (1975) ran counter to the realistic bias of post-war British fiction, turning instead to the example of JAMES JOYCE, SAMUEL BECKETT, FLANN O'BRIEN and LAURENCE STERNE. The extremity of Johnson's technical adventures occasionally provoked the charge of gimmickry, though the climate of POST-MODERNISM may well encourage a revival of interest in his work.

Johnson, Charles Richard 1948– African-American. His novels combine historical accuracy, parable, and elements of the fantastic in rendering the experience of African-Americans. They include *Faith and the Good Thing* (1974), *Oxherding Tale* (1982), *The Sorcerer's Apprentice* (1986) and *The Middle Passage* (1990), a sea tale about the members of an ancient tribe of magicians being brought to the USA as slaves. He is also the author of two plays, *Olly Olly Oxen Free: A Farce in Three Acts* (1988) and *All This and Moonlight* (1990), as well as a collection of essays, *Being and Race: Black Writing since 1970* (1988).

Johnson, Colin See MUDROOROO.

Johnson, Denis 1949– American. His novels employ stylistic experimentation to depict surrealistic journeys of consciousness in extreme circumstances. They include: *Angels* (1983); *Fiskadoro* (1985), set in a post-apocalyptic era; *The Stars at Noon* (1986); *Resuscitation of a Hanged Man* (1991); and *Already Dead: A California Gothic* (1997). *Jesus' Son* (1992) is a collection of stories.

The Incognito Lounge (1982), *The Veil* (1987), and *The Throne of the Third Heaven of the Nation's Millenium General Assembly* (1995) are collections of poetry.

Johnson, Diane 1934– American. Much of her work deals with the lives of Victorian and contemporary women. Her fiction, largely realist, includes: *Fair Game* (1968); *Burning* (1971); *The Shadow Knows* (1975), about a woman convinced she is about to be murdered; *Lying Low* (1978); *Persian Nights* (1987); *Health and Happiness* (1990); *Natural Opium: Some Traveler's Tales* (1993); and *Le Divorce* (1997). Her non-fiction includes: an account of Victorian women in *Lesser Lives* (1973); a collection of essays, *Terrorists and Novelists* (1982); a biography of DASHIELL HAMMETT (1983); and the screenplay for *The Shining* (1990), based on Stephen King's novel and co-written with the film's director, Stanley Kubrick.

Johnson, James Weldon 1871–1938 African-American. While practising law in Florida, he collaborated with his brother in writing popular songs and spirituals. 'Lift Every Voice and Sing' became known as the black anthem. His first novel, *Autobiography of an Ex-Colored Man* (1912), is about a light-skinned black man who poses as a white. *Black Manhattan* (1930) is a black history of New York. Other volumes of poetry are *Fifty Years and Other Poems* (1917), *God's Trombones: Seven Negro Sermons in Verse* (1927), *Saint Peter Relates an Incident at the Resurrection Day* (1930) and *Selected Poems* (1935). His autobiography is *Along This Way* (1933).

Johnson, Pamela Hansford 1912–81 English. Her talent for light satire is best revealed in the 'Dorothy Merlin' trilogy: *The Unspeakable Skipton* (1959), *Night and Silence, Who is Here* (1962), and *Cork Street, Next to the Hatter's* (1965). Non-fictional works include studies of IVY COMPTON-BURNETT, Proust and THOMAS WOLFE, and *On Iniquity* (1967), about the Moors Murders. With her first husband, Gordon Stewart, she wrote DETECTIVE FICTION published under the pseudonym of Nap Lombard. She married C. P. SNOW in 1950.

Johnson, Samuel See *RASSELAS*.

Johnston, George (Henry) 1912–70 Australian. His work includes *The Darkness Outside* (1959), *The Far Face of the Moon* (1964) and a trilogy of self-examining novels, *My Brother Jack* (1964; MILES FRANKLIN AWARD), *Clean Straw for Nothing* (1969; Miles Franklin Award) and *A Cartload of Clay* (1971), the last volume left incomplete at his death. Together they brilliantly present aspects of 20th-century Australian life, depicting archetypal qualities in the Australian male character. Johnston also wrote thrillers under the pseudonym of Shane Martin.

Johnston, Jennifer 1930– Irish. She is the daughter of the playwright Denis Johnston (1901–84). Her best work – *The Captains and the Kings* (1972), *How Many Miles to Babylon?* (1974)

and *The Invisible Worm* (1991) – continues the tradition of the Irish 'Big House' novel, centring on the decay of the Protestant gentry and their embattled position in modern Ireland. *Shadows on Our Skin* (1977) and *Fool's Sanctuary* (1987) depict divided loyalties in families caught up in the Northern Irish troubles. Other work includes *The Old Jest* (1979), winner of a WHITBREAD AWARD, and *The Illusionist* (1995).

Johnstone, Charles c. 1719–1800 Irish. *Chrysal: or, The Adventures of a Guinea* (1760–5), consisting of satirical episodes from contemporary life, is told by a guinea as it is passed from hand to hand. Most notable are the scenes at the Hellfire Club and the manoeuvres of an ambitious wife on behalf of her clergyman husband.

Jolley, Elizabeth 1923– Born in Britain to an English father and Austrian mother, she emigrated to Australia in 1959. She first became known for radio plays later collected in *Off the Air* (1995) and the short stories in *Five Acre Virgin* (1976), *The Travelling Entertainer* (1979) and *Woman in a Lampshade* (1983). The first two volumes were combined in *Stories* (1984). Her apparently late start as a novelist came with *Palomino* (1980), but she had already written some of her subsequently published works, including the first two volumes of her 'Vera' trilogy. She quickly won wide recognition with *The Newspaper of Claremont Street* (1981); *MISS PEABODY'S INHERITANCE* (1983); *Mr Scobie's Riddle* (1983), a comedy of old age; *Milk and Honey* (1984); and *Foxybaby* (1985) which, like *Miss Peabody's Inheritance*, is about a woman novelist and, with its play between different kinds of textual reality, also a classic of POST-MODERNISM. These were followed by the country-Gothic *The Well* (1986), which won the MILES FRANKLIN AWARD; *The Sugar Mother* (1988); *My Father's Moon* (1989), *Cabin Fever* (1990) and *The George's Wife* (1993), the 'Vera' trilogy, rooted in autobiography; and *The Orchard Thieves* (1995), a novella. *Central Mischief* (1992) is a collection of articles, speeches and essays.

Jonathan Wild the Great, The Life of A novel by HENRY FIELDING, published in 1743. It gives a fictionalized version of the life of the infamous criminal executed in 1725, ironically presenting him as an example of heroism and greatness. Wild's success in the underworld is compared to the values at work in polite society and government. Sir Robert Walpole is the chief target for this aspect of the satire. After showing an early propensity for crime, Wild becomes chief of a gang of thieves, safeguarding himself by turning over to the law any subordinates who question his leadership. He concentrates on ruining the jeweller Heartfree, his virtuous former schoolfellow. Heartfree is rescued from the scaffold by the exposure of Wild, who is hanged in his stead, a 'hero' and 'great man' to the last.

Jones, (Walter) David (Michael) 1895–1974 Welsh. Combining verse, prose, illustration and lettering, his work makes highly allusive and associative use of a variety of sources in ritual and romance. In *Parenthesis* (1937) relates the experience of Private John Ball in World War I to chivalric antecedents, and the modern waste land to Malory's *Morte Darthur*. *The Anathemata* (1952), a much wider chronicle, was admired by W. H. Auden, Kathleen Raine and EDWIN MUIR. Later works include *The Sleeping Lord and Other Fragments* (1974), *The Kensington Mass* (1975) and *The Roman Quarry and Other Sequences* (1981). *Epoch and Artist* (1959) and *The Dying Gaul* (1978) are collections of essays and articles.

Jones, James 1921–77 American. *From Here to Eternity* (1951), his first and best-known novel, is a realistic story of army life in Hawaii on the eve of the attack on Pearl Harbor. His career continued with *Some Came Running* (1957), *The Pistol* (1959), *The Thin Red Line* (1962), *Go to the Widow-Maker* (1967) and *A Touch of Danger* (1973). His short stories are collected in *The Ice Cream Headache* (1968) and *The Merry Month of May* (1971). *Viet Journal* (1974) describes a visit to Vietnam.

Jorrocks's Jaunts and Jollities A collection of 10 stories by R. S. SURTEES, published in book form in 1838, with illustrations by Hablot K. Browne ('Phiz'), and enlarged in 1869. They describe the adventures of John Jorrocks, a sporting London grocer, his vulgar wife, his friend Charlie Stubbs and his servant Binjimin. Apart from hunting, there is also racing, shooting, fishing, eating, drinking and a jaunt to France. *HANDLEY CROSS* (1843) and *HILLINGDON HALL* (1845) continue the story.

Jose, Nicholas 1952– Australian. He published two collections of short stories, *The Possession of Amber* (1980) and *Feathers and Lead* (1986), and two novels, *Rowena's Field* (1984) and *Paper Nautilus* (1987), before going to China to research Western encounters with Chinese culture. *Avenue of Eternal Peace* (1989), set in contemporary Beijing, and *The Rose Crossing* (1994), set on an island in the Indian Ocean in the 17th century, are major contributions to the recent attempt by Australian writers to engage imaginatively with Asia. He has also published a collection of essays, *Chinese Whispers* (1995).

José, F(rankie) Sionil 1924– Filipino. The foremost anglophone writer in the Philippines, he has published novels, novellas and collections of short stories. His reputation rests on the 'Rosales Quinology', consisting of *The Pretenders* (1962), *Tree* (1978), *My Brother, My Executioner* (1979), *Mass* (1982) and *Po-on* (1984). Beginning in contemporary middle-class settings, the sequence goes on to chronicle more than a century of life in every sphere of Philippine society.

Joseph Andrews A novel by HENRY FIELDING, first published in 1742. Its full title is *The History of the Adventures of Joseph Andrews, and of his Friend Mr Abraham Adams. Written in Imitation of Cervantes, Author of Don Quixote*.

Joseph is the brother of Pamela Andrews, heroine of SAMUEL RICHARDSON's *PAMELA*, and a footman to Lady Booby. When she and her companion, Mrs Slipslop, show designs on his chastity he decides to return to his sweetheart, Fanny, and takes to the road. He is accompanied by Parson Adams, an absent-minded and gullible curate intent on getting his sermons published. The pair suffer a long series of scrapes, embarrassments and encounters with rogues and hypocrites. The main characters converge for a final show-down at the Boobys' country seat. Squire Booby has meanwhile married Pamela (Joseph's sister), and the novel ends by revealing that Joseph is actually the son of a respectable couple and not Pamela's brother.

Joseph Andrews quickly outgrows the burlesque of Richardson and develops a shape of its own. Though Fielding describes himself in his 'Preface' as 'the founder of a new province of writing', his main achievement is to synthesize earlier narrative forms (epic, romance and, above all, PICARESQUE) with contemporary realism and an eye for telling detail.

Joshi, Arun 1939– Indian. He has never established a major reputation outside India but within the country his English-language fiction is regarded as both humane and modestly innovative. *The Foreigner* (1968) and *THE STRANGE CASE OF BILLY BISWAS* (1971), early novels combining the cosmopolitan and the local, are still his most widely read. Later novels include *The Apprentice* (1974), *The Last Labyrinth* (1981; awarded a SAHITYA AKADEMI prize) and *City and the River* (1990), in which, characteristically, private themes predominate over public ones.

Journal of the Plague Year, A An imaginatively reworked account, combining fact and fiction, of the Great Plague in 1664–5, written by DANIEL DEFOE and published in 1722.

The narrator is 'H. F.', a Whitechapel saddler who remains in London throughout the epidemic and provides a graphic commentary on its rise, the public reaction, the precautions taken by the authorities and the drastically changing atmosphere of the capital as it becomes depopulated. Defoe skilfully weaves plague bills of mortality, statistics, historical accounts, anecdotes and hearsay into the lively and colloquial narrative. The result is both a study in human isolation and a life-affirming work that examines a city under threat. (See also HISTORICAL FICTION.)

Joyce, James (Augustine Aloysius) 1882–1941 Irish. Born in Dublin, he was educated at Jesuit schools and University College. While an undergraduate he made the acquaintance of Yeats, Synge, Lady Gregory and George William Russell (A. E.) and others fostering the Irish cultural renaissance, but, eager to escape his family and dissatisfied with the narrowness of Irish life, he went to Paris after graduating in 1902. His mother's terminal illness obliged him to return the following year. During this visit he met Nora Barnacle, who became his permanent companion (they finally married in 1931) in a life of exile, wandering and poverty dictated by his unwavering dedication to his art. They left Ireland together in 1904 and first settled in Trieste, moving to Zurich during World War I and to Paris in 1920. During the 1930s he was increasingly beset by family worries – his daughter Lucia was diagnosed schizophrenic in 1932 – and by problems with deteriorating eyesight. The outbreak of World War II forced him to return to Zurich, where he died.

Youthful publications included an essay on Ibsen (1900) in *The Fortnightly Review* and a volume of poetry, *Chamber Music* (1907). His first significant work was DUBLINERS (1914), a collection of short stories, whose very title announced a central if paradoxical feature of his mature art: for all his Continental wanderings and cosmopolitan sensibility, his subject would always remain the city he had left. *A PORTRAIT OF THE ARTIST AS A YOUNG MAN*, begun as *Stephen Hero* in 1903, was serialized in Harriet Shaw Weaver's journal *The Egoist* in 1914–15 and published in volume form in 1916. An autobiographical novel, it used the technique of STREAM OF CONSCIOUSNESS which he had encountered in Dujardin's *Les Lauriers sont coupés* (1888).

Joyce subsequently published an unsuccessful play, *Exiles* (1918), and a slight volume of verses, *Pomes Penyeach* (1927), but these were mere asides during the creation of the two great works which occupied his remaining life. *ULYSSES*, begun in 1914 and finished in 1921, used the character of Stephen Dedalus and the technique of stream of consciousness from the *Portrait*, while subduing both to a more radically ambitious purpose: nothing less than to recreate a day in the life of Dublin in painstaking detail while also locating it in the widest possible context of history and myth. The novel was serialized in *The Little Review* from 1918 until a prosecution for obscenity in 1920, and was first published in volume form in Paris by Harriet Shaw Weaver's Egoist Press in 1922. It was banned in the USA until 1933 and in Britain until 1937. *FINNEGANS WAKE*, begun in 1923, was serialized in 12 parts as *Work in Progress* in 1928–37 and published complete in 1939. The radical experimentalism which dissolves narrative into dream and the English language into polyglot puns has given it an exaggerated reputation for inaccessibility, yet it takes its place with *Ulysses*, not just as a central text of MODERNISM, but as a work which can outlive fluctuating critical judgements of modernism.

Joys of Motherhood, The A novel by BUCHI EMECHETA, published in 1979. The ironic title refers to the struggles of Nnu Ego to raise a family over almost three decades in pre-independence Nigeria. She marries young but produces no children and is despatched to a second husband in Lagos, by whom she has nine. The eighteen chapter headings (including 'A Failed Woman', 'A Man is Never Ugly', 'Sharing a Husband', 'Woman Alone') suggest her long martyrdom, ending fittingly with a section called 'The Canonized Mother'.

Jude the Obscure A novel by THOMAS HARDY, published in 1895.

Jude Fawley, a stonemason with a talent and passion for scholarship, is trapped into marriage by Arabella Donn. When she deserts him he makes his way to Christminster (Oxford) and earns his living as a labourer while aspiring to be a student. He meets and is attracted to his cousin Sue Bridehead. She marries Phillotson, Jude's former schoolmaster, but flees his sexual advances and lives with Jude. Two children are born to them and they also take care of 'Father Time', Jude's son by Arabella. As impoverished social outcasts, they become bitterly unhappy: Sue retreats into morbid Christianity while Jude moves towards atheism. 'Father Time' kills the two children and himself. In a misguided attempt at expiation Sue returns to Phillotson. Jude declines, resentfully cared for by Arabella, and eventually dies alone.

Many contemporary readers and reviewers were outraged by the pessimism of the novel and its depiction of the 'deadly war waged between flesh and spirit'. Hardy wrote no more fiction afterwards.

Jungle, The A novel by UPTON SINCLAIR, published serially in 1905 and in book form in 1906. It portrays the appalling conditions in the Chicago stockyards and slums, as seen through the eyes of Jurgis Rudkus, a Lithuanian immigrant. He works in the fertilizer plant after being injured in the slaughterhouse, and goes to prison for attacking a foreman who has taken advantage of his wife, Ona. Blacklisted on his release, Jurgis becomes a tramp, a thief, a scab during a meat-packers' strike, a tool of a corrupt politician, and a down-and-out before discovering socialism. The novel ends by calling for reform.

Jungle Book, The and *SECOND JUNGLE BOOK, THE* Collections of short stories and poems by RUDYARD KIPLING, published in 1894 and 1895 respectively. Their core is the sequence of stories about the boy Mowgli, accidentally thrust out of the human community into the jungle. His growth to dominance over the animals and his eventual return to human service as a forest ranger provide the basic framework. The code of conduct in the animal world is severe and requires a high level of responsibility; humanity is unruly and undignified by comparison.

Juniper, Alex See HOSPITAL, JANETTE TURNER.

***Jurgen**: A Comedy of Justice* A romance by JAMES BRANCH CABELL, published in 1919. Part of his cycle set in the mythical kingdom of Poictesme, it chronicles the adventures – some of them amatory – of the pawnbroker Jurgen in search of his missing wife, Dame Lisa. He meets the Centaur Nessus, Guenevere, Thragnar, Merlin, Dame Anaitis (The Lady of the Lake) and Helen, and lives in both Hell and Heaven, before Lisa is returned to him and they resume their normal life. *Jurgen* was suppressed on grounds of obscenity from 1920 to 1922.

Just So Stories A collection of 12 stories and 12 poems by RUDYARD KIPLING, published in 1902. It was written to be read aloud by adults to children, and the interplay between human and animal worlds in the first seven stories is simpler and more playful than in THE JUNGLE BOOK. An element of teasing is most obviously apparent in such stories as 'How the Leopard Got Its Spots', in which Kipling travesties the theory of evolution.

K

Kahiga, Sam 1943– Kenyan. His childhood was overshadowed by Kenya's war of independence, and *Potent Ash* (1968), an early collection of stories written in collaboration with his brother Leonard Kibera, is critical of both colonists and freedom fighters. His other fiction includes a second collection and two novels, *Lover in the Sky* (1979) and *When the Stars are Scattered* (1979).

kailyard school A group of late 19th-century Scottish writers who wrote, often in the vernacular, about homespun topics and promoted a sentimental image of small-town life. 'Kailyard', meaning 'cabbage patch', was used by Ian Maclaren (born John Watson, 1850–1907) as the motto for a collection of his stories, *Beside the Bonnie Briar Bush* (1894). The group also included J. M. BARRIE and S. R. Crockett (1860–1914), author of *The Stickit Minister* (1893).

Kanga, Firdaus 1959– Indian. *Trying to Grow* (1989) is an autobiographical novel dealing with his Parsee childhood in Bombay and his disability (he was born with brittle bones). *Heaven on Wheels* (1991) is an account of his journeys round Britain, where he now lives, and *A Kind of Immigrant* (1992) is a play about homosexual love.

Kangaroo A novel by D. H. LAWRENCE, published in 1923. Set in Australia, it is principally a vehicle for Lawrence's reactions to the country and to post-World War I politics. Richard Lovat Somers, a writer, and his wife Harriet meet Benjamin Cooley ('Kangaroo'), a Jewish barrister and leader of a radical political party, who tries unsuccessfully to enlist Somers's support for his programme, a combination of fascism and Lawrentian 'blood consciousness'. After a meeting in Canberra Hall has been violently disrupted, the couple leave for America.

Katiyo, Wilson 1947– Zimbabwean. *A Son of the Soil* (1976) and *Going to Heaven* (1979) follow the story of Alexio's life in white-dominated Rhodesia. The first describes his father's death and his schooldays in Salisbury. The second describes the death of his wife and child, when their village is razed, and the political persecution which makes him flee to London, the ironic 'heaven' of the title.

Katz, Stephen 1935– American. Innovative and experimental, his fiction is often parodic of American culture in its humorous depiction of bizarre circumstances in everyday life. His work includes *The Exaggerations of Peter Prince* (1968), *Creamy and Delicious* (1970), *Moving Parts* (1977), *Weir and Pouce* (1984), *Stolen Stories* (1984), *Florry of Washington Heights* (1987), *43 Fictions* (1991) and *Swanny's Ways* (1995).

Kavanagh, Dan See BARNES, JULIAN.

Kavanagh, Julia 1824–77 Irish. She spent much of her early life in France, drawing on her knowledge of the country in *Woman in France during the Eighteenth Century* (1850) and in several of her novels. These were influenced by CHARLOTTE BRONTË, particularly in their portrayal of independent-minded women faced with restrictive conventions, and were also praised by Brontë, who became the author's friend. They include: *Madeleine* (1848), about a girl in the Auvergne; *Nathalie* (1850), probably Kavanagh's best work; *Adele* (1858); and *Bessie* (1872).

Kaye-Smith, Sheila 1887–1956 English. *The Tramping Methodist* (1908) started a series of rural novels focusing on a Sussex family, the Alards. The best known are *Sussex Gorse* (1916), *Tamarisk Town* (1919), *Green Apple Harvest* (1920), *Joanna Godden* (1921) and *The End of the House of Alard* (1923). Later work includes *The History of Susan Spray* (1931), *Ember Lane* (1940), *Mrs Gailey* (1951) and an autobiography, *Three Ways Home* (1937).

Keane, Molly 1904–96 Anglo-Irish. She began her career writing under the pseudonym of M. J. Farrell. *The Knight of Cheerful Countenance* (1926), *Young Entry* (1928), *Devoted Ladies* (1934), *Mad Puppetstown* (1931) and *The Rising Tide* (1937) deal with the fox-hunting Anglo-Irish ascendancy into which she had been born. The horrors of sectarian violence and a divided Ireland shape *Two Days in Aragon* (1941). Her plays include *Spring Meeting* (1938), about a spinster secretly addicted to gambling. The death of her husband was followed by three decades of silence, broken by *Good Behaviour* (1981) and then *Time after Time* (1983) and *Loving and Giving* (1988). Their moral acuity, blend of the comic and the macabre and evocation of the Irish past won her a new audience.

Keary, Annie 1825–79 English. She wrote several notable children's books: *Mia and Charles* (1856), *The Heroes of Asgard* (with her sister Eliza Keary; 1857) and *Sidney Grey* (1857), a school story. Her adult novels include: *Janet's Home* (1863); *Oldbury* (1869); *Castle Daly* (1875), her greatest success, set in the Irish famine; and *A Doubting Heart* (1879), unfinished at her death.

Keillor, Garrison 1942– American. His radio programme, 'A Prairie Home Companion', introduced a long-running series of tales, gently comic and confidentially anecdotal, about the fictional Minnesota town of Lake Wobegon. These have been collected in *Happy To Be Here* (1985), *Lake Wobegon Days* (1985), *Leaving Home* (1987) and, with other short fiction, essays and verse, *We are Still Married* (1989). *WLT: A Radio*

Romance (1992) is a novel and *The Book of Guys* (1993) a collection of stories.

Kelley, William Melvyn 1937– American. Concerned with the lives and identities of contemporary African-Americans, his fiction draws on oral culture and often uses satire to portray the contrast between his protagonists and 'white' society. It includes *A Different Drummer* (1962), *Dancers on the Shore* (1964), *A Drop of Patience* (1965), *Dem* (1967) and *Dunford Travels Everywhere* (1971).

Kelman, James 1946– Scottish. The short stories in *Not Not While The Giro* (1983) blend deadpan humour with the demotic of Scottish working-class life. Subsequent work, like the collection *Greyhound for Breakfast* (1987), has become more serious in tone. His novels include *The Busconductor Hines* (1984), *A Disaffection* (1989), which won the JAMES TAIT BLACK MEMORIAL PRIZE, and *How Late It was, How Late* (1994), an ex-convict's monologue, which won the BOOKER PRIZE.

Keneally, Thomas (Michael) 1935– Australian. His best-known work, *SCHINDLER'S ARK* (1982), about a German Catholic factory owner rescuing Jews in World War II, was conceived and written as a documentary but read sufficiently like a novel to receive the BOOKER PRIZE. It typifies Keneally's interest in journalistic research, strong storytelling and settings, contemporary or historical, of war, violence and their aftermath. This informs *Blood Red, Sister Rose* (1974), *Gossip from the Forest* (1975), *Season in Purgatory* (1976), *Confederates* (1979), *Cut-Rate Kingdom* (1980), *A Family Madness* (1986), *Towards Asmara* (1989) and *Flying Hero Class* (1991). His prolific output also includes three early Catholic novels, *The Place at Whitton* (1964), *The Fear* (1965) and *Three Cheers for the Paraclete* (1968), which won the MILES FRANKLIN AWARD. Several novels tackle typically Australian subjects: convicts in *Bring Larks and Heroes* (1967; Miles Franklin Award) and *The Playmaker* (1987), bush life in *A Dutiful Daughter* (1971), *Woman of the Inner Sea* (1992) and *A River Town* (1995), and Aborigines in *The Chant of Jimmie Blacksmith* (1972). He has also written plays and travel books.

Kenilworth A novel by SIR WALTER SCOTT, published in 1821. The story interprets events leading to the mysterious death of Amy Robsart in 1560. Secretly married to Elizabeth I's favourite, the Earl of Leicester, she is kept at Cumnor Place, near Oxford, by the villainous Richard Varney, whom her rejected suitor Edmund Tressilian believes to be her lover. Tressilian's attempts to free her finally result in her meeting the Queen at Kenilworth. Elizabeth extracts a confession of the truth from Leicester, who, suspecting Tressilian's relation with his wife, orders Varney to murder her. Tressilian arrives too late at Cumnor Place to prevent her death.

Kennedy, A(lison) L(ouise) 1965– Scottish. A bleak vision of 'small lives, easily lost' and a taste for what she has called 'nasty Scottish humour' inform two collections of stories, *Night Geometry and the Garscadden Trains* (1990) and *Now That You're Back* (1994), and *Original Bliss* (1997), a novella and stories. *Looking for the Possible Dance* (1993) and *So I am Glad* (1995) are novels, set in Glasgow, about the pain or impossibility of human relations.

Kennedy, John Pendleton 1795–1870 American. His first and best-known novel, *HORSE-SHOE ROBINSON* (1835), is set during the Revolutionary War. It was followed by *Rob of the Bowl* (1838). Kennedy had earlier produced two collections of sketches, *The Red Book* (1818–19) and, under the pseudonym of Mark Littleton, *Swallow Barn* (1832). A friend of WASHINGTON IRVING and OLIVER WENDELL HOLMES, and WILLIAM MAKEPEACE THACKERAY'S American host, he was also one of the first to recognize EDGAR ALLAN POE.

Kennedy, Margaret (Moore) 1896–1967 English. Somewhat to her exasperation, she was always best known for her second novel, *The Constant Nymph* (1924), the story of Tessa Sanger, a composer's daughter who falls in love with another composer. Kennedy collaborated in adapting the book for the stage, and it was filmed four times. *The Fool of the Family* (1930) is a sequel. The rest of her prolific output, sometimes romantic and melodramatic but also capable of a poised style and cool wit, includes: *Together and Apart* (1936), a study of divorce; *The Midas Touch* (1938); *The Feast* (1950); *Lucy Carmichael* (1951); *Troy Chimneys* (1953); and *Not in the Calendar* (1964). She also wrote a book on JANE AUSTEN (1950) and *The Outlaws on Parnassus* (1958), a study of the art of fiction.

Kennedy, William 1928– American. His fiction centres on the Irish community in Albany, New York. *The Ink Truck* (1969) is about a newspaper strike, *Legs* (1975) about the gangster Jack 'Legs' Diamond and *Quinn's Book* (1988) about pre-Civil War Albany. *Billy Phelan's Greatest Game* (1978) started a series dealing with the Phelan family, which includes his best-known novel, *Ironweed* (1983; PULITZER PRIZE), as well as *Very Old Bones* (1992) and *The Flaming Corsage* (1996). He has also written children's books with Brendan Kennedy and worked on the screenplay for Francis Ford Coppola's film *The Cotton Club* (1984).

Kentucky Cardinal, A A short novel by JAMES LANE ALLEN, published in 1894. Adam Moss, an amiable but reclusive nature lover, falls in love with his neighbour Georgiana Cobb. At her request he cages a cardinal whose trust he has gained, but the bird soon dies. They quarrel, forgive each other and plan to marry. In *Aftermath* (1895), the sequel, Georgiana dies after giving birth to their child and Adam consoles himself by returning to his first love, nature.

Kerouac, Jack 1922–69 American. *The Town and the City* (1950) was the first of his semi-autobiographical novels. *ON THE ROAD* (1957), his best-known book, describes the often aimless search for significant experience of the BEATS. *The Subterraneans* and *The Dharma Bums* (both 1958), *Tristessa* (1960), *Big Sur* (1962) and *Desolation Angels* (1965) are all products of the Beat consciousness; *Doctor Sax* and *Maggie Cassidy* (both 1959) and *Visions of Gerard* (1963) are evocations of Kerouac's boyhood. *Satori in Paris* (1966) is an account of his quest for his Breton ancestors. Other books include *Lonesome Traveller* (1960; travel sketches), *Mexico City Blues* (1959; verse) and *Book of Dreams* (1961). *Visions of Cody*, written in 1951–2, was published posthumously in 1972.

Kesey, Ken 1935– American. He is still best known for his first novel, *ONE FLEW OVER THE CUCKOO'S NEST* (1962). Subsequent novels are: *Sometimes a Great Notion* (1964), about a logging family in the Northwest; *Sailor Song* (1992), set in Alaska in the near future; and *Last Go Round* (1994). Kesey has also written for children, in *Little Trickster the Squirrel Meets Big Double the Bear* (1990) and *The Sea Lion: A Story of the Cliff People* (1991). *Kesey's Garage Sale* (1973) and *Demon Box* (1986) are collections of essays, letters, interviews, stories and drawings; *The Further Inquiry* (1990) is a memoir. TOM WOLFE's *The Electric Kool-Aid Acid Test* (1968) records Kesey's wild lifestyle in the 1960s.

Kickham, Charles J(oseph) 1828–82 Irish. A Fenian and one of the editors of *The Irish People*, he served four years in English prisons, during which he wrote *Sally Cavanagh* (1869). His real fame as a novelist depends on *Knocknagow: or, The Homes of Tipperary* (1879), a tale of depopulation, land laws and landlord greed, which became one of the most popular novels in Irish literary history.

Kidman, Fiona 1940– New Zealand. She is a popular and prolific voice of mainstream feminism. The best-selling *A Breed of Women* (1979) told the story of a woman's struggle to find a life and career for herself in New Zealand society after World War II. *Paddy's Puzzle* (1983; called *In the Clear Light* in the USA, 1985) is set in wartime Auckland, while *The Book of Secrets* (1987; winner of the NEW ZEALAND BOOK AWARD) is a family saga. *The Foreign Woman* (1993) reveals her gift for acute social observation and her eye for what marks the contemporary. *Mrs Dixon and Friend* (1982) and *True Stars* (1990) are collections of stories. *Palm Prints* (1995) is a collection of essays, speeches and occasional pieces centred on growing up in provincial New Zealand in the 1950s and 1960s. She has also published poetry, including *Wakeful Nights* (1991).

Kidnapped and *CATRIONA* A novel and its sequel by ROBERT LOUIS STEVENSON, published respectively in 1886 and 1893.

After his father's death David Balfour turns for help to his miserly uncle, Ebenezer, who has him kidnapped and put aboard a ship for the Carolinas. His subsequent adventures, with the Jacobite rebel Alan Breck, include shipwreck, accidental involvement in Colin Campbell's murder, and flight across the Highlands. Eventually Ebenezer is exposed and David's estate restored.

In the sequel David is in love with Catriona, daughter of the renegade James More. He tries to help James Stewart of the Glens, falsely accused of Colin Campbell's murder, but finds himself in danger. He survives the plot, and Alan Breck finally escapes to safety in France.

Kijewski, Karen See DETECTIVE FICTION.

Kim A novel by RUDYARD KIPLING, published in 1901. It exploits many of his childhood memories of India.

Kim (Kimball O'Hara), the orphan son of an Irish colour-sergeant and a nursemaid in a colonel's family, learns self-reliance and resourcefulness early in life on the streets of Lahore. He encounters Mahbub Ali, who works for the British Secret Service, and a Tibetan lama, on a quest to be freed from the Wheel of Life, staying in touch with them even after he is recognized by the chaplain of his father's old regiment and sent to the school for Anglo-Indian children at Lucknow. He plays an active role in the great game of imperial espionage against the Russians (see SPY FICTION), but is united with the lama at the end of the latter's quest for the sacred River of the Arrow.

Kincaid, Jamaica 1949– Caribbean/American. *Annie John* (1985) is an account of Caribbean girlhood and coming of age which has affinities with the work of JEAN RHYS, ZEE EDGELL and ERNA BRODBER. Other works include: *Lucy* (1991), a novel; *At the Bottom of the River* (1983), a collection of sketches and short stories; and *A Small Place* (1988), an essay attacking the exploitation of Antigua by colonialism and tourism. She edited *Best American Essays, 1995* (1996).

King, Francis (Henry) 1923– English. Combining fluent narrative with an interest in decadent, sometimes horrific, behaviour, his many novels include *To the Dark Tower* (1946), *The Dividing Stream* (1951; SOMERSET MAUGHAM AWARD), *The Widow* (1957), *The Custom House* (1961), *Flights* (1973), *The Action* (1979), *Act of Darkness* (1983), *Voices in an Empty Room* (1984), *The Ant Colony* (1991), *The One and Only* (1994), *Ash on an Old Man's Sleeve* (1996) and *Dead Letters* (1997). Short stories include *The Brighton Belle and Other Stories* (1968) and *Hard Feelings and Other Stories* (1976). The novella *Secret Lives* gives the title to a collaborative volume (1991) written with Tom Wakefield and Patrick Gale. King's autobiography, *Yesterday Came Suddenly* (1995), is a richly documented account of half a century of literary life. He has also published a biography of E. M. FORSTER (1978) and edited LAFCADIO HEARN's *Writings from Japan* and the diaries of J. R. ACKERLEY.

King, Stephen See GENRE FICTION and SCIENCE FICTION.

King, Thomas 1943– Canadian, of mixed Cherokee and Greek-German parentage. His fiction provides contemporary reworkings of traditional Native storytelling modes, with a particular focus on the creator/trickster figure of Coyote. *Medicine River* (1990) and *Green Grass, Running Water* (1993) are novels, *A Coyote Columbus Story* (1992) is a children's book and *One Good Story, That One* (1993) is a collection of short stories. He has been an influential figure in the development of Native Studies in Canada and the USA, and has written radio and TV dramas.

King Solomon's Mines A novel by HENRY RIDER HAGGARD, published in 1885. Sir Henry Curtis, Captain John Good RN and the narrator, Allan Quatermain, set off with their native servant, Umbopa, to find Curtis's brother George, who has gone to look for the treasure of King Solomon's mines in the lost land of the Kukuanas. After journeying over waterless desert and freezing mountains, they encounter the villainous King Twala and the witch-doctor Gagool. Umbopa turns out to be the rightful king and wins the civil war which breaks out. Twala dies in single combat with Curtis. Gagool pretends to guide the heroes to Solomon's mines but leaves them to die in an underground vault. They escape and return to civilization, finding George Curtis on the way. *ALLAN QUATERMAIN* (1887) is a sequel.

Kingsley, Charles 1819–75 English. The influence of Thomas Carlyle and F. D. Maurice, leader of the movement for Christian Socialism, is clearly apparent in Kingsley's contributions to *Politics for the People* (1848) and *The Christian Socialist* (1850–1) under the pseudonym of Parson Lot, and in his novels, *YEAST* (serial, 1848; volume, 1850) and *ALTON LOCKE* (1850), which expose the injustices suffered by agricultural labourers and workers in the clothing trade. *HYPATIA* (1843), a novel about early Christianity, is regarded by many as his finest work. *WESTWARD HO!* (1855) turned to the Elizabethan era and the landscape of his Devon childhood. *Two Years Ago* (1857) has a contemporary setting.

Other works include: *Glaucus: or, The Wonders of the Shore* (1855), a volume of natural history; *The Heroes* (1856), retelling the legends of Perseus, Theseus and Jason, and *THE WATER BABIES* (1863), a fantasy, both for children; *The Roman and the Teuton* (1864), lectures at Cambridge; *Hereward the Wake* (1866), a novel about the 'Last of the English' and his defeat by William the Conqueror at Ely; *At Last* (1871), an account of his journey to the West Indies; and *Prose Idylls* (1873), a volume of essays.

Kingsley was notable for applying Christian ethics to contemporary social problems while stopping well short of radicalism. 'Muscular Christianity', his brand of hearty Protestantism, often led him into quarrels, like the one in 1864 which prompted John Henry Newman to write *Apologia Pro Vita Sua*. His brother HENRY KINGSLEY was also a novelist; so was his daughter, Mary St Leger Kingsley Harrison, who wrote as LUCAS MALET.

Kingsley, Henry 1830–76 English. He was the younger brother of CHARLES KINGSLEY. He spent five years in Australia, the setting for the novel he published on his return, *Geoffrey Hamlyn* (1859). Subsequent works include *Ravenshoe* (1862), a romance about the mystery of the hero's birth which includes episodes set in the Crimean War; *Austin Elliott* (1863); and *The Hillyars and the Burtons* (1865), another Australian novel.

Kingston, Maxine Hong 1940– American. *The Woman Warrior* (1976) and *China Men* (1980) are partly fictionalized memoirs dealing, respectively, with her childhood and the ancestors who emigrated from China to the USA. *Tripmaster Monkey* (1989) is an intricate PICARESQUE novel set in San Francisco in the 1960s.

Kipling, Rudyard 1865–1936 English. Son of the artist John Lockwood Kipling, he was born in Bombay and sent back to England with his sister in 1871. His unhappiness at Southsea was relieved by visits to his maternal uncle, Edward Burne-Jones, who, with William Morris, inspired his move in 1878 to the United Services College at Westward Ho! in Devon. Kipling's relatively happy years there underlie his popular *STALKY & CO.* (1899). He returned to India in 1882 to work as a journalist in Lahore. His familiarity with all ranks of the Anglo-Indian community gave freshness to the poems and tales published in newspapers or as booklets by the Indian Railway Library, gathered in *Departmental Ditties* (1886), *Plain Tales from the Hills* (1888), *The Phantom Rickshaw* (1888), *Wee Willie Winkie* (1888) and *SOLDIERS THREE* (1892).

After his return to England in 1889 he rapidly established himself in literary London, winning the friendship of HENRY JAMES, HENRY RIDER HAGGARD and the poet W. E. Henley. *BARRACK-ROOM BALLADS AND OTHER VERSES* (1892), with two collections of short stories, *LIFE'S HANDICAP* (1891) and *MANY INVENTIONS* (1893), set the pattern for his major writings. Two novels, *The Light That Failed* (1891) and *The Naulahka* (with Wolcott Balestier; 1892), were relative failures. After marrying Balestier's sister, Caroline, he spent the years 1892–6 near her family in Vermont, USA, where the stories of *THE JUNGLE BOOK* (1894) and *The Second Jungle Book* (1895) were written. By the time his best-known novel, *KIM*, appeared in 1901 the family was back in England. Kipling settled in Sussex in 1902. The *JUST SO STORIES* (1902), *PUCK OF POOK'S HILL* (1906) and *Rewards and Fairies* (1910) show an unusual sympathy with children, though he continued to publish stories for adults in *Traffics and Discoveries* (1904), *Actions and Reactions* (1909), *A Diversity of Creatures* (1917), *Debits and Credits* (1926) and *Limits and Renewals* (1932). The posthumous *Something of Myself* (1937) is autobiographical.

Kipling's high reputation, as 'Poet of Empire' and the first English writer to receive the Nobel Prize for literature (1907), had begun to wane before his death. Later generations have rediscovered the craft of his poetry and the stern realism of his fiction.

Kipps: *The Story of a Simple Soul* A novel by H. G. Wells, published in 1905. Arthur Kipps's feelings for Ann Pornick, a childhood sweetheart, prove a saving grace in the years of deadening apprenticeship to Mr Shalford, a Folkestone draper. A legacy from his grandfather begins a bitterly comic process of social initiation, with Helen Walshingham, his wood-carving teacher, playing a leading part in his loss of self-esteem. He marries Ann but soon learns that his money has been embezzled by Helen's brother. The unexpected success of his friend Chitterlow's play, in which Kipps had invested, restores the fortunes of Kipps, Ann and their child.

Knight, Ellis Cornelia See *Rasselas*.

Knox, Elizabeth 1959– New Zealand. Her experimental techniques combine fantasy and realism. *After Z-Hour* (1987), her first novel, has been described as a post-modernist ghost story. *Parameta* (1989), a novella about childhood set in the Wellington suburb where she grew up, won praise for its precise and sensuous imagery. *Treasure* (1992) moves from Wellington to North Carolina and the White Steppes in an idiosyncratic blend of the metaphysical and the real. *Pomare* (1994) returns to suburban Wellington in the 1960s and the theme of children experiencing the world for the first time.

Knox, Monsignor Ronald See DETECTIVE FICTION.

Koch, Christopher 1932– Australian. He first came to the fore, with PATRICK WHITE and RANDOLPH STOW, in challenging the NATURALISM which dominated Australian fiction until the 1950s. Never a prolific writer, he is a meticulous stylist whose prose aims towards poetry in its symbolic density. His themes are an encounter with a romantic 'otherland' and an exploration of the dualities he finds at the heart of the human condition. *The Boys in the Island* (1958) and *The Doubleman* (1985) are notable for graphic evocations of his native Tasmania. *Across the Sea Wall* (1965) was inspired by his experience of India, and *The Year of Living Dangerously* (1978), generally regarded as his best work, is set in Sukarno's Indonesia. Both explore the alternative spiritual possibilities which Eastern religions and cultures offer the Australian psyche. *Highways to a War* (1995) is set against the background of American and Australian incursions into Cambodia in the 1960s; it and *The Doubleman* both won the MILES FRANKLIN AWARD. Koch has also written *Chinese Journey* (with Nicholas Hasluck; 1985) and a collection of essays, *Crossing the Gap* (1987).

Koea, Shonagh 1943– New Zealand. She stylishly portrays a combination of outward formality and inner chaos in women's lives. *The Woman Who Never Went Home* (1987) is a collection of short stories. *Staying Home and Being Rotten* (1992) shifts between present and past in the life of a widow fighting back against experiences both hilarious and appallingly sad. The stories in *Fifteen Rubies by Candlelight* (1993) are about women struggling with disappointment, loneliness and almost uniformly despicable men. In *Sing to Me Dreamer* (1994) a suburban woman learns from her Indian guru and lover that she has the power to shape her own life creatively.

Koestler, Arthur 1905–83 Born in Budapest and educated in Vienna, he lived in Palestine, worked as a journalist in Berlin, joined the Communist Party, visited the Soviet Union, reported the Spanish Civil War, and suffered imprisonment in Spain, Paris and again after his escape to Britain in 1940. His most widely read book was *Darkness at Noon* (1940), a novel condemning Stalin's totalitarianism, written in German and translated into English by another hand. His early life was essentially a paradigm of the turmoil Europe suffered in the years before World War II, and his writings were essentially a commentary, always engaged but increasingly oblique and reflective, on the nature and roots of that turmoil. His first book in English, *The Scum of the Earth* (1941), recounts these experiences; *Arrow in the Blue* (1952) and *The Invisible Writing* (1954) continue the autobiographical process. Other works, diverse yet plotting a relentless course, include: *The Yogi and the Commissar* (1945), essays about contemporary politics; *Thieves in the Night* (1946), a novel, and *Promise and Fulfilment* (1949), a work of history, both about the Jewish state; and *The Age of Longing* (1951), a novel about the threat of nuclear extermination. *The Sleepwalkers* (1959), *The Act of Creation* (1964) and *The Ghost in the Machine* (1967) are about the nature of mind. *The Roots of Coincidence* (1972) and *The Challenge of Chance* (with Sir Alister Hardy and Robert Harvie; 1973) investigate ESP. He left a bequest in his will to promote academic study of psychic phenomena.

Kogawa, Joy 1935– Japanese-Canadian. She has published several collections of poetry – *The Splintered Moon* (1967), *A Choice of Dreams* (1974) and *Jericho Road* (1977) – but is best known for *Obasan* (1981), a novel which combines documentary realism and lyrical protest against the silences of official history about the Japanese-Canadian experience. *Itsuka* (1992) is a sequel.

Koontz, Dean R. See GENRE FICTION and SCIENCE FICTION.

Kornbluth, Cyril M. See SCIENCE FICTION.

Kosinski, Jerzy 1933–91 American. An émigré from Poland, he made his fiction a rich amalgam of invention and self-referentiality exploring the dynamics of survival. He rose to fame with a supposedly autobiographical novel, *The Painted Bird* (1965), about a homeless boy's travels through war-ravaged Eastern Europe. It was followed by: *Steps* (1968), which won the National Book Award; *Being There* (1971), a comic comment on the nexus of naïvety and power; *The Devil Tree* (1973); *Cockpit* (1975); *Blind Date* (1977); *Passion Play* (1979); *Pinball* (1982); and *The Hermit of 69th Street: The Working Papers of Norbert Kosky* (1988). Non-fiction includes *The Future is Ours, Comrade* (1960).

Kroetsch, Robert 1927– Canadian. Virtually all his fiction is located in his native Alberta and concerned with the specifics of Western Canadian place and identity. Drawing heavily on classical and native Canadian myths, it frequently involves quests. Perhaps the most notable examples are *The Studhorse Man* (1969), *Gone Indian* (1973), *Badlands* (1975), *Alibi* (1983) and *The Puppeteer* (1992). Other novels are *But We are Exiles* (1965), *The Words of My Roaring* (1966) and *What the Crow Said* (1978). His many volumes of verse have been gathered into a poetic autobiography, *Field Notes* (1981, 1985, 1989). A leading critic, he has published *The Lovely Treachery of Words* (1989). Other works include: *Alberta* (1988), a travel book; *The Crow Journals* (1980), a literary diary; *Labyrinths of Voice* (1982), a book-length interview; *Excerpts from the Real World* (1986), a prose poem; and *A Likely Story* (1995), a literary autobiography. He has been an important influence on POST-MODERNISM in Canada.

Kuppner, Frank [Francis] **(Joseph)** 1951– He was born in Glasgow to a Scottish mother and West Prussian father. He has turned from poetry, such as *A Bad Day for the Sung Dynasty* (1984), to prose which constantly pushes against the conventional boundaries of the novel. It includes: *A Very Quiet Street* (1989), sub-titled 'A Novel of Sorts', bringing together autobiography, local history and reflections on the Oscar Slater case; *A Concussed History of Scotland* (1990), idiosyncratically divided into several hundred chapters, some of them less than a line long; *Something Very Like Murder* (1994), again combining reflections on a local crime – the Bertie Willcox case in 1929 – with autobiography; and *Life on a Dead Planet* (1996).

Kureishi, Hanif 1954– Anglo-Asian. Best known for his plays and the screenplay of *My Beautiful Laundrette* (filmed 1985, published 1986), he has also produced fiction. *The Buddha of Suburbia* (1990) is roistering PICARESQUE, set mainly in the south London of the 1970s where Kureishi spent his own youth. *The Black Album* (1995) is a political thriller and *Love in a Blue Time* (1997) a volume of short stories exploring love and loss.

L

La Guma, Alex 1925–85 South African. His fiction presents the iniquities of apartheid in scrupulously realistic language, while also asserting a romantic faith in his characters' potential for compassion. It includes: *A Walk in the Night* (1962), about a Cape Town slum, District Six; *And a Threefold Cord* (1964), about a shantytown; *The Stone Country* (1967), set in prison, a precise metaphor for South Africa itself; *In the Fog of the Season's End* (1972), about underground resistance; and *Time of the Butcherbird* (1979), set in a tribal area. *A Soviet Journey* (1978) is a travel book.

La Ramée, Louise de See OUIDA.

Lacombe, Patrice See FRENCH-CANADIAN NOVEL.

Lady Anna A novel by ANTHONY TROLLOPE, serialized in *The Fortnightly Review* from April 1873 to April 1874. Daniel Thwaite, a hard-working tailor from Cumberland, woos the spirited heiress Lady Anna, daughter of an earl. In spite of opposition and the advice of artistic and aristocratic friends, Anna marries Daniel and they leave for Australia.

Lady Audley's Secret A SENSATION NOVEL by MARY ELIZABETH BRADDON, serialized in 1861–2 and published in volume form in 1862. Written in haste but with a breathlessly readable plot, it has a striking central character in Lady Audley, who murders her first husband, George Talboys, on his return from Australia in order to protect her bigamous second marriage and her position as mistress of Audley Court. Her crime is uncovered by Robert Audley, Sir Michael's nephew, and she is committed to a private asylum. In a final twist to the story, Talboys turns out to be alive, having secretly left the country after surviving the attempted murder.

Lady Chatterley's Lover A novel by D. H. LAWRENCE, written and privately printed in Florence in 1928.

Constance (Connie) marries Sir Clifford Chatterley, a mineowner left paralysed and impotent by a war wound. After a superficial affair with Michaelis, a playwright, she enters into a passionate relationship with Sir Clifford's gamekeeper, Oliver Mellors, a forthright man uncontaminated by industrial society. When she becomes pregnant, Connie asks for a divorce but Sir Clifford refuses to release her. Though separated, the lovers wait hopefully for the obstacles between them to be surmounted.

Lady Chatterley was denied full publication in Britain for over 30 years. An expurgated version (1932) eliminated the four-letter words and detailed sexual descriptions. The unexpurgated text became available in 1960 after Penguin Books survived a prosecution under the Obscene Publications Act in 1959. The earlier versions of the novel have been published as *The First Lady Chatterley* (1944) and *John Thomas and Lady Jane* (1972).

Laing, B(ernard) Kojo 1946– Ghanaian. His fiction is surreal, inventive and sometimes considered obscure. *Search Sweet Country* (1986) is set in Accra in the mid-1970s, while *Woman of the Aeroplanes* (1988) and *Major Gentl and the Achimota Wars* (1992) take place in the near future. The poems in *Godhorse* (1989) also display witty combinations of imagery and formal invention.

Lamb, Lady Caroline See SILVER-FORK NOVEL.

Lamming, George 1927– Barbadian. His highly successful first novel, *IN THE CASTLE OF MY SKIN* (1953), draws on his boyhood in Barbados. Its successors include: *The Emigrants* (1954), about West Indian disillusion with life in Britain; *Of Age and Innocence* (1958), which contrasts peasant wisdom and youthful tolerance with violent, Caribbean, pre-Independence politicking; *Season of Adventure* (1960), in which the heroine painfully achieves Caribbean identity; the ambitious *Water with Berries* (1971); and his masterpiece, *Natives of My Person* (1972), set aboard a 17th-century slave ship. *The Pleasures of Exile* (1960) consists of Lamming's essays. He also edited an anthology of black writing, *Cannon Shots and Glass Beads* (1974). *Conversations* (1992) is a collection of essays, addresses and interviews.

L'Amour, Louis See GENRE FICTION.

Landon, Letitia Elizabeth 1802–38 English. One of the most popular and prolific writers of her day, she generally published under the initials L. E. L. Her poetry includes *The Fate of Adelaide* (1821), *The Improvisatrice* (1824), *The Troubadour* (1825), *The Venetian Bracelet* (1829) and *The Vow of the Peacock* (1835). Her most successful novel was *Ethel Churchill* (1837), set in the high society of the early 18th century; other novels were *Romance and Reality* (1831), *Francesca Carrara* (1834) and *Duty and Inclination* (1838).

Lang, John George 1816–64 Presumed author of the anonymous *Legends of Australia* (1842) and, as such, the first Australian-born novelist. Lang, however, lived mainly in India and Europe, contributing to many magazines, including DICKENS's *Household Words*, which published parts of his *Botany Bay; or True Tales of Early Australia* (1859). A facsimile edition of Lang's *The Forger's Wife* (1855), a novel set in Australia, appeared in 1979.

Langley, Eve 1908–74 Australian. Her quasi-autobiographical first novel, *The Pea-Pickers* (1942), was widely acclaimed for its exuberant and idiosyncratic account of two teenage sisters who disguise themselves as boys and take to the road. A sequel, *White Topee*, followed in 1954 but

Langley never fulfilled her early promise and died an eccentric recluse.

Laodicean, A: *A Story of Today* A novel by THOMAS HARDY, published in 1881. Paula Power, the Laodicean or vacillator, inherits Stancy Castle in Somerset. She falls in love with George Somerset, a young architect, but cannot agree to an engagement. She does, however, eventually accept Captain de Stancy, a member of the family which once owned the castle. He is helped by his illegitimate son, the conniving Will Dare. On discovering Dare's villainy Paula breaks her engagement and is reconciled with Somerset. Dare contrives to burn the castle to the ground.

Lardner, Ring(gold) (Wilmer) 1885–1933 American. A sports reporter, he became famous with the witty, vernacular letters he wrote as 'Jack Keefe', a newcomer to a professional baseball team. They were collected as *You Know Me, Al: A Busher's Letters* (1914). *Bib Ballads* (1915) is a volume of poetry, *Gullible's Travels* (1917) and *Treat 'em Rough* (1918) are collections of satirical stories. *The Big Town* (1921) is Lardner's only novel. He had a large and enthusiastic following by the time he published *How to Write Short Stories (with Samples)* (1924). His later works are the collections *What of It?* (1925), *The Love Nest* (1926), *Round Up* (1929) and *First and Last* (1934).

Larkin, Philip (Arthur) 1922–85 English. His reputation as a poet using traditional forms to offer a wry treatment of contemporary life rests on three major collections, *The Less Deceived* (1955), *The Whitsun Weddings* (1964), and *High Windows* (1964). The arrangement of his work in *The Collected Poems* (1988), edited by Anthony Thwaite, did not please all readers. Larkin's two understated novels, *Jill* (1946) and *A Girl in Winter* (1947), belonged to his youth and are autobiographical in origin. He also published: jazz reviews, collected in *All What Jazz?* (1970), and occasional articles and reviews, collected in *Required Writing* (1983). They are informed by the same dislike of MODERNISM which coloured his selections for *The Oxford Book of Twentieth-Century English Verse* (1973). *Collected Letters 1940–1985*, edited by Anthony Thwaite, appeared in 1992.

Larsen, Nella 1891–1964 African-American. With the encouragement of CARL VAN VECHTEN, she published two novels hailed for their contribution to the HARLEM RENAISSANCE but later overlooked. *Quicksand* (1928) follows Helga Crane's search for identity. *Passing* (1929) contrasts the lives of two childhood friends from Chicago: Irene Redfield, who (like Larsen herself) joins the Harlem middle class through marriage, and Clare Kendry, who marries a white man and passes as white.

Laski, Marghanita 1915–88 English. *The Victorian Chaise-Longue* (1953), the last of her six novels, was the most popular but *Love on the Supertax*

(1944), *To Bed with Grand Music* (1946) and *Tory Heaven* (1948) also struck a chord with their portrayal of middle- and upper-class women's subordinated, morally directionless lives in a male-dominated society. She was also a frequent radio broadcaster and a notable advocate of public funding in the arts.

Last Burden, The A novel by UPAMANYU CHATTERJEE, published in 1993. It chronicles tense relations of love and hate in an upper-class Indian extended family. The narrative proceeds by multiple flashbacks and STREAM OF CONSCIOUSNESS from the younger son, Jamun. The title refers most obviously to the old and infirm parents but also perhaps to their emotionally and economically dependent son.

Last Chronicle of Barset, The The final volume in ANTHONY TROLLOPE's BARSETSHIRE NOVELS, published in 1867.

Josiah Crawley, the intractable curate of Hogglestock, is falsely accused of stealing a £20 cheque from Lord Lufton's agent, Mr Soames. The bishop's wife, Mrs Proudie, plays a leading part in the persecution. Archdeacon Grantly's son, Major Henry Grantly, breaks with his father in insisting on becoming engaged to Crawley's daughter Grace. Mrs Arabin (the former Eleanor Harding) establishes Crawley's innocence and resolves the affair. Crawley is appointed to the parish of the late Mr Harding, and Archdeacon Grantly is won over when he meets Grace. The novel also contains the death of Mrs Proudie and follows Johnny Eames's ever-hopeful pursuit of Lily Dale.

Last Days of Pompeii, The A novel by EDWARD BULWER LYTTON, published in 1834. The action takes place just before and during the eruption of Vesuvius in AD 79. There are lively pictures of Roman life (including an early Christian sect) and a memorable villain, Arbaces, the Priest of Isis.

Last of the Barons, The A novel by EDWARD BULWER LYTTON, published in 1843. The hero is the medieval Earl of Warwick, known as 'the kingmaker'. The book was intended as a political allegory: Warwick's defeat at the Battle of Barnet represents the overthrow of the hereditary feudal order by the new commercial classes.

Last of the Mohicans, The See LEATHERSTOCKING TALES, THE.

Last Puritan, The: *A Memoir in the Form of a Novel* The only novel by the American philosopher George Santayana (1863–1952), published in 1935. It deals with the childhood and youth of Oliver Alden, the heir to a wealthy and established New England family: his upbringing by his mother; his contact with his drug-addicted father, who has already rejected the puritan values of the family heritage; his friendship with his European cousin, Mario, and courtship of another cousin, Edith; his friendship with the Englishman Jim Darnley and his unfulfilled love for Jim's sister Rose; and his death in France during World War I.

Lathen, Emma Pseudonym of Mary J. Latsis and Martha Henissart (who do not make their dates of birth public). American. *Banking on Death* (1961) launched a long-running series of DETECTIVE FICTION featuring the Wall Street banker John Putnam Thatcher and his colleague at the Sloan Guaranty Trust. At its best – in, for example, *Accounting for Murder* (1964) – it combines expertise about the world of finance and business with a wry sense of humour. Under the pseudonym of R. B. Dominic the authors have also written about the detective adventures of Ben Safford, the congressman for Ohio who first appears in *Murder Sunny Side Up* (1968).

Laurence, (Jean) Margaret 1926–87 Canadian. Her most important achievement is the 'Manawaka' sequence, five works set in a fictional Canadian small town and dealing largely with the lives of women: *The Stone Angel* (1964), *A Jest of God* (1966), *The Fire-Dwellers* (1969), *A Bird in the House* (short stories, 1970) and *THE DIVINERS* (1974), the single most impressive volume. She also published several works about Africa: *This Side Jordan* (1960), a novel set at the time of Ghanaian independence; *The Tomorrow-Tamer* (1963), short stories; *The Prophet's Camel Bell* (1963), a non-fictional account of her life in Somaliland; and *Drums and Cannons* (1968), a study of Nigerian novelists and playwrights. *Heart of a Stranger* (1976) is a collection of personal essays. *Dance of the Earth* (1989) is an autobiographical memoir.

Lavengro: *The Scholar – The Gypsy – The Priest* A fictionalized autobiography by GEORGE BORROW, published in 1851. 'Lavengro' is the gipsy name for a philologist. Borrow conceals his early family life behind irresistibly romantic portraits of his father and mother, draws a veil over his early attempts to establish himself as a writer and says nothing of Russia, where he lived in 1833–5. Instead he writes episodically and without regard for chronology about an almost penniless young man who, leaving London in 1825, wanders round England for a year or more, consorting with tinkers, innkeepers, Nonconformist ministers, eccentric old gentlemen, chaste young women and gipsies. Though many contemporaries distrusted the book, it was soon recognized as a masterpiece. *THE ROMANY RYE* (1857) is a sequel.

Lavin, Mary 1912–96 Irish. Her work deals with the small tensions of Irish middle-class life. Although she published novels, *The House in Clewe Street* (1945) and *Mary O'Grady* (1950), her preferred form was the short story. Volumes include *Tales from Bective Bridge* (1942; JAMES TAIT BLACK MEMORIAL PRIZE), *The Long Ago and Other Stories* (1944), *The Becker Wives and Other Stories*

(1946), *At Sallygap and Other Stories* (1947) and *In The Middle of the Fields* (1967). *Collected Stories* appeared in 1971 and *The Stories of Mary Lavin*, in three volumes, in 1987.

Lawless, Emily 1845–1913 Irish. Her novels, generally studies of the Irish peasantry, include *A Millionaire's Cousin* (1885), *Hurrish* (1886) and *Grania* (1892). *With the Wild Geese* (1902), a volume of poetry, was well received by contemporaries.

Lawrence, D(avid) H(erbert) (Richards) 1885–1930 English. He was born at Eastwood, Nottinghamshire. His father was a coal-miner and his mother came from a family with genteel aspirations. He left Nottingham High School in 1901 and worked as a clerk and pupil-teacher before taking a training course at University College, Nottingham. Subsequently he taught in Croydon until illness forced him to resign. His writing was first encouraged by his friend Jessie Chambers and FORD MADOX FORD, who published his poetry in *The English Review* and helped with the publication of his first novel, *THE WHITE PEACOCK* (1911). It was followed by *THE TRESPASSER* (1912), based on the experiences of his friend Helen Corke, and his first major work, the autobiographical *SONS AND LOVERS* (1913).

In 1912 Lawrence met Frieda Weekley (*née* von Richthofen), daughter of a German baron and wife of a professor at Nottingham. They went to Germany together and married after her divorce in 1914. During World War I they lived in London and Cornwall, until expelled on suspicion of spying for the Germans. By this time Lawrence had formed close friendships with, among others, DAVID GARNETT, ALDOUS HUXLEY, Bertrand Russell, Lady Ottoline Morrell, KATHERINE MANSFIELD, John Middleton Murry and RICHARD ALDINGTON. His next novel, *THE RAINBOW* (1915), was prosecuted and banned on grounds of obscenity. Its successor, *WOMEN IN LOVE*, had difficulty finding a publisher. It was finally printed privately in New York in 1920; a censored English edition followed in 1921.

In 1919 Lawrence and Frieda left England for Italy, where he wrote *The Lost Girl* (1920), *AARON'S ROD* (1922) and *Mr Noon*, an incomplete novel carrying forward his life following *Sons and Lovers*. It was eventually published in 1984. Subsequent works reflect the travels of a writer who had become a permanent exile from his native country. *KANGAROO* (1923) was written during a four-month stay in Australia, where Lawrence met M. L. Skinner (with whom he collaborated on *The Boy in the Bush*, 1924). *THE PLUMED SERPENT* (1926) was inspired by his stays in Mexico. His last novel, *LADY CHATTERLEY'S LOVER*, was published in Florence in 1928. An expurgated edition appeared in England and the USA in 1932 but the original version had to await favourable court verdicts in 1959 and 1960 respectively. The first two versions of the novel were published independently as *The First Lady Chatterley* (1944) and *John Thomas and Lady Jane* (1972).

Lawrence died of tuberculosis at Vence, in France, at the age of 44. Given the brevity of his writing career, the sheer amount of his output is remarkable. His short stories, which include some of his finest work, appeared in *The Prussian Officer* (1914), *England, My England* (1922), *The Woman Who Rode Away* (1928), *Love among the Haystacks* (1930) and *The Lovely Lady* (1933). His novellas, also among his best work, include *The Ladybird, The Fox, The Captain's Doll* (1923); *St Mawr* and *The Princess* (1925); *Sun* (1926); *The Escaped Cock* (also known as *The Man Who Died*; 1929) and *The Virgin and the Gipsy* (1930). His poetry, first collected in 1928, includes *Love Poems* (1913), *Amores* (1916), *Look! We Have Come Through!* (1917), *New Poems* (1918), *Bay* (1919), *Birds, Beasts and Flowers* (1923), *Pansies* (1929), *Nettles* (1930) and *Last Poems* (1932). In addition Lawrence wrote plays, several about mining families, collected in *The Complete Plays* (1965).

His non-fictional prose covers a broad spectrum. *Psychoanalysis and the Unconscious* (1921) and *Fantasia of the Unconscious* (1922) stand in intimate relationship to the thinking which informs his major novels. His literary criticism includes the ground-breaking *Studies in Classic American Literature* (1923) and a study of THOMAS HARDY (first published in *Phoenix*), *Reflections on the Death of a Porcupine* (1925) and *Assorted Articles* (1930) are collections of essays. His travel books include *Twilight in Italy* (1916), *Sea and Sardinia* (1921), *Etruscan Places* (1932) and *Mornings in Mexico* (1927). *Movements in European History* (1921) is a school history book written under the pseudonym of Lawrence H. Davison. Many of his uncollected stories, essays, reviews and introductions were included in *Phoenix: The Posthumous Papers* (1936) and *Phoenix II: Uncollected, Unpublished and Other Prose Works* (1968). Most of his pictures were reproduced in *The Paintings of D. H. Lawrence* (1929).

Lawrence, George Alfred 1827–76 English. *GUY LIVINGSTONE* (1857) introduced 'muscular blackguardism' (as opposed to CHARLES KINGSLEY's 'muscular Christianity') in the character of its strong and brutal hero. Eight other novels followed, including *Sword and Gown* (1859), *Barren Honour* (1862), *Breaking a Butterfly* (1869) and *Hagarene* (1874).

Lawson, Henry 1867–1922 Australian. The best of his bush ballads and stories, based on his experience of the outback in New South Wales, were written by the turn of the century. After 1901 he seemed unable to recapture his laconic humour and fine balance of style, and his later work is marred by sentimentality. Lawson's first collection was *Stories in Prose and Verse* (1894), followed by *While the Billy Boils* (1896), *On the Track* (1900) and *Joe Wilson and His Mates* (1901). A collection, *The Stories of Henry Lawson*, was edited by Cecil Mann (1965).

Le Carré, John [Cornwell, David John Moore] 1931– English. His SPY FICTION about the grey, duplicitous world of intelligence during the Cold War have increasingly come to be regarded less as thrillers than as perceptive documentations of their era. *The Spy Who Came In from the Cold* (1963), his third novel and a winner of the SOMERSET MAUGHAM AWARD, made his reputation and remains his most concentrated study. *Call for the Dead* (1961) had already introduced George Smiley, who has reappeared several times, notably in *Tinker, Tailor, Soldier, Spy* (1974) and *Smiley's People* (1980). Other novels include: *The Looking-Glass War* (1965); *A Small Town in Germany* (1968); *The Honourable Schoolboy* (1977); *The Little Drummer Girl* (1983); *The Perfect Spy* (1986); *The Russia House* (1989), in response to the end of the Cold War; and *The Tailor of Panama* (1996).

Le Fanu, (Joseph) Sheridan 1814–73 Irish. In all, he published some 20 books including novels, stories and verse, the latter including 'The Legend of the Glaive' and 'Song of the Bottle'. He is best known for his ingenious tales of mystery and terror, notably *The Cock and Anchor* (1845), *The House by the Churchyard* (1863), *UNCLE SILAS* (1864) and a volume of short stories, *IN A GLASS DARKLY* (1872).

Le Guin, Ursula K(roeber) 1929– American. Her SCIENCE FICTION includes: *The Left Hand of Darkness* (1969), about a society of hermaphrodites; *The Lathe of Heaven* (1971), about dreams which alter reality; *The Word for World is Forest* (1972), about colonialism; *The Dispossessed* (1974); and *Always Coming Home* (1986), about future inhabitants of northern California. *The Wind's Twelve Quarters* (1975), *The Compass Rose* (1982) and *Four Ways to Forgiveness* (1995) are collections of short stories and novellas. Her non-fantastic fiction, including *Orsinian Tales* (1976), *Malafrena* (1979) and *A Fisherman of the Inland Sea* (1994), is usually set in the imaginary past. Her children's books include the much-acclaimed 'Earthsea' fantasy series: *A Wizard of Earthsea* (1968), *The Tombs of Atuan* (1971), *The Farthest Shore* (1972) and *Tehanu* (1990). Her critical essays are collected in *The Language of the Night* (1979; revised 1989) and *Dancing at the Edge of the World* (1989). Her poetry includes *Wild Angels* (1975), *Hard Words and Other Poems* (1981) and *In the Red Zone* (1983). *Buffalo Gals and Other Animal Presences* (1987) mixes prose and verse.

Le Quex, William See SPY FICTION.

Le Sueur, Meridel 1900– American. Rooted in her lifelong commitment to socialism, her work has helped to establish a tradition of feminist dissent on which the women's movement of today is partly based. Her novels include *The Girl*

(1939), *Conquistadors* (1973) and *The Mound Builders* (1974); *Salute to Spring* (1940) and *Harvest and
Song for My Time* (1983) contain stories. *North Star
Country* (1945) is a history of the Midwest in
which she grew up. She has also published
poetry and books for children.

Leacock, Stephen 1869–1944 Canadian. A political economist, he spent his career at McGill
University and wrote a standard college text-
book, *Elements of Political Science* (1906).
Beginning with *Literary Lapses* (1910), he published an average of one humorous book a year
for the remainder of his life. These include *Nonsense Novels* (1911), SUNSHINE SKETCHES OF A
LITTLE TOWN (1912), *Arcadian Adventures with the
Idle Rich* (1914), *Moonbeams from the Larger Lunacy*
(1915), *Further Foolishness* (1916), *Frenzied Fiction*
(1918), *Winnowed Wisdom* (1926), *My Remarkable
Uncle* (1942) and *Last Leaves* (1945). *My Discovery of
England* (1922) and *My Discovery of the West* (1937)
grew out of highly successful lecture tours. A
master of the short sketch or extended anec-
dote, he belongs in the tradition of such North
American humorists as ARTEMUS WARD, MARK
TWAIN and, in Canada, THOMAS CHANDLER
HALIBURTON.

Leatherstocking Tales, The A series of novels by
JAMES FENIMORE COOPER, consisting of *The
Pioneers: or, The Sources of the Susquehanna* (1823),
The Last of the Mohicans: A Tale of 1757 (1826), *The
Prairie: A Tale* (1827), *The Pathfinder: or, The Inland
Sea* (1840) and *The Deerslayer: or, The First War Path*
(1841).

Set in the early frontier period of American
history, they take their name from the protagonist, Natty Bumppo, variously called
Leatherstocking, Deerslayer, Hawkeye and
Pathfinder. The chronological sequence differs
from the dates of composition. *The Deerslayer*
relates Bumppo's experiences as a young man
in upstate New York in the early 1740s. *The Last
of the Mohicans* is set during the Seven Years' War
between the French and the British in 1757. *The
Pathfinder* takes place soon after *The Last of the
Mohicans*, in the same conflict between the
French and Indians and the British colonials.
The Pioneers is set in 1793 in Otsego County, part
of the recently settled region of New York state.
The Prairie is set on the frontier of the great
plains in 1804, when Natty Bumppo is in his 80s.

Several figures emerge with almost mythic
clarity from the densely complicated romantic
plots: Bumppo himself, continually pushing forward the frontiers of a civilization which he
avoids and his creator apparently despises, and
the Red Indians, alternately noble savages and
primordial villains, memorably embodied in
Bumppo's companion, Chingachgook (Indian
John).

Lee, (Nelle) Harper 1926– American. Her only
novel is *To Kill a Mockingbird* (1960), a story of
racial prejudice set in a Southern town like her
hometown of Monroeville, Alabama. A white
lawyer, Atticus Finch, defends a black man, Tom
Robinson, falsely accused of raping a white girl.
The action is presented from the viewpoint of
Finch's six-year-old daughter, Jean Louise
('Scout').

Legend of Montrose, A A novel by SIR WALTER
SCOTT, in the third series of *Tales of My Landlord*,
published in 1819. Its setting is the rising of the
Highland clans against the Covenanters and in
support of Charles I in 1644. The novel is more
successful in its portrait of the free-booting soldier of fortune, Dugald Dalgetty, than in its
account of Allan M'Aulay's tragic love for Annot
Lyle.

Lehmann, Rosamond (Nina) 1903–90 English.
Her studies of developing womanhood and the
subtle shades of emotional relationships
include *Dusty Answer* (1927), *A Note in Music*
(1930), *Invitation to the Waltz* (1932) and its sequel
The Weather in the Streets (1936), *The Ballad and the
Source* (1944) and *The Echoing Grove* (1953). *The
Gypsy's Baby* (1946) is a volume of short stories
and *The Swan in the Evening* (1967) an autobiography.

Leiber, Fritz See SCIENCE FICTION.

Lennox, Charlotte (Ramsay) 1720–1804
Daughter of the lieutenant governor of New
York, she arrived in England at the age of 15. *The
Life of Harriot Stuart* (1750) was a SENTIMENTAL
NOVEL but she achieved success with *The Female
Quixote: or, The Adventures of Arabella* (1752), a
satire whose heroine is saturated in French
romances of the previous century. She drama-
tized it as *Angelica: or, Quixote in Petticoats* (1758).
The History of Henrietta (1758) was followed by
Sophia (1762) and *Euphemia* (1790). *The Sister*
(1769) is a play.

Leonard, Elmore (John) 1925– American. In a
long and prolific career, which has embraced
Westerns as well as DETECTIVE FICTION, he has
slowly developed both a wide reputation and a
devoted following. Earlier works, such as
Fifty-Two Pickup (1974), *Unknown Man No. 89*
(1977), *City Primeval* (1980) and *Split Images*
(1982), are tough, fast-moving thrillers distinguished by their feel for the mean streets of
Detroit. Later works, such as *Glitz* (1985), *Bandits*
(1987), *Freaky Deaky* (1988), *Get Shorty* (1990),
Maximum Bob (1991) and *Riding the Rap* (1995),
range beyond Detroit to observe the gaudiness
of America and its criminal types with genial
appreciation and a precise ear for the vernacular.

Lessing, Doris (May) 1919– Born to English parents in Persia, she was brought up in Rhodesia
and moved to Britain in 1949. Her prolific, varied output has been marked by its interest in
the private action of the mind and its willingness to challenge narrative convention. *The
Grass is Singing* (1950), reflecting her childhood
in Southern Rhodesia, was followed by *Martha*

Quest (1952), *A Proper Marriage* (1954), *A Ripple from the Storm* (1958), *Landlocked* (1965) and *The Four-Gated City* (1969), forming a sequence called *The Children of Violence*. *The Golden Notebook* (1962), hailed if not conceived as the expression of feminist politics, examines the experience of a woman writer. *Five: Short Novels* (1953) won a SOMERSET MAUGHAM AWARD.

Two experimental novels, *Briefing for a Descent into Hell* (1971) and *The Memoirs of a Survivor* (1974), anticipate *Canopus in Argos: Archives*, a series of SCIENCE FICTION (though she prefers the term 'space fiction'): *Re: Colonised Planet 5, Shikasta* (1979), *The Marriages between Zones Three, Four and Five* (1980), *The Sirian Experiments* (1981), *The Making of the Representative for Planet 8* (1982) and *Documents Relating to the Sentimental Agents in the Volyen Empire* (1983). She has since returned to realistic narrative with *The Diary of a Good Neighbour* (1983) and *If the Old Could* (originally published under the pseudonym of Jane Somers, 1984), *The Good Terrorist* (1985) and *The Fifth Child* (1988), a bleak novella. In *Love, Again* (1996) love comes late and disturbingly to an elderly woman. As well as short stories, she has also published poetry, travel books, personal writings and the first volume of her autobiography, *Under My Skin* (1994).

LETTERS An EPISTOLARY NOVEL by JOHN BARTH, published in 1979. An encyclopaedic narrative of the sort favoured by POST-MODERNISM, it presents letters exchanged between seven authors over a period of seven months. Their subjects embrace Barth's own previous work, the personal and family histories of the writers, the exploration of the American continent, the French Revolution from the perspective of a disaffected patriot and the construction of a supercomputer that will take over the planet. The format allows Barth to explore such issues as the construction of identity in writing, the relation between fiction and history, the collision between fatality and contingency, and the nature of systems of all kinds, from the numerical to the cosmological.

Lever, Charles (James) 1806–72 Irish. He made his name with a succession of lively novels about Ireland and the army: *The Confessions of Harry Lorrequer* (1837), *Charles O'Malley* (1840), *Jack Hinton the Guardsman* (1842), *Tom Burke of Ours* (1844), *Arthur O'Leary* (1844) and *The O'Donoghe* (1845). Their tone was well parodied by WILLIAM MAKEPEACE THACKERAY in *PUNCH'S PRIZE NOVELISTS*. Later novels were more subdued, partly through an attempt at greater realism and partly through fatigue; they include *Roland Cashel* (1850), *Sir Jasper Carew* (1855), *The Fortunes of Glencore* (1857), *Luttrell of Arran* (1865) and *Lord Kilgobbin* (1872).

Leverson, Ada (Esther) [née Beddington] 1862–1933 English. She contributed to *The Yellow Book* and remained a loyal friend to OSCAR WILDE during his trials and social disgrace. She published six novels, akin to the work of MAX BEERBOHM in their light and good-humoured tone: *The Twelfth Hour* (1907), *Love's Shadow* (1908), *The Limit* (1911), *Tenterhooks* (1912), *Bird of Paradise* (1914) and *Love at Second Sight* (1916). Leverson is largely forgotten but attempts to revive her reputation have been made by reprinting together *Love's Shadow*, *Tenterhooks* and *Love at Second Sight*, which all feature the engaging Edith Ottley and her husband Bruce, as *The Little Ottleys*.

Levine, Norman 1923– Canadian. His fiction evokes place and often concentrates on social outsiders, the problems of the writer's life and his own Jewish-Canadian upbringing. Volumes of short stories include *One Way Ticket* (1961), *I Don't Want to Know Anyone Too Well* (1971), *Thin Ice* (1979), *Why Do You Live So Far Away?* (1984) and *Something Happened Here* (1991). *Champagne Barn* (1984) is a collection drawn mainly from his earlier volumes. *The Angled Road* (1952) and *From a Seaside Town* (1970) are novels. Although he is best known for his fiction, he has also published poetry and an abrasive memoir, *Canada Made Me* (1958).

Lewis, Alun 1915–44 Welsh. He died in the Burma campaign from a wound which may have been self-inflicted. *Raiders' Dawn* (1942) contains poems about the identity and environment of industrial Wales, as well as love and wartime Britain. *The Last Inspection* (1942) contains wry and observant stories. Poems, stories and letters from India were collected in *Ha! Ha! Among the Trumpets* (1945), introduced by ROBERT GRAVES, and *In the Green Tree* (1948).

Lewis, C(live) S(taples) 1898–1963 English. He passed most of his academic career at Oxford, where his circle of friends ('The Inklings') included J. R. R. TOLKIEN, CHARLES WILLIAMS and Hugo Dyson. His re-conversion to Christianity, charted in his spiritual autobiography, *Surprised by Joy* (1955), was the mainspring of all his subsequent writing, starting with *The Pilgrim's Regress* (1933) and his SCIENCE-FICTION trilogy, *Out of the Silent Planet* (1938), *Perelandra* (1939) and *That Hideous Strength* (1945). The first and still most famous of his scholarly books is *The Allegory of Love* (1936), a study of courtly love, but others remain influential: *A Preface to Paradise Lost* (1942), the third volume of the Oxford History of English Literature, *English Literature in the Sixteenth Century, Excluding Drama* (1954), *Studies in Words* (1960) and *The Discarded Image* (1963). What brought him wide popularity, however, were his radio talks on Christianity during World War II (collected as *Mere Christianity*) and *The Screwtape Letters* (1942). The seven 'Narnia' stories for children, combining strong imagination and lively adventure with artfully concealed Christian parable, secured him another large audience; they began with *The*

Lion, the Witch and the Wardrobe (1950) and closed with *The Last Battle* (1956).

Lewis, Eiluned 1900–79 Welsh. Her first novel, *Dew on the Grass* (1934), was a best-selling account of her childhood on the Welsh border. *The Captain's Wife* (1943) portrays her mother's girlhood in 19th-century Pembrokeshire. Her interest in rural traditions is reflected in the 'Countrywoman's Notes' she contributed to *Country Life* for 35 years. Besides a third novel, *The Leaves of the Tree* (1953), she published two books of poems and two collections of essays. Selections from her unfinished memoirs appeared posthumously in *A Companionable Talent* (1996). Unassuming and quietly humorous, her writing is never sentimental; she is an unusual instance of a rural writer at home in the literary world of the metropolis.

Lewis, M(atthew) G(regory) 1775–1818 English. After serving as attaché at the British Embassy at The Hague, he entered Parliament in 1796, the same year he published his GOTHIC NOVEL, *THE MONK*. Its sensational success earned him the nickname of 'Monk' Lewis and encouraged him to seek out the company of the rich, titled and famous. It is now almost the only work by which he is remembered, but Lewis wrote other novels (*The Bravo of Venice*, 1804; *Feudal Tyrants*, 1806), plays (*The Castle Spectre*, 1796; *The East Indian*, 1799; *Alphonso, King of Castile*, 1801; *The Wood Demon*, 1807) and several volumes of verse – though his best poem, 'Alonzo the Brave and the Fair Imogine', appeared in *The Monk*. His *Journal of a West Indian Proprietor*, posthumously published in 1834, describes his efforts to manage the Jamaican sugar plantations he had inherited and to improve conditions for the slaves.

Lewis, (Harry) Sinclair 1885–1951 American. His first success, *MAIN STREET* (1920), is a satirical portrayal of small-town Midwestern life which looks back to his own roots in Sauk Center, Minnesota. *BABBITT* (1922), which continued his critique of provincial America, was followed by *Arrowsmith* (1925; PULITZER PRIZE), about an altruistic doctor, *Elmer Gantry* (1927), about a sham revivalist minister, and *DODSWORTH* (1929). In 1930 Lewis became the first American writer to receive the Nobel Prize. Though it demonstrates his continuing commitment to social and political change, his later work marked a decline in strength. *It Can't Happen Here* (1935), a warning about the possibility of fascism in the USA, was dramatized and produced by the Federal Theatre Project throughout the country with Lewis himself playing the lead. *Cass Timberlane* (1945), *Kingsblood Royal* (1947) and *The God-Seeker* (1949) return to the Minnesota setting of *Main Street*.

Lewis, (Percy) Wyndham 1882–1957 Born in the USA, of an American father and English mother, he was brought up in Britain. As the leading spirit of vorticism, a term coined by Ezra Pound for their version of MODERNISM, he conducted its short-lived journal, *Blast* (1914–15). His first novel, *Tarr* (1918), is an intellectual comedy set in pre-war Paris. *The Childermass* (1928), a fantasy located in a waste land outside heaven's gate, began a sequence eventually continued by *Monstre Gai* and *Malign Fiesta* (both 1955) and called *The Human Age*. *The Apes of God* (1930), a satire mocking the fashionable racket of art and literature in the London of the 1920s, is often considered his best work. *The Revenge for Love* (1937) is set against the background of the Spanish Civil War. *Self Condemned* (1954), his last major novel, is semi-autobiographical. It reflects the disillusionment and isolation to which Lewis was increasingly condemned, not just by his fascist sympathies in the 1930s but by his gift for making enemies among his contemporaries. His political and critical essays, which embody this gift quite as markedly as his fiction, include *The Art of Being Ruled* (1925), *Time and Western Man* (1927), *Men without Art* (1934), *The Mysterious Mr Bull* (1938) and *The Writer and the Absolute* (1952). His short stories were collected in *The Wild Body* (1927) and *Rotting Hill* (1951). Chapters of his autobiography were published in *Blasting and Bombardiering* (1937) and *Rude Assignment* (1950).

Leyner, Mark 1956– American. His kinetic, pastiche-like novels satirize American popular culture, politics, education and middle-class morality. The experimental technique is 'hypertextual' in that textual elements seem randomly presented and bear multiple connections to each other. Leyner's titles suggest his satirical bent: *I Smell Esther Williams* (1986), *My Cousin, My Gastroenterologist* (1990), *Et tu, Babe* (1992), *Tooth Imprints on a Corn Dog* (1995) and *The Tetherballs of Bougainville* (1997).

Libra A novel by DON DELILLO published in 1988. In a room by himself a retired CIA operative, Nicholas Branch, researches but does not start to write an encyclopaedic history of John F. Kennedy's assassination, based on secret information as well as the publicly available documents. Parallel narratives trace the record of known facts about Lee Harvey Oswald – his service in the Marines, his stay in the USSR and pro-Cuban sympathies – and recreate his possible manipulation by dissident CIA operatives angered by the President's failure to take a strong enough stand against Castro. The behaviour of all the characters suggests that in an age without viable systems of belief and faith, secrets and Byzantine conspiracies fulfil the need for faith. The book takes its title from Oswald's astrological sign, Libra, whose emblem is the scales or balance.

Liddell, Robert 1908–93 English. The first phase of his career as a novelist began with *The Almond Tree* (1938) and ended with *Stepsons* (1969), which, like much of his work, harked back to an unhappy childhood. *Unreal City* (1952) reflects his love for Egypt and her most famous 20th-century poet, Cavafy. When his reputation declined, he turned to the criticism he had begun in *A Treatise on the Novel* (1947), *Some Principles of Fiction* (1953) and his study of IVY COMPTON-BURNETT (1955). *Elizabeth and Ivy* (1986) is a memoir of ELIZABETH TAYLOR and Compton-Burnett, *A Mind at Ease* (1989) a study of BARBARA PYM. He returned to fiction with *The Aunts* (1987), a portrait of childhood set in the early years of the century, which has helped to rekindle interest in his work

Life and Times of Michael K See *MICHAEL K, LIFE AND TIMES OF.*

Life in London: *or, The Day and Night Scenes of Jerry Hawthorn Esq. and His Elegant Friend Corinthian Tom, Accompanied by Bob Logic, The Oxonian, in Their Rambles and Sprees through the Metropolis* A boisterously comic description of life in Regency London by PIERCE EGAN THE ELDER, serialized in 1820–1 and published in book form in 1821, with illustrations by Robert and George Cruikshank. In a series of cheerfully coarse episodes Corinthian Tom, a Regency rake, helped by his facetious friend Bob Logic, shows the sights of the capital to his country cousin, Jerry Hawthorn. The book was enormously popular with young men who aspired to a dashing life, though Egan himself seems to have had second thoughts. In *The Finish to the Adventures of Tom, Jerry and Logic, in Their Pursuits through Life in and out of London* (1828) all the characters except Jerry come to miserable ends.

Life's Handicap: *Being Stories of Mine Own People* A collection of 27 stories by RUDYARD KIPLING, published in 1891. Almost all reflect his experiences of India. One group, which includes 'The Courting of Dinah Shadd' and 'On Greenhow Hill', deals with the characters who also appear in *SOLDIERS THREE*. Another, which includes 'The End of the Passage' and 'The Limitations of Pambe Serang', consists of horror stories.

Light in August A novel by WILLIAM FAULKNER, published in 1932. Pregnant and unwed, Lena Grove arrives in Jefferson, Mississippi, in search of Lucas Burch, her baby's father. Instead she finds Byron Bunch, a hardworking, dependable bachelor who falls in love with her. Flashback scenes provide an account of the early life of Joe Christmas, an orphan unsure of his racial origins, and of the circumstances which drive him to kill his lover Joanna Burden. He is denounced by Lucas Burch and captured. He escapes and takes refuge with Gail Hightower, a disgraced and reclusive minster, but is shot by the National Guard. Hightower withdraws again into private reverie. With her baby and Byron Bunch, Lena continues her search for Burch.

Lindsay, David 1876–1945 Scottish. He is best remembered for *A Voyage to Arcturus* (1920). Ostensibly SCIENCE FICTION, it is more precisely a symbolic morality tale grounded in the Calvinist theology he had imbibed from his father. Its innovative synthesis of space fantasy and religious allegory influenced C. S. LEWIS. *The Violet Apple* and *The Witch* appeared posthumously in 1976.

Lindsay, Jack 1900–90 The son of NORMAN LINDSAY, he was born and brought up in Australia but lived in England after 1926. He produced over 200 books, as well as editing literary journals and founding the Fanfrolico Press, and received literary awards in Australia but comparatively little recognition in his adopted country. Too restless to limit himself to a single form, he published poems, plays, translations, autobiographies, biographies and historical studies, many of them stamped by his commitment to Marxism. His 40 novels include HISTORICAL FICTION about the classical world in the trilogy consisting of *Rome for Sale* (1934), *Caesar is Dead* (1935) and *Last Days with Cleopatra* (1935), as well as *Despoiling Venus* (1935) and *Brief Light* (1939), and about Britain in the trilogy consisting of *1649* (1938), *Lost Birthright* (1939) and *Men of Forty-Eight* (1948). *We Shall Return* (1943), *Beyond Terror* (1943) and *Hullo Stranger* (1945) are novels of wartime, while *Betrayed Spring* (1953) began and *Choice of Times* (1964) closed a contemporary sequence, 'The British Way'.

Lindsay, Norman (Alfred William) 1879–1969 Australian. He first became known as an illustrator and cartoonist. His first novel, *A Curate in Bohemia* (1913), was followed by an enduring fantasy for children, *The Magic Pudding* (1918). *Redheap* (1930), *Saturdee* (1933) and *Halfway to Anywhere* (1947) form a trilogy about boyhood and adolescence. Lindsay also published three volumes of essays, *Creative Effort* (1920), *Hyperborea: Two Fantastic Travel Essays* (1928) and *Madam Life's Lovers* (1929).

Linklater, Eric 1899–1974 Scottish. His most successful novel was *Private Angelo* (1946), a comic account of post-war reorganization in Italy. *White Maa's Saga* and *Poet's Pub* (both 1929) are set in the Orkney Islands, where he spent much of his life. *Juan in America* (1931) is satirical. His work for radio includes 'conversation pieces' such as *The Great Ship* and *Rabelais Replies* and a play, *Crisis in Heaven* (all 1944). *Husband of Delilah* (1962) is the best known of his later works. *The Man on My Back* (1941) and *A Year of Space* (1953) are autobiographical.

Linton, Eliza Lynn 1822–98 English. She worked for *The Morning Chronicle*, *The Saturday Review* and DICKENS's magazine *All the Year Round*. Her best-known novels were *The True History of Joshua Davidson, Christian and Communist* (1872), tracing the career of a modern-day Jesus; *Patricia Kemball* (1873); and *The Autobiography of*

Christopher Kirkland (1885), a disguised auto-biography which attributes much of her own life to the hero. Despite an interest in creating spirited heroines, and despite her own success in leading an independent life, she was a vehement anti-feminist, as *The Girl of the Period and Other Social Essays* (1883) shows.

Lippard, George 1822–54 American. He was best known for sensational books about the immorality of large cities, such as *The Quaker City: or, The Monks of Monk Hall* (1844) and *New York: Its Upper Ten and Lower Million* (1854). He also wrote HISTORICAL FICTION, including *Blanche of Brandywine* (1846) and *Legends of Mexico* (1847).

Lister, Thomas Henry See SILVER-FORK NOVEL.

Little Dorrit A novel by CHARLES DICKENS, published in monthly parts in 1855–7 and in volume form in 1857.

Amy, 'Little Dorrit', is born in the Marshalsea, the debtors' prison where her father William Dorrit has spent so many years that he is called 'the father of the Marshalsea'. They are befriended by Arthur Clennam, recently returned from a long period abroad, whose mother employs her as a seamstress. William Dorrit inherits a fortune, leaves the Marshalsea and travels in style to Italy, where he dies, finally unable to remember anything but his years in prison. Clennam, fighting his own battles with the Circumlocution Office, becomes victim of a gigantic fraud perpetrated by the financier Merdle and is sentenced to the Marshalsea. Little Dorrit finds him there, and the couple eventually marry.

A complex sub-plot involves Clennam's mother, a gloomy and bigoted paralytic, and two villains, the Frenchman Rigaud (alias Blandois) and Jeremiah Flintwich. The latter's wife Affery is a memorable character, as are Flora Finching and 'Mr F's aunt', Little Dorrit's lovesick suitor John Chivery, the self-tormenting Miss Wade and the highly correct Mrs General.

Little Lord Fauntleroy See BURNETT, FRANCES HODGSON.

Little Women A novel by LOUISA MAY ALCOTT, published in two parts, *Little Women: or, Meg, Jo, Beth, and Amy* and *Good Wives*, in 1868 and 1869, and as a single volume, *Little Women and Good Wives*, in 1871. Meg, Jo, Beth and Amy March live with their mother (Marmee) in a small New England town. The story follows their efforts to increase the family's small income, particularly Jo's aspiration to be a writer. In the second part Meg and Amy marry, Beth dies, and Jo becomes a successful novelist and marries Dr Bhaer. The couple establish a boys' school, the subject of *Little Men* (1871) and *Jo's Boys* (1886).

Lively [née Greer], Penelope (Margaret) 1933– Born and brought up in Egypt, she settled in Britain after World War II. A preoccupation with the effect of the past on the present, often manifested in a supernatural manner, is the hallmark of her books. She began as a writer for children with *Astercote* (1970), *The Wild Hunt of Hagworthy* (1971), *The Whispering Knights* (1971), *The Ghost of Thomas Kempe* (1973), in which the ghost of a 17th-century sorcerer returns to haunt a present-day family, and *A Stitch in Time* (1976), in which the heroine becomes obsessed with a sampler embroidered more than a century before. Stories for younger children include *A House Inside Out* (1987). Her first adult novel, *The Road To Lichfield* (1977), was followed by *Judgement Day* (1980) and *According to Mark* (1984). In *Moon Tiger* (1987), which won the BOOKER PRIZE, a dying woman reflects on the relations between the academic study and the personal meaning of history. Subsequent novels include *Passing Out* (1989), *City of the Mind* (1991), *Cleopatra's Sister* (1993) and *Heat Wave* (1996). *Oleander, Jacaranda: A Childhood Perceived* (1994) is an autobiography.

Lives of Girls and Women A collection of short stories by ALICE MUNRO, published in 1971. It presents episodes from the girlhood and adolescence of Del Jordan, an artist in the making, in the fictional town of Jubilee, Ontario. Most involve an initiation or rite of passage, as she comes to terms with mortality, sexuality and the mutability of personal relationships. Taken together, the stories come close to forming a *BILDUNGSROMAN*.

Llewellyn, Richard [Lloyd, Richard Dafydd Vivian Llewellyn] 1907–83 Born in Wales, he became by his own description 'an expatriate Welshman who now lives in the world'. He achieved early success with plays, *Poison Pen* (1937) and *Noose* (1947), but gained lasting recognition with his novel, *How Green was My Valley* (1939), set in a Welsh mining community. Its blend of lyricism, realism and humour has represented something quintessentially 'Welsh' for many readers. Other novels included *None But the Lonely Heart* (1943) and *A Few Flowers for Shiner* (1950), both about the London slums. A sequence of spy novels, *The End of the Rug* (1968), *But We Didn't Get the Fox* (1969), *White Horse to Banbury Cross* (1971) and *The Night is a Child* (1972), concerned a British agent turned industrialist, Edmund Trothe. *A Night of Bright Stars* (1979), about a Brazilian pioneer aviator, was set in *fin-de-siècle* Paris.

Lodge, David (John) 1935– English. He was professor of modern English literature at the University of Birmingham from 1976 to 1987. The literary criticism in *Language of Fiction* (1966), *The Novelist at the Crossroads* (1971), *Working with Structuralism* (1981) and *After Bakhtin* (1990) combines the same fundamental adherence to a traditionally humanist definition of literature with a prolonged flirtation with structuralism and successive critical movements apparent in his fiction. Notable experiments include: *Changing Places* (1975; HAWTHORNDEN PRIZE), a CAMPUS NOVEL, and its sequel *Small World* (1983), whose structure mimics Arthurian romance; *Nice Work* (1988), self-consciously in the tradition of ELIZABETH GASKELL and the CONDITION OF ENGLAND NOVEL; *Paradise News* (1991), about tourism; and *Therapy* (1995). *How Far Can You Go?* (1980; WHITBREAD AWARD), about the problems of Catholicism, returns to an earlier mode of realism.

Lodge, Thomas See *ROSALYNDE*.

Lolita A novel by VLADIMIR NABOKOV, published by Maurice Girodias' Olympia Press in Paris in 1955 and in the USA in 1958. Between these dates it had begun its rise from the status of underground classic, supposedly pornographic in its account of Humbert Humbert's hopeless love for the underage Lolita, to that of a work exploring the discrepancies of texts, languages and cultures and belonging more to the literature of courtly love than to any other defined category. It is presented as a confession, edited and introduced by an unhelpful Freudian psychiatrist, written by Humbert before his death in prison while awaiting trial for the murder of his rival, Clare Quilty.

Lombard, Nap See JOHNSON, PAMELA HANSFORD.

London, Jack [Chaney, John Griffith] 1876–1916 American. In his restless, adventurous youth, begun on the Oakland waterfront, he sailed on a sealing voyage, agitated for socialist reform and took part in the Klondike gold rush (1897). The Klondike is the setting for his first collection of stories, *The Son of the Wolf* (1900), his first novel, *A Daughter of the Snows* (1902), and his first great popular success, *THE CALL OF THE WILD* (1903), which – like the later *White Fang* (1906) – has a dog as its hero. Subsequent collections of short stories include *Love of Life* (1907), *Lost Face* (1910), *South Sea Tales* (1911) and *The Red One* (1918). A second novel, *The Cruise of the Dazzler* (1902), was based on his experiences as an oyster pirate. *The People of the Abyss* (1903) draws on his observation of the slums of London. *THE SEA-WOLF* (1904) chronicles the voyage of a ship run by a ruthless captain. *The War of the Classes* (1905) is a socialist treatise and *The Game* (1905) a novel about prizefighting. *Before Adam* (1906) attempts to recreate a prehistoric community while *THE IRON HEEL* (1908) is set in the near future.

MARTIN EDEN (1909), more directly autobiographical, deals with his attempts to become a successful writer and to come to terms with his success. *Burning Daylight* (1910) returns to the Klondike, *Smoke Bellew* (1912) to the Yukon. *The Valley of the Moon* (1912), another socialist novel, is about a working-class couple who escape from the harshness of industrial life in Oakland to an idyllic life on the land. *John Barleycorn* (1913), an autobiographical memoir, deals with

London's struggle against alcohol. *The Star Rover* (1915) is the story of a San Quentin lifer's spiritual struggles. Hugely successful but never at ease with his success, he worked as a foreign correspondent, travelled widely and died at the age of 40, perhaps by suicide. *The Human Drift*, a socialist treatise, appeared posthumously in 1917.

London Fields A novel by MARTIN AMIS, published in 1989. Quintessentially of its decade, it describes itself variously as a true story, a murder story and a love story. The narrator is Samson Young, an American writer visiting London. He finds himself observing, recording and finally participating in events leading to the death of Nicola Six, which she meticulously plots to bring about. Characters include Keith Talent, incompetent small-time crook and would-be darts champion, and Guy Clinch, perpetually wounded decent man and parent of a monstrous child. Apocalyptic images of destruction and nuclear war insistently recur; the only redeeming emotions are parental or quasi-parental.

Lonely Londoners, The A novel by SAMUEL SELVON, published in 1956. The most significant early treatment in fiction of the post-war Caribbean migration to Britain, it uses an episodic method and an anecdotal style to convey both the attraction of the metropolis and the sense of futility its characters find in London. The book is also notable for its comic use of a form of Caribbean Creole. The central character, Moses Aloetta, reappears in *Moses Ascending* (1975) and *Moses Migrating* (1983).

Longest Journey, The A novel by E. M. FORSTER, published in 1907. The title comes from Shelley's *Epipsychidion*: 'Who travel to their home among the dead . . . / With one chained friend . . . / The dreariest and the longest journey go.' Forster applies the quotation to the unhappy marriage between the lame and delicate Frederick Elliot, nicknamed Rickie, and Agnes Pembroke, whose original fiancé, the athletic Gerald Dawes, dies in a sporting accident. On leaving Cambridge, Rickie accepts a teaching post from Agnes's brother Herbert at Sawston, a minor public school. His growing disillusionment with the values of Sawston and the Pembrokes coincides with his interest in the drunken but amiable Stephen Wonham, who turns out to be his half-brother, the son of Rickie's mother. Resolved to help Stephen, Rickie leaves Agnes but is killed trying to rescue him from an accident.

Longstreet, Augustus Baldwin 1790–1870 American. He was at various times a college president, editor of the *States Rights Sentinel* (which he founded in 1834), clergyman and jurist. He is best remembered for his *Georgia Scenes, Characters and Incidents, &c., in the First Half Century of the Republic* (1835), a collection of humorous sketches. A pioneering regionalist, he also wrote short stories and a novel, *Master William Mitten* (1864).

Looking Backward: 2000–1887 An influential Utopian novel by EDWARD BELLAMY, published in 1888. It is narrated by Julian West, a Bostonian, who falls asleep in 1887 and wakes in the year 2000 to find himself in a brilliant new society. Dr Leete explains how America came to adopt a rigorous socialist programme which has organized labour according to a system like military service. Great political, technological and sociological achievements are described in vivid detail. Edith Leete, a descendant of his former fiancée, returns his love.

Lord Jim A novel by JOSEPH CONRAD, published in 1900.

Its crux is Jim's betrayal of his duty as chief mate of the *Patna* in deserting the steamship and its cargo of pilgrims after it has struck a submerged object. In Aden the narrator, Marlow, observes Jim at the Court of Inquiry where he has elected to face the consequences of his action. Being stripped of his master's certificate brings public but not spiritual atonement. Jim takes a variety of jobs ashore but only a position as agent at the remote trading post of Patusan promises him real freedom. There he becomes Tuan, or Lord Jim, and is helped towards serenity by his relationship with Jewel. When Gentleman Brown and his fellow thieves arrive, he pledges to the elderly chief, Doramin, that they will leave without bloodshed. His misplaced trust leads to the death of Doramin's son and, accepting responsibility, Jim allows Doramin to shoot him.

Lord of the Flies WILLIAM GOLDING's first novel, published in 1954. It is an inverted Victorian boys' adventure story (referring particularly to R. M. BALLANTYE's *THE CORAL ISLAND*) with savage knowledge rather than blithe innocence at the core of the fable. Marooned on a desert island after a plane crash, a party of boys from an English public school quickly degenerates into vindictive barbarism. The roguish Jack emerges as a ruthless dictator, while the fat and clumsy Piggy is eventually killed with the Christlike Simon. It is only when the boys are rescued by a British destroyer that Piggy's well-meaning friend Ralph realizes the true extent of their depravity.

Lord of the Rings, The A three-volume novel by J. R. R. TOLKIEN, consisting of *The Fellowship of the Ring* (1954), *The Two Towers* (1954) and *The Return of the King* (1955). Paperback editions issued in the USA in the mid-1960s were best-sellers whose success instated fantasy as a paperback genre and the three-decker novel as its standard form. Tolkien spent much of his life elaborating the imaginary history and mythology of the 'Middle Earth' in which the novel is set, and his works in this vein fill supplementary volumes.

Bilbo Baggins, erstwhile hero of *The Hobbit* (1937), discovers the magic ring he acquired in that novel has awesome powers which the diabolical Sauron is avid to gain. Under the tutelage of the wizard Gandalf a disparate band of heroes is formed, led by Bilbo's son Frodo; their task is to take the ring to the Crack of Doom, in Sauron's own land of Mordor, where it may be destroyed. The company finds exotic allies to help them against a host of monstrous villains, and ultimately succeeds in defeating Sauron and restoring the dispossessed king Aragorn to his throne.

Lord Ormont and His Aminta A novel by GEORGE MEREDITH, published in 1894. The elderly Lord Ormont marries Aminta Farrell but at first refuses to present her in society because of her lowly birth. He is persuaded to change his attitude by his secretary, Matie Weyburn, but Aminta leaves him and acknowledges her love for Matie. In defiance of convention the couple go to Switzerland and open a school together. Ormont forgives them before he dies.

Lorna Doone: *A Romance of Exmoor* A novel by R. D. BLACKMORE, published in 1869. It is set on Exmoor during the late 17th century. Monmouth's rebellion and Judge Jeffreys form part of the background to the story. Young John Ridd, a yeoman, is determined to avenge his father's death at the hands of the Doones, an evil clan which pursues a career of murder and theft from a nearby valley. He also falls in love with Lorna, daughter of the clan's chieftain. He and his friends bring the Doones to account and rescue the girl. The discovery that she is really the daughter of a noble family makes him acutely aware of the difference in their positions, but his reluctance is overcome and the story ends happily. (See also HISTORICAL FICTION.)

Lothair A novel by BENJAMIN DISRAELI, published in 1870. Lothair is an orphaned nobleman whose guardians are Lord Culloden and Grandison, a clergyman who embraces Catholicism and becomes a cardinal. Lothair joins Garibaldi's campaign in Italy, where his wealth makes him a target for the Catholics. Cardinal Grandison, Clare Arundel and Monsignor Catesby try to convert him. Their influence is resisted by Lord Culloden, Lady Corisande and Theodora, who dies fighting for Garibaldi. Lothair eventually returns to England, unconverted, and marries Lady Corisande.

Love and Mr Lewisham A novel by H. G. WELLS, published in 1900. As a young schoolmaster, Lewisham dreams of being a scholar and man of influence. His ambition is matched, and appears threatened by, his attraction to the more experienced Ethel Henderson. His idealism is also offset by inadequate figures of authority in the adult world: Bonover, the shallow headmaster who dismisses him, and Ethel's father, the devious Chaffery. Later, Lewisham follows a principled pathway as a gifted student in London, although distracted by the attentions of the bluestocking, Miss Heydinger. When he meets Ethel again after a three-year gap, he sees that she is a victim of her unscrupulous father. Their courtship, Ethel's pregnancy and their marriage are traced with sympathy for the pains as well as pleasures of married life.

Lovecraft, H(oward) P(hillips) 1890–1937 American. Written in highly charged prose, his stories of fantasy, horror and SCIENCE FICTION are influenced by EDGAR ALLAN POE and preoccupied with the history of New England. The various collections which have appeared after his death, such as *Beyond the Wall of Sleep* (1943) and *The Dunwich Horror* (1945), and his novel, *The Case of Charles Dexter Ward* (1951), have earned him a cult reputation.

Lovel the Widower A story by WILLIAM MAKEPEACE THACKERAY, published in *The Cornhill Magazine* in 1860. Lovel lives with his overbearing mother-in-law, Lady Baker, and a charming governess, Miss Prior. When Lady Baker discovers that Miss Prior had been a dancer she orders her out of the house, but Lovel asks her to marry him.

Lovelace, Earl 1935– Trinidadian. Expert in varieties of Trinidadian speech, his novels penetrate serious contemporary issues. They include *While Gods are Falling* (1966), *The Schoolmaster* (1968), his masterpiece *The Dragon Can't Dance* (1979) – centred on the ways in which the role-playing associated with Trinidad's annual Carnival pervades everyday life – and *The Wine of Astonishment* (1984). *Salt* (1996), a winner of the COMMONWEALTH WRITERS PRIZE, also draws on Carnival and related folk culture to offer a rich portrait gallery of people trying to attain 'personhood' in a world which has denied their human worth. *Jestina's Calypso and Other Plays* appeared in 1984. Lovelace has also published *A Brief Conversion and Other Stories* (1988) and a dramatized version of *The Dragon Can't Dance* (1989).

Lover, Samuel 1796–1868 A Protestant Irishman, he is best remembered for 'Rory O'More', a ballad developed into a novel in 1836 and a play in 1837. *Songs and Ballads* appeared in 1839. As a humorous novelist working in the same vein as CHARLES LEVER, he scored his greatest success with *HANDY ANDY* (1842). Lover also wrote several plays, successful in their time, and stories about Irish life.

Lowndes, Marie (Adelaide) Belloc 1868–1947 The sister of HILAIRE BELLOC, she was half French by parentage but lived and worked in Britain. Most of her more than 40 novels are skilfully plotted and observed stories of crime or mystery, and several derive from real-life criminal cases. Her most famous book, *The Lodger* (1913), describes how landlady Mrs Bunting comes to realize that her genteel lodger is in fact Jack the Ripper. It inspired several film versions, including one by Alfred Hitchcock (1926).

Lowry, (Clarence) Malcolm 1909–57 British. In his youth he sailed to China as a deckhand on a merchant ship and studied at Cambridge. Then, an alcoholic and a wanderer, he lived in Mexico and British Columbia before returning to Britain. *Ultramarine* (1933) is a novel of seafaring. His second novel, *UNDER THE VOLCANO* (1947), is widely regarded as his masterpiece. A volume of short stories, *Hear Us, O Lord, from Heaven Thy Dwelling Place* (1961), *Selected Poems* (1962), *Lunar Caustic* (1968), *Dark as the Grave Wherein My Friend is Laid* (1968) and *October Ferry to Gabriola* (1971) have been published from the mass of work he left behind.

Luck of Roaring Camp and Other Sketches, The A collection of stories and sketches by BRET HARTE, published in 1870. Harte's sharply naturalistic depiction of frontier life in the American West made his popular reputation. As well as the title piece, the collection includes 'The Outcasts of Poker Flat', 'Tennessee's Partner' and 'Miggles'. Most of the stories explore the nature of the individual in frontier society, focusing on human relationships in difficult or even tragic circumstances.

Lucky Jim The first novel by KINGSLEY AMIS, published in 1954. The plot is a catalogue of the misadventures which beset Jim Dixon in the first term of his new job teaching history at a provincial university. Virtuoso comic sequences include Jim setting his bed on fire with his cigarette while staying at the home of the professor of English and his disastrous lecture to the faculty at the end of term. As well as being a work of sustained, often farcical comedy, the novel mocks 'phoniness' and pretension. (See also CAMPUS NOVEL.)

Ludlum, Robert See GENRE FICTION.

Lurie, Alison 1926– American. Her poised, witty novels explore the subversive effects of change on comfortable, middle-class Americans, often academics exposed to the world outside the campus. They include *Love and Friendship* (1962), *The Nowhere City* (1965), *Imaginary Friends* (1967), *Real People* (1970), *The War Between the Tates* (1974), *Only Children* (1979), *Foreign Affairs* (1984; PULITZER PRIZE); and *The Truth about Lorin Jones* (1988). *Women and Ghosts* (1994) is a volume of stories. *The Heavenly Zoo: Legends and Tales of the Stars* (1979), *Clever Gretchen and Other Forgotten Folktales* (1980) and *Fabulous Beasts* (1981) are children's books. Her other work includes: *Don't Tell the Grown-Ups* (1990), a study of children's literature; *The Language of Clothes* (1981), a study of fashion; and *The Oxford Book of Modern Fairy Tales* (1993).

Luska, Sidney See HARLAND, HENRY.

Lyall, Gavin See SPY FICTION.

Lyly, John See *EUPHUES*.

Lyre of Orpheus, The See *CORNISH TRILOGY, THE*.

Lytton, Edward Bulwer See BULWER LYTTON, EDWARD.

McAlpine, Rachel 1940– New Zealand. Her novels include *The Limits of Green* (1985), about ecological issues, and *Farewell Speech* (1990), a lively and purposeful novel based on the lives of three New Zealand women who struggled in the cause of women's rights. Her exuberant, strongly feminist lyrics are seen to best advantage in *Recording Angel* (1983). *Selected Poems* appeared in 1988. She has also written plays for schools and for radio; work for the stage includes *The Stationary Sixth Form Poetry Trip* (1980), *The Life Fantastic* (1982) and *Paper Towers* (1986). *Power Play* (1990) includes songs in English and Maori.

Macaulay, Dame **(Emilie) Rose** 1881–1958 English. Her urbane and witty novels, influenced by her complex relationship with Anglicanism, cover a wide range. Of her pre-war work, *Potterism* (1920) is a satire of modern journalism and commercialization, while *They were Defeated* (1932) is HISTORICAL FICTION about the poet Robert Herrick. She is chiefly remembered, however, for her two post-war novels: *The World My Wilderness* (1950), about an alienated teenager in bomb-damaged London; and *The Towers of Trebizond* (1956), in which the protagonist (whose gender is concealed until the end) visits Turkey and experiences, among other things, the confrontation between Christianity and Islam. Ruins, a central symbol in both books, are also the subject of *The Pleasure of Ruins* (1953), the most substantial of her essays and travel books.

McBain, Ed See HUNTER, EVAN.

McCaffrey, Anne See SCIENCE FICTION.

McCarthy, Cormac (Charles, Jr.) 1933– American. His novels, violent and populated by emotionally bruised and socially ostracized characters, have often been compared with the work of other Southern writers such as FAULKNER, FLANNERY O'CONNOR and CARSON MCCULLERS. They include: *The Orchard Keeper* (1965); *Outer Dark* (1968), about the consequences of a brother and sister's incest; *Child of God* (1974) and *Suttree* (1979), about wretches seeking rebirth and atonement; and *Blood Meridian, or The Evening Redness in the West* (1985), unusual because of its Western setting. *All the Pretty Horses* (1992) and *The Crossing* (1994) are the first two instalments in a projected 'Border Trilogy'.

McCarthy, Justin 1830–1912 Irish. A youthful supporter of the Young Ireland movement and an MP from 1879 onwards, he also embarked on a successful career in fiction, publishing some 20 now-forgotten novels. The best is probably *Mononia: A Love-Story of 'Forty-Eight'* (1901), reflecting the country life and political enthusiasms of his Munster youth, though *Dear Lady Disdain* (1875) and *Miss Misanthrope* (1878) were also very popular. He entered Parliament in 1879. His immensely popular *History of Our Own Times* (1879–1905), covering Queen Victoria's reign, was supplemented by *The Reign of Queen Anne* (1905) and *The History of the Four Georges and William IV* (1884–1901) and shorter studies of Peel (1891) and Gladstone (1898).

McCarthy, Mary 1912–89 American. Her best-selling novel, *The Group* (1963), follows eight Vassar women after their graduation. *The Groves of Academe* (1952) draws on her experiences as a university teacher, and *Memories of a Catholic Girlhood* (1957) describes her childhood. Her political interests are evident not just in *Vietnam* (1967) and *Hanoi* (1968) but also her travel books, *Venice Observed* (1956) and *The Stones of Florence* (1959). She also wrote literary criticism (*The Writing on the Wall*, 1970; *Ideas and the Novel*, 1981) and many more novels, short stories, and essays, including *Birds of America* (1971), *The Mask of State: Watergate Portrait* (1974), *Cannibals and Missionaries* (1979), *The Hounds of Summer and Other Stories* (1981) and *Occasional Prose: Essays* (1985). The critic Edmund Wilson was her second husband.

McClure, James See DETECTIVE FICTION.

McCullers, Carson (Smith) 1917–67 American. Usually set in the South (she was a native of Georgia), her work often deals with spiritual isolation and the attempt to overcome it through love. She was also one of the first American writers to deal openly with homosexuality. *The Heart is a Lonely Hunter* (1940), which won immediate recognition, was followed by *Reflections in a Golden Eye* (1941), *The Ballad of the Sad Café* (1951), *Clock without Hands* (1961) and *The Mortgaged Heart* (1971), a collection of stories. Edward Albee dramatized *The Ballad of the Sad Café* in 1963 and she herself dramatized *The Member of the Wedding* (1946), as well as writing another play, *The Square Root of Wonderful* (1958).

McDermid, Val See DETECTIVE FICTION.

MacDonald, George 1824–1905 Scottish. His fairy stories for children are shot through with an unmistakable blend of Christian symbolism and mystical imagination. In the most famous, *At the Back of the North Wind* (1871), a cabdriver's son called Diamond travels the world each night in the company of the North Wind, pictured as a beautiful lady. Subsequent classics include *The Princess and the Goblin* (1872), a powerful allegory of good and evil, and *The Princess and Curdie* (1883), where the miner's son Curdie again braves dangers to save the princess.

MacDonald's adult fiction – the allegorical *Phantastes* (1858) and *Lilith* (1895), and novels such as *David Elginbrod* (1863) – is less well remembered.

Macdonald, Ross Pseudonym of Kenneth Millar (1915–83). American. *The Dark Tunnel* (1944; later called *I Die Slowly*), *Trouble Follows Me* (1946; called *Night Train* in the UK), *Blue City* (1947) and *The Three Roads* (1948) – the early novels Millar published under his own name – declared his debt to the hard-boiled school of DETECTIVE FICTION. The legacy was also central to the Lew Archer novels which he went on to publish, first as John Macdonald and then as John Ross Macdonald, before settling on the final form of his pseudonym. They began with *The Moving Target* (1949) and ended with *The Blue Hammer* (1976). Like his predecessors in the work of DASHIELL HAMMETT and RAYMOND CHANDLER, Archer is a private eye in southern California – a solitary and even lonely figure as much concerned with his own private code as with the niceties of the law. Macdonald's work, however, shifts the emphasis from the underworld to the middle class, and makes the hero as much therapist as judge. *Self-Portrait: Ceaselessly into the Past* (1981), edited by Ralph Sipper, hints at the autobiographical roots of Macdonald's characteristic themes.

McElroy, Joseph 1930– American. Long regarded by critics as a major figure but largely unknown to the general public, he writes encyclopaedic narratives combining his knowledge of systems theory, history, archaeology, biology, cybernetics and media with portrayals of protagonists questing for knowledge in the chaos of 'the information age'. His work includes: *A Smuggler's Bible* (1966); *Hind's Kidnap: A Pastoral on Familiar Airs* (1969); *Ancient History: A Paraphrase* (1971); *Lookout Cartridge* (1974), about a man in search of a missing film depicting a ritualistic murder; *Plus* (1976), the story of an artificial intelligence; *Women and Men* (1987), a massive work recounting the interlocking stories and relationships of two Manhattan apartment neighbours; and *The Letter Left to Me* (1988).

McEwan, Ian 1948– English. Two collections of short stories, *First Love, Last Rites* (1975) and *In between the Sheets* (1977), and a short novel, *The Cement Garden* (1978), announced his ability to combine the graphic or shocking with a cerebral, modulated prose style. Subsequent works, increasingly more substantial, are: *The Comfort of Strangers* (1981), owing its location and claustrophobic concentration to Thomas Mann's *Death in Venice*; *The Child in Time* (1987), a study of bereavement; *The Innocent* (1990), set in Berlin during the 1950s; *Black Dogs* (1992), using the memory of Nazi atrocities for an investigation of evil; *Enduring Love* (1997), about a stalker and his victim, combining the thriller and the novel of ideas. McEwan is also the author of a TV play,

The Imitation Game (1981); an oratorio about nuclear war, *Or Shall We Die?* (1983); and the screenplay for *The Ploughman's Lunch* (1983).

MacEwen, Gwendolyn 1941–87 Canadian. A prolific writer in a wide range of forms, she was preoccupied with myth, magic and a sacrificial view of life. Her poetry includes *Selah* (1961), *The Drunken Clock* (1961), *The Shadow-Maker* (1969), *The Armies of the Moon* (1972), *The T. E. Lawrence Poems* (1982) and *Earthlight: Selected Poems 1963–1982* (1982). Other works are: *Julian the Magician* (1963) and *King of Egypt, King of Dreams* (1971), novels; *Noman* (1972), *The Honey Drum: Seven Tales from Arab Lands* (1984) and *Noman's Land* (1985), collections of stories; *The Trojan Women* (1979), a version of Euripides' play; and translations from Y. Ritsos.

McGahern, John 1934– Irish. He writes about Ireland in astringent, measured, often bleak fiction, which includes: *The Barracks* (1963); *The Dark* (1965); *The Leavetaking* (1975), about the love affair between an Irish Catholic schoolteacher and an American divorcée; *The Pornographer* (1979), contrasting the protagonist's facility at writing pornography with the gauche failure but also the tenderness of his private life; and *Amongst Women* (1990) about an ageing farmer. McGahern's economy of style lends itself ideally to short stories, gathered in *Collected Stories* (1992).

McGuane, Thomas (Francis) 1939– American. Comic and energetic, his fiction includes *The Sporting Club* (1969), *The Bushwacked Piano* (1971), *Ninety-Two in the Shade* (1973), *Panama* (1978), *Nobody's Angel* (1979), *Something To Be Desired* (1984) and *Nothing But Blue Skies* (1993). He has also written screenplays – for *Rancho Deluxe* (1973), *The Missouri Breaks* (1976) and *Tom Horn* (1980) – and *An Outside Chance: Essays on Sport* (1980).

Machen, Arthur (Llewellyn) 1863–1947 Welsh. He is chiefly remembered for supernatural tales such as *The Great God Pan* (1894) and *The Hill of Dreams* (1907), steeped in Welsh folklore and occult philosophy. He also published translations of *The Heptameron* (1886) and *The Memoirs of Casanova* (1894), and a volume of criticism, *Hieroglyphics* (1902). *Far Off Things* (1922) and *Things Near and Far* (1923) were both autobiographical. The Caerleon Edition of his works (1923) resulted from the 'rediscovery' of Machen after many years of neglect.

McIlvanney, William 1936– Scottish. Early works include *Remedy is None* (1966) and *A Gift from Nessus* (1968). His reputation rests particularly on two novels examining the Scots tradition of the 'hard man': *Docherty* (1975; WHITBREAD AWARD), about an Ayrshire miner in the early years of the century, and *The Big Man* (1985), about bare-knuckle fighting. In *The Kiln* (1996) a middle-aged man looks back to the 1950s and a summer of emotional and intellectual turmoil. *Laidlaw* (1978), *The Papers of Tony Veitch* (1983) and *Strange Loyalties* (1991) are tough and gritty DETECTIVE FICTION. McIlvanney's poetry is found in *The Longships in Harbour* (1970) and *These Words: Weddings and After* (1984).

McInerney, Jay 1955– American. He is often grouped with Bret Easton Ellis, Tama Janowitz and David Leavitt in the 'Literary Brat Pack'. His novels, about drug-using, club-hopping young New Yorkers, include *Bright Lights, Big City* (1984), *Ransom* (1985), *Story of My Life* (1988), *Brightness Falls* (1992) and *The Last of the Savages* (1996).

MacInnes, Colin 1914–76 The son of ANGELA THIRKELL and a descendant of RUDYARD KIPLING, he grew up in Australia, where his first novel, *June in Her Spring* (1952), is set. He is now remembered for his 'London trilogy' – *City of Spades* (1957), *Absolute Beginners* (1959) and *Mr Love and Justice* (1960) – which vividly evokes a London just beginning to become multi-racial and to develop a militant youth culture. MacInnes's incisive, wide-ranging essays are collected in volumes such as *England, Half English* (1961).

McKay, Claude 1890–1948 Born in Jamaica, he emigrated to the USA in 1912. A collection of poetry, *Harlem Shadows* (1922), established his popular reputation. His novels include: *Home to Harlem* (1928), about a black soldier's return to the USA; *Banjo: A Story without a Plot* (1929), about a vagabond's life on the Marseilles waterfront; and *Banana Bottom* (1933), about a black woman's return to Jamaica. Other publications include: a collection of stories, *Gingertown* (1932); an autobiography, *A Long Way from Home* (1937); and a study of the black community, *Harlem* (1940).

Mackay, Shena 1944– English. She made a precocious début with *Toddler on the Run*, a novella written when she was 15 and published with *Dust Falls on Eugene Schlumberger* in 1964. Since then she has excelled in darkly menacing descriptions of female domesticity where safety is illusory and characters live lives of quiet desperation. Her novels include: *A Bowl of Cherries* (1984); *Redhill Rococo* (1986), set in the squalid fecundity of a suburban Surrey household; *Dunedin* (1992), moving from Victorian New Zealand to south London in 1989; and *The Orchard of Fire* (1995), set in the Coronation Year of 1953. *Collected Short Stories* (1994) draws on earlier volumes: *Babies in Rhinestones* (1983), *Dreams of Dead Women's Handbags* (1987) and *The Laughing Academy* (1993).

Mackenzie, Sir (Edward Montague) Compton 1883–1972 English. The best of his many works include the grimly realistic *Carnival* (1912), the semi-autobiographical *Sinister Street* (1913–14), *Guy and Pauline* (1915), *Sylvia Scarlett* (1918), *Extraordinary Women* (1928), *Our Street* (1931), *The Four Winds of Love* (1937–45) and the well-known Scottish novels, *The Monarch of the Glen* (1941) and *Whisky Galore* (1947). He also published memoirs of his experience in the Dardanelles during World War I and the 10-volume *My Life and Times* (1963–71).

Mackenzie, Henry 1745–1831 Scottish. An Edinburgh lawyer who played a leading role in the city's learned and literary circles, he made a significant contribution to the SENTIMENTAL NOVEL with *THE MAN OF FEELING* (1771), about a man whose morality is too delicate for a harsh world. It was followed by *The Man of the World* (1773), about the selfish pursuit of happiness, and an EPISTOLARY NOVEL, *Julia de Roubigné* (1777). Mackenzie's complete works (1808) included several plays: two tragedies, *The Spanish Father* and *The Prince of Tunis*, and a comedy, *The White Hypocrite*. His *Anecdotes and Egotisms* (edited by Harold William Thompson; 1927) give a vivid picture of Edinburgh life, with gossip about the lordly and the famous.

Mackenzie, Seaforth [Mackenzie, Kenneth Ivo] 1913–54 Australian. His poetry includes *Our Earth* (1937) and *The Moonlit Doorway* (1944). Among his novels are: *The Young Desire It* (1937), drawing on his own childhood and youth; *Chosen People* (1938); and *Dead Men Rising* (first published in Britain, 1951), about a mass outbreak of Japanese prisoners of war he had witnessed during military service in World War II.

Mackintosh, Elizabeth 1897–1952 English. She wrote DETECTIVE FICTION under the pseudonym of Josephine Tey and plays and novels under the pseudonym of Gordon Daviot. *The Man in the Queue* (1929) introduced the genteel police detective Alan Grant who reappeared in several thrillers, of which the best is probably *The Daughter of Time* (1951), Grant's investigation of the character of Richard III and his supposed murder of the Princes in the Tower. *The Franchise Affair* (1948) is based on an 18th-century *cause célèbre*. The same interest in history informed Mackintosh's best-known plays as Gordon Daviot, *Richard of Bordeaux* (1932) and *Queen of Scots* (1934).

Maclaren, Ian See KAILYARD SCHOOL.

MacLaverty, Bernard 1945– Irish. His first book, *Secrets and Other Stories*, won a Scottish Arts Council award in 1977, as did the novel *Lamb* in 1980. *A Time To Dance and Other Stories* appeared in 1982, and the novel *Cal*, which deals directly with the political violence in Northern Ireland, was widely acclaimed on its publication in 1983. *Lamb* and *Cal* have been made into films. *Grace Notes* (1997), about an Ulster composer living in Scotland, was shortlisted for the BOOKER PRIZE. MacLaverty has also written children's books, including *Andrew McAndrew* (1988).

Maclean, Alistair See GENRE FICTION.

MacLennan, (John) Hugh 1907–90 Canadian. His first and best-known novels, *Barometer Rising* (1941) and *Two Solitudes* (1945), blend realism and symbolism in their examination of early 20th-century Canadian identity. Other works are *The Precipice* (1948), *Each Man's Son* (1951), *The Watch That Ends the Night* (1959), *Return of the Sphinx* (1967) and *Voices in Time* (1981). An accomplished essayist, he argued for a view of civilization in which classical humanist and contemporary materialist values are brought together.

MacLeod, Alistair 1936– Canadian. He is a meticulous stylist whose entire *oeuvre* consists of less than 20 stories, collected in *The Lost Salt Gift of Blood* (1976) and *As Birds Bring Forth the Sun* (1986). A British collection, also called *The Lost Salt Gift of Blood* (1991), includes virtually all his best work. It deals almost exclusively with the fishermen, miners and farmers of Cape Breton, probing family relationships and examining the community's Celtic heritage.

Macleod, Fiona See SHARP, WILLIAM.

McMurtry, Larry (Jeff) 1936– American. His first novel, *Horseman, Pass By*, was published in 1961 and filmed by Martin Ritt as *Hud* in 1963. Books like *The Last Picture Show* (1966), filmed by Peter Bogdanovich in 1971, *Terms of Endearment* (1975), filmed by James L. Brooks in 1983, and *Texasville* (1987) explore life in the kind of small-town Texas communities which have been mythologized into emblems of American identity in legends of the Wild West. *Lonesome Dove* (1985; PULITZER PRIZE), set in 1876, and its sequel, *Streets of Laredo* (1993), look directly at those legends. Other novels include: *Buffalo Girls* (1990); *The Evening Star* (1992), a sequel to *Terms of Endearment*; *Pretty Boy Floyd* (1994); *The Late Child* (1995); and *Dead Man's Walk* (1995).

McNeile, Herman Cyril See SPY FICTION.

McNeill, Janet 1907– Irish. She has been called Protestant Belfast's counterpart to BRIAN MOORE. Her novels, particularly strong in depicting isolation, alienation and self-doubt in the lives of middle-class Belfast women, relieve their sombre material with irony and a persistent tough-minded honesty. They include *A Child in the House* (1955), *Talk to Me* (1965), *The Small Widow* (1967), *The Maiden Dinosaur* (1964) – generally reckoned to be her best work – and *The Belfast Friends* (1966).

McNeish, James 1931– New Zealand. His central characters are beleaguered outsiders, yet his focus is on society rather than introspection. *Mackenzie: A Novel* (1970) is HISTORICAL FICTION and *The Mackenzie Affair* (1972) a documentary novel drawing on the same material about a victim of the Highland Clearances at odds with the Canterbury squattocracy. McNeish's overseas experience is vast, and used in novels which include *The Glass Zoo* (1976), about teaching in London, and *Penelope's Island* (1990), set in New Caledonia. *My Name is Paradiso* (1995) is about Sicily and Daniel Dolci, the pacifist with whom McNeish worked and whose biography he wrote in *Fire Under Ashes* (1965). *The Man from Nowhere* (1991) contains non-fiction pieces about people and places, including a trip to Berlin to gather material for a novel about Jack Lovelock, the Olympic runner. *As for the Godwits* (1977) is an autobiographical diary about the inhabitants of a remote New Zealand coastal settlement where McNeish has lived in self-imposed exile.

McNickle, D'Arcy 1904–77 Native American. *The Surrounded* (1936) is about a youth torn between his Flathead Indian and Spanish ancestry, while *Wind from an Enemy Sky* (1978) deals with the conflicts between Indian and non-Indian cultures. *Runner in the Sun: A Story of Indian Maize* (1954) is for children. McNickle also wrote a biography of Oliver LaFarge and several histories of Indian culture.

***McTeague*: A Story of San Francisco** A novel by FRANK NORRIS, published in 1899. A pioneer example of American NATURALISM in its own right, it was also indirectly influential through a powerful silent screen version, *Greed* (1924), written and directed by Erich von Stroheim.

McTeague (Mac) is a dentist absorbed in the physical pleasures of eating, drinking and smoking. His friend Marcus Schouler introduces him to Trina Sieppe, whom he courts and marries. Trina wins $5000 in a lottery and Marcus becomes jealous of Mac's good fortune. The two men fight and Marcus takes his revenge by revealing that Mac has been practising dentistry without a licence. Mac depends on Trina for money and their relationship becomes sado-masochistic. Eventually he beats her to death and flees, with her gold coins and a canary in a gold cage. Marcus, who has joined the posse searching for him, tracks him down to Death Valley. They fight and Mac kills him, but not before Marcus has handcuffed himself to Mac. The story ends with him still handcuffed to the corpse, with his canary but without water.

McWilliam, Candia 1955– English. Her style, self-consciously literary and flaunting its pleasure in unusual words, has found both admirers and detractors. Her novels include: *A Case of Knives* (1988), about the network of relationships centring on an eminent heart surgeon; *A Little Stranger* (1990), about a pregnant woman growing uneasy at the behaviour of her child's nanny; and *Debatable Land* (1994), in which memories of Scotland punctuate a voyage in the Pacific. *Wait Till I Tell You* (1997) is a collection of short stories.

Madame Delphine A short novel by GEORGE WASHINGTON CABLE, published in 1881. It is set in New Orleans. The story concerns Delphine Carraze, a quadroon and the widow of a white man. She ensures the marriage of her daughter Olive to the banker Ursin Lemaitre, against his friends' opposition, by claiming that Olive is really a white woman's child whom she had fostered. As she dies, she confesses her lie to Pere Jerome.

Maggie: *A Girl of the Streets* A novel by STEPHEN CRANE, privately printed in 1893 under the pseudonym Johnston Smith and entitled *A Girl of the Streets*. A pioneer work of American NATURALISM, it describes the sordid and almost hopeless existence of Maggie Johnson in the Bowery area of New York. Alternately neglected and abused in childhood, she is seduced and abandoned, becomes a prostitute and finally drowns herself.

magic realism A term for one manifestation of POST-MODERNISM, first applied to the large body of spectacular, fantastic fiction produced in South American countries since World War II, notably the work of Gabriel Garcia Márquez, whose *One Hundred Years of Solitude* (trans. G. Rabassa; 1970) is generally regarded as its paradigm. It juxtaposes apparently reliable, realistic reportage with extravagant fantasy, not just in a spirit of inscrutable playfulness but also in response to the manipulation of fact and information in South American politics. Indeed, magic realism assumes that truth is best viewed as a communal, collaborative construct, rather than as residing in the integrity of individual perceptions, whose authority tends merely to that of caprice and rumour. Such emphasis makes it an essentially comic genre.

Magic realism has since been identified in other literatures, including the work of the Czech novelist Milan Kundera and the Italian Italo Calvino. The chief examples in English are the novels of SALMAN RUSHDIE, ANGELA CARTER, GRAHAM SWIFT and PETER CAREY. In the European tradition, it is possible to see Rabelais and Kafka as precursors of the magic realist idiom, while Rushdie's work points back through the English novel to DICKENS and *TRISTRAM SHANDY*.

Mahy, Margaret 1936– New Zealand. She has moved from producing inventive picture-books to writing stories for older readers, vividly original in their language and plotting, which combine fantasy and magic with psychological realism. They include: *The Haunting* (1982), in which a shy young boy has to coexist with the real world and the ghosts that haunt him; *The Changeover* (1985), in which a schoolboy becomes supernaturally possessed; and *Underrunners* (1993).

Maid Marian A novel by THOMAS LOVE PEACOCK, published in 1822. It introduces the characters of Robin Hood and Richard I into a satire of oppression and extreme doctrines of social order. Coming hard on the heels of SIR WALTER SCOTT's *IVANHOE* (1819), which had portrayed Robin Hood as Robin of Locksley, it confirmed the Romantics' interest in the legendary outlaw and contributed much to his present image in popular culture.

Mail on Sunday/John Llewellyn Rhys Prize See JOHN LLEWELLYN RHYS PRIZE.

Mailer, Norman 1923– American. His war service in the Pacific prompted *THE NAKED AND THE DEAD* (1948), which made him famous on both sides of the Atlantic. His critical view of society also informed *Barbary Shore* (1951) and *The Deer Park* (1955). A pioneer of the New Journalism, he registered changes in the American sensibility in *Advertisements for Myself* (1959), *An American Dream* (1965), *Why are We in Vietnam?* (1967), *Armies of the Night* (1968; PULITZER PRIZE), *Miami and the Siege of Chicago* (1968), *Of a Fire on the Moon* (1970), *The Prisoner of Sex* (1971), *Marilyn: A Biography* (1973) and *The Fight* (1975), about Muhammad Ali. *THE EXECUTIONER'S SONG* (1979; Pulitzer Prize), recreates events surrounding the execution of Gary Gilmore. His later fiction, taking on a range of historical and political subjects, includes *Ancient Evenings* (1983), *Tough Guys Don't Dance* (1984), *Harlot's Ghost* (1991), *Oswald's Tale: An American Mystery* (1995) and *The Gospel According to the Son* (1997), which retells the New Testament from Christ's point of view.

Maillet, Antonine 1929– French-Canadian. Born in New Brunswick, she writes in Acadian French (see FRENCH-CANADIAN NOVEL). To give a worthy sense of tradition to her 'minority within a minority' she has traced the roots of Acadian colloquialisms back to the 17th-century French of Touraine and Berry, and to the work of Rabelais. This spirit is found in the earthy dramatic monologues of *La Sagouine* (1971), both a novel and a play, and in the indomitable protagonist of *Pélagie-la-Charrette* (1979; translated as *Pélagie*, 1982), about the return from exile of a group of Acadians in the 18th century. It was the first novel from outside metropolitan France to win the Prix Goncourt. The success of *La Sagouine* led her publishers to reissue her disregarded first novel, *La Pointe-aux-Coques* (1958) in 1972. Maillet's fantasy *Don l'Orignal* (1972; translated as *The Tale of Don l'Orignal*, 1978) won the Governor General's Award.

Main Street A novel by SINCLAIR LEWIS, published in 1920, and his first great success. After working as a librarian in St Paul, Minnesota, Carol Milford marries Dr Will Kennicott and moves to Gopher Prairie, where she initially rebels against the complacent small-town values but finally submits to them.

Main-Travelled Roads A collection of short stories by HAMLIN GARLAND, published in 1891 and expanded in 1899 and 1922. It depicts life in the rural Midwest as drab and monotonous. 'Under the Lion's Paw' is about the economic survival of the fittest or the most ruthless. In 'Up the Coulee' an actor returns to the Midwestern farm where he grew up. Contrasted with the harshness and squalid poverty are the 'silent heroism' of some characters and the panoramic beauty of the prairies.

Mais, Roger 1905–55 Jamaican. Concentrating on 'the dreadful condition of the working classes', he gave social-realist accounts of human despair in the Kingston slums in his collections, *Face and Other Stories* (1942) and *And Most of All Man* (1943), and the novels, *The Hills were Joyful Together* (1953) and *Brother Man* (1954). The more fluid, non-realist *Black Lightning* (1955) suggests that poverty and suffering do not totally preclude fulfilment.

Maitland, Sara 1950– English. Her fiction explores the tensions between feminism, socialism and religion, particularly Christianity. Despite its contemporary and apparently domestic setting, it is intercut with ancient voices and punctuated by magic and the supernatural. Her novels include: *Daughter of Jerusalem* (1978); *Virgin Territory* (1984); *Three Times Table* (1990), a family saga with speaking dragons; *Home Truths* (1993), drawing on African mythology. *Arky Types* (1987), with Michelene Wandor, belongs to a feminist sub-genre, Bible history pointedly told from below, also practised by MICHÈLE ROBERTS and JEANETTE WINTERSON. *A Book of Spells* (1987) and *Women Fly When Men aren't Watching* (1993) are short stories. With Roberts and ZOË FAIRBAIRNS, she belonged to the writers' group which produced *Tales I Tell My Mother* (1978) and *More Tales I Tell My Mother* (1987).

Major, Clarence 1936– African-American. *All-Night Visitors* (1969), *No* (1973), *Reflex and Bone Structure* (1975) and *Emergency Exit* (1979) are experimental works about black characters resisting the definitions and traditions imposed on them by white culture. *My Amputations* (1986), about a kidnapped novelist impersonated by a parolee, deals with his characteristic theme of black identity unrecognized. *Such was the Season* (1987), his most straightforward novel, is the narrative of a black middle-class woman about family problems after her daughter-in-law decides to run for the Georgia State Senate. Other novels include *Painted Turtle: Woman with Guitar* (1988) and *Dirty Bird Blues* (1996). Major has also published short stories and many volumes of poetry.

Malamud, Bernard 1914–86 American. His first novel, *The Natural* (1952), deals with baseball. *The Assistant* (1957), *A New Life* (1961), *The Fixer* (1966; PULITZER PRIZE) and *Pictures of Fidelman* (1969) all explore the personal struggle involved in the Jewish experience. Later novels are *The Tenants* (1971), *Dubin's Lives* (1979) and *God's Grace* (1982). Malamud's short stories are collected in *The Magic Barrel* (1958), *Idiots First* (1963) and *Rembrandt's Hat* (1973).

Malet, Lucas [Harrison, Mary St Leger Kingsley] 1852–1931 English. The daughter of CHARLES KINGSLEY, she began her own career as a novelist with *Mrs Lorimer, A Sketch in Black and White* (1882). She was best known for *The Wages of Sin* (1891), about a painter, and *The History of Sir Richard Calmady* (1901), about a handicapped baronet; in a decade of controversial fiction, they still managed to cause a considerable stir by their treatment of their heroes' sex lives.

Malgonkar, Manohar 1913– Indian. An ex-military man from a Bombay, Marathi-speaking background, he is best known for *The Princes* (1963), about the double threat to India's traditional rulers from British imperialism and the Independence movement, and for *A Bend in the Ganges* (1964), a chronicle from the beginning of the Quit India campaign up to Partition.

Mallock, W(illiam) H(urrell) 1849–1923 English. A defender of traditional values against liberal theology, the progress of science and new political ideologies, he is chiefly remembered for two satirical novels which combine the ROMAN À CLEF and the ROMAN À THÈSE in the manner of THOMAS LOVE PEACOCK. *The New Republic: or, Culture, Faith, and Philosophy in an English Country House* (1877) pits Ruskin's views against those of T. H. Huxley, Benjamin Jowett, Matthew Arnold and WALTER PATER. *The New Paul and Virginia: or, Positivism on an Island* (1878–9) takes Huxley, John Tyndall, Frederic Harrison and HARRIET MARTINEAU as its particular targets.

Malouf, David 1934– Australian. His life has alternated between Australia and Europe, while his work juxtaposes different modes of existence and perception. He achieved recognition as a poet with *Bicycle and Other Poems* (1970), *Neighbours in a Thicket* (1974), *The Year of the Foxes* (1979), *First Things Last* (1980), *Wild Lemons* (1981), *Selected Poems* (1981) and *New and Collected Poems* (1991). He has, however, become better known as a novelist. *Johnno* (1975), his most conventional novel, explores the hero's rebellion against Brisbane society in the 1940s and 1950s. *12 Edmonstone Street* (1985) contains four more autobiographical explorations. Artists play central roles in *An Imaginary Life* (1978), about Ovid, the title-novella of *Child's Play* (1982) and *Harland's Half Acre* (1984). *Fly Away Peter* (1982) and *The Great World* (1990), which won the COMMONWEALTH WRITERS PRIZE and the MILES FRANKLIN AWARD, contrast the calm of Australia with the horrors of World War I. Colonial Queensland society provides the setting for *Remember Babylon* (1993). *Antipodes* (1985) is a collection of stories.

Malzberg, Barry See SCIENCE FICTION.

Man of Feeling, The A SENTIMENTAL NOVEL by HENRY MACKENZIE, published in 1771. Harley, the quixotic hero, leaves home to seek his fortune and is educated in the harsh realities of the world by encounters with, among others, a pair of professional cardsharpers and a prostitute. In Bedlam he meets a girl who has gone mad for love. The novel is a critique of acquisitive society and a warning against being taken in by appearances, its sentimentality relieved by a pervasive, gentle irony.

Man of Property, The See FORSYTE SAGA, THE.

Man Who Loved Children, The A novel by
CHRISTINA STEAD, published in 1940. Set in the
USA (Baltimore and Annapolis) in the 1930s, it
draws on Stead's memories of her family life in
Australia a generation earlier. Sam Pollitt
relentlessly proclaims his love for his children – his daughter Louie by his first marriage
and the six others by his second wife
Henny – but is a monstrous egoist, an amalgam
of American optimism and totalitarian
self-righteousness. He fills his practically
minded wife with hatred and suicidal despair as
the family fortunes decline. Adolescent Louie
determines to poison both parents for the sake
of the children. Henny, perhaps knowingly,
drinks the poison and dies, but Sam refuses to
believe Louie's confession. She then leaves
home to seek her own path in life.

Manhattan Transfer A novel by JOHN DOS PASSOS,
published in 1925. It was the first to employ the
techniques that characterize his most important work, the trilogy *USA*. There are two central characters, Ellen Thatcher and Jimmy Herf,
who meet each other in the course of their
unfulfilled lives, marry and then separate. But
equally important are the stories of numerous
people who have in common only their status as
New Yorkers, and who come together randomly, impersonally. Each chapter begins with
passages comprising observations of city life,
slogans, snatches of dialogue, phrases from
advertisements, and newspaper headlines. They
further emphasize that *Manhattan Transfer* is a
'collective' novel.

Maniam, K. S. [Subramanian Krishnan] 1942–
An ethnic Indian (Tamil) who has spent most of
his life in Malaysia, he is widely regarded as
Malaysia's finest novelist on the basis of two
books: the highly autobiographical *The Return*
(1984), documenting the influence of an
English-language education, and *In a Far Country*
(1993), about the protagonist's search for identity in a post-colonial society. *Sensuous Horizons*
(1994) is a collection of short stories.

Manley, Delarivière (Mary) 1663–1724 She was
born in the Channel Islands. Though she wrote
a comedy, *The Lost Lover*, and a tragedy, *The Royal
Mischief* (both 1696), she is best known for pioneering the ROMAN À CLEF in English with: *The
Secret History of Queen Sarah and the Sarazians*
(1705–11); the notorious *Secret Memoirs and
Manners of Several Persons of Quality, of Both Sexes*,
usually known as *The New Atalantis* (1709), for
which she, her publisher and printer were
arrested; and *Memoirs of Europe towards the Close
of the Eighth Century* (1710). In 1711 she took over
the editorship of *The Examiner* from Jonathan
Swift, with whom she collaborated in a number
of polemical pamphlets. *The Power of Love, in
Seven Novels* (1720) is a collection of conventional
romances.

Manning, Olivia 1908–80 English. Her wartime
experiences in Bucharest, Athens, Egypt and
Jerusalem form the basis of the six novels
grouped into *The Balkan Trilogy* (*The Great Fortune*,
1960; *The Spoilt City*, 1962; *Friends and Heroes*,
1965) and *The Levant Trilogy* (*The Danger Tree*,
1977; *The Battle Lost and Won*, 1978; *The Sum of
Things*, 1980). The fate of a newly married
English couple, Harriet and Guy Pringle, is the
central thread in a narrative which gives an
ambitious and detailed portrait of the effects of
war. Other novels include *School for Love* (1951)
and *The Doves of Venus* (1955). She also published
two collections of short stories.

Mansfield, Katherine [Beauchamp, Kathleen
Mansfield] 1888–1923 Born in New Zealand,
she settled in London in 1908. There she contributed to *The New Age* and *Rhythm*, an *avant-garde*
quarterly founded by Michael Sadleir and John
Middleton Murry, who became her second husband in 1918. She died of tuberculosis in France.

Her penetrating and relentless intelligence,
balanced by a sense of form, was ideally suited
to the short story. Her first collection, *In a German Pension* (1911), was followed by *Prelude*, a
story published singly in 1918, which like much
of her best work drew on her childhood in New
Zealand and showed the influence of Chekhov.
Others appeared in *Bliss and Other Stories* (1919),
The Garden Party and Other Stories (1920) and *Other
Stories* (1922). Posthumous works included *Poems*
(edited by Murry; 1923), *Something Childish and
Other Stories* (1924) and *A Fairy Story* (1932). *The
Collected Stories of Katherine Mansfield* (1945) was
an omnibus volume. Murry also edited *The
Letters of Katherine Mansfield* (1928) and *Katherine
Mansfield's Letters to John Middleton Murry:
1913–1922* (1951).

Mansfield Park A novel by JANE AUSTEN, begun in
1811 and published in 1814.

Sir Thomas and Lady Bertram of Mansfield
Park have two daughters, Maria and Julia, and
two sons, Tom and Edmund. Fanny Price, Lady
Bertram's impoverished niece, is brought to live
at Mansfield Park where she is patronized by
three of her cousins, but finds a friend in
Edmund. When Sir Thomas leaves for the West
Indies, his children plan to stage a play
(ELIZABETH INCHBALD's *Lovers' Vows*) and engage
in flirtations, from which Fanny alone stays
aloof. Maria Bertram, though engaged to Mr
Rushworth, is attracted to Henry Crawford; his
sister Mary fascinates Edmund Bertram. But
Maria decides after all to marry Rushworth,
whereupon Henry turns his attention to Fanny.
When she refuses his proposal, Sir Thomas, now
back at Mansfield, is highly displeased at her
apparent foolishness. The unhappy Fanny visits
her own family in Portsmouth, though longing
to be back at Mansfield Park. Meanwhile Maria,
now Mrs Rushworth, runs off with Henry
Crawford. Julia elopes with a Mr Yates. Edmund,
who has taken orders, is rejected by Mary

Crawford and at last begins to see her character clearly. Edmund and Fanny eventually find happiness together.

Mantel, Hilary 1952– English. She shares with MURIEL SPARK a profound sense of the long shadow cast by sin; its eventual nemesis is frequently played out in gleefully macabre plots. Her novels include: *Every Day is Mother's Day* (1985) and its sequel, *Vacant Possession* (1986), about a mother-daughter relationship; *Eight Months on Ghazzah Street* (1988), about a young Western feminist in Jeddah; *Fludd* (1989), about the struggles of a Roman Catholic curate; *A Place of Greater Safety* (1992), about the French Revolution, a departure from her usual preference for compact elegance; *A Change of Climate* (1994) about a retired missionary couple encountering old evils; and *An Experiment in Love* (1995; HAWTHORNDEN PRIZE), set in a women's university hall of residence in the 1960s.

Manticore, The See DEPTFORD TRILOGY, THE.

Many Inventions A collection of 14 stories by RUDYARD KIPLING, published in 1893. It includes six Indian tales, of which two concern characters who also appear in *SOLDIERS THREE*. In 'His Private Honour' Ortheris's conduct is dictated by a code which transcends the army rule book. Other notable stories are: 'The Disturber of Traffic', about the delusions and growing obsession of Dowse, a lighthouse keeper in the Java Straits; 'The Finest Story in the World', in which Charlie begins to recall moments of previous lives on a Roman galley and a Viking ship; and 'The Record of Badalia Herodsfoot', a realistic account of the London slums in the 1890s.

Marble Faun, The: or, *The Romance of Monte Beni* A novel by NATHANIEL HAWTHORNE, published in 1860. In Britain it was entitled *Transformation*.

Kenyon and Hilda are Americans studying art in Rome. With Miriam, an artist, they meet Donatello, an Italian nobleman who resembles the Marble Faun sculpted by Praxiteles. Donatello falls in love with Miriam, but she is troubled by some secret from the past and dogged by a mysterious Capuchin monk. Witnessed by Hilda and perhaps encouraged by Miriam, Donatello kills the monk. Agreeing with Miriam that they must bear the consequences, he gives himself up and goes to prison. She embarks on a penitential pilgrimage. After finding relief in a Catholic confessional, Hilda marries Kenyon. The secret of Miriam's past is never revealed: a 'Postscript' claims that to seek to know whether Donatello really is a faun and who Miriam really is, would destroy the poetry and beauty of the story.

Mardi and a Voyage Thither A novel by HERMAN MELVILLE, published in 1849. It begins as an adventure story in which the narrator, Taji, and Jarl, an older seaman, desert their ship and encounter a brigantine abandoned by all except a Polynesian couple, Samoa and Annatoo. After Annatoo is drowned the three survivors arrive at the islands of Mardi, where the story becomes a kind of allegory. Taji lives happily with Yillah. When she is kidnapped he sets out to find her, accompanied by a king, a historian, a philosopher and a poet. Their search takes them to various lands, whose societies are closely observed and discussed. Dominora apparently stands for Great Britain, Porpheero for Europe and Vivenza for the USA. They eventually reach Serenia, which is ruled by Alma (Christ), but Taji insists on continuing his search alone.

Marechera, Dambudzo 1952–87 Zimbabwean. *The House of Hunger* (1978), consisting of a novella and short stories, is a cry of distress from one of the new generation of writers brought up amid war and injustice. *Black Sunlight* (1980), an intense post-modernist novel, deals with urban guerrillas. *An Articulate Anger: Dambudzo Marechera, 1952–87* (1988) contains interviews and statements. Previously unpublished, and sometimes unfinished, writings appear in *The Black Insider* (1990).

Marius the Epicurean A novel or philosophical romance by WALTER PATER, published in 1885. Set in ancient Rome, the story examines Marius' response to the philosophical influences of his time, Roman religion, the brutal spectacles of the amphitheatre and finally the growing power of Christianity. He dies to save the life of his friend Cornelius and is regarded as a martyr by the Christian church.

Markandaya, Kamala 1924– Indian, resident in Britain for most of her adult life. She won international recognition with *NECTAR IN A SIEVE* (1954), using a south Indian rural setting to which she returned in *A Handful of Rice* (1966). Other novels, about East-West cultural conflicts, are *Some Inner Fury* (1955), *A Silence of Desire* (1960), *Possession* (1962), *The Coffer Dams* (1969), *The Nowhere Man* (1972), *Two Virgins* (1973), *The Golden Honeycomb* (1977) and *Pleasure City* (1982).

Marquand, John P(hillips) 1893–1960 American. After starting with HISTORICAL FICTION set in New England, in *The Unspeakable Gentleman* (1922) and *The Black Cargo* (1925), he found his métier as an ironic observer of contemporary middle-class and upper middle-class life. *The Late George Apley* (1937; PULITZER PRIZE), *Wickford Point* (1939) and *H. M. Pulham, Esquire* (1941), republished together as *North of Grand Central* (1956), form a trilogy dealing with Boston society. *Point of No Return* (1949) reviews a banker's life. Marquand also wrote six thrillers about a Japanese intelligence agent, Mr Moto, starting with *No Hero* (1935; later retitled *Mr Moto Takes a Hand*) and finishing with *Stopover: Tokyo* (1957).

Marriage A novel by SUSAN FERRIER, published in 1818. Lady Juliana, the Earl of Courtland's daughter, soon loses her romantic illusions after she elopes with Henry Douglas, a penniless young officer. She concentrates her energy on making sure her twin daughters do not repeat her own mistake of an imprudent marriage. Mary rejects her mother's ambitious plans and settles down contentedly with the man of her choice. Adelaide allows herself to be pushed into marriage with an elderly duke but soon deserts him for a worthless man.

Marric, J. J. See DETECTIVE FICTION.

Marryat, Captain **Frederick** 1792–1848 English. He drew on his adventurous career in the navy in his early novels: *The Naval Officer: or, Scenes and Adventures in the Life of Frank Mildmay* (1829), the highly successful *Peter Simple* (1834), *Jacob Faithful* (1834) and *Mr Midshipman Easy* (1836). After *Japhet in Search of a Father* (1836) and *Snarleyyow* (1837) he turned to children's fiction with *Masterman Ready* (1841), a vigorous rebuke to Johann Wyss's romanticized *Swiss Family Robinson*. Marryat's other great success as children's writer, *The Children of the New Forest* (1847), is set in the Civil War, with heroic Royalist children hiding from their Roundhead oppressors in the forest.

Mars-Jones, Adam 1954– English. *Lantern Lecture* (1981), consisting of three long short stories, combines startling subject matter with a witty, astringent voice. Mars-Jones then turned to fostering and collecting the work of other gay authors, in *Mae West is Dead: Recent Lesbian and Gay Fiction* (1983), before publishing more stories in *Monopolies of Loss* (1992) and his first novel, *The Waters of Thirst* (1993), a sustained monologue. Directly or indirectly AIDS is a recurrent subject, as in *The Darker Proof: Stories from a Crisis* (1987), a volume of stories co-written with EDMUND WHITE.

Marsh, Dame **Ngaio** 1899–1982 New Zealand. She combined a career as a theatre producer with writing popular DETECTIVE FICTION, starting with *A Man Lay Dead* (1934), featuring Superintendent Roderick Alleyn of Scotland Yard, her equivalent of AGATHA CHRISTIE's Hercule Poirot and DOROTHY L. SAYERS's Lord Peter Wimsey. The settings are often theatrical and her plots show a tight dramatic construction. More than 30 in all, her novels include *Artists in Crime* (1938), *Died in the Wool* (1945), *Opening Night* (1951), *Killer Dolphin* (1966) and *Black as He's Painted* (1974). *A Surfeit of Lampreys* (1950) and *False Scent* (1961) are plays adapted from her own novels. Her autobiography, *Black Beech and Honeydew* (1966), is primarily about her life in the theatre.

Marshall, Alan 1902–84 Australian. His short stories continue the vernacular tradition of HENRY LAWSON, consisting of simple but reverberant sketches from everyday, most often rural, life. Among the best known and most admired are those observing children and animals. They include *Tell Us About the Turkey, Jo* (1946), *How's Andy Going* (1956), *Short Stories* (1973), *Hammers Over the Anvil* (1975) and *The Complete Short Stories of Alan Marshall* (1977). *I Can Jump Puddles* (1955), the first volume of his autobiography, won an international audience.

Marshall, Paule 1929– African-American. Born in Brooklyn, she has spent much of her life in the Caribbean; her novels reflect the experience of moving and living between two worlds. *Brown Girl, Brownstones* (1959) is the story of immigrants from Barbados struggling to survive in New York; *The Chosen Place, the Timeless People* (1969) portrays an anthropologist in the Caribbean. Other work includes: *Praisesong for the Widow* (1982), a novel; *Reena and Other Stories* (1983); *Soul Clap Hands and Sing* (1988), a collection of novellas; and *Daughters* (1991), a novel.

Martin, Violet Florence See SOMERVILLE AND ROSS.

Martin Chuzzlewit A novel by CHARLES DICKENS, published in monthly parts in 1843–4 as *The Life and Adventures of Martin Chuzzlewit, His Relatives, Friends and Enemies. Comprising All His Wills and His Ways, with an Historical Record of What He Did and What He Didn't; Shewing Moreover Who Inherited the Family Plate; Who Came in for the Silver Spoons, and Who for the Wooden Ladles. The Whole Forming a Complete Key to the House of Chuzzlewit.*

The selfish young Martin Chuzzlewit is articled to the hypocritical architect Pecksniff but dimissed at the request of his grandfather, old Martin. Jonas Chuzzlewit, old Martin's nephew, engineers his father's death, marries and maltreats Pecksniff's daughter Mercy, and draws Pecksniff into his dubious schemes. Meanwhile, Martin's disillusioning experiences in America with his irrepressible servant Mark Tapley have taught him valuable lessons. He returns to England determined to make peace with his grandfather but finds him apparently under Pecksniff's control. Eventually old Martin's purpose of testing both Pecksniff and his grandson is revealed, and Martin is able to marry Mary Graham, Chuzzlewit's companion and adopted daughter. Pecksniff is exposed and Jonas, arrested for murdering his partner in roguery, Montague Tigg, poisons himself. Pecksniff's assistant, the innocent Tom Pinch, is suitably employed by old Martin and further gratified when his beloved sister Ruth marries their friend John Westlock. Mrs Sarah Gamp, the drunken midwife, is one of Dickens's most memorable minor characters.

Martin Eden A novel by JACK LONDON, published in 1909. Martin Eden, a labourer and former sailor, educates himself and becomes a writer, aspiring to the life led by the wealthy Ruth Morse. She deserts him when a newspaper brands him a socialist but returns when his work enjoys success. He rejects her and becomes more depressed by the suicide of his friend Russ Brissenden. Despising the society that has finally honoured him, Martin kills himself during a sea voyage.

Martineau, Harriet 1802–76 English. She began by writing on religion but became interested in economics, earning a reputation as a lively expositor of Utilitarianism in *Illustrations of Political Economy* (1832–4), *Poor Law and Paupers Illustrated* (1833) and *Illustrations of Taxation* (1834). A visit to the USA prompted *Society in America* (1837), which contains her comments on slavery, and *Retrospect of Western Travel* (1838). *Deerbrook* (1839) and *The Hour and the Man* (1841), which takes Toussaint L'Ouverture as its subject, are novels. In 1853 she produced a condensed version of Comte's *Cours de philosophie positive*. Her *Autobiographical Memoir* (1877) is valuable for its comments on her contemporaries. Her brother James Martineau (1805–1900) was an influential theologian.

Mary Barton*: *A Tale of Manchester Life A novel by ELIZABETH GASKELL, published in 1848. Its close, sympathetic observation of the lives of factory workers and its portrayal of industrial unrest make it an important CONDITION OF ENGLAND NOVEL.

John Barton, an active trade unionist, is chosen by his fellows to kill Henry Carson, son of one of their employers. Carson had been paying flattering attention to Barton's daughter Mary and she had briefly been diverted from her love for Jem Wilson, a young engineer. When Jem is charged with the murder, Mary manages to establish his innocence without revealing her father's guilt. Finally Barton, on the verge of death, confesses his crime to Henry Carson's father and obtains his forgiveness.

Masefield, John (Edward) 1878–1967 English. He is chiefly remembered for the poems of the sea ('Sea Fever') and the long narrative poems which showed him untouched by MODERNISM, well underway by the time he was appointed Poet Laureate in 1930. In the course of his prolific career he also wrote plays, history books, criticism and autobiography, as well as 22 novels. Six of them were designed specifically for children; two, *The Midnight Folk* (1927) and *A Box of Delights* (1935), chronicling the adventures of young Kay Harker, have achieved the status of minor classics. His adult novels cover a broad range: tales of faraway places, such as *Multitude and Solitude* (1909) and *Sard Harker* (1924), which owe something to JOSEPH CONRAD; tales of English rural life, such as *The Hawbucks* (1929), which breathe the same atmosphere as much of his narrative poetry; tales of the sea, such as *The Bird of Dawning* (1933) and *Victorious Troy: or, The Hurrying Angel* (1935), among his best work; and, at the end of his career, HISTORICAL FICTION.

Mason, A(lfred) E(dward) W(oodley) 1865–1948 English. The best known of his popular HISTORICAL FICTION and adventure fiction is *The Four Feathers* (1902), set during the Sudan Campaign of the 1890s, in which the hero is at first branded a coward, and presented with the insulting feathers of the title, but eventually proves himself a hero. Mason is also remembered for his contribution to DETECTIVE FICTION in creating Inspector Hanaud of the Sûreté, who appeared in *At the Villa Rose* (1910), *The House of the Arrow* (1924) and *The Prisoner in the Opal* (1928).

Mason, Bobbie Ann 1940– American. She made her début with *Shiloh and Other Stories* (1982), set in rural Kentucky and peopled by humble characters coping with changes they dimly understand yet keenly feel. Her novels are: *In Country* (1985), about a 17-year-old girl trying to understand the impact of the Vietnam War on her family; *Spence + Lila* (1988), about a Kentucky farm couple; and *Feather Crown: A Novel* (1993). She has also published a second collection of stories, *Love Life: Stories* (1989), and studies of VLADIMIR NABOKOV and DETECTIVE FICTION.

Massie, Allan 1938– Scottish. Scotland's rich trove of murders provides the matter for non-fiction, in *Ill-Met by Gaslight: Five Edinburgh Murders* (1980), and HISTORICAL FICTION, in *The Hanging Tree: A Romance of the Fifteenth Century* (1990). The murderousness of power and its pursuit informs much of his fiction, including his narratives of the Roman Caesars, *Augustus* (1986), *Tiberius* (1990) and *Caesar* (1993), and *King David* (1995). The moral complexities of the recent past make the basis of: *A Question of Loyalties* (1989), about trust and betrayal in Vichy France; *The Sins of the Father* (1991), about the adult children of an Auschwitz survivor and a former Nazi; and *Shadows of Empire* (1997), about a Scottish family during World War II.

Master Humphrey's Clock A weekly miscellany begun by CHARLES DICKENS in 1840. It reintroduced Mr Pickwick and the Wellers, and served as a framework for *THE OLD CURIOSITY SHOP*, but was never in itself a commercial success. Dickens dropped the title when *BARNABY RUDGE* began to appear in 1841.

Master of Ballantrae, The*: *A Winter's Tale A novel by ROBERT LOUIS STEVENSON, published in 1889. It is set in Jacobite Scotland in the period after the 1745 Rebellion.

The narrator, Ephraim Mackellar, recounts the lifelong feud between James Durie, the Master of Ballantrae, violent, charming and unscrupulous, and his younger brother Henry, quiet, dutiful and dull. When the Master is reported killed at Culloden, Henry inherits his title, estate and sweetheart, Alison Graeme. The Master returns, embittered by his exclusion, and suffers apparent death on two more occcasions, each time at his brother's hand: first in a moonlit duel and then, when the scene has shifted to America, in a murderous attack. The shock of his last reappearance, literally from the grave, kills Henry. They are buried together.

The wild melodrama of the plot is matched by the dark subtlety of the psychology.

Masterman Ready See MARRYAT, CAPTAIN FREDERICK.

Masters, Edgar Lee 1868–1950 American. He became famous with *Spoon River Anthology* (1915), a book of epitaphs in free verse about the dead in a rural Illinois cemetery. He never repeated its success, but commanded attention with three dramatic poems, *Lee* (1926), *Jack Kelso* (1928) and *Godbey* (1931), three novels based on his youth, *Mitch Miller* (1920), *Skeeters Kirby* (1923) and *Mirage* (1924), and a hostile biographical study of Lincoln (1931). *The New Spoon River* (1924) applied the technique of his first success to urban life. *Across Spoon River* (1924) is his autobiography.

Masters, John 1914–83 English. His fast-moving, epic adventure stories about British India include *Nightrunners of Bengal* (1951), set during the Indian Mutiny, and *Bhowani Junction* (1954), about the strife immediately preceding Indian independence. Masters also wrote *Loss of Eden*, a trilogy about World War I comprising *Now, God be Thanked* (1979), *Heart of War* (1980) and *By the Green of the Spring* (1981).

Masters, Olga 1919–86 Australian. The fiction she began to write when nearly 60 orchestrates 'the violence in the human heart', offering a quiet record of malice and pain in domestic life and unremarkable places. A collection of stories, *The Home Girls* (1982), was followed by a novel, *Loving Daughters* (1984), and a collection of linked stories, *A Long Time Dying* (1985). Posthumously published works are: *Amy's Children* (1987), another novel; *The Rose Fancier* (1988), more stories; *A Working Man's Castle* (1988), a play; and *Olga Masters: Reporting Home: Her Writings as a Journalist* (1991).

Mathers, Peter 1931– Australian. His underlying belief in anarchy gives his work a comic ebullience which survives even the most dreadful events. *Trap* (1966), a winner of the MILES FRANKLIN AWARD, anticipated THOMAS KENEALLY's *The Chant of Jimmy Blacksmith* in its study of the relationship between a part-Aboriginal and the society which seeks to understand and control him. *The Wort Papers* (1972) takes up similar themes of persecution and hardship in the history of a family's relationships. After a collection of short stories, *A Change for the Better* (1984), Mathers turned to drama with *Mountain King* (1985), *Shirt Tales* (1985), *Bats* (1986), *Grigori Two* (1987), *Caught* (1987), *Urbiculture* (1987), *Travelling* (1988), *More Urbiculture* (1988), *Real McCoy* (1988) and *Caught: or In the Name of the Rose* (1988).

Mathews, Harry 1930– American. He is an exponent of POST-MODERNISM. His novels include *The Conversions* (1962) and *Tlooth* (1966), both reprinted in *The Sinking of the Odradek Stadium and Other Novels* (1975), *Cigarettes* (1987) and *The Journalist* (1994). His short stories are found in *Country Cooking and Other Stories* (1980), *Singular Pleasures* (1988), *The Way Home: Collected Longer Prose* (1989), which includes *Singular Pleasures* and *Country Cooking*, and *The American Experience* (1991). Mathews has also published poetry, memoirs, a journal and literary criticism.

Matthiessen, Peter 1927– American. His novels include: *Race Rock* (1954); *Partisans* (1955); *Raditzer* (1960); *At Play in the Fields of the Lord* (1965), about a threatened Amazonian tribe; *Far Tortuga* (1975), a seafaring narrative based on his own experiences; and *Killing Master Watson* (1990), a murder mystery. Travel books include *Under the Mountain* (1963), *The Tree Where Man was Born* (1972), *The Snow Leopard* (1978), *Blue Meridian* (1971), *In the Spirit of Crazy Horse* (1983), *Indian Country* (1984). *African Silences* (1991) and *East of Lo Monthang; In the Land of the Mustang* (1995).

Maturin, Charles Robert 1782–1824 Irish. He is remembered for MELMOTH THE WANDERER (1820), a powerful GOTHIC NOVEL. Other novels were *The Fatal Revenge* (1807), *The Wild Irish Boy* (1808), *The Milesian Chief* (1811), *Women: or, Pour et Contre* (1818) and *The Albigenses* (1824). His tragedy *Bertram* was produced with great success in 1816, but two other tragedies, *Manuel* (1817) and *Fredolfo* (1819), failed.

Maugham, W(illiam) Somerset 1874–1965 English. Born at the British Embassy in Paris, he travelled widely and from 1926 made his home in the South of France. His first novel, *Liza of Lambeth* (1897), was an experiment in NATURALISM based on his observations of slum life while qualifying as a doctor at St Thomas's Hospital. He first achieved success as a playwright, with *Lady Frederick* (1907), followed by a string of popular works which included *The Tenth Man* (1910), *Our Betters* (1917), *The Circle* (1921), *The Letter* (1927) and *For Services Rendered* (1932).

His first really successful novel was the semi-autobiographical *Of Human Bondage* (1915), charting the life of a young man in 'Blackstable' (Whitstable) and 'Tercanbury' (Canterbury). *The Moon and Sixpence* (1919), set in Tahiti, is about a Gauguinesque artist. Other novels include: *The Painted Veil* (1925), *Cakes and Ale* (1930), a light-hearted comedy which contains a fictionalized portrait of THOMAS HARDY, *The Razor's Edge* (1945) and *Catalina* (1948). His short stories, still the most widely praised aspect of his work, appeared in collections beginning with *Orientations* (1899) and ending with *Creatures of Circumstance* (1947). Particularly notable volumes are: *The Trembling of a Leaf* (1921); *Ashenden: or, The British Agent* (1928), stories based on his experience in World War I which made a major contribution to SPY FICTION; and *Six Stories in the First Person Singular* (1931).

Critics have admired Maugham's narrative skill and anti-romantic powers of observation. In his own judgement he was one of the leading 'second-raters'. His views on life and art can be found in *The Summing Up* (1938), *Strictly Personal* (1942), *A Writer's Notebook* (1949) and *Points of View* (1958).

In 1947 he endowed the SOMERSET MAUGHAM AWARD to help young British writers enrich their work by travel.

Maupin, Armistead 1944– American. Apart from *Maybe the Moon* (1992), his fiction comprises the eight volumes of his *Tales of the City* sequence: *Tales of the City* (1978), *More Tales of the City* (1980), *Further Tales of the City* (1982), *Babycakes* (1984), *Significant Others* (1988), *28 Barbary Lane: A Tales of the City Omnibus* (1990), *Sure of You* (1990) and *Back to Barbary Lane: The Final Tales of the City Omnibus* (1991). It has been praised for its light wit, Dickensian narrative multiplicity and unsentimental portrait of the gay life-style on the West Coast.

Maurice A novel by E. M. FORSTER, written in 1913–14 but not published until 1971, after his death. Maurice Hall slowly becomes aware of his homosexuality in the repressive world of public school and Cambridge. A clandestine relationship with a fellow undergraduate, Clive Durham, ends when Clive decides to become 'normal' and marries. On a visit to the newly-weds Maurice meets Alec Scudder, Clive's gamekeeper. They fall in love and Alec gives up his plan to emigrate in order to stay with Maurice. Forster's 'Terminal Note', added after the final revision in 1960, defends the happy ending and condemns the persecution of homosexuals in Britain.

Mayor of Casterbridge, The Life and Death of the: *A Story of a Man of Character* A novel by THOMAS HARDY, published in 1886. It endows the rise and fall in its hero's fortunes with the inevitability of tragic process.

Michael Henchard, an out-of-work hay trusser, gets drunk and sells his wife, Susan, and child to a sailor named Newson. After 18 years, believing her sailor-husband drowned, Mrs Newson comes with her daughter, Elizabeth-Jane, to seek out Henchard, now sober and prospering as a grain merchant and mayor of Casterbridge. He agrees to break his engagement to Lucetta Le Sueur and to marry Mrs Newson anew. She dies soon afterwards and Henchard is embittered by the discovery that Elizabeth-Jane is Newson's daughter, not his own. She goes to live with Lucetta. Donald Farfrae, an energetic young Scot whom Henchard has hired, marries Lucetta. Henchard's pig-headedness makes Farfrae set up in business for himself and he thrives as Henchard declines. The old liaison between Henchard and Lucetta is publicized and she dies of shame. Newson returns, Elizabeth-Jane and Farfrae marry, and Henchard dies on Egdon Heath cared for by the loyal Able Whittle.

Melincourt: *or, Sir Oran Haut-Ton* The second

novel by THOMAS LOVE PEACOCK, published in 1817. Rich Mr Sylvan Forester educates the orang-outang of the title so that he appears to be a charming gentleman and buys him a baronetcy and a seat in Parliament. The portrait of Forester himself owes something to Shelley. The book's targets include Wordsworth (Mr Paperstamp), Coleridge (Mr Mystic), the much-abused Poet Laureate Robert Southey (Mr Feather-nest) and William Gifford, then editor of the influential *Quarterly Review* (Mr Vamp).

Melmoth the Wanderer A GOTHIC NOVEL by CHARLES ROBERT MATURIN, published in 1820. The hero has made a pact with Satan to prolong his life, but the debt can be transferred if he can find someone else willing to assume it. This situation provides a framework for a series of episodes in which Melmoth approaches various desperate people and tries to persuade them to take on his dreadful debt. Nobody agrees and Melmoth is doomed.

Melville, Herman 1819–91 American. After working as a bank clerk, teacher and farm labourer, he became a sailor at the age of 19. He was encouraged to set down some of his more exotic experiences in *TYPEE* (1846). *OMOO* (1847), *MARDI* (1849), *REDBURN* (1849), and *WHITE-JACKET* (1850) also derived from his life at sea and won him a good deal of popular acclaim. In 1850 he and his wife moved to Pittsfield, Massachusetts, where wider reading and his friendship with NATHANIEL HAWTHORNE prompted him to write *MOBY-DICK* (1851), the whaling adventure still considered by many to be the greatest work of American fiction.

It was not well received, and from relative popularity he began to fade into obscurity. *PIERRE* (1852), a psychological and moral study based on his childhood, was followed by a short novel, *ISRAEL POTTER* (1855), *THE PIAZZA TALES* (1856), a collection of stories which includes 'Bartleby the Scrivener' and 'Benito Cereno', and his last novel, *THE CONFIDENCE-MAN* (1857). At the age of 40 he turned almost exclusively to poetry. *Battle-Pieces and Aspects of the War* (1866) was followed by *Clarel* (1876), a long poem of religious crisis, which was his last published work. *John Marr and Other Sailors* (1888) and *Timoleon* (1891) were privately printed and distributed among a small circle of acquaintances.

Additional material was published from manuscript long after his death, when his reputation began to revive. *BILLY BUDD* appeared in 1924. *Journal up the Straits* (1935), *Journal of a Visit to London and the Continent* (1948), and *Journal of a Visit to Europe and the Levant* (1955), all record his travels in the 1850s. *Weeds and Wildings* (1924) is a collection of previously unpublished poetry. His letters were published in 1960.

Memoirs of a Cavalier: *or, A Military Journal of the Wars in Germany, and the Wars in Eng-*

land, from the Year 1632 to the Year 1648 A novel by DANIEL DEFOE, published in 1724. Andrew Newport, an English gentleman, accompanies the imperial army during the Thirty Years War and, after the sack of Magdeburg, joins the opposing army of Gustavus Adolphus, King of Sweden. After the king's death at the Battle of Lutzen in 1632, Newport returns to England and fights for Charles I, taking the narrative to the Battle of Naseby and the end of the Civil War.

Memoirs of a Woman of Pleasure *(Fanny Hill)* See CLELAND, JOHN.

Men at Arms See SWORD OF HONOUR.

Meredith, George 1828–1909 English. The son of a naval outfitter in Portsmouth, he was articled to a London solicitor but quickly turned to writing. In 1849 he married Mary Ellen Nicholls, widowed daughter of THOMAS LOVE PEACOCK, who deserted him for the painter Henry Wallis in 1857. Her death in 1861 left him free to marry Mary Vulliamy. In 1864 he moved to Flint Cottage at Box Hill in Surrey, his home for the rest of his life.

After working as a journalist and publisher's reader (in which capacity he encouraged both THOMAS HARDY and GEORGE GISSING), Meredith published *Poems* (1851), which contained the first version of 'Love in the Valley'. After two fantasies, *The Shaving of Shagpat* (1856) and *Farina* (1857), came THE ORDEAL OF RICHARD FEVEREL (1859) and EVAN HARRINGTON (1861), the novels which established his distinctive voice, at once thoughtful and comic, wryly questioning and exuberant. *Modern Love* (1862) earned him a permanent place as a poet. Over the next 20 years he published a steady flow of novels: SANDRA BELLONI (first called *Emilia in England*; 1864); RHODA FLEMING (1865); VITTORIA (1867), a sequel to *Sandra Belloni*; THE ADVENTURES OF HARRY RICHMOND (1871); BEAUCHAMP'S CAREER (1876); THE EGOIST (1879), the work that best exemplifies his epigrammatic wit and mastery of comic form; THE TRAGIC COMEDIANS (1880); and DIANA OF THE CROSSWAYS (1885). *Poems and Lyrics of the Joy of Earth* appeared in 1883.

With good reason, OSCAR WILDE described Meredith as 'a prose Browning'. His condensed and loaded prose, discovered in all his novels, is particularly notable in later works: ONE OF OUR CONQUERORS (1891), LORD ORMONT AND HIS AMINTA (1894) and THE AMAZING MARRIAGE (1895). His critical essay *On Comedy and the Uses of the Comic Spirit* (1897) is a highly regarded study. Further volumes of poetry included *Poems and Ballads of Tragic Life* (1887), *A Reading of Life* (1909) and *Last Poems* (1909).

Metcalf, John 1938– Canadian. Born in Britain, he emigrated to Canada in 1962. His fiction uses a disciplined, sometimes spare, poetic style to capture the beauty and absurdity of modern life. Collections of stories include *The Lady Who Sold Furniture* (1970), *The Teeth of My Father* (1975), *Selected Stories* (1982), and *Adult Entertainment* (1986). Two novels, *Going Down Slow* (1972) and *General Ludd* (1980), satirize academic life. *Girl in Gingham* (1978) contains two novellas. *Kicking Against the Pricks* (1982), critical essays, and *Writers in Aspic* (1988), an anthology, express his irritation at the Canadian literary establishment.

Michael K, Life and Times of A novel by J. M. COETZEE, published in 1983. It won a CNA LITERARY AWARD in South Africa and the BOOKER PRIZE in Britain. A bleak and apocalyptic work, it takes place during a South African civil war and combines in Michael K the figures of Kafka's K and Christ. Michael K is a hare-lipped gardener who tries to take his ailing mother from Cape Town to her birthplace in the Karoo. She dies on the way but he continues, his journey becoming a quest for survival as he struggles to avoid detention camps. The novel examines the predicament of people in a repressive society and celebrates the independence and liberty of the individual.

Michener, James A(lbert) 1907–1997 American. To the surprise of some critics, he won a PULITZER PRIZE for his first book, *Tales of the South Pacific* (1947), which served as the basis for the Rodgers and Hammerstein musical *South Pacific*. It was followed by *The Fires of Spring* (1948), *Sayonara* (1954), about the love affair between an American soldier and a Japanese woman, and *The Bridges at Toko Ri* (1953), about a pilot in the Korean War. Thereafter Michener devoted himself to bulky, heavily researched best-sellers taking the history of a region or nation as their theme; they include *Hawaii* (1959), *The Source* (about Israel; 1965), *Iberia* (about Spain; 1968), *Centennial* (about the USA; 1974), *Chesapeake* (1978), *The Covenant* (about South Africa; 1980) and *Space* (1982). *The World Is My Home* (1992) is his autobiography.

Middlemarch: *A Study of Provincial Life* A novel by GEORGE ELIOT, published in 1871–2.

Initially the narrative concentrates on the blighted marriage of the wealthy young Puritanical idealist, Dorothea Brooke, to the middle-aged pedant, Dr Edward Casaubon, labouring fruitlessly on his *Key to All Mythologies*. Upon his death, affection develops between Dorothea and her former husband's cousin, Will Ladislaw, whom she eventually marries. Another strand traces the career of the equally idealistic Dr Tertius Lydgate, devotee of scientific progress and the new medicine, and his marriage to the local mayor's daughter, Rosamund Vincy, whose foolish social ambitions ruin his life. A third narrative depicts the down-to-earth relationship between Rosamund's brother Fred and Mary Garth, daughter of the honest estate manager, Caleb

Garth. The affairs of Bulstrode, the rich hypocritical banker who harbours a grim secret, are also followed to their humiliating end.

These narratives involve many sharply observed minor characters: Dorothea's uncle Mr Brooke, a characteristic early-19th-century landowner and source of much unintentional humour; Mrs Cadwallader, the witty wife of the Rector, himself hardly a fisher of souls; Sir James Chettam, a stolid local squire who marries Dorothea's sister, Celia; Mrs Bulstrode, a woman of dignity and integrity, and the billiard-playing vicar, Camden Farebrother. Beyond them is a huge gallery of briefer portraits of servants, auctioneers, clergymen, businessmen, housewives, labourers, tenants, medical men, schoolmistresses, children and apothecaries.

Even those who appear fleetingly are fused into a portrait of English economic, social, and religious life during the pre-Reform years 1829–32. All the characters and the narrative strands in which they play their part serve George Eliot's purpose of examining the 'web of society' and asking whether it merely destroys or is eventually improved by ardent but flawed souls like Dorothea and Lydgate.

Middleton, Stanley 1919– English. During a career as a Nottingham schoolmaster, he has produced a succession of quietly observed, 'implacably domestic' novels set in his native Potteries. They include *Holiday* (BOOKER PRIZE; 1974), *Entry into Jerusalem* (1982), *Valley of Decision* (1985), *Beginning to End* (1991), *A Place to Stand* (1992) and *Brief Hours* (1997).

Midnight's Children A novel by SALMAN RUSHDIE, published in 1981 and awarded the BOOKER PRIZE and, in 1993, voted the 'Booker of Bookers'. Its garrulous and unreliable narrator, Saleem Sinai, is one of a thousand and one children born in India at midnight on the moment of its declaration of independence and thereby endowed with magical powers. The novel extends the conceit of a country born without a history, and therefore fated to make it up as it goes along, into a fabulous and teeming display of tall-story-telling, a major example of MAGIC REALISM.

Miles Franklin Award An annual award for a novel portraying 'Australian life in any of its phases', established by a bequest from the estate of MILES FRANKLIN. Since its inception it has been won by: PATRICK WHITE's *Voss* (1957); RANDOLPH STOW's *To the Islands* (1958); VANCE PALMER's *The Big Fellow* (1959); 'Elizabeth O'Connor''s *The Irishman* (1960); White's *Riders in the Chariot* (1961); THEA ASTLEY's *The Well-Dressed Explorer* and George Turner's *The Cupboard Under the Stairs* (1962); Sumner Locke Elliot's *Careful, He Might Hear You* (1963); GEORGE JOHNSTON's *My Brother Jack* (1964); Thea Astley's *The Slow Natives* (1965); PETER MATHERS's *Trap* (1966); THOMAS

KENEALLY's *Bring Larks and Heroes* (1967); Thomas Keneally's *Three Cheers for the Paraclete* (1968); George Johnston's *Clean Straw for Nothing* (1969); Dal Stiven's *A Horse of Air* (1970); DAVID IRELAND's *The Unknown Industrial Prisoner* (1971); Thea Astley's *The Acolyte* (1972); no award in 1973; Ronald McKie's *The Mango Tree* (1974); XAVIER HERBERT's *Poor Fellow My Country* (1975); David Ireland's *The Glass Canoe* (1976); Ruth Park's *Swords and Crowns and Rings* (1977); JESSICA ANDERSON's *Tirra Lirra by the River* (1978); David Ireland's *A Woman of the Future* (1979); Jessica Anderson's *The Impersonators* (1980); PETER CAREY's *Bliss* (1981); RODNEY HALL's *Just Relations* (1982); no award in 1983; TIM WINTON's *Shallows* (1984); CHRISTOPHER KOCH's *The Doubleman* (1985); ELIZABETH JOLLEY's *The Well* (1986); Glenda Adams's *Dancing on Coal* (1987); no award in 1988 (period of award altered); Peter Carey's *OSCAR AND LUCINDA* (1989); Tom Flood's *Oceana Fine* (1990); DAVID MALOUF's *The Great World* (1991); Tim Winton's *Cloudstreet* (1992); Alex Miller's *The Ancestor Game* (1993); Rodney Hall's *The Grisly Wife* (1994); 'Helen Demidenko''s *The Hand That Signed the Paper* (1995); Christopher Koch's *Highways to a War* (1996); and DAVID FOSTER's *The Glade Within the Grove* (1997).

In 1994 novels by prominent writers, including some previous winners, were excluded from consideration because of a narrow interpretation of the requirement to present Australian life. A more liberal approach was signalled by the award of the prize in 1995 to *The Hand That Signed the Paper*, about Ukranian collaboration in the Holocaust. 'Demidenko' was subsequently identified as Helen Darville, the daughter of British immigrants, and repeated calls were made for the judges to resign.

Mill on the Floss, The A novel by GEORGE ELIOT, published in 1860.

Maggie and Tom Tulliver are the children of the miller of Dorlcote, an honest but unimaginative man, and his weak and foolish wife. In this oppressive environment Maggie's intelligence, scholarly competence and wide-ranging imagination become liabilities, especially in a woman. She responds to Philip Wakem, the deformed son of the leading lawyer in the nearby town of St Ogg's. Tulliver regards the lawyer Wakem as his enemy and Tom, blindly supporting his father's cause, makes Maggie give up Philip's friendship. After Tulliver's death Maggie goes to St Ogg's to stay with her cousin Lucy, who is to marry Stephen Guest. He is attracted to Maggie and his irresponsible behaviour on a boating expedition compromises her reputation. Tom turns her out of his house and she is ostracized by local society, except for Lucy, Philip and the rector, Dr Kenn. Autumn brings a flood which threatens the mill, and Maggie attempts to rescue Tom. She fails, and brother and sister are drowned together, but not before they have briefly recaptured the affection they felt for each other as children.

Response to *The Mill on the Floss* has been divided between admiration of the skill with which George Eliot evokes rural background to Maggie and Tom's childhood and criticism of the rushed and arbitrary ending.

Millar, Kenneth See MACDONALD, ROSS.

Miller, Henry (Valentine) 1891–1980 American. His most famous work, *Tropic of Cancer* (1934), describes his promiscuous life in Paris. Considered pornographic, it was not published in the USA until 1961. *Black Spring* (1936), ten autobiographical stories, and *Tropic of Capricorn* (1939), about his years working for Western Union, were also suppressed. *The Colossus of Maroussi* (1941) is a travel book about Greece, while *The Air-Conditioned Nightmare* (1945) and *Remember to Remember* (1947) decry the spiritual and cultural desolation of his native land. Other works include *The World of Sex* (1940), *The Plight of the Creative Artist in the United States of America* (1944), *Books in My Life* (1951), *The Time of the Assassins: A Study of Rimbaud* (1956) and a trilogy – *Sexus* (1949), *Plexus* (1953; first published in French, 1952) and *Nexus* (1960) – collectively titled *The Rosy Crucifixion*.

Miller, Walter M. See SCIENCE FICTION.

Millhauser, Steven 1943– American novelist and short story writer. His novels deal with the interplay between art and life and the artist's role in shaping culture and sensibility. *Edwin Mullhouse: The Life and Death of an American Writer, 1943–1954* (1972) is a parody of literary biography in which an 11-year-old writes about a friend and rival. *Portrait of a Romantic* (1977) ironically examines adolescence as a period of *angst* and turbulence. *From the Realm of Morpheus* (1986) is a contemporary ALICE'S ADVENTURES IN WONDERLAND. *Martin Dressler: The Tale of an American Dreamer* (1996; PULITZER PRIZE) offers a classic American type, the commercial entrepreneur, as a symbol of culture. *In the Penny Arcade* (1987) and *The Barnum Museum* (1991) are collections of stories.

Millin, Sarah Gertrude 1889–1968 South African. *Adam's Rest* (1922), *God's Stepchildren* (1924), *Mary Glenn* (1925) and *The Sons of Mrs Aab* (1931) made a major contribution to South African fiction during the inter-war period. Her novels show an awareness of the realities and complexities of racial conflict, a subject explored further in her study, *The South Africans* (1926, revised 1934). She also published biographies of Rhodes (1933) and Smuts (1936).

Mills, Martin See BOYD, MARTIN.

Milne, A(lan) A(lexander) 1882–1956 English. An assistant editor of *Punch*, he won additional good opinions with his plays, *Wurzel-Flummery* (1917), *Mr Pim Passes By* (1919; published, 1922), *The Truth about Blayds* (1921; published, 1922)

and *The Dover Road* (1921; published, 1922). His great success, however, came with children's books. *When We were Very Young* (1924) and *Now We are Six* (1927) were verses about his young son Christopher Robin. The works by which he will always be remembered are *Winnie-the-Pooh* (1926) and *The House at Pooh Corner* (1928), based on the imaginary conversations and adventures of Christopher Robin's toys. Each is given a distinctive characteristic: Pooh's greediness, Eeyore's misanthropy, Tigger's bounciness and Piglet's timidity. The stories are perfectly adapted to young readers' interests, concentrating on topics such as birthday presents, the quest for food and mini-adventures involving bad weather, mysterious footprints or getting lost. Pooh's 'hums' (or verses) and E. H. Shepard's illustrations are also memorable.

Milne came to resent the success of these little books at the expense of his adult work. This includes: *The Red House Mystery* (1922), his solitary contribution to DETECTIVE FICTION; two novels, *Two People* (1931) and *Chloë Marr* (1946); a plea against war, *Peace with Honour* (1934); and an autobiography, *It's Too Late Now* (1939). His last triumph was a stage adaptation of KENNETH GRAHAME'S *THE WIND IN THE WILLOWS* as *Toad of Toad Hall* (1929).

The Mimic Men A novel by V. S. NAIPAUL, published in 1967. It takes the form of a first-person memoir by its central character, Ralph Singh, a former Caribbean politician now living in a suburban London hotel. His unchronological narrative reviews his life: as a student in England, when he married the English Sandra; as a child on the (fictional) island of Isabella; as one of a new generation of Caribbean politicians and, after his fall from power, as an exile in London.

Misfortunes of Elphin, The A romance by THOMAS LOVE PEACOCK, published in 1829. He uses Welsh Arthurian legends to satirize literary affectations and political movements. Elphin succeeds to the kingdom of Ceredigion, which has suffered through Seithenyn's negligence. He is imprisoned by a neighbouring prince, Maelgon, but the bard Taliesin secures his release by appealing to King Arthur. The book contains many songs and set-piece speeches; some of them adapt or translate Welsh sources, while others, like 'The War-Song of Dinas Vawr', are original.

Miss Peabody's Inheritance A novel by ELIZABETH JOLLEY, published in 1983. Miss Peabody is a London office-worker whose sterile life caring for her bedridden mother is relieved only by the work in progress she receives from novelist Diana Hopewell in Australia. She idolizes Diana and eagerly awaits each new episode in the adventures of Miss Arabella Thorne, an eccentric headmistress who is taking her intimates and one of her 'gels' on a tour of Europe. Miss Peabody even expects to run into these characters in London, and her repressions lift in anticipation. After her mother's death, she journeys to Australia, only to find that Diana is dead and that she was another bedridden old lady. The now-liberated Miss Peabody's inheritance is Diana's manuscript and, as its only reader, she is now set to beome its author.

Miss Ravenel's Conversion From Secession to Loyalty A novel by JOHN DE FOREST, published in 1867. Dr Ravenel moves from New Orleans to New Boston (based on New Haven, where De Forest lived), but the sympathies of his daughter Lillie, remain with the Confederates. Her conversion begins when she is wooed by two Union officers. She marries the dashing and aristocratic Carter but he proves unfaithful. After he dies in battle she marries his virtuous rival, Colbourne, thus completing her conversion to Abolitionism. The novel is memorable for battle scenes which anticipate those of STEPHEN CRANE.

Mistry, Rohinton 1952– Born in Bombay, he emigrated to Canada in 1975. The overlapping stories in *Tales from Firozsha Baag* (1987) may be read as a single novel. SUCH A LONG JOURNEY (1991), Mistry's first novel proper and a winner of the COMMONWEALTH WRITERS PRIZE, intertwines the political events leading to the creation of Bangladesh with a study of thwarted aspirations. *A Fine Balance* (1996), another winner of the Commonwealth Writers Prize, has a deliberately unspecific Indian setting with echoes of the State of Emergency period (1976–7).

Mitchell, James Leslie See GIBBON, LEWIS GRASSIC.

Mitchell, Margaret See GONE WITH THE WIND.

Mitchell, W(illiam) O(rmond) 1914– Canadian. A popular raconteur and humorist with his roots in oral storytelling, he is a seminal figure in the development of recent western Canadian writing. His first novel, *Who Has Seen the Wind* (1947), is a classic account of a Prairie boyhood. *Jake and the Kid* (1961) collects 13 of the original stories from the more than 300 scripts he wrote for his series on Canadian Broadcasting Corporation radio in 1951–8. Other works include *The Kite* (1962), *The Vanishing Point* (1973), *How I Spent My Summer Holidays* (1981), *Ladybug, Ladybug* (1988), *According to Jake and the Kid* (1989), *Roses are Difficult* (1990), *The Black Bonspiel of Willie MacCrimmon* (1993), and the plays *The Devil's Instrument* (1973) and *Back to Beulah*, published in *Dramatic W. O. Mitchell* (1982).

Mitchison, Naomi (Mary Margaret) 1897– Scottish. A passion for history, science and politics informs her prolific output. She made her reputation with novels and stories of ancient Greece, notable for their relaxed account of male homosexuality; they include *The Conquered* (1923), *Black Sparta* (short stories; 1928) and *The Corn King and the Spring Queen* (1931). *We Have Been Warned* (1935) expresses her anti-totalitarian beliefs, while *The Blood of the Martyrs* (1939) is set in ancient Rome. Novels such as *The Bull Calves* (1947) draw on her Scottish ancestry and interest in Scottish identity; *Early in Orcadia* (1987) is about prehistoric Orkney.

A scientist from a family of scientists (her brother was J. B. S. Haldane), she has also written SCIENCE FICTION, including *Memoirs of a Spacewoman* (1962), which enjoys cult status, and *Solution Three* (1975). Her knowledge of Africa informs *Images of Africa* (1981) and other works. She has produced a series of invaluable autobiographies, including *All Change Here* (1975), *You May Well Ask* (1979) and *As It Was* (1988).

Mitford, Mary Russell 1787–1855 English. The charming *Our Village: Sketches of Rural Life, Character and Scenery* began as a series of contributions to *The Lady's Magazine* in 1819 and appeared in five volumes in 1824–32. The village is Three Mile Cross, near Reading, which itself became the subject of *Belford Regis: Sketches of a Country Town* (1835). A novel, *Atherton and Other Tales* (1854), was less successful. Miss Mitford's plays include *The Foscari* (1826), *Rienzi* (1828) and *Charles I* (1834). *Recollections of a Literary Life* (1852) comments on her contemporaries.

Mitford, Nancy (Freeman) 1904–73 English. She was the daughter of the 2nd Baron Redesdale; her younger sister, Jessica, wrote an account of their family life in *Hons and Rebels* (1960). Nancy Mitford's novels generally describe Bohemian life in upper-class society, combining a satiric tone with a sharp ear for dialogue. The most successful include *The Pursuit of Love* (1945), *Love in a Cold Climate* (1949) and *The Blessing* (1951). Her biographies include *Madame de Pompadour* (1954), *Voltaire in Love* (1957), *The Sun King* (1966), and *Frederick the Great* (1970). With A. S. C. Ross she edited and contributed to *Noblesse Oblige* (1956), a collection of satirical essays on snobbery which gave the terms 'U' and 'non-U' to the language. She also edited family correspondence in *The Ladies of Alderley* (1938) and *The Stanleys of Alderley* (1939).

Mittelholzer, Edgar 1909–65 Guyanese. His 23 novels helped to create a genuine Caribbean consciousness incorporating Guyanese history and landscape. The Kaywana novels – *Children of Kaywana* (1952; including *Kaywana Heritage*, separately published from 1976), *The Harrowing of Hubertus* (1954; later published as *Kaywana Stock*) and *Kaywana Blood* (1958) – are a family saga covering the years 1612–1953. Other works include: *Corentyne Thunder* (1941), about the Indian peasantry in Guyana; *A Morning at the Office* (1950), about Jamaican race relations; *Shadows Move among Them* (1952) and *The Mad MacMullochs* (1959), both about ideally free, sexually liberated communities; *Latticed Echoes* (1960); *The Life and Death of Sylvia* (1953); *The*

Pilkington Drama (1965), which ends with a suicide by fire prefiguring the manner of Mittelholzer's own death.

Mo, Timothy 1950– He was born in Hong Kong of English and Cantonese parents. *The Monkey King* (1978), set in Hong Kong, and *Sour Sweet* (1982; HAWTHORNDEN PRIZE), set in London's Chinese community, have been followed, more ambitiously, by: *An Insular Possession* (1986), about the Opium Wars; *The Redundancy of Courage* (1991), about a guerrilla movement in a fictional country modelled on the Philippines; and *Brownout on Breadfruit Boulevard* (1995).

Moby-Dick: *or, The Whale* A novel by HERMAN MELVILLE, published in New York and London in 1851. The British title was *The Whale*.

The central narrative thread is Ishmael's account of his whaling voyage from Nantucket on the *Pequod*. Before he goes aboard he befriends Queequeg, a harpooner from the South Sea Islands, and hears Father Mapple's sermon about Jonah. The crew of the *Pequod*, castoffs and refugees of all races and lands, is a microcosm of humanity. The harpooners are Queequeg, Tashtego (a Gay Head Indian) and Daggoo (an African); the three mates are Starbuck, Stubb and Flask. The mysterious Captain Ahab appears only after several days at sea, to reveal that he sees the purpose of the voyage as being to kill the white sperm whale known as Moby-Dick, which took off his leg on a previous voyage. The crew are drawn into his monomaniacal plan; only the business-like Starbuck demurs. The story culminates in a three-day chase of Moby-Dick, which ends when the enraged whale charges the ship. Ahab is caught in his harpoon line and drowned. The *Pequod* sinks, taking all the whaling boats and their crews down in the suction. The only survivor is Ishmael, clinging to the coffin that had been made for Queequeg.

The novel is by turns naturalistic and fantastic. Large sections dwell on the history and technique of whaling, the anatomy of whales, and the mythic significance of the whale, shaping these subjects – as well as virtually every aspect of life on board the *Pequod* – into obscure parables. The result, turbulent and highly complex, elevates Ahab's mad quest to the level of epic and tragedy.

Modern Chivalry A novel by HUGH HENRY BRACKENRIDGE, published between 1792 and 1815. Captain John Farrago and his Irish servant, Teague O'Regan, American versions of Don Quixote and Sancho Panza, travel around Pennsylvania, their adventures providing the occasion for satirical observations about post-Revolutionary American life and manners. Farrago devotes much of his energy to discouraging or preventing the untrained, uneducated Teague from taking advantage of the opportunities offered by the new American society – as preacher, Indian treaty maker, potential husband for a well-bred young lady and pupil to a French dancing master. The tensions between them thus dramatize the problem of authority and leadership in a democracy.

Modern Instance, A A novel by WILLIAM DEAN HOWELLS, serialized in 1881 and published in volume form in 1882. He referred to it as his 'New Medea', a 'modern instance' of what would happen to a gradually estranged couple. Marcia Gaylord's marriage to Bartley Hubbard, a Boston journalist, fails and she leaves him. They are eventually divorced and he dies in Arizona. She is courted by Ben Halleck, who nevertheless cannot decide whether or not to leave the ministry for her. The novel ends without giving his final decision.

modernism The term for an international tendency in the arts brought about by a creative renaissance during the last decade of the 19th century and lasting into the years following World War I. Strictly speaking, modernism cannot be reliably characterized by a uniform style or even described as a 'movement', since it embraced a wide range of artistic movements, including Symbolism, impressionism, postimpressionism, futurism, constructivism, imagism, vorticism, expressionism, dada, and surrealism. Technically, modernism was distinguished by its challenge to traditional representation and its highly self-conscious manipulation of form. Conventional narrative gave way to STREAM OF CONSCIOUSNESS and conventional poetic form to free verse. Such experiments were conducted with strong awareness of pioneering studies in other disciplines: in psychology, William James's *Principles of Psychology* (1890) and Freud's *The Interpretation of Dreams* (1899); in physics, Einstein's *General Principles of Relativity* (1915); and in anthropology, Sir James Frazer's *The Golden Bough* (1890–1915).

The most notable landmarks in English literature are commonly understood to include HENRY JAMES's *THE AMBASSADORS* (1903), JOSEPH CONRAD's *NOSTROMO* (1904), and JAMES JOYCE's *ULYSSES* (1922) and, in poetry, T. S. Eliot's *The Waste Land* (1922). The fiction of FORD MADOX FORD, VIRGINIA WOOLF and, in America, WILLIAM FAULKNER, as well as the poetry of Ezra Pound and William Butler Yeats, could be added to a list which would still be far from exhaustive.

Moggach, Deborah 1948– English. *Close to Home* (1979) draws on her knowledge of north London, *Hot Water Man* (1982) on her experience of Pakistan. Other work has been concerned with the endlessly diverse permutations of family life. It includes *Porky* (1983), about father-daughter incest; *To Have and To Hold* (1986), about surrogate motherhood; *Driving in the Dark* (1988), about the bonds between a father and his illegitimate son; *Stolen* (1990), about the children of a mixed marriage involved in a custody battle; *Seesaw* (1996), about a kidnapping; and *Close Relations* (1997).

Moir, David Macbeth 1798–1851 Scottish. He contributed regularly to *Blackwood's Edinburgh Magazine* and other periodicals, signing his name with the Greek capital delta. His best-remembered book, *The Life of Mansie Wauch, Tailor in Dalkeith* (1828) is an imaginary autobiography containing much wry observation. It is dedicated to JOHN GALT.

Molesworth, Mary Louisa 1839–1921 English. She published *Lover and Husband* (1869) and several other novels under the pseudonym Ennis Graham before turning to children's books with great popular success. The publishing firm of Macmillan made a practice of issuing a book by Mrs Molesworth every Christmas, sometimes illustrated by Walter Crane. Among more than 100 titles are *The Cuckoo Clock* (1877), *The Tapestry Room* (1879), *The Adventures of Herr Baby* (1881), *The Children of the Castle* (1890), *The Carved Lions* (1895), *Peterkin* (1902), *The Little Guest* (1907) and *The Story of a Year* (1910).

***Moll Flanders**: The Fortunes and Misfortunes of the Famous* A novel by DANIEL DEFOE, published in 1722.

Moll herself narrates the story of her life. Born in Newgate, she is taken in by the mayoress of Colchester, from whom she passes to another gentlewoman, whose son seduces her. She leads an adventurous love life and eventually marries. In Virginia with her husband, she finds her mother and discovers that her husband is in fact her brother. She leaves him and her children for England, where she falls into bad company and becomes a thief. Transported to Virginia, she renews her liaison with a former husband on the way. Moll inherits her mother's plantation and prospers. When their sentence runs out, she and her husband return to England, where she looks back from the age of 70 over 'the wicked lives we have lived'.

Moll Flanders owes much of its success and its importance in the development of English fiction to the fact that it is a novel of character rather than an adventurous romance. It may not be neat or shapely, but Moll herself is made an identifiable personality.

Momaday, N(atachee) *[Navarre]* **Scott** 1934– Native American. He received a PULITZER PRIZE for his first novel, *House Made of Dawn* (1968), about a young man's flight from the reservation. He has since published a second novel, *The Ancient Child* (1989), as well as a collection of Kiowa folk-tales, *The Way to Rainy Mountain* (1969), a memoir, poetry and *In the Presence of the Sun: Stories and Poems 1961–91* (1993)

Monastery, The A novel by SIR WALTER SCOTT, published in 1820. It is more interesting for its evocation of Kennaquhair, a monastery based on Melrose Abbey, in the time of Elizabeth I than for the romantic plot, which concerns the rivalry of Sir Piercie Shafton and the brothers Edward and Halbert Glendinning in their love for Mary Avenel. *The Abbot* (1820), set in the reign of Mary, Queen of Scots, was intended as a sequel.

Monk, The A GOTHIC NOVEL by M. G. LEWIS, published in 1796. It relies on horror rather than terror, and allows supernatural events to remain without natural explanation. The theme is the sexual repression at the heart of asceticism. Ambrosio, a devoted young monk, is tempted into depravity and eventually damned by his association with Matilda, the model for his own much beloved portrait of the Virgin Mary but in fact the Devil's emissary. Sub-plots compound the horror of a tale which many found both ridiculous and indecent, though it also enjoyed considerable popularity.

Monsarrat, Nicholas (John Turney) 1910–79 English. He is chiefly remembered for his novel of World War II, *The Cruel Sea* (1951), made into a successful film. Other works, never quite outgrowing the formulae of adventure fiction, include *The Tribe That Lost Its Head* (1956) and *Richer Than All His Tribe* (1968), racial allegories prompted by the conflicts he had observed in South Africa. *Life is a Four-Letter Word* (1966–70) is his autobiography.

Montana Book Award and Montana New Zealand Book Award See NEW ZEALAND BOOK AWARD and GOODMAN FIELDER WATTIE BOOK AWARD.

Montague, C. E. See SPY FICTION.

Montgomery, L(ucy) M(aud) 1874–1942 Canadian. *ANNE OF GREEN GABLES* (1908), a children's book, was an immediate popular success. *Anne of Avonlea* (1909) and numerous other titles followed the scapegrace heroine's career from teaching college to marriage and domesticity, but without recapturing the charm of the original book. Other novels include *The Blue Castle* (1926), *Kilmeny of the Orchard* (1910) and the melancholy, semi-autobiographical *Emily of New Moon* (1923), *Emily Climbs* (1925) and *Emily's Quest* (1927).

Moodie, Susanna [née Strickland] 1803–85 She emigrated from Britain to Canada in 1832. *Enthusiasm and Other Poems* (1831) was followed by other volumes written to help the family finances, including the novels *Mark Hurdlestone and the Gold Worshipper* (1853), *Geoffrey Monckton* (1853) and *Flora Lyndsay* (1854). Her most enduring works are *Roughing It in the Bush: or, Life in Canada* (1852) and *Life in the Clearings versus the Bush* (1853). Her sisters, Agnes Strickland (1796–1874) and Catharine Parr Traill (1802–99), were also writers.

Moonstone, The A novel by WILKIE COLLINS, published in 1868. It uses features of the SENSATION NOVEL to create a pioneering example of

DETECTIVE FICTION. The story is told through eye-witness accounts by the characters, a method Collins favoured in much of his fiction.

Franklin Blake presents the Moonstone diamond, stolen from a Hindu holy place, to Rachel Verinder but it disappears by the next morning. Sergeant Cuff investigates the mystery. Suspicion falls variously on three Hindus lurking in the neighbourhood, the servant Rosanna Spearman and Rachel herself. She inexplicably turns against Franklin Blake and becomes engaged to the philanthropist Godfrey Ablewhite. Ezra Jennings, the local doctor's assistant, demonstrates that Blake unknowingly removed the diamond while under the influence of opium. The diamond, meanwhile, is traced to a London bank and Cuff exposes Ablewhite as the thief, but not before Ablewhite has been killed and the diamond retrieved by the Hindus.

Moorcock, Michael 1939– English. He became editor of *New Worlds* in 1964, making it a forum for surreal, modernist SCIENCE FICTION. Among his own works are: the 'Jerry Cornelius' stories, including a tetralogy, *The Final Programme* (1968), *A Cure for Cancer* (1971), *The English Assassin* (1972) and *The Condition of Muzak* (1977); *Behold the Man* (1969); the 'Dancers at the End of Time' series, including *An Alien Heat* (1972), *The Hollow Lands* (1974) and *The End of All Songs* (1976); and many fantasy novels, including the Elric series. *Gloriana* (1978), *Blood* (1995) and *Fabulous Harbours* (1995) are more sophisticated. His mildly surrealistic non-fantasy novels include *The Brothel in Rosenstrasse* (1982), *Byzantium Endures* (1983), *The Laughter of Carthage* (1984), *Mother London* (1988), *Casablanca* (1989) and *Jerusalem Commands* (1992).

Moore, Brian 1921– Born in Belfast, he emigrated to Canada in 1928 and then to the USA in 1959. His experience of Catholicism and a divided Ireland frequently provides him with themes for novels whose unflinchingly realistic surfaces belie an underlying engagement with phantasmagora, myth and ritual. Works include: *Judith Hearne* (1955; retitled *The Lonely Passion of Judith Hearne*), about a Belfast spinster's descent into delusion; *The Feast of Lupercal* (1957); *The Luck of Ginger Coffey* (1960); *An Answer from Limbo* (1962); *The Emperor of Ice Cream* (1965); *I Am Mary Dunne* (1968), perhaps his best book, a study of imperilled identity; *Catholics* (1972); *The Great Victorian Collection* (1975); *The Mangan Inheritance* (1979); *Cold Heaven* (1983), about earthly reincarnation; *Black Robe* (1985), about 17th-century Jesuits and Canadian Indians; *The Colour of Blood* (1987), about Communist Poland; *Lies of Silence* (1990), a thriller about Ireland; and *No Other Life* (1993); *The Statement* (1996), about the legacy of the Occupation in France; and *The Magician's Wife* (1997), about the conflict between Europe and Islam in 19th-century Algeria.

Moore, George (Augustus) 1852–1933 Anglo-Irish. Born in Ireland and educated in Birmingham, he spent ten years in Paris, studying painting and publishing two books of verse, *Flowers of Passion* (1878) and *Pagan Poems* (1881). After his arrival in London in 1880 he published poems, plays, essays, art criticism, an autobiography and a stream of novels which clearly showed the influence of Zola's NATURALISM: *A Modern Lover* (1883), *A Mummer's Wife* (1885), *A Drama in Muslin* (1886), *A Mere Accident* (1887), *Spring Days* (1888), *Mike Fletcher* (1889) and *Vain Fortune* (1891). He achieved a major success with *ESTHER WATERS* (1894), generally acknowledged as his finest work.

His years in Ireland (1899–1911) are described in *Hail and Farewell* (1911–14), a trilogy of reminiscence valuable for its portrait of the Irish literary revival and the establishment of the Abbey Theatre. Back in London, he acquired a reputation as a literary sage. His last period as a writer was announced by *The Brook Kerith* (1916), a painstaking novel about Jesus. Other works include two more novels, *Héloïse and Abelard* (1921) and *Aphrodite in Aulis* (1930), and plays, *The Making of an Immortal* (1927) and *The Passing of the Essenes* (1930; a revised version of *The Apostle*, 1911).

Moore, Lorrie 1957– American. Replete with irony, wit and word-play, her work includes two story collections, *Self-Help* (1985) and *Like Life* (1990), and two novels, *Anagrams* (1986) and *Who Will Run the Frog Hospital?* (1994).

Moorhouse, Frank 1938– Australian. As co-founder (with MICHAEL WILDING) and editor of the alternative fiction magazine *Tabloid Story*, he has had an influence beyond his own writing. This he began by describing as 'discontinuous narrative'. More traditional than some Australian POST-MODERNISM, his work uses forms reflecting the fragmentation of contemporary urban life. His books include *Futility and Other Animals* (1969), *The Americans, Baby* (1972), *The Electrical Experience* (1974), *Conference-Ville* (1976), *Tales of Mystery and Romance* (1977), *The Everlasting Secret Family and Other Secrets* (1980), *Room Service* (1986), *Forty Seventeen* (1988), *Lateshows* (1990), *Grand Days* (1994) and *Loose Living* (1995). He has edited an important anthology of Australian contemporary fiction, *The State of the Art: The Mood of Contemporary Australia in Short Fiction* (1983). *Days of Wine and Rage* (1980) documents the 1970s. He has also written several screenplays.

More, Hannah 1745–1833 English. She was a friend of Joshua Reynolds, Samuel Johnson, David Garrick, HORACE WALPOLE and a member of the bluestocking circle of intellectual women centred on Elizabeth Montagu. Though she began by writing plays – *The Search after Happiness* (1773), *Inflexible Captive* (1774), *Percy* (1777) and *The Fatal Falsehood* (1779) – her strong

Evangelical convictions caused her to abandon the theatre and devote herself to didactic writing. It was aimed largely at the poorer classes she perceived as vulnerable to the ideas spread by the French Revolution. *Village Politics* (1793) was followed by the popular series of *Cheap Repository Tracts* (1795–8), which included her most famous story, 'The Shepherd of Salisbury Plain'. The Religious Tract Society was formed to continue her work, while she herself went on to support William Wilberforce in his campaign against slavery, to pioneer the Sunday School movement and to write a didactic novel, *Coelebs in Search of a Wife* (1809). Her *Letters* appeared in 1834.

More, St Thomas See *UTOPIA*.

Morgan, Charles (Langbridge) 1894–1958 English. His fiction, once greatly admired but nowadays neglected, is often concerned with the relation between art and life and often takes the artist as a central character. It includes: *Portrait in a Mirror* (1929); *The Fountain* (1932; HAWTHORNDEN PRIZE), sometimes considered his most successful work; *Sparkenbroke* (1936); *The Voyage* (1940); *The Judge's Story* (1947), a fable about the struggle between spiritual and material values, echoed in a collection of essays, *Liberties of the Mind* (1951); and *Challenge to Venus* (1957). His plays include: *The Flashing Stream* (1938); *The River Line* (1952), from his 1949 novel of the same title; and *The Burning Glass* (1954). He also wrote a tribute to his friend GEORGE MOORE (1935) and *Ode to France* (1942), a country where he enjoyed a high reputation.

Morgan, Lady Sydney [née Owenson] ?1783–1859 Irish. She was known for Irish romances, the best being *The Wild Irish Girl* (1806), *O'Donnel* (1814) and *The O'Briens and the O'Flahertys* (1827). She wrote two lively books on France and Italy, and a life of Salvator Rosa.

Morier, James Justinian *c.* 1780–1849 English. Service with Sir Hartford Jones's mission to Persia led to his *Journey through Persia, Armenia and Asia Minor* (1812) and the more notable *Second Journey through Persia* (1818). Morier also used his experiences in several Oriental romances, of which the most successful is *The Adventures of Hajji Baba of Ispahan* (1824), a PICARESQUE novel whose uncomplimentary account of Persian society drew a protest from the Persian minister in London, printed in a sequel, *The Adventures of Hajji Baba of Ispahan in England* (1828).

Morrieson, Ronald Hugh 1922–72 New Zealand. Virtually unknown at the time of his death, he passed his whole life in the small town of Taranaki. From it he created a bizarre and funny fictional world, marrying literature and popular culture in a vigorous, original style that has been called 'Taranaki Gothic'. His four novels are *The Scarecrow* (1963), *Came a Hot Friday* (1964), *Predicament* (1975) and *Pallet on the Floor* (1976).

Morris, William See *DREAM OF JOHN BALL, A*; *NEWS FROM NOWHERE*; and *WELL AT THE WORLD'S END, THE*.

Morris, Wright 1910– American. Preoccupied with the American Edenic myth and the influences of American history, his novels include *My Uncle Dudley* (1942), *The Man Who was There* (1945), *The World in the Attic* (1949), *The Works of Love* (1952), *A Field of Vision* (1956, National Book Award), *Love Among the Cannibals* (1957), *Ceremony in Lone Tree* (1960), *Cause for Wonder* (1963), *In Orbit* (1967), *Fire Sermon* (1971), *A Life* (1973), *The Fork River Space Project* (1977) and *Plains Song* (1980). *Collected Stories: 1948–1986* appeared in 1986. He has published literary criticism and three volumes of memoirs, *Will's Boy: A Memoir* (1981), *Solo: An American Dreamer in Europe, 1933–34* (1983) and *A Cloak of Light: Writing My Life* (1985).

Morrison, Arthur 1863–1945 English. He spent most of his life in the East End of London, the setting for his best work. *Tales of Mean Streets* (1894) and two novels, *A CHILD OF THE JAGO* (1894) and *THE HOLE IN THE WALL* (1902), portray the working people and criminals of the slums without sentimentality or didacticism. Despite the debt to Zola and GEORGE MOORE, they are works of considerable originality in their clear-eyed realism and unadorned prose style. Morrison's DETECTIVE FICTION – *Martin Hewitt, Investigator* (1894), *Chronicles of Martin Hewitt* (1895) and *Hewitt: Third Series* (1896) – enjoyed a brief popularity in the wake of the SHERLOCK HOLMES STORIES. More interesting, and now equally little known, is a novel of witchcraft and smuggling in Napoleonic times, *Cunning Murrell* (1900). He also published an early and influential study, *The Painters of Japan* (1911).

Morrison, John (Gordon) 1904– Australian. His polished, realistic stories bridge the gap between HENRY LAWSON and 20th-century Australian fiction. 'The Incense Burner' and 'North Wind' are touchstones in the development of Australian writing. Collections are *Sailors Belong Ships* (1947), *Black Cargo* (1955) and *Twenty-Three* (1962). Selections include *The Best Stories of John Morrison* (1988). His novels are *The Creeping City* (1949) and *Port of Call* (1950).

Morrison, Toni [Wofford, Chloe] 1931– African-American. She has won wide recognition for novels reaching back into the black American experience, particularly as it has affected women: *The Bluest Eye* (1970), about a year in the life of a young black girl who declines into insanity; *Sula* (1973), about the friendship between two young black women; *Song of Solomon* (1977), about Milkman Dead's exploration of his family history; *Tar Baby* (1981), about motherhood and the relationships between black and white cultures; *BELOVED* (1987; PULITZER PRIZE); *Jazz* (1992), *Race-ing Justice,*

En-gendering Power (1992), Playing in the Dark (1992) and Paradise (1997) are non-fiction; interviews can be found in Conversations with Toni Morrison (1994), edited by Danielle Taylor-Guthrie. She was awarded the Nobel Prize for Literature in 1993.

Mortimer, John (Clifford) 1923– English. A barrister, he made his literary reputation with plays such as The Dock Brief (1958), Come As You Are (1970) and Heaven and Hell (1976), notable for their cool and witty tone. His highly successful TV career includes the creation of Rumpole, a splendidly disreputable barrister introduced in a volume of stories, Rumpole of the Bailey (1978); his reappearances include The Trials of Rumpole (1979), Rumpole for the Defence and Rumpole's Return (1980), the misleadingly titled Rumpole's Last Case (1987) and Rumpole à la Carte (1990). Comic novels about the unlovely consequences of Thatcherism include Paradise Postponed (1985) and Titmuss Regained (1990). His autobiography, In Character (1983), extends the story begun in his play, A Voyage round My Father (1970).

Mosley, Nicholas [Lord Ravensdale] 1923– English. His works include Accident (1966), filmed by Joseph Losey from a screenplay by Harold Pinter in 1967, and an abstract, experimental sequence consisting of Catastrophe Practice: Plays Not for Acting, and Cypher: A Novel (1979), Imago Bird (1980), Serpent (1981), Judith (1986, revised 1992) and Hopeful Monsters (1990; WHITBREAD AWARD). He has also written a study of the poet Julian Grenfell (1976), a biography of his parents Sir Oswald and Lady Cynthia Mosley (1982–3), and a typically scrupulous autobiography, Efforts at Truth (1994).

Mosley, Walter 1952– African-American. An important new voice in DETECTIVE FICTION, he has created Ezekiel ('Easy') Rawlins, a black detective living largely by his wits in Los Angeles during the post-war years. Devil in a Blue Dress (1990), A Red Death (1991), White Butterfly (1992), Black Betty (1994) and A Little Yellow Dog (1996) follow his fortunes. The novels revisit the territory of RAYMOND CHANDLER's Philip Marlowe in order to view it through the eyes of the marginal and the dispossessed.

Motley, Willard 1912–65 American. His observation of the slums of Chicago served as material for his first novel, Knock on any Door (1947). We Fished All Night (1951) and Let No Man Write My Epitaph (1958) are also critical examinations of the urban environment. Let Noon be Fair (1966) traces the gradual corruption of a Mexican tourist town.

Mottram, R(alph) H(ale) 1883–1971 English. He first achieved recognition with The Spanish Farm (1924; HAWTHORNDEN PRIZE), the first part of a trilogy continued in Sixty-four, Ninety-four (1925) and The Crime at Vanderlynden's (1926). It is set on a farm near the Front during World War I. Many of his later novels are set in East Anglia, where he spent most of his life.

Mowatt, Anna Cora 1819–70 American. Born to American parents in Bordeaux, she married a New York lawyer at the age of 15. After publishing a verse romance, Pelayo (1836), and a verse satire, Reviewers Reviewed (1837), she turned her hand to novels of New York social life, including The Fortune Hunter (1844) and Evelyn: or, A Heart Unmasked (1845). The success of her play Fashion (1845), a comedy about the newly rich Mr and Mrs Tiffany, encouraged her to go on the stage herself. She toured for nine years, retiring to write her Autobiography of an Actress (1854), Mimic Life (1856) and Twin Roses (1857) – romantic narratives of life in the theatre – and various historical sketches.

Mphahlele, Es'kia [Ezekiel] 1919– South African. His stories of the ghetto and the black experience in Man Must Live (1947), The Living and the Dead (1961) and In Corner B (1967), selected in The Unbroken Song (1981), sound a rising note of political protest. The Wanderers (1971), Chirundu (1979) and Father Come Home (1984) are novels, the last an affecting tale of dispossessed and scattered African families. However, his narrative skill is seen at its best in his vivid autobiography, Down Second Avenue (1959). Afrika My Music: An Autobiography 1957–1983 (1984) is less compelling. Mphahlele's influential criticism includes The African Image (1962, revised edition 1974) and Voices in the Whirlwind (1972).

Mr Badman, The Life and Death of A religious allegory by the Nonconformist preacher and writer John Bunyan (1628–88), published in 1680. It consists of a dialogue between Mr Wiseman and Mr Attentive about Mr Badman, who has recently passed over into damnation. The book shows a considerable degree of realism, especially in its vivid representation of a 17th-century market town and the lively credibility of Mr Badman's own character, making an unmistakable contribution to the development of the novel. For Bunyan, see also THE HOLY WAR and THE PILGRIM'S PROGRESS.

Mr Britling Sees It Through A novel by H. G. WELLS, published in 1916. Strongly autobiographical, it captured the national mood as World War I took its toll. Through Britling, a mature and successful writer, we are given a picture of Wells's early enthusiasm for the war and his growing disillusionment, as well as glimpses of his marital infidelities, generally considered among the novelist's less discreet reflections on his life.

Mr Gilfil's Love Story See SCENES OF CLERICAL LIFE.

Mr Midshipman Easy See MARRYAT, CAPTAIN FREDERICK.

Mr Polly, The History of A novel by H. G. WELLS, published in 1910. At the age of 37, Alfred Polly seems trapped in his unprofitable shop and his marriage to Miriam, but he escapes for a life on the road. Rural England, around the Potwell Inn and its plump landlady, prove a haven from the pressures of his class and its failed commercial prospects. Polly is able to settle at the Inn only after proving his manhood in a fight with the criminal Uncle Jim, and after Miriam has been awarded life insurance for the husband she thinks dead.

Mr Scarborough's Family A novel by ANTHONY TROLLOPE, serialized in 1882–3 and published in volume form in 1883. The plot concerns the disappointment of Mr Scarborough who, after the birth of a son, Mountjoy, marries his wife again before the birth of a second son, Augustus, to ensure that he can declare the latter his heir, should Mountjoy not prove of responsible character. The novel is enlivened by the characters of Mr Grey, Scarborough's attorney, and his daughter, Dolly, who refuses to marry because all the men she meets compare unfavourably with her father.

Mr Sponge's Sporting Tour A novel by R. S. SURTEES, published in 1853 with illustrations by John Leech. Probably his best novel, it has more form and balance than the others and the central character is convincingly developed. Sponge lives up to his name by forcing himself on rich men and making up to their daughters, but his skill on horseback and genuine love of hunting redeem him. *Mr Facey Romford's Hounds* (1865) is a sequel.

Mrs Dalloway A novel by VIRGINIA WOOLF, published in 1925. Clarissa Dalloway, the wife of Richard Dalloway MP and a fashionable London hostess, is to give an important party. Her character is gradually revealed through her thoughts during the day and her memories of the past, rendered by STREAM OF CONSCIOUSNESS. The other people who have touched her life are her one-time suitor Peter Walsh, lately returned from India; her childhood friend Sally Seton; her daughter Elizabeth and spinster tutor Miss Kilman; and a political hostess, Lady Bruton. A complementary character is Septimus Warren Smith, a shell-shocked veteran whose presence locates the book in the shadow cast by the suffering of World War I. He has retreated into a private world and ends the day by committing suicide.

Mudrooroo [Johnson, Colin] 1939– Aboriginal Australian. He was one of a number of Aborigines who changed their names in protest against the bicentennial celebrations. He is still best known for his first novel, *Wild Cat Falling* (1965), a brief but intense book focusing on a 19-year-old half-Aboriginal, half-white 'anti-hero'. *Doin Wildcat* (1988) describes the filming of the novel. His other fiction includes *Long Live Sandawara* (1979), *Doctor Wooreddy's Prescription for Enduring the Ending of the World* (1983), *Master of the Ghost Dreaming* (1990) and *Wildcat*

Screaming (1992). His verse includes *The Song Circle of Jacky and Selected Poems* (1986) and *Dalwurra: A Poem Cycle* (1988). He has written the first theorizing account of Aboriginal literature, *Writing from the Fringe* (1990), and co-edited *Paperbark* (1990), the main collection of Aboriginal writings. His play, *The Aboriginal Protesters Confront the Declaration of the Australian Republic on 26 January 2001 with the Production of 'The Commission' by Heiner Müller* (1983), was produced in 1995.

Muir, Edwin 1887–1959 Scottish. He is remembered for the verse, increasingly allegorical and bearing the stamp of his idiosyncratic philosophy, gathered in *Collected Poems 1921–1958* (1960). Before committing himself fully to poetry, he wrote three novels, all to some degree autobiographical: *The Marionette* (1927), set in contemporary Salzburg; *The Three Brothers* (1931), a BILDUNGSROMAN set in 16th-century Scotland; and *Poor Tom* (1932), set in Glasgow before World War I. His declared autobiography, *The Story and the Fable* (1940), was revised as *An Autobiography* (1954). Muir also published criticism and, with his wife Willa, translations of Kafka.

Mulgan, John 1911–45 New Zealand. He and his one novel, *Man Alone* (1939), have become part of the mythology of New Zealand masculine identity. The hero, Johnson, is an ex-soldier alienated from society between the wars. His inability to fit in and his experiences in the Auckland riots subvert the myth of New Zealand as 'God's Own Country', a myth Mulgan's father Alan had helped to promote. His struggle to survive alone in the bush is a test of manhood, from which he emerges into a kind of redemption through mateship as he joins other men going off to fight in the Spanish Civil War. *Report on Experience* (1945) is a posthumously published account of Mulgan's experiences in peace and war.

Mulock, Dinah Maria [Mrs Craik] 1826–87 English. *The Ogilvies* (1849), *Olive* (1850), *The Head of the Family* (1852) and *Agatha's Husband* (1853) were followed by her most popular work, *JOHN HALIFAX, GENTLEMAN* (1856). Set in Tewkesbury (called Norton Bury), it is a CONDITION OF ENGLAND NOVEL, concerned with class and industrial conflict. Later novels included *A Life for a Life* (1859), *Christian's Mistake* (1865), *The Woman's Kingdom* (1869) and *Young Mrs Jardine* (1879). She also published poetry and some sensible and penetrating essays, including 'A Woman's Thoughts about Women' (1853).

Mungoshi, Charles 1947– Zimbabwean. His best-known novel, *Waiting for the Rain* (1975), is set in rural, pre-independence Zimbabwe and draws on Shona and Christian traditions for its portrait of spiritual, political and material drought, as well as inter-generational conflicts. Other writing in English includes the stories in *Coming of the Dry Season* (1972), banned before

Zimbabwean independence, and *Some Kinds of Wounds and Other Short Stories* (1980). *One Day, Long Ago* (1991), consisting of stories rendered from Shona, won the NOMA AWARD. Work in Shona includes three novels and a play.

Munonye, John 1929– Nigerian. He admits to being influenced by CHINUA ACHEBE, whose Igbo cultural background he shares. His most substantial achievement is a trilogy, *The Only Son* (1966), *Obi* (1969) and *Bridge to a Wedding* (1978), covering three generations of Igbo life. Other novels include *The Oil Man of Obange* (1971), the philosophical *A Wreath for the Maidens* (1973) and the PICARESQUE *A Dancer of Fortune* (1974).

Munro, Alice 1931– Canadian. Her low-key, understated stories question notions of 'normality' and make her provincial towns mythical places in which universal dramas are enacted. She is both an acute observer of small-town Canadian cultural codes – in particular how women are socialized – and a writer who describes patterns of growing up and behaviour that are common across cultures. Two books, *LIVES OF GIRLS AND WOMEN* (1971) and *Who Do You Think You Are?* (1978; as *The Beggar Maid* in Britain), are collections of short stories with common protagonists who provide a sense of novelistic unity. Other collections – *Dance of the Happy Shades* (1968), *Something I've been Meaning to Tell You* (1974), *The Moons of Jupiter* (1982), *The Progress of Love* (1987), *Friend of My Youth* (1990) and *Open Secrets* (1994) – are unified by recurrent themes and motifs.

Munro, Hector Hugh See SAKI.

Murdoch, Dame **Iris (Jean)** 1919– English. The casual humour of *Under the Net* (1954) was followed by the growingly emphatic symbolism of *The Flight from the Enchanter* (1955), *The Sandcastle* (1957) and *The Bell* (1958), widely considered her most successful novel, about a declining religious community. Her prolific output has continued with *A Severed Head* (1961), *An Unofficial Rose* (1962), *The Unicorn* (1963), *The Italian Girl* (1964), *The Red and the Green* (1965), *The Time of the Angels* (1966), *The Nice and the Good* (1968), *Bruno's Dream* (1969), *A Fairly Honourable Defeat* (1970), *An Accidental Man* (1971), *The Black Prince* (1972), *The Sacred and Profane Love Machine* (1974), *A Word Child* (1975), *Henry and Cato* (1977), *The Sea, The Sea* (1978; BOOKER PRIZE), *The Philosopher's Pupil* (1983), *The Book and the Brotherhood* (1987), *Message to the Planet* (1989), *The Green Knight* (1993) and *Jackson's Dilemma* (1995). Her philosophical works include *Sartre: Romantic Rationalist* (1953), *The Sovereignty of Good* (1970) and *The Fire and the Sun: Why Plato Banned the Artists* (1977).

Murnane, Gerald 1939– Australian. His fiction draws on closely held autobiographical experience, distanced and made objective by the nov-

elist's craft, which itself becomes the object of passionate attention. Novels include *Tamarisk Row* (1974), *A Lifetime on Clouds* (1976), *The Plains* (1982) and *Inland* (1988). *Landscape with Landscape* (1985), *Velvet Waters* (1990) and *Emerald Blue* (1995) are collections of stories.

Mwangi, Meja (David) 1948– Kenyan. He belongs to a generation deeply affected by the Mau Mau emergency of the early 1950s, the subject of *Carcase for Hounds* (1974), filmed as *Cry Freedom*, and *Taste of Death* (1975). His later fiction, most famously *Going Down River Road* (1976), has generally been concerned with social conditions in post-independence Kenya. Other books include *Kill Me Quick* (1973), *The Cockroach Dance* (1979), *The Bushtrackers* (1979), *Bread of Sorrow* (1987), *Weapon for Hunger* (1989), *The Return of Shaka* (1989) and *Striving for the Wind* (1990).

My Àntonia A novel by WILLA CATHER, published in 1918. It takes the form of a memoir by Jim Burden about his childhood friend Àntonia Shimerda, daughter of a Bohemian farming family in Black Hawk, Nebraska. Àntonia takes a series of menial jobs before being seduced and abandoned by a railroad man, Larry Donovan. She returns to her mother's farm, gives birth to a daughter and marries Anton Cuzak. When Jim, who has moved East, returns 20 years later he finds Àntonia on the farm she and her husband have built, worn down but satisfied with her lot.

Myers, L(eopold) H(amilton) 1881–1944 English. He is best known for a tetralogy set in 16th-century India at the court of the Mogul emperor Akbar: *The Near and the Far* (1929), *Prince Jali* (1931), *The Root and the Flower* (1935) and *The Pool of Vishnu* (1940), republished in one volume as *The Near and the Far* in 1943. It uses a past and idealized society to explore the poverty of contemporary existence, particularly its failure to reconcile material and spiritual values.

Mysteries of Udolpho, The A GOTHIC NOVEL by ANN RADCLIFFE, published in 1794. The setting is Gascony and the Italian Apennines at the end of the 16th century. Emily de St Aubert becomes the ward of her tyrannical aunt, Madame Cheron, who marries the sinister Montoni. She is carried off to Udolpho, Montoni's castle in the Apennines, where frightening and apparently supernatural occurrences are frequent. She manages to escape, however, and returns to Gascony and her lover, the Chevalier de Valancourt. Montoni is captured and brought to justice. The combination of terrifying incident and lavishly PICTURESQUE setting made *Udolpho* one of the most popular of all Gothic novels.

mystery fiction See DETECTIVE FICTION.

Mystery of Edwin Drood, The See *EDWIN DROOD, THE MYSTERY OF*.

Nabokov, Vladimir 1899–1977 Born in St Petersburg, he followed his family into exile, studying at Cambridge in 1919–22 and producing critically acclaimed poems, stories and novels written in Russian while living in Berlin and Paris. In the USA he published his first novels in English, *The Real Life of Sebastian Knight* (1941) and *Bend Sinister* (1947), and a memoir, *Conclusive Evidence* (1951; expanded and revised as *Speak, Memory*, 1966). The success of *LOLITA* (1955) enabled him to move to Switzerland. While working on his translation of Pushkin's *Eugene Onegin* (1964), he wrote three more novels: *Pnin* (1957), a CAMPUS NOVEL about an émigré teacher as baffled by the USA as the hero of *Lolita*; *Pale Fire* (1962), which explores the discrepancies between John Shade's autobiographical poem and the commentary by its posthumous editor, Charles Kinbote; and *Ada, or Ardor: A Family Chronicle* (1969), another 'edited' text of maze-like design, set in Amerussia on the planet Antiterra. *Nabokov's Dozen* (1958) and *Nabokov's Quartet* (1966) are collections of stories. He also supervised the translation of his Russian novels by his son Dimitri. *The Enchanter* (1987) is a belatedly published novella.

Nagarajan, K(rishnaswamy) 1893–1986 Indian. He is best known for *Athavar House* (1937), a chronicle of an Indian joint family which recalls JOHN GALSWORTHY's *THE FORSYTE SAGA*, and for *Chronicles of Kedaram* (1961), the ironic account of a small Coromandel coast town in the 1930s. *Cold Rice*, a collection of short stories, appeared in 1945.

Nahal, Chaman 1927– Indian. He is best known for *AZADI* (1975; awarded a SAHITYA AKADEMI prize), a novel about Partition, and the Gandhian trilogy, *The Crown and the Loincloth* (1981), *The Salt of Life* (1990) and *The Triumph of the Tricolour* (1993). Nahal has also written: a satirical novel, *The English Queens* (1979); two love stories, *My True Faces* (1973) and *Into Another Dawn* (1977); and a volume of stories, *The Weird Dance* (1965).

Naipaul, Shiva(dhar) S(rinivasa) 1945–85 Trinidadian. His novels are *Fireflies* (1970), *The Chip-Chip Gatherers* (1973) and the despairing *A Hot Country* (1983). *North of South* (1978) reports on Africa, *Black and White* (1980) on American subcultures and the People's Temple mass suicides in Guyana. *Beyond the Dragon's Mouth* (1984) collects journalism, autobiography and stories. He was the younger brother of V. S. NAIPAUL.

Naipaul, Sir V(idiadhar) S(urajprasad) 1932– Trinidadian, of Indian descent. He has lived in Britain since 1950. The genial satire of Trinidadian life in *The Mystic Masseur* (1957; JOHN LLEWELLYN RHYS PRIZE), *The Suffrage of Elvira* (1958) and *Miguel Street* (1959) culminated in his comic masterpiece, *A HOUSE FOR MR BISWAS* (1961). Novels set in England are *Mr Stone and the Knights Companion* (1963), about the city, and *The Enigma of Arrival* (1987), about the countryside. While keeping his fastidious, sardonic tone, Naipaul has developed his preoccupation with 20th-century uncertainties and the damaging effects of imperialism in *THE MIMIC MEN* (1967), *In a Free State* (1971; BOOKER PRIZE); *Guerrillas* (1975) and *A Bend in the River* (1979), a work of tragic scope. *A Flag on the Island* (1967) collects his short stories, while *A Way in the World* (1994) consists of linked stories and prose pieces.

His non-fiction, largely based on his travels and closely related to his novels, includes: *The Middle Passage* (1962) and *The Loss of El Dorado* (1969), about the Caribbean; *An Area of Darkness* (1964), *India: A Wounded Civilization* (1977) and *India: A Million Mutinies Now* (1990); *A Turn in the South* (1989), about the American South; and *Among the Believers* (1981), about Islam. *Finding the Centre* (1984) contains a memoir of his father, while *The Overcrowded Barracoon* (1972) and *The Return of Eva Perón* (1980) collect shorter pieces.

Naked and the Dead, The A novel by NORMAN MAILER, published in 1948. Set on a Pacific island during World War II, it focuses on 13 soldiers, whose civilian lives are recalled through flashbacks. Mailer's cynicism about America's past and his doubts about its post-war future are expressed largely through the clash between the rigid General Cummings and the liberal Lieutenant Hearn. Rough in language, violent in action, and hostile towards mainstream American values, the book foreshadows much of Mailer's later writing.

Namjoshi, Suniti 1941– Indian. After spending the first half of her life in India and the second half outside, she is now one of the most significant representatives of the Indian *diaspora* in Britain. She is best known for *Feminist Fables* (1981), revisions of various myths and traditional tales. *The Conversations of Cow* (1985), *The Blue Donkey Fables* (1988) and *The Mothers of Maya Diip* (1989) maintain her satirical, subversive perspective.

Narayan, R(asipuram) K(rishnaswami) 1907– Indian. His early novels – *Swami and Friends* (1935), *The Bachelor of Arts* (1937), *The Dark Room* (1938) and *The English Teacher* (1945; as *Grateful to Life and Death* in the USA, 1953) – are largely autobiographical. A mature middle phase includes *Mr Sampath* (1949; as *The Printer of Malgudi* in the USA, 1955), *The Financial Expert* (1952), *Waiting for the Mahatma* (1955), *THE*

GUIDE (1958), awarded a SAHITYA AKADEMI prize, and *The Man-Eater of Malgudi* (1962). Later novels are *The Sweet Vendor* (1967; as *The Vendor of Sweets* in the USA), *The Painter of Signs* (1976), *A Tiger for Malgudi* (1983) and *Talkative Man* (1986). Deceptively simple English and an ironic outlook make him particularly accessible to Western readers, though the unobtrusive, wry moral thrust of his fiction also aligns it with traditional Indian story-telling. He has also published many volumes of short stories and a genial autobiography, *My Days* (1975).

Nasby, Petroleum V(esuvius) [Locke, David Ross] 1833–88 American. A humorist in the style of ARTEMUS WARD and Josh Billings, he specialized in facetious letters to the editor. *The Nasby Papers* (1864) ridiculed the Confederate cause in the Civil War by proclaiming its righteousness in the silliest way possible. Abraham Lincoln was among its admirers. Locke also wrote a political novel, *The Demagogue* (1881).

Nashe [or **Nash**]**, Thomas** See *UNFORTUNATE TRAVELLER, THE*.

Native Son A novel by RICHARD WRIGHT, published in 1940. Bigger Thomas, a black from the Chicago ghetto, goes to work as chauffeur to a wealthy white family, accidentally kills the daughter, Mary, and in his panicked flight, kills his girlfriend. Awaiting trial in prison, he feels a sense of freedom for the first time. His Communist lawyer, Max, shows him what real emotional connection with a white person can be. Max tries to make him talk about the social conditions which led to his acts, but Bigger is too proud to do anything more than affirm that 'what I killed for, I am!'

naturalism A term generally applied to art which seeks to adhere to nature. More strictly, it refers to the scientifically based extension of REALISM propounded by Émile Zola in the 1870s and 1880s. In naturalist writing, medical and evolutionary theories of 19th-century science inform readings of human character and social interactions, which are seen as being genetically and historically determined. The struggle of the individual to adapt to environment, the fight for the spouse and the Darwinian idea of the survival of the fittest become central concerns. The resulting mood is usually bleak, with the characters often appearing victims of circumstance, heredity or instinct.

In Britain naturalism had no dedicated champion to rival Zola, but it nevertheless discernibly influenced GEORGE GISSING, GEORGE MOORE, notably in *ESTHER WATERS* (1894) and THOMAS HARDY, notably in *JUDE THE OBSCURE* (1895), as well as leaving its mark on ARTHUR MORRISON, ARNOLD BENNETT and the young SOMERSET MAUGHAM. It played a more important role in American fiction, where FRANK NORRIS, THEODORE DREISER, JACK LONDON and STEPHEN CRANE were all notable exponents.

Plays indebted to naturalism include J. M. Synge's *Riders to the Sea* (1904) and JOHN GALSWORTHY's *Strife* (1909).

Naylor, Gloria 1950– African-American. Her novels deal with African-American women and families. *The Women of Brewster Place* (1982) is the story of seven women exploring their memories and their sexuality in a closed circle of intimacy; *Mamaday* (1988) is about the relationship between a woman and her great-aunt. Other novels include *Linden Hills* (1985) and *Bailey's Café* (1992).

Nazareth, Peter 1940– Ugandan. Born of Goan parents and long resident in the USA, he has written two novels about political systems in post-independence Africa: *In a Brown Mantle* (1972) and *The General is Up* (1984). Nazareth's importance as a critic has been established by *Literature and Society in Modern Africa* (1972), *The Third World Writer: His Social Responsibility* (1978) and *Literature of the African People* (1984).

Ndebele, Njabulo S(imakahle) 1949– South African. In both his critical work, collected in *Rediscovery of the Ordinary* (1991), and his stories, some of which are collected in *Fools and Other Stories* (1983), he tries to move beyond the representation of what he calls the 'spectacular' aspects of life under apartheid to depict the 'ordinary', by which he means the daily routines, individual experiences and inner feelings which survive despite deprivation and horror. His fiction for children includes *Bonolo and the Peach Tree* (1992), dedicated to 'all the young dreamers in the world'.

Nectar in a Sieve A novel by KAMALA MARKANDAYA, published in 1954. The story is told by Rukmani, wife of a south Indian peasant and mother of seven children. The family live in unspeakable poverty on land owned by an absentee landlord. Their existence is disrupted by the building of a tannery, seen by Rukmani as the beginning of a process which will destroy the 'sweet quiet of village life'.

Nesbit, E(dith) 1858–1924 English. After doing literary hack work, she discovered her talent for writing lively stories for children unburdened with moralizing. Her first success, *The Story of the Treasure Seekers* (1899), was about the Bastable children and their mini-adventures. Succeeding books mixed fantasy with reality, most successfully in *The Phoenix and the Carpet* (1904) and *The Story of the Amulet* (1906), both involving time-travel. Her most famous novel, *The Railway Children* (1906), has a more realistic setting. The title characters retreat to the countryside after their father is arrested on a trumped-up charge, and make friends with the local railway porter, Perks. The story involves a political refugee, theft, misplaced charity and fierce family loyalty – powerful ingredients for young readers, balanced by romantic adventures, fortunate coincidences and happy endings.

New Atlantis, The An unfinished Utopian fiction by the philosopher and essayist Sir Francis Bacon (1561–1626), posthumously published in 1627. English mariners discover the Pacific island of Bensalem, a high civilization of great antiquity which has isolated itself from the world to preserve its integrity. The chief purpose of the story is to introduce Bacon's ideal design for a college of sciences, here called Salomon's House or the College of the Six Days' Works. It represents the kind of institution that Bacon hoped James I would establish to carry out the programme of experiments suggested in *Sylva Sylvarum* (1627), following the methods of scientific enquiry laid out in *The Advancement of Learning* (1605) and the *Novum organum* (1620). His proposals were revived in the 1650s and in some measure fulfilled by the foundation of the Royal Society in 1660.

New Grub Street A novel by GEORGE GISSING, published in 1891. Its bleak portrait of the literary world is drawn from Gissing's own discouraging struggle.

Despite writing two fine books, Edward Reardon is hampered by poverty and an unsympathetic wife, Amy. Her desertion of him, coupled with his failure, sends him to the grave. Alfred Yule is an unappreciated and embittered scholar. His daughter Marian falls in love with Jasper Milvain, a self-interested reviewer, but he abandons her when her expected legacy does not materialize, marries the widowed Amy and becomes, in worldly terms, a success. Other characters include Harold Biffen, earnestly polishing a novel of absolute realism, and Whelpdale, a failure who becomes an 'adviser to literary aspirants'.

New Zealand Book Award The best-known award for New Zealand writing, inaugurated in 1976 and amalgamated in 1996 with the Montana Book Award, which had already taken over the GOODMAN FIELDER WATTIE BOOK AWARD in 1994. The resulting Montana New Zealand Book Award is managed by Booksellers New Zealand and supported by the Book Publishers Association of New Zealand and the New Zealand Society of Authors.

Winners of the New Zealand Book Award for fiction were: MAURICE GEE, *A Glorious Morning Comrade* (1976) and O. E. Middleton, *Selected Stories* (1976); IAN WEDDE, *Dick Seddon's Great Dive* (1977); M. K. Joseph, *The Time of Achamoth* (1978); Maurice Gee, *Plumb* (1979); JANET FRAME, *Living in Maniototo* (1980); MAURICE SHADBOLT, *The Lovelock Version* (1981); Maurice Gee, *Meg* (1982); VINCENT O'SULLIVAN, *Dandy Edison for Lunch* (1982); Sue McCauley, *Other Halves* (1983); KERI HULME, *THE BONE PEOPLE* (1984); MARILYN DUCKWORTH, *Disorderly Conduct* (1985); C. K. STEAD, *All Visitors Ashore* (1985); Peter Hooper, *People of the Long Water* (1986); PATRICIA GRACE, *Potiki* (1987); FIONA KIDMAN, *The Book of Secrets*

(1988); Janet Frame, *The Carpathians* (1989); John Cranna, *Visitors* (1990); Maurice Gee, *The Burning Boy* (1991); Peter Wells, *Dangerous Desires* (1992); Fiona Farrell, *The Skinny Louie Book* (1993); DAMIEN WILKINS, *The Miserables* (1994); C. K. Stead, *The Singing Wakapapa* (1995).

Winners of the Montana New Zealand Book Award for fiction have been: Sheridan Keith, *Zoology* (1996); and ALAN DUFF, *What Becomes of the Broken Hearted?* (1997).

Newby, P(ercy) H(oward) 1918–97 English. Though well received by critics and fellow-novelists, his work never quite found the wider audience it deserves. Many of the 19 novels he published between 1945 and 1991 were shaped by his experience of Egypt, where he served in World War II and later worked as a university teacher. They include: *Picnic at Sakkara* (1955) and *A Guest at His Going* (1960), whose treatment of British colonialism and Egyptian nationalism earned comparison with E. M. FORSTER's *A PASSAGE TO INDIA*; *Something To Answer For* (1968), set in Port Said during the Suez crisis, which won the BOOKER PRIZE; and *Coming in with the Tide* (1991), HISTORICAL FICTION with a Welsh setting.

Newcomes, The: *Memoirs of a Most Respectable Family* A novel by WILLIAM MAKEPEACE THACKERAY, published in parts in 1853–5. The narrator is Arthur Pendennis, the hero of *PENDENNIS*, who appears again as the narrator of *THE ADVENTURES OF PHILIP*.

Colonel Thomas Newcome is a simple and honourable gentleman. His son Clive is in love with his cousin Ethel, daughter of the wealthy banker, Sir Brian Newcome. Their union is opposed by her relatives – notably her snobbish brother Barnes and her grandmother, the Countess of Kew – though she resists their pressure to marry her cousin, Lord Kew, or Lord Farintosh. Clive is manoeuvred into marrying Rosey, daughter of the scheming Mrs Mackenzie. When Colonel Newcome loses his fortune he is so bullied and reproached by Mrs Mackenzie that he takes refuge in the Greyfriars almshouse, where he dies. Clive's fortunes are restored by the discovery of a will, and his wife's death leaves him free to marry Ethel.

Newgate novel A school of crime fiction popular in the 1830s. It took real-life cases as the source for plots and, by way of citing a respectable precedent, pointed to the treatment of crime in HENRY FIELDING's *JONATHAN WILD* (1743), John Gay's *The Beggar's Opera* (1728) and Hogarth's engravings. Critics alleged that it sentimentalized or glamorized the criminal, making him the victim of social circumstances in EDWARD BULWER LYTTON's *Paul Clifford* (1830), a conscience-stricken philosopher in the same author's *EUGENE ARAM* (1832) and a romantic outlaw in WILLIAM HARRISON AINSWORTH's *Rookwood* (1834), about the highwayman Dick

Turpin, and *Jack Sheppard* (1839), about the 18th-century prison-breaker. Controversy grew more heated when Benjamin Courvoisier, the manservant executed for the murder of Lord William Russell in 1840, claimed to have been prompted to his crime by reading *Jack Sheppard*.

DICKENS'S *OLIVER TWIST* (1837–8) and THACKERAY'S early work *CATHERINE* (1839–40) were intended to counter the immoral tendencies of Newgate fiction, or at least to avoid the charges levelled at it, by offering a harshly realistic view of crime and a deliberately unglamorous view of criminals.

News from Nowhere: or, *An Epoch of Rest, being Some Chapters from a Utopian Romance* A prose work by the artisan, poet and socialist William Morris (1834–96), published in 1890. He dreams of waking amid a communist society in the early 21st century. The central chapters comprise a discussion with an aged historian, in which the course of history from the 19th century through violent socialist revolution and up to the Utopian present is described. The society envisaged is based on 'the religion of humanity', the sanctity of labour and its inseparability from art. In the concluding chapters Morris journeys up the Thames from London to Kelmscott for the hay-making season.

For Morris, see also *A DREAM OF JOHN BALL* and *THE WELL AT THE WORLD'S END*.

Ngcobo, Lauretta [née Gwina] 1931– South African. *Cross of Gold* (1981), written while she was in political exile, deals with the question whether – given the constraints of apartheid – a black South African could effect real choice. *And They Didn't Die* (1990) explores the life of a woman who rebels against the migrant system. Ngcobo has also edited an anthology of essays by black women in Britain, *Let It Be Told* (1987).

Ngugi wa Thiong'o [Ngugi, James] 1938– Kenyan. He has lived in exile since 1982. His novels, progressing from freshly written accounts of youthful idealism and disillusion to complex political analysis, include: *Weep Not, Child* (1964), *The River Between* (1965), *A GRAIN OF WHEAT* (1967), *Petals of Blood* (1977), *Devil on the Cross* (originally published in Gikuyu; 1982) and *Matigari* (originally published in Gikuyu; 1987). *Secret Lives* (1975) is a collection of short stories. His plays dramatize peasant, proletarian and national struggles. *Detained* (1981) describes his year-long detention after the banning of *Nhaahika Ndeenda* (with Ngugi wa Mirii, 1977; English version, *I Will Marry When I Want*, 1982). *Homecoming* (1972), *The Writer and Politics* (1981) and *Barrel of a Pen* (1983) are collections of essays.

nichol, b p 1944–88 Canadian. He first attracted attention with the 'concrete poetry' in *The Year of the Frog* (1967), *Ballads of the Restless Are* (1968) and *Dada Lama* (1968). He later used a wide variety of modes – publicly performed sound-poetry, free verse and STREAM OF CONSCIOUSNESS prose among them – to challenge commonly held assumptions about language and the creative process. His best-known work is *The Martyrology*, a continuing poem in several parts, of which the first two books appeared in 1972 and the last book, as *gIFTS*, in 1990. Other works include *Two Novels* (1969), *Still Water* (1970), *ABC: The Aleph Beth Book* (1971), *Love: A Book of Remembrances* (1974), *Craft Dinner* (1978), *Journal* (1978) and *extreme positions* (1981).

Nicholas Nickleby A novel by CHARLES DICKENS, published in monthly parts in 1838–9 and in volume form in 1839 as *The Life and Adventures of Nicholas Nickleby, Containing a Faithful Account of the Fortunes, Misfortunes, Uprisings, Downfallings, and the Complete Career of the Nickleby Family*. Loosely structured, with frequent excursions into sentiment and melodrama, it is nevertheless informed by the joyful energy that typifies his early work.

After the death of Nicholas Nickleby senior, his widow and children Nicholas and Kate turn for help to his brother Ralph, an unscrupulous financier. Kate is apprenticed to a dressmaker, Madame Mantalini, and Nicholas sent to teach at Dotheboys Hall in Yorkshire. He rebels against Wackford Squeers's ill-treatment of the pupils, particularly the half-witted orphan Smike. Nicholas and Smike run away, working where they can and travelling with Vincent Crummles's company of actors. Kate, meanwhile, is exposed to the unwelcome attentions of Ralph Nickleby's business associates, including Sir Mulberry Hawk. Alerted to her danger by Newman Noggs, Ralph's eccentric clerk, Nicholas returns to London with Smike, obtains a post in the business of the amiable Cheeryble brothers and thrashes Sir Mulberry. Squeers and Ralph Nickleby conspire to injure Nicholas through Smike, but their plan fails when Smike dies. Newman Noggs and the Cheerybles help defeat the villains completely and, with the revelation that Smike had been his own son, Ralph hangs himself.

Nigger of the 'Narcissus', The A novel by JOSEPH CONRAD, published in 1897. The preface is frequently cited as a manifesto of literary Impressionism and its chief aim: 'before all, to make you see'. Narrated by an anonymous seaman, the story reveals the tensions on board the *Narcissus* on its way from Bombay to London. Captain Alistoun and the veteran Singleton, primarily concerned with their duties, are increasingly at odds with the younger Donkin and the title character, Wait. During a storm which puts the safety of the entire ship at risk, five men chance their lives to save Wait from the cabin where he lies ill. In the end the captain calmly reasserts a seaman-like authority over Donkin, and Singleton's belief that Wait will die at the first sight of land comes true.

Nightmare Abbey A satirical novel by THOMAS LOVE PEACOCK, published in 1818. Its principal target is the contemporary literary intelligentsia, particularly the Romantic poets and critics, with their predilection for morbid subjects and unworldly philosophical systems.

Mr Glowry is the master of Nightmare Abbey on the edge of the Lincolnshire Fens, where he lives with his philosophical son Scythrop (Shelley) and a retinue of servants chosen for their depressing appearance or dismal names. He keeps open house for his fellow spirits and relatives. The most persistently mocked character is Mr Flosky (Coleridge), though Mr Cypress (Byron) is also derided for his misanthropy and Scythrop for his illuminist politics. Their modish melancholy contrasts with the enthusiasm of the scientist Mr Asterias, dedicated to capturing a mermaid, and of Mr Hilary, whose protests against the prevailing 'conspiracy against cheerfulness', and advocacy of nature, Mozart and the life-affirming wisdom of the ancient Greeks, appear to have the author on their side.

Nin, Anaïs 1903–77 American. She was born in Paris, to which she returned in 1923–39, becoming a friend of HENRY MILLER. The elegant sparsity of her *Diary* (1966–83), begun in 1931, and her volumes of erotica, *Delta of Venus: Erotica* (1977) and *Little Birds* (1979), are as much at odds with Miller's style as her fiction. Influenced by D. H. LAWRENCE (of whom she wrote a study in 1932) and psychoanalysis, this includes: *House of Incest* (Paris, 1936; USA, 1947); *The Winter of Artifice* (Paris, 1939; USA, 1942), a collection of three novelettes; *Under a Glass Bell* (1944), a volume of short stories; *Cities of Interior*, a five-part sequence (1946–58); and *Collages* (1964).

Nineteen Eighty-Four A novel by GEORGE ORWELL, first published in 1949. In 1984 Britain has become Airstrip One in the superstate Oceania, perpetually at odds with Eurasia and Eastasia. It is ruled by the Party under the aegis of the possibly non-existent Big Brother, whose agents constantly rewrite history and redesign the language to control people's thoughts absolutely. A minor Party operative, Winston Smith, commits thought-crimes by keeping a secret diary and loving Julia, but is seduced into self-betrayal by his superior, O'Brien. Interrogation ultimately breaks his spirit. This brilliant, bitter ROMAN À THÈSE provides a heavily ironic commentary on the state of the world in 1948. The development of world politics between then and 1984 did nothing to soothe the anxieties with which it plays.

1919 See *USA*.

Njau, Rebeka 1934– Kenyan. In addition to a play, *The Scar* (1965), she has published *Ripples in the Pool* (1975), a novel dealing with the conflict between traditional values and the quest for affluence and power in the post-independent state. *The Hypocrite* (1980) is a collection of stories.

Nkosi, Lewis 1936– South African. He worked on the staff of *Drum* magazine before leaving South Africa in 1961 for the USA, Britain and Zambia. *Mating Birds* (1986) is a novel about the interaction between sexual and racial politics in South Africa. His eloquent, often provocative essays about township life, the generation of 1950s writers in South Africa, apartheid, exile, and African literature were collected in *Home and Exile* (1964). A later collection, *Tasks and Masks* (1981), is concerned with contemporary African writing. He has also written *Rhythm of Violence* (1965), one of the first English-language plays by a black South African.

Noma Award A prize founded in 1980 by Schoichi Noma, former president of the Japanese publisher Kodansha Ltd, to encourage African writing. Open to works in any African language, indigenous or European, it has twice been won by fiction in English: CHENJERAI HOVE's *Bones* (1988) and CHARLES MUNGOSHI's *One Day, Long Ago* (1991), honoured in 1989 and 1992 respectively.

Norris, (Benjamin) Frank(lin) 1870–1902 American. Born in Chicago, he was partly brought up in San Francisco, where he later worked as a journalist. He also reported on the Boer War from South Africa and the Spanish-American War from Cuba. Early works such as his sea story, *Moran of the Lady Letty* (1898), first appeared in a San Francisco magazine, *The Wave*.

Norris is chiefly remembered for his contributions to NATURALISM in *McTeague* (1899) and his projected trilogy, *The Epic of the Wheat*, of which two volumes, THE OCTOPUS (1901) and THE PIT (1903), were completed before his early death from an appendix operation. The third part, *The Wolf*, which would have told of a wheat famine in Europe, was never written. Also published posthumously were *The Responsibilities of the Novelist* (1903), describing the type of naturalistic writing he had derived from Zola, and *Vandover and the Brute* (1914), a novel which he had started in 1895.

North and South A novel by ELIZABETH GASKELL, serialized in DICKENS's magazine *Household Words* in 1854–5 and published in volume form in 1855.

Margaret Hale leaves the south and goes with her father to the grim industrial city of Milton-Northern, where he teaches aspiring millowners. She takes the side of the workers and confronts the millowner John Thornton. He is strongly drawn to her despite the difference in their views, but she coldly rejects his proposal of marriage. Their relationship is further complicated by his mistaken jealousy. Eventually Thornton's business problems modify his attitude to the workers, and the pair come together.

An important CONDITION OF ENGLAND NOVEL

for its portrait of the contrast between the comfortable south and industrial north, the book also has in Margaret a tough, wilful and self-confidently proud heroine, reflecting the influence of CHARLOTTE BRONTË.

Northanger Abbey A novel by JANE AUSTEN, published posthumously in 1818, though it had been begun in 1798 and accepted by a publisher in 1803. Her shortest major work, it makes fun of the fashion for the GOTHIC NOVEL, particularly the work of ANN RADCLIFFE.

A guest of Mr and Mrs Allen at Bath, Catherine Morland meets the eccentric General Tilney, his son Henry and his daughter Eleanor. She is invited to their home, Northanger Abbey, where she imagines various gruesome secrets surrounding the General and his house. Henry proves that her suspicions are groundless but the General orders her out of the house. She returns home and is followed by Henry, who explains that the General had, mistakenly, come to believe her penniless. Restored to a sensible humour by the truth, the General finally consents to Henry's marriage to Catherine.

Norton, The Hon. Mrs Caroline (Elizabeth Sarah) 1808–77 English. The grand-daughter of the playwright Richard Brinsley Sheridan, she pursued a literary career with many volumes of poetry and three novels, including *Stuart of Dunleath* (1851), *Lost and Saved* (1863) and *Old Sir Douglas* (1867). Though successful, her writings brought her less fame than the public failure of her marriage to George Chapple Norton, who in 1836 brought an unsuccessful suit against Lord Melbourne for alienating her affections. Her marital wrongs prompted her to write *English Laws for Women* (1853) and other powerful pamphlets on women's rights. The object of much abuse and much admiration, she is said to have provided GEORGE MEREDITH wth the model for the heroine of *DIANA OF THE CROSSWAYS*.

Norton, Mary 1903–92 English. Her first novels for children, *The Magic Bedknob* (1943) and *Bonfires and Broomsticks* (1947), reissued together as *Bedknob and Broomstick* (1970), concern the adventures of three children and Miss Price, a village spinster who is also studying to be a witch. *The Borrowers* (1952) was the first in a series of five books about a family of tiny people who flee when they are discovered by the 'human beans' and embark on an epic journey across the countryside.

Nostromo: A Tale of the Seaboard A novel by JOSEPH CONRAD, published in 1904.

It is set in the coastal province of Sulaco, the wealthiest region of the South American republic of Costaguana. Along with the San Tomé silver mine, the Englishman Charles Gould has inherited the instability of a civil war between Ribiera's legal government and Montero's populist party. To save the silver from the rebels he entrusts it to the journalist Martin Decoud and the Italian Nostromo ('our man'), Capataz de Cargadores, a local hero, who smuggle it out into the gulf. When they are forced to run aground on nearby islands, the Isabels, they hide the silver and Nostromo returns to Sulaco. Left alone, Decoud drowns himself. Though Dr Monygham persuades him to summon loyal forces to save Sulaco, Nostromo has been shocked into awareness that he is exploited by his employers. He allows people to believe that the silver has been lost and makes secret visits to retrieve it from the Isabels, where the lighthouse keeper is now Giorgio Viola, the father of his betrothed, Linda. Nostromo finds himself in love with Linda's sister Giselle. When Giorgio mistakes him for an intruder and shoots him, the secret of the silver is lost forever.

novel of sensibility See SENTIMENTAL NOVEL.

Novels by Eminent Hands See PUNCH'S PRIZE NOVELISTS.

Noyes, Alfred 1880–1958 English. His poetry – which includes the epic in blank verse *Drake* (1906–8) and famous shorter poems like 'The Barrel Organ' ('Come down to Kew in lilac time') and 'The Highwayman' – was vigorously traditional. *The Torch-Bearers*, an ambitious trilogy about science and Christianity consisting of *The Watchers of the Sky* (1922), *The Book of Earth* (1925) and *The Last Voyage* (1930), reflected a growing preoccupation with religion. Notable among his novels are the ventures into fantasy in *Walking Shadows* (1918), *The Hidden Player* (1924) and *The Last Man* (1940). *Two Worlds for Memory* (1953) is autobiographical.

Nwapa, Flora (Nwanzuruahal) 1931–94 Nigerian. *Efuru* (1966) and *Idu* (1969) established her as Nigeria's first woman novelist. Both study the lives of women in rural society and give the particular flavour of Igbo culture. Nwapa moved closer to popular romance in later books such as *This is Lagos and Other Stories* (1971), *Wives at War and Other Stories* (1981), *One is Enough* (1981), *Never Again* (1984) and *Women are Different* (1986), often dealing with urban women who have rejected traditional mores. She also wrote children's literature.

Nye, Robert (Thomas) 1939– English. Chiefly known as a poet, he was also one of the first contemporary authors to explore the possibility of fictional 'memoirs' by famous figures from history, literature and legend. *Falstaff* (1976), a best-seller which won the HAWTHORNDEN PRIZE, has been followed by *Merlin* (1978), *Faust* (1980), *The Memoirs of Lord Byron* (1989), *The Life and Death of My Lord Gilles de Rais* (1990) and *Mrs Shakespeare* (1993).

O

O. Henry Awards See HENRY, O.

O Pioneers! A novel by WILLA CATHER, published in 1913. Alexandra Bergson, eldest daughter of Swedish immigrants living on the Nebraska Divide, makes a success of her portion of the family farm by her innovative techniques. She becomes rich enough to send her youngest brother Emil to college. On his return he has an affair with Alexandra's friend Marie Tovesky. Marie's husband shoots the lovers in a rage. Hearing of the tragedy, Alexandra's childhood sweetheart, Carl Linstrum, returns from California and marries her.

Oakley, Barry (Kingham) 1931– Australian. His many plays, often distinctly literary in their bias, range through vaudeville, buffoonery, naturalism, realism, dream and satire. Satire is also a recurrent mode in his stories, *Walking Through Tiger Land* (1977), while *pícaro* characters (see PICARESQUE) are often used to criticize contemporary society in his novels. They include *A Wild Ass of a Man* (1967), *A Salute to the Great McCarthy* (1969), *Let's Hear it for Prendergast* (1970) and *Craziplane* (1989). *Scribbling in the Dark* (1985) is a collection of essays.

Oates, Joyce Carol 1938– American. Her intense, often violent vision has led her to incorporate elements of romance, the GOTHIC NOVEL and DETECTIVE FICTION. It is perhaps most powerfully expressed in *Wonderland* (1971), based on LEWIS CARROLL'S *ALICE'S ADVENTURES IN WONDERLAND*, and in the loosely arranged trilogy, *A Garden of Earthly Delights* (1967), *Expensive People* (1968) and *Them* (1969). Other works, many focusing on the pathology of families and individuals, include *Childwold* (1976), *Bellefleur* (1980), *Angel of Light* (1981), *A Bloodsmoor Romance* (1982), *Mysteries of Winterhurn* (1984), *Solstice* (1985), *Marya: A Life* (1986), *You Must Remember This* (1987), *American Appetites* (1989), *Because It is Bitter, Because It is My Heart* (1990), *Black Water* (1992), based on Edward Kennedy's accident at Chappaquiddick, *Foxfire: Confessions of a Girl Gang* (1993), *What I Lived For* (1994), *We were the Mulvaneys* (1996) and *First Love: A Gothic Tale* (1996). Short-story collections include *By the North Gate* (1963), *The Wheel of Love* (1970), *The Goddess and Other Women* (1974), *Crossing the Border* (1976), *Last Days* (1984), *The Assignation* (1988), *Heat and Other Stories* (1991), *Haunted: Tales of the Grotesque* (1994), and *Will You Always Love Me? and Other Stories* (1996). She has also written mystery and horror novels under the pseudonym of Rosamond Smith, including *The Lives of Twins* (1987), *Soul-Mate* (1990), *Nemesis* (1990), *Snake Eyes* (1992), *You Can't Catch Me* (1995) and *Double Delight* (1997). Her poetry and non-fiction includes *Contraries: Essays* (1981), *On Boxing* (1987), and *(Woman) Writer: Occasions and Opportunities* (1988).

O'Brian, Patrick 1914– Anglo-Irish. He is best known for a meticulously researched sequence of historical novels following the fortunes of Captain John Aubrey and his ship's surgeon Stephen Maturin during the Napoleonic Wars. Begun in *Master and Commander* (1970), it includes *H.M.S. Surprise* (1973), *The Mauritius Command* (1977), *Desolation Island* (1978), *The Far Side of the World* (1984) and *The Yellow Admiral* (1997). O'Brian's short stories can be found in *The Last Pool* (1950), *The Walker* (1953), *Lying in the Sun* (1956), *The Chian Wine* (1974) and *Collected Short Stories* (1994). He has also published translations from the French and biographies of Picasso (1976) and the 19th-century naturalist Joseph Banks (1987).

O'Brien, Edna 1932– Irish. Much of her work is concerned with the position of women: their lack of fulfilment and the repressive nature of their upbringing. *The Country Girls* (1960), *The Lonely Girl* (1962) and *Girls in Their Married Bliss* (1963) follow the quest for 'life' of two Irish girls, 'Kate' Brady and 'Baba' Brennan. Other novels, often bleak but lightened by a lyrical quality associated with nostalgia for Ireland, include *August is a Wicked Month* (1965), *Casualties of Peace* (1966), *A Pagan Place* (1971), *Night* (1972), *Johnny I Hardly Knew You* (1977), *The High Road* (1988), *House of Splendid Isolation* (1994) and *Down by the River* (1996). Collections of stories include *The Love Object* (1968), *A Scandalous Woman and Other Stories* (1974), *Mrs Reinhardt and Other Stories* (1978; called *A Rose in the Heart* in the USA) and *Lantern Slides* (1990).

O'Brien, Fitz-James c. 1828–62 Born in Ireland, he emigrated to the USA and established a reputation for short stories in the fantastic vein. The most famous was 'The Diamond Lens' (1858). He also published a play, *A Gentleman from Ireland* (1858).

O'Brien, Flann [O'Nolan, Brian] 1911–66 Irish. As 'Myles na Gopaleen' he also contributed a column to *The Irish Times* from 1940, in which he constantly argued against the use of clichés about Ireland. A collection, *The Best of Myles*, appeared in 1968. His first and most important novel, *At Swim-Two-Birds* (1939), combines realism and fantasy in a manner which places it in a direct line of descent from JOYCE's *ULYSSES*. Other novels include *The Hard Life* (1961), *The Dalkey Archive* (1964), and *The Third Policeman* (1967). A novel in Gaelic, *An Béal Bocht* (1941), was translated by P. C. Power as *The Poor Mouth* (1973).

O'Brien, Tim (William Timothy) 1946– American. His experiences in the Vietnam War inform his fiction. It includes: *If I Die in a Combat Zone, Box Me Up and Ship Me Home* (1973), about a young draftee; *Northern Lights* (1975), about a veteran returning home; *Going After Cacciato* (1978), his best-known work, the dream journey of an infantryman; *The Nuclear Age* (1981), about an anti-war protester; and *In the Lake of the Woods* (1994). *The Things They Carried: A Work of Fiction* (1990) is a series of interconnected fictions narrated by a character named 'Tim O'Brien'.

O'Connor, Flannery 1925–64 American. Before her early death she made a strong impression on the literary scene with her portrayal of spiritual struggle in the rural South. Using grotesque humour and unnerving irony, her work exposes the religious poverty and crippled intellect of the modern world – a vision which reflects her own devout Catholicism. Her novels are *WISE BLOOD* (1952), about the lonely and self-tortured prophet of a 'church of Christ without Christ', and *The Violent Bear It Away* (1960). Equally influential are the stories collected in *A Good Man is Hard to Find* (1955; as *The Artificial Nigger and Other Stories* in Britain, 1959) and *Everything That Rises Must Converge* (1965).

O'Connor, Frank [O'Donovan, Michael Francis] 1903–66 Irish. Although he produced translations of Irish verse, plays for the Abbey Theatre (of which he was a director), novels and literary criticism, his reputation rests chiefly on the realistic short stories published in *Guests of the Nation* (1931), *The Saint and Mary Kate* (1932), *Bones of Contention* (1936), *Three Old Brothers* (1937), *The Big Fellow* (1937), *Crab Apple Jelly* (1944), *The Common Chord* (1947), *Traveller's Samples* (1950), *Domestic Relations* (1957) and *My Oedipus Complex* (1963). *An Only Child* (1961) and the unfinished *My Father's Son* (1968) are autobiographical.

***Octopus, The**: A Story of California* The first volume of FRANK NORRIS's unfinished trilogy *The Epic of the Wheat*, published in 1901. The second volume is *THE PIT* (1903); the third volume was never written. The octopus is the Pacific and Southwestern Railroad, which in the course of the story dispossesses the wheat farmers of California. The chief antagonists are Behrman, a railroad agent who is suffocated when he falls into the wheat he has plundered, and Magnus Derrick, a farmer eventually ruined when his son Lyman betrays him. Other characters include: Dyke, a railroad engineer who wants to be a farmer; Shelgrim, the railroad president; and the protesting poet, Presley.

***Odd Women, The** A novel by GEORGE GISSING, published in 1893. Dr Madden's death leaves his three daughters stranded with very little money and no training of any kind. Their loneliness and poverty in London lodgings and their desperate maintenance of middle-class respectability are conveyed with considerable pathos. In contrast to them is Rhoda Nunn, an active feminist who believes in preparing women for some fate other than marriage.

O'Dell, Scott 1903–89 American. His most famous work for children, *Island of the Blue Dolphin* (1960), tells how Karana, an Indian girl, survives for 18 years alone on a tiny island. *The King's Fifth* (1966), describes how foreign adventurers looted South America.

Odle, E. V. See SCIENCE FICTION.

O'Faolain, Sean 1900–91 Irish. *A Nest of Simple Folk* (1933), *Bird Alone* (1936) and *Come Back to Erin* (1940) are novels dealing with the tyranny and pathos of Irish life and politics, particularly the oppression of Irish Catholicism. *Midsummer Night Madness* (1932) is a book of short stories. He also wrote biographies of several leading Irish figures, literary criticism and an autobiography, *Vive-moi!* (1964).

Officers and Gentlemen See *SWORD OF HONOUR*.

O'Flaherty, Liam 1897–1984 Irish. He is best known for his unsentimental short stories, many of them about his native Aran Islands. Volumes include *Spring Sowing* (1926) and *The Fairy Goose* (1929), collected in *The Short Stories of Liam O'Flaherty* (1956). *The Informer* (1925; JAMES TAIT BLACK MEMORIAL PRIZE), generally considered his best novel, is about the last day of Gypo Nolan, a destitute Irish revolutionary who betrays a comrade. *The Martyr* (1927), *The Assassin* (1928), *The Puritan* (1931) and *Famine* (1937) are equally uncompromising and realistic accounts of the Irish condition. *Two Years* (1930), *I Went to Russia* (1931) and *Shame the Devil* (1934) are autobiographies which document O'Flaherty's wide travels.

Ogot, Grace 1930– Kenyan. Her stories have appeared in *Land without Thunder* (1968), *The Other Woman and Other Stories* (1976) and *The Island of Tears* (1980). *The Promised Land* (1970) and *The Graduate* (1980) are novels. Her writing reflects a wide-ranging experience of contemporary social, political and economic problems, together with an interest in the pre-colonial culture of her Luo ancestors.

O'Hara, John 1905–70 American. His novels include: *Appointment in Samarra* (1934), about the suicide of Julian English in the stratified society of 'Gibbsville', based on the author's hometown of Pottsville, Pennsylvania; *Butterfield 8* (1935), about the experiences of a Manhattan newspaperman; and *Pal Joey* (1940), which he adapted as a musical in the same year, a comic series of letters from a nightclub entertainer. Like O'Hara's novels, the short stories collected in volumes stretching from *The Doctor's Son* (1935) to *Waiting for Winter* (1967) often focus on questions of class and social privilege. O'Hara also worked as a screenwriter in Hollywood and published *Five Plays* (1961).

Okara, Gabriel (Imomotimi Gbaingbain) 1921–

Nigerian. His short political allegory, *The Voice* (1964), has been widely noticed for its attempt at a form of English which incorporates the structural principles of the Ijaw language. Though he has published little and did not issue his first collection of poetry, *The Fisherman's Invocation*, until 1978, he enjoys a high reputation for lyrics rooted in the oral tradition.

Okpewho, Isadore 1941– Nigerian. In addition to a critical study, *The Epic in Africa* (1979), he has published: *The Victims* (1970), about a family consumed by guilt, hatred and poverty; *The Last Duty* (1976), about the effects of the Nigerian Civil War on six characters who interpret their duty differently; and *Tides* (1993), an EPISTOLARY NOVEL confronting the issue of environmental pollution.

Okri, Ben 1959– Nigerian. He belongs to a small group of younger writers who have largely abandoned the concerns of CHINUA ACHEBE's generation for a more personal, introspective mode. His prodigious if slightly unwieldy talent was announced in two apparently autobiographical novels, *Flowers and Shadows* (1980) and *The Landscapes Within* (1981), and two collections of stories, *Incidents at the Shrine* (1986) and *Stars of the New Curfew* (1988). THE FAMISHED ROAD (1991), which won the BOOKER PRIZE, was followed by a quasi-sequel, *Songs of Enchantment* (1993), and *Astonishing the Gods* (1995).

Old Creole Days A collection of seven stories by GEORGE WASHINGTON CABLE, published in 1879. The chief setting is the old French quarter of New Orleans, populated by Creoles, Cubans, Spaniards and Santo Domingan refugees as well as Germans, Irish and Sicilians. Cable is fluent in the various dialects, though his plots often take a sentimental or melodramatic turn. The stories are 'Café des Exiles', 'Belle Demoiselle Plantation', 'Posson Jone', 'Tite Poulette', 'Sieur George', 'Jean-ah Poquelin' and 'Madame Délicieuse'. The last concerns a quarrel between Madame Délicieuse's forward-looking fiancé, Dr Mossy, and his father, General Villivicencio, who is waging a campaign for public office to purge New Orleans of Yankee ideals. Madame Délicieuse, a Creole beauty, engineers a reconciliation. *MADAME DELPHINE* was added to later editions of the volume.

Old Curiosity Shop, The A novel by CHARLES DICKENS, serialized in *MASTER HUMPHREY'S CLOCK* in 1840–1 and published in volume form in 1841. The prolonged deathbed sufferings of Little Nell made it immensely popular with contemporaries, though today it is among the least regarded of Dickens's works.

Little Nell (Nell Trent) lives in the shop of the title with her grandfather. When he falls into the clutches of the moneylender Daniel Quilp, an evil dwarf, they quit the shop and roam the countryside together, reduced to beggary. Quilp sets out in pursuit, while Kit Nubbles, the errand boy at the shop, does his best to find and help them. Nell's great-uncle, returned from abroad, succeeds in tracing them only when it is too late. Exhausted by her troubles, Nell dies a lingering death, followed soon afterwards by her grandfather. Trying to evade arrest, Quilp drowns in the Thames.

Old Mortality A novel by SIR WALTER SCOTT, the second in the first series of his *Tales of My Landlord*, published in 1816 and for many years one of his most admired works. The title is the nickname of Robert Paterson who, at the end of the 18th century, wandered round Scotland caring for the graves of the Cameronians, or strict Covenanters. His stories of the 17th-century Covenanters persecuted by John Graham of Claverhouse form the basis of the novel.

The hero is Henry Morton, driven to join the Covenanters by unjust treatment after he shelters John Balfour without knowing him to be involved in murdering the Archbishop of St Andrews. Against this background are set the vicissitudes of Morton's love for Edith Bellenden, who belongs to a royalist family, and his relations with his rival, Lord Evandale.

Old Wives' Tale, The A novel by ARNOLD BENNETT, published in 1908. It follows the lives of two sisters, Constance and Sophia Baines, from 1860 to their deaths in about 1906. Constance remains in Bursley, marries the family apprentice, Samuel Povey, and is left in lonely widowhood when her son Cyril goes to London. Sophia has a more adventurous but equally frustrated life. She elopes with Gerald Scales, a glamorous commercial traveller, but he deserts her in Paris, where she achieves independence as proprietor of the Pension Frensham. In old age she returns to Bursley to live with her sister. Sophia's journey to Manchester, where she is too late to speak to the dying Scales, strikes a grim keynote to the concluding section, 'What Life Is'.

Oldtown Folks A novel by HARRIET BEECHER STOWE, published in 1869, and set in the fictional Oldtown, Massachusetts, during the post-Revolutionary period. Horace Holyoke tells the story of two runaway children who find happiness in spite of their oppressive upbringing in a leading Oldtown family. Henry becomes an Anglican minister. Tina marries first the dashing Davenport and then, after he dies in a duel, Holyoke himself. Other memorable citizens are Parson and 'Lady' Lothrop, and Sam Lawson, whose commentary provides a comic perspective.

Oliphant, Laurence 1829–88 English. Born in Cape Town, he qualified as a barrister in Ceylon (Sri Lanka) and became one of the most remarkable travellers of his age, publishing *Journey to Khatmandu* (1852), *The Russian Shores of the Black Sea* (1853), *Minnesota and the Far West* (1855) and a *Narrative of the Earl of Elgin's Mission to China and*

Japan in the Years 1857, 58, 59 (1859). As a correspondent for *The Times* he covered aspects of the Crimean War, the Indian Mutiny, the Risorgimento and the Franco-Prussian War. *Piccadilly* (1866) is an amiably satirical novel about London life. In 1867 Oliphant became a disciple of the American 'prophet' Thomas Lake Harris. After this disillusioning experience he founded a community of Jewish immigrants at Haifa, where he wrote a second novel, *Altiora Peto* (1883), and, with his wife, the curious *Sympneumata* (1885), which they believed to have been dictated by a spirit. The autobiographical *Episodes of a Life of Adventure* appeared in 1887, and his cousin MARGARET OLIPHANT wrote his biography.

Oliphant, Margaret 1828–97 English. One of the most popular authors of her day, she wrote more than 100 books and some 200 contributions to *Blackwood's Edinburgh Magazine*. Of the *Chronicles of Carlingford*, a series of novels about Scottish life, *Salem Chapel* (1863) and *Miss Marjoribanks* (1866) received particular praise. Other Scottish novels included *The Minister's Wife* (1869), *Effie Ogilvie* (1886) and *Kirsteen* (1890). She also wrote histories, biographies (notably a life of her cousin LAURENCE OLIPHANT, 1892) and an *Autobiography* (1899).

Olive Schreiner Prize A South African literary award established in 1961 by Die Suid-Afrikaanse Akademie vir Wetenskap en Kuns (The South African Academy of Science and the Arts) and named in honour of OLIVE SCHREINER. Its administration was taken over in 1971 by the English Academy of Southern Africa. The prize is awarded annually, rotating between poetry, drama and prose. Writers in English from South Africa and neighbouring countries are eligible providing they are not yet established. Novels which have won the prize include Anna M. Louw's *20 Days That Autumn: 21st March – 9th April 1960* in 1964, M. F. Roebuck's *Nyitso: A Novel of West Africa* in 1967, Sheila Fugard's *The Castaways* in 1973, Rose Zwi's *Another Year in Africa* in 1982, MÉNAN DU PLESSIS' *A State of Fear* in 1985 and John Conyngham's *The Arrowing of the Cane* in 1988. Collections of short stories include Sherila Roberts; *Outside Life's Feast* in 1976, AHMED ESSOP's *The Hajji and Other Stories* in 1979 and Ivan Vladislavic's *Missing Persons* in 1991.

Oliver Twist: *or, The Parish Boy's Progress* A novel by CHARLES DICKENS, serialized in 1837–9 and published in book form in 1838. One of its aims was to correct the glamorous portrayal of criminals in the NEWGATE NOVEL of the day; another was to attack the inhumane New Poor Law of 1834.

Oliver's mother dies soon after giving birth to him in the workhouse. He outrages Mr Bumble, the parish beadle, by daring to 'ask for more' and is apprenticed to an undertaker, where he is no better used. He runs away to London and meets the Artful Dodger (Jack Dawkins), who takes him to the den where Fagin has a stable of boys trained as thieves. Fagin's associates are the burglar Bill Sikes and Nancy, a prostitute. Oliver is rescued by the benevolent Mr Brownlow but, prompted by the villainous Monks, the thieves kidnap him. When they send him out on a burglary with Bill Sikes, he is wounded and cared for by the inhabitants of the house, Mrs Maylie and her adopted daughter Rose. Nancy visits Rose to warn her that Monks is bribing Fagin to corrupt Oliver. With Mr Brownlow's help enquiries are begun. Nancy's betrayal is discovered and Bill Sikes murders her. In the hue and cry he accidentally hangs himself, and Fagin and the rest are taken. Monks is revealed to be Oliver's half-brother, seeking an inheritance of which Oliver was ignorant for himself, while Rose Maylie is Oliver's aunt. Fagin is hanged and Oliver is adopted by Mr Brownlow.

Olsen, Tillie 1913– American. *Tell Me a Riddle* (1962) draws on her experience as a working-class wife, mother, wage-earner and labour activist in San Francisco. *Yonnondio: From the Thirties* (1974) tells the story of a poor family's journey to the slums of an industrial city in an unsuccessful search for a way out of poverty and despair. *Silences* (1978), a collection of essays, explains how social and economic pressures prevent members of oppressed groups from becoming writers. Other non-fiction includes *Mother to Daughter, Daughter to Mother, Mothers on Mothering: A Reader* (1984) and *Mothers and Daughters: That Special Quality* (1987), essays with Julie Olsen Edwards and Estelle Jussim.

Omoo: *A Narrative of Adventures in the South Seas* A novel by HERMAN MELVILLE, published in 1847. A sequel to *TYPEE*, it proved equally controversial in its depiction of the failure of missionary work in Tahiti. After his flight from the Marquesas the narrator signs on with the crew of the *Julia*, an unseaworthy ship with a sick and unstable captain. The crew mutinies in Tahiti, and the narrator and the doctor, Long Ghost, find work on a plantation in Imeeo and then become beachcombers. The narrator finally ships out on the whaler *Leviathan*.

Omotoso, Kole 1943– Nigerian. He moved from realism in *The Edifice* (1971) to allegory in *The Combat* (1972) and *Sacrifice* (1974), besides using the conventions of DETECTIVE FICTION in *Fella's Choice* (1974) and *The Scales* (1976). *To Borrow a Wandering Leaf* (1978) and *Memories of Our Recent Boom* (1982) expose corruption and abuse of power in modern Nigeria while his most ambitious novel, *Just Before Dawn* (1988), combines fact and fiction in a panorama of Nigerian life since the 1880s.

On the Road A semi-autobiographical novel by

JACK KEROUAC, published in 1957. One of the most popular statements by the BEATS, it tells of a group of friends travelling around America in search of new and intense experiences. The headlong style of Sal Paradise's narrative captures the chaos, exhilaration and despair of their quest. Several characters are modelled on Kerouac's friends: Dean Moriarty is Neal Cassady and Carlo Marx is Allen Ginsberg.

Ondaatje, Michael 1943– Canadian, born in Sri Lanka. He first received critical acclaim for *The Dainty Monsters* (1967), *The Man with Seven Toes* (1969) and *Rat Jelly* (1973), poetry characterized by a surreal vision in which macabre imagery and unexpected conjunctions force readers to reassess their habitual ways of viewing the world. Later volumes are *There's a Trick with a Knife I'm Learning to Do* (1979) and *The Cinnamon Peeler* (1990), a collection which brings together much of the best of his earlier poetry. *The Collected Works of Billy the Kid* (1970), *Coming through Slaughter* (1979) and *Running in the Family* (1982) experiment with a form combining prose, poetry and visual representation in discontinuous narratives. Two novels, *In the Skin of a Lion* (1987), set in Toronto during the 1920s and 1930s, and *THE ENGLISH PATIENT* (1992), co-winner of the BOOKER PRIZE, are considered his finest works to date.

One Flew over the Cuckoo's Nest A novel by KEN KESEY, published in 1962. The story is told from the viewpoint of a Native American, Bromden, who pretends to be deaf and dumb. He is an inmate in a psychiatric ward ruled by Big Nurse. A new arrival, the defiant McMurphy, encourages them to rebel but is lobotomized by the doctors. Bromden smothers him out of rage and pity and escapes.

One of Our Conquerors A novel by GEORGE MEREDITH, published in 1891. Nesta Victoria is the illegitimate daughter of Victor Radnor and Natalia Dreighton. Her suitor, the Hon. Dudley Sowerby, is unenthusiastic when he learns the story of her birth and of her determination to continue her friendship with the hapless Mrs Marsett, mistress of an army officer. Natalia falls ill during the crisis and dies only a few hours before Victor receives news of the death of his wife (whose existence he has kept a secret); the irony unhinges his mind. Nesta eventually marries a more worthy suitor, Dartrey Fenellan.

Opie, Amelia [née Alderson] 1769–1853 English. The wife of the painter John Opie, and a friend of WILLIAM GODWIN and MARY WOLLSTONECRAFT, she produced much popular fiction and poetry. Her novels included *Father and Daughter* (1801), *Adeline Mowbray* (suggested by Wollstonecraft's life; 1802), *Simple Tales* (1806), *Valentine's Eve* (1816) and *Madeline* (1822). She abandoned fiction after becoming a Quaker in 1825, devoting much of her energy to the Bible Society and the Anti-Slavery Society. Her last book, a volume of poetry, was *Lays for the Dead* (1833).

Oppenheim, E. Phillips See GENRE FICTION and SPY FICTION.

Orange Prize A recently established annual prize for the best novel written in English by a woman of any nationality. The exclusion of male writers, and the fact that the award is (at £30,000) the most valuable annual literary prize awarded in Britain, have generated both controversy and publicity. It owes its name to its sponsor, the telecommunications company. The first award was to HELEN DUNMORE for *A Spell in Winter* (1995), from Britain; the second was to Anne Michaels for *Fugitive Pieces* (1996), from Canada.

Oranges Are Not the Only Fruit A novel by JEANETTE WINTERSON, published in 1985. It won a WHITBREAD AWARD for First Novel. Jeanette, the narrator, describes a Lancashire childhood dominated by her adoptive mother, a Christian fundamentalist who is portrayed as one of modern fiction's great maternal monsters. The book moves constantly between farce and terror, as the adolescent Jeanette's emerging lesbianism brings her into conflict with her mother's co-religionists. Reading books, including the Bible, takes Jeanette into wide and more generous worlds; studying them eventually takes her to Oxford.

Orczy, Baroness (Emma Magdalena Rosalia Marie Josefa Barbara) 1865–1947 Born in Hungary, she arrived in London at the age of 15. *The Scarlet Pimpernel* (1905), which she and her husband successfully dramatized, introduced Sir Percy Blakeney and his exploits rescuing victims of the French Revolution. Its many popular sequels included *I Will Repay* (1906) and *The Elusive Pimpernel* (1908). Baroness Orczy also wrote DETECTIVE FICTION, notably stories about 'The Old Man in the Corner' in *The Case of Miss Elliott* (1905), *The Old Man in the Corner* (1909) and *Unravelled Knots* (1925).

Ordeal of Richard Feverel, The A novel by GEORGE MEREDITH, published in 1859.

Deserted by his wife, Sir Austin Feverel brings up his son Richard according to his own system. Richard falls in love with Lucy Desborough, a farmer's niece whom Sir Austin thinks too humble. The couple marry in secret. Sir Austin ruthlessly manipulates Richard's feelings to separate him from Lucy, sending him to London where Lord Mountfalcon, who has designs on Lucy, puts him in the path of a 'fallen' woman. Richard is easily seduced and goes abroad in shame. He hurries home on learning that he is a father and that Sir Austin is at last reconciled to Lucy. Just when happiness seems within his grasp, he discovers Lord Mountfalcon's villainy, challenges him to a duel and is seriously wounded. Lucy loses her reason and dies.

Orlando*: *A Biography A novel by VIRGINIA

WOOLF, published in 1928. Dedicated to VITA SACKVILLE-WEST, it used her ancestral home at Knole in Kent as its setting. The deliberately fanciful story traces the career of the androgynous Orlando from the late 16th century to the present day. He begins as an Elizabethan poet and playwright, and becomes Ambassador Extraordinary to Constantinople under Charles II, an 18th-century lady of high society, a mother, and, in the present day, a woman poet.

Orley Farm A novel by ANTHONY TROLLOPE, issued in monthly parts in 1861–2. Sir Joseph Mason's will leaves his estate to Joseph, his son by his first wife, and in a codicil reserves Orley Farm for Lucius, his son by his second wife. Though Joseph originally contests the codicil, the widowed Lady Mason and Lucius live comfortably at the Farm for 20 years until Dockwrath, a discontented attorney, persuades Joseph to revive his challenge. Mr Chaffanbrass appears successfully for Lady Mason in the suit, but afterwards she confesses her forgery to her elderly lover, Sir Peregrine Orme. Orley Farm reverts to Joseph Mason.

Oroonoko: or, The Royal Slave A novel by APHRA BEHN, published c. 1678 and included in *Three Histories* (1688). It was the first expression in English literature of sympathy for the plight of slaves. Thomas Southerne adapted it for the stage in 1695.

Oroonoko, grandson and heir of an African king, loves the beautiful Imoinda, daughter of the king's general. The old king himself falls in love with Imoinda and commands that she be taken to his harem, then sells her as a slave. Captured and sold by an English slaver, the grieving Oroonoko finds Imoinda in Surinam, where he rouses the other slaves to escape. They are eventually induced to surrender to Byam, the deputy governor, who has Oroonoko flogged. Determined to exact retribution but knowing he cannot escape its consequences, Oroonoko kills Imoinda, is discovered near her body and is cruelly executed.

Ortiz, Simon 1941– Native American. His work reflects a strong concern for Native American civil rights and the preservation of Native American culture. His stories include *Fightin': New and Collected Stories* (1983). His volumes of poetry include *Naked in the Wind* (1970), *Going for the Rain* (1976), *Fight Back: For the Sake of the People, For the Sake of the Land* (1980), *From Sand Creek* (1981) and *Woven Stone* (1992).

Orwell, George [Blair, Eric Arthur] 1903–50 English. He went from Eton into the Burmese Imperial Police and then to a deliberately chosen state of 'fairly severe poverty' described in *Down and Out in Paris and London* (1933). *Burmese Days* (1934), a novel, expressed his dislike of imperialism. A second novel, *A Clergyman's Daughter* (1935), is about a middle-class woman's brief period of freedom among tramps and hop-pickers. The aspirations and humiliations of Gordon Comstock, the hero of *Keep the Aspidistra Flying* (1936), closely paralleled Orwell's own. *Coming Up for Air* (1939) was written in the shadow of World War II.

The Road to Wigan Pier (1937), a documentary account of unemployment in the north of England commissioned for the Left Book Club, was a milestone in literary journalism. It established Orwell's political outlook as an unaligned democratic socialist, a position emphasized by *Homage to Catalonia* (1938), about his experiences in the Spanish Civil War, and the stream of lucid and colloquial journalistic essays he produced throughout the 1930s and 1940s. Originally reprinted in such volumes as *Inside the Whale* (1940), *Critical Essays* (1946) and *Shooting an Elephant* (1950), they were gathered in the four volumes of *Collected Essays, Journalism and Letters* edited by his second wife, Sonia Orwell, and Ian Angus (1968). ANIMAL FARM (1945) and NINETEEN EIGHTY-FOUR (1949), his pessimistic satires about the threat of political tyranny, have remained his most popular works.

Oscar and Lucinda A novel by PETER CAREY, published in 1988 and awarded both the BOOKER PRIZE and the MILES FRANKLIN AWARD. Ostensibly a pastiche of Victoriana (DICKENS, GEORGE ELIOT and Edmund Gosse among others), it appeared in Australia's bicentennial year and satirizes many of the myths of 'nation-building'. Oscar Hopkins, son of a Nonconformist preacher, runs away from home and becomes an Anglican priest and a compulsive gambler, before he arrives in Sydney. Lucinda Lepiastrier grows up in the colony, inherits a fortune and, a gambler herself, invests in a glassworks. To win Oscar's hand, she wagers all on his overland expedition to transport a prefabricated glass church to a remote settlement. Oscar perishes at the end of the journey, but not before he impregnates a governess, enabling the story of the unrequited lovers to be told by a descendant.

Osofisan, Femi (Babafemi Adeyemi) 1946– Nigerian. He is chiefly known as the most talented and productive figure in the Nigerian theatre after WOLE SOYINKA, treating social and political issues both seriously and satirically in *A Restless Run of Locusts* (1975), *The Chattering and the Song* (1977), and *Who's Afraid of Solarin?* (1978). His single novel, *Kolera Kolej* (1975), is a satire of political machinations in a post-independent African country.

O'Sullivan, Vincent 1937– New Zealand. His early poetry, in *Our Burning Time* (1965), *Revenants* (1969) and *Bearings* (1973), repeatedly turns to myth. *Butcher and Co.* (1977) and *The Butcher Papers* (1982) show his flair for drama and satire, as well as his mastery of vernacular, qualities also apparent in his short stories, *The Boy, the*

Bridge, the River (1978), *Dandy Edison for Lunch* (1981), *Survivals* (1985) and *The Snow in Spain* (1990). His novels include the satirical *Miracle* (1976) and *Let the River Stand* (1993), set in rural New Zealand from the 1920s to the 1950s. *Dandy Edison for Lunch* won the NEW ZEALAND BOOK AWARD, *The Boy, the Bridge, the River* won the GOODMAN FIELDER WATTIE BOOK AWARD, and *Let the River Stand* won the Goodman Fielder Wattie Book Award after it became the Montana Book Award. Later poetry includes *The Pilate Tapes* (1986). He has also written plays, including *Shuriken* (1985) and *Billy* (1990), published a study of the New Zealand poet James K. Baxter (1976) and co-edited the letters of KATHERINE MANSFIELD (1985–93).

Ouida [de la Ramée, Marie Louise] 1839–1908 She was born in Britain, of a French father and English mother, she took her pen-name from a childhood mispronunciation of her given name Louise. *Under Two Flags* (1867), her most famous work, is a story of the Foreign Legion. Among the rest of her 45 novels were *Tricotin* (1869), *Puck* (1870), *Two Little Wooden Shoes* (1874), *Moths* (1880) and *In Maremma* (1882). Her vivid brand of hot-house romanticism kept her novels popular until the 1890s.

Our Mutual Friend CHARLES DICKENS's last complete novel, published in monthly parts in 1864–5 and in volume form in 1865.

The chief of its several plots centres on John Harmon, thought drowned but in fact secretly evaluating Bella Wilfer, the girl he must marry if he is to receive his inheritance. As John Rokesmith, he becomes secretary to Mr Boffin (known as Noddy and the Golden Dustman), heir to the property if John does not marry Bella. When Harmon falls in love with Bella but is scornfully rejected, the worthy Boffin affects a miserly unpleasantness which eventually succeeds in reconciling her with Harmon. A second plot concerns Lizzie Hexam, daughter of the dishonest waterman Gaffer Hexam, who is accused of murdering Harmon. She is passionately loved by Bradley Headstone, schoolmaster of her brother Charley, but loves the indolent barrister Eugene Wrayburn, a friend of Mortimer Lightwood. The jealous Headstone tries to kill his rival but Lizzie saves him. Rogue Riderhood blackmails Headstone and they kill each other in a fight. Other characters enforcing a bleak and comprehensive vision of contemporary society include the faded aristocrats and parvenus gathered at the Veneerings' dinner table, the pauperized Betty Higden and the greedy Silas Wegg.

Ozick, Cynthia 1928– American. Her short stories include *The Pagan Rabbi and Other Stories* (1971), *Bloodshed and Three Novellas* (1976) and, reflecting her interest in mysticism and the supernatural, *Levitation: Five Fictions*. Novels include *Trust* (1981), *The Cannibal Galaxy* (1983) and *The Messiah of Stockholm* (1987). *The Shawl* (1991) brings together a novella and a short story about the ordeal of a Holocaust survivor in later life. *Art and Ardor* (1983), *Metaphor and Memory* (1989), *What Henry James Knew and Other Essays on Writers* (1993) and *Fame and Folly* (1996) are collections of essays.

P

Page, Thomas Nelson 1853–1922 American. Much of his writing – which extended to essays and biographies as well as fiction – sentimentalized the aristocratic Old South. His fiction includes *In Ole Virginia: or, Marse Chan and Other Stories* (1887), *On Newfound River* (1891) and *Red Rock: A Chronicle of Reconstruction* (1898); the last, about the hardships suffered by southerners during Reconstruction, became a best-seller. Page was appointed US ambassador to Italy in 1913.

Pair of Blue Eyes, A A novel by THOMAS HARDY, published in 1872. The setting, as well as the characters of Stephen Smith and Elfride Swancourt, echoes the circumstances of Hardy's courtship of Emma Gifford, who became his first wife.

Elfride, the daughter of the vicar of Endelstow on the north Cornish coast, falls in love with Stephen, a young architect who comes to restore the church. Her father opposes the marriage because of Stephen's humble origins. Elfride at first agrees to run away, then vacillates and in Stephen's absence becomes engaged to his friend and patron, the idealistic Henry Knight. When he learns of her previous engagement Knight leaves her heartbroken. When Stephen and Knight meet, they resolve their differences and hurry down to Cornwall, but their train also carries the corpse of Elfride, being transported home for burial after her marriage to a man she did not love.

Hardy apparently modelled the character of Knight on Sir Leslie Stephen (for whom, see VIRGINIA WOOLF), who also served as the original for Vernon Whitford in GEORGE MEREDITH'S *THE EGOIST*.

Palace of the Peacock A novel by WILSON HARRIS, published in 1960. Like JOSEPH CONRAD'S *HEART OF DARKNESS* and PATRICK WHITE'S *VOSS*, it uses a journey into a physical interior as a metaphor for a voyage of psychic discovery. A multi-racial crew travels upriver into the heartland of Guyana (then British Guiana), led by the imperialist Donne, who is seeking Amerindian labour for his plantation. Their journey retraces that of an earlier crew, all of whom died, and more generally the conquest of the country by colonizers.

Paley, Grace 1922– American. Her stories deal with the frustrations, failures, and limitations of working-class lives. *The Little Disturbances of Man* (1959) presents carefully crafted stories rooted in character, but *Enormous Changes at the Last Minute* (1974) offers open-ended, seemingly plotless structures. Subsequent volumes are *Later the Same Day* (1985), *Long Walks and Intimate Talks* (1991) and *The Collected Stories* (1994).

Palliser, Charles 1947– American, resident in Britain. *The Quincunx: The Inheritance of John Huffam* (1989) recreates the Victorian novel on a scale comparable to WILKIE COLLINS for its plot and DICKENS for its moral ambition. By contrast *The Sensationist* (1991), about an alienated foreigner in Glasgow, rejoices in condensation. Technical virtuosity is given full play in *Betrayals* (1994), with ten chapters which tell the same story in ten different ways.

Palliser Novels, The A sequence of novels by ANTHONY TROLLOPE, about political and Parliamentary life. Plantagenet Palliser – the Liberal politician who first appeared in one of the BARSETSHIRE NOVELS, *THE SMALL HOUSE AT ALLINGTON* – and his wife Glencora are central presences. The sequence consists of *CAN YOU FORGIVE HER?* (1864–5), *PHINEAS FINN* (1867–9), *THE EUSTACE DIAMONDS* (1871–3), *PHINEAS REDUX* (1873–4), *THE PRIME MINISTER* (1875–6) and *THE DUKE'S CHILDREN* (1879–80).

Palmer, Vance (Edward Vivian) 1885–1959 Australian. Eager to promote and contribute to a national literature, he first attempted to establish himself as a popular writer with plays and fiction. *The Man Hamilton* (1928) began his career as a serious novelist, continued by *Men are Human* (1930), *The Passage* (1930), *Daybreak* (1932) and *The Swayne Family* (1934). Later work included a trilogy about the mining community of Mount Isa, *Golconda* (1948), *Seedtime* (1957) and *The Big Fellow* (1959), the last of which won the MILES FRANKLIN AWARD. Palmer also published poetry, essays, criticism and collections of short stories, among them *Let the Birds Fly* (1955) and *The Rainbow-Bird* (1957).

Paltock, Robert 1697–1767 English. He is remembered for a fantasy, *The Life and Adventures of Peter Wilkins* (1751). The hero is shipwrecked in the far south and reaches a country inhabited by people who can fly. He falls in love with one of them, Youwarkee, marries her and rises to importance in the kingdom.

Pamela*: or *Virtue Rewarded An EPISTOLARY NOVEL by SAMUEL RICHARDSON, its first part published in 1740 and its second part in 1741.

Pamela Andrews is a teenage maidservant in a household where her mistress has just died. The lady's son, Mr B., conceives a passion for her and, helped by his servants Mrs Jewkes and Monsieur Calbrand, tries to take advantage of her position. Pamela is partly revolted and partly attracted by Mr B., but at length his persistence makes her leave the house. Part of Pamela's journal which has been stolen by Mrs Jewkes enables Mr B. better to understand her character. He writes asking her to return and at length proposes marriage. The second, less inspiring part of the book depicts Pamela's acclimatization to her new position, the changing attitudes of Mr B.'s family, her husband's wayward behaviour and the dignified way she handles married life.

Pamela was the 18th-century equivalent of a runaway best-seller. An early example of the unified novel of character, it owed its success largely to the plight of the heroine and the strongly evocative atmosphere of domestic tension which Richardson creates. HENRY FIELDING was the most memorable of the contemporary parodists of Richardson, both in *An Apology for the Life of Mrs Shamela Andrews* (1741), a skilful burlesque on the values and mannerisms of the first part of *Pamela*, and in his use of Pamela's brother Joseph as the central character in *JOSEPH ANDREWS*.

Panter-Downes, Mollie (Patricia) 1906– English. She is probably best known for non-fiction such as *Ooty Preserved* (1967), about an Indian hill-station beloved by the British Raj, and *At the Pines* (1971), about the old age of the poet Swinburne in Putney with THEODORE WATTS-DUNTON. Although she has written five novels, beginning with *The Shoreless Sea* (1923), and many uncollected short stories, she herself holds her fiction in small regard. Her reputation as a novelist rests on a single, flawless work, *One Fine Day* (1947), following the daily routine of an 'ordinary' middle-class housewife in post-war England.

Parade's End A tetralogy of novels by FORD MADOX FORD, consisting of *Some Do Not . . .* (1924), *No More Parades* (1925), *A Man Could Stand Up* (1926) and *Last Post* (1928). It describes the struggle for survival by Christopher Tietjens in pre-war London and in action during World War I. Events enter into Christopher's consciousness impressionistically, and the impersonal narrator, using many time-shifts, is faithful to the characters' inner constructions of reality.

Paretsky, Sara 1947– American. V. I. Warshawski, a Chicago private eye, is the heroine of highly praised DETECTIVE FICTION which shows Paretsky fluent in the hard-boiled conventions established by DASHIELL HAMMETT and RAYMOND CHANDLER but also determined to rework them from a feminist perspective. The series includes *Indemnity Only* (1982), *Deadlock* (1984), *Killing Orders* (1986), *Bitter Medicine* (1987), *Blood Shot* (1988, called *Toxic Shock* in UK), *Burn Marks* (1990), *Guardian Angel* (1992) and *Tunnel Vision* (1994).

Park, Ruth 1922– Australian. Her adult fiction includes: the trilogy formed by *The Harp in the South* (1948) and *Poor Man's Orange* (1949), set in a working-class inner suburb of Sydney, and their prequel *Missus* (1985); *The Witch's Thorn* (1951); *A Power of Roses* (1953); *Pink Flannel* (1955); *Once-a-Pecker, Two-a-Pecker* (1957); *The Good Looking*

Woman (1961); and *Swords and Crowns and Rings* (1977). As a prolific writer for children, she is best known as the creator of the Muddle-headed Wombat series. She has also published two acclaimed volumes of autobiography, *A Fence Around the Cuckoo* (1992) and *Fishing in the Styx* (1993).

Parker [Rothschild], Dorothy 1893–1967 American. Her writings are characterized above all by sardonic wit and irreverent sophistication. She contributed reviews, articles, columns, poems and short stories to magazines such as *Vogue, Vanity Fair, Esquire, The New Yorker, The Nation, The New Republic, Cosmopolitan, The Saturday Evening Post* and *The American Mercury*. Her first, best-selling book of verse, *Enough Rope* (1926), was followed by two more volumes, *Sunset Gun* (1928) and *Death and Taxes* (1931), and her collected poems, *Not So Deep As a Well* (1936). Her short stories appeared in *Laments for the Living* (1930), *After Such Pleasure* (1933) and *Here Lies* (1939). She collaborated with Elmer Rice on the play *Close Harmony* (1929) and with Arnaud d'Usseau on *Ladies of the Corridor* (1953).

Parker, Robert B(rown) 1932– American. The avowed influences on his DETECTIVE FICTION are DASHIELL HAMMETT, RAYMOND CHANDLER and ROSS MACDONALD, the subjects of his doctoral dissertation at Boston University in 1971. *The Godwulf Manuscript* (1973) introduced Spenser, the private-eye hero of a series, still continuing, which has increasingly attempted to reconcile the traditional tough guy and the 'new man'. Parker has also completed the fragment of the novel which Chandler left behind at his death, in *Poodle Springs* (1989), and continued the story of *The Big Sleep* in *Perchance to Dream* (1991).

Parks, Tim(othy) (Harold) 1954– English. His evangelical Christian background informs his first novel, *Tongues of Flame* (1985). Physical and emotional violence in families and between intimates has often formed the matter of his subsequent work, which includes *Loving Roger* (1986; JOHN LLEWELLYN RHYS PRIZE), *Cara Massimina* (1990, published under the pseudonym of John MacDowell in the UK; called *Juggling the Stars* in the USA) and *Mimi's Ghost* (1995). In *Europa* (1997) a coachload of British delegates travel to the European Parliament in Strasbourg. Parks brings to his sombre subjects keen irony, gleeful humour and a determination to be accessible.

Passage to India, A A novel by E. M. FORSTER, published in 1924 and awarded the JAMES TAIT BLACK MEMORIAL PRIZE.

Adela Quested visits Chandrapore with Mrs Moore to make up her mind whether to marry Mrs Moore's son Ronny, a narrow-minded magistrate. Adela's desire to understand the 'real India', shared by Mrs Moore, annoys the white community apart from the liberal Cyril Fielding, principal of the government college.

Fielding's friend Dr Aziz takes Mrs Moore and Adela to visit the Marabar Caves. Mrs Moore suffers a nihilistic psychic experience and Adela believes she has been sexually assaulted by Aziz. He is arrested and committed to prison to await trial. Only Fielding continues to assert his innocence, but their friendship is irrevocably compromised. Mrs Moore dies on the voyage home, and Adela, under extreme psychological pressure, admits that she was mistaken. Some time afterwards, Aziz and Fielding meet for the last time and discuss the future of India. Aziz insists that he and Fielding can be friends only when the British are driven out of India.

Patchen, Kenneth 1911–72 American. His experimental verse, with its proletarian stance, influenced the work of the BEATS. It appeared in *Before the Brave* (1936), *First Will and Testament* (1939), *The Teeth of the Lion* (1942), *Cloth of the Tempest* (1943), *Pictures of Life and Death* (1946), *To Say If You Love Someone* (1948), *Hurrah for Anything* (1957), *Because It Is* (1960) and *Collected Poems* (1968). His fiction includes: *The Journal of Albion Moonlight* (1941), a surrealist allegory; *Memoirs of a Shy Pornographer* (1945), a satire; *Sleepers Awake* (1946); and *See You in the Morning* (1948). *Panels for the Walls of Heaven* (1947) and *The Famous Boating Party* (1954) are prose poems.

Pater, Walter (Horatio) 1839–94 English. A diffident Oxford don, he secured his reputation as leader of the Aesthetic Movement with *Studies in the History of the Renaissance* (1873). It was followed by a novel, *MARIUS THE EPICUREAN* (1885), *Imaginary Portraits* (1887), the unfinished *Gaston de Latour* (1888), *Appreciations with an Essay on Style* (1889), *Plato and Platonism* (1893), *The Child in the House* (1894) and several posthumous publications, *Miscellaneous Studies* (1895), *Greek Studies* (1895) and *Essays from 'The Guardian'* (1896). 'Appreciation' was a byword with Pater, whose criticism rarely took an opposing stance. To him an understanding and an apprehension of beauty were paramount, as was a melancholy recognition of the brevity of human life. Disciples often misrepresented him as a hedonistic voice of 'Art for Art's sake' but he never wholly relinquished the ethical implications of aestheticism. The morbid side to his work, most apparent in *Gaston de Latour*, was seized on by followers in the 1890s.

Paterson, A(ndrew) B(arton) 1864–1941 Australian. 'Banjo' Paterson is remembered less for his journalism and novels, which include *The Outback Marriage* (1906), than for the ballads he published in his best-selling *The Man from Snowy River* (1895). He also collected authentic bush ballads, gathered in an anthology, *Old Bush Songs* (1905). His *Collected Verse* appeared in 1921. Their slangy idiom and infectious rhythms make Paterson's own poems, and the ones he collected, immediately memorable; everyone in the English-speaking world knows 'Waltzing Matilda', which he adapted from a traditional source. *Happy Dispatches* (1934) is a volume of reminiscences.

Pathfinder, The See LEATHERSTOCKING TALES, THE.

Paton, Alan (Stewart) 1903–88 South African. The account of black living conditions in *Cry, the Beloved Country* (1948) alerted world opinion to South Africa's racial inequalities. It was followed by an altogether more accomplished novel about Afrikaner inflexibility, *Too Late the Phalarope* (1953), *Debbie Go Home: Stories* (1961; as *Tales from a Troubled Land* in the USA, 1965), and *Ah, But Your Land is Beautiful* (1981), an uneasy combination of 'experimental' fiction and 1950s history. Two biographies, *Hofmeyr* (1964) and *Apartheid and the Archbishop* (1973), both won the CNA LITERARY AWARD. *Towards the Mountain* (1981) is his autobiography.

Paton Walsh, Jill [Gillian] 1937– English. Most of her fiction uses a historical setting. Adult novels include *Farewell the Great King* (1972), *Lapsing* (1986), *A School for Lovers* (1989), *The Knowledge of Angels* (1994), retelling the fable of the wolf-child, and *The Serpentine Cave* (1997). She has embarked on DETECTIVE FICTION with *The Wyndham Case* (1993) and *A Piece of Justice* (1995). Children's novels include *The Emperor's Winding-Sheet* (1974), *A Parcel of Patterns* (1983), *The Dolphin Crossing* (1967), *Fireweed* (1969) and *A Chance Child* (1978), mixing history with fantasy. *Goldengrove* (1972) and its sequel *Unleaving* (1976) deal with the problems of adolescence.

Paul, Phyllis 1903–73 English. In the tradition of the GOTHIC NOVEL, her work deals with hallucinations and clairvoyance, uses flashback and synchronized narrative, and evokes an atmosphere of unease and a haunting sense of place (especially outer London). The plight of the insane and their relatives is presented in *Constancy* (1951) and *A Little Treachery* (1962). *Camilla* (1949) and *A Cage for the Nightingale* (1957) focus on the death of children, *Twice Lost* (1960) and *Pulled Down* (1964) on mysterious disappearances. *Rox Hall Illuminated* (1956) is about a religious cult. Although she was admired by such contemporaries as ELIZABETH BOWEN, JOHN COWPER POWYS and REBECCA WEST, Paul has yet to achieve more general popularity.

Payn, James 1830–98 English. After contributing to DICKENS's magazine *Household Words*, he made his mark with a SENSATION NOVEL, *Lost Sir Massingberd* (1865). Many of his subsequent novels were in the same vein; others, such as *Married Beneath Him* (1865), were domestic love stories in the manner of ANTHONY TROLLOPE. All were written on the avowed principle that one first-rate novel would earn him less than three second-rate ones.

Peacock, Thomas Love 1785–1866 English. A modest inheritance enabled him to live as private scholar and man of letters, and he was not obliged to seek regular employment until he was in his thirties, when he obtained a senior post at the East India Company. He remained at India House until his retirement in 1856.

His development as a writer was inseparable from his friendship with the poet Shelley, who gave him confidence in his powers and drew him into a wider literary circle. By the time Peacock made his début as a novelist his manner was already that of the informed insider. *HEADLONG HALL* (1816), *MELINCOURT* (1817) and *NIGHTMARE ABBEY* (1818) all presuppose a reader versed in contemporary intellectual controversy and capable of identifying the proponents of different positions. Although the books are supreme examples of the *ROMAN À CLEF*, the primary target of Peacock's urbane satire is not the individuals portrayed but the philosophical, social and political attitudes they typify. To this extent, they are also in the tradition of the *ROMAN À THÈSE*. His most characteristic formal device is the suspension of narrative for a kind of wickedly parodied Socratic dialogue or Platonic symposium, in which the characters argue each other under the well-laden tables of their hosts. Discussion is leavened by farce, witty songs and love-plots ending in incongruous marital alliances. *MAID MARIAN* (1822) and *THE MISFORTUNES OF ELPHIN* (1829) combine topical satire with historical romance, but *CROTCHET CASTLE* (1831) returns to his earlier, and perhaps more congenial, form. Many readers regard *GRYLL GRANGE* (1860-1), a satire on the mid-Victorian age, as his masterpiece.

Peacock's poetry includes *Rhododaphne* (1818), which anticipates Keats's *Lamia*; lyrical pieces such as 'Long Night Succeeds the Little Day' (1826) and 'Newark Abbey' (1842); and *The Paper Money Lyrics* (1837), a satire on political economy and the banking fraternity. His most systematic critical writings are the fragmentary *Essay on Fashionable Literature* (1818) and *The Four Ages of Poetry* (1820), which provoked Shelley to write *A Defence of Poetry*. The two-part *Memoirs of Shelley* appeared in 1858-60.

Peake, Mervyn (Laurence) 1911-68 English. He showed himself a master of the grotesque with his first novel, *Titus Groan* (1946), a minutely detailed Gothic fantasy set in an ancient castle peopled by monumental and bizarre figures. *Gormenghast* (1950) and *Titus Alone* (1959) followed; all were reissued as a trilogy in 1967. Peake's verse includes *Rhymes without Reason* (1944), *The Glassblowers* (1950) and *The Rime of the Flying Bomb* (1962), a ballad of the blitz. He illustrated most of his work himself, as well as providing drawings for editions of Coleridge's *The Rime of the Ancient Mariner* in 1943, and ROBERT LOUIS STEVENSON's *TREASURE ISLAND* in 1949. *A Book of Nonsense* was published posthumously in 1972.

Pelham: or, The Adventures of a Gentleman A SILVER-FORK NOVEL by EDWARD BULWER LYTTON,

published in 1828. The hero is a fashionable dandy, whose habit of wearing black for dinner started a trend which has lasted to the present day. He succeeds in clearing a friend from suspicion of a vicious murder (based on the Thurtell case of 1824).

Pendennis, The History of A novel by WILLIAM MAKEPEACE THACKERAY, published in monthly parts in 1848-50. A leisurely *BILDUNGSROMAN*, often compared to DICKENS's *DAVID COPPERFIELD*, it has strongly autobiographical elements.

Arthur Pendennis is brought up by his widowed mother, who lives with her adopted daughter Laura Bell. His worldly uncle, Major Pendennis, saves him from an imprudent marriage to an actress, Miss Fotheringay, daughter of the tipsy Captain Costigan. Pen goes to Oxbridge, where he becomes idle and extravagant. Back at home he flirts with the shallow Blanche Amory, daughter of the second wife of Sir Francis Clavering, and dutifully proposes to Laura, who rejects him. In London, where he lodges with George Warrington, he starts to write for the *Pall Mall Gazette* and publishes a successful novel. He meets Blanche again and becomes attracted to a porter's daughter, Fanny Bolton. She nurses him when he is ill and his mother wrongly suspects her of being his mistress. Mother and son are reconciled before her sudden death. Major Pendennis uses his knowledge of family scandal to try to arrange a worldly marriage between Pen and Blanche. When Pen discovers the scandal, that Blanche's father is alive and a criminal, he repudiates the arrangement but decides to honour his engagement. She, however, has transferred her affections to his friend Harry Foker. Pen proposes to Laura, whom he has come to love, and she accepts him.

Arthur Pendennis reappears in Thackeray's fiction as the narrator of *THE NEWCOMES* (1853-5) and *THE ADVENTURES OF PHILIP* (1862).

Percy, Walker 1916-90 American. Most of his novels are about Southerners, usually alienated people in search of fulfilment. They include: *The Moviegoer* (1961), about a New Orleans stockbroker; *The Last Gentleman* (1966) and its sequel *Second Coming* (1980); *Love in the Ruins* (1971), a satire about a scientist; *Lancelot* (1977); and *The Thanatos Syndrome* (1987). Percy's essays on language were collected in *The Message in the Bottle* (1975).

Peregrine Pickle, The Adventures of The second novel by TOBIAS SMOLLETT, published in 1751. The story is farcical and violent, and its reception was mixed enough to make Smollett issue an expurgated version (1758).

Peregrine is an ungovernable youth who goes from bad to worse before being tamed by disillusion and imprisonment. He is released by the good offices of those to whom he has formerly been generous and is rewarded by the hand of Emilia, whom he has treated badly, despite their mutual love.

The novel has two unusual features. One is the interpolated story of the widowed Lady Vane's remarriage and subsequent adulteries, which she is believed to have paid Smollett to publish. The other (Chapter 95) is Peregrine's purchase of a beggar girl, whom he tries to make a fine lady. The parallels with GEORGE BERNARD SHAW's *Pygmalion* have been noted.

Perelman, S(idney) J(oseph) 1904–79 American. A sharp observer of American society, he published some 20 books, mostly collections of humorous pieces which had appeared in *The New Yorker*, beginning with *Dawn Ginsbergh's Revenge* (1929). In Hollywood he wrote scripts for the Marx brothers and the screenplays for *Ambush* (1939) and *The Golden Fleecing* (1940), both with his wife Laura Weinstein, the sister of NATHANAEL WEST. He also wrote travel books, including *Westward Ha! or Around the World in Eighty Clichés* (1948) and *Eastward Ha!* (1977).

Persuasion JANE AUSTEN's last completed novel, published in 1818. Though written when her health was rapidly failing, it shows no loss of power: the social comedy is deftly handled and the overriding tone is one of serious and profound reflection.

The snobbish Sir Walter Elliot of Kellynch Hall has three daughters: the haughty, unmarried Elizabeth; Mary, married to Charles Musgrove, the local squire's son; and the admirable but neglected Anne. When Sir Walter is forced to let Kellynch to Admiral and Mrs Croft, Anne again meets Captain Frederick Wentworth, Mrs Croft's brother, whose proposal she had refused eight years before on the advice of her godmother, Lady Russell. Anne, who still loves Wentworth, is at once disappointed and relieved when he appears to care for her no longer. Wentworth soon becomes a favourite with the Musgrove family, particularly Charles's two high-spirited sisters, Louisa and Henrietta. Anne's suspicion that he is attracted to Louisa seems to be confirmed by his concern when she suffers an accident during a jaunt to Lyme Regis. In Bath, where her father and sister have settled, Anne is courted by William Elliot, her cousin and father's heir, but discovers his scheming nature. Unexpected news arrives of Louisa Musgrove's engagement to Captain Benwick, and soon afterward Wentworth appears, anxious to renew his addresses to Anne but uncertain of his reception. He is finally emboldened to make a declaration and the couple are at last united.

Peters, Lenrie 1932– Gambian. One of the calmest and least doctrinal voices in contemporary African literature, he has urged the need for a pan-African outlook. Best-known for his highly accessible poetry, he has also published an early

novel, *The Second Round* (1965), portraying the predicament of a young doctor returning to Sierra Leone.

Peril of the Peak A novel by SIR WALTER SCOTT, first published in 1823. Its background is religious strife in the reign of Charles II. The Royalist Sir Geoffrey Peveril and the Puritan Major Bridgenorth, two neighbouring Derbyshire gentlemen who have managed to live through the Civil War as friends, quarrel when their children, Julian Peveril and Alice Bridgenorth, fall in love.

Philip, The Adventures of A novel by WILLIAM MAKEPEACE THACKERAY, serialized in *The Cornhill Magazine* in 1861–2 and published in book form in 1862. Narrated by Arthur Pendennis, it completes the trio of interconnected and semi-autobiographical novels begun with THE HISTORY OF PENDENNIS and THE NEWCOMES.

Philip Firmin is the son of Dr Brand Firmin, the 'Brandon' of *A SHABBY GENTEEL STORY*, who has since married a wealthy woman, Lord Ringwood's niece. Her death leaves Philip rich and his independent spirit wins Lord Ringwood's approval. He suspects his father's shady past and discovers that he is being blackmailed by Tufton Hunt, the dissolute clergyman who officiated at the sham wedding between Brandon and Caroline Gann in the earlier story. Dr Firmin loses Philip's fortune by speculation and flees to America. The rest of the novel deals with Philip's rejection by his cousin Agnes Twysden in favour of a wealthy suitor, his marriage to Charlotte Baynes, his early career as a journalist, and the kindness shown him by Arthur and Laura Pendennis, as well as Caroline. The discovery of Lord Ringwood's will restores him to prosperity.

Phillips, Caryl 1958– Born in St Kitts, he has lived in Britain since childhood. His plays include *Strange Fruit* (1980), about generational conflicts in a family, and *Where There is Darkness* (1982). Since the mid-1980s he has mainly written fiction: *The Final Passage* (1985), about a small islander who migrates to Britain; *A State of Independence* (1986), about a West Indian's return home at the time of his country's independence; *Higher Ground* (1989), a panoramic account of the black diaspora; *Cambridge* (1991), about Caribbean plantation society near the end of the slave era; and *CROSSING THE RIVER* (1993). *The European Touch* (1987) is a non-fictional reflection on travels in Europe.

Phillips, Jayne Anne 1952– American. She blends realistic and surrealistic detail in stories of rural and domestic life, childhood, and altered states of consciousness. *Black Tickets* (1979) and *Fast Lanes* (1987) are short-story collections. Her novels include *Machine Dreams* (1985) and *Shelter* (1994), which takes place during 24 hours in a rural girls' camp.

Phillpotts, Eden 1862–1960 English. He wrote

well over 200 books, the best of them novels about Dartmoor like *Children in the Mist* (1898), *The Secret Woman* (1905), *The Thief of Virtue* (1910) and *Widecombe Fair* (1913). The DETECTIVE FICTION he published under his own name and as Harrington Hext has been largely forgotten. He collaborated with his daughter Adelaide on two successful stage comedies, *The Farmer's Wife* (1924) and *Yellow Sands* (1926), as well as on several shorter pieces.

Phineas Finn: The Irish Member A novel by ANTHONY TROLLOPE, serialized in 1867–9 and published in volume form in 1869. The second of his PALLISER NOVELS, and the first to deal with Parliament itself, it is thought to portray aspects of BENJAMIN DISRAELI in Mr Daubeny and of Gladstone in Mr Gresham.

The story follows the fortunes of the charming Irish barrister and MP, Phineas Finn. Despite his commitment to Mary Jones, he wins the love of Lady Laura Standish, who continues to help his career after marrying Robert Kennedy. Phineas's interest in Violet Effingham provokes a duel with Lord Chiltern, though the two men are reconciled and Violet marries Chiltern. The background to these intrigues is the new reform bill which the Liberals are trying to steer through Parliament. Phineas is forced to resign his post as junior minister when he supports Irish tenant rights. He refuses the hand and fortune of the widowed Madame Max Goesler, the Duke of Omnium's companion, and returns to Ireland, where he marries Mary Jones and becomes Inspector of the Cork Poor Houses.

Phineas Redux The fourth of ANTHONY TROLLOPE'S PALLISER NOVELS, serialized in 1873–4 and published in volume form in 1873.

Now widowed, Phineas Finn re-enters Parliament. His attempt to mediate between Lady Laura Kennedy and her increasingly insane husband aggravates matters and is publicized in its worst light by his old enemy Quintus Slide, a radical journalist. More scandal ensues when Phineas quarrels publicly with a cabinet minister, Mr Bonteen, who is afterwards murdered. Phineas is arrested and brought to trial but acquitted with the help of his lawyer, Chaffanbrass, and Madame Max Goesler. Suspicion falls on Mr Emilius, Lady Eustace's estranged husband, who escapes prosecution through lack of evidence. Disillusioned with public life, Phineas refuses a government post and finally marries Madame Max. The death of the old Duke of Omnium enables Plantagenet Palliser's cousin Adelaide to marry her penniless suitor Gerard Maule. The novel's pessimism is balanced by the rise of Plantagenet Palliser, the new Duke of Omnium, as Trollope's ideal statesman.

Piazza Tales, The A volume of six stories by HERMAN MELVILLE, published in 1856. It is introduced by 'The Piazza', Melville's descriptive recollection of his Massachusetts farmhouse, to which he added a piazza.

The two most important stories are 'Benito Cereno' and 'Bartleby the Scrivener'. In the former, set in 1799, Amasa Delano encounters a Spanish ship apparently commanded by the enfeebled Benito Cereno but in fact controlled by his Senegalese valet Babo, who has led his fellow slaves in a mutiny. 'Bartleby the Scrivener' is about an enigmatic copyist whose response to any unwelcome request is 'I would prefer not to'.

Other stories in the collection are: 'The Bell Tower', about an over-reaching artist named Bannadonna; 'The Lightning-Rod Man', about a man who refuses an insistent lightning-rod salesman because he believes that man should not fear acts of God; and 'The Encantadas: or, Enchanted Isles', about the Galapagos Islands.

picaresque A term derived from the Spanish *pícaro*, originally a low-life character who lived dishonestly by his wits but later anyone at odds with, or outside, society. The picaresque novel, an episodic narrative describing the progress of the *pícaro*, began with the anonymous *Lazarillo de Tormes* (1554) and Mateo Alemán's *Guzmán de Alfarache* (1559), translated into English by James Mabbe. In Europe the tradition was consolidated by a French writer, Le Sage, in *Gil Blas* (1715–35), set in Spain.

In English literature the tradition began with THOMAS NASHE'S *THE UNFORTUNATE TRAVELLER* (1594) and RICHARD HEAD'S *The English Rogue* (1665). In the 18th century, it continued in the work of DANIEL DEFOE (notably *MOLL FLANDERS*, 1722), TOBIAS SMOLLETT (notably *RODERICK RANDOM*, 1748) and HENRY FIELDING (notably *TOM JONES*, 1749). Nashe, Head, Defoe and Smollett make their heroes to some degree amoral, and generally maintain an atmosphere of cheerful savagery which is still within harking distance of their Spanish originals. Fielding, however, pointed the way to the future by his insistence on the essential good-heartedness of his hero in *Tom Jones*, even if he did leave him rather too free in his sexual appetites to commend him to Victorian taste.

By the 19th century the picaresque novel in Britain had virtually forgotten its origin in the literature of roguery. Only in a work such as WILLIAM MAKEPEACE THACKERAY'S *BARRY LYNDON* (1844) does the hero retain more than a discreet touch of the *pícaro*, and even this Thackeray thought it prudent to modify when he revised the book for republication in 1852. Otherwise, novels such as DICKENS'S *PICKWICK PAPERS* (1836–7) and *NICHOLAS NICKLEBY* (1838–9), which are often loosely called 'picaresque', are picaresque only in the general sense that they tell an episodic story in which the hero goes on a journey. The protagonists are models of amiable innocence or resolute virtue.

In America, writers such as HERMAN MELVILLE and MARK TWAIN maintained a more active interest in roguery, and particularly in the confidence trickster. But even there, from Twain's HUCKLEBERRY FINN (1884) onwards, the picaresque novel is increasingly subsumed into the literature of the journey and the open road. That tradition, investigating the ambiguities of freedom as enjoyed by the outsider, has continued in the 20th century with works such as J. D. SALINGER's THE CATCHER IN THE RYE (1951) and JACK KEROUAC's ON THE ROAD (1957).

Pickwick Papers, The CHARLES DICKENS's first novel, formally titled The Posthumous Papers of the Pickwick Club, published in monthly parts in 1836-7.

It takes its loose, easy structure from the travels to Ipswich, Rochester, Bath and elsewhere of Samuel Pickwick and his fellow members of the Pickwick Club, Tracy Tupman, Augustus Snodgrass and Nathaniel Winkle. Mr Pickwick's innocent and trusting nature repeatedly makes him the butt of comic adventures. In the book's most prolonged episode he gives his landlady Mrs Bardell the impression that he wishes to marry her, and so provokes a suit for breach of promise. Interspersed among these adventures are moral and melodramatic stories – 'The Bagman's Story', 'The Convict's Return', 'The Stroller's Tale' and others – which counterbalance the prevailing comedy of the book.

Most memorable among the wide variety of characters are: Sam Weller, Pickwick's sharp-witted Cockney servant, and his coachman father Tony; the glib strolling player Alfred Jingle and his rascally servant Job Trotter; the medical student Bob Sawyer; and the good-natured Wardles. The rapacious Dodson and Fogg, the pompous Serjeant Buzfuz and others connected with Mrs Bardell's lawsuit hint – like Pickwick's own experiences in prison near the end of the novel – at the darker vision Dickens's later work would explore.

Picture of Dorian Gray, The A novel by OSCAR WILDE, published in 1890. Once regarded as daringly modern in its portrayal of fin-de-siècle decadence, it draws on traditional motifs to create a powerful GOTHIC NOVEL. Dorian sells his soul to keep his youth and beauty. His tempter is the amoral Lord Henry Wotton and his good angel, or conscience, is the portrait painter Basil Hallward, whom he murders. The story highlights the tension between the polished surface and the secret vices of high life.

Piercy, Marge 1937– American. Most of her work deals with women's assigned place in a male-dominated society. Woman on the Edge of Time (1976) is a dystopian feminist fantasy. Other novels include Going Down Fast (1969), Dance the Eagle to Sleep (1970), Small Changes (1973), Vida (1979), Braided Lives (1982), Fly Away Home (1984), Gone to Soldiers (1987), He, She, and It (1991), Body of Glass (1992) and The Longings of Women (1994). Her poetry includes Breaking Camp (1968), Hard Loving (1969), 4-Telling (1971), To be of Use (1973), Living in the Open (1976), The Twelve-Spoked Wheel Flashing (1978), The Moon is Always Female (1980), Circles on the Water: Selected Poems (1982), Stone, Paper, Knife (1983) and Mars and Her Children (1992).

Pierre: or, The Ambiguities A novel by HERMAN MELVILLE, published in 1852. Pierre Glendinning, the son of a wealthy widow in upstate New York, abandons his fiancée, Lucy Tartan, for Isabel, who claims to be his illegitimate half-sister. At first he believes his motive is merely protective, though he allows the world to think he has married her. Later he is forced to realize his true feelings. Pierre kills his cousin, Glen, in a violent confrontation and is arrested. Lucy and his mother die of grief. Torn by conflicting emotions about their forbidden love, Pierre and Isabel commit suicide in his prison cell.

Pilgrim's Progress, The: From this World to That Which is to Come A religious allegory by the Nonconformist preacher and writer John Bunyan (1628–88), published in two parts (1678 and 1684).

Presented as the author's dream, Part I recounts Bunyan's own experience of conversion in figurative terms. He sees Christian with a book in his hand and a burden on his back, in great distress because the book tells him he lives in the City of Destruction and will suffer death and judgement. Leaving behind his wife and children, Christian follows Evangelist's advice to flee towards a Wicket Gate. His pilgrimage takes him through the Slough of Despond, past the Burning Mount, thence to the Wicket Gate, the Interpreter's House, the Cross (where his burden rolls away), the Hill Difficulty, the House Beautiful, the Valley of Humiliation, the Valley of the Shadow of Death, Vanity Fair, Lucre Hill, the River of the Water of Life, By-Path Meadow, Doubting Castle, the Delectable Mountains, the Enchanted Ground and the country of Beulah, until he finally passes over the River into the Celestial City. On the way he is helped by Faithful, who is put to death in Vanity Fair, and then Hopeful, who accompanies him into the Celestial City. They encounter enemies (the fiend Apollyon, Lord Hategood and Giant Despair) and unreliable friends (Mr Worldly Wise-man, Ignorance, Talkative and By-ends).

The greater number and variety of pilgrims in Part II make it more like a social novel. Christian's wife Christiana follows him, with her children and their neighbour Mercy. Greatheart, who joins them at the Interpreter's House, slays Giant Despair and various other giants and monsters. Fellow pilgrims include Mr Feeble-mind, Mr Ready-to-halt, Mr Honest,

Valiant-for-truth, Mr Stand-fast, Mr Despondency and his daughter Much-afraid. At the end they pass over the River.

From the moment of its publication *The Pilgrim's Progress* has appealed to an extraordinarily wide readership. It has appeared in innumerable editions and been translated into well over 100 languages. The book's popularity owes much to the beauty and simplicity of Bunyan's prose, the vividness of his allegorical characters, and the deftness with which he renders colloquial speech. Though allegorical in form, the work is also profoundly realistic, particularly in its portrayal of the pilgrims striving to hold to their beliefs in a hostile and uncomprehending world.

For Bunyan, see also THE HOLY WAR and THE LIFE AND DEATH OF MR BADMAN.

Pioneers, The See LEATHERSTOCKING TALES, THE.

Pirate, The A novel by SIR WALTER SCOTT, published in 1822. It is set in the 17th century in a remote part of Zetland (Shetland), where the shipwreck of the buccaneer, Cleveland, disrupts the life of Mordaunt and his relations with Minna and Brenda, daughters of the wealthy Magnus Troil. Mordaunt finally foils Cleveland's attempt to capture Magnus and his daughters, and marries Brenda.

Pirsig, Robert (Maynard) 1928– American. *Zen and the Art of Motorcycle Maintenance* (1974) is an account of a cross-country trip with his son which combines autobiography, fiction and philosophical reflection. It caught the mood of its time and earned Pirsig a cult reputation, not renewed by his only subsequent work, *Lila: An Inquiry into Morals* (1991).

Pit, The: *A Story of Chicago* The second volume of FRANK NORRIS's unfinished trilogy *The Epic of the Wheat*, posthumously published in 1903. The first volume is THE OCTOPUS (1901); the third volume was never written.

The pit is the Chicago stock exchange, where Curtis Jadwin speculates successfully in the wheat market and is driven almost to madness by his obsession with money. His material success is paralleled by the decline of his marriage to Laura Dearborn, who resumes an old relationship with the aesthete Sheldon Corthell. She returns to Jadwin at the end, after a glut in the market has destroyed his fortune.

Plaatje, Solomon Tshekisho 1877–1932 South African. Newspaper editor and first Secretary of the African National Congress (1912), he attacked the 1913 Natives Land Act for turning blacks into pariahs in *Native Life in South Africa* (1916). *Mhudi*, written about 1917 but published in 1930, was the first novel to present pre-colonial African society sympathetically. Plaatje's *Boer War Diary* was discovered and published in 1972.

Plath, Sylvia 1932–63 American. Her short life and early death by suicide continue to fascinate biographers and generate controversy. Born in Boston, she came to Britain and married the poet Ted Hughes in 1957. *The Colossus and Other Poems* (Britain, 1960; USA, 1962) was the only volume of poetry to appear during her lifetime. Posthumous volumes include *Ariel* (1965), *Crossing the Water* (Britain, 1971; USA, 1972) and *Winter Trees* (Britain, 1971; USA, 1972). Though her work has clear affinities with confessional poetry, she often uses irony to distance herself from her personal subject matter. Her only novel, *The Bell Jar* (Britain, 1963; USA, 1971), is partly autobiographical and shows unmistakable affinities with her poetry. Her prose is collected in *Johnny Panic and the Bible of Dreams: Short Stories, Prose, and Diary Excerpts* (1979). *The Journals of Sylvia Plath* appeared in 1982.

Plomer, William (Charles Franklyn) 1903–73 Born in South Africa, he travelled widely before settling in Britain. Racism is the subject of his first, angry novel, *Turbott Wolfe* (1926). The poems in *Notes for Poems* (1927), *The Family Tree* (1929), *The Fivefold Screen* (1932), *Visiting the Caves* (1936), *The Dorking Thigh* (1945), *Collected Poems* (1960) and *Celebrations* (1972) are divided between serious work and satire. Besides editing Francis Kilvert's diaries (1938–40) and HERMAN MELVILLE's poems, Plomer collaborated with Benjamin Britten as librettist for *Gloriana* (1953) and his three 'church operas'.

Plumed Serpent, The A novel by D. H. LAWRENCE, published in 1926. Kate Leslie, an Irish widow, visits Mexico in search of some quality that will renew her life. She meets General Don Cipriano Viedma, a pure-bred Indian, and Don Ramón Carrasco, scholar and political leader, whose mission is to revive the old cult of Quetzalcoatl, the plumed serpent. Attracted by Don Cipriano's sexual energy and the cult's violent, elemental power, she takes on the role of Malintzi, a fertility goddess and bride of Cipriano, now elevated by Don Ramón to the status of war god, Huitzilopochtli.

Plumptre, Anne 1760–1818. English. Her novels, which include *Antoinette* (1796), *The Rector's Son* (1798), *The Western Mail* (1801), *Something New* (1801) and *The History of Myself and a Friend* (1813), were largely unnoticed. Her most ambitious translations, from the German playwright Kotzebue in the 1790s, were overshadowed by the work of ELIZABETH INCHBALD and Sheridan. She attracted more attention with two travel books: *Narrative of Three Years' Residence in France* (1810), based on a trip begun in the company of AMELIA OPIE, and *Narrative of a Residence in Ireland* (1817). The former is remembered for its defence of Napoleon, though it also contains sharp comments on fellow radicals. *Tales of Wonder, of Honour and of Sentiment* (1818) is a moralistic work for children written jointly with her sister Annabella.

Poe, Edgar Allan 1809–49 American. Born in Boston, he spent an apparently unhappy childhood with the foster-father from whom he took his middle name. Several years in England (1815–20) were followed by unsuccessful spells at university and in the army. His career in journalism shuttled him backwards and forwards between Richmond in Virginia, Philadelphia and New York, though he never ceased to regard himself as a Southerner. His child-bride, Virginia Clemm, whom he married in 1836, died an early death in 1847. Poe himself died at Baltimore in squalid and partly unexplained circumstances.

In the course of this makeshift and itinerant life, increasingly complicated by poverty, nervous disorder and alcoholism, he still managed to produce a steady stream of writing. The title work of *The Raven and Other Poems* (1845), his chief popular success as a poet, prompted him to write 'The Philosophy of Composition' (1846), which – together with his lecture, 'The Poetic Principle' (which was posthumously published, 1850) – constitutes his chief aesthetic statement. The emphasis on calculated craftsmanship and intensity of effect is reflected in the stories partly collected in *Tales of the Grotesque and Arabesque* (1840) and *Tales* (1845). Leading titles include 'Ligeia', 'The Fall of the House of Usher', 'William Wilson', 'The Masque of the Red Death', 'The Pit and the Pendulum', 'The Tell-Tale Heart', 'The Black Cat', and 'The Cask of Amontillado'. Three stories, 'The Murders in the Rue Morgue', 'The Purloined Letter' and 'The Mystery of Marie Roget', had a decisive influence on the development of DETECTIVE FICTION.

All his work begins by borrowing the conventions, and usually the European settings, of the GOTHIC NOVEL but creates its own distinctive milieu of private horror, psychological rather than physical, observed with clinical, even grimly humorous detachment. His only novel, *The Narrative of Arthur Gordon Pym* (1838), belongs to the same world as the stories, while an ambitious treatise, *Eureka* (1848), wrestles with its philosophical implications.

Pohl, Frederik 1919– American. He began his career in SCIENCE FICTION writing novels in collaboration with C. M. Kornbluth, including *The Space Merchants* (1953), a prophetic satire about advertising agencies. His many solo novels include: *Man Plus* (1976); the 'Heechee' series begun with *Gateway* (1977); *Chernobyl* (1987), a drama-documentary account; *Mining the Oort* (1992); and *The Voices of Heaven* (1994). Notable collections of stories include *The Case against Tomorrow* (1957), *The Man Who Ate the World* (1960), *Day Million* (1970), *In the Problem Pit* (1976), *The Years of the City* (1984) and *The Day the Martians Came* (1988). *The Singers of Time* (with Jack Willamson; 1991) dramatizes modern cosmological theories.

Poor White A novel by SHERWOOD ANDERSON, published in 1920. It tells how late 19th-century technology changes the lives of the inhabitants of Bidwell, Ohio, and particularly that of Hugh McVey, a telegraph operator who begins as a shy, inhibited 'poor white' but becomes rich and famous, as well as isolated, through the success of his inventions. Disillusioned, he finally realizes the negative effects of industrial progress.

Porter, Anne Maria 1780–1832 English. She was the younger sister of the more successful JANE PORTER. The most popular of her many novels was *The Hungarian Brothers* (1807), about the French Revolutionary war.

Porter, Hal 1911–84 Australian. Although he worked in many genres, he is best known for his three volumes of autobiography, *The Watcher on the Cast-Iron Balcony* (1963), *The Paper Chase* (1966) and *The Extra* (1975), and his precise, carefully crafted stories. They are collected in *Short Stories* (1942), *A Bachelor's Children* (1962), *The Cats of Venice* (1965), *Mr Butterfry and Other Tales of New Japan* (1970), *Fredo Fuss Love Life* (1974) and *The Clairvoyant Goat* (1981). He was both one of Australia's finest prose stylists and a chronicler of uncelebrated aspects of the country's social life. His novels – *A Handful of Pennies* (1958), *The Tilted Cross* (1961) and *The Right Thing* (1971) – are sympathetic towards loners and eccentrics. Other works include three plays, *The Tower* (1963), *The Professor* (1966) and *Eden House* (1969), and several volumes of poetry, *The Hexagon* (1956), *Elijah's Ravens* (1968) and *In an Australian Country Graveyard* (1974).

Porter, Jane 1776–1850 English. Highly successful in her day, she wrote some of the earliest HISTORICAL FICTION. *The Scottish Chiefs* (1810), about William Wallace and Robert Bruce, and ending with the Battle of Bannockburn, appeared before SIR WALTER SCOTT began his Waverley novels. Her younger sister was ANNE MARIA PORTER.

Porter, Katherine Anne 1890–1980 American. She is best remembered for *Ship of Fools* (1962), an ambitious, allegorical novel set on a German passenger ship sailing from Mexico in 1931. Her shorter fiction was gathered in *The Collected Stories of Katherine Anne Porter* (1965; PULITZER PRIZE). Her other publications include *Collected Essays and Occasional Writings* (1970) and *The Never-Ending Wrong* (1977), an account of the infamous Sacco-Vanzetti trial and execution.

Portnoy's Complaint A novel by PHILIP ROTH, published in 1969. It takes the form of an account by Alexander Portnoy to his analyst of his relationship with his suburban Jewish family. Portnoy's guilty responses to his family's needs alternate with self-conscious rebellion: he masturbates, refuses to get married and has affairs with gentile women. In Israel he finds himself impotent with an Israeli girl, who confronts him with the contradictions of his existence and embodies for him a noble, self-sacrificing model of Jewishness.

Portrait of a Lady, The A novel by HENRY JAMES, serialized in 1880-1 and published in volume form in 1881.

Isabel Archer, a young American girl, arrives in England to stay with her aunt and uncle, Mr and Mrs Touchett, and their tubercular son, Ralph. Ralph persuades Mr Touchett to include her in his will, so his death makes her rich. To preserve her freedom, Isabel has turned down proposals of marriage from Casper Goodwood, an American, and Lord Warburton. In Florence with Mrs Touchett and her friend, Madame Merle, she meets and marries the American expatriate Gilbert Osmond, only to discover him to be a selfish and sterile dilettante interested in her money. He forbids her to visit the dying Ralph in England; she goes, after learning that Madame Merle is the mother of his daughter Pansy. Casper Goodwood makes a last attempt to gain Isabel but she returns to Osmond and Pansy in Italy.

Portrait of the Artist as a Young Man, A An autobiographical novel by JAMES JOYCE, serialized by *The Egoist* in 1914-15 and published in volume form in 1916. It was developed from *Stephen Hero*, begun in 1904. Part of the earlier work survived and was edited by T. Spencer in 1944.

Stephen Dedalus, an intelligent but frail child, struggles towards maturity in Ireland. The novel traces his intellectual, moral, and artistic development from babyhood to the completion of his education at University College, Dublin. His individuality is stifled by many levels of convention, dictated by the family, Catholicism and Irish nationalism. He finally embraces the wider and more rewarding world of literature, philosophy and aesthetics, and frees himself from the claims of family, church and state. He resolves to leave Ireland for Paris to forge 'the uncreated conscience' of his race. He reappears in ULYSSES.

post-modernism An international movement, affecting all the contemporary arts, which has succeeded MODERNISM. In literature, and particularly the novel, it rejects realism in favour of a heightened sense of artifice, a delight in games and verbal pyrotechnics, a suspicion of absolute truth and a resulting inclination to stress the fictionality of fiction. All these traits were already present in modernist works such as JOYCE's FINNEGANS WAKE but they re-emerged with special force in early American examples of post-modernism such as VLADIMIR NABOKOV's *Pale Fire* (1962), THOMAS PYNCHON's *V* (1963), KURT VONNEGUT JR's *SLAUGHTERHOUSE-FIVE* (1969) and JOHN BARTH's *LETTERS* (1979).

Its distrust of traditional mimetic genres, allied to the philosophical climate of structural-ism and deconstruction, has also encouraged post-modernism to embrace popular forms, such as DETECTIVE FICTION (Umberto Eco's *The Name of the Rose*, 1983), SCIENCE FICTION (DORIS LESSING's *Canopus in Argos* sequence) and fairy tale (a recurrent source in the work of ANGELA CARTER). Equally post-modernist is the blurring of boundaries between the novel and journalism in TRUMAN CAPOTE's *In Cold Blood* (1966), the New Journalism of TOM WOLFE and others, and ROBERT PIRSIG's *Zen and the Art of Motorcycle Maintenance* (1974). The fiction of SALMAN RUSHDIE, probably the most striking British practitioner, would seem to confirm the link between post-modernism and the post-colonial experience already suggested by the MAGIC REAL-ISM of Gabriel García Márquez.

Potter, (Helen) Beatrix 1866-1943 English. To enliven her otherwise dull life with well-to-do parents in Kensington, she kept a journal in code (edited by Leslie Linder; 1966) and painted. A letter to a young friend illustrated with drawings of animals grew into *The Tale of Peter Rabbit* (privately printed, 1901), followed by *The Tailor of Gloucester* (1902).

Subsequent picture-books, issued during a long and profitable association with the publisher Frederick Warne, include: *The Tale of Squirrel Nutkin* (1903), *The Tale of Benjamin Bunny* (1904), *The Tale of Two Bad Mice* (1904), *The Tale of Mrs Tiggy-Winkle* (1905), *The Tale of Jeremy Fisher* (1906), *The Story of a Fierce Bad Rabbit* (1906), *The Story of Miss Moppet* (1906), *The Tale of Tom Kitten* (1907), *The Tale of Jemima Puddle-Duck* (1908), *The Tale of the Flopsy Bunnies* (1909), *The Tale of Mrs Tittlemouse* (1910), *The Tale of Timmy Tiptoes* (1911) and *The Tale of Pigling Bland* (1913). They range from adventure stories to charming, eventless catalogues of animal domesticity, illustrated with a minute eye for detail.

After her marriage in 1913 she lived in the Lake District, the setting for many of her books. There she put most of her energies into sheep farming and conservation, leaving 4000 acres of land to the National Trust. *The Tale of Little Pig Robinson* (1930) was the only story of note to appear in her declining years.

Powell, Anthony (Dymoke) 1905- English. His early novels - *Afternoon Men* (1931), *Venusberg* (1932), *From a View to a Death* (1933), *Agents and Patients* (1936), and *What's Become of Waring?* (1939) - are polished, elliptical satires which made critics link his name with that of EVELYN WAUGH. His main achievement is *A DANCE TO THE MUSIC OF TIME*, a 12-volume ROMAN FLEUVE beginning with *A Question of Upbringing* (1951) and ending with *Hearing Secret Harmonies* (1975), which amounts to a leisurely survey of English society as Powell has experienced it. Later, more eccentric novels are *O, How the Wheel Becomes It!* (1983) and *The Fisher King* (1986). He has also published a biographical study of John Aubrey

(1948) and a selection from *Brief Lives* (1949), as well as two collections of book reviews, *Miscellaneous Verdicts* (1990) and *Under Review* (1992). *To Keep the Ball Rolling* (1976–82) is a four-volume autobiography. *Journals: 1982–86* (1995) provoked fury and delight.

Powell, Dawn 1897–1965 American. Thanks in part to the advocacy of GORE VIDAL, her fiction is currently being rescued from neglect; its satirical bent has prompted comparison with DOROTHY PARKER and, more pertinently, MURIEL SPARK. Early novels such as *She Walks in Beauty* (1928) and *Dance Night* (1930) are set in her native Midwest. *Turn, Magic Wheel* (1936) announces her abiding interest in New York, particularly the café society of Greenwich Village. The best of her work includes *A Time to be Born* (1942), drawing on her childhood, and two gleefully sharp studies of literary and bohemian pretensions, *The Locusts Have No King* (1948) and *The Wicked Pavilion* (1954). *The Golden Spur* (1962) was her last novel. Powell also wrote short stories, plays and screenplays.

Power and the Glory, The A novel by GRAHAM GREENE, published in 1940 and awarded the HAWTHORNDEN PRIZE the following year. It is set in Mexico, which Greene had visited to observe and comment on the persecution of the Catholic Church. His visit also prompted a travel book, *The Lawless Roads* (1939).

A lapsed priest, drunk and lecherous, rediscovers his original commitment despite (or perhaps because of) being banned. His life is contrasted with that of a fellow priest, Padre Jose, who has capitulated to the regime, and a 'gringo' thief and murderer, hunted by the police. His opponent, a good and honourable police lieutenant, finally corners the priest at the bedside of the dying 'gringo'. The priest's execution is imbued with Christlike implications, and the novel closes on a subdued note of triumph.

Power of Sympathy, The An EPISTOLARY NOVEL by WILLIAM HILL BROWN, published anonymously in 1789 and generally considered to be the first American novel. It warns young women of the danger from would-be seducers by telling a tragic tale based in part on an actual scandal in Boston society. Harrington is determined to win Harriot Fawcet, unaware that she is his half-sister. When the truth of her parentage is revealed, she collapses and dies soon afterwards, while the grief-stricken Harrington eventually commits suicide.

Powys, John Cowper 1872–1963 English. He was the brother of LLEWELYN POWYS and T. F. POWYS. Although he worked for much of his life as a lecturer in the USA, his writings are imbued with the atmosphere of the West Country, where he spent his boyhood, and Wales, where he lived on his return to Britain. He published poetry, essays on literature, religion and philosophy,

and an early group of romances: *Wood and Stone* (1915), *Rodmoor* (1916) and *Ducdame* (1925).

However, his reputation – still controversial – depends on ambitious, esoteric novels which combine folklore and the supernatural with elements of the epic: *Wolf Solent* (1929); *A Glastonbury Romance* (1932); *Weymouth Sands* (1934; revised as *Jobber Skald* in 1935 but restored to its original form in 1963), about the intense relationship between Jobber, his lover Perdita and his enemy Dog Cattistock; *Maiden Castle* (1936), set among the excavations of the Dorchester fort; and *Morwy: or, The Vengeance of God* (1937), about man's inhumanity to man. Later novels include: *Owen Glendower* (1940) and *Porius: A Romance of the Dark Ages* (1951), historical romances; *The Inmates* (1952), about madness; *Atlantis* (1954), a fantastic tale about Odysseus; and *The Brazen Head* (1956), about the medieval philosopher and scientist Roger Bacon.

Powys, Llewelyn 1884–1939 English. He was the brother of JOHN COWPER POWYS and T. F. POWYS. His many books include: *Ebony and Ivory* (1923), based on his experiences in Kenya; *Skin for Skin* (1925), about the tuberculosis which eventually killed him; and other loosely autobiographical works such as *Love and Death: An Imaginary Autobiography* (1939). *Earth Memories* (1934) and *Dorset Essays* (1935) were his best-known volumes. *Confessions of Two Brothers* (with John Cowper Powys; 1916) and *Damnable Opinions* (1935) show the independent-mindedness that characterized all three brothers. *Black Laughter* (1924) and *Apples be Ripe* (1930) are novels.

Powys, T(heodore) F(rancis) 1875–1953 English. The brother of JOHN COWPER POWYS and LLEWELYN POWYS, he is best known for two allegorical fantasies which explore paradoxes about good and evil: *Mr Weston's Good Wine* (1927), in which God and the archangel Michael visit the village of Folly Down in the person of Mr Weston, wine merchant, and his junior partner; and *Unclay* (1931), in which John Death visits the village of Dodder with orders from God to kill various inhabitants. Other works include *An Interpretation of Genesis* (1907) and *Soliloquies of a Hermit* (1916), showing his preoccupation with religion, and many volumes of short stories, among them *The Left Leg* (1923), *Black Bryony* (1923), *Mr Tasker's Gods* (1924) and *Bottle's Path* (1946), one of his very few books after 1940.

Praed, Mrs Campbell 1851–1935 Australian. *My Australian Girlhood* (1902) is the story of her early years in Queensland. After settling in Britain in 1876 she produced some 40 novels, frequently drawing on her experience of Australia and contrasting refined English gentlemen with crude, spiky Australians whose qualities prove more enduring. Titles include *An Australian Heroine* (1880), *Policy and Passion* (1881), *Miss Jacobsen's Chance* (1886), *The Romance of a Station* (1889), *Mrs*

Tregaskiss (1895), *Nulma* (1897), *The Maid of the River* (1905), *Opal Fire* (1910) and *Sister Sorrow* (1916).

Prairie, The See LEATHERSTOCKING TALES, THE.

Pratchett, Terry [Terence] **(David John)** 1948– English. His comic fantasies set on Discworld, cleverly subverting the clichés of genre fantasy and other kinds of imaginative fiction, began with *The Colour of Magic* (1983), achieved best-seller status with *Mort* (1987), and rapidly extended at the rate of two a year to *Interesting Times* (1995) and *Maskerade* (1995). They are enormously popular with teenagers, and much of Pratchett's other work is aimed specifically at a younger audience. *Truckers* (1989) began a trilogy about tiny extraterrestrials marooned on Earth. *Only You Can Save Mankind* (1992) and *Johnny and the Dead* (1993) are moral fables.

Prichard, Katherine Susannah 1883–1969 Born in Fiji, she published her first novel, *The Pioneers* (1915), while working as a journalist in London. In Australia she took pains to familiarize herself with the background of novels such as *Working Bullocks* (1926), about teamsters, *Coonardo* (1929) – her best novel – about a cattle station, and *Haxby's Circus* (1930). A trilogy, *The Roaring Nineties* (1946), *Golden Miles* (1948), and *Winged Seeds* (1950), is set in the goldfields of Western Australia. Her poetry includes *Clovelly Verses* (1913) and *The Earth Lover and Other Verses* (1932).

Pride and Prejudice A novel by JANE AUSTEN, written in 1796–7 under the title 'First Impressions', revised and finally published in 1813.

Mr and Mrs Bennet of Longbourn are an ill-matched couple, he detached and ironic, she gossipy and absorbed in finding husbands for their five daughters. Jane, the eldest, falls in love with the wealthy Charles Bingley but her sister, the witty and high-spirited Elizabeth, dislikes Bingley's still wealthier friend, FitzWilliam Darcy, for his coldness and arrogance. Her prejudice is confirmed by George Wickham, an engaging militia officer who describes the injustices he has suffered from Darcy. Finding the Bennets vulgar, Darcy and Bingley's sisters persuade him to abandon Jane. Elizabeth is briefly wooed by William Collins, a clergyman who will inherit Mr Bennet's property. He marries her friend, Charlotte Lucas, instead. On a visit to the couple Elizabeth again meets Darcy, staying with his aunt and Collins's patron, Lady Catherine de Bourgh. He falls in love with her but proposes so condescendingly that she refuses. In a letter he defends himself and exposes Wickham as an adventurer. The couple meet again when she visits his seat, Pemberley, during a tour of Derbyshire. His charm and grace begin to impress her. When her sister Lydia elopes with Wickham, Darcy helps to trace them and ensure that they marry. Bingley renews his courtship of Jane and, despite interference from Lady Catherine,

Darcy persists in his courtship of Elizabeth. Both couples are finally united.

Priestley, J(ohn) B(oynton) 1894–1984 English. He wrote over 60 books and more than 40 plays. His wide-ranging interest in England and the English character, and his appeal to 'the man in the street', made him one of the most popular 'middlebrow' authors of his day. His first success was *The Good Companions* (1929), a novel about three people who join a concert party. *Angel Pavement* (1930) is a more sombre tale of London. His best-known works for the stage are *Dangerous Corner* (1932), *I Have been Here Before* (1937) and *Time and the Conways* (1937), known collectively as the 'Time' plays because of the use they made of theories from J. W. Dunne's *An Experiment with Time* (1927). *Postscripts* (1940), *Britain Speaks* (1940) and *All England Listened* (1968) are selections from wartime broadcasts. Post-war publications include novels (*Festival at Farbridge*, 1951; *Saturn over the Water*, 1961; *It's an Old Country*, 1967) and criticism, including *The Art of the Dramatist* (1957) and *Literature and Western Man* (1960), influenced by Jung. *Martin Released* (1962) and *Instead of the Trees* (1977) are autobiographical.

Prime Minister, The The fifth of ANTHONY TROLLOPE'S PALLISER NOVELS, serialized in 1875–6 and published in volume form in 1876.

Emily Wharton defies her father to marry Ferdinand Lopez but discovers his dishonesty. Plantagenet Palliser, Duke of Omnium, becomes Prime Minister of an insecure coalition government, which Lady Glencora helps to sustain with lavish entertaining at Gatherum Castle. Her foolish encouragement of Lopez associates the duke with his affairs until Phineas Finn silences the gossip with an effective speech in the Commons. Meanwhile the financial affairs of Lopez and his partner deteriorate, and he commits suicide. In due course Emily marries Arthur Fletcher, her father's first choice for her, and the duke's coalition government falls. Too thin-skinned for party politics, the duke is a model of integrity, Trollope's 'perfect gentleman'.

Prime of Miss Jean Brodie, The A novel by MURIEL SPARK, published in 1961. Miss Jean Brodie, a schoolmistress in Edinburgh during the 1930s, fascinates her pupils at the Marcia Blaines School for Girls with her vigorously eccentric approach to teaching. Her 16-year-old charges, the 'Brodie set', are increasingly drawn into Miss Brodie's emotional life and her relationships with the two fellow masters, Teddy Lloyd and Gordon Lowther. Sandy Stranger has an affair with Lloyd during the summer of 1938 and betrays Miss Brodie to the headmistress, Miss Mackay, who dismisses her for teaching Fascism. The 'Brodie set' leave school to meet different and in some cases tragic fates but the colourful, morally ambiguous influence of

'Miss Jean Brodie in her prime' endures long after her death.

Prince and the Pauper, The: A Tale for Young People of All Ages A novel by MARK TWAIN, published in England in 1881 and in the USA in 1882. In the last years of Henry VIII's reign, Prince Edward and Tom Canty, a pauper, exchange places by mistake. Edward sees at first hand the wretchedness of the poor and the cruelty of the law. He manages to establish his identity in time for his coronation after Henry's death, and during his brief reign does his best to keep in mind his experiences as a pauper.

Prince of Abyssinia, The See RASSELAS.

Princess Casamassima, The A novel by HENRY JAMES, serialized in 1885–6 and published in volume form in 1886.

Set in London in the 1880s, it portrays characters from all classes. The hero is Hyacinth Robinson, an orphan brought up by a poor dressmaker, Miss Pynsent. He meets Paul Muniment, a proletarian revolutionary, and joins a secret society, through which he also comes into contact with Christina, the Princess Casamassima, an American expatriate separated from her Italian husband. (She had previously appeared in an earlier novel, RODERICK HUDSON.) European travels alter his views, but he is ordered to assassinate a duke. The Princess Casamassima visits his apartment to offer to take his place, but Hyacinth has already killed himself.

Prisoner of Zenda, The A novel by ANTHONY HOPE, published in 1894. It follows the swashbuckling adventures of Rudolf Rassendyll, an Englishman whose striking resemblance to the King of Ruritania helps thwart a plot to usurp the throne by Black Michael and Rupert of Hentzau. *Rupert of Hentzau* (1898) is a sequel.

Pritchett, Sir V(ictor) S(awdon) 1900–97 English. Although he also published travel books, journalism and biographies, he is best known for the short stories collected in such volumes as *The Spanish Virgin and Other Stories* (1932), *You Make Your Own Life* (1938), *It May Never Happen* (1945), *When My Girl Comes Home* (1961) and *The Camberwell Beauty* (1974). *Dead Man Leading* (1937) and *Mr Beluncle* (1951) are novels. His criticism includes studies of GEORGE MEREDITH (1970), Balzac (1973) and Turgenev (1977), and *The Complete Essays* (1991). *A Cab at the Door* (1968) is a notable autobiography.

Private Memoirs and Confessions of a Justified Sinner, The A novel by JAMES HOGG, published in 1824. It is the most ambitious, and now the most widely read, of his prose works.

Set in late 17th-century Scotland, the story is divided into two main parts. The first contains the 'editor's narrative' of the strife-torn marriage of the Lord of Dalcastle and the murder of his son and heir, George Colwan, in circumstances pointing to the complicity of his half-brother Robert Wringhim, a Calvinist bigot. The second part consists of Wringhim's own memoir, discovered in his grave a century after his presumed suicide. It reveals how, with the aid of a malign *alter ego*, or *doppelgänger*, who persuaded him he was doing God's work, he murdered first a preacher, then his brother, and then apparently his mother. Wringhim gradually realizes that the companion is really the Devil, who appears to have claimed him in the end.

Private Papers of Henry Ryecroft, The A semi-autobiographical novel by GEORGE GISSING, published in 1903. It takes the form of a journal kept by a recluse who has been helped by a legacy from a friend to withdraw from the London literary world where he had failed as a writer.

Professor, The CHARLOTTE BRONTË's first completed novel, written in 1846 but not published until 1857. It draws on the same experiences that she later used more successfully in *VILLETTE*. An Englishman, William Crimsworth, goes to Brussels as a schoolmaster and falls in love with Frances Henri, a fellow teacher and Anglo-Swiss girl.

Proulx, E(dna) Annie 1935– American. Her only collection of short fiction, *Heart Songs and Other Stories* (1988), is set in the harsh regions of northern New England. *Postcards* (1992), her first novel, evokes the life of Loyal Blood, heir to a New England farm he has left behind in favour of thirty years' wandering. *The Shipping News* (1993; PULITZER PRIZE), is set in Newfoundland, to which, Quoyle, a failed journalist, moves with his daughters after his wife's accidental death in a car crash. *Accordion Crimes* (1996), rich in the social and cultural observation which characterizes all her work, is about a series of immigrants who successively own an accordion made by an Italian immigrant before he died at the hands of gangsters. Proulx has also published non-fiction dealing with gardening, wine-making and bartering.

Provost, The A novel by JOHN GALT, published in 1822. An essay in sustained irony, it displays his rich humour, ready sympathy and fine command of the Scots vernacular. The story is narrated by Mr Pawkie, who has three times reached the office of provost (mayor). He unwittingly reveals his own canny nature as he reflects on his progress through public life and contrasts the sophistication of the wider world of business and politics with the manners and speech of provincial Scotland.

Puck of Pook's Hill A collection of 10 stories and accompanying poems by RUDYARD KIPLING, published in 1906. It was intended for both adults and children. The meeting of two children, Dan and Una (loosely modelled on Kipling's own children), with the nature spirit Puck provides the framework for tales reaching back in

English history, past the Normans and Saxons to the Roman invaders. Most show individuals who are able to illuminate their historical predicaments, and point to the capacity of civilization to renew itself. A sequel, *Rewards and Fairies* (1910), followed a similar format. Both volumes contain some of Kipling's best-known verse. 'A St Helena's Lullaby', 'The Way through the Woods' and 'If', in the latter volume, have been much admired.

Pudd'nhead Wilson, The Tragedy of A novel by MARK TWAIN, published in 1894.

The title character is a lawyer, David Wilson, called 'Pudd'nhead' by a community – Dawson's Landing, Missouri, in the 1830s – which ridicules his eccentric ideas. The story of confused identities chiefly concerns Tom (son of the slave-owner Percy Driscoll) and Chambers (son of the slave Roxana and a Virginian gentleman). Roxana She switches the two when they are babies, and on the death of Percy his brother Judge Driscoll adopts Chambers, believing him to be Tom. Chambers grows up to be a bully, a liar and a coward. Finally he murders Judge Driscoll and popular opinion fixes the crime on Luigi, one of a pair of aristocratic Italian twins who have recently arrived in the town. Using fingerprints, Wilson uncovers the real facts of the case, establishes the true identities of Chambers and Tom, and becomes a town celebrity. The disgraced Chambers is sold down the river as a slave and Roxy is supported by her surrogate son, Tom.

Pulitzer Prizes A group of American literary prizes awarded annually to works published the previous year, in the following categories: fiction, drama, poetry, history, biography and general non-fiction (or journalism). They were founded in 1917 as part of the bequest with which the newspaper proprietor Joseph Pulitzer (1847–1911) established the Columbia University School of Journalism. The prizes for poetry and for journalism were added to the original categories in 1921 and 1962 respectively. The original terms of the fiction prize were relaxed in 1932 to allow novels without a specifically American setting to be considered and in 1947 to embrace collections of short stories as well as novels.

The first award was made in 1918 to a forgotten writer, Ernest Poole, for a forgotten novel, *His Family*, published the previous year. Major novelists among the subsequent prize-winners included EDITH WHARTON for *THE AGE OF INNOCENCE* (published in 1920), WILLA CATHER for *One of Ours* (1922), SINCLAIR LEWIS for *Arrowsmith* (1925), THORNTON WILDER for *The Bridge of San Luis Rey* (1927), as well as twice more for his plays, and JOHN STEINBECK for *THE GRAPES OF WRATH* (1939). Any list of prescient choices would mention the award to ROBERT PENN WARREN for *All the King's Men* (1946), yet several major writers have been acknowledged only belatedly: ERNEST HEMINGWAY had to wait until *The Old Man and the Sea* (1952) and WILLIAM FAULKNER until *A Fable* (1954), while F. SCOTT FITZGERALD was never honoured. Conservative attitudes sometimes created a preference for safe best-sellers, such as EDNA FERBER's *So Big* (1924), Margaret Mitchell's *GONE WITH THE WIND* (1936), JOHN HERSEY's *A Bell for Adano* (1944), JAMES A. MICHENER's *Tales of the South Pacific* (1947), Herman Wouk's *The Caine Mutiny* (1951) and Allen Drury's *Advise and Consent* (1959).

Latterly, however, awards have sometimes also been made to more daring works. Winners in recent decades include WILLIAM STYRON's *The Confessions of Nat Turner* (1967), N. SCOTT MOMADAY's *House Made of Dawn* (1968), WALLACE STEGNER's *Angle of Repose* (1971), EUDORA WELTY's *The Optimist's Daughter* (1972), THOMAS PYNCHON's *GRAVITY'S RAINBOW* (1973), SAUL BELLOW's *Humboldt's Gift* (1975), NORMAN MAILER's *THE EXECUTIONER'S SONG* (1979), JOHN KENNEDY TOOLE's *A Confederacy of Dunces* (1980), JOHN UPDIKE's *Rabbit is Rich* (1981) and *Rabbit at Rest* (1990), ALICE WALKER's *The Color Purple* (1982), WILLIAM KENNEDY's *Ironweed* (1983), ALISON LURIE's *Foreign Affairs* (1984), LARRY MCMURTRY's *Lonesome Dove* (1985), PETER TAYLOR's *A Summons to Memphis* (1986), TONI MORRISON's *BELOVED* (1987), ANNE TYLER's *Breathing Lessons* (1988), OSCAR HIJUELOS' *The Mambo Kings Play Songs of Love* (1989), JANE SMILEY's *A Thousand Acres* (1991), ROBERT OLEN BUTLER's *A Good Scent from a Strange Mountain* (1992), E. ANNIE PROULX's *The Shipping News* (1993), CAROL SHIELDS's *The Stone Diaries* (1994), RICHARD FORD's *Independence Day* (1995) and STEVEN MILLHAUSER's *Martin Dressler* (1996).

Punch's Prize Novelists Parodies of contemporary novelists by WILLIAM MAKEPEACE THACKERAY, published in *Punch* in 1847 and later retitled *Novels by Eminent Hands*. The targets include BULWER LYTTON, JAMES FENIMORE COOPER, G. P. R. JAMES, CHARLES LEVER and BENJAMIN DISRAELI, whose *CONINGSBY* is mocked in 'Codlingsby'. Thackeray's playful critique throws light on his intentions and achievements in *VANITY FAIR*, written at the same time.

Purdy, James 1923– American. Much of his fiction focuses on small-town provincial America. It includes: *63: A Dream Palace* (1956); *Malcolm* (1959); *The Nephew* (1960); *Cabot Wright Begins* (1964); *Eustace Chisholm and the Works* (1967); *I am Elijah Thrush* (1972); a trilogy, *Sleepers in Moon-Crowned Valleys*, comprising *Jeremy's Version* (1970), *The House of the Solitary Maggot* (1974) and *Mourners Below* (1981); *On Glory's Course* (1984); *In the Hollow of His Hand* (1986); *Garments the Living Wear* (1989); *Out With the Stars* (1992); and *Gertrude of Stony Island Avenue* (1997). He has also published poetry, plays and short stories, collected as *The Candle of Your Eyes* (1987).

Pym, Barbara (Mary Crampton) 1913–80 English. After success with novels such as *Excellent Women* (1952) and *A Glass of Blessings* (1958) she fell out of favour until, with the publication of *Quartet in Autumn* (1977), her work was championed by PHILIP LARKIN. *The Sweet Dove Died* (1979) was followed by four post-humous novels, *A Few Green Leaves* (1980), *An Unsuitable Attachment* (1982), *Crampton Hodnet* (1985) and *An Academic Question* (1986). Her books are wistful, delicate comedies with an unsparingly sad undertow; frustration in love is their common theme and the intrigue-ridden world of middle-class churchgoing a distinctive milieu.

Pynchon, Thomas 1937– American. Though he is not prolific, his work is inventive and highly regarded for its contribution to POST-MODERNISM. It includes: *V.* (1963), a long, dark-toned fantasy; *The Crying of Lot 49* (1966), about the attempts of the modern mind to organize an apparently chaotic universe; *GRAVITY'S RAINBOW* (1973; PULITZER PRIZE); *Vineland* (1990), a shorter and more conventional narrative; and *Mason & Dixon* (1997), about the surveying expedition by Charles Mason and Jeremiah Dixon in the 18th century. *Slow Learner* (1984) is a collection of stories.

Q See QUILLER-COUCH, SIR ARTHUR.

Queen, Ellery The pseudonym which the American writers Frederic Dannay (1905–82) and Manfred B(ennington) Lee (1905–71) used for DETECTIVE FICTION. Together they published 30 novels and many short stories about a detective bearing the same name they had chosen as their pseudonym. *The Roman Hat Mystery* (1929) and other early novels are thickly plotted Golden Age puzzles which make Ellery Queen a light-hearted dilettante owing a good deal to S. S. VAN DINE's Philo Vance. Later novels – notably in the period announced by *Calamity Town* (1942) and ended with *The Finishing Stroke* (1958) – aimed at greater realism. The most enduring achievement connected with their name, however, may well be *Ellery Queen's Mystery Magazine*, which under Dannay's editorship from 1941 until his death achieved an unsurpassed record for publishing short stories by new and established writers. Dannay and Lee also collaborated as Barnaby Ross, and Dannay published an autobiographical novel, *The Golden Summer* (1953), as Daniel Nathan.

Quentin Durward A novel by SIR WALTER SCOTT, published in 1823. Its background is the rivalry between Louis XI and Charles the Bold, Duke of Burgundy, in 15th-century France. Quentin Durward, a young Scot in the king's guard, conducts the Burgundian heiress, Isabelle de Croye, to the protection of the Bishop of Liège. Their journey is beset by dangers from the duke and also from the villainy of the king's servant, William de la Marck, the Wild Boar of the Ardennes. Quentin kills de la Marck and wins Isabelle's hand, and Louis outwits the duke.

Question of Power, A A novel by BESSIE HEAD, published in 1973. She acknowledged its strongly autobiographical nature. Focused entirely on the inner world of the protagonist Elizabeth, it documents her journey through mental illness to recovery. Her consciousness is filled with a cast of characters personifying good and evil, drawn from various mythologies and religions, who alternately torment and teach her. Running parallel to this nightmare world is the daytime world of Elizabeth's life in her Botswanan village. She eventually asserts the primacy of the ordinary over those who maintain power over others for whatever reason.

Quiet American, The A novel by GRAHAM GREENE, published in 1955. The narrator is Thomas Fowler, a cynical, middle-aged English journalist in Vietnam during the French war against the Vietminh. His story concerns the murder of Alden Pyle (the Quiet American), a naive and high-minded idealist. It alternates between the aftermath of Pyle's death and the events leading up to it. Pyle has stolen Fowler's mistress, Phuong, and become involved in subversive politics. When Fowler learns of his part in a bomb explosion in a local café, he lays information which prompts Pyle's murder. At the end, Fowler finds himself in a position to marry Phuong, but is left wishing that 'there existed someone to whom I could say that I was sorry'.

Quiller-Couch, Sir Arthur 1863–1944 English. He was better known by his pseudonym, Q. After working in journalism he returned to his native Cornwall in 1892 and used it as background for novels which include *Dead Man's Rock* (1887), *Troy Town* (1888), *The Splendid Spur* (1889) and *The Ship of Stars* (1899). Volumes of poetry include *Verses and Parodies* (1893), *Poems and Ballads* (1896) and *The Vigil of Venus* (1912). *The Oxford Book of English Verse* (1900) was the first of several famous anthologies he compiled for Oxford University Press. He was knighted for political services in 1910 and appointed the first King Edward VII Professor of English Literature at Cambridge in 1912. Two volumes of lectures, *On the Art of Writing* (1916) and *On the Art of Reading* (1920), enjoyed great popularity.

R

Rabbit tetralogy Four novels by JOHN UPDIKE, published at ten-year intervals, tracing the life and trials of Harry (Rabbit) Angstrom through four decades of contemporary American history. *Rabbit Run* (1960) tells the story of Rabbit's quest for identity amidst the conformism of the 1950s. *Rabbit Redux* (1971) deals with Rabbit's failing marriage and his relationship to Skeeter, a black revolutionary. In *Rabbit is Rich* (1981) an affluent Rabbit is forced to examine his relationship to his son and lost love in the inflationary 1970s. In *Rabbit at Rest* (1990) Rabbit, beset by his obsessions and an overriding sense that he has lived only on the surface, experiences an epiphanic perception of the significance of his life at the moment of death. *Rabbit is Rich* and *Rabbit at Rest* both won the PULITZER PRIZE.

Radcliffe, Ann 1764–1823 English. Although she did not originate the GOTHIC NOVEL, she established herself as its best-known and most popular exponent with six works: *The Castles of Athlin and Dunbayne* (1789), *A Sicilian Romance* (1790), *The Romance of the Forest* (1791), THE MYSTERIES OF UDOLPHO (1794), *The Italian* (1797) and the posthumously published *Gaston de Blondeville* (1826). Her persecuted heroines, wild and lonely settings, cliff-hanging chapter endings and apparently supernatural events became widely imitated conventions. Mrs Radcliffe also wrote verse, included in her novels and collected in two volumes (1834). *A Journey Made in the Summer of 1794 through Holland and the Western Frontier of Germany* (1795) shows the same mastery of landscape description as her novels.

Ragged Trousered Philanthropists, The: *Being the Story of Twelve Months in Hell, Told by One of the Damned* A novel published in 1914 under the pseudonym of 'Robert Tressall' (as the name was then spelled). It is the work of Robert Noonan (1870–1911). During its complex publishing history the book appeared in various mutilated and increasingly truncated forms. The first reliable text – restoring the author's preferred spelling of his pseudonym, as 'Robert Tressell' – was published in 1955.

A passionate and bitter satire, the book was originally hailed as the first great British working-class novel, although it later emerged that Noonan was not working-class. The 'philanthropists' of the title are the building workers of Mugsborough (a thinly disguised Hastings, where Noonan worked) who 'donate' their skill, labour, health and the well-being of their families to the capitalist bosses who exploit them. Frank Owen, a skilled decorator and self-educated socialist, tries to open his fellow-workers' eyes to their unwitting part in a brutal and corrupt social order. Offered the chance of working on a grand new house which is, in fact, a shoddy sham, he is torn between principle and the desire to make something of genuine beauty. The town, the house and the workers assume mythic proportions and become the stuff of tragedy.

Ragtime A novel by E. L. DOCTOROW, published in 1975. Its portrait of the years leading up to World War I deals with both the fluidity of American culture and its stifling insistence on racial conformity. The competing central narratives contrast the rise of a Jewish socialist immigrant, Tateh, who becomes a film-maker with the fate of a black piano player, Coalhouse Walker, Jr, finally driven to attack J. P. Morgan's library. The richly anecdotal course of the book embraces historical events such as the shooting in 1906 of the architect Stanford White by the millionaire Harry K. Thaw, in a jealous quarrel over Thaw's wife Evelyn Nesbit, and appearances by historical figures such as Harry Houdini, Freud and Jung, Scott Joplin, J. P. Morgan, Henry Ford, Emma Goldman, Thomas Edison, Booker T. Washington, Emiliano Zapata and Archduke Ferdinand.

Railway Children, The See NESBIT, E.

Rainbow, The A novel by D. H. LAWRENCE, published in 1915. It chronicles the lives of three generations of the Brangwen family in Nottinghamshire during a period which spans the transition from rural to urban culture.

Tom Brangwen inherits Marsh Farm in the Erewash Valley and marries a Polish widow, Lydia, who already has a daughter, Anna. Tom becomes devoted to Anna but estranged from his wife, even after the birth of two sons, Tom and Fred. Anna marries Will Brangwen, Tom's nephew, but after a rapturous honeymoon the couple grow apart and Anna devotes herself to her children. The narrative concentrates increasingly on the growth of the oldest child, Ursula. She goes to university and becomes a teacher, and has an unsatisfactory affair with Anton Skrebensky, an army officer. They are separated by the end of the novel and Ursula is left, alone and recovering from illness, to contemplate a rainbow: 'the earth's new architecture' symbolically sweeping away 'the old, brittle corruption of houses and factories'. Ursula and her younger sister Gudrun reappear in WOMEN IN LOVE.

Although Lawrence's publisher had forced him to make changes to his original text, *The Rainbow* was prosecuted and banned for obscenity; unsold copies were destroyed. A scene involving the pregnant Anna gave particular offence. The novel was reissued in 1926 from an American edition which had been further censored.

Raj Quartet, The See SCOTT, PAUL.

Rand, Ayn 1905–82 Born in St Petersburg, she emigrated to the USA in 1926. She first attracted a popular audience with a novel, *The Fountainhead* (1943), whose hero owed something to the personality of the architect Frank Lloyd Wright. She advocated her belief that humans are rational, self-interested and pledged to individualism in a variety of works: *Atlas Shrugged* (1957), a novel about the dangers of altruism; *The Objectivist*, a journal she founded in 1962; and *The Ayn Rand Letter* (1971–82). Her views earned her a cult following among libertarians. Critical works include *For the New Intellectual* (1961), *The Virtue of Selfishness* (1965) and *The New Left: The Anti-Industrial Revolution* (1971).

Ransome, Arthur (Michell) 1884–1967 English. His work in Russia produced *Old Peter's Russian Tales* (1916) and an account of the Bolshevik Revolution, *Six Weeks in Russia* (1919). *Swallows and Amazons* (1931) was the first in a series of children's adventure stories reflecting his enthusiasm for sailing, the outdoor life and those parts of England (the Lake District, the Norfolk Broads) which favour such activities. Other titles in this vein included *Pigeon Post* (1936), *We Didn't Mean to Go to Sea* (1938), *The Big Six* (1940), and *Great Northern?* (1947). Ransome also wrote *Racundra's First Cruise* (1923) and *Mainly about Fishing* (1959). Rupert Hart-Davis edited *The Autobiography of Arthur Ransome* (1976).

Rao, Raja 1908– Indian. His early stories were in Kannada and English, the latter published as *The Cow of the Barricades* (1947) and *The Policeman and the Rose* (1978). His expansive novels include *Kanthapura* (1938), THE SERPENT AND THE ROPE (1960; awarded a SAHITYA AKADEMI prize), *The Cat and Shakespeare* (1965) and *Comrade Kirillov* (1976; in French translation, 1965). Later works, such as *The Chessmaster and His Moves* (1988) and *On the Ganga Ghat* (1989), a collection of stories, require stamina and patience.

Rasselas, Prince of Abyssinia, The History of A philosophical romance by Samuel Johnson (1709–84), scholar, critic, lexicographer, poet and man of letters. Published in 1759, as *The Prince of Abyssinia: A Tale*, it is said to have been written in the evenings of a single week to pay for his mother's funeral. The exotic setting ensured it instant success.

The book tackles Johnson's habitual theme of the 'choice of life'. Rasselas, son of the Abyssinian Emperor, determines to seek the world outside the luxurious 'happy valley' to which he has been confined, setting out full of theoretical hopes and fruitless meditations with his sister Nekayah and the elderly philosopher Imlac. His romantic notions are contradicted by the miseries, hardships and disappointments of the real world. The plot itself is slender, but the whole work is invigorated by Johnson's robust common sense and occasional glints of humour. Idealism and innocence, the pastoral values, are gently deflated. 'The Conclusion, in which Nothing is concluded' illustrates the book's deliberate structure, and affirms Johnson's conviction that action is superior to introspection.

Ellis Cornelia Knight (1757–1837), associated with Johnson and his circle in her youth, provided a romantic continuation of *Rasselas* in *Dinarbas* (1790).

Rattlin the Reefer A novel by the English writer Edward Howard (?1791–1841), published in 1836. The story resembles the more famous novels of the sea by CAPTAIN FREDERICK MARRYAT, whose shipmate Howard had been. Marryat himself thought enough of the book to prepare it for publication, describing it as 'Edited by the author of *Peter Simple*'.

Raven, Simon 1927– English. A prolific writer, whose rakish wit quickly earned him a name as an *enfant terrible*, he consolidated his reputation with two ROMANS FLEUVES: the 10-volume *Alms for Oblivion*, beginning with *Fielding Gray* (1967) and ending with *The Survivors* (1976); and the 7-volume *The First-born of Egypt*, beginning with *Morning Star* (1984) and ending with *The Troubadour* (1992). His work for television includes an adaptation of TROLLOPE'S PALLISER NOVELS (1974).

Raymond, Derek See COOK, ROBIN.

Read, Piers Paul 1941– English. He is the son of the critic and poet Sir Herbert Read (1893–1968). Coloured by his Catholicism, his novels are sternly moralistic and almost Victorian, not just in their assiduously realized social colour and probing of conscience but also in their extravagant plot contrivance. *A Married Man* (1979) is a study of a barrister in mid-life crisis, while *The Upstart* (1973) is a BILDUNGSROMAN. His interest in European affairs has prompted: *Polonaise* (1976), about Nazi collaboration in Poland; *A Season in the West* (1988), about a dissident Czech writer seeking asylum in Britain; and *Knights of the Cross* (1997), about a German plot for mastery of a United Europe.

Reade, Charles 1814–84 English. The various offices he held at Magdalen College, Oxford, did not distract him from a vigorous career in literature. His interest in theatre management led to collaboration with Tom Taylor in several plays, beginning with *Masks and Faces* (1852), which he turned into a novel, *Peg Woffington* (1853). His first success as a novelist came with *It is Never Too Late to Mend* (1856), intended to reform prisons. Other ROMANS À THÈSE included: *Hard Cash* (1863), attacking abuses in private lunatic asylums; *Foul Play* (1868), about abuses at sea; *Put Yourself in His Place* (1870), attacking

Trade Union closed shops; *A Terrible Temptation* (1871), returning to the attack on private asylums; and *A Woman-Hater* (1877), about the disadvantages of village life.

Still involved in the theatre, he dramatized several of his novels, including *Griffith Gaunt* (1866), which he considered his best work, and collaborated with Dion Boucicault. Ill-health made him turn to short stories but did not prevent him writing *Hang in Haste, Repent at Leisure* (1877), a series of letters which led to the reprieve of four people condemned to death for murder, and adapting Zola's *L'Assommoir* for the English stage as *Drink*. Unflaggingly energetic, fiercely polemical and cannily commercial, he was ranked with DICKENS and GEORGE ELIOT in his day. Now he is remembered, if at all, for *THE CLOISTER AND THE HEARTH* (1861), his most carefully researched foray into HISTORICAL FICTION.

Reade, (William) Winwood 1838–75 English. The nephew of CHARLES READE, he made his name with *The Martyrdom of Man* (1872), a history of civilization frankly hostile to religion. It remained popular for some years after his early death. His novels, fantastically plotted and often attacked by reviewers for their handling of both sex and religion, are *Charlotte and Myra: A Puzzle in Six Bits* (1859), *Liberty Hall, Oxon.* (1860), *See Saw* (1865) and *The Outcast* (1875), debating matters of faith and doubt. His travel books deal with his experiences in Africa, where he studied the habits of the gorilla.

realism A term first used in France in the 1850s for literature concerned with representing the world as it is rather than as it ought to be. Realism observes and documents contemporary life and everyday scenes as objectively as possible in low-key, unrhetorical prose and reproduces the flavour of colloquial speech in its dialogue. Though realist writers may portray characters from all social levels, they often look to the lowest social classes and take cruelty or suffering as their subject.

Realism became the dominant mode of the 19th-century European novel and, from the late 1880s, the theatre as well. The great works of European realist fiction include Flaubert's *Sentimental Education*, Tolstoy's *Anna Karenina* and Dostoevsky's *Crime and Punishment*. Accurate observation and attention to the structures of society make GEORGE ELIOT's *MIDDLEMARCH* a notable English example. The chief American realists are WILLIAM DEAN HOWELLS and SINCLAIR LEWIS, while the line of English realist writing continues in the 20th century via ARNOLD BENNETT to the post-World War II evocations of English middle-class life by ANGUS WILSON and the Northern working-class fiction of the 1950s. Realism in drama – associated with the names of Ibsen and Strindberg – played an important part in reviving the English theatre in the first decade of this century (Harley Granville-Barker, JOHN GALSWORTHY) and again in the 1950s (John Osborne and his generation). In Ireland Sean O'Casey and in America Eugene O'Neill and Arthur Miller developed native versions of dramatic realism. See also NATURALISM.

Rebecca of Sunnybrook Farm See WIGGIN, KATE DOUGLAS.

Rebel Angels, The See CORNISH TRILOGY, THE.

Rechy, John (Francisco) 1934– American. His work generally portrays the homosexual communities of major cities such as New York and Los Angeles. It includes *City of Night* (1963), *Numbers* (1967), *This Day's Death* (1969), *The Vampires* (1971), *The Fourth Angel* (1973), *Rushes* (1979), *Bodies and Souls* (1983), *Marilyn's Daughter* (1988), *The Miraculous Day of Amalia Gómez* (1991) and *Our Lady of Babylon* (1996). He has also published a study of urban homosexual lifestyles, *The Sexual Outlaw* (1977).

Red Badge of Courage, The A novel by STEPHEN CRANE, published in 1895. Set during the American Civil War, it contrasts the frightening realities of battle with conventional war narratives. Eager for glory, Henry Fleming enlists in the Union army but flees from his second encounter with the enemy into the forest. There he attempts to find solace in Nature, but fails to justify his desertion in his own eyes. A meeting with a dying soldier sparks his anger at the injustices of war. He returns, marked by the 'red badge' of a soldier who has fought, and behaves heroically but without pride in his heroics. He remains haunted by the memory of the 'tattered' soldier, a wounded man deserted on the field.

Redburn: His First Voyage A novel by HERMAN MELVILLE, published in 1849. It draws on his own first voyage as an apprentice seaman. Wellingborough Redburn ships from New York on the *Highlander*, a trader bound for Liverpool. He is treated with indifference and cruelty by Captain Riga and his fellow seamen, particularly Jackson. After finding appalling poverty in Liverpool, Redburn goes to London with Harry Bolton, a spendthrift aristocrat. The pair join the *Highlander* for its return voyage to America. Jackson's treacheries continue, though he dies as they near New York. Captain Riga cheats Harry and Redburn out of their wages.

Redgauntlet An EPISTOLARY NOVEL by SIR WALTER SCOTT, published in 1824. The background to the story is the supposed return to Scotland of the Young Pretender after the defeat of the 1745 rebellion. Herries of Birrenswork (Sir Edward Redgauntlet), a fanatical Jacobite, kidnaps Sir Arthur Darsie Redgauntlet, his nephew and the head of the family, but Alan Fairford sets out to rescue his friend. The novel includes 'Wandering Willie's Tale', a classic ghost story.

Reed, Ishmael (Scott) 1938– African-American. Combining surrealism and angry satire, his novels aspire to break the cycle of oppression of

American minorities. They include *The Free-Lance Pall-Bearers* (1967), *Yellow Back Radio Broke-Down* (1969), *Mumbo-Jumbo* (1972), *The Last Days of Louisiana Red* (1974), *Flight to Canada* (1976), *The Terrible Twos* (1982), *Reckless Eyeballing* (1986), *The Terrible Threes* (1989) and *Japanese by Spring* (1993). His poetry includes *Catechism of D Neo-American HooDoo Church* (1970), *Chattanooga* (1973), *A Secretary to the Spirits* (1978) and *New and Collected Poems* (1988). *Shrovetide in New Orleans* (1978), *God Made Alaska for the Indians* (1982) and *Airing Dirty Laundry* (1993) are collections of essays.

Reed, Jeremy 1954– English. He established himself as a poet but has also produced prose combining fiction, biography, autobiography and criticism. His preoccupation with Decadent and often homosexual authors inspires *Isidore* (1991), about Lautréamont, *When the Whip Comes Down* (1992), about the Marquis de Sade, and *Chasing Black Rainbows* (1994), about Antonin Artaud. Connections between sexual ambivalence, drugs and art inform *The Lipstick Boys* (1984) and *Inhabiting Shadows* (1990), as well as unconventional biographies of Rimbaud (1991) and Lou Reed (1994). *Diamond Nebula* (1994) uses SCIENCE FICTION to transcend rigid categories of gender, sexuality and identity.

Reed, Talbot Baines 1852–93 English. *The Fifth Form at St Dominic's* (1887), *Cock House at Fellsgarth* (1891) and *The Master of the Shell* (1894) are boys' stories glamorizing public-school life.

Reeve, Clara 1729–1807 English. She earned herself an important place in the development of the GOTHIC NOVEL with *The Champion of Virtue* (1777; republished as *The Old English Baron*, 1778). Other novels were *The Two Mentors* (1783), *The Exiles* (1788), *The School for Widows* (1791), *Memoirs of Sir Roger de Clarendon* (1793) and *Destination* (1799).

Reid, Forrest 1875–1947 Irish. Most of his 16 novels are centred on childhood and set their values against those of the decaying commercial society of north-east Ulster. *Peter Waring* (1937) is widely regarded as his best work, although the Tom Barber trilogy, *Uncle Stephen* (1931), *The Retreat* (1936) and *Young Tom* (1944), is almost as well known. His autobiographies, *Apostate* (1926) and *Private Road* (1940), are steeped in the nostalgia which characterizes the best of his fiction.

Reid, Captain (Thomas) Mayne 1818–83 Born in County Down (Ireland), he travelled in the USA and fought in the Mexican-American war before settling in Britain. He drew on his American adventures in popular novels for boys, notably *The Rifle Rangers: or, Adventures in Southern Mexico* (1850), *The Scalp Hunters: or, Romantic Adventures in Northern Mexico* (1851), *The Boy Hunters* (1853), *The Maroon* (1862), *The Cliff-Climbers* (1864), *Afloat in the Forest* (1865), *The Headless Horseman* (1866), *The Castaways* (1870) and *Gwen-Wynne* (1877). *The Quadroon: or, A Lover's Adventure in Louisiana*

(1856) was adapted for the stage by Dion Boucicault as *The Octoroon* (1859). He also wrote travel books, poetry, plays and a book on croquet (1863).

Reid, V(ictor) S(tafford) 1913–87 Jamaican. With ROGER MAIS and the sculptress Edna Manley, he was a member of the Focus group which helped to promote a sense of cultural nationalism in Jamaica in the 1940s. His first novel, *New Day* (1949), was seminal in the development of Caribbean fiction. The first work to use Creole as its narrative medium, it describes changes in Jamaican society between 1865, the date of the Morant Bay rebellion, and 1944, when a new constitution was introduced. Reid's other novels include: *The Leopard* (1958), set in Kenya at the time of the Mau Mau freedom fighters' struggle; *Sixty-Five* (1960), a children's novel about the Morant Bay rebellion; *Peter of Mount Ephraim* (1971); and *The Jamaicans* (1976).

Renault, Mary [Challans, Eileen Mary] 1905–83 English. She emigrated to South Africa in 1948. Her reputation rests mainly on her lively but learned HISTORICAL FICTION about the ancient world: *The Last of the Wine* (1956), *The King Must Die* (1958) and *The Bull from the Sea* (1962; winner of the CNA LITERARY AWARD), about Theseus; *The Lion in the Gateway* (1964), for young people; *The Mask of Apollo* (1966), *Fire from Heaven* (1970), *The Persian Boy* (1972) and *Funeral Games* (1981), about Alexander; and *The Praise Singer* (1978). *The Charioteer* (1953) is about servicemen and homosexuality during World War II.

Rendell, Ruth [Baroness Rendell] 1930– English. She has established a reputation with talented and prolific DETECTIVE FICTION which falls into several categories. A popular series, begun in *From Doon with Death* (1965) and still continuing with *Road Rage* (1997), features Detective Chief Inspector Reginald Wexford of the Kingsmarkham police. In contrast to its conventional reliance on police procedure, other novels have treated crime in deliberately unsettling ways. Notable titles have included *To Fear a Painted Devil* (1965), *One Across, Two Down* (1971), *The Face of Trespass* (1974), *A Demon in My View* (1976), *Make Death Love Me* (1979), *Master of the Moor* (1982) and *The Bridesmaid* (1989). Similar preoccupations have been yet more freely treated in the novels Rendell has published under the pseudonym of Barbara Vine; they include *A Dark-Adapted Eye* (1986), *A Fatal Inversion* (1987), *The House of Stairs* (1988) *Gallowglass* (1990), *King Solomon's Carpet* (1991), *Asta's Book* (1993), *No Night is Too Long* (1994) and *The Brimstone Wedding* (1996). She was made a life peer in 1997.

Return of the King, The See LORD OF THE RINGS, THE.

Return of the Native, The A novel by THOMAS HARDY, published in 1878. It is set on Egdon Heath.

Damon Wildeve, an engineer turned landlord of 'The Quiet Woman', carries on an affair with Eustacia Vye but marries the gentle Thomasin Yeobright. Clym Yeobright, Thomasin's cousin, wearies of life in Paris and returns to the heath intending to become a schoolmaster. He marries Eustacia, but his sight fails and he is reduced to furze-cutting for a livelihood. In despair she renews her association with Wildeve and becomes partially responsible for the death of Clym's mother. She leaves home and drowns herself in Shadwater Weir; Wildeve dies trying to save her. The remorseful Clym becomes an open-air preacher and Thomasin marries Diggory Venn, the 'isolated and weird' reddleman who moves in and out of the narrative.

Rhoda Fleming A novel by GEORGE MEREDITH, published in 1865. Rhoda and Dahlia, daughters of the widowed Farmer Fleming, come to London under the protection of their uncle, Anthony Hackbut. Edward Blancove seduces and deserts Dahlia. Her shame is deepened by a miserable marriage to the bigamous Sedgett and she attempts suicide. The self-willed, determined Rhoda marries an ex-soldier and farm-assistant, Robert Eccles. Several down-to-earth characters – among them Master Gammon, Mrs Sumfit and Mrs Boulby – enliven a sombre story.

Rhys, Jean 1894–1979 Born in Dominica, she came to Britain in 1909 and spent most of the inter-war years in Paris. Appearing after a long period of silence and artistic oblivion, her finest novel, WIDE SARGASSO SEA (1966), invents the tragic story of Rochester's mad wife in CHARLOTTE BRONTË's JANE EYRE. The same painful clarity in portraying personal, sexual and social exploitation marks her other writing. Earlier work includes the stories in The Left Bank (1927) and the novels Postures (1928; as Quartet in the USA, 1929 and subsequently), After Leaving Mr Mackenzie (1930), Voyage in the Dark (1934) and Good Morning, Midnight (1939). Later work includes Tigers are Better-looking (1968) and a finely designed collection of stories, Sleep It Off Lady (1976). Smile Please: An Unfinished Autobiography appeared in 1979, Letters 1931–1966 in 1984.

Rhys, John Llewellyn See JOHN LLEWELLYN RHYS PRIZE.

Ricci, Nino 1959– Canadian, of Italian parentage. Lives of the Saints (1990) is set in a remote village in the Italian Apennines and, through the eyes of the young narrator Vittorio, exposes the hypocrisy and superstition that underlie its veneer of Catholicism. In a Glass House (1993) is a sequel in which Vittorio goes to Canada and is reunited with his estranged father.

Rice, Anne 1941– American. Interview with the Vampire (1976) was the most successful of several late-1970s novels which reinterpreted the vampire as a heroic figure beset by existential angst. Her subsequent 'vampire chronicles', The Vampire Lestat (1985), Queen of the Damned (1988), The Tale of the Body Thief (1992) and Memnoch the Devil (1995), became best-sellers and inspired a curious cult of life-style fantasists. Her attempts to rework other traditional motifs of horror fiction in The Mummy, or Ramses the Damned (1989) and The Witching Hour (1990) were less successful. She has also published novels under the pseudonyms Anne Rampling and A. N. Roquelaure.

Rice, Elmer 1892–1967 American. He was primarily known as the author of more than 50 plays which experiment with theatrical devices, as well as embodying his devotion to social justice and liberal causes. On Trial (1914), his first, is often credited with introducing the technique later called flashback, while The Adding Machine (1923) helped to pioneer expressionism in the American theatre. Street Scene (1929) evokes a day in the life of a New York tenement. In addition, Rice wrote several novels. The first, A Voyage to Purilia (1930), is a dystopian fantasy prompted by his disillusioning experiences in Hollywood. It enjoyed a greater success in Britain than in the USA. Other novels include Imperial City (1937), about New York, and The Show Must Go On (1949), drawing on his knowledge of theatrical life.

Riceyman Steps A novel by ARNOLD BENNETT, published in 1923 and awarded the JAMES TAIT BLACK MEMORIAL PRIZE. It concentrates on the life of Henry Earlforward in and around the antiquarian bookshop he has inherited in Clerkenwell. In middle age he courts and marries Violet Arb but she fails to bring warmth into a household dominated by his miserliness. Only when he is near death can he acknowledge the effects of his life-denying passion. A contrast is offered by the life of the maidservant Elsie, who nurses and marries the shell-shocked Joe.

Rich Like Us A novel by NAYANTARA SAHGAL, published in 1985 and awarded a SAHITYA AKADEMI prize in 1986. Set during Indira Gandhi's State of Emergency (1976–7), it tells the story of Sonali, a conscientious civil servant exiled to a remote outpost, and of Rose, cockney mistress (later wife) of a Hindu business tycoon, who is murdered on the initiative of her stepson, in league with the new political bosses.

Richard Mahony, The Fortunes of A trilogy of novels by HENRY HANDEL RICHARDSON, consisting of Australia Felix (1917), The Way Home (1925) and Ultima Thule (1929), first published together in 1930.

Richard Townshend Mahony gives up his medical practice and emigrates to join the Australian gold rush in the 1850s. When prospecting proves fruitless, he opens a 'Diggers' Emporium', which prospers until he refuses to support the diggers in militant action against the authorities. His wife, Mary, persuades him to return to medicine, but he fails and retreats into himself, turning first to religion and then to spiritualism. When things seem at their lowest ebb some shares in a dubious mine soar in value and Mahony can return to Europe with Mary. Back in Australia, he learns that he is ruined because his agent has absconded. Hiding the full truth from Mary, he is eventually driven to mental and physical collapse. Mary, resolute and uncomplaining, works as a postmistress in a remote settlement, nursing her husband in the last weeks of his life.

Richards, David Adams 1950– Canadian. He has written about his native Maritime Canada and the tightly knit, often intense lives of its inhabitants in *The Coming of Winter* (1974), *Blood Ties* (1976) and the more ambitious *Lives of Short Duration* (1981). *Dancers at Night* (1978) is a volume of short stories. *Nights below Station Street* (1988) and *Evening Snow* (1990) are the first two books in a trilogy.

Richardson, Dorothy M(iller) 1873–1957 English. She is remembered for *Pilgrimage*, a sequence of novels tracing the life of its heroine, Miriam Henderson, which made an early use of STREAM OF CONSCIOUSNESS. The individual volumes are: *Pointed Roofs* (1915), *Backwater* (1916), *Honeycomb* (1917), *Interim* (1919), *The Tunnel* (1919), *Deadlock* (1921), *Revolving Lights* (1923), *The Trap* (1925), *Oberland* (1927), *Dawn's Left Hand* (1931), *Clear Horizon* (1935), *Dimple Hill* (1938) and the posthumously published *March Moonlight* (1967).

Richardson, Henry Handel [Richardson, Ethel Florence] 1870–1946 Australian. Born in Melbourne, she studied music in Germany and finally settled with her husband in London. Music supplies the background for *Maurice Guest* (1908) and *The Young Cosima* (1939). *The Getting of Wisdom* (1910) draws on her adolescence in Australia. She revisited the country only once, to ensure the authenticity of *Australia Felix* (1917), the first part of a trilogy completed in *The Way Home* (1925) and *Ultima Thule* (1929) and published as *THE FORTUNES OF RICHARD MAHONY* (1930). An autobiography, *Myself When Young* (1948), appeared after her death.

Richardson, Samuel 1689–1761 English. Although he was born in Derbyshire, his father was a London joiner and the family had returned to the capital by 1700. His father could not afford the classical education needed to make Richardson a clergyman, and he was bound apprentice to a printer in 1706. He proved diligent, marrying his master's daughter and setting up in business by himself as a master printer in 1721, and continued to prosper throughout his life. In 1754 he was elected Master of the Stationers' Company and in 1760 he purchased a share of the patent of the printer to the king. In later years he suffered from ill health which he considered nervous in origin. His virtues were those of the industrious apprentice; his weakness was agreed to be his vanity.

The Apprentice's Vade Mecum (1733), urging the ambitious youth to diligence, sobriety and self-denial, was followed by a didactic version of *Aesop's Fables*, an edition of *The Negotiations of Sir Thomas Roe in his Embassy to the Ottoman Port for the years 1621 to 1628 Inclusive* and an anonymous continuation of DANIEL DEFOE's *A Tour through the Whole Island of Great Britain*. His three works of fiction are all EPISTOLARY NOVELS, a form he did not invent but brought to a new height of sophistication, as he did the novel of common life, avoiding 'the improbable and the marvellous'. *PAMELA* (first part 1740; second part 1741) made him famous and *CLARISSA* (1747–8), his masterpiece, consolidated his reputation as both a celebrant of female virtue and a subtle psychologist. *THE HISTORY OF SIR CHARLES GRANDISON* (1753–4), a portrait of male virtue, was influential in its day but is now less well remembered. Taking up a hint from his friend Samuel Johnson, he also published *A Collection of the Moral and Instructive Sentiments, Maxims, Cautions and Reflections, Contained in the Histories of Pamela, Clarissa and Sir Charles Grandison, Digested under Proper Heads* (1755).

HENRY FIELDING's mockery was expressed in *An Apology for the Life of Mrs Shamela Andrews* (1741) and *JOSEPH ANDREWS* (1742), but otherwise Richardson's reputation stood high during his lifetime. He attracted a wide circle of admirers, typically female, which included two sisters, Lady Bradshaigh and Lady Echlin, whose correspondence with him survives. Johnson, though admitting that 'if you were to read Richardson for the story your impatience would be so much fretted that you would hang yourself', also affirmed that 'there is more knowledge of the human heart in one letter of Richardson's than in all of *TOM JONES*'. During the 19th century, Richardson's supposedly effeminate preoccupations were denigrated by comparison with Fielding's manliness, but his greatness has now been once more acknowledged.

Richler, Mordecai 1931– Canadian. His early work – notably *The Apprenticeship of Duddy Kravitz* (1959) – is broadly comic, satirizing Canadian sacred cows and showing an ambivalent attitude to his Jewish heritage. *St Urbain's Horseman* (1971), a product of his years in England, is centred on the experience of a Jewish-Canadian in London. His finest work to date, *SOLOMON GURSKY WAS HERE* (1989), has a rich gallery of comic characters and an unconventional view of Canadian history. It won the COMMONWEALTH WRITERS PRIZE. His other novels include *Son of a Smaller Hero* (1955), *A Choice of Enemies* (1957), *Cocksure* (1968), *Joshua Then and Now* (1980) and *Barney's Version* (1997). *This Year in Jerusalem*

(1994) is an account of a journey to Israel in which Richler reflects on contemporary Jewishness and his own upbringing. He has also written screenplays, essays, sketches and children's books, including *Jacob Two-Two Meets the Hooded Fang* (1975) and *Jacob Two-Two and the Dinosaur* (1988).

Riders, The A novel by TIM WINTON, published in 1994 and shortlisted for the BOOKER PRIZE. After living in Europe for some years, manual worker Fred Scully, his artistically ambitious wife Jennifer, and their young daughter Billie decided to buy a farm in Ireland. Jennifer returns to Australia with Billie to sell their house. When Scully goes to Shannon airport to take them to their new home he finds Billie there alone; Jennifer had left the plane in London. Father and daughter begin a search that takes them across Europe. While Jennifer's whereabouts and why she has disappeared remain mysterious, Scully, who returns to Ireland with Billie, comes to new realizations about himself and his relationship with the old world.

Ridley, James 1736–65 English. He is remembered for *The Tales of the Genii: or, The Delightful Lessons of Horan, the Son of Asmar* (1764), originally presented as a translation from the Persian but in fact a lively exercise in Orientalism modelled on *The Arabian Nights*. It proved immensely popular and was many times reprinted, sometimes in censored versions for children.

Rienzi: The Last of the Tribunes A novel by EDWARD BULWER LYTTON, published in 1835. The hero is Cola di Rienzo, a visionary idealist who briefly succeeded in subduing the warring factions of 14th-century Rome and in establishing a republic with himself as tribune. He was eventually torn to pieces in the streets. The story thus had a message about the dangers of liberty in post-Reform Bill England.

Riley, Joan 1958– Jamaican/British. In *The Unbelonging* (1985), *Waiting in the Twilight* (1987) and *Romance* (1988) she writes about women who have migrated from the Caribbean to Britain and struggle to build a decent life in the face of discrimination and marginalization. *A Kindness to the Children* (1992) returns to Jamaica. Using suggestions from members of the black community as her basis, Riley has evolved a method which reads like a fictional equivalent of oral history.

Ringuet See FRENCH-CANADIAN NOVEL.

Rippingale, C(uthbert) E(dward) 1825–97 English. Born into a Nonconformist manufacturing family, he rejected both aspects of his background in his early work. *Robert Higden: or, The Sweat Shop* (1851) attacks conditions in the clothing trade and *The Lion Yard Meeting* (1852) the hypocrisies of evangelical religion. *Can These Bones Live?* (1859), his only other novel of the 1850s, suggests a spiritual crisis. Later novels,

such as *The Testing of Sir Richard Fortescue* (1865) and *The Trials of Sir Clarence* (1872), combined High Anglican fervour with a love of medieval chivalry.

Rise of Silas Lapham, The A novel by WILLIAM DEAN HOWELLS, serialized in 1884–5 and published in volume form in 1885. Colonel Silas Lapham, makes a fortune manufacturing paint, moves his family from Vermont to Boston and urges his wife and daughters to enter fashionable society. The family does not fit in and Lapham gets drunk at the Coreys' dinner party. His business speculations fail but he resists his partners' suggestion that he sell some property to a British firm despite knowing it to be worthless. Bankrupt, disgraced but morally restored, he returns to Vermont. His older daughter Penelope and Tom Corey run away together to Mexico to escape the social barriers that made them unhappy in New England.

Ritchie, Anne (Isabella) Thackeray, Lady 1837–1919 English. She was the elder daughter of WILLIAM MAKEPEACE THACKERAY. Of her eight novels, *Old Kensington* (1873) and *Mrs Dymond* (1885) are still remembered. Although VIRGINIA WOOLF and others have paid tribute to their impressionistic charm, Lady Ritchie's most enduring work was as a memorialist of the Victorian writers she had known, notably in *Records of Tennyson, Ruskin and Robert and Elizabeth Browning* (1892), *Chapters from Some Memoirs* (1894), and her introductions to the 13-volume 'Biographical Edition' of her father's works (1894–8). She is portrayed as Mrs Hilbery in Woolf's *Night and Day*.

Rob Roy A novel by SIR WALTER SCOTT, published in 1817. Set in the early 18th century, it follows the adventures of Frank Osbaldistone. At the home of his uncle, Sir Hildebrand, in the north of England he falls in love with Diana Vernon and meets the malicious Rashleigh, Sir Hildebrand's youngest son, who is plotting to ruin Frank and his father. Frank goes to the Highlands with Bailie Nicol Jarvie and is helped by the outlaw Rob Roy MacGregor in thwarting Rashleigh, who eventually dies at Rob Roy's hand.

The historical Rob Roy (1671–1734), a drover, became a powerful and dangerous outlaw when he and his clan were proscribed as Jacobite sympathizers. A ruthless opponent of the government, he was famous for disinterested kindness and sympathy with the oppressed.

Robbins, Tom (Thomas Eugene) 1936– American. He is often compared to other West Coast authors such as KEN KESEY and RICHARD BRAUTIGAN. Eccentric in its narrative structure, his fiction is preoccupied with Eastern mysticism. It includes *Another Roadside Attraction* (1971), *Even Cowgirls Get the Blues* (1976), *Still Life with Woodpecker* (1980), *Jitterbug Perfume* (1984), *Skinny Legs and All* (1990) and *Half Asleep in Frog Pajamas* (1994).

Robert Elsmere A novel by MRS HUMPHRY WARD, published in 1888. It describes the hero's spiritual pilgrimage. He begins as a young Anglican clergyman of untroubled faith but is exposed to the unsettling influences of modern thought, particularly in the library of the local squire, Roger Wendover. Elsmere's studies gradually lead him to abandon his faith in miracles and in Christ as anything more than a symbol of the divine spirit at work in humanity, a position which estranges him from his orthodox wife. Eventually he founds the New Brotherhood of Christianity, an educational settlement in the London slums. The fact that the novel was commonly supposed to offer portraits of T. H. Green, WALTER PATER and Mark Pattison ensured its topical success. Gladstone's lengthy review boosted its sales yet further.

Roberts, Sir Charles G(eorge) D(ouglas) 1860–1943 Canadian. Called 'the father of Canadian literature', he was a prolific writer, producing poetry, several romances and 18 collections of short stories, including *Earth's Enigmas* (1896), *The Kindred of the Wild* (1902), *The Watchers of the Trails* (1904) and *Kings in Exile* (1909). These are largely about animals, scientifically observed to create what Roberts himself called 'psychological romance'. Of his 10 books of poetry, the earlier volumes such as *In Divers Tones* (1886) and *Songs of the Common Day* (1893) are generally thought his best. *Selected Poems* appeared in 1936.

Roberts, Michèle 1949– English. Her mother was French, and critics have often compared her work to that of Colette. The rich and dangerous attractions of Christianity, particularly Catholicism, inform: *A Piece of the Night* (1978); *The Visitation* (1983), in which Mary gives her version of bearing Christ; *The Wild Girl* (1984), about Mary Magdalene; and *The Book of Mrs Noah* (1987). Spiritualism, psychoanalysis, ghost stories and legendary murders run through *In the Red Kitchen* (1990). *Daughters of the House* (1992) is set mainly in Occupied France. *Flesh and Blood* (1994) involves a series of tales within a tale, regressing through time. With SARA MAITLAND and ZOË FAIRBAIRNS, Roberts belonged to the writers' group which produced *Tales I Tell My Mother* (1978) and *More Tales I Tell My Mother* (1987).

Robertson, Olivia 1917– Anglo-Irish. She produced a small but distinctive body of work beginning with *St. Malachy's Court* (1946), sketches based on her experiences as a social worker in Dublin. *Field of the Stranger* (1948), and *Miranda Speaks* (1950) combine satirical observation with a sense of the mysterious and magical. In 1976 she and her brother, Baron Strathloch, founded The Fellowship of Isis; her experiences as priestess are described in works such as *The Call of Isis* (1975) and *Ordination of a Priestess* (1977).

Robinson, Marilynne 1944– American. Her single novel, *Housekeeping* (1980), is a lyrical *BILDUNGSROMAN* detailing not only growth but female independence and self-definition. *Mother Country* (1989) examines Britain's nuclear power industry and its dangerous disposal of nuclear waste.

Robinson, 'Perdita' (Mary) 1758–1800 English. She achieved fame as an actress and notoriety as the mistress of the future George IV, who addressed her in amorous letters as 'Perdita'. Her reputation helped the popularity of her writing, which included: poems, notably a collection of sonnets, *Sappho and Phaon* (1796); several insignificant plays; and a succession of romances beginning with a GOTHIC NOVEL, *Vancenza* (1792). She was a friend of WILLIAM GODWIN and MARY WOLLSTONECRAFT, who encouraged her to write *Thoughts on the Condition of Women* (1798).

Robinson Crusoe A novel by DANIEL DEFOE, published in 1719 as *The Life and Strange Surprising Adventures of Robinson Crusoe, of York, Mariner. Written by Himself*. Although it subsequently assumed a near-mythological status, the story is based squarely on the true account published by Alexander Selkirk, a fugitive sailor who went to sea in 1704 and was put ashore at his own request on an uninhabited Pacific island, where he survived until his rescue in 1709.

In Defoe's imaginative reworking, Crusoe is a mariner who takes to the sea despite parental warnings, suffers misfortunes at the hands of Barbary pirates and the elements, and is shipwrecked off South America. A combination of systematic salvaging, resourcefulness and good fortune enables him to survive on his island for some 28 years, two months and 19 days, according to the painstaking journal in which the adventures are recorded. During this time he needs to adapt to his alien environment, demonstrate the self-sufficiency so admired by Defoe himself, and come to terms with his own spiritual listlessness. If *Robinson Crusoe* now seems inconsistent and even unconvincing as a psychological study of isolation, it should be remembered that it owes more to Puritan spiritual autobiographies and allegories than to the novel, then still in its infancy. It is at any rate a deliberate amalgam of the specific and the general, combining typical characteristics of the adventure story with the exotic fables of travel literature.

Robinson Crusoe enjoyed instant and permanent success, and has become one of those classics of English literature which (like GULLIVER'S TRAVELS, perhaps, or THE PILGRIM'S PROGRESS) appeal at various levels to adults and children alike. It draws its strength from a combination of disparate echoes and shapes: Jonah, Job, Everyman, the Prodigal Son, the colonial explorer and the proto-industrialist are all elements in Crusoe's character. Defoe continued the story in *The Farther Adventures of Robinson Crusoe* (1719), in which he revisits the island and loses Friday in an attack by savages, and *The Serious Reflections . . . of Robinson Crusoe* (1720), neither of which has achieved wide recognition.

Roderick Hudson A novel by HENRY JAMES, serialized in 1875, published in volume form in 1876 and revised in 1879.

Roderick Hudson, an amateur sculptor, is taken to Europe by the wealthy connoisseur Rowland Mallet. In Rome his work suffers when he becomes fascinated by the American expatriate Christina Light. Rowland brings Roderick's mother and fiancée, Mary Garland, from New England and their presence has the desired effect until Christina marries Prince Casamassima. Rowland attempts to rekindle Roderick's work by taking him, Mrs Hudson and Mary to Switzerland but he borrows money to follow Christina. After a quarrel in which Rowland calls him an ungrateful egoist, Roderick dies in the mountains, perhaps by suicide. Christina reappears in a later novel, *THE PRINCESS CASAMASSIMA*.

Roderick Random, The Adventures of The first novel by TOBIAS SMOLLETT, published in 1748. Modelled on Le Sage's *Gil Blas* (1715–35), it has the savage energy of true PICARESQUE. The hero describes a violent, adventurous life which includes a spell as surgeon's mate in the navy, shipwreck, service as a footman, fortune-hunting for an heiress with his friend and companion in roguery Hugh Strap, and time in debtors' prison. He finally encounters his long-lost, but now wealthy, father and marries his true love, Narcissa. Strap marries her maid. Episodes frequently draw on the author's own youthful experience of life at sea and in the theatrical world of London.

Unlike later novelists in the English tradition – including those whom he strongly influenced, such as DICKENS – Smollett saw no need to soften the roguery of his villains or temper the coarseness of their adventures. *Roderick Random* does not seek to engage the reader's sympathy or moral approval, but commands attention by the unabashed vitality of the writing.

Rogers, Jane 1952– English. She won immediate recognition with her first novel, *Separate Tracks* (1983), about alienated young people in Thatcher's Britain. Subsequent work includes: *Her Living Image* (1984), about the conflict between family and the world of friends, work and politics; *The Ice is Singing* (1987), in which a beleaguered woman drives across England in flight from memories; *Mr Wroe's Virgins* (1991), set in early 19th-century Lancashire, about seven women in the household of a self-proclaimed messiah; and *Promised Lands* (1995), linking the Australian past and present.

Rolfe, Frederick William 1860–1913 English. He also styled himself Baron Corvo and Fr. (i.e. Father) Rolfe. His paranoid sensibility and ornate prose style are best displayed in *Hadrian the Seventh* (1904), the story of how George Arthur Rose, a failed priest, is elected Pope. Rose is clearly modelled on the author, a Catholic convert and rejected candidate for the priesthood. Other works include *Stories Toto Told Me* (1898) and *In His Own Image* (1901), collections of stories. *Chronicles of the House of Borgia* (1901) is a collection of essays showing the fascination with late medieval and Renaissance Italy which also informs two romances, *Don Tarquinio* (1905) and *Don Renato* (1909). Two posthumously published works are extravagantly fictionalized autobiography. *The Desire and Pursuit of the Whole* (1934) takes savage revenge on his friends and patrons, and *Nicholas Crabbe* (1958) is based on the unhappy years at the start of his writing career. A. J. A. Symons's *The Quest for Corvo* (1934) gives a classic account of the difficulty in separating the reality of Rolfe's life from the lies and fantasy in which he shrouded it.

roman à clef A 'novel with a key', in which real people appear under fictitious names, lightly disguised but still recognizable. The form was pioneered in English by DELARIVIÈRE MANLEY in *The Secret History of Queen Sarah and the Sarazians* (1705–11) and the notorious *Secret Memoirs and Manners of Several Persons of Quality, of Both Sexes*, usually known as *The New Atalantis* (1709), for which she, her publisher and printer were arrested. Commercial fiction still periodically aims to achieve this sort of *succès de scandale*. Otherwise, the purpose of the *roman à clef* is often satiric, if only mildly so. The fiction of THOMAS LOVE PEACOCK provides a rich portrait-gallery, with witty commentary, of his leading contemporaries among the Romantic movement. Peacock's achievement remains unrivalled, though ALDOUS HUXLEY came close to reviving its spirit in *Crome Yellow* (1921). Huxley's *Point Counter Point* (1928) contains an admiring portrait of his friend D. H. LAWRENCE, another 20th-century writer who, without aiming at novels to be read with the use of a key, included in *WOMEN IN LOVE* (1920) recognizable portraits of friends and contemporaries such as Lady Ottoline Morrell, Bertrand Russell and members of the BLOOMSBURY GROUP.

roman à thèse A 'thesis novel' or, in the Victorian phrase, 'novel with a purpose', intended to popularize or propagate an idea or cause. Their urgent preoccupation with social and economic problems, coupled with their debt to the polemics of Thomas Carlyle, led many 19th-century novelists to adopt the form, notably BENJAMIN DISRAELI, CHARLES KINGSLEY in *ALTON LOCKE* and others associated with what came to be called the CONDITION OF ENGLAND NOVEL, as well as CHARLES READE and, in his later career, WILKIE COLLINS.

Alongside this tradition of protest and warning, there also flourished a tradition of the *roman à these* as practised by THOMAS LOVE PEACOCK and W. H. MALLOCK. It dealt in debate about current ideas – whether in politics, aesthetics or philosophy – and, by its readily identifiable portraits of thinkers of the day, allied itself with the *ROMAN À CLEF*. In *Crome Yellow* (1921) ALDOUS HUXLEY showed himself as the 20th-century heir to this tradition, though in *BRAVE NEW WORLD* he found fable and SCIENCE FICTION a natural vehicle for the novel of ideas – as GEORGE ORWELL did in *ANIMAL FARM* and *NINETEEN EIGHTY-FOUR*, and, indeed, writers have done ever since Thomas More wrote *UTOPIA*.

roman fleuve A sequence of novels in which the individual books are linked by recurrent characters. It may describe a social milieu, as in TROLLOPE'S BARSETSHIRE NOVELS and PALLISER NOVELS, or a family, as in JOHN GALSWORTHY'S *THE FORSYTE SAGA*. However remotely or modestly, these works echo Honoré de Balzac's aim that the interconnections between novels and stories written over a 20-year period (1827–47) should bind them together as a single *Comédie humaine*. Another prototype for the *roman fleuve*, further removed from the conventional architecture of the 'family saga', is Marcel Proust's *A la recherche du temps perdu* (1913–27), made influential in English through Scott Moncrieff's translation (1922–31). Here the novelist adopts a loosely autobiographical approach, making each new volume in the sequence contribute to an evolving portrait of his life and times. The closest English counterpart to Proust's approach is probably ANTHONY POWELL'S *A DANCE TO THE MUSIC OF TIME*, though C. P. SNOW undertook a similar project in *Strangers and Brothers* (1940–70).

Romany Rye, The GEORGE BORROW's sequel to *LAVENGRO*, published in 1857. It continues the story of the author's life after 1825 in the same unchronological, episodic, open-ended way. The book contains some of Borrow's best writing, not least the enigmatic conclusion to the Isopel Berners episode, a tale which soon established itself as a classic of prose romance. Instead of giving the book a conventional structure, Borrow abruptly broke off the account of his life in mid-career and added the 'Appendix', a powerful invective against 'gentility nonsense' and critics of *Lavengro*.

Romola A novel by GEORGE ELIOT, published in *The Cornhill Magazine* in 1862–3 and in book form in 1863. It is set in Florence during the 1490s.

Tito Melema, an unscrupulous young Greek, ingratiates himself with the blind scholar Bardo de' Bardi and marries his high-minded daughter Romola. When her love is replaced by contempt, Romola turns for spiritual guidance to the fundamentalist friar Savonarola. Tito is eventually killed by his adoptive father, Baldassare. Romola finds fulfilment in caring for the sick during an outbreak of plague and in looking after her children and Tessa, a peasant girl Tito had betrayed. The fanatical Savonarola is burned at the stake for heresy. Other characters include Machiavelli, Piero di Cosimo and 50 or more lesser figures of the time. George Eliot spent months researching the historical background, which abounds with details of almost every aspect of life in Renaissance Florence. (See also HISTORICAL FICTION.)

Room with a View, A A novel by E. M. FORSTER, published in 1908.

Lucy Honeychurch and her chaperone, the genteel Miss Bartlett, are frustrated in their hopes of obtaining a room with a view at the Pensione Bertolini in Florence. Miss Bartlett accepts the offer of an exchange with Mr Emerson and his son, George, after being reassured by a respectable acquaintance, the Rev. Mr Beebe. But George, after rescuing Lucy when she has witnessed a street murder, impulsively embraces her during a visit to Fiesole. Affronted, she and Miss Bartlett take themselves off to Rome and then return to Surrey. Here she becomes engaged to the cultured but shallow Cecil Vyse but breaks off the engagement when she realizes that she loves George, who has come to live nearby. The novel ends with George and Lucy on their honeymoon at the Pensione Bertolini.

Rosalynde A prose romance by Thomas Lodge (?1557–1625), pamphleteer, poet and playwright, published in 1590. Based on the 14th-century *Tale of Gamelyn*, it offered a popular blend of pastoral, EUPHUISM and Arcadian romance. The story of the usurping brothers Torismond and Saladyne, and the banished lovers Rosalynde and Rosader in the forest, gave Shakespeare his main source for *As You Like It*. Other prose romances by Lodge are *Frobonius and Prisceria* (1584), *Robert Second Duke of Normandy* (1591), *William Longbeard* (1593) and *A Margarite of America* (1596).

Ross, (James) Sinclair 1908–96 Canadian. He achieved wide recognition with his first novel, *AS FOR ME AND MY HOUSE* (1941), a classic of Western Canadian fiction which portrays the repressive nature of prairie life from the point of view of a small-town minister's wife. It was followed by *The Well* (1957), *The Lamp at Noon and Other Stories* (1968), *Whir of Gold* (1970), *Sawbones Memorial* (1974) and *The Race and Other Stories* (1982).

Roth, Henry 1906–95 American. His reputation is largely based on *Call It Sleep* (1934), about a Jewish boy, David Schearl, growing up in New York. *A Star Shines Over Mount Morris Park* (1994), *A Diving Rock in the Hudson* (1995) and *From Bondage* (1996) are instalments in a six-volume *ROMAN FLEUVE* called *Mercy of a Rude Stream. Nature's First*

Green (1979) is a volume of memoirs and *Shifting Landscapes* (1987) a collection of shorter writings.

Roth, Philip 1933– American. Jewish-American life in particular, and modern American society in general, are the subjects of his comedies of manners, which include *Goodbye, Columbus* (a novella and stories; 1959), *Letting Go* (1962), *When She was Good* (1967), *PORTNOY'S COMPLAINT* (1969), *The Breast* (1972), *The Great American Novel* (1973), *My Life as a Man* (1974) and *The Professor of Desire* (1977). *Our Gang* (1971) is a satire on the Nixon administration. Later work, eliding the boundaries between fiction and autobiography, includes: *The Ghost Writer* (1979), *Zuckerman Unbound* (1981), *The Anatomy Lesson* (1983) and *The Counterlife* (1986), forming a semi-autobiographical sequence about the education, sudden fame, and subsequent disillusion of a writer; *Deception* (1990); *Operation Shylock: A Confession* (1993); *Sabbath's Theater* (1995); and *American Pastoral* (1997). He has also published two volumes of memoirs, *The Facts* (1988) and *Patrimony: A True Story* (1991), an essay about his father.

Rowson, Susanna Haswell *c.* 1768–1824 Born in England, she went to America with her family as a child and began to write after her return to England in 1777. She produced several books of verse and SENTIMENTAL NOVELS. The most famous was *CHARLOTTE TEMPLE* (1791, US publication 1794), the first American best-seller. After she and her husband returned to the USA in 1793 to pursue stage careers, she turned her hand to comedies and romances: *Slaves in Algiers* (1794), *The Female Patriot* (1794), *The Volunteers* (1795), *A Kick for a Bite* (1795), *Trials of the Human Heart* (1795), and *Americans in England* (1796). Latterly she devoted herself to didactic works for youth, including *Charlotte's Daughter: or, The Three Orphans* (1828), a sequel to *Charlotte Temple*.

Roxana: *or, The Fortunate Mistress* A novel by DANIEL DEFOE, published in 1724. It is presented as the autobiography of the beautiful Mlle Beleau, daughter of Huguenot refugees in England.

Ambitious for a more exciting life, she deserts her husband after squandering his fortune and producing five children. Nicknamed Roxana, she becomes a high-class kept woman moving between 'protectors' across England, Holland and France. Her faithful maid Amy accompanies her progress. After amassing a considerable fortune, Roxana marries a wealthy Dutch merchant but he discovers her deviousness. She receives only a pittance from his will and is left in penury and penitence. Despite its sometimes unconvincing psychology and anticlimactic ending, the book has unmistakable energy and narrative strength.

Rubens, Bernice (Ruth) 1928– English. Her work customarily treats themes of loneliness and rejection. The context is social and domestic in *Go Tell the Lemming* (1973) and *Birds of Passage* (1981). Her personal knowledge of musical families and child prodigies finds expression in *Madame Sousatzka* (1962) and *Spring Sonata* (1979), the monologue of a soon-to-be stillborn baby, which moves toward allegory. With *The Elected Member* (1970; BOOKER PRIZE) and *Our Father* (1987), the context is explicitly metaphysical. The Jewish experience informs much of her work, including *Set on Edge* (1960) and a historical saga about 17th-century Hassidim, *Brothers* (1983) and *Kingdom Come* (1990). In *Yesterday in the Back Lane* (1995) an old murder casts a long shadow. *The Waiting Game* (1997) is a dark comedy about the multi-layered workings of blackmail.

Rudd, Steele [Davis, Arthur Hoey] 1868–1935 Australian. His broad comic sketches about the hapless Rudd family, set in the Darling Downs, were gathered in several collections: *On Our Selection* (1899), *Sandy's Selection* (1904), *Back at Our Selection* (1906), *Dad in Politics* (1908), *On an Australian Farm* (1910), *We Kaytons* (1921) and *Me an' th' Son* (1924).

Rule, Jane 1931– Canadian, born in the USA. Canada's best-known lesbian writer, she has produced several novels: *Desert of the Heart* (1964), *This is Not for You* (1970), *Against the Season* (1971), *The Young in One Another's Arms* (1977), *Contract with the World* (1980), *Memory Board* (1987) and *After the Fire* (1989). Her short stories include *Theme for Divers Instruments* (1975) and *Inland Passage* (1985). She has also written *Lesbian Images* (1975), a study of GERTRUDE STEIN, Colette and VITA SACKVILLE-WEST among others, and *Outlander* (1980), a collection of essays and short stories.

Runyon, (Alfred) Damon 1884–1946 American. The New York scene provided the material for his unique vernacular humour: athletes, show people, gamblers, hustlers, crooks and their women are transformed into recognizable types. His volumes of stories include *Guys and Dolls* (1931), which gave its name to a highly successful musical inspired by his work, followed by *Blue Plate Special* (1934), *Take It Easy* (1938), *Furthermore* (Britain 1938, USA 1941), *Runyon à la Carte* (1944), *Short Takes* (1946) and *Runyon on Broadway* (1950). He also wrote a successful farce, *A Slight Case of Murder* (1940), in collaboration with Howard Lindsay.

Rushdie, (Ahmed) Salman 1947– Born in Bombay, he emigrated to Britain in 1965. An important example of MAGIC REALISM, his fiction attempts to reshape the history of his time to make it congruent with identities fractured by imperialism and questions how fiction dare undertake so colossal a task. *Grimus* (1975), an extravagant fable, was followed by *MIDNIGHT'S CHILDREN* (1981), which won the BOOKER PRIZE, about India, and *Shame* (1983), about Pakistan. Nothing in his previous success prepared

Rushdie or his publishers for the reception of *THE SATANIC VERSES* (1988), whose oblique but energetic consideration of religion – particularly Islam – provoked an *affaire* raising questions of censorship and freedom of expression. Islamic protest against the novel's 'blasphemy' culminated in the *fatwa*, or death sentence, pronounced against the author by the Ayatollah Khomeini of Iran in February 1989. Rushdie was forced into hiding, from which he has given occasional interviews and published: a children's story, *Haroun and the Sea of Stories* (1990); a volume of essays, *Imaginary Homelands* (1991); a monograph on the film version of *The Wizard of Oz* (1992); a collection of short stories, *East, West* (1994); and a novel, *The Moor's Last Sigh* (1995), which, like *The Satanic Verses*, won a WHITBREAD AWARD. *The Jaguar Smile* (1987) is a travel book about Nicaragua under the Sandinistas.

Russ, Joanna See SCIENCE FICTION.

Ruth A novel by ELIZABETH GASKELL, published in 1853.

Ruth Hilton, an innocent seamstress, is seduced and abandoned in Wales during her pregnancy by Henry Bellingham, a country gentleman. Thurstan Benson, a dissenting parson, and his sister Faith take her to his northern parish of Eccleston, where she lives as their widowed relative, Mrs Denbigh, and gives birth to a son, Leonard, and works as governess to the Bradshaws. When Bellingham (now calling himself Donne) reappears as the local parliamentary candidate, he proposes marriages but Ruth refuses. When her secret becomes public, she, Leonard and the Bensons are treated as pariahs. She rehabilitates herself by brave deeds during a cholera epidemic and, in a last gesture, nurses Bellingham back to health before falling ill and dying herself. A sub-plot deals with the attachment between Bradshaw's daughter Jemima and his partner Walter Farquhar.

Rutherford, Mark See WHITE, WILLIAM HALE.

Sackville-West, Vita [Victoria] **(Mary)** 1892–1962 English. She wrote some 50 books. They include: *Knole and the Sackvilles* (1922; revised 1958), an account of her family and the family home in Kent; *The Land* (1926), a long pastoral poem set in the Weald of Kent; studies of Teresa of Avila, the Spanish mystic, and Thérèse of Lisieux, the 'Little Flower' of France in *The Eagle and the Dove* (1943); a biography of 'La Grande Mademoiselle', *Daughter of France* (1959); and books on gardening derived from the weekly columns she contributed to *The Observer* and her work at Sissinghurst, her home with her husband Harold Nicolson. Several of her novels are among her most enduring work. They include: *Challenge* (1923), based on her affair with Violet (Keppel) Trefusis; *The Edwardians* (1930), a story of upper-class life in which Knole is depicted as 'Chevron'; and *All Passion Spent* (1931), a moving study of the widowhood of Lady Slane. Vita Sackville-West's friend VIRGINIA WOOLF used her as the model for the androgynous hero of *ORLANDO*.

Sacred Fount, The A short novel by HENRY JAMES, published in 1901.

During a weekend party at the country house of Newmark the narrator observes that his hostess, Grace Brissenden, though much older than her husband, Guy, seems the more youthful and energetic of the two. He speculates that Guy is the 'sacred fount' from which his wife draws her new vitality, leaving him correspondingly devitalized. He then applies this theory to another pair of guests, Gilbert Long and May Server. He further decides that Gilbert and Grace, the dominant partners of their respective marriages, and Mary and Guy, the weaker partners, are drawing closer together. But Grace, whom he takes into his confidence, tells him that he has imagined the whole thing. The reader is left uncertain.

Sad Fortunes of the Reverend Amos Barton, The See *SCENES OF CLERICAL LIFE*.

Sahgal, Nayantara 1927– Indian. As Nehru's niece, she was close to Gandhian idealism before Independence and to subsequent political in-fighting, experiences reflected in elegantly written novels such as *A Time to be Happy* (1958), *This Time of Morning* (1965), *Storm in Chandigarh* (1969) and *The Day in Shadow* (1971). Her later novels, including *A Situation in New Delhi* (1977), *RICH LIKE US* (1985; awarded a SAHITYA AKADEMI prize), *Plans for Departure* (1986) and *Mistaken Identity* (1988) are more experimental. *Prison and Chocolate Cake* (1954) and *From Fear Set Free* (1962) are autobiograph-

ical pieces. Sahgal's biography of her cousin Indira Gandhi (1982) is highly critical.

Sahitya Akademi, The A national academy of letters established by the Indian government in 1954. It awards annual prizes to literary works in any of 22 languages, including English. Novels in English to have won the prize are (with the year of their nomination): R. K. NARAYAN, *THE GUIDE* (1960); RAJO RAO, *THE SERPENT AND THE ROPE* (1963); BHABANI BHATTACHARYA, *Shadow from Ladakh* (1967); MULK RAJ ANAND, *Morning Face* (1971); CHAMAN NAHAL, *AZADI* (1977); ANITA DESAI, *Fire on the Mountain* (1978); ARUN JOSHI, *The Last Labyrinth* (1982); NAYANTARA SAHGAL, *Rich Like Us* (1986); VIKRAM SETH, *The Golden Gate* (1988); AMITAV GHOSH, *THE SHADOW LINES* (1989); SHASHI DESHPANDE, *That Long Silence* (1990); I. ALLAN SEALY, *THE TROTTER-NAMA* (1991); and Ruskin Bond, *Our Trees Still Grow in Dehra* (1992).

St Ronan's Well A novel by SIR WALTER SCOTT, published in 1824. It abandons his usual historical settings for a fashionable Scottish spa in the early 19th century. The enmity of two half-brothers, sons of the late Earl of Etherington, is inflamed by their vexed and tragic relationship with Clara Mowbray, daughter of the laird of St Ronan's. Scott's portrait of Meg Dods, a down-to-earth landlady, has been praised.

Saki [Munro, Hector Hugh] 1870–1916 English. His first book, *The Rise of the Russian Empire* (1899), was his only serious work. Thereafter he adopted the name of the cup-bearer in Edward FitzGerald's *The Rubáiyát of Omar Khayyám* and published collections of short stories: *Reginald* (1904), *Reginald in Russia and Other Sketches* (1910), *The Chronicles of Clovis* (1912) and *Beasts and Superbeasts* (1914). Whimsical in their plots and light-heartedly cynical in their tone, they are also given a darker side by memories of his unhappy childhood with his maiden aunts in Devon. He also wrote two novels, *The Unbearable Bassington* (1912) and *When William Came* (1913), the latter a satirical fantasy subtitled 'A Story of London under the Hohenzollerns'. Two further collections appeared after Munro's death in World War I, *The Toys of Peace and Other Papers* (1919) and *The Square Egg and Other Sketches* (1924).

Salinger, J(erome) D(avid) 1919– American. His only novel has been the highly successful *THE CATCHER IN THE RYE* (1951), narrated by a teenager in rebellion against the adult world. *Nine Stories* (entitled *For Esmé – With Love and Squalor* in Britain; 1953) introduces the Glass family, who reappear in *Franny and Zooey* (1961), *Raise High the Roofbeam, Carpenters* (1963) and *Seymour: An Introduction* (1963). Further brief instalments in their history have appeared in magazines but Salinger has since announced that he now writes only for personal diversion.

Salkey, (Felix) Andrew (Alexander) 1928– Jamaican. His children's novels include *Hurricane* (1964), *Earthquake* (1965), *Drought* (1966), *Riot* (1967), *Jonah Simpson* (1969) and *The River That Disappeared* (1980). Adult novels like *A Quality of Violence* (1959) and *The Late Emancipation of Jerry Stover* (1968) stress the aridity of Caribbean experience. English society proves no less bleak and inhospitable in *Escape to an Autumn Pavement* (1960), *The Adventures of Catullus Kelly* (1969) and *Come Home, Michael Heartland* (1976). *Havana Journal* (1971) and *Georgetown Journal* (1972) are travel books. Salkey has also published poetry and edited anthologies of Caribbean writing. *Anancy's Score* (1973), *One* (1985) and *Anancy, Traveller* (1992) are all collections of stories about Anancy, the Caribbean spider trickster-hero.

Sanchez, Thomas 1942– Chicano. *Rabbit Boss* (1973) won acclaim as an epic, often hallucinatory narrative of the Washo Indians over four generations. Other novels include *The Zoot-Suit Murders* (1978), set in Los Angeles during the 1940s, and *Mile Zero* (1989), set in Key West. Sanchez has also published a collection of essays on Southern California, *Angels Burning: Native Notes from the Land of Earthquake and Fire* (1987).

Sanditon An unfinished novel which JANE AUSTEN worked on during the early months of 1817, the year of her death. It was first published in 1925. Charlotte Heywood is a guest of the Parker family at Sanditon, a seaside village rapidly developing into a fashionable resort. There she meets Lady Denham and her nephew and niece, Sir Edward and Miss Denham.

Sandra Belloni A novel by GEORGE MEREDITH, published in 1864 as *Emilia in England*. Emilia Sandra Belloni, an Italian with a fine singing voice, leaves her father and is taken up by the Pole family, whose spineless son, Wilfred, falls in love with her. Pole tries to marry Wilfred to Lady Charlotte Chillingworth but she sees through the young man and exposes him to Emilia. Merthyr Powys and his sister take her under their wing and, as she leaves for the Milan conservatory, she and Merthyr look forward to their probable marriage. The story continues in *VITTORIA*.

Sansom, William 1912–76 English. His first collection of stories, *Fireman Flower* (1944), drawing on his experiences in wartime London, was followed by *South* (1948), *Something Terrible, Something Lovely* (1948), *The Passionate North* (1950), *A Touch of the Sun* (1952), *Lord Love Us* (1954), *A Contest of Ladies* (1956), and *Among the Dahlias* (1957). Sansom also wrote novels, travel books, film scripts, television plays and lyrics.

Santayana, George See LAST PURITAN, THE.

Sapper (McNeile, Herman Cyril) See SPY FICTION.

Sardines A novel by NURUDDIN FARAH, published in 1981. It tells the story of a group of Somali intellectuals (Farah coins the term 'privilegentsia') struggling to give their lives meaning in a Mogadiscio held in the tyrannical grasp of the General, a thinly disguised portrait of Siyad Barre. At the centre is Median, writer and journalist, with her precocious young daughter Ubax and estranged husband Sabater, unenthusiastic holder of various portfolios in the repressive and nepotistic government.

Sargeson, Frank 1903–82 New Zealand. His first collection, *Conversations with My Uncle and Other Sketches* (1936), showed his skill at using the language of the ill-educated and semi-literate. *Collected Stories, 1935–1963* appeared in 1964 and *The Stories of Frank Sargeson* in 1973. His novels include: *I Saw in My Dream* (1949); *Memoirs of a Peon* (1965), the PICARESQUE recollections of a man enslaved by literature and lust; *The Hangover* (1967); *Joy of the Worm* (1969); *Man of England Now* (1972); *Sunset Village* (1976); and *En Route* (1979).

Saro-Wiwa, Ken(ule Beeson) 1941–95 Nigerian. The author of numerous short stories for children and adults, he is best known for his novel of the Nigerian Civil War, *Sozaboy: A Novel in Rotten English* (1985), the first serious, full-length prose narrative from Nigeria to be written entirely in Pidgin and other popular registers. After a murder trial in 1995, regarded internationally as a travesty, Saro-Wiwa was executed by Nigeria's military regime.

Saroyan, William 1908–81 American. His first collection of short stories, *The Daring Young Man on the Flying Trapeze* (1934), typifies his genial vision. Other collections include *Inhale and Exhale* (1936), *Three Times Three* (1936), *The Trouble with Tigers* (1938), *My Name is Aram* (1940) and *Dear Baby* (1944). *The Human Comedy* (1943), *The Adventures of Wesley Jackson* (1946), *Rock Wagram* (1951), *Mama, I Love You* (1956), *Papa, You're Crazy* (1957) and *One Day in the Afternoon of the World* (1964) are novels. Saroyan perhaps achieved greatest fame with his plays, which include *My Heart's in the Highlands* (1939), *The Time of Your Life* (1939), *Love's Old Sweet Song* (1941), *The Beautiful People* (1942), *Across the Board on Tomorrow Morning* (1942), *Hello Out There* (1943), *Don't Go Away Mad* (1949) and *The Cave Dwellers* (1957). *The Bicycle Rider in Beverly Hills* (1952), *Here Comes, There Goes, You Know Who* (1961) and *Obituaries* (1979) are autobiographical.

Sarton, May 1912–95 American. Her work addresses moral and political issues in a distinct and localized idiom. Novels include *The Single Hound* (1938), *The Birth of Grandfather* (1957), *The Small Room* (1961), *Mrs Stevens Hears the Mermaids Singing* (1965), *Kinds of Love* (1970), *As We are Now* (1973), *Anger* (1982) and *The Education of Harriet Hatfield* (1990). Her verse is gathered in

Collected Poems (1974). Autobiographical writings include *I Knew a Phoenix* (1959), *Plant Dreaming Deep* (1968), *Journal of Solitude* (1973), *Recovering* (1980), *Honey in the Hive* (1988), *Endgame: A Journal of the Seventy-Ninth Year* (1992) and *Encore: A Journal of the Eightieth Year* (1993).

Satanic Verses, The A novel by SALMAN RUSHDIE, published in 1988. It won a WHITBREAD AWARD. The narrative announces its assault on certainty in the opening image of Gibreel Farishta and Saladin Chamcha plummeting earthwards after their airliner has been blown apart. The byzantine plot follows their fortunes on landing, often transmuting them into other identities, notably the exiled Imam waiting to return to his decadent homeland of Sodom and the prophet-figure Mahound. Islamic outrage was also provoked by an imaginary brothel scene in which the girls are named after the prophet's 12 wives and another dream sequence dramatizing the question of whether disputed verses in *The Koran* may have been written by the Devil rather than God. Such criticism ignores Rushdie's deliberately combative irony and the ostentatious fictiveness of his whole project. Energetic, comic and self-questioning, *The Satanic Verses* is anything but polemical or categorical.

Satchell, William 1860–1942 New Zealand. Born in London, he emigrated to New Zealand in the 1880s. His first novel of New Zealand life, *The Land of the Lost*, appeared in 1902. Others were *The Toll of the Bush* (1905), *The Elixir of Life* (1907) and the highly praised *The Greenstone Door* (1914), about Anglo-Maori relations.

Saunders, Hilary St George See SPY FICTION.

Savage, Marmion 1803–72 Anglo-Irish. Editor of *The Examiner*, he published six novels, including *Falcon Family* (1845), a satire on the Young Ireland party.

Sayers, Dorothy L(eigh) 1893–1957 English. Her reputation rests on her DETECTIVE FICTION about the elegant and apparently light-hearted amateur detective, Lord Peter Wimsey: *Whose Body?* (1923), *Clouds of Witness* (1926), *Unnatural Death* (1927), *The Unpleasantness at the Bellona Club* (1928), *Strong Poison* (1930), which also introduced Harriet Vane, *The Five Red Herrings* (1931), *Have His Carcase* (1932), *Murder Must Advertise* (1932), set in an advertising agency, *The Nine Tailors* (1934), set in the Fens, *Gaudy Night* (1935), with Wimsey and Vane in Oxford, and *Busman's Honeymoon* (1937), in which Wimsey and Vane are married. The later novels in the series determinedly introduce a new note of seriousness. Her only detective novel without Wimsey is *The Documents in the Case* (with Robert Eustace; 1930). Other work includes a sequence of radio plays about the life of Christ, *The Man Born to be King* (1941–2) and translations of Dante's *Inferno* (1949), *Purgatorio* (1955) and *Paradiso* (completed by Barbara Reynolds; 1962) and of *The Song of Roland* (1957).

Scarlet Letter, The A novel by NATHANIEL HAWTHORNE, published in 1850. An introductory section describes his work in the Salem Custom House. The novel itself is set in 17th-century Boston.

Charged with adultery, Hester Prynne refuses to reveal the identity of her lover and the father of her illegitimate baby. She is condemned to wear a scarlet 'A' on her breast but, as the years pass, finds a place in society by helping other outcasts and unfortunates. Her daughter, Pearl, develops into a mischievous 'elfin' child. Meanwhile her husband, who arrived in time to witness her public humiliation, adopts the name Roger Chillingworth and swears her to secrecy about his identity. He guesses correctly that her lover was the young minister, Arthur Dimmesdale, and under the guise of giving medical help torments Dimmesdale with veiled allusions to his guilt. Hester begs Dimmesdale to escape with her to Europe. He briefly yields to the temptation, and Hester even removes the letter from her breast, before the moment passes. Having delivered a powerful Election Day Sermon, Dimmesdale bids Hester and Pearl to join him on the pillory, publicly confesses his sin and dies in her arms. Hester and Pearl leave Boston. Pearl settles in Europe but Hester voluntarily returns, resumes her scarlet 'A' and continues her life of penance.

Scenes of Clerical Life Three tales by GEORGE ELIOT, serialized in 1857 and published together in volume form in 1858.

'The Sad Fortunes of the Reverend Amos Barton' concerns the well-meaning but maladroit curate of Shepperton, who acquires the sympathy and understanding of his parishioners only after the death of his wife, Milly. 'Mr Gilfil's Love-Story' centres on the tragic life of an earlier clergyman of the same parish, Shepperton. Maynard Gilfil falls in love with a talented singer, Caterina Sarti (Tina), but she loves the feckless Captain Anthony Wybrow and becomes dangerously unbalanced when he dies. Gilfil seeks her out, restores her to health and marries her, but her spirit is so broken that she dies soon afterwards, leaving him to a lonely old age. 'Janet's Repentance' tells the tragic story of the hostility of the drunken, braggard lawyer, Robert Dempster, towards the conscientious Rev. Edgar Tryan of Milby. Dempster is joined in the hostility by his wife, Janet, also addicted to drink. But Tryan helps her when she is forced to flee her home and, now able to resist the temptation of alcohol, she is at his bedside when he dies, exhausted by his work for the parish.

Schindler's Ark A novel by THOMAS KENEALLY, published in 1982 and called *Schindler's List* in the USA. A 'faction' of the sort Keneally had experimented with in previous work, it uses 'the textures and devices of a novel' to probe the ambiguities and contradictions of recent history.

Oskar Schindler opportunistically establishes himself as an industrialist in Poland after the German invasion, but soon finds himself protecting rather than exploiting his Jewish workers. As the business expands, his list of 'essential' personnel ensures that over a thousand escape the gas chambers, even though his factory does not produce a single shell. He is escorted by a Jewish bodyguard to Switzerland at the end of the war, and eventually declared a 'Righteous Person' by Israel and buried in Jerusalem.

Steven Spielberg based his award-winning film *Schindler's List* (1993) on the book.

Schreiner, Olive 1855-1920 South African. She moved to Britain in 1881 and achieved success with *The Story of an African Farm* (1883), originally published under the pseudonym of Ralph Iron, attacking the heroic image of the frontier and presenting a heroine who makes the novel an important feminist document. *Trooper Peter Halket of Mashonaland* (1897) attacks Cecil Rhodes and his Chartered Company's treatment of blacks in 'Rhodesia'. Two novels she often reworked appeared posthumously as *From Man to Man* (1926) and *Undine* (1929).

She saw herself less as a novelist than a writer trying to transform an uncaring society – hence such works as *Dreams* (1891) and *Dream Life and Real Life* (1893). Her polemical writings championed the victims of injustice: the Boer republics in *A South African's View of the Situation* (1898), unfranchised South African blacks in *A Letter on the South African Union and the Principles of Government* (1909) and women in *Woman and Labour* (1911). The OLIVE SCHREINER PRIZE is named in her honour.

Schulberg, Budd (Wilson) 1914– American. The son of the film pioneer B. P. Schulberg, he was brought up in Hollywood and wrote screenplays for two films directed by Elia Kazan, *On the Waterfront* (1954) and, from one of his own short stories, *A Face in the Crowd* (1957). His novels, which cultivate a fast filmic pace and sometimes take Hollywood as their subject, include: *What Makes Sammy Run?* (1941), about a film mogul; *The Harder They Fall* (1947), based on the career of the boxer Primo Carnera; *The Disenchanted* (1951), which contains a disguised portrait of F. SCOTT FITZGERALD; *Sanctuary* (1970); and *Everything That Moves* (1981). His short stories are collected in *Some Faces in the Crowd* (1954) and *Love, Action, Laughter and Other Sad Tales* (1989).

Schwartz, Delmore 1913-66 American. His principal concern was with the complex relationship between the private self and the outside world. *In Dreams Begin Responsibilities* (1938), *Genesis, Book One* (1943) and *Vaudeville for a Princess, and Other Poems* (1950) combine poetry and prose. *Shenandoah* (1941) is a verse play and

The Imitation of Life (1941) a collection of essays. *The World is a Wedding* (1948) consists of stories dealing with the problems of Jewish life in America. *Summer Knowledge: New and Selected Poems 1938-58* appeared in 1959 and *Successful Love, and Other Stories* in 1961.

science fiction Fiction set in the future, or in a contemporary setting disrupted by an imaginary device such as a new invention or the introduction of an alien being. It differs from other kinds of fantastic narrative in claiming that it respects the limits of scientific possibility, and that its innovations are plausible extrapolations from present knowledge, though relatively few examples are genuinely conscientious in this respect.

Although elements of science fiction appear in many stories of imaginary voyages, it was not until the 19th century that the advancement of science inspired a good deal of work in this vein. MARY SHELLEY's *FRANKENSTEIN* (1818) is an early example, and science-fictional themes appear in the work of EDGAR ALLAN POE and NATHANIEL HAWTHORNE. GEORGE CHESNEY's account of an imaginary invasion, *The Battle of Dorking* (1871), helped a spate of future war stories (see also SPY FICTION), and Jules Verne popularized tales of flying machines, submarines and spaceships. Movements for political reform and the theory of evolution encouraged speculation about the future. These various threads were drawn together by H. G. WELLS in *THE TIME MACHINE* (1895), *The Island of Dr Moreau* (1896), *The Invisible Man* (1897), *THE WAR OF THE WORLDS* (1898), *When the Sleeper Wakes* (1899), *The First Men in the Moon* (1901) and *The War in the Air* (1908). Other important works before World War I were M. P. SHIEL's *The Purple Cloud* (1901), WILLIAM HOPE HODGSON's *The House on the Borderland* (1908), *The Hampdenshire Wonder* (1912) by J. D. Beresford (1873-1947), ARTHUR CONAN DOYLE's *The Lost World* (1912) and, in the USA, JACK LONDON's *THE IRON HEEL* (1907).

After World War I British futuristic fiction was dominated by the idea that a new war could and probably would obliterate civilization. It appears in *People of the Ruins* (1920) by Edward Shanks (1892-1953) and *Theodore Savage* (1922) by Cicely Hamilton (the pseudonym of Cicely Mary Hamill, 1872-1952), as well as the work of prolific new writers like W. OLAF STAPLEDON, S. Fowler Wright (1874-1965), Neil Bell (the pseudonym of Stephen Southwold, 1887-1964) and John Gloag (1896-1981). Wells's *The Shape of Things to Come* (1933) reaches an optimistic conclusion, but only after describing devastation by war and plague. A frequent corollary was that man must ultimately be replaced by a new species, an idea at its most extravagant in Stapledon's *Last and First Men* (1930) and *Odd John* (1935) but also informing *The Clockwork Man* (1923) by E. V. Odle (1890-1942), Gloag's

Tomorrow's Yesterday (1930), Shiel's *The Young Men are Coming!* (1937) and Beresford's '*What Dreams May Come . . .* ' (1941). Utopian speculation was not entirely stifled but undermined and opposed by a cynicism most comprehensively expressed in *The Question Mark* (1923) by Muriel Jaeger (?1893–) and ALDOUS HUXLEY's *BRAVE NEW WORLD* (1932).

The USA, by contrast, was relatively untouched by World War I and its futuristic fictions were haunted by no such anxieties. Space adventure stories, contemptuously dubbed 'space operas' by their critics, were encouraged by the gaudy fantasies of EDGAR RICE BURROUGHS and the magazines introduced by Hugo Gernsback, who first popularized the term 'science fiction'. But with the anxieties bred by the Depression in the 1930s the magazine editor John W. Campbell Jr encouraged a more sober and realistic approach. The new generation of writers he recruited – ISAAC ASIMOV, ROBERT A. HEINLEIN, Clifford D. Simak (1904–88), Theodore Sturgeon (1918–85), A. E. VAN VOGT and Fritz Leiber (1910–92) – brought a measure of intellectual sophistication to science fiction while retaining its imaginative fertility and adventurousness. Many notable American works of the 1940s were magazine series subsequently assembled into book form: these include Asimov's robot stories (*I, Robot*, 1950) and *Foundation* trilogy (1951–3), Heinlein's 'Future History' series and the series collected in Simak's *City* (1952).

The British tradition of scientific romance petered out after World War II, its last notable practitioners being C. S. LEWIS and Gerald Heard (the pseudonym of H. F. Heard, 1889–1971). Its pessimistic tone (further encouraged by Hiroshima) culminated in GEORGE ORWELL's *NINETEEN EIGHTY-FOUR* (1949) and Aldous Huxley's *Ape and Essence* (1949). The best of the British writers of futuristic fiction who came to prominence after the war combined serious and anxious concerns with the greater imaginative scope and ideative playfulness of science fiction. They included JOHN WYNDHAM, BRIAN ALDISS, John Brunner (1934–95) and J. G. BALLARD, all of whom retained a strong interest in the catastrophist tradition in their best works. The most successful of the British postwar writers of science fiction, ARTHUR C. CLARKE, is more strongly affiliated to the American optimistic tradition, but shows marked Stapledonian influences in *Childhood's End* (1953) and *The City and the Stars* (1956).

In the USA the popularity of science fiction increased dramatically with the advent of paperbacks, shifting the form towards novels and, eventually, novel series. Most of the best writers of the 1950s, though, made their names with clever short stories, and some of the apologists for the genre who helped it to gain respect-

ability – notably KINGSLEY AMIS – argued that science fiction works best in short-story form because its strengths lie with the ingenious development of ideas rather than with elaborate characterization. Significant American works of the 1950s and 1960s include RAY BRADBURY's *The Martian Chronicles* (1950) and *Fahrenheit 451* (1953), *The Space Merchants* (1953) by FREDERICK POHL and Cyril M. Kornbluth (1923–58), *The Demolished Man* (1953) and *The Stars My Destination* (1956) by Alfred Bester (1913–87), *A Case of Conscience* (1958) by James Blish (1921–75) and *A Canticle for Leibowitz* (1960) by Walter M. Miller (1922–). The last two show a preoccupation with religion which has – rather paradoxically and perhaps surprisingly – become noticeable in modern science fiction. Even where religion is not explicitly evoked, a fascination with the relationship between moral and metaphysical issues still survives.

The mid-1960s saw a modishly experimental phase in both Britain and the USA. In Britain a 'new wave' was promoted by MICHAEL MOORCOCK, who converted the magazine *New Worlds* into an Arts Council-supported *avant-garde* periodical. In America Harlan Ellison (1934–) promoted a series of anthologies begun with *Dangerous Visions* (1967). Moorcock's tetralogy of novels featuring Jerry Cornelius (1968–77) exemplified his new approach, while Ellison's graphic short fictions are best displayed in *I Have No Mouth and Must Scream* (1967). The best of the experimental new writers were Roger Zelazny (1937–95), SAMUEL R. DELANY, Barry Malzberg (1939–), John Sladek (1937–) and THOMAS M. DISCH – all American, though the last two were first received more enthusiastically in Britain. Their most impressive works include Delany's *Dhalgren* (1975) and Disch's *Camp Concentration* (1968). Alongside this *avant-garde*, however, great commercial success was achieved by many more conventional science-fiction writers. Writers like Pohl and ROBERT SILVERBERG found new success as novelists. Asimov, Clarke and Heinlein all attained best-seller status, as did FRANK HERBERT with *Dune* (1965) and KURT VONNEGUT JR with *SLAUGHTERHOUSE-FIVE* (1969). Following Vonnegut's success the American academic establishment began to pay serious attention to science fiction, helping to boost the reputations of PHILIP K. DICK and URSULA LE GUIN. The former attracted attention because of his ingenuity in presenting images of artificial and hallucinatory worlds which dissolve into confusion, the latter because of her moral earnestness and purity of style.

The feminist movement in America helped several new female writers to emerge in the 1970s, including Joanna Russ (1937–) and the pseudonymous James Tiptree Jr (Alice Sheldon,

1915–87)). In recent years science fiction has been partly displaced in the marketplace by heroic fantasy, following the extraordinary success of US paperback editions of J. R. R. TOLKIEN's *THE LORD OF THE RINGS*. The two genres overlap in the work of best-selling writers like Anne McCaffrey (1926–) and Piers Anthony (1934–). The situation has been further complicated by a resurgence of interest in horror fiction, with best-selling writers such as Stephen King (1947–) and Dean R. Koontz (1945–) frequently borrowing science-fictional ideas to mingle with traditional supernatural motifs.

The boundaries of the genre are now more difficult to outline than ever before. Its imagery has diffused throughout contemporary culture to become familiar in some measure to everyone. This familiarity has enabled some writers and individual works to escape stigmatization, and has helped make the products of the scientific imagination available to reputable writers. THOMAS PYNCHON's *GRAVITY'S RAINBOW* (1973), DON DELILLO's *Ratner's Star* (1976), GORE VIDAL's *Kalki* (1978), DORIS LESSING's *Canopus in Argos: Archives* series (1979–83) and PAUL THEROUX's *O-Zone* (1986) are examples of 'mainstream' novels which use science-fictional elements. The 1990s saw a remarkable proliferation of 'alternative history' stories, which spilled out of the genre to include such best-sellers as *Fatherland* (1992) by Robert Harris (1957–) and *1945* (1995) by the American politician Newt Gingrich (1943–) and William R. Fortschen. The difficulty of achieving elaborate characterization and density of environmental detail in futuristic and hypothetical settings still prevents even the best science-fiction novels from living up to the expectations of traditionally minded literary critics, but the excellence of fabulists like Vonnegut and Disch is helping to change hidebound expectations of what novels can and ought to be.

Scott, Paul (Mark) 1920–78 English. His principal achievement is the Raj Quartet, consisting of *The Jewel in the Crown* (1966), *The Day of the Scorpion* (1968), *The Towers of Silence* (1972) and *A Division of the Spoils* (1974). It covers the final years of British India (1942–7), as the British are progressively shown to be governing an alien, often violently antagonistic land. *Staying On* (1977), a coda which won the BOOKER PRIZE, is a sanguine comedy about Tusker and Lucy Smalley, minor characters from the Quartet, living out a bleak retirement in India. Like the Quartet, Scott's earlier novels show a dense, painstaking realism and are set in either India or Malaya, except for *The Bender* (1963), which takes place in London. The best is generally thought to be *The Birds of Paradise* (1962), which illustrates his preoccupation with the process of history and the shifting perspectives of the past.

Scott, Sir Walter 1771–1832 Scottish. Born and educated in Edinburgh, he was admitted to the Scottish Bar in 1792 and married Margaret Charlotte Carpenter (Charpentier) in 1795. Absorbed in folklore and the supernatural, he entered literature through poetry, most notably with *Minstrelsy of the Scottish Border* (1802–3), an edition of old and new ballads. He made his name with *The Lay of the Last Minstrel* (1805), a poem based on an old border narrative, which launched a series of verse romances taking history or legend as their subject: *Marmion* (1808), *The Lady of the Lake* (1810), *The Vision of Don Roderick* (1811), *Rokeby* and *The Bridal of Triermain* (both 1813), *The Lord of the Isles* and *The Field of Waterloo* (both 1815), and *Harold the Dauntless* (1817). During these years Scott was also involved in editorial work with *Original Memoirs Written during the Great Civil War* (1806), an edition of Dryden's poetry (1808), *Memoirs of Captain George Carleton* (1808), *The State Papers of Sir Ralph Sadler* (1809) and *The Secret History of James I* (1811). After writing reviews for the Whig *Edinburgh Review*, he took an active part in establishing the Tory *Quarterly Review* in 1809.

By 1811 Scott's always muddled business interests, which included printing and publishing agreements with John and James Ballantyne, brought him near bankruptcy. He was rescued by Archibald Constable, who published *WAVERLEY* in 1814. One reason for attempting fiction was the astonishing success in 1810 of the first two cantos of Byron's *Childe Harold's Pilgrimage*, whose sophistication quite eclipsed the once successful romance narratives in which he excelled. The fact that Scott issued *Waverley* anonymously implies caution, but its immediate and enormous popularity decisively turned his career from poetry to fiction. A torrent of novels, merely identified as being by 'the author of *Waverley*', poured forth: *GUY MANNERING* (1815), *THE ANTIQUARY* (1816), *The Black Dwarf* and *OLD MORTALITY* (both 1816 and constituting the first series of *Tales of My Landlord*), *ROB ROY* (1817), *THE HEART OF MIDLOTHIAN* (1818; second series of *Tales of My Landlord*), *THE BRIDE OF LAMMERMOOR* and *A LEGEND OF MONTROSE* (1819; third series of *Tales of My Landlord*), *IVANHOE* (1819), *THE MONASTERY* and *The Abbot* (both 1820), *KENILWORTH* and *THE PIRATE* (both 1821), *THE FORTUNES OF NIGEL* (1822), *PEVERIL OF THE PEAK*, *QUENTIN DURWARD* and *ST RONAN'S WELL* (all 1823), *REDGAUNTLET* (1824), *The Betrothed* and *THE TALISMAN* (as *Tales of the Crusaders*, 1825) and *WOODSTOCK* (1826).

Scott was still busy with editions, antiquarian studies and literary criticism, including an edition of Swift (1814), *Memories of the Somervilles* (1815), *The Border Antiquities of England and Scotland* (1814–17), and *Lives of the Novelists*, contributed to Ballantyne's Novelists' Library (1821–4). He was also entertaining on a baronial scale at his country house, Abbotsford, enjoying the role of laird, and working at the law as well as letters. It is not surprising that his health was considerably undermined. In 1825–6 a financial crisis involving Ballantyne and Co. and Archibald Constable left him with a debt of £130,000. Honourably disdaining bankruptcy, he set to work at an even more furious pace to produce CHRONICLES OF THE CANONGATE, with The Two Drovers, The Highland Widow and The Surgeon's Daughter in its first series (1827) and St Valentine's Day: or, The Fair Maid of Perth in the second (1828), Anne of Geierstein (1829), and Count Robert of Paris and Castle Dangerous (1832) in the fourth series of Tales of My Landlord. The merciless toil finally overwhelmed him while he was recuperating in Italy and he returned to die at Abbotsford.

Few authors have enjoyed a higher reputation than Scott once did. In his lifetime and for nearly a century after his death he was not merely an immensely popular writer but a major cultural force. Single-handedly he not merely pioneered HISTORICAL FICTION but made it seem, to most of his Victorian successors, the very summit of the novelist's art. His Scottish novels, particularly Waverley and Rob Roy, did much to rescue that country from the low esteem it had acquired after the 1745 rebellion and to make it at once respectable and romantic. The descriptions of landscape and ruins with which his books abound helped to shape Romanticism. Above all, his use of history confirmed the taste for medievalism which lasted throughout the 19th century, and the conduct of his historical figures served as the model of the chivalric code by which Victorian gentlemen attempted to live. Yet today Scott is forgotten as a poet and neglected as a novelist. The immense bulk of his writing and the sheer length of his individual works intimidate. Current neglect overlooks his humour, his gift for memorably eccentric characters, his erudite and down-to-earth mastery of folklore and, most important, the underlying seriousness of his preoccupation with history and the processes of social and political change.

Sea-Wolf, The A novel by JACK LONDON, published in 1904. Humphrey Van Weyden is thrown overboard when two ferry boats collide in San Francisco Bay. A sealing schooner, the Ghost, saves him but its brutal captain, Wolf Larsen, presses him into service. In the sealing grounds off Japan they pick up Maude Brewster, who joins him in the struggle against Larsen. The pair flee the ship and reach a deserted island, where the Ghost is driven ashore. Deserted by his crew and suffering from cerebral cancer, Larsen dies, still defiant. Van Weyden and Maude make the Ghost seaworthy and set out for civilization.

Sealy, I(rwin) Allan 1951– Anglo-Indian. Born and raised in India, he studied in the USA and Canada, and now lives in New Zealand. THE TROTTER-NAMA (1988), awarded a SAHITYA AKADEMI prize, uses a traditional narrative form. Hero (1991) studies a characteristically Indian hybrid, the film star who has turned politician.

Second Jungle Book, The See JUNGLE BOOK, THE.

Secret Agent, The: A Simple Tale A novel by JOSEPH CONRAD, published in 1907. The sub-title establishes the ironic tone of a story about revolutionary politics in contemporary London which has exercised a major influence over later approaches to SPY FICTION by writers such as GRAHAM GREENE.

Mr Verloc works as a double agent, infiltrating the anarchist underworld to supply information to Inspector Heat of Scotland Yard and the Russian agent provocateur, Vladimir. Frustrated by English complacency, Vladimir orders Verloc to blow up the Greenwich Observatory. Verloc equips himself with explosives from the sinister 'Professor' and recruits his weak-witted stepson Stevie as his innocent accomplice. Stevie's horrifying death in Greenwich Park drives Verloc's wife Winnie to kill him. She plans to leave the country with the anarchist Ossipon, but he deserts her on learning of the murder. Driven to madness, she jumps overboard from a Channel ferry.

Secret Garden, The See BURNETT, FRANCES HODGSON.

Sedgwick, Catharine Maria 1789–1867 American. Her first novel, A New England Tale (1822), which traces the growth of the orphaned Jane Elton, became one of America's first bestsellers. Redwood (1824), about another orphan, Ellen Bruce, brought its author a popularity equal to that of JAMES FENIMORE COOPER and WASHINGTON IRVING. Hope Leslie (1827) is about relations between whites and Indians in 17th-century New England. Other works include Clarence (1830), The Linwoods (1835) and a trilogy consisting of Home (1835), The Poor Man and the Rich Man (1836), and Live and Let Live (1837). Her last novel, Married or Single? (1857), reflects her awareness of the social difficulties faced by unmarried women.

Selby, Hubert, Jr 1928– American. His best-known work, the collection of stories entitled Last Exit to Brooklyn (1964), deals with homosexuality, prostitution and brutality, while exploring human isolation in the city. It was the subject of a much-publicized obscenity trial in Britain. Selby has also published three novels – The Room (1971), The Demon (1976) and Requiem for a Dream (1978) – and a volume of short stories, Song of the Silent Snow (1986).

Selvon, Samuel (Dickson) 1923–94 Trinidadian, of Indian and Scottish descent. He emigrated to Britain in 1950 and to Canada in the early 1980s. He pioneered the use of Caribbean Creole dialect for other than merely comic effects in his 'London' novels. Works with a Trinidadian settings are *A Brighter Sun* (1952), *An Island is a World* (1955), *Turn Again, Tiger* (1958), *I Hear Thunder* (1963), *The Plains of Caroni* (1970) and *Those Who Eat the Cascadura* (1973). His sharp-edged accounts of West Indian settlement in Britain include *THE LONELY LONDONERS* (1956) and *The Housing Lark* (1965). British racism and its concomitant Black Power protests are satirical targets in the more pungent *Moses Ascending* (1975) and *Moses Migrating* (1983), which complete a trilogy about the protagonist of *The Lonely Londoners*. He also wrote short stories, collected in *Ways of Sunlight* (1958), and many radio plays, from *Lost Property* (1965) to *Zeppi's Machine* (1977). *Eldorado West One* (1988) is a collection of seven one-act plays about characters who first appeared in *The Lonely Londoners*. *Highway in the Sun* (1988) brings together four of his longer plays. *Foreday Morning* (1989) is a selection of his prose.

Senior, Olive 1941– Jamaican. The stories in *Summer Lightning* (1986), which won the COMMONWEALTH WRITERS PRIZE, draw on her own broad experience of Jamaican society, examining issues of race, class, colour and gender in a variety of styles that span the full range of the Jamaican linguistic continuum. A second collection, *Arrival of the Snake Woman* (1989), again contains stories written from a child's perspective, as well as pieces which reflect the discontent of adults who look nostalgically back to their childhood. She has also published: *The Message is Change* (1972), about the 1972 Jamaican General Elections; *A–Z of Jamaican Heritage* (1983), a valuable source of information about folk customs and traditions; two collections of verse, *Talking of Trees* (1985) and *Gardening in the Tropics* (1995); *Working Miracles: Women's Lives in the English-Speaking Caribbean* (1991), a sociological study; and a third collection of stories, *The Discerner of Hearts* (1995).

sensation novel A type of Victorian novel which took mystery and crime as its subject and suspense as its narrative method. Like the earlier GOTHIC NOVEL, it appealed directly to the reader's sensations by seeking to induce fear, excitement and curiosity, but it preferred a modern setting – the world of the railway and the telegraph – and it sometimes included criticism of current social abuses. Like the earlier NEWGATE NOVEL, it sometimes borrowed details from real-life criminal cases and could draw accusations of encouraging immorality (most memorably from John Ruskin in his essays on 'Fiction Fair and Foul'). The plots, which often hinge on falsely assumed identities or wills and legal questions of inheritance, are intricate and developed in a leisurely fashion to fill the requisite three volumes.

The sensation novel enjoyed its heyday in the 1860s, with the work of WILKIE COLLINS, partic-

ularly his hugely successful *THE WOMAN IN WHITE* (1860), and with MARY ELIZABETH BRADDON's *LADY AUDLEY'S SECRET* (1862). These books owed at least a part of their success to their memorable villains, who have obvious affinities with the stage melodrama of the period. DICKENS was influenced by sensation fiction, most obviously in *THE MYSTERY OF EDWIN DROOD* (1870), while the young THOMAS HARDY exploited it in his first published novel, *DESPERATE REMEDIES* (1871). Soon its attributes would merge with DETECTIVE FICTION as pioneered by ARTHUR CONAN DOYLE, whose early work includes *The Firm of Girdlestone* (1890), a novel looking directly back to sensation fiction.

Sense and Sensibility JANE AUSTEN's first published novel (1811). It originated in a story, 'Elinor and Marianne' (1795), which she began to rewrite in 1797.

When Henry Dashwood dies the estate of Norland Park in Sussex passes to John, his son by his first marriage, with the recommendation that he take care of the second Mrs Dashwood and her daughters. But John and his wife, encouraged by her mother, Mrs Ferrars, selfishly ignore the obligation. The second Mrs Dashwood and her daughters retire to a cottage in Devonshire. Marianne, the embodiment of 'sensibility', falls in love with the charming and penniless John Willoughby, who abandons her for an heiress. Elinor, the embodiment of 'sense', loves Mrs John Dashwood's brother Edward Ferrars. Her self-control enables her to conceal her distress at learning that he has for some time been secretly engaged to Lucy Steele. News of the engagement causes Mrs Ferrars to disinherit him in favour of his brother Robert. Lucy transfers her attention to Robert, freeing Edward from a commitment he regretted and allowing him to marry Elinor instead. The staunch and generous Colonel Brandon wins Marianne.

Sentimental Journey through France and Italy, by Mr Yorick, A A novel by LAURENCE STERNE, published in 1768. He had travelled through France and Italy from 1765–6 to help his tuberculosis. For the resulting fiction he adopted the character of Yorick from *TRISTRAM SHANDY*. Hastily undertaken, Yorick's journey whisks the reader across the Channel on the first page but never reaches Italy: the narrative breaks off with memorable suddenness when he is still short of Lyons. Indifferent to tourist sights, Yorick is a virtuoso of emotion, continually finding experiences that affect his delicate sensibilities, stimulate his benevolence, arouse his libido or cause comic confusion. TOBIAS SMOLLETT, whom Sterne met in Italy, is caricatured as the learned Smelfungus.

sentimental novel [novel of sensibility] A style of fiction, fashionable from the mid-18th century onwards, reflecting a belief that the natural emotions were good, kindly and innocent, and that society, law and civilization were to blame for corrupting man. The highly charged emotional world of SAMUEL RICHARDSON's PAMELA (1740), CLARISSA (1747–8) and SIR CHARLES GRANDISON (1753–4) contributed to its rise, though the sentimental novel reached full expression in works such as HENRY BROOKE's THE FOOL OF QUALITY (1766–72), LAURENCE STERNE's A SENTIMENTAL JOURNEY THROUGH FRANCE AND ITALY (1768) and HENRY MACKENZIE's THE MAN OF FEELING (1771), in all of which effusive emotion is celebrated as evidence of a good heart. Oliver Goldsmith's THE VICAR OF WAKEFIELD (1776) is frequently included among the hundreds of sentimental novels produced in the period, though it is arguably an early parody. In a later generation, writers as diverse as MARY WOLLSTONECRAFT, HANNAH MORE and JANE AUSTEN all reacted against the uncontrolled excesses of sentimentalism.

Serpent and the Rope, The A novel by RAJA RAO, published in 1960 and awarded a SAHITYA AKADEMI prize in 1963. Ramaswamy, a Brahmin from Mysore living with his French wife in Aix-en-Provence, is writing a thesis on Cathar heresy. The novel is in the form of a spiritual quest, taking the protagonist back to India and later to Cambridge. Its metaphysical structure is underlined by the title, which refers to a complex passage about the self as the only reality and the illusory nature of everything beyond it.

Seth, Vikram 1952– Born in India, he was educated in Britain, the USA and China. His collections are: *The Humble Administrator's Garden* (1985), quiet, graceful pieces influenced by THOMAS HARDY and PHILIP LARKIN; *The Golden Gate* (1986), a novel in verse about Californian life; and *All You Who Sleep Tonight* (1990). *From Heaven Lake* (1983) is an account of his journey through Sinkiang and Tibet to Nepal. *A SUITABLE BOY* (1993), which claims to be the longest serious 20th-century novel in English, won the COMMONWEALTH WRITERS PRIZE.

Sewell, Anna 1820–78 English. Born into a family of Norfolk Quakers, she sometimes assisted her mother, who wrote verses and stories for children. Not until she was 50, when she had become an invalid, did she begin writing her only novel, BLACK BEAUTY. This enduringly popular story of a horse appeared in 1877, a few months before her death.

Shabby Genteel Story, A A story by WILLIAM MAKEPEACE THACKERAY, serialized in 1840 and published in book form in 1852. 'George Brandon', a fashionable young gentleman fleeing his creditors, lodges with the shabby genteel Gann family at Margate and seduces the youngest daughter, Caroline, into a mock marriage. The unfinished story is developed in THE ADVENTURES OF PHILIP, where 'Brandon' reappears under his real name, Firmin.

Shadbolt, Maurice 1932– New Zealand. Prolific but uneven, he has often tackled large public themes. Collections of short stories include *The New Zealanders* (1959), *Summer Fires and Winter Country* (1963) and *Figures in Light* (1978). Novels include: *Among the Cinders* (1965); *Strangers and Journeys* (1972), a realistic work taking in events such as the Depression and the 1951 waterfront strike; *A Touch of Clay* (1974); *Danger Zone* (1976), about French nuclear testing in the Pacific; *The Lovelock Version* (1980), which breaks with realistic narrative conventions; *Season of the Jew* (1986), about the rebellion of the 19th-century Maori leader Te Kooti; *Monday's Warriors* (1990); and *The House of Strife* (1993), about Hone Heke's rebellion in 19th-century North Auckland. *One of Ben's* (1993) is an autobiography. *The Lovelock Version* won the NEW ZEALAND BOOK AWARD and the GOODMAN FIELDER WATTIE BOOK AWARD; *Strangers and Journeys* and *The Season of the Jew* also won the Goodman Fielder Wattie.

Shadow Lines, The A novel by AMITAV GHOSH, published in 1988 and awarded a SAHITYA AKADEMI prize in 1989. It follows the protagonist's account of an uneventful Calcutta childhood, mostly lived vicariously through his more cosmopolitan relatives. The reminiscences gradually form an intimate family chronicle, moving between Calcutta, Delhi, London and Dhaka (Bangladesh) over four generations. The 'shadow lines' of the title refer to political frontiers, which (it is implied) are less substantial than the contours of individual memory.

Shamela Andrews, An Apology for the Life of Mrs See PAMELA and FIELDING, HENRY.

Shanks, Edward See SCIENCE FICTION.

Shapcott, Thomas (William) 1935– Australian. *Selected Poems 1956–1988* (1989) is the best introduction to the range of a poet who has shown his commitment to both traditional and experimental forms in many volumes, beginning with *Time on Fire* (1961). He turned to fiction in the 1980s. *Flood Children* (1981), *The Birthday Gift* (1982), *White Stag of Exile* (1984), *Hotel Bellevue* (1986) *The Search for Galina* (1989) and *Mona's Gift* (1993) are novels; *Limestone and Lemon Wine* (1988) and *What You Own* (1991) are stories. *Holiday of the Icon* (1984), *Mr Edmund* (1990) and *His Master's Ghost* (1990) are children's books. Shapcott has tried to define the direction of Australian verse in a succession of influential anthologies. He has also published *Biting the Bullet: A Literary Memoir* (1990).

Sharp, William 1855–1905 Scottish. Under his own name he produced novels, including *The Sport of Chance* (1888) and *The Children of Tomorrow* (1889) and several volumes of poetry: *The Human Inheritance, The New Hope, Motherhood and Other Poems* (1882), *Earth's Voices* (1884), *Romantic Ballads and Poems of Phantasy* (1888) and *Sospiri di Roma* (1891). This work is less interesting than the rhapsodic verse and prose romances on

Celtic themes which he represented as being by Fiona Macleod, less a pseudonym then a second literary personality whose identity he kept a closely guarded secret. They include *Pharais* (1894), *The Mountain Lovers* (1895), *The Sin-Eater and Other Tales* (1895), *The Washer of the Ford* (1895) and a collection of articles, *The Winged Destiny* (1904).

Sharpe, Tom [Thomas] **(Ridley)** 1928– English. His exuberant, defiantly tasteless comedy works best when harnessed to angry satire of apartheid in *Riotous Assembly* (1971) and *Indecent Exposure* (1973) and of Oxbridge venality in *Porterhouse Blue* (1974). Softer targets – decaying aristocrats, decadent public schools, ruthless developers – make for enjoyably boisterous tales; some feature Wilt, the luckless polytechnic lecturer of *Wilt* (1976), *The Wilt Alternative* (1979) and *Wilt on High* (1984). *Grantchester Grind: A Porterhouse Chronicle* (1995) returns to the scene of Sharpe's earlier triumph, while *The Midden* (1996) follows the fortunes of Timothy Bright, super-crook *manqué*.

Shaw, George Bernard 1856–1950 Irish. He is, of course, best remembered for his long succession of witty and provocative plays, beginning with *Widowers' Houses* (1892), and including, among many others, *Mrs Warren's Profession* (written 1893, produced 1902), *Arms and the Man* (1894), *Candida* (1897), *The Devil's Disciple* (1897), *You Never Can Tell* (1899), *Man and Superman* (1905), *Major Barbara* (1905), *Doctor's Dilemma* (1906), *Caesar and Cleopatra* (1907), *Misalliance* (1910), *Androcles and the Lion* (1913), *Pygmalion* (1913), *Heartbreak House* (1920), *Back to Methuselah* (1922), *Saint Joan* (1923), *The Apple Cart* (1929) and *The Millionairess* (1936).

Between 1879 and 1883, before he had started his career in the theatre and before he had even made his mark as a music and drama critic, he made a false start as a novelist. None of the five novels he produced found a publisher easily or quickly. In the order of their composition, they are: *Immaturity* (1931), a title, he later said, of 'merciless fitness'; *The Irrational Knot* (1926), effectively his first study of sex and marriage; *Love Among the Artists* (1916); *Cashel Byron's Profession* (serialized in 1884, published in book form in 1886), the most interesting, about prizefighting; and *An Unsocial Socialist* (1887). Though he later congratulated himself on his narrow escape from being a successful novelist, he did return intermittently to prose fiction – notably in his socio-political parable, *The Adventures of a Black Girl in Her Search for God* (1932).

***She**: A History of Adventure* A novel by HENRY RIDER HAGGARD, published in 1887.

The scholar Horace Holly, who narrates the story, goes to Africa with his ward, Leo Vincey, on a quest to avenge Leo's first ancestor, Kallikrates, murdered by an unknown woman. They discover the underground tombs of Kôr,

ruled over by a mysterious queen who has the secret of eternal life: She-Who-Must-Be-Obeyed, or Ayesha. She recognizes Leo as the reincarnation of Kallikrates, whom she murdered because he would not accept her love. Leo and Holly are taken to the Place of Life, an underground cavern where they may step into the Fire of Life and be made immortal. When Ayesha herself enters the Fire she becomes immeasurably old and then monkey-like before dying. Shattered and transformed by their experience, the heroes set out for Tibet, where they hope to encounter Ayesha again.

Haggard wrote two sequels, *Ayesha* (1905) and *Wisdom's Daughter* (1923), both lacking the haunting power of the original.

Shelley, Mary (Wollstonecraft) 1797–1851 English. She was the only daughter of WILLIAM GODWIN and MARY WOLLSTONECRAFT, who died a few days after her birth. At 16 she ran away to France and Switzerland with the poet Shelley, marrying him in 1816 on the death of his wife Harriet. Her most famous work, FRANKENSTEIN: *or, The Modern Prometheus* (1818), was begun on Lake Geneva in the summer of 1816 as her contribution to a ghost-story competition devised by Byron, Shelley and Byron's friend Polidori.

She returned to England after Shelley's death and devoted herself to the welfare of their only surviving child, Percy Florence, and to her career as a writer. None of her later novels matched the power, originality, and mythical sweep of her legendary first work. Of more abiding interest, however, are: *Mathilde*, an unfinished novel begun in 1819 (published in 1959), which draws strongly on her relations with Godwin and Shelley; *Valperga* (1823), a romance set in 14th-century Italy which portrays the lovelessness and destructiveness of personal political ambition; and *The Last Man* (1826), a vision of the end of human civilization, set in the 21st century. She also edited the first authoritative edition of Shelley's poems (1839). *Rambles in Germany and Italy, in 1840, 1842 and 1843* (1844), was well received.

Sheridan, Frances 1724–66 Anglo-Irish. The mother of the playwright Richard Brinsley Sheridan (1751–1816), she moved from Dublin to London in 1754 with her husband, the actor-manager Thomas Sheridan. She launched her career as a novelist with the popular *Memoirs of Miss Sidney Biddulph: Extracted from Her Own Journal* (1761), heavily influenced by SAMUEL RICHARDSON's *PAMELA*, and followed her heroine's further tribulations in a *Continuation of the Memoirs* (1767). Her other novels were *The History of Nourjahad* (1767) and *Eugenia Adelaide*, her first effort, not published until 1791. Three plays, *The Discovery* (1763), *The Dupe* (1764) and *A Trip to Bath* (1765), were produced at Drury Lane.

Sherlock Holmes stories Four novels and 56

short stories by SIR ARTHUR CONAN DOYLE. They are not just the most famous and enduring contribution to DETECTIVE FICTION but also probably the most imitated, parodied and adapted literary works in the language.

Holmes and his colleague Dr Watson first appear in two novels, *A Study in Scarlet* (published in *Beeton's Christmas Annual* for 1887) and *The Sign of Four* (1890), but did not reach a wide readership until Doyle began the short stories for *The Strand Magazine* collected as *The Adventures of Sherlock Holmes* (1892) and *The Memoirs of Sherlock Holmes* (1894). To free himself from his creation Doyle killed Holmes off in the last story, 'The Final Problem', but the resulting outcry forced him to return to a subject which he increasingly saw as a distraction from his serious work. *The Hound of the Baskervilles* (1902) narrates an early case of the dead detective's, but 'The Adventure of the Empty House', in *The Return of Sherlock Holmes* (1905), reveals how Holmes had in fact survived apparent death at Moriarty's hands. Holmes appeared in a further novel, *The Valley of Fear* (1915), and two more collections, *His Last Bow* (1917) and *The Case-Book of Sherlock Holmes* (1927).

Doyle's literary model was EDGAR ALLAN POE's stories about Dupin, from which he elaborated the brilliant but eccentric detective, the admiring friend who narrates the story, the cases which are puzzling and fantastic as much as sensationally criminal, and the dramatically revealed solution. To them he added a strong feeling for late Victorian and Edwardian London, witty dialogue and a chivalric concern for the unjustly oppressed. Such qualities are perhaps best displayed in the early short stories, particularly 'A Scandal in Bohemia', 'The Red-Headed League' and 'The Adventure of the Speckled Band'. Of the novels, *The Hound of the Baskervilles*, mainly set on Dartmoor, is the most firmly constructed. The first of many actors to play Holmes was William Gillette, who toured for over 30 years in his melodrama, *Sherlock Holmes* (1899).

Sherwood, Mary Martha 1775–1851 English. The best remembered of her many pious stories and tracts aimed at children is *The History of the Fairchild Family* (1818), about the misadventures of Lucy, Emily and Henry Fairchild. In a notorious passage Mr Fairchild shows them a rotting corpse hanging on a gibbet as a warning against family disputes.

Shiel, M(atthew) P(hipps) 1865–1947 English. He wrote DETECTIVE FICTION in *Prince Zaleski* (1895) and horror stories *Shapes in the Fire* (1896) before cashing in on the boom in SCIENCE FICTION and future war stories with *The Yellow Danger* (1898). A fervent believer in social and evolutionary progress, he combined a quasi-Nietzschean interest in 'overmen' with insistence on the necessity of altruism. His masterpiece is *The*

Purple Cloud (1901), which visits catastrophe on the earth to test the faith of a modern Job. His philosophy is most comprehensively displayed in later novels such as *How the Old Woman Got Home* (1928) and *Dr Krasinski's Secret* (1929) and a last scientific romance, *The Young Men are Coming!* (1937).

Shields, Carol 1935– Canadian. Born in a Chicago suburb, she has mainly lived in Winnipeg since 1957. She was over 40 before her first novel, *Small Ceremonies* (1976), appeared but quickly established a reputation as one of Canada's leading novelists. Like *Small Ceremonies*, *The Republic of Love* (1992) is a complex study of a woman on the brink of changing her life in early middle age. *The Stone Diaries* (1993; PULITZER PRIZE) is typical of her fiction in constantly suggesting the extraordinariness latent in a supposedly ordinary woman's life. Other novels are *The Box Garden* (1977), *Happenstance* (1980), *A Fairly Conventional Woman* (1982), *Swann: A Mystery* (1987; retitled *Mary Swann* in the UK, 1990) and *Larry's Party* (1997). She has also published short stories, in *Various Miracles* (1985) and *The Orange Fish* (1989), and two collections of verse.

Shirley A novel by CHARLOTTE BRONTË, published in 1849. A CONDITION OF ENGLAND NOVEL, it is set in Yorkshire during the Luddite riots.

Robert Gérard Moore, a millowner, falls into conflict with his workers in trying to install new machinery. His brother, Louis, is tutor to the wealthy Keeldar family and, even though he loves the rector's niece, Caroline Helstone, Robert proposes to Shirley Keeldar. She rejects him with contempt. The end of the Napoleonic war frees him from his difficulties and the devoted Caroline accepts him. Shirley, meanwhile, is drawn to Louis. The character of Shirley, which made the Christian name popular, is believed to have been modelled on EMILY BRONTË.

Shorthouse, Joseph Henry 1834–1903 English. He is remembered for *JOHN INGLESANT* (privately printed, 1880; published, 1881), HISTORICAL FICTION evoking religious and political tensions during the English Civil War. It also reflects Shorthouse's preoccupation with Victorian tensions between Anglicans and Roman Catholics in the aftermath of the Oxford Movement. Apart from other novels, he also wrote *The Platonism of Wordsworth* (1882) and edited George Herbert's *The Temple* in 1882.

Shute, Nevil [Norway, Nevil Shute] 1899–1960 English by birth and education, he settled in Australia. His fiction often exploited his expertise as an aircraft engineer: *No Highway* (1948) makes metal fatigue into the stuff of mystery and suspense. Other novels include *Marazan* (1926), *So Disdained* (1928), *Lonely Road* (1932), *Ruined City* (1938), *What Happened to the Corbetts* (1939), *Pied Piper* (1942), *Pastoral* (1944), *The Far*

Country (1952), *In the Wet* (1953), *The Breaking Wave* (1955), *On the Beach* (1957) and *The Trustee from the Toolroom* (1960). *A Town Like Alice* (1949), his best-known novel, invests its bleak Australian setting with romance and adventure.

Sidhwa, Bapsi 1938– Pakistani. Sidhwa's fiction has been coloured by her Parsee background and her first-hand experience of Indian Partition. Her first novel, *The Crow Eaters* (1978), is a satirical account of a Parsee community in Lahore. *The Bride* (1983) is about a city-educated woman trying to flee from an arranged marriage with a northern tribesman. *Ice-Candy-Man* (1988) is a partly autobiographical account of Partition, seen through the eyes of a young girl.

Sidney, Sir Philip See ARCADIA.

Silas Marner: The Weaver of Raveloe A novel by GEORGE ELIOT, first published in 1861.

Falsely judged guilty of theft, Silas Marner leaves his dissenting community and, as the novel opens, has been living for 15 years as a linen-weaver in Raveloe, lonely but increasingly wealthy. Squire Cass has two sons: Godfrey, attracted to Nancy Lammeter but secretly married to the opium-ridden Molly Farren, and the good-for-nothing Dunstan (Dunsey). Dunstan steals Marner's gold and disappears. Molly dies in the snow-covered fields trying to reach the squire's residence to disclose her marriage. Their little girl, Eppie, toddles away from her dying mother to the threshold of Marner's cottage, where she is cared for by the lonely weaver. In his eyes she becomes more precious than his lost gold. The narrative moves forward 16 years to the discovery of the skeleton of Dunstan Cass with Silas's gold in a newly drained stone-pit. This revelation prompts Godfrey Cass to admit to Nancy, now his wife but childless, that Eppie is his daughter. They try to adopt the young girl, but neither Eppie nor Silas wish to be separated, and the novel concludes with her marriage to the worthy Aaron Winthrop. The story is spiced with rustic humour and forceful village characters.

Silko, Leslie Marmon 1948– American. Of Laguna Pueblo ancestry, she draws on traditional Laguna sources to explore Native American cultures and identities. *Ceremony* (1977), a novel about a mixed-blood Laguna haunted by his experiences in the Pacific during World War II, remains her best-known work. Other work includes: *Laguna Woman* (1974), a collection of poems; *Storyteller* (1981), poetry and short fiction; *Almanac of the Dead* (1991), a novel; *Sacred Water* (1993), narratives and pictures; and *Yellow Woman and the Beauty of the Spirit* (1996), a collection of essays.

Sillitoe, Alan 1928– English. He remains best known for his novel *Saturday Night and Sunday Morning* (1958) and the title story of *The Loneliness of the Long-Distance Runner* (1959; HAWTHORNDEN PRIZE), working-class fiction which linked his name with that of other provincial realists of the late 1950s and early 1960s such as JOHN BRAINE and STAN BARSTOW.

silver-fork novel A mocking name for early 19th-century novels of fashionable life and manners. Authors included Lady Charlotte Bury (1775–1861), THEODORE HOOK, LADY BLESSINGTON, Lady Caroline Lamb (1785–1828), EDWARD BULWER LYTTON, BENJAMIN DISRAELI, FRANCES TROLLOPE, Thomas Henry Lister (1800–42), Robert Plumer Ward (1765–1846), CATHERINE GORE and SUSAN FERRIER.

Silverberg, Robert 1935– American. He has produced more than 100 works of SCIENCE FICTION, more than 60 works of non-fiction and various works in other genres. His finest achievement is a series, including *Thorns* (1967), *The Man in the Maze* (1969), *A Time of Changes* (1971), *Dying Inside* (1972) and *Shadrach in the Furnace* (1976), using the science-fictional vocabulary of ideas to model situations of extreme psychological alienation. Other novels include *Downward to the Earth* (1970), *Son of Man* (1971), *Gilgamesh the King* (1984), *Lord of Darkness* (1985), *Kingdoms of the Wall* (1992) and *Hot Sky at Midnight* (1994). *The Reality Trip and Other Implausibilities* (1972), *Born with the Dead* (1974) and *The Conglomeroid Cocktail Party* (1984) are among his many collections of short stories.

Simak, Clifford D. See SCIENCE FICTION.

Simms, William Gilmore 1806–70 American. His 30 novels, immensely successful in their day, depicted the Old South and helped to propagate the Southern myth of perfectibility. The best-known is *THE YEMASSEE: A Romance of Carolina* (1835), about the 1715 uprising by the Yemassee Indians against the English colonists. Others include: *Martin Faber* (1833), a study of a murderer; *Guy Rivers: A Tale of Georgia* (1834), a romance of the Southern frontier; *The Partisan: A Tale of the Revolution* (1835); *Mellichampe: A Legend of the Santee* (1836), also about the Revolutionary War; and *Woodcraft: or, Hawks about the Dovecote* (1854; originally published as *The Sword and the Distaff: or, 'Fair, Fat, and Forty'*, 1852). As well as short stories, many books of verse and much ephemeral journalism, he also published several works of non-fiction: the essay 'Slavery in America' (1837), *The History of South Carolina* (1840), *The Geography of South Carolina* (1843) and *The Life of Francis Marion* (1844).

Simple Story, A A novel by ELIZABETH INCHBALD, published in 1791. Dorriforth, a priest, and his ward, Miss Milner, fall in love but cannot marry until he inherits a peerage and is released from his vows. When she resumes an affair with a former suitor, Dorriforth (now Lord Elmwood) banishes her and their daughter Matilda. Lady Elmwood dies of remorse and Elmwood's feelings are revived when Matilda is abducted by a libertine. He restores her to her home and position. The character of Dorriforth/Elmwood was apparently based on the actor John Philip Kemble.

Simpson, Helen See DANE, CLEMENCE.

Sinclair, Iain 1943– English. He was already an established poet when he published *White Chappell, Scarlet Tracings* (1987), one of many novels of its decade inspired by Jack the Ripper. It is distinguished by the ferocious exuberance of Sinclair's imagination and by his encyclopaedic knowledge of London. The same qualities inform: two subsequent, highly praised novels, *Downriver (or, The Vessels of Wrath): A Narrative in Twelve Tales* (1991), which won the JAMES TAIT BLACK MEMORIAL PRIZE, and *Radon Daughters: A Voyage, between Art and Terror, from the Mound of Whitechapel to the Limestone Pavements of the Burren* (1994); and the 'excursions' in *Lights Out for the Territory* (1997).

Sinclair, May [Mary] **(Amelia St Clair)** 1863–1946 English. *The Three Sisters* (1914), about middle-class women in the repressive society of Victorian and Edwardian Britain, was the first of her 'psychological' novels, showing the influence of Freud, Jung and Havelock Ellis. She was also an admirer of DOROTHY RICHARDSON's *Pilgrimage* and became a leading exponent of STREAM OF CONSCIOUSNESS. *The Three Sisters* was followed by *Mary Oliver* (1919), an intense study of a mother-daughter relationship, and *The Life and Death of Harriet Frean* (1922). In all, she wrote 24 novels as well as short stories and literary criticism.

Sinclair, Upton 1878–1968 American. *THE JUNGLE* (1906), an exposé of the meat-packing industry in Chicago, remains his best-known work and perhaps the most famous of all 'muckraking novels'. Sinclair went on to publish more than 100 books, including a series of pamphlets on American life: *The Profits of Religion* (1918); *The Brass Check* (1919), on journalism; *The Goslings* (1924), on education; *Money Writes!* (1927), on art and literature; and *The Flivver King* (1937) on the motor industry. *World's End* is an 11-volume *ROMAN FLEUVE* following the life of Lanny Budd, the illegitimate son of a munitions tycoon, from the eve of World War I through the turbulence of inter-war politics to World War II and the anti-Communist climate in the USA after the war. Its individual volumes are *World's End* (1940), *Between Two Worlds* (1941), *Dragon's Teeth* (1942; PULITZER PRIZE), *Wide is the Gate* (1943), *The Presidential Agent* (1944), *Dragon Harvest* (1945), *A World to Win* (1946), *A Presidential Mission* (1947), *One Clear Call* (1948), *O Shepherd, Speak!* (1949) and *The Return of Lanny Budd* (1953). Sinclair published a selection from his correspondence, *My Lifetime in Letters* (1960), and an autobiography (1962).

Singh, Khushwant 1915– A London-trained lawyer of Sikh background, he began his literary career while holding a diplomatic post in Canada. *TRAIN TO PAKISTAN* (1956; as *Mano Majra*

in the USA) is a powerful account of Partition as reflected in a border village. *I Shall Not Hear the Nightingale* (1959) tells the story of a Punjabi Sikh family in the 1940s, while *Delhi* (1989) provides a massive chronicle of the city. Singh has also published four collections of short stories.

Sir Charles Grandison, The History of An EPISTOLARY NOVEL by SAMUEL RICHARDSON, published in 1753–4.

Harriet Byron arrives in London society and excites the desires of the wealthy, dishonourable Sir Hargrave Pollexfen. When she repeatedly refuses him, he has her abducted and packed off to his country estate in a carriage. She is saved by the intervention of the wealthy and gallant Sir Charles Grandison, and the pair fall in love. While in Italy, though, Sir Charles had become attached to Clementina della Porretta, daughter of a noble family. Clementina suffers a mental breakdown and her parents beg Sir Charles to return urgently to Italy, to save her at any price. The lady recovers when he arrives, but the hero's honour is saved from a difficult dilemma by Clementina's decision that their different religions constitute too great an impediment. With a clear conscience Sir Charles returns to England and marries Harriet.

Sir Harry Hotspur of Humblethwaite A novel by ANTHONY TROLLOPE, serialized in 1870 and published in volume form in 1871. A study in ancestral pride and the stubbornness born of high breeding and noble feelings, it has a tragic power and concentration unique in Trollope's work.

Sir Harry Hotspur, a wealthy Cumberland squire, prefers to leave his property to his daughter Emily rather than George Hotspur, a distant cousin. The rakish George wins Emily's heart and her father refuses his consent. Pressed by creditors and the threat of legal action, George undertakes never to see Emily again in return for payment of his debts and an annuity. Emily is taken to Italy by her parents, where she learns of George's marriage to his mistress and dies broken-hearted.

Sir Launcelot Greaves, The Life and Adventures of A novel by TOBIAS SMOLLETT, published in volume form in 1762. His fourth novel, it is generally regarded as one of his weakest. Sir Launcelot Greaves is an 18th-century Don Quixote, riding about England in armour with his ludicrous squire, Timothy Crabshaw. The humour is harsh and the main interest of the book lies in its picture of England before the Industrial Revolution and in a few of its characters: the rogue Ferret, Mrs Gobble, a justice's wife and Captain Crowe, a naval knight-errant.

Sister Carrie A novel by THEODORE DREISER, published in 1900. Carrie Meeber, a Midwestern country girl, moves to Chicago and becomes the mistress of Charles Drouet, a salesman, before taking up with his friend George Hurstwood, a middle-aged, married restaurant manager. He embezzles money and elopes with Carrie to New York, where he opens a saloon. It fails and Carrie begins a successful career when she is forced to work as a chorus girl to support them. She deserts Hurstwood, who ends up a drunken beggar on Skid Row, eventually committing suicide.

Sitwell, Sir (Francis) Osbert (Sacheverell) 1892–1969 English. The brother of Edith and Sacheverell Sitwell, he wrote variously and prolifically. His poetry includes political and pacifist satires in *The Winstonburg Line* (1919), the text for William Walton's choral work, *Belshazzar's Feast* (1931), and *Demos the Emperor* (1949), a 'Secular Oratorio'. *Before the Bombardment* (1926) is the best-known of several novels. He is most likely to be remembered for his autobiography: *Left Hand, Right Hand* (1945), *The Scarlet Tree* (1946), *Great Morning!* (1948), *Laughter in the Next Room* (1949) and *Noble Essences* (1950). A later volume was *Tales My Father Taught Me* (1962).

Sketch Book of Geoffrey Crayon, Gent., The A book of essays and tales by WASHINGTON IRVING, serialized in 1819–20. Most pieces are descriptive and thoughtful essays on England, though two of the most famous tales, 'The Legend of Sleepy Hollow' and 'Rip Van Winkle', are set in America. *The Sketch Book* made Irving the first American author to receive international recognition.

Sladek, John See SCIENCE FICTION.

Slaughterhouse-Five A novel by KURT VONNEGUT JR, published in 1969. Billy Pilgrim is kidnapped by alien Tralfamadorians, taken to a distant planet and put on display. He learns that time is an illusion; things occur simultaneously. The narrative moves between significant events in his life: particular emphasis falls on his experiences in World War II, when he is captured by the Germans and survives the Allies' bombing of Dresden in a converted slaughterhouse. He marries his way into a profession as an optometrist, lives through a plane crash, loses his wife in a car accident, and is assassinated at a convention on flying saucers. Prefaced by Vonnegut's account of his own experience of the bombing of Dresden, the novel is a chilling indictment of war.

Small House at Allington, The The fifth of ANTHONY TROLLOPE'S BARSETSHIRE NOVELS, serialized in 1862–4 and published in book form in 1864.

The widowed Mrs Dale lives with her daughters Lily and Bell at the Small House at Allington as tenant of her brother-in-law Squire Dale. Lily falls in love with a civil servant, Adolphus Crosbie, but he jilts her for an unhappy and unsuccessful marriage to Lady Alexandrina De Courcy. Lily's love for him prevents her marrying the devoted Johnny Eames. A related plot deals with Eames's romantic and financial entanglements in London; the public thrashing he gives Crosbie makes him a local hero. Lily's sister resists an advantageous match with her cousin Bernard and instead marries a local physician, Dr Crofts.

The saddest of the Barsetshire novels, it established Lily Dale as a favourite heroine with the public. Plantagenet Palliser, a central character in the PALLISER NOVELS, first appears in *A Small House at Allington*.

Smart, Elizabeth 1913–86 Canadian. She spent most of her adult life in England. Her long liaison with GEORGE BARKER prompted *By Grand Central Station I Sat Down and Wept* (1945), a passionate love-poem in prose. She also published a second short novel, *The Assumption of the Rogues and Rascals* (1978), as well as two collections of poems, *A Bonus* (1977) and *Eleven Poems* (1982), and a collection of poetry and prose, *In the Mean Time* (1984). As an expatriate writer, her closest affinities were with English poetry.

Smedley, Francis Edward 1818–64 English. He was known for novels blending romance with sport and adventure. The most popular was *Frank Fairleigh: or, Scenes from the Life of a Private Pupil* (1850); others were *Lewis Arundel* (1852) and *Harry Coverdale's Courtship* (1855).

Smiley, Jane 1949– American. Often set in the Midwest, her fiction examines the dynamics of family life. It includes: *Barn Blind* (1980); *At Paradise Gate* (1981); *Duplicate Keys* (1984), a mystery novel set in New York; *The Greenlanders* (1988) is ambitious HISTORICAL FICTION based on Viking sagas and the colonization of Greenland; *Ordinary Love and Good Will* (1989), two novellas; *A Thousand Acres* (1991; PULITZER PRIZE), her best-known book, reworking *King Lear* from a feminist perspective; and *Moo* (1995), a sprawling satire of academic life (see CAMPUS NOVEL). *The Age of Grief* (1987) and *The Life of the Body* (1990) are collections of stories.

Smith, Ali(son) (May) 1962– Scottish. *Free Love* (1995) is a collection of short stories considering the many faces of love. *Like* (1997), a novel set partly in Smith's native Inverness, explores relations between England and Scotland in the 1980s through two contrasting narratives.

Smith, Charlotte 1749–1806 English. She was known as a poet and, chiefly, as a novelist. *Emmeline: or, The Orphan of the Castle* (1788), her first novel, is a sentimental romance. *Desmond* (1792), *The Banished Man* (1794) and *The Young Philosopher* (1798) chart her changing reactions to the revolution in France, where she and her husband had taken refuge to avoid his creditors in Britain. *The Old Manor House* (1793) is a work of more sober realism, admired by SIR WALTER SCOTT.

Smith, Iain Crichton 1928– Scottish. He writes in English and Gaelic and translates his own work and that of other Scottish Gaelic poets. The Gaelic language and the landscape and people of the Scottish islands and Highlands figure prominently in his writing. Fiction includes: *Consider the Lilies* (1968), a poignant evocation of an elderly woman caught up in the Highland Clearances; *A Field Full of Folk* (1982); *The Tenement* (1985); *The Dream* (1990); *Selected Stories* (1990) and *An Honourable Death* (1992). Verse, gathered in *Collected Poems* (1992), includes the sequence 'Shall Gaelic Die?' and the much-anthologized 'Old Woman'. Selected essays appear in *Towards the Human* (1986).

Smith, Pauline (Janet) 1882–1959 South African. Though she lived mostly in Britain, the austere, rigorously crafted short stories in *The Little Karoo* (1925), and her novel about late 19th-century Boer peasant life, *The Beadle* (1926), show a sensitive grasp of Afrikaner culture. *A.B.* (1933) is a tribute to ARNOLD BENNETT, who first encouraged her.

Smith, Rosamond See OATES, JOYCE CAROL.

Smith, Stevie [Florence Margaret] 1902–71 English. Known for her distinctive and deceptively 'simple' verse, gathered in *Collected Poems* (1975), she also wrote three novels which are rarely accorded their rightful place in the ranks of experimental fiction. *Novel on Yellow Paper* (1936) is the first-person narrative, using STREAM OF CONSCIOUSNESS, of Pompey Casmilus, the apparently scatty secretary of a publishing magnate. He reappears in *Over the Frontier* (1938), darker-toned in its confrontation with fascism and anti-semitism. Smith's last novel and her own favourite, *The Holiday* (1949), is set during World War II.

Smither, Elizabeth 1941– New Zealand. Emily Dickinson, Wallace Stevens and William Empson are acknowledged influences on the spare, often witty lyrics, which have appeared in such volumes as *Here Come the Clouds* (1975), *You're Very Seductive William Carlos Williams* (1978), *Casanova's Ankle* (1981), *Professor Musgrove's Canary* (1986) and *A Pattern of Marching* (1989). Her fiction is characterized by urbane and shimmering prose: plot and theme matter less than stylistic surface in *First Blood* (1983) and *Brother-love Sister-love* (1986). Her short stories appear in *Night at the Embassy* (1990) and *Mr Fish and Other Stories* (1993).

Smollett, Tobias (George) 1721–71 Scottish. Born at Leven, near Loch Lomond, he studied at Glasgow and Edinburgh universities and became a surgeon's mate in the navy, serving under Admiral Vernon at the siege of Cartagena in 1741. His youthful writing included poetry – *The Tears of Scotland* (1746), about the Duke of Cumberland's reprisals after the 1745 rebellion, and the satirical *Advice* (1746) and *Reproof* (1747) – and a stubbornly unperformed play about James I of Scotland, *The Regicide*, which he published in 1749.

His first novel, *THE ADVENTURES OF RODERICK RANDOM* (1748), drew on his naval experience and theatrical disappointments. *THE ADVENTURES OF PEREGRINE PICKLE* (1751) continued the vein of violent, hard-bitten PICARESQUE for which his novels are known. Though he obtained the degree of Doctor of Physic in 1752, he soon abandoned his practice in Bath for London, where he earned an insecure living from literary hack work. *THE ADVENTURES OF FERDINAND COUNT FATHOM* appeared in 1753 and his translation of *Don Quixote* in 1755. A comedy, *The Reprisal: or, The Tars of Old England*, was staged in 1757 at Drury Lane by David Garrick, whom he had caricatured as Marmoset in *Roderick Random*. As editor of the *Critical Review or Annals of Literature* in 1756–63 he was relentlessly quarrelsome with other authors and spent three months in prison for libel. While there, he wrote *THE LIFE AND ADVENTURES OF SIR LAUNCELOT GREAVES*, printed in *The British Magazine* (which he edited 1760–1) and in volume form in 1762. His *Complete History of England Deduced from the Defeat of Julius Caesar to the Treaty of Aix-la-Chapelle, 1748* (1758) brought him some financial success. *The Briton*, the journal he started in 1762 to defend the Earl of Bute, the Prime Minister, prompted John Wilkes to reply with *The North Briton*. The controversy dissolved their friendship, without preventing Bute's resignation or earning Smollett his gratitude.

Smollett went to France and Italy for his health in 1764. *Travels through France and Italy* (1766) confirmed his reputation for ill-temper and prompted LAURENCE STERNE to caricature him in *A SENTIMENTAL JOURNEY* as 'the learned Smelfungus'. *Adventures of an Atom* (1769) is a political satire. A journey, again in search of health, to Edinburgh and Inverary in 1770 contributed impressions to his last and arguably most accomplished novel, *THE EXPEDITION OF HUMPHRY CLINKER* (1771). He died at Leghorn.

Snow, C(harles) P(ercy), 1st Baron Snow of Leicester 1905–80 English. His career as scientist and eventually politician is mirrored in his ROMAN FLEUVE, *Strangers and Brothers* (1940–70). It follows the career of Lewis Eliot in a leisurely manner, permitting a wide survey of contemporary life, in *Strangers and Brothers* (1940; later retitled *George Passant*), *The Light and the Dark* (1947), *Time of Hope* (1949), *The Masters* (1951), *The New Men* (1954), *Homecomings* (1956), *The Conscience of the Rich* (1958), *The Affair* (1959), *Corridors of Power* (1963), *The Sleep of Reason* (1968) and *Last Things* (1970). His influential *The Two Cultures and the Scientific Revolution* (1959), arguing that literary intellectuals and scientists had ceased to communicate, was savagely attacked by F. R. Leavis for its utilitarian approach to the study of the humanities. *Science and Government* (1961) examined the power factor in government-sponsored research. *Public Affairs* (1971) deals with the dangers as well as the benefits of technology. *A Variety of Men* (1967) presents biographical studies. Snow married PAMELA HANSFORD JOHNSON in 1950.

Soldiers Three A collection of 13 stories by RUDYARD KIPLING, published in 1888 alongside the booklets entitled *Under the Deodars*, *The Phantom Rickshaw* and *Wee Willie Winkie* and reprinted with them in a two-volume collection (1892). The stories depict the soldierly virtues necessary to sustain the Empire and the daily life of the British fighting man on the alert against potential invaders from Afghanistan. Elements of farce and melodrama are most evident in the short episodes of battle and skirmish. But the strongest ingredients are the atmosphere of the brooding landscape and the men's stoicism, companionship and ability to survive a tedious, emotionally cheerless routine.

Solomon Gursky was Here A novel by MORDECAI RICHLER, published in 1989. It won the COMMONWEALTH WRITERS PRIZE in 1990. His most ambitious novel, it interweaves a number of stories, moving between the 19th-century London underworld, the Franklin expedition to discover the North-West passage, the Canadian Prairies during the Depression and contemporary Quebec. Moses Berger, the central figure, sets out to discover the truth about the mysterious Solomon Gursky and his family. The trail he follows yields many comic surprises, including the discovery that Solomon's grandfather Ephraim survived the Franklin expedition, leaving traces of Jewish artefacts in the Arctic.

Somerset Maugham Award A British literary prize awarded annually to up to four works of any type except drama. It was endowed by W. SOMERSET MAUGHAM in 1947 to help young British writers to travel and gain experience of foreign countries. The first winner, in 1948, was A. L. BARKER with *Innocents* (1947). Subsequent fiction-winners, with their dates of publication, have included: FRANCIS KING's *The Dividing Stream* (1951), DORIS LESSING's *Five* (1953), John le Carré's *The Spy Who Came in from the Cold* (1963), MICHAEL FRAYN's *The Tin Men* (1965), B. S. JOHNSON's *Trawl* (1966), SUSAN HILL's *I'm the King of the Castle* (1970), WILLIAM BOYD's *A Good Man in Africa* (1981), Matthew Kneale's *Whore Banquets* (1987), Helen Simpson's *Four Bare Legs in a Bed* (1990), Lawrence Norfolk's *Lemprière's Dictionary* (1991), Alan Warner's *Morven Caller* (1995) and Philip Hensher's *Kitchen Venom* (1996).

Somerville, Edith See SOMERVILLE AND ROSS.

Somerville and Ross [Somerville, Edith Anna Oenone (1858–1949) and Martin, Violet Florence (1862–1915)] Anglo-Irish. The most popular of the cousins' work represents the tradition of exploiting the humours of the true Irish in relation to the owners of the big houses and estates. It includes: *An Irish Cousin* (1889), their first book; *The Real Charlotte* (1894), their most

ambitious novel; *The Silver Fox* (1898), a novel about hunting; and the enormously popular *Some Experiences of an Irish RM* (1899), stories about a resident magistrate in Ireland, continued in *Further Experiences of an Irish RM* (1908). Edith Somerville continued to use the pseudonym of Somerville and Ross after Violet Martin's death, for *The Big House of Inver* (1925) among other works.

Sons and Lovers A novel by D. H. LAWRENCE, published in 1913. Largely autobiographical, it is based on his childhood and youth.

Gertrude Coppard, a schoolteacher, marries Walter Morel, a miner, but he drinks heavily and resists her efforts to change him. She concentrates her energies on her children and, after the death of her oldest son, William, makes Paul Morel the focus of her emotions and aspirations. Walter Morel is scorned and excluded by his family. Paul works as a junior clerk in Nottingham and paints in his spare time. He falls in love with Miriam Leivers, an intense, reserved and 'spiritual' girl. Mrs Morel is jealous. Later Paul has an affair with Clara Dawes, a married woman, and is also powerfully drawn to her husband, Baxter. Mrs Morel suffers a long and painful illness, which Paul relieves by administering morphia. After her death he determines to set out and make his own life.

Sontag, Susan 1933– American. She is best known for her essays on *avant-garde* film and for her literary criticism, collected in *Against Interpretation* (1966), *Styles of Radical Will* (1969) and *Under the Sign of Saturn* (1980). Influential longer studies are: *On Photography* (1977); *Illness as Metaphor* (1977), written after she contracted cancer; and *AIDS and its Metaphors* (1989). Her surreal and experimental novels include *The Benefactor* (1963), *Death Kit* (1967) and *The Volcano Lover* (1992), about Nelson. *I, etcetera* (1978) is a collection of short fiction. She has also written two filmscripts, *Duet for Cannibals* (1969) and *Brother Carl* (1971), and a play, *Alice in Bed* (1993).

Sorrentino, Gilbert 1929– American. His experimental fictions range from the encyclopaedic *Mulligan's Stew* (1979), written in the mode of JAMES JOYCE's ULYSSES and FINNEGANS WAKE, to *The Orangery* (1978), a poetry sequence consisting of variations on the word 'orange'. Other novels and fictions include *Steelwork* (1970), *The Actual Quality of Imaginative Things* (1971), *Splendide-Hôtel* (1973), *Aberration of Starlight* (1980), *Crystal Vision* (1981), *Blue Pastoral* (1983), *Odd Number* (1985), *Rose Theater* (1987), *Misterioso* (1989), *Under the Shadow* (1991), *Red the Fiend* (1995) and *Pack of Lies* (1997).

Sound and the Fury, The A novel by WILLIAM FAULKNER, published in 1929.

The decline of the Compson family, and the crucial role played by the daughter, Caddy, who ran away, is evoked in four separate sections, largely reliant on STREAM OF CONSCIOUSNESS. The first three are narrated by Caddy's brothers: Benjy, an 'idiot'; Quentin, who kills himself while a freshman at Harvard; and the embittered Jason. The final section concentrates on the Compsons' black servant, Dilsey, and her grandson, Luster. An appendix which Faulkner added in 1946 reviews the history of the Compson family from 1699 to 1945 and ends with this assessment of the blacks who served the Compsons: 'They endured.'

South Wind The most popular novel by NORMAN DOUGLAS, considered *risqué* when it was published in 1917. It is set on the Mediterranean island of Nepenthe (based on Capri), where the Bishop of Bambopo, Thomas Heard, is visiting his cousin Mrs Meadows during the season of the *sirocco*, or south wind. The plot revolves around a series of Rabelaisian conversation pieces involving Nepenthe's exotic inhabitants, including the Duchess of San Martino (an aspiring Catholic), Don Francesco ('a thoroughgoing pagan'), Mr Keith (a heretical eccentric) and Freddy Parker, the Commissioner. Caught under the spell of the south wind, the Bishop finds himself condoning much that he should not, including a murder.

Southern, Terry 1924–95 American. He once enjoyed cult status for the role he played in the iconoclasm and the drug culture of the 1960s. The eroticism of *Candy*, co-written with Mason Hoffenberg, made it an underground classic after it was published by Maurice Girodias' Olympia Press in Paris in 1958; it did not appear in the USA until 1964. The reference in its title to Voltaire's *Candide* is borne out by the satire of *Flash and Filigree* (1958), about the medical profession, and *The Magic Christian* (1959), about an eccentric millionaire, Guy Grand. The best memorial to Southern's time in Hollywood is not his novel *Blue Movie* (1970) but the screenplays he co-wrote for Stanley Kubrick's *Dr Strangelove* (1963), Tony Richardson's film of EVELYN WAUGH's *The Loved One* (1965) and Dennis Hopper's *Easy Rider* (1968). *Red Dirt Marijuana and Other Tastes* (1967) brings together stories and essays in the style of New Journalism associated with TOM WOLFE and Hunter S. Thompson.

Soyinka, Wole 1934– Nigerian. He is primarily a playwright, ranging from geniality to angry farce and satire in such works as *The Trials of Brother Jero* (*Three Plays*, 1963) and *The Lion and the Jewel* (1963). Yoruba cosmography and culture, explicated in *Myth, Literature and the African World* (1976), are also prominent in *The Road* (1965) and *Death and the King's Horseman* (1975). Initially turning to fiction for want of a stage outlet, he has written two novels: *THE INTERPRETERS* (1965) and the powerful *Season of Anomy* (1973), an allegory of political upheavals in a thinly disguised post-Independence Nigeria. He writes about his imprisonment during the Nigerian Civil War in a prose journal, *The Man Died* (1973), and verse collections, *Poems from Prison* (1969) and *A Shuttle in the Crypt* (1972). *Aké: The Years of Childhood* (1981) and its sequel, *Ibadan: The Penkelmes Years* (1994), are memoirs. Other works include *Art, Dialogue and Outrage: Essays on Literature and Culture* (1988). Soyinka received the Nobel Prize for Literature in 1986.

Spark, Muriel (Sarah) 1918– Scottish. She established her talent for irony and black humour in *The Comforters* (1957), *Memento Mori* (1959) and *The Ballad of Peckham Rye* (1960). She is perhaps best known for *THE PRIME OF MISS JEAN BRODIE* (1961), successfully filmed, and *Girls of Slender Means* (1963), set in Kensington. Other novels include *The Mandelbaum Gate* (1965), *The Public Image* (1968), *The Driver's Seat* (1970), *The Take-Over* (1976), *Loitering with Intent* (1981), *A Far Cry from Kensington* (1988), *Symposium* (1990) and *Reality and Dreams* (1996). *Collected Stories* and *Collected Poems* both appeared in 1967. *Curriculum Vitae* (1992) is an autobiography.

Spillane, Mickey 1918– American. He is best known for tough-guy DETECTIVE FICTION featuring Mike Hammer, in a series begun with *I, the Jury* (1947), *My Gun is Quick* (1950) and *Vengeance is Mine!* (1950). Frequently attacked for their sex and violence – as well as their unthinking reflection of the anti-Communism of the 1950s – the Mike Hammer novels stand in a direct line of descent from the comic strips (for which Spillane once wrote scripts) and the stories in 'pulp' magazines such as *Black Mask*.

Spiritual Quixote, The: *or, The Summer's Ramble of Mr Geoffry Wildgoose: A Comic Romance* A novel by RICHARD GRAVES, published in 1773.

Enthusiastic about Methodism, Geoffry Wildgoose sets off with the cobbler Jerry Tugwell on a summer tour to preach the Gospel and meet his hero, George Whitefield (whom Graves had known at Oxford). He encounters life on the road in 18th-century England. The Methodists generally, and Whitefield in particular, are satirized.

Spoils of Poynton, The A short novel by HENRY JAMES, serialized in 1896 as *The Old Things*, and published in volume form in 1897.

Poynton Park is the home of Owen Gereth and the 'spoils' are the antiques and *objets d'art* with which his mother has filled it. Mrs Gereth tries to prevent Owen from marrying the tasteless Mona Brigstock by interesting him instead in her kindred spirit, Fleda Vetch. He is increasingly attracted to Fleda, thus reassuring his mother's worries about the fate of the spoils, but Mona insists on the marriage. Owen writes to Fleda from abroad, asking her to choose from Poynton whatever object she would like. She arrives just as the house and its contents inexplicably go up in flames.

Spy, The: *A Tale of the Neutral Ground* A novel by JAMES FENIMORE COOPER, published in 1821.

His first successful book, set during the American Revolution. The complicated plot, introducing elements which SPY FICTION would later make familiar, centres on the activities of Harvey Birch, a supposed loyalist who is actually a spy for George Washington in the 'neutral ground' of Westchester County, New York. Washington appears several times disguised as 'Mr Harper'.

spy fiction A type of fiction which deals with espionage, either by following the activities of professional agents and members of the intelligence services in their attempts to obtain or protect covert information, or by following the adventures of ordinary people caught up in conspiracies against national security. Beyond this simple generalization, it grows difficult to isolate spy fiction as a distinct sub-genre because of the territory it shares with others types of GENRE FICTION, such as thrillers and adventure stories in its reliance on suspense and physical incident, DETECTIVE FICTION in its preoccupation with puzzles and codes, and even SCIENCE FICTION in its interest in technological innovation. A distinctive feature of the spy novel, however, is its intimate relationship to contemporary political events: a relationship which may variously be interpretative or exploitative, but which has accounted for the major phases of its development as well as its popularity with a mass audience.

Spies themselves sometimes like to claim their profession is as old as prostitution. Literary critics seeking antique precedents for the spy novel can point to the Old Testament story of Moses sending spies to check on the Promised Land in advance of the Israelites. In practical terms, however, the development of the spy novel is considerably more recent. Its beginning can be found in JAMES FENIMORE COOPER's *THE SPY* (1821), which weaves a true story from the American War of Independence into a complicated plot full of hints for later writers in its use of double agents, disguise and duplicity of motive.

After Cooper the USA contributed surprisingly little to the development of spy fiction, and most of the writers who took up his hints were British. They were encouraged to do so by a combination of factors dominating the political climate in the early years of the twentieth century: the perceived threat to the Empire, the defeat suffered in the Boer War, tensions in central Europe, the presence in Britain of political exiles engaged in conspiracy, and the confirmation offered by the Dreyfus Affair in France of the role espionage had come to play in political and diplomatic relations. All these different elements combined to give spy fiction a special relevance.

One response, immortalized by RUDYARD KIPLING's *KIM* (1901), was the novel celebrating the 'great game' of espionage on the North-West frontier. Another, rooted in anxiety about Germany's rise to power, was the novel prophesying war and invasion. Its provenance already stretched back to SIR GEORGE TOMKYNS CHESNEY's *The Battle of Dorking* (1871), but it was given new life by ERSKINE CHILDERS in *The Riddle of the Sands* (1903), a cunningly crafted story about German plans for invasion by sea, and by William Le Quex (1864–1927) in *The Invasion of 1910* (1905). A vivid writer of pulp fiction, Le Quex brought a new and highly influential degree of versimilitude to his subject by introducing what purported to be facsimiles of agents' reports, drawings and secret instructions from Berlin.

When war did actually come, it had a profound impact on a form whose possibilities writers had just begun explore. JOHN BUCHAN's *The Thirty-Nine Steps* (1915) introduced Richard Hannay, a hero whose status would, in a succession of novels, move from amateur to professional and whose career would span the pre-war period of invasion scares, World War I itself and the post-war years. After the war popular writers such as E. Phillips Oppenheim (1866–1946), best known for *The Great Impersonation* (1920), quickly grasped that espionage made a convenient focus for novels appealing to a fascination with high society, fashionable life and exotic locations (the Côte d'Azur being the favourite choice). This durable formula still produces best-sellers today.

Quantitatively speaking, the years from 1914 to 1939 were the most productive in the history of spy fiction, though qualitatively speaking they were hardly its golden age. From all the mass of work two broad traditions emerged: the romantic and the realistic. Romantic spy fiction, whose heroes were usually amateurs drawn accidentally into the world of conspiracy and intrigue, was produced by EDGAR WALLACE, Sydney Horler (1888–1954), who aspired to inherit Wallace's mantle, and a host of lesser names, such as C. E. Montague (1867–1928), Francis Beeding (the pseudonym of John Palmer, 1888–1944) and Hilary St George Saunders (1898–1951), author of stories about Colonel Alastair Granby. Typical of the better known practitioners was Sapper (Herman Cyril McNeile, 1888–1937), with his tales – the first appeared in 1920 – of Bulldog Drummond and his battle against the arch-villain Carl Petersen.

The realistic approach, by contrast, tended to deal with professional agents rather than amateurs. Its chosen locations might sometimes have been foreign and even potentially exotic, but it was their seediness which counted. Above all, it presented espionage not in terms of heroic struggle, much less heroic game, but in terms of moral obliquity, deceit and betrayal. All these elements, of course, were already present in JOSEPH CONRAD's *THE SECRET AGENT* (1907) – a book which has served several generations of writers as a model for realistic spy fiction. Those who profited from Conrad's example between the wars include: W. SOMERSET MAUGHAM, in *Ashenden* (1928), a series of interlinked stories based on his wartime experience as a spy in Switzerland and Russia; ERIC AMBLER, who in early works such as *Epitaph for a Spy* (1938), *The Mask of Dimitrios* (1939; called *A Coffin for Dimitrios* in the USA) and *Journey into Fear* (1940), brought both expertise and a studiously neutral tone to his handling of European politics; GEOFFREY HOUSEHOLD in *Rogue Male* (1939), a novel in the overlapping territory between spy and adventure fiction; and the young GRAHAM GREENE in *Stamboul Train* (1932; called *Orient Express* in the USA), *A Gun for Sale* (1936; called *This Gun for Hire* in the USA) and *The Confidential Agent* (1939).

Greene's career as a spy novelist continued after World War II, reinforced by his wartime experience of espionage, in *The Third Man* (1950), *The Quiet American* (1955), *Our Man in Havana* (1958) and *The Human Factor* (1978). The post-war years, in fact, mark another major phase in the development of spy fiction, stimulated by the Cold War. The political climate might have changed since the 1920s and 1930s, yet the response by novelists only confirmed the gulf between the romantic and realistic traditions. The romantic tradition was most memorably maintained by IAN FLEMING. Beneath their determinedly modern fascination with technological gimmickry, his James Bond novels owed debts to the patriotic vigour of Buchan and the sophisticated veneer of Oppenheim, while their arch-villains placed them in a direct line of descent from Sapper. Apart from Graham Greene himself, the realistic tradition in the Cold War years passed into the hands of JOHN LE CARRÉ, notably in *The Spy Who Came in from the Cold* (1963); LEN DEIGHTON, notably in *The Ipcress File* (1963); and a host of others including John Bingham (Lord Clanmorris, 1908–88), Ted Allbeury (1917–), Gavin Lyall (1932–), Brian Freemantle (1936–) and, in the USA, Richard Condon (1915–96) with *The Manchurian Candidate* (1959).

So completely did the spy novel – whether in the hands of Ian Fleming or of John Le Carré – digest the atmosphere of the Cold War that, with its end, rash prophets foresaw an end to spy novels as well. Yet politics is always fertile in creating tensions and anxieties which grip the public mood and lend themselves to the purposes of spy fiction. International terrorism and the threat of political instability from the Arab states present themselves as appropriate subjects, and have already provided the matter for best-sellers on both sides of the Atlantic. Those who did not wish to be so aggressively

contemporary had ample encouragement from the general revival of HISTORICAL FICTION to attempt a marriage between the spy novel and the historical novel, as Robert Harris (1957–) has done in *Fatherland* (1992) and *Enigma* (1995).

There were deeper reasons why spy fiction did not die. Even before the end of the Cold War, it had begun to relax its concentration on the intrigues of East-West conflict. In Britain the cases of George Blake, Kim Philby and Anthony Blunt had already prompted novelists to consider the maze-like impenetrability of the intelligence establishment itself, as a world where concepts of loyalty or truth quickly lose their meaning. In the USA the conspiracy theories flourishing in the aftermath of the Kennedy assassination had led writers down a similar path. A novel such as DON DELILLO's *LIBRA* (1988) is typical of the result. Here the maze-like intricacies of espionage and the traditional plot complications of spy fiction blend easily with the ethos of POST-MODERNISM, in which meaning has become forever unstable, endlessly elusive, capable of infinite re-writing and infinite re-reading.

Stacpoole, Henry de Vere 1863–1951 English. He wrote well over 50 novels, of which the first commercial successes were *The Crimson Azaleas* (1907) and *The Blue Lagoon* (1908). The latter, a romantic story of a boy and girl shipwrecked on a Pacific island, has been compared to J. M. BARRIE's *Peter Pan* and Maeterlinck's *The Blue Bird*. It was later filmed. Stacpoole wrote four more 'Blue Lagoon' novels: *The Beach of Dreams* (1919), *The Garden of God* (1923), *The Gates of Morning* (1925) and *The Girl of the Golden Reef* (1929). He was also a poet and a translator of Sappho and Villon.

Stafford, Jean 1915–79 American. She was part of the literary circle which included Robert Lowell (her former husband), DELMORE SCHWARTZ and Randall Jarrell. Her novels are *Boston Adventure* (1944), *The Mountain Lion* (1947) and *The Catherine Wheel* (1952). Her characteristic preoccupation with loneliness, and particularly with lonely, outcast women, was more naturally suited to the highly crafted stories which appeared in volumes such as *Children are Bored on Sunday* (1953) and *Bad Characters* (1964) and were gathered in *The Collected Stories of Jean Stafford* (1969; PULITZER PRIZE).

Stalky & Co. A collection of nine stories by RUDYARD KIPLING, published in 1899. Five other tales, originally scattered in separate collections, were added to *The Complete Stalky & Co.* (1929). Kipling drew on his boyhood experiences at the United Services College at Westward Ho! in Devon. Stalky, M'Turk and Beetle (a loose self-portrait of Kipling) conduct a battle of wits with the masters and other boys. It is notable that the authority of the headmaster, 'Prooshian' Bates, is never seriously questioned and that the trio affirms the laws of social responsibility and self-discipline. In the final story the ex-schoolboys continue their exploits in India.

Stapledon, W(illiam) Olaf 1886–1950 English. His SCIENCE FICTION presents ideas about ethics and evolution. The most famous are *Last and First Men* (1930), a history of man's descendants extending over billions of years, and *Star Maker* (1937), a spectacular vision of the whole universe and its creator. His more orthodox scientific romances – *Odd John* (1935), *Sirius* (1944), *The Flames* (1947) and *A Man Divided* (1950) – deal with exceptional individuals doomed to personal failure.

Stead, C(hristian) K(arlson) 1932– New Zealand. He has published critical studies of MODERNISM, in *The New Poetic* (1964) and *Pound, Yeats, Eliot and the Modernist Movement* (1986), as well as being influenced by it in his own verse. Collections include *Whether the Will is Free* (1962), *Crossing the Bar* (1972), *Walking Westward* (1979), *Poems of a Decade* (1983) and *Voices* (1990). His novels, often markedly political, include *Smith's Dream* (1971; winner of the GOODMAN FIELDER WATTIE BOOK AWARD), *All Visitors Ashore* (1984; winner of the NEW ZEALAND BOOK AWARD), *The Death of the Body* (1986) and *Sister Hollywood* (1989). *The End of the Century at the End of the World* (1993) combines romance, academic mystery and a satirical examination of radical politics in the 1960s. *The Singing Wakapapa* (1994; winner of the New Zealand Book Award) is a historical detective story about a Pakeha (European) family whose ancestor arrived in New Zealand in 1834. *Five for the Symbol* (1981) is a collection of stories.

Stead, Christina (Ellen) 1902–83 Australian. She lived abroad between 1928 and 1974, in Britain, France and the USA, and set only one major work, *Seven Poor Men of Sydney* (1934), in Australia. As a result, though internationally recognized, she was at first not seen as an Australian writer and not properly acknowledged in her own country. Her gift for minute, objective observation of experience is perhaps seen at its best in three novels: *THE MAN WHO LOVED CHILDREN* (1940); *For Love Alone* (1944), about her fight to get to Britain; and *The Dark Places of the Heart* (1966; retitled *Cotter's England* in the UK, 1967), about Britain during the Cold War.

Other works include: *The Salzburg Tales* (1934), a collection of stories; *The Beauties and Furies* (1936) and *The House of All Nations* (1938), set in Paris; *Letty Fox: Her Luck* (1946), *A Little Tea, a Little Chat* (1948) and *The People with the Dogs* (1952), set in America; *The Little Hotel* (1973); *Miss Herbert (The Suburban Wife)* (1976); *The Puzzleheaded Girl* (1967), four novellas; *Ocean of Story* (1985), a posthumous collection of stories; and the unfinished *I'm Dying Laughing* (1986). Two collections of letters have appeared (1992).

Stegner, Wallace (Earle) 1909–93 American. He began a long and prolific career with a novella, *Remembering Laughter* (1937). Memories of his childhood in the North-West filled the epic proportions of *The Big Rock Candy Mountain* (1943). He won a PULITZER PRIZE for *Angle of Repose* (1971), a documentary novel recreating, from her papers, the life of the author and illustrator Mary Hallack Foote (1847–1938). Subsequent work included *The Spectator Bird* (1976), a short novel about old age and memory, and *Crossing to Safety* (1987), about friendship. His shorter fiction can be found in *Collected Stories* (1990).

Stein, Gertrude 1874–1946 American. From 1903 until her death she lived in France, remaining in Paris except for the period of Nazi occupation. With her companion, Alice B. Toklas, she became the hostess to a circle of painters and writers, including Picasso, Braque, Matisse, Juan Gris, SHERWOOD ANDERSON, ERNEST HEMINGWAY and F. SCOTT FITZGERALD. Altogether she produced over 500 titles: novels, poems, plays, articles, portraits of famous people and memoirs. *Three Lives: Stories of the Good Anna, Melanctha, and the Gentle Lena* (1909), introduced her highly experimental style, with repeated phrases, sentences and paragraphs, and little punctuation. *The Autobiography of Alice B. Toklas* (1933), probably her best-known work, is a fictionalized account of her own life from her companion's point of view. Others include: *Composition as Explanation* (1926), a critical study; *Lucy Church Amiably* (1930), a novel; *Four Saints in Three Acts* (1929), a lyric drama staged as an opera (with music by Virgil Thompson) in 1934; *Lectures in America* (1935); *Everybody's Autobiography* (1937), which is her own autobiography; *Wars I Have Seen* (1945), a memoir; and *Brewsie and Willie* (1946), a novel about American soldiers in France during and immediately after World War II.

Steinbeck, John 1902–68 American. He came to prominence with *Tortilla Flat* (1935), a vivid portrait of life among the *paisanos* in Monterey. The tone of his work changed with *In Dubious Battle* (1936), a novel about a strike among migratory workers in the California fruit orchards, *Of Mice and Men* (1937), the story of two itinerant farm workers who yearn for some sort of home, and *The Long Valley* (1938), 13 stories set in Salinas Valley. His best-known work is *THE GRAPES OF WRATH* (1939), about a family fleeing from the Oklahoma dust bowl to California. It was followed by *The Moon is Down* (1942), a short novel about Norwegian resistance to the Nazi occupation, *Cannery Row* (1945), in which he returned to the *paisanos* of Monterey, and *The Wayward Bus* (1947), in which passengers on a stranded bus in California become a microcosm of contemporary American frustrations. Among his other novels are *The Pearl* (1947), *East of Eden* (1952), *Sweet Thursday* (1954) and *The Winter of Our*

Discontent (1961). His non-fiction includes *Bombs Away: The Story of a Bomber Team* (1942), *The Log of the Sea of Cortez* (1951), a selection of his dispatches as a war correspondent, *Once There was a War* (1958), and *Travels with Charley* (1962), about his personal rediscovery of America. He received the Nobel Prize for literature in 1962.

Stephen Hero See PORTRAIT OF THE ARTIST AS A YOUNG MAN, A.

Stephens, James 1882–1950 Irish. He became famous with a prose fantasy, THE CROCK OF GOLD (1912). *The Demi-Gods* (1914) is in the same vein, while *Deirdre* (1923) again took Celtic legend for its subject. Stephens had begun his career with *Insurrections* (1909), the first of several volumes of verse later gathered in *Collected Poems* (1926, enlarged 1954). Collections of stories include *Here are Ladies* (with poems; 1913), *In the Land of Youth* (1924), *Etched in Moonlight* (1928) and *Irish Fairy Tales* (1920). An active Sinn Feiner, he also edited the poems of his friend and colleague Thomas MacDonagh, executed in the Easter Rising of 1916, and published *The Insurrection in Dublin* (1916).

Sterne, Laurence 1713–68 English. The son of an army subaltern, he was born in Tipperary, brought up in garrison towns and educated for eight years in Halifax until his father's death in 1731 left the family penniless. A cousin helped him to enter Jesus College, Cambridge, as a 'sizar' (poor scholar). He received his degree in 1737 and then took orders, becoming vicar of Sutton-on-the-Forrest in Yorkshire in 1738 and later prebendary of York Minster. After marrying Elizabeth Lumley in 1741 he moved to Stillington, another Yorkshire parish. His wife suffered an emotional breakdown in 1758, when he was involved in a number of 'sentimental' dalliances with local ladies.

The first two volumes of his novel, *TRISTRAM SHANDY*, appeared in 1760, immediately catapulting him to literary fame; further volumes appeared in 1761, 1762, 1765 and 1767. In London Sterne was lionized by fashionable society, an experience he relished. Taking a flamboyant delight in playing the parts of his own characters in real life, he became a cult figure, the subject of outlandish anecdotes and, to some, the object of disapproval. His new recognition brought him the perpetual curacy of Coxwold, near his other Yorkshire parishes, where he named his home Shandy Hall. He adopted the persona of the parson in *Tristram Shandy* for *The Sermons of Mr Yorick*, of which successive volumes appeared in 1760, 1766 and 1769. They were extremely well subscribed, despite their lack of doctrinal content and infrequent attention to such devotional topics as faith. In 1762–4 Sterne lived abroad at Toulouse, with his depressed wife and his daughter Lydia, spending much of his remaining life in Continental travel intended to relieve his tuberculosis. A seven-month tour of France and Italy during 1765 resulted in *A SENTIMENTAL JOURNEY* (1768), a second novel as arresting and fragmentary as his first. During 1767 Sterne formed an attachment to Eliza Draper, the wife of an East India Company officer for whose eyes he kept a journal published after his death as *Letters from Yorick to Eliza* (1775).

Despite the immense popularity of *Tristram Shandy*, in particular, during Sterne's lifetime, his full importance has been acknowledged only since his death. Samuel Johnson, SAMUEL RICHARDSON and Oliver Goldsmith were among contemporaries to denounce his whirling, anarchic method or take offence at his playful indecency. Yet Sterne's oddity is neither accidental nor perverse; it is the strategy of an inventive, thoughtful comic talent. His work points the way to later experiments (by JAMES JOYCE and exponents of POST-MODERNISM, for example), though not all of these would be conducted with the vein of good humour, delicate yet often dark, which runs so riddlingly through his work.

Stevenson, Robert Louis 1850–94 Scottish. Poor health did not prevent him being an enthusiastic traveller. *An Inland Voyage* (1878), describing a canoe tour of France and Belgium, was followed by the enduringly popular *Travels with a Donkey in the Cevennes* (1879). *The Amateur Emigrant* (posthumously published, 1895) described his journey to California in 1879. In America he married Mrs Fanny Osbourne, for whose son Lloyd he first devised *TREASURE ISLAND* (1883). Back in England determined to make his living by writing, he devoted much of his energy to carefully crafted essays and short stories, collected in *Virginibus Puerisque* (1881), *Familiar Studies of Men and Books* (1882), *New Arabian Nights* (1882), *The Merry Men* (1887), *Memories and Portraits* (1887), *Across the Plains* (1892) and *Island Nights' Entertainments* (1893).

The list of his novels mixes popular romance with steadily developing psychological intensity. In addition to *Treasure Island*, it includes *Prince Otto* (1885), THE STRANGE CASE OF DR JEKYLL AND MR HYDE (1886), *KIDNAPPED* (1886) and its sequel, *Catriona* (1893), THE BLACK ARROW (1888), THE MASTER OF BALLANTRAE (1889), and *The Wrong Box* (1889) and *The Wrecker* (1892), both with Lloyd Osbourne. He left unfinished *WEIR OF HERMISTON* (1896) and *St Ives* (1897 and 1898), completed by SIR ARTHUR QUILLER-COUCH.

Other work includes books of poems, *A Child's Garden of Verses* (1885) and *Underwords* (1887), and several fustian dramas, *Deacon Brodie* (1880), *Admiral Guinea* (1884), *Beau Austin* (1885) and *Macaire* (1885), written with W. E. Henley. Stevenson left England in 1888 and finally settled in Samoa, where he enjoyed a period of comparative health and productivity before his early death. *In the South Seas* (1896) and *A Footnote to History* (1892) document his indignation at European exploitation of the Polynesian islands. Even more important are his two novellas: *The Beach of Falesá*, so inimical to his readers that, though a version was included in *The Island Nights' Entertainments*, its full text was not published until 1984, and *The Ebb-Tide* (1894), prefiguring JOSEPH CONRAD's *HEART OF DARKNESS*.

Long categorized merely as a belletrist and children's writer, Stevenson is now being widely revalued and his novels are beginning to take their rightful place in the adult tradition of early MODERNISM. 'Victor Hugo's Romances' (1874), 'A Gossip on Romance' (1883) and 'A Humble Remonstrance' (1884) – a reply to HENRY JAMES's 'The Art of Fiction' which led to a lifelong friendship between the two writers – show his search for a fiction which would avoid the trap of representationalism, his focus on 'incident' as a type of narrative epiphany, and his use of old forms for new purposes.

Stewart, J(ohn) I(nnes) M(ackintosh) 1906–94 Scottish. Under his own name he wrote novels and critical studies, notably *Eight Modern Writers* (1963). But he is better known for his long career writing DETECTIVE FICTION as Michael Innes, beginning with *Death at the President's Lodging* (1936; as *Seven Suspects* in the USA), *Hamlet, Revenge!* (1937), *Lament for a Maker* (1938) and *Stop Press* (1939). Ingenious, urbane and playful, they remain classics. Their policeman hero, John (later Sir John) Appleby, later featured in chase novels – notably *The Secret Vanguard* (1940), *From London Far* (1946), *The Journeying Boy* (1949) and *Operation Pax* (1951; as *The Paper Thunderbolt* in the USA) – as well as fantastic adventures, such as *The Daffodil Affair* (1942) and *Appleby's End* (1945).

Stoker, Bram [Abraham] 1847–1912 Irish. He worked as a civil servant and drama critic in Dublin before becoming personal manager to Sir Henry Irving. *DRACULA* (1897) is the most famous of his 15 works of fiction. He also wrote the two-volume *Personal Reminiscences of Henry Irving* (1906).

Stone, Louis 1871–1935 Born in Britain, he was taken to Australia by his parents in 1884. *Jonah* (1911), a realistic account of the life of a working-class larrikin ('street rowdy' or 'Jack the lad'), is now highly regarded as the first classic novel of Sydney life, though it failed to win recognition when it first appeared. He produced only one further novel, *Betty Wayside* (1915), which describes the fortunes of a woman pianist in Sydney.

Stone, Robert (Anthony) 1937– American. *A Hall of Mirrors* (1968) follows three shiftless people to New Orleans, where a right-wing political rally explodes into violence. *Dog Soldiers* (1975) is about heroin smuggling on the Californian border. *A Flag for Sunrise* (1981), his most praised and also his most Conradian novel, chronicles a popular uprising in Central America. *Children of Light* (1986) is a satire on Hollywood, and *Outerbridge Reach* (1992) is a narrative of the sea in which the protagonist tests himself against others and the forces of nature.

Storey, David 1933– English. The grim, rawly realistic portrait of a Rugby League footballer in *This Sporting Life* (1960) prefigures the more extreme depictions of isolated men in crisis in *Radcliffe* (1963) and *Pasmore* (1972). *Saville* (1976), which won the BOOKER PRIZE, *A Prodigal Child* (1982) and *Present Times* (1985), continue Storey's two major themes: the loss of working-class roots and the crises of marriage and career arising out of mid-life stasis. His realistically set but tangentially plotted plays include: *The Contractor* (1970), about the putting-up of a marquee at a wedding; *Home* (1970), set in a mental home; and *The Changing Room* (1972), about football. *Collected Poems* appeared in 1992.

Story of a Country Town, The A novel by E. W. HOWE, published in 1883. The story is told by Ned, the son of John Westlock, a minister-farmer and later businessman, who eventually deserts his family. The important people in Ned's life are: his uncle Jo Erring, driven to murder Clinton Bragg by his jealous love for Mateel Shepherd; the young schoolteacher Agnes Deming, whom Ned marries; and the miller Damon Barker, who makes him aware of the rich and varied world beyond the country town of Twin Mounds.

Stout, Rex (Todhunter) 1886–1975 American. He owed his reputation as a writer of DETECTIVE FICTION to almost 40 novels about Nero Wolfe, beginning with *Fer-de-Lance* (1935) and finishing with *A Family Affair* (1975). Their enduring attraction lies in Stout's unusual mixture of ingredients. Nero Wolfe himself is an eccentric great detective in the classic mould established by SIR ARTHUR CONAN DOYLE, but Archie Goodwin, the Watson-like assistant and narrator, owes a good deal to the hard-boiled tradition pioneered by DASHIELL HAMMETT and RAYMOND CHANDLER.

Stow, Randolph 1935– Australian. He established his reputation with five novels: *A Haunted Land* (1956) and *The Bystander* (1957), linking poetic feeling for landscape with an account of turbulent, emotional lives; *To the Islands* (winner of the MILES FRANKLIN AWARD; 1958, revised edition 1982), a symbolic fable reminiscent of PATRICK WHITE's *Voss*; the densely symbolic *Tourmaline* (1963); and the more realistic *The Merry-Go-Round in the Sea* (1965). He then wrote a popular children's book, *Midnite: Stories of a Wild Colonial Boy* (1967), and continued with the poetry collected in *A Counterfeit Silence* (1969). From 1971 to 1981 he wrote for musical theatre with the composer Peter Maxwell Davies. He returned to the novel with one of his finest books, *Visitants* (1979), followed by *Girl Green as*

Elderflower (1980) and *The Suburbs of Hell* (1984), both set in East Anglia, where he has lived for some years.

Stowe, Harriet Beecher 1811–96 American. She was the daughter of Lyman Beecher, rector of the First Church in Litchfield, Connecticut, and later president of the Lane Theological Seminary in Cincinnati, Ohio. Her brother, Henry Ward Beecher, became an influential preacher and her sister Catharine a prominent writer and ideologue of domesticity, female education and woman's separate sphere. Her husband, Calvin E. Stowe, whom she married in 1836, was a professor at Lane and then at Bowdoin College, Maine.

Here she wrote her first novel, *Uncle Tom's Cabin* (1851–2). Its attack on slavery made it an immediate and controversial best-seller both in the USA and abroad. Triumphal tours of Europe in 1853, 1856 and 1859 forged friendships with George Eliot and Elizabeth Barrett Browning, and provided material for *Sunny Memories of Foreign Lands* (1854). *The Key to Uncle Tom's Cabin* (1853) defended the accuracy of her portrait of the South. A second anti-slavery novel, *Dred: A Tale of the Great Dismal Swamp* (1856), told the story of a dramatic attempt at a slave rebellion, attacking ministers who failed to oppose slavery and again demonstrating the redemptive powers of Christian womanhood, white and black.

She turned away from political controversy in: *The Minister's Wooing* (1859), about love and marriage in the shadow of Calvinist uncertainty; *Agnes of Sorrento* (1862), set in the Catholic Italy of Savonarola; *The Pearl of Orr's Island* (1862), exploiting the local colour of the New England shore; and three novels of New York society, *Pink and White Tyranny* (1871), *My Wife and I* (1871) and its sequel, *We and Our Neighbours* (1875). *Oldtown Folks* (1869) and *Oldtown Fireside Stories* (1871), drew on her husband's childhood memories, and *Poganuc People* (1878), her last novel, on her own.

She also wrote children's books, travelogues, works of theology, temperance tracts and practical articles about housekeeping, decoration and the 'servant problem', including the highly influential *The American Woman's Home* (1869), co-written with her sister Catharine.

Strange Case of Billy Biswas, The See *Billy Biswas, The Strange Case of*.

Strange Case of Dr Jekyll and Mr Hyde, The See *Dr Jekyll and Mr Hyde, The Strange Case of*.

stream of consciousness A technique used by novelists to represent a character's thoughts and sense impressions without conventional syntax or logical sequence. The term was first used by William James in his *Principles of Psychology* (1890) to describe the random flux of conscious and sub-conscious thoughts and impressions in the mind. A parallel description

can be found in Henri Bergson's account (1889) of the *élan vital*, popularized in England by George Bernard Shaw.

Literature can show examples before James and Bergson – notably Laurence Sterne's *Tristram Shandy* (1767), a work profoundly influenced by contemporary theories of mental 'association'. But it was the rise of modernism, bringing with it a determination among novelists to capture the realities of mental life, which encouraged the regular use of stream of consciousness and established its determining features. James Joyce, who preferred the term *monologue intérieur* and claimed to have discovered the technique in Edouard Dujardin's *Les Lauriers sont coupés* (1888), experimented in *Ulysses* (1922) with modes ranging from the telegrammatic brevity of Leopold Bloom's reflections, whose content and sequence is usually dictated by passing sensory impressions, to the largely unpunctuated soliloquy by Molly Bloom which closes the book. Other examples include the work of Virginia Woolf, particularly her later fiction, and of lesser writers such as Dorothy Richardson and May Sinclair. In the USA the most significant experiments are by William Faulkner, particularly in *The Sound and the Fury* (1929) and *As I Lay Dying* (1930). The opening section of the former novel, focused on the thoughts and impressions of the idiot Benjy, constitutes a bravura performance to compare with Molly Bloom's soliloquy.

Streatfeild, Noel 1895–1986 English. *Ballet Shoes* (1936), her first and best book for children, describes a family of orphans who eventually make good in the ballet and theatre world. Other 'career' novels include *Tennis Shoes* (1937) and *White Boots* (1951), about skating. *The Bell Family* (1954) chronicles the domestic adventures of a gently idealized middle-class family which first featured in plays for BBC radio's *Children's Hour*.

Strong, L(eonard) A(lfred) G(eorge) 1896–1958 English. *Dewer Rides* (1929), set on Dartmoor, launched his career as a novelist. *Travellers* (1945) won the James Tait Black Memorial Prize. Versatile and fluent, Strong wrote plays and radio scripts, compiled anthologies, and produced several biographies and autobiographies. *The Body's Imperfection* (1957), a collection of verse, shows him pausing more reflectively than his vast output usually allowed.

Stuart, Francis 1902– Irish. A lifelong Republican, he married Iseult, daughter of Maud Gonne, the Irish nationalist loved by Yeats. In 1939 he went to Germany and remained there during World War II, nominally as a teacher but also as a broadcaster under the Reich's patronage. From *Women and God* (1931) onwards, his fiction had always been to some degree autobiographical. In considering his experience of the war, it grew urgently more so, in *The Pillar of Cloud* (1948), *Redemption* (1949), *The Flowering Cross* (1950) and, most notably, *Black List, Section H* (1971), a 'fictional memoir' which first had difficulty finding a publisher but then was largely responsible for his rehabilitation. *Memorial* (1973), *A Hole in the Head* (1977) and *The High Consistory* (1981) form a trilogy dealing variously with the Irish political crisis.

Sturgeon, Theodore See SCIENCE FICTION.

Sturgis, Howard (Overing) 1855–1920 Novelist. The son of an American businessman, he was born in Britain and raised in a family which numbered many writers, English and American, among its friends. His cousin was George Santayana (for whom, see THE LAST PURITAN). HENRY JAMES admired his first novel, *Tim* (1891), a school-story of boyish loves. *All That was Possible* (1895), an EPISTOLARY NOVEL, is about a 'good' though 'fallen' woman who forms an attachment to a 'virtuous' man. His clear if gentle censure of conventional morality paved the way for the more searching analysis of *Belchamber* (1904), the book universally recognized as Sturgis's best, and one of the most outstanding Edwardian novels. It provides a grim commentary on the venality and cruelty of much Edwardian high society. Henry James, who had interfered ceaselessly in its composition, disliked the finished work, but E. M. FORSTER and VIRGINIA WOOLF were among its many admirers. Thereafter Sturgis published nothing, though various short stories were found among his papers after his death – including a sketch about a Jamesian critic who drove unfortunate authors to suicide.

Styron, William 1925– American. His work, preoccupied with all the various forms of oppression, includes *Lie Down in Darkness* (1951), *The Long March* (1952), *Set This House on Fire* (1960), *The Confessions of Nat Turner* (1967; PULITZER PRIZE), about a black slave rebellion, and *Sophie's Choice* (1979), about the consequences of the Holocaust. *This Quiet Dust* (1982) is a collection of essays and *Darkness Visible* (1990) an account of his battle with depression. Drafts of *Lie Down in Darkness* appear in *Inheritance of Night* (1993), edited by James L. W. West III.

Such a Long Journey A novel by ROHINTON MISTRY, published in 1991. Set in 1971 – when East Pakistan, with Indian support, won political independence as Bangladesh – it chronicles the lives of a group of apartment tenants in a Parsee enclave of Bombay. It includes Gustad Noble, an unassuming bank clerk and family man, who becomes unwittingly involved in fraud, corruption and the political intrigues of the day. The novel was awarded the COMMONWEALTH WRITERS PRIZE.

Suitable Boy, A A novel (or, strictly, trilogy of novels) by VIKRAM SETH, published in 1993. It won the COMMONWEALTH WRITERS PRIZE. Often compared in its ambition and sheer size (more than 1800 pages) to one of the great panoramic novels of the 19th century, it is set against the backdrop of modern India's journey towards Independence and Partition and encompasses the country's bewildering array of castes, faiths, families and traditions. The story takes places in the fictional city of Brahmpur. Ending as it begins, with a wedding, it follows a single love story – Lata's long quest for her 'suitable boy' – and the intertwined fates of four families linked by marriage. Through them and scores of supporting characters, ranging from maharajahs, administrators and merchants to poets, peasant farmers and rickshaw wallahs, Seth builds a vivid portrait of an ancient society poised on the brink of momentous change – serious matter conveyed with affection, vigour and humour.

Sun Also Rises, The A novel by ERNEST HEMINGWAY, published in 1926. The British edition (1927) was entitled *Fiesta*. It deals with the 'lost generation' of American and English expatriates in Paris. The narrator is Jake Barnes, an American journalist rendered impotent by a wound in World War I and hence unable to consummate his relationship with Lady Brett Ashley. Jake's self-taught emotional pragmatism is contrasted with the self-pitying sentimentalism of his acquaintance Robert Cohn.

Sunshine Sketches of a Little Town A collection of interlinked short stories by STEPHEN LEACOCK, published in 1912. Its portrait of a quintessential Canadian small town, Mariposa (based on Orillia, Ontario, where Leacock had a summer home), blends sentimentality and irony. This ambivalence prefigures representation of small-town life in the fiction of ALICE MUNRO, ROBERTSON DAVIES and SANDRA BIRDSELL.

Surfacing A novel by MARGARET ATWOOD, published in 1972. The unnamed narrator-protagonist journeys with her lover Joe and two friends to northern Quebec in search of her missing father. It becomes clear that the novel is more centrally about a quest for her own past, particularly its repressed aspects, which she comes to terms with when she dives into a lake and discovers her father's drowned body. 'Surfacing' with a new-found awareness, she regresses into an animal-like state of existence that enables her to free herself from the negative cultural influences of her past. The end sees her emerging from this state, possibly about to go back to the city with Joe.

Surgeon's Daughter, The See CHRONICLES OF THE CANONGATE.

Surtees, R(obert) S(mith) 1805–64 English. He came of a long line of country gentlemen in County Durham. After qualifying in the law, he started writing for the *Sporting Magazine* and founded the *New Sporting Magazine* with Rudolph Ackermann in 1831, editing it until 1836, when he retired to the family property.

His major works were: his trilogy about John Jorrocks, the foxhunting grocer, *JORROCKS'S JAUNTS AND JOLLITIES* (1838; enlarged, posthumous version, 1869), *HANDLEY CROSS* (1843; enlarged version, 1854) and *HILLINGDON HALL* (1845; *MR SPONGE'S SPORTING TOUR* (1853); *Ask Mamma* (1858); *Plain or Ringlets?* (1860); and *Mr Facey Romford's Hounds*, a sequel to *Mr Sponge's Sporting Tour* which was being serialized when he died and appeared in book form in 1865. They are loosely, sometimes carelessly, constructed. What gives them life are the hard-bitten, talkative, closely observed characters taken from the whole spectrum of country life. The foxhunting episodes ring true and the notation of speech, especially North Country dialect, is masterly.

Sutcliff, Rosemary 1920–92 English. *The Chronicles of Robin Hood* (1950) was the first of more than 30 novels for children showing her strong and sophisticated grasp of history. Classics include: *The Eagle of the Ninth* (1954), about the Roman occupation of Britain; *Songs for a Dark Queen* (1978), a savage novel about Boadicea; and *The Light Beyond the Forest* (1979), beginning a cycle about King Arthur. *Blue Remembered Hills* (1983) tells the story of her own early life.

Swan, Susan 1945– Canadian. Her first novel, *The Biggest Modern Woman of the World* (1983), is the fictionalized autobiography of Swan's namesake and possible ancestor, Anna Haining Swan, an exhibit in the showman P. T. Barnum's American Museum in New York. It is a tall tale which blends bizarre fantasy with historical fact. *Last of the Golden Girls* (1991) and *The Wives of Bath* (1993) also portray unconventional women.

Swift, Graham 1949– English. The preoccupation with history and memory announced by *The Sweet-Shop Owner* (1980) and *Shuttlecock* (1981) has continued in subsequent work: *Waterland* (1983), an ambitious Fenland saga which has much in common with MAGIC REALISM and the early fiction of Günter Grass; *Out of This World* (1987); *Ever After* (1992), again exploring inheritance and family history; and *Last Orders* (1996), which won the BOOKER PRIZE and the JAMES TAIT BLACK MEMORIAL PRIZE. *Learning to Swim* (1982) is a collection of stories.

Swift, Jonathan See *GULLIVER'S TRAVELS* and *TALE OF A TUB, A.*

Swinnerton, Frank (Arthur) 1884–1982 English. His novel *Nocturne* (1917) was a critical and commercial success which he felt overshadowed subsequent work. This consisted of nearly 40 novels and 20 critical books. To his work as publisher (responsible for 'discovering' DAISY ASHFORD's *The Young Visiters*) and critic for *The Evening News* and *The Observer*, he added the dimension of close personal contact. Living to the age of 98, he became an important link between the Georgian literary scene and later writing.

Sword of Honour A trilogy by EVELYN WAUGH, comprising *Men at Arms* (1952), *Officers and Gentlemen* (1955) and *Unconditional Surrender* (1961), published as a single work in 1965.

It follows the experiences of Guy Crouchback, a Catholic and man of honour, in World War II. The comedy of *Men at Arms*, much concerned with an eccentric fellow officer, Apthorpe, gives way to the disillusioning accounts of action in Alexandria and Crete in *Officers and Gentlemen* and Italy and Yugoslavia in *Unconditional Surrender*. The portraits of Virginia Troy, Guy's ex-wife, her second husband, Tommy Blackhouse, and the extraordinary Brigadier Ritchie-Hook blend nostalgia with satire.

Sybil: or, The Two Nations A novel by BENJAMIN DISRAELI, published in 1845. The earliest and in some ways the best CONDITION OF ENGLAND NOVEL (see also ROMAN À THÈSE), it is notable for its account of Chartist agitation and its description of the miserable living and working conditions of the poor.

The story contrasts the lives of a spurious aristocracy, ennobled by monastic plunder and commercial greed, with the noble aspirations of the journalist, Stephen Morley, and his friend, Walter Gerard, thoughtful representatives of the working class. Walter's daughter, Sybil, is a Catholic who wishes to take the veil but eventually marries a member of the 'aristocracy' and herself turns out to be the heir to an ancient title.

Sylvia's Lovers A novel by ELIZABETH GASKELL, published in 1863. Set in Monkshaven (Whitby) during the late 18th century, it combines a realistic portrait of whaling and the cruelties of the press gangs with an increasingly melodramatic plot.

Sylvia Robson loves Charley Kinraid, a 'spectioneer' (harpooner), and is loved by her earnest cousin Philip. When Kinraid is taken by the press gang Philip fails to deliver his parting message of constancy to Sylvia and allows her to suppose him dead. Her father Daniel is hanged for his part in a riot against the press gangs. She contracts a loveless marriage with Philip. When Kinraid returns three years later, she refuses to go away with him but disdains her husband for his dishonesty. Philip leaves in disgrace, enlists in the navy and encounters Kinraid, whose life he saves. Eventually Philip returns to Monkshaven, sick and friendless, and is reconciled with Sylvia before his death.

Symons, Julian (Gustave) 1912–94 English. After a hesitant start with *The Immaterial Murder Case* (1945), his DETECTIVE FICTION shifted the emphasis from unravelling puzzles to considering the psychological roots, the social context and the consequences of crime in novels such as *The Thirty-First of February* (1950), *The Broken Penny* (1953), *The Narrowing Circle* (1954), *The Colour of Murder* (1957), *The Progress of a Crime* (1960), *The*

Killing of Francie Lake (1962; called *The Plain Man* in the USA), *The End of Solomon Grundy* (1964), *The Man Who Killed Himself* (1967), *The Man Whose Dreams Came True* (1968), *The Man Who Lost His Wife* (1970) and *The Players and the Game* (1972). *The Blackheath Poisonings* (1978), *Sweet Adelaide* (1980) and *The Detling Murders* (1982; called *The Detling Secret* in the USA) use Victorian settings.

Bloody Murder (1972; revised edition 1992; originally called *Mortal Consequences* in the USA) is both a reliable history of detective fiction and a persuasive argument for his own view of the form. Symons also wrote poetry, popular histories and biographies of, among others, DICKENS (1951) and Thomas Carlyle (1952).

T

Tagore, Rabindranath 1861–1941 Indian. He helped to inspire the Bengali literary revival with poems, short stories and popular songs. To the wider world his appeal came through his own English translations of his work. His versions of the novels *The Home and the World* (1919) and *Gora* (1924) may be regarded as imaginative 'transcreations' rather than mere translations. In 1913 he became the first Asian to receive the Nobel Prize for Literature.

Tale of a Tub, A A prose satire by Jonathan Swift (1667–1745), poet, pamphleteer and satirist. His first major work, it was written *c.* 1696 and published in 1704.

The principal narrative is the 'fable of the coats', an allegory following the fortunes of three brothers each left a coat by their father with strict instructions never to alter it. Peter (the Catholic Church), Martin (the Anglican) and Jack (the Calvinist) all exercise ingenuity in treating what they have inherited as they please and the fable traces the resulting squabble. More interesting are the many digressions – on, for example, critics, madness and digressions – designed to carry the main satiric force of the book. The title itself (as well as meaning 'flim-flam') refers to the practice of throwing tubs off the back of ships to distract the attention of whales; the digressions act in similar fashion. The chief targets of this most complex and accomplished of Swift's early works include religious fanaticism, pedantry, scientific credulity, quackery and self-delusion.

Tale of Two Cities, A A novel by CHARLES DICKENS, serialized in his magazine *All the Year Round* and published in volume form 1859. Set in London and Paris at the time of the French Revolution, it marked a more determined approach to HISTORICAL FICTION than the earlier *BARNABY RUDGE*. It is most alive in its descriptions of mob violence.

After being imprisoned for 18 years in the Bastille, Dr Manette is released and comes to England. His daughter Lucy loves Charles Darnay, an honourable man cursed by his descent from the Evrémondes, and is hopelessly loved by the wastrel Sydney Carton. After his marriage to Lucy, Darnay returns to France and is arrested by the revolutionaries but released through Manette's intercession. When he is arrested again the evidence against him is a denunciation of the Evrémondes written by Manette during his imprisonment. Darnay is condemned to death but saved by the heroic self-sacrifice of Carton, who exploits his physical resemblance to Darnay and takes his place at the guillotine. Minor characters include the fanatical Madame Defarge, the upright Miss Pross and Jerry Cruncher, part-time grave robber.

Talisman, The A novel by SIR WALTER SCOTT, the second of his *Tales of the Crusades*, published in 1825. The talisman of the title has a historical basis in the amulet, known as the Lee-penny, brought back from the Crusades by Sir Simon Lockhart and kept in the possession of his heirs, the Lockharts of the Lee. In Scott's novel the talisman is given to the hero, Sir Kenneth, the Knight of the Leopard, during his adventures in the Holy Land at the time of Richard I. The book once rivalled Scott's *IVANHOE* in popularity.

Tan, Amy 1952– Asian-American. Her novels, which portray the lives and experiences of Chinese and American women, include *The Joy Luck Club* (1989), *The Kitchen God's Wife* (1991) and *The Hundred Secret Senses* (1995).

Tancred: or, The New Crusade A novel by BENJAMIN DISRAELI, published in 1847. The third in the trilogy begun by *CONINGSBY* and *SYBIL*, it draws together characters from the earlier books and reintroduces the enigmatic Sidonia, now revealed as an international negotiator. Tancred, Lord Montacute, retraces the journey made by his Crusader ancestors to Jerusalem to find the roots of Christianity. There he becomes an unwitting pawn in political machinations, is kidnapped, discovers a community worshipping the old Greek gods, and falls in love with Eva, an acute theologian who lectures him on the history of Mediterranean civilization. She refuses his proposal of marriage and swoons at the moment his parents come from England to claim him.

Largely a *ROMAN À THÈSE*, the book is a piece of special pleading for Jewish culture by and about a 19th-century Christian who cannot revert to Judaism, however deep his nostalgia.

Tarkington, (Newton) Booth 1869–1946 American. His first novel, *The Gentleman from Indiana* (1899), was a realist study in the manner of WILLIAM DEAN HOWELLS and his second, *Monsieur Beaucaire* (1900), a historical romance. Subsequent works include: *The Turmoil* (1915); *The Magnificent Ambersons* (1918; PULITZER PRIZE) and *The Midlander* (1924), published together as *Growth* (1927), about the effects on society of the rise of the *nouveau riche* businessman; and *Alice Adams* (1921; Pulitzer Prize), an ironic novel of manners about a girl who seeks but fails to marry a rich man. Among his nostalgic novels of boyhood and adolescence for children are *Penrod* (1914), *Seventeen* (1916), *Penrod and Sam* (1916) and *Penrod Jashber* (1929). Plays include an adaptation of *Monsieur Beaucaire* (1901), *The Man* *from Home* (1908), *The Country Cousin* (1921), *The Intimate Strangers* (1921), *The Wren* (1922) and *Bimbo, the Pirate* (1926).

Tasma See COUVREUR, JESSIE.

Taylor, Bayard (James) 1825–78 American. *Views A-Foot* (1846), about Europe, and *Eldorado: or, Adventures in the Path of Empire* (1850), about the California Gold Rush of 1849, were followed by more travel books describing further adventures: *A Journey to Central Africa* (1854), *The Lands of the Saracen* (1855), *A Visit to India, China and Japan in the Year 1853* (1855), *Northern Travel* (1857), *Travels in Greece and Russia* (1859) and *At Home and Abroad* (1860). His international experience and varied tastes also inform his many volumes of verse, which include *Rhymes of Travel, Ballads and Poems* (1849), *Lars: A Pastoral of Norway* (1873) and *The Echo Club and Other Literary Diversions* (1876). His novels, by contrast, are concerned with America; they include *Hannah Thurston* (1863), *John Godfrey's Fortunes* (1864), *The Story of Kennett* (1866) and *Joseph and His Friend* (1870), the last two set in rural Pennsylvania, where he had been born and brought up. *Beauty and the Beast and Tales of Home* (1872) brings together a diverse collection of stories.

Taylor, Elizabeth 1912–75 English. Her novels, written with simplicity and precision, include: *At Mrs Lippincote's* (1946), a gentle study of bourgeois life; *Palladian* (1947); *A Wreath of Roses* (1950), about a middle-aged woman and a younger man; *The Soul of Kindness* (1963); *Mrs Palfrey at the Claremont* (1972), about old age; and *Blaming* (1976), about a young woman's turmoil after her husband's death. *Hester Lilly* (1954), *The Blush* (1958), *A Dedicated Man* (1965) and *The Devastating Boys* (1962) contain short stories. *Mossy Trotter* (1967) is for children.

Taylor, Peter 1917– American. Nashville, St Louis and Memphis, as well as the fictional town of Thornton, Tennessee, are the setting of many of his works, which frequently centre on the conflict between the values of small-town Southern life and those of an urban culture. *A Woman of Means* (1950) is a novella; *A Summons to Memphis* (1986; PULITZER PRIZE) and *In the Tennessee Country* (1994) are novels. He has published many collections of stories: *A Long Fourth and Other Stories* (1948), *The Widows of Thornton* (1954), *Happy Families are All Alike* (1959), *Miss Leonora When Last Seen* (1963), *The Collected Stories of Peter Taylor* (1969), *In the Miro District and Other Stories* (1977), *The Old Forest and Other Stories* (1985) and *The Oracle at Stoneleigh Court* (1993).

Tenant of Wildfell Hall, The ANNE BRONTË's second novel, published in 1848.

Helen Graham, the tenant of Wildfell Hall, is young, beautiful and said to be a widow. Markham, a neighbouring farmer who narrates the story, falls in love with her and defends her reputation against local gossip until he overhears her in affectionate conversation with her landlord, Frederick Lawrence. Helen's diary shows that she loves Markham but also reveals her secret. She is married to Arthur Huntingdon, a drunkard who made her life so miserable that her brother, Lawrence, offered her Wildfell Hall as a refuge. She tells Markham the truth, and then has to return to her husband, now dangerously ill. His death frees Helen to marry Markham.

Although the novel was a popular success, its frank portrait of Huntingdon's alcoholism and of Helen's struggle to free herself from such a husband struck some contemporaries as offensive. Anne Brontë was unrepentant.

Tender is the Night The last complete novel by F. SCOTT FITZGERALD, published in 1934. A revised edition (1948) reorganized the action into chronological order, but most modern editions follow the original version, which begins on the Riviera.

It is about the decline of Dick Diver, a promising young American psychiatrist studying in Zurich. He marries a beautiful American patient, Nicole Warren, but grows frustrated by their leisurely, sociable life on the Riviera. He becomes infatuated with Rosemary Hoyt, an American actress much younger than himself, and starts to drink heavily. Nicole falls in love with Tommy Barban, a French mercenary and member of their Riviera circle, and eventually divorces Dick. His failure is complete when he returns to a small-town medical practice in America.

Tennant, Emma 1937– English. Her most original work, such as *The Bad Sister* (1978), *Wild Nights* (1980) and *Faustine* (1992), explores extreme psychological states and alternative notions of reality through fantasy, dreams and STREAM OF CONSCIOUSNESS. *Queen of Stories* (1982), *Woman Beware Woman* (1983), *The House of Hospitalities* (1987) and *A Wedding of Curiosity* (1988), the last two beginning a projected sequence called *Cycle of the Sun*, are more conventional. She has also written continuations of JANE AUSTEN's *PRIDE AND PREJUDICE*, in *Pemberley* (1993), and *EMMA* in *Emma in Love* (1996).

Tennant, Kylie 1912–88 Australian. Irony, a talent for the swift evocation of atmosphere and an inclination to value the country more than the city characterize her novels: *Tiburon* (1935), *Foveaux* (1939), *The Battlers* (1941), *Ride on Stranger* (1943), *Time Enough Later* (1945), *Lost Haven* (1946), *The Joyful Condemned* (1953), *The Honey Flow* (1956), *Tell Morning This* (1967) and *Tantavallon* (1983). Other work includes: a children's book, *All the Proud Tribesmen* (1959); a study of Aborigines, *Speak You So Gently* (1959); and an autobiography, *The Missing Heir* (1986).

Tess of the d'Urbervilles: A Pure Woman Faithfully Presented A novel by THOMAS HARDY, published in 1891. It provoked a controversy, continued by *JUDE THE OBSCURE*, which encouraged him to abandon fiction for poetry.

Learning of his descent from the ancient Norman family of d'Urbervilles, poor John Durbeyfield of Marlott joins his wife Joan in encouraging their daughter Tess to seek the kinship of the parvenu Stoke d'Urbervilles. She is seduced by the vulgar Alec d'Urberville and bears a child who dies. To make a fresh start, she goes to work in southern Wessex at the fertile Talbothays farm. There she meets Angel Clare, younger son of a parson, and accepts his offer of marriage. On their wedding night Tess confesses her unhappy past to Angel, who recoils in puritanical horror. He goes off to Brazil and she works at the grim upland farm of Flintcomb Ash. There she is again approached by Alec, now an itinerant preacher. Angel returns to England, weakened but wiser, and traces Tess to Sandbourne, where she is living as Alec's wife. In her despair she kills Alec and, after a brief idyllic period with Angel, is arrested at Stonehenge, tried, and hanged in Wintoncester (Winchester) jail.

Tey, Josephine See MACKINTOSH, ELIZABETH.

Thackeray, William Makepeace 1811–63 Novelist. Born in Calcutta of Anglo-Indian parents, he came to England in 1817 to be educated at private schools and, in 1822–8, at Charterhouse. In 1830 he left Trinity College, Cambridge, after two spendthrift years. He travelled on the Continent, dabbled in journalism, studied law in a desultory manner and, when most of his patrimony was swallowed up in the Indian bank failures of 1833, studied painting in London and Paris. In 1836 he published his first book, lithograph caricatures of the ballet 'La Sylphide' entitled *Flore et Zéphyr*, and, on the strength of his post as Paris correspondent of *The Constitutional*, married Isabella Shawe. By 1840 the signs of her insanity were unmistakable and she was confined, leaving him to care for his daughters: Anne, born in 1837, later ANNE THACKERAY RITCHIE, and Harriet Marian ('Minny'), born in 1840, future first wife of Sir Leslie Stephen (for whom, see VIRGINIA WOOLF).

Three early travel books – *The Paris Sketch Book* (1840), *The Irish Sketch Book* (1843) and *Notes of a Journey from Cornhill to Grand Cairo* (1846) – anticipate his later manner less clearly than the stream of reviews, comic sketches, parodies and satires he contributed to periodicals, often with his own illustrations and under colourful pseudonyms. For *Fraser's Magazine* he wrote *THE YELLOWPLUSH PAPERS* (1837–8), *CATHERINE* (1839–40), *A SHABBY GENTEEL STORY* (1840), *THE GREAT HOGGARTY DIAMOND* (1841) and *The Fitz-Boodle Papers* (1842–3). George Savage Fitz-Boodle reappears as the editor of Thackeray's first real novel, *BARRY LYNDON*, serialized in *Fraser's* in 1844. His growing reputation was consolidated by his work for *Punch*

from 1842 onwards, particularly *The Book of Snobs* (1846–7). His social awareness, and the discontent with contemporary fiction evident in his masterly parody, *PUNCH'S PRIZE NOVELISTS* (1847), inform the satirical, anti-heroic vision of his first major novel, *VANITY FAIR* (1847–8).

An immediate popular and critical success, *Vanity Fair* was followed by a semi-autobiographical *BILDUNGSROMAN*, *THE HISTORY OF PENDENNIS* (1848–50), and *THE HISTORY OF HENRY ESMOND* (1852), carefully planned HISTORICAL FICTION whose melancholy tone reflects his pain at the end of his platonic relationship with Jane Brookfield the previous year. His growing interest in the reign of Queen Anne and the 18th-century is reflected in *The English Humorists of the Eighteenth Century*, casual, anecdotal lectures delivered in 1851, published in 1853, and made the basis of his first American lecture tour in 1852–3. *THE NEWCOMES* (1853–5), a panoramic novel of English social life, was followed by *The Rose and the Ring* (1855), the last and best of his six Christmas Books. On a second visit to the United States in 1855–6 he lectured on *The Four Georges* (1860), treating the Hanoverian kings in the same gossipy manner he had used to discuss the writers of the period. *THE VIRGINIANS*, a historical novel continuing the Esmond family saga, appeared in 1857–9. Thackeray became the founding editor of *The Cornhill Magazine*, a monthly journal launched by the publisher George Smith in 1860. His last works were published in the *Cornhill*: a short novel, *LOVEL THE WIDOWER* (1860), the discursive essays gathered as *The Roundabout Papers* (1860–3), and his last complete novel, *THE ADVENTURES OF PHILIP* (1861–2). *DENIS DUVAL* (1864) was unfinished.

Thackeray's reputation rests on *Vanity Fair*, *Henry Esmond*, and, less securely, *Pendennis* and *The Newcomes*. The authorial garrulity of his later fiction and essays has not always been fashionable, but recent critics have rediscovered the keen satirical eye and comic irreverence of his early works, which have the energy of the 18th-century writers he admired. His sceptical, ironic but compassionate vision of a society dominated by the power of money and class gives his best work the authority of major art.

Tharoor, Shashi 1956– Indian. After beginning his education in India, he received higher degrees in the USA and then worked for the United Nations. *THE GREAT INDIAN NOVEL* (1989) is an epic of modern India. *Show Business* (1994) is a satirical account of the Bombay film industry.

Their Eyes were Watching God A novel by ZORA NEALE HURSTON, published in 1937. Janie Crawford refuses to settle for drudgery and deprivation. She leaves her first husband for a handsome visionary, Joe Starks, and together they establish Florida's first all-black town.

After Joe's death Janie falls in love with the younger, penniless Vergible Woods, known as Tea Cake. When he dies she returns, saddened but victorious, to the town she and Joe had founded.

Thelwell, Michael 1939– Jamaican/American. He is best known for *The Harder They Come* (1980), a novel inspired by Perry Henzell's 1972 film of the same name. Both follow the exploits of a man on the run whose exploits enact cinematic fantasies and make him a folk-hero among Jamaica's urban poor. Thelwell's collection of essays, *Duties, Pleasures and Conflicts* (1987), and many of his short stories deal with the American Civil Rights Movement.

Theron Ware, The Damnation of A novel by HAROLD FREDERIC, published in 1896. Its British title was *Illumination*. It tells the story of a talented young Methodist minister's growing disillusionment with conservative, small-town life in upstate New York, and his interest in exotic, sophisticated ideas. He becomes increasingly detached from his wife and congregation, and increasingly drawn to the beautiful and free-spirited Celia, a Catholic church organist, whom he follows to New York. Humiliated by their encounter, he falls ill. When he recovers, he and his wife go west to Seattle, where he will try to go into business and perhaps into politics.

Theroux, Paul 1941– Born in Massachusetts, USA, he now lives in Britain. *The Great Railway Bazaar* (1975), *The Old Patagonian Express* (1978) and *Riding the Iron Rooster* (1988) are travel books about train journeys. *The Kingdom by the Sea* (1983) tours the coast of the British Isles, while *The Happy Isles of Oceania* (1992) explores the South Pacific. His witty, stylish fiction essays many genres. *Girls at Play* (1969) and *Jungle Lovers* (1971) are tales of naive Westerners in Africa; *The Family Arsenal* (1976) is an atmospheric thriller; *The Consul's File* (1977) and *The London Embassy* (1982) are collections of stories about expatriates in Malaya and London. *The Mosquito Coast* (1981) is a graphic parable set in the Honduran jungle; *O-Zone* (1986) flirts with SCIENCE FICTION; and *My Secret History* (1989) an ambitious *BILDUNGSROMAN*. Other fiction includes *Saint Jack* (1973), *Picture Palace* (1978; WHITBREAD AWARD), *Doctor Slaughter* (1985), *Chicago Loop* (1990) and *My Other Life: A Novel* (1996).

Things Fall Apart CHINUA ACHEBE's first novel, published in 1958. Translated into more than 50 languages, it remains probably the single most influential and widely read novel yet written by an African.

It tells the story of Nigeria from the inside by depicting the arrival of British missionaries and colonial administrators at Umuofia, an Igbo village, at the end of the 19th century. Okonkwo, originally a wealthy elder, becomes progressively discredited until he is imprisoned for

his role in burning the new church. He kills a messenger sent by the District Commissioner and commits suicide. Achebe's depiction of an intricate, finely balanced social structure and his ironic portrayal of the colonial encounter set an influential new pattern for African writing.

Thirkell, Angela 1890–1960 English. The granddaughter of the painter Edward Burne-Jones and the mother of COLIN MACINNES, she was launched by financial necessity on a prolific and popular career as a writer – like her fictional *alter ego* Mrs Morland, who first appeared in *High Rising* (1933). She became best known for comedies of English social life (located, with increasing insistence, in ANTHONY TROLLOPE's fictional Barsetshire) such as *Wild Strawberries* (1934), *August Folly* (1936) and *Summer Half* (1937), probably her most satisfying work. The anti-semitism of *Cheerfulness Breaks In* (1940) signalled a growing snobbishness, and the novels of her last decade, from *The Duke's Daughter* (1951) to *Three Score and Ten* (completed by C. A. Lejeune, 1961), show her invention flagging.

Thomas, Audrey 1935– Born in the USA, she moved to England before emigrating to Canada in 1959. She has also lived in Africa. Her fiction is eclectic, influenced by POST-MODERNISM and strongly feminist in its exploration of women's ambitions and self-contradictions. Collections of short stories include *Ten Green Bottles* (1967), *Real Mothers* (1981), *Goodbye Harold, Good Luck* (1986) and *The Wide Blue Yonder* (1990). Her novels include *Mrs Blood* (1970), *Songs My Mother Taught Me* (1973) and *Blown Figures* (1975), a trilogy centred on one female protagonist, and *Latakia* (1979), *Intertidal Life* (1985) and *Graven Images* (1993).

Thomas, D(onald) M(ichael) 1935– English. He remains best known for a controversial novel, *THE WHITE HOTEL* (1981). Other fiction includes *The Flute Player* (1979), *Birthstone* (1980), a *Russian Quartet* consisting of *Ararat* (1983), *Swallow* (1984), *Sphinx* (1986) and *Summit* (1987), *Lying Together* (1990), *Flying into Love* (1992), about the Kennedy assassination, and *Pictures at an Exhibition* (1993). A poet before he became a novelist, Thomas has published several volumes of verse, including *Selected Poems* (1983), and translations from the Russian of Anna Akhmatova, Yevtushenko and Pushkin. *Memories and Hallucinations* (1988) is a sexually candid autobiography.

Thomas, Dylan (Marlais) 1914–53 Welsh. He is chiefly remembered for his verse 'play for voices', *Under Milk Wood* (1953), and for poems such as 'And Death Shall Have No Dominion', 'Do Not Go Gentle into That Good Night' and 'Fern Hill', gathered in *Collected Poems* (1953). Though less important, his prose fiction developed in step with his poetry and deploys the same richly impacted style. The sketches and stories, some of them originally written for radio, in *Portrait of the Artist as a Young Dog* (1940), *Quite Early One Morning* (1954) and *A Prospect of the Sea* (1955) are largely autobiographical. *Adventures in the Skin Trade* (1955) consists of three chapters of an unfinished novel. *The Death of the King's Canary* (1976), written with John Davenport in 1940, is nominally DETECTIVE FICTION hinging on the murder of the Poet Laureate but really an excuse for satire of the literary scene and parody of contemporary poets.

Thompson, Jim [James] **(Myers)** 1906–77 American. A writer of DETECTIVE FICTION, he published nearly 30 novels which first appeared only in cheap paperback editions and now enjoy a cult following. *Nothing More Than Murder* (1949) pays tribute to JAMES M. CAIN, but Thompson's special métier lay in creating the psychopathically unreliable narrators of *The Killer Inside Me* (1952), *A Hell of a Woman* (1954) and *Pop. 1280* (1964). *The Getaway* (1959) was memorably filmed by Sam Peckinpah in 1973, and French cinema continues to pay regular homage to his work. Thompson also co-wrote the screenplays for two films by Stanley Kubrick, *The Killing* (1956) and *Paths of Glory* (1957).

Three Clerks, The A novel by ANTHONY TROLLOPE, published in 1858. It offers a lively picture of the Victorian Civil Service and also a self-portrait of the young Trollope in Charley Tudor.

Harry Norman and Alaric Tudor, of the prestigious Weights and Measures office, and Alaric's cousin Charley Tudor are regular visitors at the home of the widowed Mrs Woodward and her three daughters. Alaric marries the eldest, Gertrude, but is tried and imprisoned for embezzlement. Harry marries the second Woodward girl, Linda, and settles down as a country squire. Charley, an honest scapegrace, extricates himself from debt and an imprudent entanglement with an Irish barmaid, Norah Geraghty, marries Katie Woodward and wins promotion to the Weights and Measures office.

Through the Looking-Glass and What Alice Found There A fantasy by LEWIS CARROLL, published in 1871. Like its predecessor, *ALICE'S ADVENTURES IN WONDERLAND*, it was illustrated by Sir John Tenniel. Alice enters the back-to-front land behind the mirror, where she meets characters caught up like herself in a cosmic chess game. Favourites among them include the Red Queen, the White Queen, Tweedledum and Tweedledee, the White Knight, the Walrus and the Carpenter and Humpty Dumpty. Poems include the memorable, slightly sinister 'Jabberwocky'.

Thurber, James (Grover) 1894–1961 American. Gently satirical, his work expresses the dilemma of the moral innocent in a complex modern world. Many of his most famous cartoons and writings first appeared in *The New Yorker*, including his short story, 'The Secret Life of Walter Mitty' (1932). Collections include *The Owl in the Attic, and Other Perplexities* (1931), *The Seal in My Bedroom, and Other Predicaments* (1932), *Let Your Mind Alone* (1937), *My World – And Welcome to It!* (1942) and *The Beast in Me, and Other Animals* (1948). Thurber wrote *Is Sex Necessary?* (1929) with E. B. WHITE and a successful comedy, *The Male Animal* (1940), with Elliot Nugent. *My Life and Hard Times* (1933) is autobiographical, and *The Years with Ross* (1959) a memoir of his years on the staff of *The New Yorker*. *The Thirteen Clocks* (1950) is one of several books for children.

Time Machine, The A short novel by H. G. WELLS, developed from a series of speculative articles and twice serialized before book publication in 1895. The Time Traveller invents a machine for travelling through time to investigate the destiny of the human species. In the year 802,701 the meek and beautiful Eloi are living in apparently idyllic circumstances, but they are prey to the degenerate Morlocks, descendants of labourers who have lived underground for centuries. In later eras the Time Traveller sees the life-forms which survive the extinction of man, and 30 million years hence he is witness to the world's final decline as the sun cools.

Tiptree, James See SCIENCE FICTION.

Tlali, Miriam (Masoli) 1933– South African. *Muriel* (edited version, 1975; fuller version, 1979) is about a hire-purchase clerk who becomes aware of racism and capitalist exploitation, and *Amandla* (1981) about the Soweto schoolchildren's rebellion of 1976. Both novels were banned in South Africa, as was her story, 'The Point of No Return'. It was reprinted in *Mihloti* (1984) with journalism and interviews about black women under apartheid. *Footprints in the Quag: Stories and Dialogues from Soweto* (1989; called *Soweto Stories* in Britain) moves away from her documentary mode and introduces a more strongly feminist note.

To Kill a Mockingbird See LEE, HARPER.

To Let See *FORSYTE SAGA, THE*.

To the Is-land The first volume of an autobiography by JANET FRAME, published in 1982, and continued in *An Angel at My Table* (1984) and *The Envoy from Mirror City* (1985). The trilogy was republished as one volume in 1990. *To the Is-land* covers the period from her birth until 1942, when she left school, evoking a childhood combining pleasure in nature and an imaginative life fostered by literature with the traumas of poverty, illness and death in the family. *An Angel at My Table* covers the years spent in mental hospitals as a misdiagnosed schizophrenic. *The Envoy from Mirror City* describes the period from 1956 onwards, when her literary reputation was established and she lived abroad. The trilogy has been praised as an evocative account of an artist's struggle for survival against a narrow and punitive society and as a demonstration of how language and memory work to constitute identity.

To the Lighthouse A novel by VIRGINIA WOOLF, published in 1927. It works through STREAM OF CONSCIOUSNESS and imagery to create an atmospheric record of the characters' moment-by-moment experiences.

Mr Ramsay (clearly modelled on Woolf's father, Sir Leslie Stephen) is a tragic and self-pitying philosopher while Mrs Ramsay (modelled on her mother, Julia) is warm, creative and intuitive, the centre of the household. The first section, 'The Window', describes a day during their summer holiday on the west coast of Scotland, where their guests include: a painter, Lily Briscoe; an ageing poet, Augustus Carmichael; a scientist, William Bankes; and a priggish young academic, Charles Tansley. The action focuses on the conflict arising from young James Ramsay's desire to visit the lighthouse, and his father's quenching of this hope. In the second section, 'Time Passes', Mrs Ramsay has died, her eldest son, Andrew, has been killed in World War I, and the daughter, Prue, has died in childbirth. The Ramsays' seaside house lies deserted and desolate, but at the end of the section Lily Briscoe and Augustus Carmichael arrive to reawaken life. Lily Briscoe assumes the 'visionary' mantle left by Mrs Ramsay, and during the final section ('The Lighthouse') Mr Ramsay and his son, James, at last make the long-delayed voyage to the lighthouse. Lily completes a painting which had been inspired by Mrs Ramsay.

Tolkien, J(ohn) R(onald) R(euel) 1892–1973 Born in South Africa, he lived and worked in Britain, ending his long association with Oxford as Merton Professor of English (1945–59). His expertise in Anglo-Saxon literature, particularly epic and folklore, and his fluency in medieval languages formed a natural background to his imaginative writing. *The Hobbit* (1937) is a children's story about Bilbo Baggins, an amiable type of gnome required to destroy a menacing dragon. The same characters and a similar quest to destroy evil – this time reluctantly undertaken by the hobbit Frodo – appear in THE LORD OF THE RINGS (1954–5), a more ambitious three-volume work which seeks to create a history and mythology for an unspecified period of the past which Tolkien calls 'Middle Earth'. A posthumous sequel, *The Silmarillion* (1977), did not enjoy the same popularity.

Tom Brown's Schooldays A novel by THOMAS HUGHES, published in 1857. Written when its author was still young enough to remember his own days at Rugby, it describes the experiences of an upper middle-class boy progressing from shyness to self-confidence. His two best friends are the gentle, idealistic Arthur and the mischievous, irreverent East. When younger boys are bullied by Flashman, it is East and Tom who stand up to him. The story ends with Tom as Head Boy under the kindly tutelage of Thomas Arnold (in real life headmaster of Rugby from 1828 to 1841).

The first great school story, Hughes's novel helped to found a long tradition of uncritical acceptance for public-school values and practices in children's literature. A sequel, *Tom Brown at Oxford* (1861), has never enjoyed the same popularity. The character of Flashman has been wittily appropriated in a series of novels by GEORGE MACDONALD FRASER.

Tom Jones, A Foundling, The History of A novel by HENRY FIELDING, published in 1749.

A foundling brought up by the rich and benevolent Mr Allworthy, Tom is torn between his love for Sophia Western, a neighbouring squire's daughter, and the more available charms of Molly Seagrim, the gamekeeper's daughter. His enemies include his tutor Thwackum, the philosopher Square, and the mean-spirited Blifil, Allworthy's nephew and heir. Blifil uses Tom's affair with Molly to discredit him in Allworthy's eyes. Banned from his home, Tom takes to the road with Partridge, the schoolmaster. He encounters Sophia, who has run away from her father because he insists that she marry Blifil, and follows her to London. His adventures on the way allow Fielding to portray a rich gallery of characters. In London Tom drifts into an affair with Lady Bellaston, thus further offending Sophia. When he apparently kills his opponent in a duel, Lady Bellaston and her friend Lord Fellamar arrange his arrest and imprisonment. Fortunately, Tom's opponent does not die, and it is revealed that Blifil knows the secret of Tom's birth. He is the son of Allworthy's sister Bridget and hence Allworthy's proper heir. Sophia forgives him his infidelities, and they are married.

The novel is Fielding's masterpiece. The introductory chapters that preface each of the novel's 18 books cultivate the reader in a way then unprecedented in English fiction, establishing a narrative voice satisfying contemporary fondness for moral commentary. The tangled comedies of coincidence are offset by the neat, architectonic structure of this most shapely novel. The portrait of the virtuous Sophia is triumphantly free from stereotypes while Tom Jones himself is both a vital and a fallible hero.

Tom Sawyer, The Adventures of A novel by MARK TWAIN, published in 1876. Tom lives with his respectable Aunt Polly in the Mississippi River town of St Petersburg, Missouri. An intelligent and imaginative boy who is nevertheless careless and mischievous, he prefers the outdoor and parentless life of his friend Huck Finn, with whom he enjoys various comic adventures. They culminate in exposing Injun Joe for murdering the town doctor and in finding his buried treasure. THE ADVENTURES OF

HUCKLEBERRY FINN (1884) continues the boys' story in a different vein.

Tomlinson, H(enry) M(ajor) 1873–1958 English. He is chiefly remembered for *All Our Yesterdays* (1930), a novel encompassing the years 1900–19; its anti-war theme and descriptions of the trenches were drawn from his experience as a correspondent in France during World War I. His first novel, *Gallions Reach* (1927), had already confirmed the fascination with the sea which runs through most of his writing, including his travel books. Subsequent novels are: *The Snows of Helicon* (1933); *All Hands* (called *Pipe All Hands* in the USA; 1937); *The Day Before* (1939), dealing with the years from the Boer War to World War I; *Morning Light: The Islanders in the Days of Oak and Hemp* (1946); and *The Trumpet Shall Sound* (1957), set near the end of World War II. *A Mingled Yarn* (1953) brings together autobiographical essays.

Tono-Bungay A novel by H. G. WELLS, published in 1909. Often regarded as a latter-day CONDITION OF ENGLAND NOVEL, it follows the narrator George Ponderevo's quest for moral and intellectual certainties.

After a childhood at Bladesover, a country house where his mother is housekeeper, he becomes apprentice to the narrow-minded Evangelical baker, Nicodemus Frapp. His uncle, Edward Ponderevo, makes him salesman for 'Tono-Bungay', a quack medicine which makes the family a fortune. George's marriage to Marion Ramboat, like his experience of religion and commerce, is a failure. His real destiny is with science, and he becomes a student of aeronautics. Uncle Edward's fortunes decline and George's expedition to an island off Africa to collect 'quap', a radioactive material, fails. George's perpetual quest continues amid recurring disillusions. He flies his dying uncle to France to save him from imprisonment and has a love affair with the Hon. Beatrice Normandy. Eventually, he emerges as the harbinger of inexorable change with his latest invention, a destroyer.

Toole, John Kennedy 1937–69 American novelist. *A Confederacy of Dunces* is a satirical comedy about his native New Orleans. Appearing in 1980, 11 years after Toole's suicide, it won a PULITZER PRIZE. Another posthumous work, *The Neon Bible* (1989), was subsequently made into a film.

Toomer, Jean (Nathan Eugene) 1894–1967 African-American. He played a central part in the HARLEM RENAISSANCE. His most widely read work, *Cane* (1923), is a mixture of stories and poems partly based on his work at a black school in rural Georgia. The mystic Georges Gurdjieff influenced later work such as *Essentials* (1931), a collection of philosophical aphorisms. *The Wayward and the Seeking* (edited by Darwin T. Turner; 1980) gathers previously unpublished poems, stories, and autobiographical sketches.

Tourgée, Albion W(inegar) 1838–1905 American. A Northerner, he moved to North Carolina in 1864 and served as a judge of its Supreme Court in 1868–74. His commitment to Reconstruction and the reform of the South is reflected in novels such as *Toinette* (1874; republished as *A Royal Gentleman*, 1881) and *A Fool's Errand* (1879), which began an attack on the Ku Klux Klan continued in *Bricks without Straw* (1880), published the year after he left the South, and in *Our Continent*, the journal he edited in 1882–4. Of his later novels, *Hot Plowshares* (1882), *Black Ice* (1888) and *Eighty-Nine: or, The Grand Master's Story* (1891) return to the theme of Republican reform of the South. Tourgée served as US consul in Bordeaux from 1897 until his death.

Townsend, Sue [Susan] (Lilian) 1946– English. She is best known for the solemn, bookish hero whose accidentally comic adventures are chronicled in *The Secret Diary of Adrian Mole Aged 13¾* (1982) and its several sequels. *The Queen and I* (1992) follows the fortunes of a dethroned royal family in a republican Britain. *Ghost Children* (1997) is a novella about abortion. Her work for the stage includes adaptations of *The Secret Diary of Adrian Mole Aged 13¾* (1985) and *The Queen and I* (1994).

Traffics and Discoveries A collection of 11 stories and 11 poems by RUDYARD KIPLING, first published in 1904. The stories range in subject matter from mystery and the supernatural ('Mrs Bathurst', 'They', 'Below the Mill Dam' and 'Wireless') to the Boer War ('A Sahib's War').

Tragic Comedians, The A novel by GEORGE MEREDITH, published in 1880. Clotilde, a nobleman's daughter, wants to marry Alvan in the face of her family's wrath but is deceived into accepting the suitor of their choice, Marko. Alvan dies in a duel with Marko, whose marriage to Clotilde goes ahead. Meredith based the story on Helene von Donniges's account of her love affair with the German socialist, Ferdinand Lassalle.

Train to Pakistan A novel by KUSHWANT SINGH, published in 1956 and called *Mano Majra* in the USA. It is set in an ethnically mixed frontier village at the time of Partition. The shadow of sectarian violence looms with the arrival of a train from neighbouring Pakistan full of butchered Sikh and Hindu refugees. The Sikh villagers are about to ambush a Pakistan-bound train in reprisal when they are thwarted, at the cost of his own life, by a young Sikh whose Muslim sweetheart is on the train.

Travels into Several Remote Nations of the World, in Four Parts, by Lemuel Gulliver See *GULLIVER'S TRAVELS*.

Traven, B. The pseudonym of the novelist and short-story writer best remembered for *The Treasure of the Sierra Madre*. An elusive figure, he is usually identified with Otto Fiege, who was born in 1882 at Zwiebodzin (then in Germany, now in Poland) and died under the name of Hal Croves in Mexico in 1969. His works were published in German and then translated into English, often by himself and his publisher's editor. *The Treasure of the Sierra Madre* (1934; originally *Der Schatz der Sierra Madre*, 1927) is an adventure story of greed and desperation indebted to JACK LONDON and the American school of NATURALISM. It was filmed by John Huston in 1947. Other works include *Die Baumwollpflücker* (1926; *The Cottonpickers*, 1956), *Das Totenschiff* (1926; *The Death Ship*, 1934), *Die Brücke im Dschungel* (1929; *The Bridge in the Jungle*, 1938) and *Die Rebellion der Gehenkten* (1936; *The Rebellion of the Hanged*, 1952). *Trozas* (in German, 1977; in English, 1994) is a long-lost novel about Mexican slave labour in the mahogany trade.

Trease, (Robert) Geoffrey 1909–98 English. *Bows against the Barons* (1934), about Robin Hood, and *Comrades of the Charter* (1934) are HISTORICAL FICTION for children written from a left-wing viewpoint. His many subsequent books, less politically motivated but still ahead of their time in the determination to write for and about ordinary children, include *No Boats on Bannermere* (1949), *Follow My Black Plume* (1963) and *Song for a Tattered Flag* (1992).

Treasure Island An adventure novel for children by ROBERT LOUIS STEVENSON, serialized as *The Sea Cook: or, Treasure Island* by 'Captain George North' in 1881–2 and published in book form in 1883. Though Stevenson himself did not take it seriously, it has always been his most popular work.

Jim Hawkins, the landlady's son at the Admiral Benbow inn, acquires a map showing where Captain Flint's treasure is buried from Billy Bones, an old pirate hunted by his former confederates. Squire Trelawney and Dr Livesey charter a schooner and set sail for Treasure Island with Jim. He discovers that the crew includes the pirates, led by the ship's one-legged cook, Long John Silver. The rest of the story, telling how the pirates are defeated and the treasure found, takes second place to the interest Stevenson finds in Silver, embodying every young boy's image of what a pirate should be. The character is said to have been modelled on the poet and editor W. E. Henley.

Treece, Henry 1911–66 English. A founder of the New Apocalypse movement, he published several volumes of poetry, including *The Black Seasons* (1945) and *The Exiles* (1952). Critical works include *How I See Apocalypse* (1946) and the first book on DYLAN THOMAS (1949). *The Legion of the Eagle* (1954) began his HISTORICAL FICTION for children, dealing mostly with the Vikings and Romans. *The Children's Crusade* (1958), widely translated and probably his best book, deals with one of the most baffling episodes of medieval history. Treece also wrote thrillers for children.

Trelawny, Edward (John) 1792–1881 English. His experiences as a midshipman in the Royal Navy form the basis of his autobiographical novel, *Adventures of a Younger Son* (1831), in which he claims to have deserted in India and assumed command of a French privateer. In 1822 he surfaced in Pisa where he became a member of the circle round Byron and Shelley. He supervised the cremation of Shelley's body on the beach at Viareggio and accompanied Byron to Greece, where he was married, for the second time, to a Greek girl in 1824. *Recollections of the Last Days of Byron and Shelley* (1858; republished as *Records of Byron, Shelley and the Author*, 1878) gives an extremely lively and readable account of this period, though it is none too scrupulous with the facts. Trelawny sustained his reputation as an adventurer by his elopement in 1841 with the married Lady Augusta Goring. A larger-than-life figure, he had become the monument of the Byronic age by the end of his long life.

Tremain, Rose 1943– English. She is preoccupied with the links between fiction and people's need to tell the stories of their lives. Her novels include: *Sadler's Birthday* (1976), *Letter to Sister Benedicta* (1978) and *The Cupboard* (1981), all with ageing or elderly narrators; *The Swimming Pool Season* (1985); *Restoration* (1989), her best-known work, set in Charles II's reign; *Sacred Country* (1992); and *The Way I Found Her* (1997). Her short fiction is found in *The Colonel's Garden and Other Stories* (1984), *The Garden of the Villa Mollini and Other Stories* (1987) and *Evangelista's Fan and Other Stories* (1994). She has also written plays for radio and television.

Tremblay, Michel 1942– French-Canadian. Born in Montréal, he writes in the street patois *joual* (see FRENCH-CANADIAN NOVEL). A self-advertised homosexual, he deals with the outcasts of society – male prostitutes, transvestites, homosexuals and incestuous lovers – in the working-class districts. *Les Belles-Soeurs* (1968) marked his emergence as the most successful contemporary French-Canadian playwright. His most important novels are *La Grosse Femme d'à côté est enceinte* (1978; translated as *The Fat Woman Next Door is Pregnant*, 1981) and *Thérèse et Pierrette à l'école de saints-anges* (1980; translated as *Thérèse and Pierrette at the Ecole des Saintes Anges*, 1980). Tremblay has also written short stories and reminiscences of childhood.

Trespasser, The A novel by D. H. LAWRENCE, first published in 1912. The story follows Helena Verden's intense, though largely non-sexual, affair with her ex-violin teacher, Siegmund MacNair. She cannot give herself to him completely and he cannot bring himself to desert his wife and children for her. He finally commits suicide. The novel ends a year after his death, with Helena turning to her would-be suitor Cecil Byrne for 'rest and warmth'.

Tressell, Robert See *RAGGED TROUSERED PHILANTHROPISTS, THE*.

Trevor, Glen See HILTON, JAMES.

Trevor, William [Cox, William Trevor] 1928– Anglo-Irish. Much of it set in Ireland, his fiction shows a penchant for settings of faded gentility and often deals with the corruption or destruction of innocence, represented by childhood and old age. Novels include: *The Old Boys* (1964); *Mrs Eckdorf in O'Neill's Hotel* (1969); *Elizabeth Alone* (1973); *The Children of Dynmouth* (1976; WHITBREAD AWARD), about a psychopathic teenager menacing a retirement resort; *Fools of Fortune* (1983; Whitbread Award); and *The Silence in the Garden* (1988). *FELICIA'S JOURNEY* (1994) won him his third Whitbread Award. His prolific output of shorter fiction includes a collected volume (1983), *The News from Ireland* (1986), *Family Sins* (1989), *Two Lives* (1991), a pair of novellas, and *After Rain* (1996). *Excursions in the Real World* (1993) is his autobiography.

Trilby A novel by GEORGE DU MAURIER, published in 1894 with his own illustrations. Trilby is an artist's model who, manipulated by Svengali, becomes a famous singer. Svengali has given his name to the language; Trilby's name survives as that of a man's felt hat, dented across the crown.

Tristram Shandy, Gentleman, The Life and Opinions of A novel by LAURENCE STERNE, published in instalments: Volumes I and II in 1760, III and IV in 1761, V and VI in 1762, VII and VIII in 1765 and Volume IX in 1767. Its immediate popularity was surprising for a novel which defies convention at every turn. *Tristram Shandy* distributes its narrative content across a bafflingly idiosyncratic time-scheme interrupted by digressions, authorial comments and interferences with the printed fabric of the book.

The story does manage to start *ab ovo*, with the narrator-hero describing his own conception, but he is not actually born for several volumes and disappears from the book in Volume VI. His father is Walter Shandy, the science-smitten but benevolent head of Shandy Hall, where he lives in continuous exasperation with his wife. 'My uncle Toby' is an old soldier wounded in the groin at the siege of Namur, who passes his time recreating military sieges, helped by the devoted Corporal Trim. These are some of the characters whose behaviour can be understood in terms of their personal 'hobby-horses'. Dr Slop is the man-midwife delayed in delivering the infant Tristram, the Widow Wadman is the neighbour with amorous designs on Uncle Toby, and Yorick is the amiable local parson. After Tristram is born, Volume IV opens with the story of Slawkenbergius (a mock-encomium on noses) and an account of how the baby mistakenly came to be christened 'Tristram'. After

Trim's discourse on morality in Volume V there is a fine dialogue between Tristram's parents in Volume VI, about the 'breeching' (or dressing) of their child, and the sentimental story of Le Fevre. The novel then follows the author's adult travels to France, returning to an account of the Widow Wadman's designs on Uncle Toby in Volume IX.

With its black pages, wiggly lines, misplaced chapters and other surprises, *Tristram Shandy* stands in part against the idea of literature as finished product, its surfaces capable of reflecting the conditions of life. That is one reason why it has proved so fertile an influence on 20th-century fiction. Yet it was also very much in keeping with the mood of an age caught up in the cults of 'sensibility' (see SENTIMENTAL NOVEL) and the picturesque. And, aside from his debt to John Locke's theory of the association of ideas, Sterne was working in a long tradition of intellectual satire embracing Montaigne, Rabelais, Erasmus and Jonathan Swift, as well as drawing on PICARESQUE and travel literature. In turn, a book which could strike a contemporary like Samuel Johnson as 'odd' and hence not destined to last, has grown into a respected precedent and a recurrent influence in the age of POST-MODERNISM.

Trollope, Anthony 1815–82 English. He was educated at Harrow and Winchester, where his family's poverty exposed him to humiliation and unhappiness vividly remembered in his *Autobiography* (1883). The Trollopes' fortunes improved when his mother, FRANCES TROLLOPE, embarked on a successful literary career. Trollope himself worked in the Post Office from the age of 19, making an inauspicious start reflected in his novel, *THE THREE CLERKS* (1858). He later travelled widely, worked in Ireland and invented the pillar box, though he felt that his superiors did not properly recognize his services.

By the time he resigned in 1867 he was already a successful and respected novelist. Recognition came with his fourth novel, *THE WARDEN* (1855), which inaugurated the BARSETSHIRE NOVELS, about clergymen and their families in a fictional western county: *BARCHESTER TOWERS* (1857), *DOCTOR THORNE* (1858), *FRAMLEY PARSONAGE* (1860), *THE SMALL HOUSE AT ALLINGTON* (1862–4), and *THE LAST CHRONICLE OF BARSET* (1866–7), Trollope's favourite in the series. With their recurrent characters in a familiar, unfolding community, these books marked a new departure for the English regional novel; their realistic presentation of middle-class domestic relationships proved highly congenial to the reading public.

His other great sequence was the political or PALLISER NOVELS. Political interests are peripheral in the first, *CAN YOU FORGIVE HER?* (1864–5), and the third, *THE EUSTACE DIAMONDS* (1871–3), but *PHINEAS FINN* (1867–9), *PHINEAS REDUX* (1873–4), *THE PRIME MINISTER* (1875–6) and *THE DUKE'S CHILDREN* (1879–80) paint an unrivalled portrait of parliamentary political society in the high Victorian period. The series owes much to the steadily deepening presentation of Plantagenet Palliser and his wife Glencora, the characters on whom, with Mr Crawley of *The Last Chronicle*, Trollope believed his reputation with posterity would rest. The pessimistic vision of *Phineas Redux* reflects his own experience as unsuccessful Liberal candidate for Beverley in 1868, also treated in a separate novel, *Ralph the Heir* (1870–1). A broader pessimism informs *THE WAY WE LIVE NOW* (1874–5), a wide-ranging social satire which many consider his masterpiece.

His best-known works – the Barsetshire Novels, the Palliser Novels and *The Way We Live Now* – make up less than a quarter of his fictional output. It also includes: *THE BERTRAMS* (1859), *CASTLE RICHMOND* (1860), *ORLEY FARM* (1861–2), *THE BELTON ESTATE* (1865–6), *THE CLAVERINGS* (1866–7), *HE KNEW HE WAS RIGHT* (1868–9), *THE VICAR OF BULLHAMPTON* (1869–70), *SIR HARRY HOTSPUR OF HUMBLETHWAITE* (1870), *LADY ANNA* (1873–4), *THE AMERICAN SENATOR* (1876–7), *DR WORTLE'S SCHOOL* (1880), *AYALA'S ANGEL* (1881), and *MR SCARBOROUGH'S FAMILY* (1882–3). The indifferent reception of *Nina Balatka* (1866–7) and *Linda Tressel* (1867–8), which he published anonymously, confirmed his suspicion that 'a name once earned carried with it too much favour'. Trollope also produced travel books on *The West Indies and the Spanish Main* (1859), *North America* (1862), *Australia and New Zealand* (1873) and *South Africa* (1878); wrote biographies of Cicero (1880) and Lord Palmerston (1882), a politician congenial to his own position as an 'advanced conservative liberal'; and a study of THACKERAY (1879), the novelist he considered his master.

Few of Trollope's works are without interest. His productivity meant that he relied unduly on the entanglements of romantic plot-making (for which he professed indifference) and cultivated an even professionalism of style which can lull the reader into ignoring the subtle and varied understanding of human nature on which his best work is based. To this strength should be added his understanding of the institutions of mid-Victorian England and the unobtrusive irony which informs his sympathetic vision of human fallibility.

Trollope, Mrs Frances 1780–1863 English. She married Thomas Anthony Trollope in 1809. Two of their six children, ANTHONY TROLLOPE and T. ADOLPHUS TROLLOPE, became novelists. Her husband's scheme to set up a fancy goods emporium in Cincinnati failed but a book about her American experiences, *Domestic Manners of the Americans* (1832), made her a best-selling author

at the age of 52. Driven by family debts, she published 40 more volumes in the next 25 years, mainly novels but also several travel books. Two novels have a place in the history of Victorian fiction: the anti-evangelical novel *Vicar of Wrexhill* (1837), an early contribution to the novel of religious controversy, and *The Life and Adventures of Michael Armstrong, the Factory Boy* (1840), one of the first Victorian 'industrial' novels.

Trollope, Joanna 1943– English. She is a descendant of ANTHONY TROLLOPE. Set in the upper middle-class Home Counties or Cotswolds, *The Choir* (1988), *A Village Affair* (1989), *The Rector's Wife* (1991), *The Men and the Girls* (1992), *The Best of Friends* (1995) and *Next of Kin* (1996) examine the crises of vocation and self-respect that afflict outwardly comfortable lives. Trollope has also written *Britannia's Daughters* (1983), a study of women in the British Empire, and published historical romances under the pseudonym of Caroline Harvey.

Trollope, T(homas) Adolphus 1810–92 English. The eldest son of FRANCES TROLLOPE and elder brother of ANTHONY TROLLOPE, he settled in Florence in 1843 and Rome in 1873. He published 60 books of history, travel and fiction. Many of his novels are set in Italy and some, such as *Filippo Strozzi* (1860), are HISTORICAL FICTION. None has the abiding interest of his autobiography, *What I Remember* (1887–9), which is valuable for its picture of expatriate life in Italy in mid-Victorian times, and for its reminiscences of DICKENS, Elizabeth Barrett Browning, Robert Browning, GEORGE ELIOT and G. H. Lewes.

Trotter-Nama, The A novel by I. ALLAN SEALY, published in 1988 and awarded a SAHITYA AKADEMI prize in 1991. Set in the Trotter family home of Sans Souci and structured as a *nama*, or traditional Indian narrative form, it follows the history of an Anglo-Indian clan from the 18th century to Indian Independence. Sealy's emphasis is on the themes of displacement and exile.

Trumpet-Major, The A novel by THOMAS HARDY, published in 1880. His only venture into full-dress HISTORICAL FICTION, it is set during the Napoleonic wars – the period which would also provide him with the subject of his epic poem, 'The Dynasts'.

Anne Garland and her mother live in one part of Overcombe Mill. The other part is occupied by Miller Loveday, who has two sons: Robert, a sailor, and John, trumpet-major of a regiment of Dragoons. Anne is loved by John but does not return his affection, and does not welcome the attentions of the buffoonish Festus Derriman. John rescues his brother from the clutches of Matilda Johnson. Robert eventually marries Anne. Mrs Garland succumbs to the charms of Miller Loveday. John leaves 'to blow his trumpet till silenced for ever upon one of the bloody battle-fields of Spain'.

Turn of the Screw, The A short novel by HENRY

JAMES, published in 1898. A governess takes charge of two children, Miles and Flora, at the lonely country house of Bly. She sees the ghosts of the former steward, Peter Quint, and governess, Miss Jessel. Her suspicion that the children are in touch with the ghosts is confirmed by their evasiveness when questioned. In a final confrontation, she is determined to free Miles from Quint's malign influence, but the boy dies in her arms. The fact that, after a brief introductory section, the story is told from the point of view of the governess raises doubts about whether the ghosts are 'real' or merely her hallucinations.

Tutuola, Amos 1920–97 Nigerian. He inaugurated West African literature in English with *The Palm-Wine Drinkard* (1952), a sequence of 30 episodes of quest, endurance and the achievement of wisdom, adapted mainly from Yoruba folk tales and written in the best English his scanty schooling permitted. His other books are: *My Life in the Bush of Ghosts* (1954), *Simbi and the Satyr of the Dark Jungle* (1955), *The Brave African Huntress* (1958), *Feather Woman of the Jungle* (1962), *Ajaiyi and His Inherited Poverty* (1967), *The Witch-Herbalist of the Remote Town* (1981) and *The Wild Hunter in the Bush of Ghosts* (1989).

Twain, Mark [Clemens, Samuel Langhorne] 1835–1910 American. Born in Florida, Missouri, and brought up in the Mississippi River town of Hannibal, he spent his youth as a river pilot, journeyman printer, soldier in the Confederate Army and silver prospector in Nevada. In San Francisco he worked as a journalist with BRET HARTE.

He adopted the name of Mark Twain in 1863 and made it famous with *THE CELEBRATED JUMPING FROG OF CALAVERAS COUNTY*, a short story which gave its name to a collection published in 1867. A trip to Europe and the Holy Land prompted his first major work, *The Innocents Abroad* (1869). After he settled in the East and married in 1870, he confirmed his popularity with: *Roughing It* (1872), a humorous narrative of his early travels out West; *THE GILDED AGE* (1873), a satirical novel of the post-Civil War era co-written with CHARLES DUDLEY WARNER; *THE ADVENTURES OF TOM SAWYER* (1876); and *A Tramp Abroad* (1880). The last works of what might be called Twain's optimistic period were *THE PRINCE AND THE PAUPER* (1882), a romance set in the time of Henry VIII, and *Life on the Mississippi* (1883), part history, part geography, part memoir and part travel book.

After unwise investment made him bankrupt he published *THE ADVENTURES OF HUCKLEBERRY FINN* (1884), which has a moral dimension lacking in *Tom Sawyer*, followed by *A CONNECTICUT YANKEE IN KING ARTHUR'S COURT* (1889) and *THE TRAGEDY OF PUDD'NHEAD WILSON* (1894), both deeply pessimistic. *The American Claimant* (1892), *Tom Sawyer Abroad* (1894), and *Tom Sawyer,*

Detective (1896) sought to recapture the innocent fun of his early works, but *The Man That Corrupted Hadleyburg* (1900) and *What is Man?* (1906) furthered the journey into pessimism. Recovered from bankruptcy but afflicted by family sorrows, Twain continued to lecture widely in the USA and abroad. At his death he left a wealth of unpublished material, including *The Mysterious Stranger* (1916) and *Letters from the Earth* (1962). His *Autobiography* was published in 1924.

Two Drovers, The See CHRONICLES OF THE CANONGATE.

Two on a Tower A novel by THOMAS HARDY, published in 1882. Swithin St Cleeve, a young astronomer, meets Lady Viviette Constantine, some 10 years his senior, and secretly marries her when news comes of Sir Blount Constantine's death in Africa. Then they learn that Sir Blount, although now dead, was alive when they married, thus rendering the union void. Under pressure from Viviette, Swithin claims an inheritance which is contingent on his remaining single until he is 25. He travels abroad. Discovering that she is pregnant, Viviette marries the Bishop of Melchester, who dies soon afterwards. When Swithin returns and proposes again, she dies of the shock.

Two Towers, The See LORD OF THE RINGS, THE.

Tyler, Anne 1941– American. *The Accidental Tourist* (1985), about a lonely writer of guide books for business travellers, typifies her work in its oddball characters, whimsical tone and emphasis on family life. Other novels include *If Morning Ever Comes* (1964), *A Slipping-Down Life* (1970), *Celestial Navigation* (1974), *Searching for Caleb* (1976), *Morgan's Passing* (1980), *Dinner at the Homesick Restaurant* (1982), *Breathing Lessons* (1988; PULITZER PRIZE), *Saint Maybe* (1991) and *Ladder of Years* (1995).

Tyler, Royall 1757–1826 American. He combined writing with a distinguished legal career. His reputation rests largely on *The Contrast* (1787), the first comedy by a native American writer to be professionally produced. It was followed, less successfully, by several lost plays and four unproduced works. *The Island of Barrataria* is a farce based on an episode from Cervantes; *The Judgment of Solomon*, *The Origin of the Feast of Purim* and *Joseph and his Brethren* are sacred verse dramas. *THE ALGERINE CAPTIVE* (1797) was his only novel. *The Yankey in London* (1809) is a collection of essays and sketches.

Tynan, Katharine 1861–1931 Irish. A close friend and associate of Yeats in the Irish literary revival, she published more than 200 books. The best-remembered are the verses gathered in *Collected Poems* (1930), but she also published many novels, beginning with *The Way of a Maid* (1893), and volumes of short stories, beginning with *A Cluster of Nuts: Being Sketches Among My Own People* (1894). Set in both England and Ireland, her fiction on the whole avoids the political tensions and conflicts of Irish life and deals instead in elaborate romantic plots.

Typee: *A Peep at Polynesian Life. During a Four Months' Residence in a Valley of the Marquesas* HERMAN MELVILLE's first novel, published in 1846.

It is based on his own experiences in the South Seas. Tommo and Toby jump ship in the Marquesas Islands, where they meet the Typees.

Left alone with the tribe, Tommo finds it friendly and criticizes the destructive effects of white missionary efforts – an aspect of the book which provoked controversy. However, he becomes increasingly homesick for the Western world and, seeing evidence of ritual cannibalism, begins to fear that he will be the next victim. He decides to flee the valley and is rescued by the boat of an Australian whaler. *Omoo* is a sequel.

U

Ulysses A novel by JAMES JOYCE, serialized in *The Little Review* from 1918 until a prosecution for obscenity in 1920, and first published in volume form in Paris by Harriet Shaw Weaver's Egoist Press in 1922. It was banned in the USA until 1933 and in Britain until 1937.

The action takes place in Dublin on a single day, 16 June 1904. Its main protagonists are: Leopold Bloom, a Jewish advertisement canvasser; his unfaithful wife Molly, a concert singer; and Stephen Dedalus, from *A PORTRAIT OF THE ARTIST AS A YOUNG MAN*, now a discontented schoolteacher. In the course of the book's 3 sections and 18 chapters, Bloom and Stephen wander separately through the city on errands which are largely trivial. However, Bloom's presence at Paddy Dignam's funeral (in Chapter 6, 'Hades') and the presence of both men at the Holles Street Hospital for Mrs Purefoy's lying-in (Chapter 14, 'Oxen of the Sun') indicates the book's preoccupation with the cycle of birth and death, though not necessarily in that order. They finally meet at the end of the day (Chapter 15, 'Circe' or 'Nighttown') when Bloom rescues Stephen from a scuffle with two British soldiers and takes him home to Eccles Street for a cup of cocoa. Their encounter may or may not alter the sense of futility, frustration and loneliness which possesses them both. In Stephen that sense has focused on his alienation from Catholicism and his father, Simon Dedalus. In Bloom it has focused on the death of his infant son, Rudy, some years before.

Joyce's minutely detailed account of the mundane, and occasionally sordid, episodes of the day, and of the topography of Dublin, would seem to place *Ulysses* at the extreme edge of REALISM. A different purpose is implied by the systematic allusion to Homer's *Odyssey* which dominates the book's manifold references to literature, music, philosophy, history and myth and gave the original titles to its chapters. According to this scheme Bloom represents Odysseus (Ulysses), Molly is Penelope and Stephen is Telemachus. The Homeric parallel has a double and deliberately contradictory purpose: making satire, or at least mock-heroic, of the contrast between ancient grandeur and pitiful modernity but also asserting that the present can provide valid material for epic.

Joyce's relentlessly experimental method answers this complex challenge. He uses STREAM OF CONSCIOUSNESS (notably in Molly Bloom's soliloquy, which forms the final chapter, 'Penelope') but does not rely on it to sustain a book whose vast resources also embrace parody (of newspaper language in Chapter 7,

'Aeolus', women's magazine fiction in Chapter 13, 'Nausicca', and of the whole history of English prose style in 'Oxen of the Sun') and expressionist drama in 'Circe'.

Uncle Remus See HARRIS, JOEL CHANDLER.

Uncle Silas: *A Tale of Bartram-Haugh* A suspense novel by SHERIDAN LE FANU, published in 1864. Maud Ruthyn becomes the ward of her sinister uncle Silas at his remote house, Bartram-Haugh, Derbyshire. He tries to force her into marrying his unpleasant son, Dudley, and then plots her murder. The web of intrigue tightens with the introduction of the grotesque French governess, Madame de la Rougierre. In the event, Dudley kills the governess by mistake and Maud makes her escape.

Uncle Tom's Cabin: *or, Life among the Lowly* A best-selling anti-slavery novel by HARRIET BEECHER STOWE, serialized in 1851–2 and published in book form in 1852.

Uncle Tom, a saintly and faithful slave, is separated from his family and sold to a slave trader when his owners, the Shelbys, fall into financial difficulties. Young George Shelby vows to redeem him one day. On his voyage down the Mississippi Tom saves the life of Eva St Clare ('little Eva'), whose father buys him out of gratitude. In New Orleans he grows close to Eva and her black friend Topsy, but little Eva dies, her father is killed in an accident and Tom is sold to the villainous Simon Legree. He is finally whipped to death for refusing to betray two escaped slaves. George Shelby arrives as Tom is dying, and vows to fight for the Abolitionist cause.

Unconditional Surrender See SWORD OF HONOUR.

Under the Greenwood Tree: *or, The Mellstock Quire* A novel by THOMAS HARDY, published in 1872. Termed 'a rural painting of the Dutch school', it is set in and about Mellstock (Stinsford) and concerns the love of Dick Dewey, a tranter, for the flighty but charming Fancy Day, whom he finally marries against the rivalry of Farmer Shiner and Parson Maybold. The sunny tone is touched with regret at the changing of the old rural order as the village band is replaced by a 'cabinet-organ'.

Under the Volcano A novel by MALCOLM LOWRY, published in 1947. A year after the event Jacques Laruelle recalls the last day in the life of Geoffrey Firmin, the British Consul in Cuernavaca, Mexico, in 1938. The alcoholic Firmin, his estranged wife Yvonne (who has had an affair with Laruelle) and Firmin's brother Hugh visit the festival of the Day of the Dead: Yvonne is killed by a runaway horse which the Consul has unleashed, and Firmin is murdered by fascist thugs. Dense with symbol and allusion, the narrative can be read as an unparalleled evocation of extreme alcoholism, a synthesis of arcane myth systems or an unforced allegory of a world on the brink of war.

Under Western Eyes A novel by JOSEPH CONRAD, published in 1911.

The narrator, an elderly English teacher of languages in Geneva, tells the story of the Russian student Razumov, using Razumov's diary as well as his own observation. Razumov's quiet life in St Petersburg is disrupted when Victor Haldin, a revolutionary idealist who has just assassinated a minister of state, seeks shelter with him. He betrays Haldin, only to find that the autocracy now regards him as a suspect. Dispatched to Geneva as a secret agent, he is repelled by revolutionaries like the grotesque Peter Ivanovitch and made more guilty by the admiration of Haldin's mother and sister, Natalia, who think him a revolutionary hero. When he confesses to Natalia (whom he loves) and to the revolutionaries, they burst his eardrums. He is struck down and crippled by a tram he cannot hear.

Unfortunate Traveller, The A prose tale by Thomas Nashe (or Nash; 1567–1601), satirist, pamphleteer and playwright. Published in 1594, it is now his best remembered and most admired work, largely for its claim to be the first PICARESQUE novel in English. The story follows the Continental adventures of Jack Wilton, a young English page in the reign of Henry VIII, from his tricks at the English camp during the siege of Tournai to his hair-raising experiences in Italy, where he is involved in rapes, murders, revenges and schemings. Nashe is nowhere more brutal or sensational in his writing, perhaps in an attempt to burlesque the stock situations and tone of popular Elizabethan journalism.

university novel See CAMPUS NOVEL.

Unsworth, Barry 1930– English. Early works were *The Partnership* (1966) and *The Greeks Have a Word For It* (1967), based on his experiences teaching English in Greece and Turkey, *The Hide* (1970) and *Mooncranker's Gift* (1973). *Pascali's Island* (1980) and *The Rage of the Vulture* (1982), about the dying days of the Ottoman Empire, announced his fascination with the paradoxical strangeness and familiarity of the past. That tension has informed subsequent work: *Stone Virgin* (1985), set in Venice; *Sugar and Rum* (1988); *Sacred Hunger* (1992; BOOKER PRIZE), about the human and moral cost of the slave trade in 18th-century Britain; and *Morality Play* (1995), set in the 14th century among a band of travelling players. *After Hannibal* (1996) returns to the present day and to Italy, where he now lives.

Untouchable A novel by MULK RAJ ANAND, published in 1935. Set in a British Army regiment, it follows 24 hours in the life of Bakha, a young latrine cleaner of the lowest caste. His life is briefly transformed at a political rally attended by the great Gandhi, but the ideology behind Anand's fierce indictment of caste and class is more often Marxist than nationalist.

Updike, John (Hoyer) 1932– American. He established a reputation as a keen observer of modern American life with the novel *Rabbit Run* (1960), whose central character, Harry Angstrom, reappears in *Rabbit Redux* (1971), *Rabbit is Rich* (1981; PULITZER PRIZE) and *Rabbit at Rest* (1990; Pulitzer Prize), the sequence forming the *RABBIT* TETRALOGY. Assured, urbane and ironic, Updike's fiction is as versatile as it is prolific. It includes: *The Centaur* (1963); *Couples* (1968); *Bech: A Book* (1970) and its sequel *Bech is Back* (1982); *A Month of Sundays* (1975), the first novel in the 'Scarlet Letter Trilogy', completed by *Roger's Version* (1986) and *S.* (1988); *Marry Me* (1976); *The Coup* (1978); *The Witches of Eastwick* (1982); *Brazil* (1994); and *In the Beauty of the Lilies* (1996). His collections of short stories include *The Same Door* (1959), *Pigeon Feathers* (1962), *Museums and Women and Other Stories* (1972), *Trust Me* (1987) and *The Afterlife and Other Short Stories* (1994). He has also published poetry, children's books, art criticism in *Just Looking* (1989) and autobiography in *Self-Consciousness* (1989). His reviews and essays are gathered in *Assorted Prose* (1965), *Picked-Up Pieces* (1978), *Hugging the Shore* (1983), *Odd Jobs* (1991) and *Golf Dreams: Writings on Golf* (1996).

Upfield, Arthur W(illiam) 1888–1964 Australian. After emigrating from Britain, he worked as an itinerant trapper, a miner and a geologist. His experience served him well in writing DETECTIVE FICTION, which consisted chiefly of 29 novels about the part-Aboriginal Detective Inspector Napoleon Bonaparte ('Bony') of the Queensland Police. The first, *The Barrakee Mystery* (called *The Lure of the Bush* in the USA), appeared in 1929; the last, *The Lake Frome Monster* (1966), was completed by J. L. Price and Dorothy Strange after Upfield's death. They are notable for a feeling for the Australian outback and an interest, unusual for their date, in Aboriginal culture.

Upward, Edward (Falaise) 1903– English. A lifelong friend of CHRISTOPHER ISHERWOOD, he joined the Communist Party in the 1930s. *Journey to the Border* (1938) is a Kafkaesque political allegory about a private tutor's progress towards radicalism and the Workers' Movement. Like many radicals of his generation, Upward was caught in the trap of Party dogmatism during the Stalin era. *The Spiral Ascent* – a trilogy consisting of *In the Thirties* (1962), *Rotten Elements* (1969) and *No Home but the Struggle* (1977) – chart his political soul-searching and personal struggles during the years of silence. Collections of stories include *The Railway*

Accident and Other Stories (1969), *The Night Walk and Other Stories* (1987), *An Unmentionable Man* (1994) and, with Isherwood, *The Mortmere Stories* (1994).

Urquhart, Fred(erick) (Burrows) 1912– Scottish. The remarkably open attitude to male homosexuality evident in his first novel, *Time Will Knit* (1938), and a subsequent volume of short stories, *I Fell for a Sailor* (1940), has characterized much of his work. His short fiction makes fine use of Scottish dialect and gives affectionate but clear-sighted depictions of working-class women and men who work the land, qualities much in evidence in the stories which give their titles to the two volumes of his collected stories, *The Dying Stallion* (1967) and *The Ploughing Match* (1968).

Urquhart, Jane 1949– Canadian. In *The Whirlpool* (1986), a novel set around Niagara Falls, a 19th-century woman's journal reflects the competing claims of Old and New World cultures. *Changing Heaven* (1990) engages in a dialogue with EMILY BRONTË's *WUTHERING HEIGHTS*. *Away* (1993) is about an Irish settler family. In the *Underpainter* (1997) a minimalist painter sees art as justifying exploitation and manipulation. Urquhart has also published *Storm Glass* (1987), a collection of short stories, and *False Shuffles* (1982) and *The Little Flowers of Madame de Montespan* (1983), collections of verse.

USA A trilogy of novels by JOHN DOS PASSOS, consisting of *The 42nd Parallel* (1930), *1919* (1932) and *The Big Money* (1936). One of the most ambitious as well as saddest and most angry works the USA has yet produced, it aims to chronicle the essential experience of the first 30 years of the 20th century. Only its immense length has prevented it finding a permanent readership.

The most conventional, and least satisfactory, of its several approaches follows the lives of various 'typical' fictional characters, ending in disaster or disappointment. Their individual stories are supplemented by: 'Camera Eye' sections, written in STREAM OF CONSCIOUSNESS, which present the experiences of a young boy growing to manhood; 'Newsreels', or montages, of slogans, newspaper headlines, popular songs and political speeches; and, most fruitful of all, incisive miniature biographies of historical figures, who include Eugene V. Debs, Randolph Bourne, Thorstein Veblen, Thomas Edison, Frank Lloyd Wright, Theodore Roosevelt, Woodrow Wilson, Henry Ford, Isadora Duncan and Rudolph Valentino.

Utopia A prose work by St Thomas More (1477–1535), humanist, politician and Roman Catholic martyr. Written in Latin, it was published at Louvain in 1516 as *Libellus vere aureus, nec minus salutaris quam festivus, de optimo reipublicae statu deque nova insula Utopia* ('A truly golden little book, no less beneficial than entertaining, about the best state of a commonwealth and the new island of Utopia'). Ralph Robinson's English version appeared in 1551 and Gilbert Burnet's translation in 1684.

In Book I More meets the traveller Raphael Hythlodaeus at Antwerp and discusses the state of European society with him. Book II (which was written first) contains Raphael's description of the happy island state of Utopia, where all things are held in common, gold is despised and the people live communally. Interpretations of *Utopia* (the name plays on two Greek words *eutopos*, 'a good place', and *outopos*, 'no place') are many and diverse. It has been seen as a programme for an ideal state, a vision of the ideal to be contemplated (like Plato's *Republic*), a satire of contemporary European society, and a humanist *jeu d'esprit*.

Models for More's island state can be found in earlier literature and its influence can be felt in Francis Bacon's *NEW ATLANTIS* (1627), one of many such works in the 17th century, when 'Utopian' became current as an adjective. The ambiguities of More's island, whether it is ideal, possible or even desirable, continue in subsequent Utopian literature, as does the use of imagined strange lands for satirical purposes (Swift's *GULLIVER'S TRAVELS*, SAMUEL BUTLER'S *EREWHON*). 'Dystopian' was first used as an adjective in the late 19th century by John Stuart Mill, to suggest an imagined state which was not desirable. But the desirability of Utopia is deliberately open to question even in More's work. ALDOUS HUXLEY's *BRAVE NEW WORLD* and GEORGE ORWELL's *NINETEEN EIGHTY-FOUR* describe apparent Utopias that reveal themselves to be dystopian.

V

Vachss, Andrew 1942– American. *Flood* (1985) introduces Burke, ex-convict turned vigilante in the violent underworld of New York, who reappears in works such as *Strega* (1987), *Blue Belle* (1988), *Hard Candy* (1989), *Blossom* (1990) and *Sacrifice* (1991). Burke belongs to the 'enforcer' tradition identified with MICKEY SPILLANE's Mike Hammer. The preoccupation with child abuse which permeates the books reflects Vachss's work as criminal lawyer.

van der Post, Sir Laurens (Jan) 1906–96 South African. *In a Province* (1934), his first and most convincing novel, is an early indictment of white South African racism. Of his later novels, both *The Seed and the Sower* (1963) and *The Hunter and the Whale* (1967) won the CNA LITERARY AWARD. Elsewhere his narrative skills are most successful in non-fictional works expressing his openness to other cultures, the intuitive and the mythopoeic, derived from childhood exposure to San (Bushman) and other African societies. These influences, reinforced by the friendship with Jung dealt with in *Jung and the Story of Our Time* (1976), are charted in *Venture to the Interior* (1952), about exploration in Malawi, and *The Lost World of the Kalahari* (1958), *The Heart of the Hunter* (1961), *A Mantis Carol* (1975) and *Testament to the Bushman* (with Jane Taylor; 1984), records of surviving San culture. More specifically autobiographical writings include *Yet Being Someone Other* (1982) and *About Blady: A Pattern Out of Time* (1991).

Van Dine, S. S. Pseudonym of Willard Huntington Wright (1880–1939). American. Under his own name Wright published art criticism and a novel, *The Man of Promise* (1916). As S. S. Van Dine he published DETECTIVE FICTION, achieving an immense popular success, which eventually embarrassed him, with 12 Philo Vance novels: the series began with *The Benson Murder Case* (1926) and *The Canary Murder Case* (1927) and ended with *The Winter Murder Case* (1939). The plots are intricate puzzles constructed according to 'rules of fair play' as exacting as those formulated by Monsignor Ronald Knox in Britain; the hero is as relentlessly learned and facetious as British counterparts like DOROTHY L. SAYERS's Lord Peter Wimsey. Although the books ushered in the Golden Age of detective fiction in the USA (encouraging ELLERY QUEEN, for example), they quickly fell from fashion: Philo Vance, Ogden Nash famously suggested, 'Needs a kick in the pance'.

Van Herk, Aritha 1954– Canadian. *Judith* (1978), about a woman who leaves the city to run a pig farm, has affinities with the work of MARIAN ENGEL's *The Bear*. In *The Tent Peg* (1981) a woman disguises herself to work as cook to an all-male mining expedition, while the PICARESQUE *No Fixed Address: An Amorous Journey* (1987) has an underwear saleswoman as protagonist. The 'geografictione' *Places far from Ellesmere* (1990) and *In Visible Ink* (1991) challenge boundaries between fiction and autobiography, poetry and criticism, geographical and creative writing. *A Frozen Tongue* (1992) is a collection of critical essays and 'ficto-criticism'.

Van Vechten, Carl 1880–1966 American. He is best known for novels such as *Peter Whiffle* (1922), *The Blind Bow-Boy* (1923), *Firecrackers* (1925) and *Parties* (1930), which deal with the cultural life of New York in the 1920s. *Nigger Heaven* (1926), his most highly acclaimed work, is set in Harlem. Other novels include a satire of Hollywood, *Spider Boy* (1928), and *The Tattooed Countess* (1924), set in his home state of Iowa. He was also a music and drama critic and wrote several memoirs, including *Sacred and Profane Memoirs* (1932) and an account of GERTRUDE STEIN, published as an introduction to her *Three Lives* (1909).

van Vogt, A(lfred) E(lton) 1912– Born in Canada, he moved to the USA in 1944. As a colourful pulp writer of SCIENCE FICTION he produced many stories whose harassed heroes gradually achieve control of awesome superhuman powers, including *Slan* (1940; in book form, 1948), *The World of Null-A* (1945; in book form, 1946; revised, 1965) and the two stories in *Masters of Time* (1950). His intellectual substance is perhaps best displayed in his non-fantasy novel about brainwashing, *The Violent Man* (1962). His writing career was interrupted when he became a follower of L. Ron Hubbard's Scientology.

Vanderhaeghe, Guy 1951– Canadian. The stories in his first collection, *Man Descending* (1982), chronicle the disillusionment and pain of daily life in the contemporary world. Earlier stories were gathered in *The Trouble with Heroes and Other Stories* (1983). His novel, *My Present Age* (1984), further explores isolation while *Homesick* (1989), like many recent Canadian novels, deals with a female protagonist's need to return to and connect with her origins. *The Englishman's Boy* (1996) brings together two narratives which point the difference between the Canadian Wild West of the 1870s and its mythologized version in a 1920s Hollywood film.

Vanity Fair: A Novel without a Hero A novel by WILLIAM MAKEPEACE THACKERAY, published in monthly parts in 1847–8 and in volume form in 1848.

A vast satirical panorama of a materialistic

society and a landmark in the history of REAL-ISM, it is set during the period of Waterloo. The plot traces the destinies of two contrasted hero-ines: the poor but resourceful Becky Sharp and her affectionate, trusting friend Amelia Sedley. Thwarted in her attempt to trap Amelia's brother Jos into marriage, Becky becomes gov-erness to the Crawley family. Sir Pitt Crawley proposes to her, only to find that she has already married his soldier son, Rawdon. The news alienates the wealthy aunt on whom Rawdon depends, and the couple live by their wits. Amelia's fortunes decline: her stockbroker father is ruined and her love affair with the vain George Osborne is opposed by his purse-proud father. Although in love with Amelia himself, George's friend William Dobbin persuades him to marry her. The principal characters move with the army to Brussels and George is killed at Waterloo. The grieving Amelia dotes on her son, Georgy, and the memory of George.

Becky neglects her son, Rawdon, in favour of a life of fashion, abruptly ended when her hus-band finds her in a compromising situation with Lord Steyne. She flees to the Continent, where she is discovered by Amelia, whose for-tunes have revived with the return of Dobbin and Jos from India and Georgy's adoption by his wealthy grandfather. The meeting leads to the revelation that George had proposed to elope with Becky on the eve of Waterloo, thus destroy-ing the sentimental memories which prevented Amelia marrying the faithful Dobbin. Becky regains her hold over Jos, who dies in suspicious circumstances. Rawdon dies abroad and his son inherits the Crawley estate. Becky ends in the guise of a pious widow.

Vansittart, Peter 1920– English. A distinctive though often neglected writer, preoccupied with language rather than narrative, he has often used historical settings: ancient Rome in *The Wall* (1990), Luther's Germany in *The Friends of God* (1963) and *A Safe Conduct* (1995). Legends underpin *Lancelot* (1978), *The Death of Robin Hood* (1981) and *Parsifal* (1988). Other novels include *I am the World* (1942), *Broken Canes* (1950), *A Little Madness* (1953), *Carolina* (1961), *Quintet* (1976) and *Aspects of Feeling* (1986). *Paths from the White Horse* (1985) is his autobiography.

Vassanji, Moyez G(ulamhussein) 1950– Born in Kenya, he now works in Canada. THE GUNNY SACK (1989) and *The Book of Secrets* (1994) deal with the experience of Asian muslims in East Africa. *No New Land* (1991), a much smaller novel, is about Asian immigrants in Toronto. *Uhuru Street* (1992) is a collection of stories set in Dar es Salaam.

Vathek: *An Arabian Tale* A novel by WILLIAM BECKFORD, written in French and first published in English in 1786. The translation, probably by Samuel Henley, may have been undertaken at Beckford's request and with his help, but was presented as Henley's own version from the Arabic. Corrupted by power and his thirst for forbidden knowledge, Caliph Vathek becomes a servant of Eblis, the devil. He finally realizes the vanity of earthly treasures and wonders but not before he and his companions are condemned to eternal torment: their bodies will remain intact but their hearts will burn for ever inside them.

Although Beckford's fantasy owes much to the fashion for the GOTHIC NOVEL, its setting allies it with the Orientalism already apparent in Samuel Johnson's *RASSELAS* and later to reach its full flowering in the work of Byron and Thomas Moore.

Vein of Iron A novel by ELLEN GLASGOW, pub-lished in 1935. It deals with the Scottish-Irish Fincastle family, ministers and leaders in Shut-In Valley in the Virginia mountains since Colonial times. The story focuses on Ada, fol-lowing her from childhood through the years of the Depression. With her 'vein of iron', her undaunted pride and courage, she overcomes the community's rejection of her because of her affair with Ralph McBride, marries him, goes back to work after he is paralysed in a car acci-dent and eventually buys back the family home after her father's death.

Vicar of Bullhampton, The A novel by ANTHONY TROLLOPE, serialized in 1869–70 and published in volume form in 1870. Frank Fenwick's vigor-ous, practical Christianity shows in his concern for the children of the local miller Jacob Brattle. When Sam Brattle is accused of complicity in the murder of a local farmer, Fenwick helps to bring the real murderers to trial. He also rescues Sam's fallen sister Carry, restoring her to her father's home and forgiveness. Love-interest is provided by the hopeless passion of the local squire, Harry Gilmore, for Mary Lowther and her eventual marriage to her cousin Walter Marrable.

Vicar of Wakefield, The The only novel by the playwright and poet Oliver Goldsmith (?1730–74), written in 1761 or 1762 but not pub-lished until 1766.

The Vicar, Dr Primrose, tells the story of his family's fall from contentment. Their hardships begin when he loses his personal fortune in the bankruptcy of a merchant company. He finds a new living through the patronage of Squire Thornhill but the Squire persuades the eldest daughter, Olivia, into a false marriage cere-mony and then deserts her. She is found by her father and brought back home. When his vicar-age burns down and his debts are called in, Dr Primrose is thrown into prison. He is joined by George, his son, who has challenged Thornhill to a duel. The younger daughter, Sophia, is abducted and the deserted Olivia, so the Vicar is told, has died of grief. Dr Primrose endures all these blows with stoicism. A kind-hearted but apparently seedy gentleman, calling himself Mr Burchell but in fact the Squire's uncle Sir William, rescues Sophia, and proves that Olivia's marriage was after all a true one and that she is not dead. George is able to marry his love, Arabella Wilmot, and Dr Primrose's fortune is restored to him by the reformation of the swindler, Ephraim Jenkinson

Whether it is read as a SENTIMENTAL NOVEL or mild parody of the form, the story has the perennial charm of a fairy tale: the rural setting is cosy, the characters are divided into stereotypes of good and evil, and their sufferings can be magically relieved by a happy ending. It incorporates three notable short poems: 'The Hermit: or, Edwin and Angelina', 'When Lovely Woman Stoops to Folly' and 'Elegy on the Death of a Mad Dog'.

Victory A novel by JOSEPH CONRAD, published in 1915.

The story is set in Indonesia. On a rare impulse the cynical Axel Heyst helps Morrison, the captain of a trading brig, by paying his fines. He is offered a share in the Tropical Belt Coal Company and becomes its owner when Morrison dies. The Company fails but Heyst remains on the island of Samburan, alone except for his servant Wang. Schomberg, the hotel keeper in Sourabaya, circulates rumours that Heyst murdered Morrison and has secreted a fortune on the island. His malignancy increases when Heyst, on a rare visit, rescues an English girl, Lena, from his unwanted attentions. Schomberg invites a trio of desperadoes to raid Heyst's island: 'plain Mr Jones', Ricardo, and Pedro. Lena is mortally wounded trying to baffle their plans. She dies in Heyst's arms with the smile of private 'victory' on her lips. Heyst commits suicide in despair.

Vidal, Gore 1925– American. *Williwaw* (1946) and *In a Yellow Wood* (1947) made use of his experiences in World War II. *The City and the Pillar* (1948, revised 1965), a best-seller dealing frankly with homosexuality, started the pattern of controversy he continued with, for example, *Myra Breckenridge* (1968) and *Myron* (1974). *Washington DC* (1964) started the satire on politics continued in long, exhaustively researched novels scrutinizing famous lives and epochs from American history: *Burr* (1973), *1876* (1976), *Lincoln* (1984), *Empire* (1987) and *Hollywood* (1989). *Kalki* (1978) and *Live from Golgotha* (1992) postulate false Messiahs and imminent Armageddon; *Duluth* (1983) ridicules TV soap opera. Popular culture, right-wing politics and fundamentalist religion are also favourite targets of the essays in *Homage to Daniel Shays: Collected Essays, 1952–1972* (1972), *Matters of Fact and Fiction: Essays, 1973–1976* (1977), *Armageddon? Essays, 1983–1987* (1987), *A View from the Diners Club: Essays, 1987–1991* (1991) and *Virgin Islands: A Dependency of United States: Essays, 1992–1997*

(1997). He has also written DETECTIVE FICTION under the pseudonym of Edgar Box.

Villette A novel by CHARLOTTE BRONTË, published in 1853. It develops material already used in her first novel, *THE PROFESSOR*.

Lucy Snowe goes to teach at a girls' school in Villette, a Belgian town based on the author's experience of Brussels, and proves her worth to Madame Beck, the headmistress. She is condescendingly befriended by a pupil, Ginevra Fanshawe, whose admirers include Dr John Bretton, the son of Lucy's godmother. Lucy represses her own feelings for him and Bretton, realizing Ginevra's vanity, falls in love with Paulina Home. Lucy buries herself in her work but gradually awakens to the fascination of the professor, Paul Emmanuel, a waspish man who finds in her a response that mellows and softens him. When he is obliged to go to the West Indies he leaves Lucy in charge of his school, promising to return in three years.

Vine, Barbara See RENDELL, RUTH.

Virginian, The: *A Horseman of the Plains* A romantic novel of the old West by OWEN WISTER, published in 1902. Set mostly in the Wyoming cattle country of the 1870s, it portrays a society which combines the unrefined manly life of the cowboys with signs of advancing civilization. The plot builds toward the wedding day of the pretty Vermont schoolteacher, Miss Molly Wood and the Virginian, when the hero is forced to kill his sworn enemy, Trampas. The novel's influence beyond the printed page was assured when the role of the Virginian was played by Gary Cooper in the 1929 Hollywood film.

Virginians, The A novel by WILLIAM MAKEPEACE THACKERAY, published in parts in 1857–9 and in book form in 1858–9. Stately and rather static HISTORICAL FICTION, it continues the story of the Esmond family from *THE HISTORY OF HENRY ESMOND* by following the fortunes of Esmond's twin grandsons, George and Harry Warrington.

George, the elder, is reported killed in action against the French. Harry visits England, becomes a favourite of his aunt (the Beatrix of *Henry Esmond*, now the Baroness Bernstein) and falls in love with his middle-aged cousin, Lady Maria Esmond. He falls into debt but is rescued by George, escaped from French imprisonment. Now that Harry is no longer the heir, Maria releases him from his engagement. George settles in London, turns to writing plays and, to his mother's disapproval, marries the middle-class Theo Lambert. On the death of his English uncle, Sir Miles Warrington, he succeeds to the title and the Warrington estates in England. Meanwhile Harry serves with General Wolfe at the capture of Quebec, buys an estate in Virginia and marries the daughter of his mother's companion. The brothers find themselves on opposing sides during the Revolution and George, who has fought for the King, resigns his Virginian estate to Harry and retires to England.

Virtue, Noel 1947– New Zealand. At first more highly regarded in Britain, his first novel, *The Redemption of Elsdon Bird* (1987), was published in New Zealand in 1992. Like *In the Country of Salvation* (1990), it deals with a young boy's struggle to cope with social and religious pressures in small-town New Zealand in the 1950s. Other novels include *Always the Islands of Memory* (1991), about two sisters coping with past memories, and *Sandspit Crossing* (1994), which returns to small-town life and fundamentalist religion. *Once a Brethren Boy: An Autobiography* (1995) explains how his homosexuality is the central force shaping his identity.

Vittoria A novel by GEORGE MEREDITH, published in 1867. It continues the story begun in *SANDRA BELLONI*. Sandra Belloni, who sings under the name of 'Vittoria', supports the Italian independence movement inspired by Mazzini. Suspicion falls on her because her English friend, Wilfred Pole, is an officer in the Austrian army. She marries the patriot Carlo Ammiani, but the enmity of Violetta d'Isorella and Anna von Lenkenstein endangers Vittoria, Carlo and Wilfred and Carlo is killed. She is comforted by the arrival of her friend Merthyr Powys.

Vivian Grey The first novel by BENJAMIN DISRAELI, published in 1826. The scrappily plotted narrative follows the fortunes of Vivian, a clever and manipulative young man much like his creator. The most interesting character is Essper George, a conjuror who becomes Vivian's servant and entertains him with tall stories. The book may owe something to the tradition of HENRY FIELDING's *TOM JONES* and TOBIAS SMOLLETT's *PEREGRINE PICKLE*, with their scapegrace heroes accompanied by faithful servants.

Vizenor, Gerald 1934– Native American. His volumes of English haiku poetry include *Raising the Moon* (1964), *Seventeen Chirps* (1964), *Two Wings the Butterfly* (1967) and *Matsushima: Haiku* (1984). Although his first novel, *Darkness in Saint Louis Bearheart* (1978), is a self-reflexive exercise in POST-MODERNISM, it shows the same interest in Native American culture which informs its successors, *Griever: An American Monkey in China* (1990), *Bearheart* (1990) and *The Heirs of Columbus* (1991), as well as his non-fictional writing. Vizenor has also published *Landfill Meditation: Crossblood Stories* (1991).

Vollmann, William T(anner) 1959– American. His elaborate, innovative fiction has often been compared to the work of THOMAS PYNCHON. It includes: *You Bright and Risen Angels: A Cartoon* (1987), about a war between insects and the inventors of electricity; *Whores for Gloria; or, Everything was Beautiful until the Girls Got Anxious* (1991), a 'documentary novel'; *Butterfly Stories* (1993); and *The Atlas* (1996). *The Ice-Shirt* (1990)

began a projected seven-volume sequence, *Seven Dreams: A Book of North American Landscapes* about the supposed colonization of North America by the Vikings; it has been continued in *Fathers and Crows* (1992) and *The Rifles* (1994). Vollmann's short stories are found in *The Rainbow Stories* (1989) and *Thirteen Stories and Thirteen Epitaphs* (1991).

Vonnegut, Kurt, Jr 1922– American. His novels are ironic jeremiads combining dark humour with unashamed sentimentality. *Player Piano* (1952) is a dystopian novel about automation. *The Sirens of Titan* (1959) is satirical SCIENCE FICTION, introducing the Tralfamadorian aliens who reappear in his most substantial work *SLAUGHTERHOUSE-FIVE: or, The Children's Crusade* (1969). *Cat's Cradle* (1963) and *Galapagos* (1985) are sarcastic apocalyptic fantasies.

Vonnegut's non-fantastic novels, including *Mother Night* (1961), *God Bless You, Mr Rosewater* (1965), *Jailbird* (1979), *Deadeye Dick* (1985) and *Hocus Pocus* (1991), are character studies with innocent, unlucky protagonists. Other novels include *Breakfast of Champions: or, Goodbye Blue Monday!* (1973), *Slapstick: or, Lonesome No More* (1976) and *Bluebeard* (1987). His short fiction is collected in *Welcome to the Monkey House* (1968). Plays include *Happy Birthday, Wanda June* (1960) and *Timesteps* (1979). His non-fiction is collected in *Wampeters, Foma and Granfalloons* (1974) and two volumes of 'autobiographical collage', *Palm Sunday* (1981) and *Fates Worse Than Death* (1991).

Voss A novel by PATRICK WHITE, published in 1957 and the first novel to win the MILES FRANKLIN AWARD. White's source was the journals of the Australian explorers Leichhardt and Eyre.

The first part, set in Sydney in the 1840s, describes preparations for an expedition into the Australian interior. The long central section, which employs a dense, metaphorical style, is the story of the journey itself and of how the megalomaniac explorer Voss gradually comes to acknowledge humility. The final section returns to Sydney and deals ironically with the making of the myth of Voss, who has perished, along with all the members of the expedition except one. Voss's actual journey is complemented by the metaphorical journey of Laura Trevelyan, who remains in Sydney but functions as his anima and 'spiritual wife'.

Voyage Out, The VIRGINIA WOOLF's first novel, written in 1912–13 but not published until 1915. Unlike her later works, it is realistic in form, though it contains passages of lyrical intensity.

Rachel Vinrace, an innocent young woman, sails to South America on her father's ship, accompanied by her aunt, Helen Ambrose, and uncle Ridley. At Lisbon she meets Richard and Clarissa Dalloway (who reappear in *MRS DALLOWAY*). In South America she falls in love with Terence Hewet, an aspiring writer interested in women's experiences and concerned about their position in society. They determine to establish their future marriage on a new basis of equality, but Rachel is taken ill and dies. The novel ends with the English party at the hotel retiring to bed.

Waddell, Helen (Jane) 1889–1965 English. She is remembered for: her moving novel *Peter Abelard* (1933), about the medieval French theologian (1079–1142) and his tragic love affair with Héloïse; *The Wandering Scholars* (1927), a pioneering study of European learning in the 12th century and the sometimes ribald goliardic verse associated with it; and the verse translations in *Medieval Latin Lyrics* (1933).

Wain, John 1925–94 English. His most famous novel is his first, *Hurry On Down* (1953), a PICARESQUE comedy which identified him as a leader of the ANGRY YOUNG MEN. Later novels include *The Contenders* (1958), *Strike the Father Dead* (1962), *The Smaller Sky* (1968), *A Winter in the Hills* (1971), *Young Shoulders* (1982; WHITBREAD AWARD) and two BILDUNGSROMANEN, *Where the River Meets* (1988) and *Comedies* (1990). *Nuncle* (1960) and *Death of the Hind Legs* (1966) contain short stories. His cerebral, witty verse is collected in *Poems 1949–79* (1981). He also wrote a biography of Samuel Johnson (1974), literary criticism and radio plays.

Walker, Alice 1944– African-American. She is best known for her novels: *The Third Life of Grange Copeland* (1970); *The Color Purple* (1982; PULITZER PRIZE), an EPISTOLARY NOVEL about a black woman raped by the man she believed to be her father; *Meridian* (1977); *The Temple of My Familiar* (1989); and *Possessing the Secret of Joy* (1992). Her short fiction appears in *In Love and Trouble: Stories of Black Women* (1973) and *You Can't Keep a Good Woman Down* (1981). She has also published many volumes of verse, children's books and non-fiction, which includes *Warrior Marks* (1993), a harsh exploration of female circumcision, and the essays and speeches in *Anything We Love Can Be Saved: A Writer's Activism* (1997).

Wallace, David Foster 1962– American. Often compared to figures such as THOMAS PYNCHON and WILLIAM GADDIS, he writes satiric and encyclopaedic compendiums of contemporary American life-styles, music, New Age philosophies and drug culture. His first novel, *The Broom of the System* (1987), won him immediate recognition; it was followed by *Girl with Curious Hair* (1989), a collection of stories, and *Infinite Jest* (1996), a novel. *A Supposedly Funny Thing I'll Never Do Again* (1997) is a collection of essays.

Wallace, (Richard Horatio) Edgar 1875–1932 English. His prodigious writing career began with *The Four Just Men* (1906) and extended to nearly 100 more popular novels – embracing DETECTIVE FICTION, SPY FICTION and adventure stories – as well as more than 50 volumes of short stories, nearly 30 plays, four volumes of verse, many miscellaneous books and a

demanding schedule of newspaper work. The 1[?] books featuring the adventures of 'Sanders o[f] the River' were among his most popular works[.] Of his detective fiction, the stories about J. G[.] Reeder were particularly successful: *Room 1[3]* (1924), *The Mind of Mr J. G. Reeder* (1925), *Terro[r] Keep* (1927), *Red Aces* (1929) and *The Guv'no[r]* (1932). Wallace died while working in Holly[-] wood on the storyline for *King Kong* (1933).

Wallace, Lew(is) 1827–1905 American. As well a[s] the enormously successful BEN-HUR (1880), h[e] wrote: *The Fair God* (1873), a novel about th[e] Spanish conquest of Mexico; *The Boyhood of Chris[t]* (1888); *The Wooing of Malkatoon* (1897), a tragi[c] poem; and an autobiography. After fightin[g] with distinction in the Mexican War and th[e] Civil War, he practised law and served as gover[-] nor of New Mexico and US minister to Turkey.

Wallant, Edward (Lewis) 1926–62 American. *Th[e] Pawnbroker* (1961), his most acclaimed work, i[s] about Sol Nazerman, a Polish Jew who owns [a] pawnshop in Harlem, where he relives the ho[r-] rors of a Nazi concentration camp in nigh[t] mares and flashbacks. Wallant's first novel, *Th[e] Human Season* (1960), is the story of [a] middle-aged immigrant Jew after his wife'[s] death. *The Tenants of Moonbloom* (1963) and *Th[e] Children at the Gate* (1965) appeared pos[t-] humously.

Walmsley, Leo 1892–1966 English. His novel[s] portray the austere and often dangerous lives o[f] Yorkshire fishermen. They include *Three Feve[rs]* (1932), *Foreigners* (1935) and *Sally Lunn* (1937[;] later dramatized.

Walpole, Horace, 4th Earl of Orford 1717–9[7] English. His place in the history of English fi[c-] tion was assured by a single work, THE CASTLE O[F] OTRANTO (1764), an exercise in medievalis[m] which began the taste for the GOTHIC NOVEL. Ye[t] Walpole intended *The Castle of Otranto* merely a[s] a *jeu d'esprit*. His only other literary venture wa[s] equally modest and equally odd: a blank-vers[e] tragedy, *The Mysterious Mother* (1768), whic[h] made the protagonist's remorse for incest it[s] central theme and so was not thought suitab[le] for presentation on stage. Both works we[re] by-products of the career of a man who, thoug[h] youngest son of the Prime Minister Sir Rober[t] Walpole, largely preferred the life of a connoi[s-] seur.

His first contribution to art studies was *Aede[s] Walpolianae*, an annotated catalogue of th[e] family collection of paintings. It appeared i[n] 1747, the same year he moved to Twickenha[m] and started to Gothicize his house, Strawber[ry] Hill, an activity which absorbed him for near[ly] 25 years. The fame of Strawberry Hill, aided b[y] his *Description of the Villa of Horace Walpole* (1774), was a major factor in the Gothic Revival in architecture. The *Description* was printed on his own press, which he also used to issue an edition of poems by his friend Thomas Gray (1757) and his own *Catalogue of the Royal and Noble Authors of England* (1758), a combination of bibliography, antiquarianism and criticism. Other books were his reworking of the antiquary George Vertue's manuscripts as *Anecdotes of Painting in England* (1762–71), *Catalogue of Engravers Who Have Been Born or Resided in England* (1763), *Historic Doubts of the Life and Reign of Richard III* (1768), *Essay on Modern Gardening* (1785) and an edition of Lucan's *Pharsalia* (1760). Walpole's political connections and his own career as an MP led to several posthumous works: *Memoirs of the Last Ten Years of the Reign of George the Second* (1822), *Memoirs of the Reign of George the Third* (1845) and *Journal of the Reign of King George the Third from the Year 1771 to 1783* (1859).

Yet all these activities are insignificant by comparison with the letters Walpole wrote throughout his life. Over 4000 survive, now gathered in the monumental 48-volume Yale edition (1937–83). Addressed to many correspondents and clearly written with an eye to publication, they discuss antiquarian matters, politics, literature, architecture, painting and the gossip of the day with *brio* and playful but unflagging intelligence. Together they constitute both a continual source of delight and a major social document of their age.

Walpole, Sir Hugh (Seymour) 1884–1941 English. In all, he wrote over 40 popular novels which made him one of the best-known writers of his day. They include: *Mr Perrin and Mr Traill* (1911), based on his own brief experiences as a teacher; *Fortitude* (1913); *The Duchess of Wrexe* (1914); *The Dark Forest* (1916) and *The Secret City* (1919), the first novel to win the JAMES TAIT BLACK MEMORIAL PRIZE, both based on his experiences with the Russian Red Cross in World War I; and *The Herries Chronicle*, a family saga set in Cumberland, consisting of *Rogue Herries* (1930), *Judith Paris* (1931), *The Fortress* (1932) and *Vanessa* (1933).

Walsh, Jill [Gillian] Paton See PATON WALSH, JILL [Gillian].

Walwicz, Ania 1951– Australian. Her sense of herself as outsider, both as woman and migrant from Poland, and her late encounter with the language in which she now writes, left her free to break through structural formalities. The work in *Writing* (1982), *Boat* (1989) and *Red Roses* (1992) can be described as both poetry and prose: using no punctuation, it piles up apparently illogical connections which nevertheless accumulate profound rationality of meaning. Her plays are *Girlboytalk* (1986), *Dissecting Mice* (1989) and *Elegant* (1990).

War of the Worlds, The A novel by H. G. WELLS, serialized in 1897 and published in book form in 1898. A classic story of alien invasion, it provided a model for countless cruder imitations; Orson Welles's famous radio adaptation in the USA in 1938 was realistic enough to cause panic. In the first part missiles from Mars land in England, arousing only mild interest until they disgorge fearful war machines. Panic spreads as resistance fails and London is destroyed. In the second part survivors of the catastrophe live in hiding. Finally, the Martians prove unprotected against earthly bacteria, which succeed where men's best efforts failed in destroying them.

Ward, Artemus [Browne, Charles Farrar] 1834–67 American. He wrote mock letters to the editor of *The Cleveland Plain Dealer* in 1857–9 and pioneered the comic lecture (a form MARK TWAIN would later adopt), attacking Abolitionists, Mormons, Shakers, feminists, temperance advocates and anyone else he considered hypocritical or ineffectual. As staff member and then editor of *Vanity Fair*, he became known as the 'unofficial dean of American humour'. His publications include *Artemus Ward, His Book* (1862), *Artemus Ward, His Travels* (1865) and, after his death during a lecture tour of England, the posthumous *Artemus Ward in London and Other Papers* (1867).

Ward, Mrs Humphry (Mary Augusta) 1851–1920 English. The niece of Matthew Arnold, she married Thomas Humphry Ward, Oxford don and later art critic of *The Times*. Acquaintance with Oxford figures such as J. R. Green, T. H. Green, Benjamin Jowett, Mark Pattison and WALTER PATER encouraged her academic interests and her adoption of an unorthodox religious position, close to that of Matthew Arnold, which abandoned belief in the historical truth of the Gospels and concentrated on applying the spiritual truths of Christianity to humanitarian work. Her novel *ROBERT ELSMERE* (1888) records the intellectual and emotional implications of such a pilgrimage. The next phase of her life showed its practical results, particularly in her work for the Passmore Edwards Settlement, opened in Bloomsbury in 1897. Despite her support for higher education for women, she became president of the Women's Anti-Suffrage League in 1908.

Apart from *Robert Elsmere*, the most notable of her 25 novels are *The History of David Grieve* (1892) and *Helbeck of Bannisdale* (1898) for their treatment of religious issues, and *Marcella* (1894) and *Delia Blanchflower* (1915) for their debate of social and political issues. *England's Effort* (1916), *Towards the Goal* (1917) and *Fields of Victory* (1919) describe the Allied effort during World War I. *A Writer's Recollections* (1918) provides interesting accounts of the many major literary figures she had met and a record of the social and intellectual life of Oxford in her early years. Her translation of the *Journal Intime* of the Swiss mystic Henri Amiel (1885) long remained the standard English edition.

Ward, Robert Plumer See SILVER-FORK NOVEL.

Warden, The The first of ANTHONY TROLLOPE'S BARSETSHIRE NOVELS, published in 1855.

The Bishop of Barchester appoints Septimus Harding, a gentle and unworldly clergyman, warden of the almshouse of Hiram's Hospital. A local reformer, John Bold, and the *Jupiter* newspaper (*The Times*) attack the discrepancy between Harding's comfortable annual salary and the small weekly allowance given to the old men. Bold abandons the campaign at the request of Harding's youngest daughter, Eleanor, whom he marries. But the battle continues between reformers and conservatives, led by Archdeacon Grantly, and the warden resigns.

One of Trollope's finest and most characteristic works, the novel contains an implicit defence of his own art and moral vision in portraits of Thomas Carlyle as Dr Pessimist Anticant and DICKENS as Mr Popular Sentiment.

Warner, Charles Dudley 1829–1900 American. He is best remembered for THE GILDED AGE (1873), his first published novel, written in collaboration with MARK TWAIN. Its theme of greed and corruption is developed in the trilogy of novels he went on to write, consisting of *A Little Journey in the World* (1889), *The Golden House* (1894) and *That Fortune* (1899), about the fate of the fortune amassed by the Henderson family. Warner also produced several collections of essays, including *Summer in a Garden* (1870), *Being a Boy* (1878) and *The Relation of Literature to Life* (1896).

Warner, Rex 1905–86 English. *Poems* (1937) was inspired by the same anti-totalitarian fervour which animated W. H. Auden, CHRISTOPHER ISHERWOOD and other writers of his generation during the 1930s. *The Wild Goose Chase* (1937) and *The Professor* (1938) are bleak novels showing the influence of Kafka. *The Aerodrome* (1941), his best-known novel, depicts the conflict between the aerodrome, whose personnel believe in cleanliness, health and discipline, and an unnamed but quintessentially English village. Warner's many translations include: Euripides' *Medea* (1944), *Hippolytus* (1950) and *Helen* (1951); Aeschylus' *Prometheus Bound* (1947); Xenophon's *Anabasis* (1949); Thucydides (1954); Plutarch (1958); and the poetry of George Seferis (1960). His studies of classical subjects include *The Young Caesar* (1958) and *Pericles the Athenian* (1963).

Warner, Sylvia Townsend 1893–1978 English. Her poetry, influenced by THOMAS HARDY, includes *The Espalier* (1925), *Time Importuned* (1928), *Opus 7* (1931) and *Rainbow* (1932). Her novels include: *Lolly Willowes* (1926), a supernatural story; *Mr Fortune's Maggot* (1927), about a missionary; and *The True Heart* (1929), a story of love set in the Essex marshes, which shows her at her imaginative and lyrical best. *A Garland of Straw* (1943) and *Museum of Cheats* (1947) are volumes of short stories.

Warren, Robert Penn 1905–89 American. A member of the Southern literary group known as the Fugitives, he helped to found and edit its magazine, *The Fugitive* (1922–5), contributed to its manifesto, *I'll Take My Stand: The South and the Agrarian Tradition* (1930), and became editor of *The Southern Review* with Cleanth Brooks in 1935. His poetry and fiction are marked by a brooding, philosophical intelligence, and he wrote perceptively on writers with a similar cast of mind, notably JOESPH CONRAD and WILLIAM FAULKNER. His many volumes of verse include *Selected Poems 1923–1943* (1944), *Selected Poems: New and Old 1923–1966* (1966) and *New and Selected Poems 1923–1985* (1985). *A Robert Penn Warren Reader* (1988) is a useful anthology of his poetry and prose. As a novelist he remains best known for *All the King's Men* (1946; PULITZER PRIZE), the story of a corrupt Southern politician, Willie Stark, apparently modelled on Governor Huey Long of Louisiana. Other works include *New and Selected Essays* (1989) and several volumes of criticism and creative writing edited in collaboration with Cleanth Brooks, notably *Understanding Poetry: An Anthology for College Students* (1938; revised editions 1950, 1960 and 1976) and *Understanding Fiction* (1943; revised editions 1959 and 1979). He became the first Poet Laureate of the USA in 1986.

Warren, Samuel 1807–77 English. His melodramatic *Passages from the Diary of a Late Physician* appeared in *Blackwood's Edinburgh Magazine* in 1830–7. *Ten Thousand a Year* (1841) led some reviewers to compare him favourably with DICKENS. Packed with sensational incident and portraits of the legal profession and high society, it describes the rise and fall of Mr Tittlebat Titmouse. *Now and Then* (1847) was less successful and Warren, a qualified barrister who later became a Conservative MP, turned to writing legal textbooks.

Washington Square A short novel by HENRY JAMES, serialized in 1880 and published in volume form in 1881. Catherine Sloper, the daughter of a wealthy New York physician, leads a bleak existence until she is courted by Morris Townsend. Believing Morris to be a fortune-hunter, Dr Sloper opposes their engagement and takes Catherine to Europe for a year. Morris returns 17 years later, after Dr Sloper has died, and proposes again. She rejects him and settles down to the life of a spinster in the family house in Washington Square.

Waten, Judah 1911–85 Australian. The son of Russian Jews, he established his reputation as a pioneering writer of migrant experience with his story-cycle *Alien Son* (1952). The theme combines with that of political activism (again based on personal experience) in his novels, *The Unbending* (1954), *Shares in Murder* (1957), *Time of Conflict* (1961), *Distant Land* (1964), *Season of Youth* (1966), *So Far No Further* (1971) and *Scenes from Revolutionary Life* (1982).

Water-Babies, The: *A Fairy Tale for a Land Baby* A fantasy for children by CHARLES KINGSLEY, serialized in 1862–3 and published in volume form in 1863. Tom, a young chimney-sweep, runs away from his brutal employer, Grimes. In his flight he falls into a river and is transformed into a water baby. Thereafter, in the river and the seas, he meets all sorts of creatures and learns a series of moral lessons.

Waterhouse, Keith (Spencer) 1929– English. He made his name as a novelist with *Billy Liar* (1959), which mixed whimsy with the provincial realism of contemporaries such as JOHN BRAINE and STAN BARSTOW. Its successors include a sequel, *Billy Liar on the Moon* (1976), *Maggie Muggins* (1981) and *Unsweet Charity* (1992). His collaborative work for stage, screen and television with Willis Hall includes an adaptation of *Billy Liar* (1960), *Celebration* (1961), *All Things Bright and Beautiful* (1963) and *Say Who You Are* (1965). *Jeffrey Bernard is Unwell* (1989) is a stage adaptation of Jeffrey Bernard's *Spectator* columns.

Watership Down A novel by RICHARD ADAMS, published in 1972. A long and intricately plotted anthropomorphic fantasy about a community of rabbits who set out to found a new warren, it found a large adult readership only after initial success as children's literature. While its allegory of human society extends to the semimystical overtones of an enigmatic God-rabbit, El-a-H'rairah, Adams's novel is also notable for its authentic account of rabbit behaviour and its sensitive evocation of the Berkshire Downs.

Watson, Sheila 1919– Canadian. Her novel *THE DOUBLE HOOK* (1959) received much critical and popular attention. Rejecting the rural NATURAL-ISM of much Canadian literature, it draws on native myths to create one of the few masterpieces of MODERNISM in Canada. *Five Stories* was published in 1984. *Deep Hollow Creek* (1992), written in the 1930s, is based on Watson's experiences as a schoolteacher in the interior of British Columbia.

Watts-Dunton, (Walter) Theodore 1832–1914 English. Born Theodore Watts, he published contributions to *The Athenaeum*, some Shakespearean criticism, a volume of poetry and *Aylwin* (1898), a novel which includes a thinly disguised portrait of Dante Gabriel Rossetti. Also a student of gypsy-life, he edited GEORGE BORROW's *LAVENGRO* (1893) and *THE ROMANY RYE* (1900). His literary aspirations outpaced his abilities, and Watts-Dunton is usually remembered for taking care of Swinburne during the last 30 years of the poet's life.

Waugh, Alec [Alexander] **(Raban)** 1898–1981 English. He was the elder brother of EVELYN WAUGH. Successes in the course of his long career as a middlebrow novelist include *The Loom of Youth* (1917), a precocious first novel about public-school homosexuality, and *Island in the Sun* (1956), a steamy account of sexual and racial tensions in the Caribbean.

Waugh, Evelyn (Arthur St John) 1902–66 English. Son of the publisher Arthur Waugh and younger brother of ALEC WAUGH, he was educated at Lancing and Hertford College, Oxford. In 1928 he married Evelyn Gardner (whom he divorced in 1930) and was received into the Catholic Church. *DECLINE AND FALL* (1928), *Vile Bodies* (1930), *Black Mischief* (1932), *A HANDFUL OF DUST* (1934), *Scoop* (1938) and *Put Out More Flags* (1942) caught the witty and cynical mood of his generation and established him as its leading satirical novelist. His wide travels also produced several books: *Labels: A Mediterranean Journal* (1930), *Remote People* (about Africa; 1931), *Ninety-Two Days* (about South America; 1934), *Waugh in Abyssinia* (about Mussolini's invasion; 1936), and *Robbery under Law: The Mexican Object Lesson* (1939). His last travel book was *A Tourist in Africa* (1960).

In 1937 Waugh married Laura Herbert and settled in the West Country. *Work Suspended* (1942), two chapters of an unfinished novel, was followed by *BRIDESHEAD REVISITED* (1945), marking a change from his earlier satirical mode. *Men at Arms* (1952), *Officers and Gentlemen* (1955) and *Unconditional Surrender* (1961) make up a trilogy, *SWORD OF HONOUR*, published together in 1965. Its account of World War II echoes Waugh's own disillusioning experiences, particularly with the British Military Mission to Yugoslavia in 1944. *The Loved One* (1948) is a black little fable about Hollywood and the California funeral industry. *Helena* (1950), HISTORICAL FIC-TION set in the Rome of the Emperor Constantine, was Waugh's favourite work, but not his readers'. *The Ordeal of Gilbert Pinfold* (1957) is a frankly autobiographical account of a middle-aged writer who suffers a nervous breakdown. *A Little Learning* (1964) began an autobiography which he did not live to complete. It has been supplemented by editions of his *Diaries* (1976) and *Letters* (1980).

Waverley SIR WALTER SCOTT's first novel, published anonymously in 1814. It is set during the 1745 rebellion.

When young Edward Waverley goes to join his regiment in Scotland he finds himself attracted both to the gentle Rose Bradwardine and the beautiful Flora, who, like her brother Fergus Mac-Ivor, is an ardent Jacobite. Waverley's romantic vacillation corresponds to a political vacillation between loyalty to the Crown and interest in the Jacobite cause. Unfairly blamed for an incipient mutiny, cashiered from his regiment and saved from prison only by Rose's intervention, he is driven to join the Jacobites. After the rebels are defeated Fergus Mac-Ivor is executed but Waverley, who has saved the life of Colonel Talbot, is pardoned. Rejected by Flora, who enters a convent, he eventually marries Rose.

The novel's success, which confirmed Scott in changing from poetry to fiction, did much to foster a romantic interest in Scotland and Scottish history among English readers.

Waves, The A novel by VIRGINIA WOOLF, published in 1931. Her most experimental novel, it uses STREAM OF CONSCIOUSNESS to trace the lives of six characters – Bernard, Susan, Rhoda, Neville, Jinny and Louis – from childhood, when they share a house together, to their reunions in later life and finally to their old age. Each character's life story is revealed incidentally and, although there is no differentiation in their speech, their individual personalities are revealed by recurring phrases and images. Italicized passages record the ascent and descent of the sun, the rise and fall of the waves, and the passing of the seasons. The novel is often considered Woolf's masterpiece.

Way of All Flesh, The A semi-autobiographical novel by SAMUEL BUTLER, posthumously published in 1903.

The narrator, Overton, follows four generations of the Pontifex family and particularly the career of Ernest Pontifex. After an unhappy childhood with his tyrannical and strictly religious father, Ernest becomes a clergyman, lands up in prison and makes a disastrous marriage, from which he is freed when his drunken wife turns out to be already married. Anxious to avoid repeating the Pontifex paternal tyranny, he farms out the children of his union. Having inherited an income from his aunt Alethea, he embarks upon a solitary life, literary vocation and eclectic interests much resembling Butler's own adult career.

The fortunes of the Pontifex family are designed to show that personal happiness stems from the liberating effect of acting on inherited and largely unconscious stores of vitality. The play between the conscious and unconscious also fuels the thrust of the novel's attack upon the conventions and hypocrisies of Victorian family life.

Way We Live Now, The A novel by ANTHONY TROLLOPE, serialized in 1874–5 and published in volume form in 1875. Undervalued in his own day, it is now recognized as one of his finest works, a satire comparable in scope to WILLIAM MAKEPEACE THACKERAY's *VANITY FAIR* and DICKENS's *LITTLE DORRIT*.

At its centre is the fitfully heroic figure of Augustus Melmotte, a wealthy financier of obscure origins. Courted by impecunious aristocrats eager to get on the boards of his companies, he quickly rises to social prominence and enters the House of Commons. The bubble bursts with the discovery of fraud and he commits suicide. A related plot involves Lady Carbury's efforts to arrange a marriage between her son, Sir Felix, and Melmotte's daughter Marie, which collapse when Felix gambles away the money Marie has obtained for their elopement. The only character to denounce the widespread corruption is Lady Carbury's cousin Roger Carbury, a middle-aged country squire in love with her daughter Hetta. Another plot concerns Roger and his friend Paul Montague, the erstwhile lover of Winifred Hurtle, a passionate American. Although the marriage of Paul and Hetta provides the conventional happy ending, the loneliness and disappointment of Mrs Hurtle and Roger Carbury ensure that the mood of Trollope's most sombre novel is sustained to the end.

Webb [*née* Meredith], **(Gladys) Mary** 1881–1927 English. *Precious Bane* (1924) became a best-seller after it had been praised by the Prime Minister, Stanley Baldwin, who wrote an introduction to the 1928 edition. Its stark descriptions of the Shropshire countryside, infused with a romantic and often naive passion, were brilliantly parodied by Stella Gibbons in *COLD COMFORT FARM* (1932). Mary Webb's other novels include *The Golden Arrow* (1916), *Gone to Earth* (1917), *The House in Dormer Forest* (1920) and *Seven for a Secret* (1922).

Wedde, Ian 1946– New Zealand. A leading exponent of open form, informal language and verbal collage, he was strongly influenced by modern American poetry. Collections include: *Homage to Matisse* (1971); *Earthly: Sonnets for Carlos* (1975); *Spells for Coming Out* (1977); *Castalay* (1980), which contains *Pathway to the Sea* (1975); *Tales of Gotham City* (1984), *Tendering* (1988) and *The Drummer* (1993). His introduction to *The Penguin Book of New Zealand Verse* (1985), which he co-edited, is an important sequel to Allen Curnow's introduction to the previous Penguin anthology (1960). His fiction includes: *Dick Seddon's Great Dive* (1976), which won the NEW ZEALAND BOOK AWARD; *Symmes Hole* (1986), a richly allusive account of New Zealand past and present with which he made his mark as a novelist; and *Survival Arts* (1988). *The Shirt Factory* (1981) is a volume of short stories. *How to be Nowhere: Essays and Texts 1971–1994* (1995) collects occasional pieces about literature and the visual arts.

Weir of Hermiston An unfinished novel by ROBERT LOUIS STEVENSON. Although the fragment published posthumously in 1896 does little more than set the scene and introduce the chief characters, it is generally acknowledged as a potential masterpiece.

The formidable hanging judge, Adam Weir, Lord Hermiston, banishes his son Archie to the remote and uncivilized village of Hermiston, where he lives as a recluse with his devoted housekeeper, Kirstie. Her four nephews, the 'Black Elliotts', are notorious for their ruthless hunting-down of their father's murderer. Archie falls in love with their sister Christina. The couple's meetings become known to Kirstie and Frank Innes, Archie's treacherous friend. Archie tells Christina that their relationship must end. The fragment ends here, but Stevenson's plans show that Archie would kill Innes in a quarrel and be tried by his father before being rescued by the 'Black Elliotts'. He would escape to America with Christina, while Lord Hermiston would die from the shock of having sentenced his own son to death.

Welch, Denton (Maurice) 1915–48 British. He published many poems, 60 short stories and three largely autobiographical novels: *Maiden Voyage* (1943), introduced by Edith Sitwell, *In Youth is Pleasure* (1945) and *A Voice through a Cloud* (1950). His *Journals* (1952) give a vivid account of a life increasingly restricted by a severe spinal injury.

Welch, James 1940– Native American. His first novel, *Winter in the Blood* (1974), is about a young Indian trying to make sense of his heritage. Though set in the contemporary Midwest, *The Death of Jim Loney* (1979) is concerned with the traditional codes of behaviour found in the mythic stories of the Gros Ventres. *Fool's Crew* (1986) is set in the Two Medicines Indian region of Montana in the 1870s. *The Indian Lawyer* (1990) is a political thriller. Other work includes poetry, *Riding the Earthboy Forty* (1976), and historical non-fiction, *Killing Custer: The Battle of the Little Bighorn and the Fate of the Plains Indians* (1994).

Weldon, Fay 1933– English. Her prolific output has alternated between television plays and vigorous, resourceful novels articulating a contemporary feminist consciousness. These include: *Female Friends* (1975); *Praxis* (1978); *Puffball* (1980), an extended evocation of the process of conception; *The President's Child* (1982) and *The Life and Loves of a She-Devil* (1983), caustic satires of male-dominated society; *The Rules of Life* (1987), a novella; *The Hearts and Lives of Men* (1987); *Darcy's Utopia* (1990); *Growing Rich* (1992); *Life Force* (1992); and *Affliction* (1993), about therapy's part in marriage-breaking. Her dissection of the painful aspects of intimacy is continued in *Splitting* (1995) and *Worst Fears* (1996).

Well at the World's End, The A prose romance by the artisan, poet and socialist William Morris (1834–96), published in 1896. Ralph, youngest son of King Peter of Upmeads, sets out on a quest for the 'Well at the World's End', whose waters give the drinker long life and an ever-youthful 'lucky' appearance. He falls in love with the Lady of Abundance who has drunk from the Well, but she is killed before she can lead him to it. After a period of despair Ralph's quest finds a parallel in his search for Ursula, his first love. Together they reach the Well, drink from it and eventually return to rule Upmeads and live in peace.

With Morris's other prose romances – *The Wood beyond the World* (1894) and the posthumously published *The Water of the Wondrous Isles* and *The Sundering Flood* (both 1897) – it influenced the poetry of W. B. Yeats, and subsequently found a new readership among devotees of J. R. R. TOLKIEN and C. S. LEWIS. For Morris, see also *A DREAM OF JOHN BALL* and *NEWS FROM NOWHERE*.

Well-Beloved, The: *A Sketch of a Temperament* A novel by THOMAS HARDY, serialized as *The Pursuit of the Well-Beloved* in 1892 and substantially revised for book publication in 1897. It is set on the Isle of Slingers (Portland), where the sculptor Jocelyn Pierston pursues his ideal Well-Beloved by courting, successively, a mother, daughter and grand-daughter all named Avice. With illness and encroaching age the ideal recedes and he marries another old flame, Marcia Bencomb.

Weller, Archie (Irving Kirkwood) 1957– Part-Aboriginal Australian. He is also known as Kirk Weller. His novel *The Day of the Dog* (1981) gives a vivid picture of the violence and want endured at the margins of urban society. *Going Home* (1986) explores the same settings, showing a mastery of the European short-story form as a frame for Aboriginal material. He has written film scripts and two plays, *Sunset and Shadows* (1989) and *Nidjers* (1990), and co-edited *Us Fellas* (1988), essays and short stories by Aboriginal writers.

Wells, H(erbert) G(eorge) 1866–1946 English. The son of an unsuccessful Bromley tradesman, he won a scholarship to the Normal School of Science (now Imperial College), London, in 1884. The teaching of T. H. Huxley, Darwin's most articulate supporter, was a profound influence. Wells's literary career began with SCIENCE FICTION: *THE TIME MACHINE* (1895), *The Wonderful Visit* (1895), *The Island of Dr Moreau* (1896), a grim parable of the blind and bestial forces underlying civilization, *The Invisible Man* (1897), *THE WAR OF THE WORLDS* (1898), *When the Sleeper Wakes* (1899), *The First Men in the Moon* (1901) and *The War in the Air* (1908). Their implicit note of warning about the impact of alien races or advanced science on established society prefigures his later concern with social and political realities. His interest in the changing social order reappears in *A Modern Utopia* (1905), which, with other works such as the later 'discussion' novel, *The New Machiavelli* (1911), displays his didactic tendency. A quarrelsome member of the Fabian Society, he frequently engaged in public controversy with leading thinkers of the day, notably GEORGE BERNARD SHAW.

Wells's major novels with a bias towards social realism drew heavily on his own youthful experiences. *LOVE AND MR LEWISHAM* (1900) and *KIPPS* (1905) were followed by *TONO-BUNGAY* (1909), his most ambitious novel, and *THE HISTORY OF MR POLLY* (1910). *Ann Veronica* (1909) was considered scandalous for its portrayal of an emancipated woman. Later works, less distinguished though still popular, were *MR BRITLING SEES IT THROUGH* (1916), *Mr Blettsworthy on Rampole Island* (1928) and *The Bulpington of Blup* (1932). Wells's public reputation survived the disgrace which attached to his views on sexual freedom and his widely reported liaison with REBECCA WEST during his second marriage. He continued to see himself as a popular educator, in works like *The Outline of History* (1920), and resisted despair in the face of the Great War and the rise of fascism, though World War II prompted a pessimistic last work, *Mind at the End of Its Tether* (1945). *Experiment in Autobiography* (1934) is a lively and engaging self-portrait.

Welsh, Irvine 1958– Scottish. *Trainspotting* (1993), a novel and the basis for a film which has achieved cult status, is about the Edinburgh underclass for whom drugs and violence form the fabric of everyday life. It is written in a mixture of standard English, Scots and phonetically rendered street-slang. Welsh's other work includes: *The Acid House* (1994), consisting of short stories and a novella; *Maribou Stork Nightmares* (1995), set ostensibly in Africa but also in a nightmare landscape of remembered or imagined violence; and *Ecstasy: Three Tales of Chemical Romance* (1996), making playful contrasts between the drug culture and other less expected worlds.

Welty, Eudora 1909– American. She established herself as a major Southern writer with fiction often set in her native territory of rural Mississippi. It includes *A Curtain of Green, and Other Stories* (1941), *The Wide Net, and Other Stories* (1943), *The Golden Apples* (1949), *The Bride of the Innisfallen, and Other Stories* (1955) and *The Collected Stories of Eudora Welty* (1985). She also wrote novels in the Southern Gothic tradition, among them *The Robber Bridegroom* (1942), *Delta Wedding* (1946), *The Ponder Heart* (1954), *Losing Battles* (1970) and *The Optimist's Daughter* (1972; PULITZER PRIZE). Her literary autobiography, *One Writer's Beginnings*, appeared in 1984.

Wendt, Albert 1939– Western Samoan. The one writer from the South Pacific with an international reputation, he is best known for *Leaves of the Banyan Tree* (1979), which won the GOODMAN FIELDER WATTIE BOOK AWARD. A three-generation saga of Western Samoan life, it corrects sentimentalized Western versions of the 'South Seas'. Wendt's earlier novels were *Sons for the Return Home* (1973) and *Pouliuli* (1977). *Ola* (1991) moves for the first time outside the South

Pacific. *Black Rainbow* (1992) is a futuristic satire on the quest for cultural identity in New Zealand. *Flying-Fox in a Freedom Tree* (1974) and *The Birth and Death of the Miracle Man* (1986) are collections of short stories. *Inside Us the Dead* (1976) and *Shaman of Visions* (1984) are volumes of poetry. Wendt also founded the first literary journal in the South Pacific, *Mana*, and edited the first anthology of Pacific writing, *Lali* (1980).

Wescott, Glenway 1901–87 American. His first publication was *The Bitterns* (1920), a book of verse influenced by imagism. His best-known works were published while he was an expatriate in France in the 1920s. They include *The Apple of the Eye* (1924) and his most successful novel, *The Grandmothers* (1926). Both are stories of frontier life in Wisconsin, offering a lyrical evocation of the past, a deeply felt assessment of Wescott's heritage. *Good-Bye Wisconsin* (1928) is a collection of stories. His last notable publication was *The Pilgrim Hawk* (1940).

Wessex The name borrowed by THOMAS HARDY from Anglo-Saxon history for the West Country setting of most of his novels and many of his poems. It was first used in *FAR FROM THE MADDING CROWD*. Unlike the historic Wessex, Hardy's Wessex is centred on Dorset and particularly Dorchester, whose fictional name is Casterbridge. The slight transposition is typical of Hardy's treatment of real placenames to create a 'partly real, partly dream' landscape.

West, Nathanael [Weinstein, Nathan Wallenstein] 1903–40 American. His preoccupation with the barrenness of contemporary life dominates his best-known work. *Miss Lonelyhearts* (1933) is the story of a newspaperman who writes an advice-to-the-lovelorn column, *A Cool Million: The Dismantling of Lemuel Pitkin* (1934) is a satire of the American Dream and *The Day of the Locust* (1939) exposes the squalid hidden world of Hollywood, where West worked as a scriptwriter for a minor studio from 1935.

West, Paul 1930– American, born in Britain. Although he has written poetry, memoirs and literary criticism, he is primarily a novelist. *Tenement of Clay* (1965) is a remarkable harbinger of the POST-MODERNISM informing his entire oeuvre. *Alley Jaggers* (1966), *I'm Expecting to Live Quite Soon* (1970) and *Bela Lugosi's White Christmas* (1972) form a trilogy about a working-class family in West's native northern England. *The Very Rich Hours of Count von Stauffenberg* (1980), *Rat Man of Paris* (1986), *Lord Byron's Doctor* (1989), *The Women of Whitechapel and Jack the Ripper* (1991) and *Sporting with Amaryllis* (1996) are elaborate reinventions of history.

West, Dame Rebecca 1892–1983 Novelist and journalist. Born Cicily Isobel Fairfield, she had a brief career as an actress (her role in Ibsen's *Rosmersholm* suggesting the name she was to adopt). She then became a journalist and outspoken advocate of women's rights. Her relationship with H. G. WELLS resulted in the birth of a son, Anthony West, in 1914. Her first novel, *The Return of the Soldier* (1918), was about a shell-shock victim. Others include *The Judge* (1922), *The Strange Necessity* (1928), *Harriet Hume* (1929), *The Thinking Reed* (1936), *The Fountain Overflows* (1957), *The Birds Fall Down* (1966), *This Real Night* (1984), a sequel to *The Fountain Overflows*, and *Sunflower* (1986). Recent studies have applauded the strong characterization of her heroines. Her other works include a study of Yugoslavia, *Black Lamb and Grey Falcon* (1941–2), and *The Meaning of Treason* (1949, revised 1952 and 1965), an account of the treason trials following World War II, revised to include later espionage trials.

Westmacott, Mary See CHRISTIE, AGATHA.

Westward Ho! A novel by CHARLES KINGSLEY, published in 1855. Now remembered chiefly as children's literature, it was Kingsley's most ambitious novel and his most ambitious attempt at HISTORICAL FICTION: an epic of England's heroic victory over Spain and the fear of Catholic domination in the 16th century. The story is packed with incident and clotted with pedantry and preaching: Drake, Sir Walter Raleigh, Edmund Spenser and other real-life heroes crowd the pages, as do references to the chronicler of British seafaring, Richard Hakluyt. Its heady mixture of patriotism, sentiment and romance set the attitudes of English children for several generations.

Wetherell, Elizabeth [Warner, Susan Bogert] 1819–85 American. She launched her career producing moral and sentimental novels for children with two best-sellers, *The Wide Wide World* (1850) and *Queechy* (1852), both about orphans. In some of her work she collaborated with her sister Anna Bartlett Warner (1826–1915).

Weyman, Stanley (John) 1855–1928 English. He began his highly successful historical romances with *The House of the Wolf* (serialized in 1888–90; published in book form, 1890). *A Gentleman of France* (1893), set in the period of Henry of Navarre, was praised by ROBERT LOUIS STEVENSON. It was followed by *Under the Red Robe* (1894; successfully dramatized in 1896), *The Red Cockade* (1895), *The Castle Inn* (1898), *Count Hannibal* (1901), about the Massacre of St Bartholomew, *Chippinge* (1906), set at the time of the Reform Bill, and many others. (See also HISTORICAL FICTION.)

Wharton, Edith (Newbold) 1862–1937 American. Born into a wealthy New York family, she moved to France with her husband in 1907, remaining there after her divorce in 1913. Her close friendship with HENRY JAMES was a major influence on her work, acknowledged in *The Writing of Fiction* (1925). *THE HOUSE OF MIRTH* (1905) was her first popular success. *Madame de Treymes* (1907) tackled a characteristic theme, the difference between American and European social customs, though her range extended to the study of rural New England which made *ETHAN FROME* (1911) enduringly popular. *The Reef* (1912) and *The Custom of the Country* (1913) attacked the hypocrisies of New York society. *The Marne* (1918) and *A Son at the Front* (1923) are about World War I. *THE AGE OF INNOCENCE* (1920) made her the first woman to receive a PULITZER PRIZE. *The Mother's Recompense* (1925), *Twilight Sleep* (1927) and *The Children* (1928) deal with inter-generational differences in families. *Hudson River Bracketed* (1929) and *The Gods Arrive* (1932) examine the artistic temperament through the character of Vance Western, a struggling novelist. At her death she was working on *The Buccaneers* (1938), set in Saratoga in the 1860s. The best-known of her 11 collections of short stories is probably *Xingu and Other Stories* (1916). *A Backward Glance* (1934) is autobiographical.

Wharton, William Pseudonym of Albert du Aime (1925–). American. The absurdity of human conflicts is the theme of his first novel, *Birdy* (1979), and his most accomplished novel, *A Midnight Clear* (1982), based on his experience of World War II. He is also preoccupied with identity and self-definition: *Pride* (1986), like *Birdy*, uses an animal metaphor to underscore its story of a man's gradual reclamation of his honour. Other novels include *Dad* (1981), *Scumbler* (1984), *Tidings* (1987), *Franky Furbo* (1989) and *Last Lovers* (1991). *Ever After: A Father's True Story* (1995) is a memoir of his daughter's fatal car accident in 1988, while *Houseboat on the Seine* (1996) describes moving to Paris and building the houseboat where he has lived for more than 20 years.

What Maisie Knew A novel by HENRY JAMES, published in 1897. Though written in the third person, it is told from the point of view of the perceptive but somewhat naive Maisie.

Her parents, Beale and Ida Farange, divorce when she is six and it is arranged that she spend half the year with her father and half with her mother. Beale marries Miss Overmore, who had been Maisie's governess; Ida marries Sir Claude but still has a succession of lovers. Her two new step-parents become attracted to one another and eventually marry. Maisie is abandoned by Beale and Ida to the care of her new governess, Mrs Wix. Sir Claude invites her to live with him and the former Miss Overmore who, unfortunately, cannot abide Mrs Wix, the one 'safe' adult whom Maisie absolutely trusts. The novel ends with Maisie refusing to live with Sir Claude and his new wife in Boulogne and departing for England with Mrs Wix.

What's Bred in the Bone See CORNISH TRILOGY, THE.

Wheatley, Dennis See GENRE FICTION.

Where Angels Fear to Tread The first novel by E. M. FORSTER, published in 1905.

The widowed Lilia Herriton visits Italy with her friend Caroline Abbott and falls in love with Gino Carella, a dentist's son. Mrs Herriton, her mother-in-law, dispatches Philip, her brother-in-law, but he arrives to find that Lilia has married Gino. The marriage fails and Lilia dies in childbirth. Philip is again dispatched, with his sister Harriet, to join Caroline in rescuing the baby. Philip and Caroline begin to succumb to the charm of Italy but Harriet, refusing to admit defeat, steals the baby. It dies in a carriage accident. Gino assaults Philip and the three English characters return home. On the journey, Philip discovers that he has fallen in love with Caroline, she with Gino.

Whetstone, George ?1544–?1587 English. *The Rock of Regard* (1576) is mainly a collection of prose and verse tales, largely drawn from Italian sources. His unacted play *Promos and Cassandra* (1578) takes a story from Cinthio's *Hecatommithi* which reappears, with other work by Cinthio, in his collection of prose romances, *An Heptameron of Civil Discourses* (1582). One or other version, or perhaps both, served as the main source for Shakespeare's *Measure for Measure*. Whetstone's other works are a verse eulogy commemorating George Gascoigne (1577) and a series of biographical elegies of distinguished contemporaries, including Sir Philip Sidney (with whom he had fought at Zutphen).

Whitbread Awards A group of annual awards to works by writers who have been resident in Britain or the Republic of Ireland for at least three years. When it was inaugurated in 1971, prizes were given in three categories: fiction, biography and poetry. In subsequent years an award for children's books and the Whitbread First Novel Award have been added, and since 1985 winners in all categories have been entered for the Whitbread Book of the Year Award.

The first novel to win the fiction prize was *The Destiny Waltz* (1971) by Gerda Charles (Edna Lipson). Subsequent winners have included WILLIAM MCILVANNEY's *Docherty* (1975), PAUL THEROUX's *Picture Palace* (1978), JENNIFER JOHNSTON's *The Old Jest* (1979), DAVID LODGE's *How Far Can You Go?* (1980), Maurice Leitch's *Silver's City* (1981), CHRISTOPHER HOPE's *Kruger's Alp* (1984), PETER ACKROYD's *Hawksmoor* (1985), Lindsay Clarke's *The Chymical Wedding* (1989), JANE GARDAM's *The Queen of the Tambourine* (1991), ALASDAIR GRAY's *Poor Things* (1992) and BERYL BAINBRIDGE's *Every Man for Himself* (1996). SALMAN RUSHDIE has been twice honoured, for *THE SATANIC VERSES* (1988) and *The Moor's Last Sigh* (1995). WILLIAM TREVOR has won three times, for *The Children of Dynmouth* (1976), *Fools of Fortune* (1983) and *FELICIA'S JOURNEY* (1994), which also won the Book of the Year Award. Other novels to have been chosen as Book of the Year include KAZUO ISHIGURO's *An Artist of the Floating World*

(1976), NICHOLAS MOSLEY's *Hopeful Monsters* (1990) and JOAN BRADY's *Theory of War* (1993).

Recipients of the Whitbread First Novel Award include: WILLIAM BOYD's *A Good Man in Africa* (1981), BRUCE CHATWIN's *On the Black Hill* (1982), JEANETTE WINTERSON's *ORANGES ARE NOT THE ONLY FRUIT* (1985), Paul Sayers's *The Comforts of Madness* (1988), JAMES HAMILTON-PATERSON's *Gerontius* (1989), Gordon Burn's *Alma Cogan* (1991), Jeff Torrington's *Swing Hammer Swing!* (1992), Rachel Cusk's *Saving Agnes* (1993) and Kate Atkinson's *Behind the Scenes at the Museum* (1995), which was also voted Book of the Year.

White, Antonia 1899–1980 English. Her first novel, *Frost in May* (1933), is a largely autobiographical account of Nanda Grey's convent education. Clara Batchelor, the heroine of *The Lost Traveller* (1950), *The Sugar House* (1952) and *Beyond the Glass* (1954), suffers in her relationships with men, is confined in an asylum, and eventually returns to the faith which she had rejected early in life. The conclusion echoes *The Hound and the Falcon* (1965), Antonia White's account of her own reconversion to Catholicism. She also translated works by Colette.

White, E(lwyn) B(rooks) 1899–1985 American. He became a writer and contributing editor for *The New Yorker* in 1926. His long-term friendship with JAMES THURBER included a collaboration, *Is Sex Necessary?* (1929). Other works include *Alice Through the Cellophane* (1933), *Quo Vadimus? Or the Case for the Bicycle* (1938), *One Man's Meat* (1942), *The Second Tree from the Corner* (1954) and *The Points of My Compass* (1962). His contribution to children's literature includes two notable books, *Stuart Little* (1945) and *Charlotte's Web* (1952).

White, Edmund 1940– American. He is best known for a loose trilogy of autobiograhical novels, consisting of: *A Boy's Own Story* (1982) and *The Beautiful Room is Empty* (1988), about growing up gay in America, and *The Farewell Symphony* (1997), which uses the departing musicians in Haydn's work as a metaphor for the devastation wrought by AIDS in the gay community. He has also published: *Forgetting Elena* (1973); *Nocturnes for the King of Naples* (1978); *Caracole* (1985); and *Skinned Alive* (1995). *The Darker Proof: Stories from a Crisis* (1987) is a volume of stories co-written with ADAM MARS-JONES. He has investigated gay communities in *States of Desire: Travels in Gay America* (1980) and written a biography of the French writer Jean Genet (1993). David Bergman has edited *The Burning Library: Writings on Art, Politics and Sexuality 1969–93* (1994).

White, Patrick 1912–90 Australian. He came from a wealthy Australian family but was born and educated in Britain. He returned to live in Australia after World War II. The rediscovery of his Australianness ultimately led to three of his finest novels: *The Tree of Man* (1955), covering a period from pioneer settlement to suburbanization, *Voss* (1957) and *Riders in the Chariot* (1961), which contains a powerful indictment of Australian suburban life. Both *Voss* and *Riders in the Chariot* won the MILES FRANKLIN AWARD. Other novels include *The Happy Valley* (1939), *The Living and the Dead* (1941), *The Aunt's Story* (1948), *The Solid Mandala* (1966), *The Vivisector* (1970), *The Eye of the Storm* (1973), *A Fringe of Leaves* (1976) and *The Twyborn Affair* (1979), which he declared would be his last. He broke his resolution in 1986 with *Memoirs of Many in One* 'by Alex Xenophon Demirjian Gray, edited by Patrick White'.

The Burnt Ones (1964) and *The Cockatoos* (1974) are collections of short stories. Plays such as *The Season at Sarsaparilla* (1961), *Night on Bald Mountain* (1962) and *Signal Driver* (1983) established him as one of Australia's finest non-naturalistic dramatists. His autobiography, *Flaws in the Glass* (1981), openly acknowledged his homosexuality. *Patrick White Speaks* (1990) is a collection of essays and speeches, often campaigning, from 1958 to 1988.

He was awarded the Nobel Prize for Literature in 1973.

White, T(erence) H(anbury) 1906–64 English. His early work was hardly successful, though aficionados of DETECTIVE FICTION still sometimes remember *Darkness at Pemberley* (1932), and *England Have My Bones* (1937), in praise of the English countryside, had its admirers. Profoundly affected by Sir Thomas Malory's *Le Morte D'Arthur*, which, as a pacifist, he considered 'a quest for an antidote to war', he made a major contribution to Arthurian literature with his quirky, humorous retelling of the legend in *The Sword in the Stone* (1939), *The Witch in the Wood* (1940), *The Ill-Made Knight* (1941) and *The Candle in the Wind* (1958). The series was revised as *The Once and Future King* (1958). A fifth volume, *The Book of Merlyn*, was posthumously discovered and published in 1977. Other works included *Mistress Masham's Repose* (1946), about descendants of the Lilliputians from GULLIVER'S TRAVELS; *The Goshawk* (1951), about training a pet hawk; *The Book of Beasts* (1954), a translation from a medieval bestiary; and *The Master* (1957), part parable and part SCIENCE FICTION.

White, William Hale 1831–1913 English. He was born into a Dissenting family in Bedford and began to train as an Independent minister but was expelled for raising issues of biblical criticism. He worked as a journalist and civil servant but in his fifties began to publish in two distinct, though for him related, fields: fiction, published under the pseudonym of Mark Rutherford, and philosophy. *The Autobiography of Mark Rutherford, Dissenting Minister* (1881) relates, in thinly veiled form, his own spiritual pilgrimage from orthodoxy through Unitarianism, theism and agnosticism to stoic resignation. What distinguishes his account both here and in the sequel, *Mark Rutherford's Deliverance* (1885), is the narrator's air of absolute fidelity to the truth,

however drab, sombre or inconvenient to the demands of fictional structure. These two novels, together with *The Revolution in Tanner's Lane* (1887), provide a portrait of 19th-century dissent where nostalgia for the past glories of Puritanism informs the astringent analysis of its present decay.

Under his own name White published studies of John Bunyan, Wordsworth and Spinoza. His other writings – the novels *Catherine Furze* (1893), *Miriam's Schooling and Other Papers* (1893) and *Clara Hopgood* (1896), and the essays and stories published in *Pages from a Journal* (1900), *More Pages from a Journal* (1910) and *Last Pages from a Journal* (1915) – confirm the picture of a deeply self-critical moral earnestness schooling an innately depressive temperament for survival in an uncongenial world.

White Hotel, The A controversial best-selling novel by D. M. THOMAS, published in 1981. It attracted passionate support and notoriety in equal measures for its sexual explicitness and direct treatment of Nazi war atrocities. Beginning with a virtuoso pastiche of a Freudian case history, the novel ultimately shows the neuroses of the patient and protagonist, Lisa Erdman, to have been premonitory of her eventual mutilation and murder in the Babi Yar massacre.

White-Jacket: or, *The World in a Man-of-War* A novel by HERMAN MELVILLE, published in 1850. It describes the homeward voyage of the frigate *Neversink* from Peru eastward round the Horn to Virginia, emphasizing the degrading conditions the men live in and the tyrannies practised by the captain and officers. The criticism of flogging was timely, and copies of the book were sent to Congress during its debate of the issue. The title refers to the nickname which the narrator earns by making himself a white jacket from scraps of cloth.

White Peacock, The D. H. LAWRENCE's first novel, published in 1911. Told by Cyril Beardsall, the story follows the relationships of his sister, Lettie, with George Saxton, a tenant farmer's son, and Leslie Tempest, heir of a wealthy mineowner. Lettie flirts with both but marries Tempest for material security. Tormented by the knowledge that he could have won her, Saxton instead marries the commonplace Meg. Cyril himself shows a mild romantic interest in Saxton's sister, Emily, but nothing comes of it. The most striking figure is the gamekeeper, Annable, precursor of Mellors in LADY CHATTERLEY'S LOVER.

Whitehead, Charles 1804–62 English. He wrote several popular works: a poem, *The Solitary* (1831); two romantic novels, *Jack Ketch* (1834) and *Richard Savage* (1842); and a verse drama, *The Cavalier* (1836). His career was blighted by drunkenness, and he ceased writing in about 1850, dying in Australia.

Whiteing, Richard 1840–1928 English. *The Island* (1888) and its sequel, *Number 5 John Street* (1889), depict social unrest in late Victorian Britain and criticize accepted values. A series of satirical articles dating from Whiteing's time in Paris appeared in *The Evening Star* from 1866.

Whyte-Melville, G(eorge) J(ohn) 1821–78 English. He published some 23 novels on historical, romantic and sporting subjects. His sporting novels, such as *Market Harborough* (1861), have survived best, being perceptive, vivid and curiously undated. He was killed, characteristically, in a hunting accident.

Wide Sargasso Sea A novel by JEAN RHYS, published in 1966, long after her other major novels. It rewrites CHARLOTTE BRONTË's *JANE EYRE* by telling the story of the 'first Mrs Rochester', the madwoman in the attic at Thornfield Hall, here called Antoinette rather than Bertha. Using an impressionistic narrative mode which has its roots in the STREAM OF CONSCIOUSNESS favoured by MODERNISM, Rhys relocates her heroine in the Caribbean of her childhood and early womanhood, explaining the causes of her alleged madness while also giving expression to Rochester's view of the ill-fated marriage. Much of the novel's vivid imagery responds directly to *Jane Eyre*.

Wideman, John Edgar 1941– African-American. He grew up in the Homewood neighbourhood of Pittsburgh, the setting for many of his novels about African-American lives and history. They include: *A Glance Away* (1967); *Hurry Home* (1970); *The Lynchers* (1973); *The Homewood Trilogy*, consisting of *The Hiding Place* (1981), *Damballah* (1981) and *Sent for You Yesterday* (1983); *Reuben* (1987); *Philadelphia Fire* (1990); and *The Cattle Killing* (1996). He has also written two memoirs: *Brothers and Keepers* (1995), an account of his brother's conviction and life imprisonment for murder, and *Fatheralong: A Meditation on Fathers and Sons, Race and Society* (1994).

Wiebe, Rudy (Henry) 1934– Canadian. His first novel, *Peace Shall Destroy Many* (1962), has been followed by works notable for their revisionist accounts of the history of Canadian minorities: Mennonites in *The Blue Mountains of China* (1970), Cree Indians in *The Temptations of Big Bear* (1973) and the Métis population of Manitoba in *The Scorched-Wood People* (1977). *A Discovery of Strangers* (1994) describes an encounter between the Franklin expedition to discover the North-West Passage and a group of Yellow Indians. His other novels are *First and Vital Candle* (1966), *The Mad Trapper* (1980) and *My Lovely Enemy* (1983). *Where is the Voice Coming From?* (1974) and *The Angel of the Tar Sands* (1982) are collections of stories. *Playing Dead* (1989) is 'a contemplation concerning the Arctic'.

Wieland*: or, *The Transformation A GOTHIC NOVEL by CHARLES BROCKDEN BROWN, published in 1798 and generally recognized as one of America's first major novels.

In a letter Clara, only surviving member of the Wieland family, tells how the mystical Wieland senior died of spontaneous combustion. Following his wife's death, their children, Clara and Wieland Jr, are cared for by Catherine Pleyel, whom Wieland eventually marries. When Catherine's brother Henry arrives, Clara falls in love with him and the four enjoy each other's company insulated from the outside world. The arrival of the mysterious Carwin destroys their peace. Disembodied voices tell of the death of Henry's fiancée, encouraging him to fall in love with Clara, but then suggest that Clara and Carwin are having an affair. Henry finds his fiancée alive and marries her. The voices eventually drive Wieland to murder his wife and children. He is confined in an asylum but escapes on the very evening when Carwin confesses to Clara that he himself has created the voices by ventriloquism. When the voices order him not to kill his sister, Wieland commits suicide instead. Carwin disappears. After his wife's death Henry finally marries Clara.

Wiggin [*née* Smith], **Kate Douglas** 1856–1923 American. Her first novels for children were written to raise money for her free nursery school in San Francisco, but her great best-seller, *Rebecca of Sunnybrook Farm* (1903), came many years later. It describes the conflict between the lively heroine and her spinster aunt, Matilda Sawyer, in small-town Maine. Other works include the autobiographical *My Garden of Memory* (1923).

Wilcox, James 1949– American. His novels are comedies of manners set in the fictional town of Tula Springs, Louisiana. They include: *Modern Baptists* (1983), about tangled affections and confusions of identity; *North Gladiola* (1985), about the tensions and pretensions of small-town life; *Miss Undine's Living Room* (1987), about the solution of a mystery; *Sort of Rich* (1989), about an outsider who moves to Tula Springs; *Polite Sex* (1991); and *Guest of a Sinner* (1993). Wilcox has been favourably compared to WILLIAM FAULKNER.

Wilde, Oscar (Fingal O'Flahertie Wills) 1854–1900 Irish. The son of Sir William Wilde and Jane Francesca Wilde, he studied at Trinity College, Dublin, and later at Magdalen College, Oxford, where he declared himself a disciple of WALTER PATER and the Aesthetic Movement as well as distinguishing himself in classical studies. His first volume of poetry appeared in 1878. In 1882 he toured the USA as a lecturer, though his play *Vera* flopped in New York in 1883. *The Happy Prince and Other Tales* (1888) are fairy stories written for the two sons by his marriage in 1884. A similar collection, *A House of Pomegranates*, followed in 1891, together with *Lord Arthur Savile's Crime and Other Stories* and *The*

Duchess of Padua, an uninspired verse tragedy. Altogether more important was the insolently epigrammatic wit, and the fascination with the relations between serene art and decadent life, expressed in THE PICTURE OF DORIAN GRAY (1890). Wilde found his true theatrical voice with *Lady Windermere's Fan* (1892), *A Woman of No Importance* (1893), *An Ideal Husband* (1895) and his masterpiece, *The Importance of Being Earnest* (1895). *Salome*, written in French, was published in 1894 in an English translation by Lord Alfred Douglas.

Wilde's homosexuality was an open secret. When the Marquess of Queensberry, Lord Alfred's father, publicly insulted him, Wilde sued for libel but lost his case. He was prosecuted and imprisoned for homosexual acts in 1895. His bitter letter of reproach to Lord Alfred was published incomplete as *De Profundis* (1905), though his poem, *The Ballad of Reading Gaol* (1898), is a more characteristic, because more generous, reaction to his imprisonment. On his release in 1897 he went to France, calling himself 'Sebastian Melmoth', and died in Paris after, it is said, being received into the Catholic church. ROBERT HICHENS's *The Green Carnation* (1894) remains the best attempt at parody of a literary style which invited imitation while remaining confident of its inimitability.

Wilder, Laura Ingalls 1867–1957 American. She was over 60 before she began to write children's stories remembered from her own pioneering childhood. *Little House in the Big Woods* (1932) describes life in a log cabin, with Laura herself appearing in the third person. *Little House on the Prairie* (1935) tells how Laura's father takes his family out West. In *The Long Winter* (1940) the family finally settles in a small town, where their hardships are again described with compassionate realism. Subsequent novels take Laura to marriage and a teaching career.

Wilder, Thornton (Niven) 1897–1975 American. His best-known novel is *The Bridge of San Luis Rey* (1927; PULITZER PRIZE), a study of the role of destiny, or providence, in the death of five travellers when the bridge near Lima collapses in 1714. Other novels are: *The Cabala* (1926); *The Woman of Andros* (1930), set in ancient Greece; *Heaven's My Destination* (1934), about the fortunes of a good and simple man during the Depression; *The Ides of March* (1948), about the last days of Julius Caesar; and two late works, *The Eighth Day* (1967) and *Theophilus North* (1973).

The six one-act sketches in *The Long Christmas Dinner and Other Plays* (1931) mingle realism with experimentation, notably expressionism, designed to 'shake up' the American theatre. His reputation as a playwright rests primarily on three works: *Our Town* (1938; Pulitzer Prize); *The Skin of Our Teeth* (1942; Pulitzer Prize), about mankind's precarious survival; and *The Matchmaker* (1955), revised from an earlier play

called *The Merchant of Yonkers* (1939) and later the basis for the musical comedy *Hello Dolly!* (1963). Several of Wilder's essays on the theatre are included in *American Characteristics and Other Essays* (1979).

Wilding, Michael 1942– Australian, born and educated in Britain. An energetic champion of *avant-garde* fiction, he founded the magazine *Tabloid Story* with FRANK MOORHOUSE and the publishing imprint of Wild and Woolley. His short-story collections are *Aspects of the Dying Process* (1972), *The West Midland Underground* (1975), *Scenic Drive* (1976), *The Phallic Forest* (1978), *Reading the Signs* (1985) and *The Man of Slow Feeling* (1985), *Great Climate* (1991), selected from the previous volumes, and *This is For You* (1994). *Under Saturn* (1988) is a collection of four novellas. His novels are *Living Together* (1974), *The Short Story Embassy* (1975), *Pacific Highway* (1982) and *The Paraguayan Experiment* (1985). Critical works include studies of Milton's *Paradise Lost* (1969) and MARCUS CLARKE (1977), *Political Fictions* (1980) and *Dragon's Teeth: Literature in the English Revolution* (1987).

Wilhelm, Peter 1943– South African. His fiction explores alienation and suffering; his characters are victims who make a fragile attempt at transcendence through love. His first novel, *The Dark Wood* (1977), portrays two Afrikaner brothers whose contrasting responses to the system are equally ineffective. *Summer's End* (1984), SCIENCE FICTION for young readers, is uncharacteristically optimistic. *The Healing Process* (1988) is excruciating in its portrayal of illness, poverty, violence and moral decay. *The Mask of Freedom* (1994) eschews optimism following the birth of South African democracy, instead exposing the fragility of transition in a dystopian narrative set in the near future. *LM and Other Stories* (1975), *At the End of a War* (1981) and *Some Place in Africa* (1987) are short-story collections. Wilhelm's poetry has been collected in *Falling into the Sun: Poems* (1993).

Wilkins, Damien 1963– New Zealand. *The Veteran Perils* (1990) is a collection of short stories and *The Idles* (1993) a collection of poems. His first novel, *The Miserables* (1994), works from the hero's introspection about the present to a wider New Zealand context and a coolly clinical exploration of the past. It won the NEW ZEALAND BOOK AWARD. *Little Masters* (1995) follows the fortunes of young New Zealanders abroad.

Williams, Charles (Walter Stansby) 1886–1945 English. Imbued with his Christian faith, his writings deal with man's relation to God and the problem of good and evil. *Thomas Cranmer of Canterbury* and *The House of the Octopus* are among the verse dramas written in 1936–41 and collected in John Heath-Stubbs's edition (1963). Equally characteristic is the intense, sometimes obscure contribution to Arthurian literature in two volumes, *Taliessin through Logres* (1938) and

The Region of the Summer Stars (1944), admired by C. S. LEWIS. Williams's novels, or 'metaphysical thrillers', include *War in Heaven* (1930), *Many Dimensions* (1931), *Descent into Hell* (1937) and *All Hallows' Eve* (1945). *He Came down from Heaven* (1937) and *The Descent of the Dove* (1939) are works of theology. His literary criticism includes a study of Dante (1943).

Williams, Denis 1923–90 Guyanese. *Other Leopards* (1963), the finest novel about a Caribbean journey back to Africa, describes the 'mulatto' situation of an archaeological draughtsman working in the Sudanic belt. *The Third Temptation* (1968), set in Wales, is a more abstract meditation on perception and perspective. Williams, who was also a painter and the curator of an archaeological museum in Georgetown, also published *Image and Idea in the Arts of Guyana* (1970) and *A Study of Sacred and Secular Forms of African Classical Art* (1974), as well as *Giglioli in Guyana* (1973), a biography of the man who eradicated the malarial mosquito from the country.

Williams, Helen Maria ?1762–1827 English. She mixed in London's literary and bluestocking circles in the 1780s. *Poems* (1786) contained the 'Sonnet to Twilight' which prompted Wordsworth to his first published poem, 'Sonnet, On Seeing Miss Helen Maria Williams Weep at a Tale of Distress'. In 1788 she went to France, where she spent most of her remaining life, her liberalism growing into support of the Revolution. Her various *Letters from France* covering the years 1790–5 made English conservatives regard her as the embodiment of dangerous extremism. *Julia* (1790) is a SENTIMENTAL NOVEL; its successor, *Perourou, the Bellows-Mender* (1801), was adapted for the stage by EDWARD BULWER LYTTON as *The Lady of Lyons* (1838). She also published *A Tour of Switzerland* (1798) and translations of Saint-Pierre's *Paul et Virginie* and Humboldt's travels.

Williams, John (Alfred) 1925– African-American. *The Angry Ones* (1960) is about an artist who fights a personal war against racism, while in *Night Song* (1961) a musician uses his jazz to combat discrimination. Williams's voice is increasingly militant in *Sissie* (1963), *The Man Who Cried I Am* (1967), *Sons of Darkness, Sons of Light* (1969) and *Captain Blackman* (1972). *Mothersill and the Foxes* (1975), *The Junior Bachelor Society* (1976), *Click Song* (1982), *The Berhama Account* (1985) and *Jacob's Ladder* (1987) are less radical, though still firmly emphasizing black unity. *If I Stop I'll Die* (1991), co-authored with his son Dennis A. Williams, is drawn from the life of Richard Pryor. His non-fiction includes a study of RICHARD WRIGHT, *The Most Native of Sons* (1970).

Williams, Nigel 1948– English. A prolific author, he is best known for his fiction, which began with accomplished and witty examples of the BILDUNGSROMAN, such as *My Life Closed Twice*

(1977), and has continued with energetically plotted black comedies in an implacably suburban setting: *The Wimbledon Poisoner* (1990), *They Came from SW19* (1992), *East of Wimbledon* (1993), *Scenes from a Poisoner's Life* (1994) and *Stalking Fiona* (1997).

Williams, Raymond (Henry) 1921–88 Welsh. He was chiefly known as a critic. *Culture and Society 1780–1950* (1958), *The Long Revolution* (1961) and *Keywords* (1976) advocated the socially responsible ideal of a 'common culture'. *Communications* (1962) and *Television: Technology and Cultural Form* (1974) broadened the analysis from literature to other media. Always an active socialist, he moved closer to Marxism in his later work, including *Orwell* (1971), *The English Novel from Dickens to Lawrence* (1971), *The Country and the City* (1973), *Marxism and Literature* (1977) and *Culture* (1981). His drama criticism is found in *Drama from Ibsen to Eliot* (1952; revised as *Drama from Ibsen to Brecht*, 1968) and *Modern Tragedy* (1966).

The social and cultural concerns of his critical writing also inform his fiction, though they are located more specifically in the context of his relationship with his native Wales. His novels are *Border Country* (1960), *Second Generation* (1964), *The Volunteers* (1978), *The Fight for Manod* (1979), *Loyalties* (1985); *The Beginning* (1989) and *The Eggs of the Eagle* (1990) form the first two volumes of an ambitious trilogy, *People of the Black Mountains*, cut short by his death.

Williamson, Henry 1895–1977 English. He is best remembered for *Tarka the Otter* (1927; HAWTHORNDEN PRIZE), a minutely observed and moving tale of animal life which became a popular classic. Like *The Peregrine's Saga* (1923), *The Old Stag* (1926), *Salar the Salmon* (1935), *The Phasian Bird* (1948) and *Tales of Moorland and Estuary* (1953), it reflects his debt to RICHARD JEFFERIES. His other pre-war writings include *The Wet Flanders Plain* (1929) and *A Patriot's Progress* (1930), about World War I, and *The Flax of Dreams*, a sequence of novels comprising *The Beautiful Years* (1921), *Dandelion Days* (1922), *The Dream of Fair Women* (1924) and *The Pathway* (1928). After World War II, during which he was briefly interned because of his fascist sympathies, he published *A Chronicle of Ancient Sunlight*, a partly autobiographical 15-novel sequence beginning with *The Dark Lantern* (1951) and concluding with *The Gale of the World* (1969).

Wilson, A(ndrew) N(orman) 1950– British. His prolific output of fiction began with baleful comedies, such as *The Sweets of Pimlico* (1977), a winner of the JOHN LLEWELLYN RHYS PRIZE, and *Unguarded Hours* (1978). However, his reputation rests mainly on *The Healing Art* (1980), *Who was Oswald Fish?* (1981) and *Wise Virgin* (1982), intricately plotted tragicomedies which confront perplexing moral dilemmas. Subsequent novels include *Scandal* (1983) and *Gentlemen in England* (1985). *A Watch in the Night* (1996) completed 'The

Lampfitt Chronicles', begun with *Incline Our Hearts* (1988), *A Bottle in the Smoke* (1990), *Daughters of Albion* (1991) and *Hearing Voices* (1995). Disenchantment with the Church and monarchy have inspired recent non-fiction, including *Against Religion* (1991), *Jesus* (1993) and *The Rise and Fall of the House of Windsor* (1993). He has also published biographies of SIR WALTER SCOTT (1980), Milton (1983), HILAIRE BELLOC (1984), Tolstoy (1988) and C. S. LEWIS (1990). *Penfriends from Porlock* (1988) collects his stringent literary criticism.

Wilson, Sir Angus (Frank Johnstone) 1913–91 English. The realistic surface of his work and its determined if sceptical engagement with moral values made comparison with E. M. FORSTER inevitable, though in fact he challenged the tradition of liberal humanism. Novels include: *Hemlock and After* (1952), about a writer's attempt to establish a literary colony; *Anglo-Saxon Attitudes* (1956), about middle age; *The Middle Age of Mrs Eliot* (1958), about widowhood; *Late Call* (1964), about the spiritual desolation of a new town in the Midlands; *No Laughing Matter* (1967), about the Matthews family from 1912 to 1967; *As If by Magic* (1973), about a world-ranging quest for meaning; and *Setting the World on Fire* (1980), contrasting the lives of two brothers. *The Old Men at the Zoo* (1961) is a bizarre and violent fable about the near future. Equally important are the short stories in *The Wrong Set* (1949), *Such Darling Dodos* (1950) and *A Bit off the Map* (1957). Other work included studies of Zola (1950), DICKENS (1970) and RUDYARD KIPLING (1977), and *Diversity and Depth in Fiction: Selected Critical Writings* (1983). As professor of English literature at the University of East Anglia from 1966, he presided with MALCOLM BRADBURY over Britain's only notable university course in creative writing. MARGARET DRABBLE has written his biography (1995).

Wilson, Colin (Henry) 1931– English. He shot to fame with *The Outsider* (1956), an enthusiastic, disorganized study of alienation hailed by some as a manifesto of the ANGRY YOUNG MEN generation. Wilson survived his subsequent abrupt rejection by critics and has, by his prolific output, to some extent succeeded in removing himself from their influence. The first of his 'psychological thrillers' was *Ritual in the Dark* (1960), based on the Jack the Ripper case. Other novels include *The Mind Parasites* (1967), *The Killer* (1970), *The Black Room* (1975) and *The Janus Murder Case* (1984). Numerous works of non-fiction deal with literature, philosophy (particularly existentialism), psychology, the occult and the paranormal, and crime. *Autobiographical Reflections* appeared in 1988.

Wilson, Ethel 1890–1980 Canadian. She was born in South Africa and spent part of her childhood in Britain. Her first novel, *Hetty Dorval* (1947), was followed by *The Innocent Traveller* (1949),

Swamp Angel (1954) and *Love and Salt Water* (1956), developing her gift for poised studies of human relationships, their modest surface and apparently traditional structure belying a keen ironic intelligence. *The Equations of Love* (1952) brings together two novellas, and *Mrs Golightly and Other Stories* (1961) most of her important short stories.

Wind in the Willows, The A novel for children by KENNETH GRAHAME, published in 1908. Helped in its popularity by the illustrations of E. H. Shepard and Arthur Rackham, it has enjoyed a second, equally enduring life on the stage, usually in A. A. MILNE's adaptation as *Toad of Toad Hall* (1929).

Three bachelor animals live easy lives on the banks of the Thames: the timid but friendly Mole, the forceful Water Rat and the irresponsible Toad, owner of Toad Hall. When Toad is imprisoned for enthusiastically dangerous driving, Toad Hall is invaded by the stoats and weasels who normally live in the Wild Wood beyond. Escaping from prison dressed as a washerwoman, Toad recaptures his ancestral home with his two friends and the curmudgeonly Badger. The book's strength lies in its animal characterizations and the charming descriptions of the countryside, which include a meeting with the god Pan.

Winesburg, Ohio A collection of 23 stories by SHERWOOD ANDERSON, published in 1919. Partly based on the author's hometown in Ohio, they explore American small-town life and are given further unity by the character of George Willard, a reporter for the local newspaper who has literary ambitions and to whom all the other characters gravitate in the course of the book.

Wings of the Dove, The A novel by HENRY JAMES, published in 1902. Kate Croy and Merton Densher are secretly engaged. She becomes friends with the wealthy Milly Theale, whose death from a mysterious illness can be postponed only by happiness. Kate encourages Merton to take an interest in Milly, hoping that they will get married and that he will soon be a rich widower. Milly learns of the true relationship between Kate and Merton from the fortune-hunting Lord Mark and dies soon afterwards. When Merton learns that Milly has made him rich enough to marry Kate he offers to marry her only if she agrees not to accept the money. Kate declines and they separate.

Winnie-the-Pooh See MILNE, A. A.

Winterson, Jeanette 1959– English. *ORANGES ARE NOT THE ONLY FRUIT* (1985), a first novel which won a WHITBREAD AWARD, evokes her Evangelical upbringing in Lancashire. Winterson has since distanced herself from *Boating for Beginners* (1986), a hasty feminist reworking of the story of Noah's Ark, by calling it a 'comic book'. *The Passion* (1987), which won the JOHN

LLEWELLYN RHYS PRIZE, weaves myths around historical figures and places, chiefly Napoleon and Venice. *Sexing the Cherry* (1989) is an intermittently successful fantasy about a mythical Dog-Woman, while *Written on the Body* (1992) experiments with an ungendered narrator of the sort developed by MAUREEN DUFFY. *Art and Lies* (1994), which provoked charges of pretentiousness, centres on late 20th-century namesakes of Sappho, Handel and Picasso. *GUT Symmetries* (1997), in which the abbreviation stands for Grand Unified Theory, enlists recent physics and popular science in its exploration of human relations. She has also published *Art Objects: Essays on Ecstasy and Effrontery* (1995).

Winthrop, Theodore 1826–61 American. None of his books was published before his death in the Civil War. His novels include *Cecil Dreeme* (1861), *Edwin Brothertoft* (1862) and *John Brent* (1862), his best-known work, which exploits its Western setting to produce a melodramatic plot involving kidnappings and unscrupulous Mormons. *Life in the Open Air* (1863) and *The Canoe and the Saddle* (1863) are travel books.

Winton, Tim(othy) (John) 1960– Australian. His fiction lovingly records the land and seascape of Western Australia and the communities of its small towns, concentrating with particular compassion on the lives of the inarticulate. His novels are *An Open Swimmer* (1982), *Shallows* (1984; MILES FRANKLIN AWARD), *That Eye, The Sky* (1986), *In the Winter Dark* (1988), the ambitious *Cloudstreet* (1991; Miles Franklin Award) and *THE RIDERS* (1994), shortlisted for the 1995 BOOKER PRIZE. *Scission* (1985) and *Minimum of Two* (1987) are collections of short stories. *Jesse* (1989), *Lockie Leonard, Human Torpedo* (1990) and *The Bugalugs Bum Thief* (1991) are children's books.

Wise Blood A novel by FLANNERY O'CONNOR, published in 1952. Hazel Motes is obsessed by the idea that redemption is impossible and that the whole notion of Jesus as saviour is suspect. Setting himself up as a preacher of non-belief, he meets a variety of outcasts and social misfits – notably, the false preacher Asa Hawkes (who has supposedly blinded himself out of religious fervour) and his daughter Sabbath Lily. He is finally driven to murder and self-mutilation, from which he dies.

Wise Children A novel by ANGELA CARTER, published in 1991. A PICARESQUE story encompassing almost a century of English theatrical life is held together by septuagenarian twins, Dora Chance, the narrator, and her sister Nora. Illegitimately fathered by Sir Melchior Hazard, bastion of the 'legitimate' theatre, the twins work as variety artistes, the Lucky Chances. From these basic oppositions between high and low culture, legitimacy and bastardy, Carter weaves a dazzling tale about the nature of art, the benign and baleful functions of illusion, and the gleeful delights of women growing old disgracefully. Familiar as these themes are from Carter's earlier work, *Wise Children* shares with *Nights at the Circus* (1984) in particular an emphasis on the life-giving, and sometimes life-threatening, forces of anarchy and carnival.

Wiseman, Adele 1928–92 Canadian. *The Sacrifice* (1956), a modern version of the Abraham and Isaac story, and the more experimental *Crackpot* (1974) deal with the Jewish experience on the Canadian Prairies. She also wrote two plays, a children's book and *Old Woman at Play* (1978), a fragmentary memoir of her mother. *Memoirs of a Book Molesting Childhood* (1987) is a collection of essays.

Wister, Owen 1860–1938 American. *Red Man and White* (1896), *Lin McLean* (1896) and *The Jimmyjohn Boss* (1900) are collections of stories set in the Western cattle country which he had first visited for reasons of health. His best-known novel, *THE VIRGINIAN* (1902), was an enormous popular success. Its hero set the mould for the Western hero in countless novels and movies. Wister then turned to the East for his subjects. *Philosophy Four* (1903) is about undergraduate life at Harvard; *Lady Baltimore* (1906) is set in Charleston. He also wrote a biography of Ulysses S. Grant (1900) and reminiscences of Theodore Roosevelt (1930), the boyhood friend to whom he had dedicated *The Virginian*.

With the Procession A novel by HENRY BLAKE FULLER, published in 1895. Set in Fuller's native Chicago, it tells the story of David Marshall and his family of social climbers. Exhausted by the demands made upon him – to build a new house, to be a philanthropist, to cut a public figure – he dies, sacrificed to the family's ambition to march 'with the procession'.

Wives and Daughters The last novel by ELIZABETH GASKELL, almost complete at her untimely death in 1865. It was serialized in 1864–6 and published in book form in 1866.

At the centre of its various skilfully interwoven plots is Molly Gibson's development from a confused, insecure girl to a poised young woman. The daughter of the local doctor in Hollingford, she extricates her step-sister Cynthia Kirkpatrick from an unwise commitment to the land agent Preston, is a ministering angel at the home of the old-fashioned Squire Hamley and finally marries Hamley's younger son Roger, a respected scientist who had been briefly engaged to the magnetic Cynthia. Socially, the novel ranges from the Lord and Lady Cumnor, the Hamleys and the Gibsons down to mob-capped spinsters, tenant farmers and ordinary labourers to register a lively, informative picture of early 19th-century England. A host of lesser characters contribute a leavening humour, a dramatic moment or a small turn to the plot. *Wives and Daughters* is an enduring work as narrative, social history and psychological study.

Wodehouse, Sir P(elham) G(renville) 1881–1975 English. Beginning in 1902, he published well over 100 books, as well as contributing lyrics to a number of successful musical comedies with Cole Porter, Irving Berlin and George Gershwin. Set in leisured upper-class society, his comic novels and short stories are sustained by romantic, gently farcical plots and a carefully wrought prose style which combines literary allusion, the slang of the day and the occasional audacious simile. Jeeves and Bertie Wooster, the omni-competent manservant and his amiably incompetent master, have proved his most enduring creations. Introduced in *The Man with Two Left Feet* (1917), they appear in a long series of novels and collections of short stories bearing such expressive titles as *The Inimitable Jeeves* (1923), *Carry On, Jeeves!* (1925) and *Right Ho, Jeeves* (1934). *Blandings Castle* (1935) began a similar series centred on the eccentric Lord Emsworth.

Wolfe, Gene (Rodman) 1931– American. His SCIENCE FICTION is multi-layered and sometimes deliberately cryptic. *The Fifth Head of Cerberus* (1972) is a meditation on the philosophy of identity. The four-volume 'Book of the New Sun' begun with *The Shadow of the Torturer* (1980) and concluded with *The Citadel of the Autarch* (1983) offers a baroque vision of a decadent far future whose main motifs are carefully inverted in *Soldier of the Mist* (1986) and *Soldier of Arete* (1989), set in an equally remote imaginary past. *Nightside the Long Sun* (1993) began a second sequence of far-future novels. His short-story collections include *Gene Wolfe's Book of Days* (1981) and *Endangered Species* (1989).

Wolfe, Thomas (Clayton) 1900–38 American. Though now overlooked, his generous, sprawling novels enjoyed a considerable reputation in the years after their publication. *Look Homeward, Angel* (1929), his strongly autobiographical first novel, follows the early life of Eugene Gant. His story is continued in *Of Time and the River* (1935), in which he attends Harvard and leaves for Europe after a disappointing love affair. Wolfe also wrote a collection of stories, *From Death to Morning* (1935), several plays and *The Story of a Novel* (1936), a critical examination of his own work. The mass of manuscript he left at his death was edited by Edward C. Aswell as *The Web and the Rock* (1939) and *You Can't Go Home Again* (1940). Another volume of short stories, *The Lost Boy*, was published in 1965.

Wolfe, Tom [Thomas] (Kennerly) 1930– American. A major proponent of the New Journalism, he has explored society, politics and contemporary culture in *The Kandy-Kolored Tangerine Flake Streamline Baby* (1966), *The Pump House Gang* (1968), *Radical Chic and Mau-Mauing the Flak-Catchers* (1971), *The Painted Word* (1975), *Mauve Gloves and Madmen, Clutter and Vine and Other Stories* (1976), *The Right Stuff* (1979), *In Our Time* (1980), *From Bauhaus to Our House* (1982) and *The Purple Decades* (1982). *The Electric Kool-Aid Acid Test* (1968) describes the wild life-style of KEN KESEY and his friends. Despite his earlier strictures against fiction, he scored a popular success with *THE BONFIRE OF THE VANITIES*, a novel originally serialized in *Rolling Stone* magazine in 1984–5 but heavily revised for its book publication in 1987. *Ambush at Fort Bragg* (1997), a novella, was issued directly as an audio cassette rather than being published as a book.

Wollstonecraft, Mary 1759–97 English. *Thoughts on the Education of Daughters* (1787) and two children's books resulted from her experience running a school at Newington Green. The self-pitying *Mary: A Fiction* (1788) was written while working in Ireland as governess to Lord Kingsborough's daughters. Her *Vindication of the Rights of Men* (1790) replied to Edmund Burke's *Reflections on the Revolution in France*. In it she identifies herself with the democratic programmes of the European Enlightenment and deplores both the complacency of British society and its trivialization of women. The latter theme is taken up at greater length in her most famous work, *A Vindication of the Rights of Woman* (1792), a sometimes chaotically written but rhetorically powerful plea for fundamental change in society's perception of the function, place and potential of women.

She travelled alone to France in 1792 and published the still largely approving *History and Moral View of the Origin and Progress of the French Revolution* in 1794. In Paris she fell in love with GILBERT IMLAY and bore him a daughter. An unlikely solo journey to Scandinavia is described in *Letters Written during a Short Residence in Sweden, Norway and Denmark* (1796). WILLIAM GODWIN, with whom she had formed an attachment, encouraged her to begin her last novel, *The Wrongs of Woman*, developing the themes of her *Vindication*. They married but she died eleven days after the birth of their daughter, the future MARY SHELLEY. In 1798 Godwin published his *Memoirs* of his wife and edited her *Posthumous Works*, which included letters to Imlay, a fragment of autobiographical fiction, *The Cave of Fancy*, and the unfinished *Wrongs of Woman*. He also portrayed her in his novel *St Leon* (1799). By this time, conservative reaction had set in in England, and she was much attacked as an unsexed woman, 'a hyena in petticoats' and a 'philosophizing serpent'.

Woman in White, The A novel by WILKIE COLLINS, serialized in 1859–60 and published in volume form in 1860. One of the most popular SENSATION NOVELS of its day, it shows Collins at the height of his powers.

The story is told through eyewitness accounts by the main characters. At Limmeridge House in Cumberland the new drawing master, Walter Hartright, meets the pretty Laura Fairlie and her ugly, intelligent half-sister Marian

Halcombe. He falls in love with Laura but she insists on marrying Sir Percival Glyde despite the warnings of Anne Catherick, the mysterious woman in white who has escaped from the mental asylum to which Sir Percival has committed her. Marian continues the investigation. Sir Perceval enlists the help of the charming but sinister Count Fosco to gain control of Laura's fortune. They exploit the resemblance between Laura and Anne Catherick, now dead, to bury Anne under Laura's name and commit Laura to an asylum as Anne. Marian helps her escape and is joined by Walter. They discover that Sir Percival is illegitimate; he dies attempting to destroy the parish register revealing his secret. Fosco admits his part in the conspiracy before being killed by the Italian secret societies he has betrayed. Laura and Walter marry.

Women in Love A novel by D. H. LAWRENCE, first published in 1920. Ursula and Gudrun Brangwen, from THE RAINBOW, are central characters in what is not strictly a sequel but rather a continuation of Lawrence's inquiry into the possibilities that human relationships hold amid the unpromising circumstances of modern industrial culture.

Ursula falls in love with Rupert Birkin, a school inspector. Gudrun is drawn into a tense relationship with Gerald Crich, son of the local mineowner. Birkin and Gerald are close friends, though Gerald rejects Birkin's attempt to establish a closer intimacy between them. Ursula and Birkin marry. Gudrun's destructive relationship with Gerald reaches its climax when the four go to Innsbruck together. Gudrun flirts with a decadent German sculptor, Loerke. Gerald attacks them before wandering off to die alone in the snow. Birkin grieves for Gerald and attempts to explain to a sceptical Ursula his vision of a male love to complement his love for her.

Though far from being a systematic ROMAN À CLEF, the novel contains recognizable portaits of Lawrence's contemporaries among the minor characters: Lady Ottoline Morrell as the neurotic Hermione Roddice, Bertrand Russell as Sir Joshua and members of the BLOOMSBURY GROUP as the artists with whom Birkin associates in London.

Wongar, Banumbir Aboriginal name used by Streten Bozic (1936–), who was born in Yugoslavia and emigrated to Australia in 1960. His novels evoke Aboriginal culture and its bitter dilemma in the face of a still hostile society. They include: *The Trackers* (1978); *Walg* (1983), *Karan* (1985) and *Gabo Djara* (1987), making up *The Nuclear Trilogy*; and *Marngit* (1991). He has also published several volumes of stories – *The Sinners* (1972), *The Track to Bralgu* (1978), *Babaru* (1982) and *The Last Pack of Dingoes* (1993) – and a collection, *Aboriginal Myths* (with Alan Marshall; 1972).

Wood, Mrs **Henry (Ellen)** 1814–87 English. Although her mixture of sentiment, melodrama and piety did not command universal admiration, she achieved world-wide fame with her second novel, *EAST LYNNE* (1861). Its many successors included *Mrs Halliburton's Troubles* (1862), *The Channings* (1862), *Verner's Pride* (1862–3) and *Roland Yorke* (1869). She considered *The Shadow of Ashlydat* (1863) her best novel. Much of her work was serialized in *The Argosy*, a journal she bought in 1867 and edited thereafter. A memoir by her son appeared in 1894.

Woodlanders, The A novel by THOMAS HARDY, published in 1887.

Socially ambitious for his daughter Grace, the timber merchant George Melbury regrets committing her to the rustic Giles Winterbourne, and uses Winterbourne's financial and legal misfortunes as an excuse to end their relationship. Melbury insists that Grace marry Dr Edred Fitzpiers though she, knowing about Fitzpiers's dalliance with Suke Damson, is not enthusiastic. Fitzpiers forms a liaison with Felice Charmond of Hintock Manor House and goes with her to the Continent, where they quarrel and part. The shadowy figure of the 'gentleman from South Carolina' kills Mrs Charmond in a jealous rage. Supported by her father's vain hope that she can obtain a divorce, Grace encourages Giles and is forced to seek shelter at his cottage in bad weather. Out of propriety he takes to a hopelessly inadequate outdoor retreat and dies of exposure. Grace is reunited with Fitzpiers, and the ever-faithful Marty South is left to mourn Giles.

Woodstock: *or, The Cavalier. A Tale of the Year 1651* A novel by SIR WALTER SCOTT, published in 1826. The story concerns the escape of the future Charles II after the Battle of Worcester to Woodstock, where an old Cavalier, Sir Henry Lee, is ranger. His daughter Alice loves her cousin Everard, but Lee disdains him because Everard serves Cromwell and has earned his favour. Charles falls in love with Alice, Everard behaves honourably and Cromwell appears in the story. On his escape Charles leaves a parting message reconciling Sir Henry and Everard, who is now able to marry Alice.

Woolf, Leonard (Sidney) 1880–1969 English. After Cambridge, where he became a member of the Apostles and was profoundly influenced by G. E. Moore, he entered the Ceylon Civil Service. On his return to England he became an active member of the Fabian Society and a focal member of the BLOOMSBURY GROUP. He married VIRGINIA WOOLF in 1912. As well as writing for various political journals, he published two novels, *The Village in the Jungle* (1913), about Ceylon, and *The Wise Virgins* (1914). Other works are about politics and international affairs. *Sowing* (1960), *Growing* (1961), *Beginning Again* (1964), *Downhill All the Way* (1967) and *The Journey*

Not the Arrival Matters (1969) are highly regarded volumes of autobiography.

Woolf, (Adeline) Virginia 1882–1941 English. She was born Virginia Stephen, the daughter of Sir Leslie Stephen (1832–1904), critic, scholar and first editor of the *Dictionary of National Biography* – by his second wife, Julia Duckworth. The Bloomsbury house she shared with her sister Vanessa (later the wife of the art critic Clive Bell) and her brothers Thoby and Adrian after their father's death in 1904 became the original meeting-place of the BLOOMSBURY GROUP. She married one of the Group's members, LEONARD WOOLF, in 1912. Together they founded the Hogarth Press, which published *Two Stories* in 1917 ('The Mark on the Wall' by Virginia, and 'Three Jews' by Leonard), KATHERINE MANSFIELD's *Prelude* (1918), T. S. Eliot's *Poems* (1919) and *The Waste Land* (1923).

By this time she was herself a published novelist, though the appearance of her first work, *THE VOYAGE OUT*, completed in 1913, was delayed until 1915 by one of the mental breakdowns from which she suffered throughout her life. *Night and Day* (1919) is a realistic novel set in London, contrasting the lives of two friends, Katherine and Mary. *JACOB'S ROOM* (1922), based on the life and death of Thoby, broke away from traditional REALISM. Like *MRS DALLOWAY* (1925) it fulfilled the purpose laid down in her essay 'Modern Fiction' (1919), to capture as faithfully as possible the reality which she described as 'a luminous halo, a semi-transparent envelope surrounding us from the beginning of consciousness to the end.' With *TO THE LIGHTHOUSE* (1927) and *THE WAVES* (1931) she fully established herself as a leading exponent of MODERNISM. Her greatest commercial success was *ORLANDO* (1928), a fantastic biography tracing its androgynous protagonist through four centuries. It was dedicated to her intimate friend VITA SACKVILLE-WEST. Another 'biography', *Flush* (1933), revolves around the life of Elizabeth Barrett Browning's pet spaniel. *THE YEARS* (1937) was more conventional, but her last novel, *BETWEEN THE ACTS*, posthumously published in 1941, returned to the experimental. It was completed just before the final attack of mental illness which drove her to suicide.

Virginia Woolf is now generally acknowledged as one of the major innovative novelists of the 20th century, best known, perhaps, for her use of STREAM OF CONSCIOUSNESS. Her contribution to feminist criticism has been widely recognized: *A Room of One's Own* (1929) and its still more radical sequel, *Three Guineas* (1938), are now established classics. Her critical essays, notably those in *The Common Reader* (1925) and *The Second Common Reader* (1932), were reprinted in *Collected Essays of Virginia Woolf* (1966–7). Her letters, edited by Nigel Nicolson

and J. Trautmann (1975–80), include correspondence with nearly everyone associated with the Bloomsbury Group. Her diaries, edited by Anne Olivier Bell and A. McNeillie (1977–84), give an invaluable picture of her creative method.

Woolrich, Cornell (George Hopley) 1903–1968. American. He also published under the pseudonyms George Hopley and William Irish. The leading works in his 'Black Series' include *The Bride Wore Black* (1940), *Phantom Lady* (1942), *Deadline at Dawn* (1944), *Night Has a Thousand Eyes* (1945) and several collections of short stories. Much of his writing first appeared in 'pulp' magazines such as *Black Mask* and, in turn, provided material for the Hollywood *film noir* and directors such as Alfred Hitchcock and François Truffaut. These associations have sometimes led Woolrich to be classed as a writer of hard-boiled DETECTIVE FICTION. In fact, he dealt in suspense rather than detection; his preoccupation with a private nightmare world of fear, helplessness and obsession identified him with the tradition of American Gothic stemming from the non-detective stories of EDGAR ALLAN POE.

Woolson, Constance (Fenimore) 1840–94 American. Her wide knowledge of the USA is reflected in: *Castle Nowhere: Lake-Country Sketches* (1875); *Rodman the Keeper: Southern Sketches* (1880); *Anna* (1882), about a girl from Mackinac Island, Michigan, in New York; *For the Major* (1883), set in North Carolina; *East Angels* (1886), set in Florida; and *Jupiter Lights* (1889), about the conflict between North and South. *Horace Chase* (1894) is about a woman who discovers, almost too late, the sterling character of her self-made husband. *Dorothy, and Other Italian Stories* (1896), her last book, concerns Americans in Europe.

Workers in the Dawn The first novel by GEORGE GISSING, published in 1880. It is about rich and poor, degradation, drink, destitution and the effects of heredity. Two solutions are proposed: revolution, which the author rejects, and education, which he endorses. But to educate the masses is seen as a hard struggle. The noble Helen, who has embraced the doctrines of 'Schopenhauer, Comte and Shelley', wears herself out giving free lessons in adult literacy and dies of inherited consumption. Arthur, in love with Helen, carelessly marries Carrie, a woman of low morals, and is defeated by misfortune.

World of Wonders See *DEPTFORD TRILOGY, THE.*

Wren, P(ercival) C(hristopher) 1885–1941 English. The most famous of his many popular novels of romance and adventure is *Beau Geste* (1924), about the Foreign Legion. It was followed by more stories about the three Geste brothers, *Beau Sabreur* (1926), *Beau Ideal* (1928) and *Good Gestes* (1929). Other titles include *Dew and Mildew* (1912), *The Wages of Virtue* (1916), *Valiant Dust* (1932), *Sinbad the Sailor* (1935), *Rough Shooting* (1938) and *The Uniform of Glory* (1941).

Wright, Richard 1908-60 African-American.

NATIVE SON, the novel which won him recognition, appeared in 1940, the year he left the USA, first for Mexico and then for Paris. His other novels are *The Outsider* (1953), chronicling a black intellectual's search for identity, *Savage Holiday* (1954) and *The Long Dream* (1958). *Eight Men* (1961) gathers short stories, radio plays, a novella, and an autobiography. Wright's non-fictional work includes an illustrated folk history of American blacks, *Twelve Million Black Voices* (1941), an acclaimed autobiography, *Black Boy* (1945), and its sequel, *American Hunger* (1977). He also published three books of social criticism inspired by his travels: *Black Power* (1954), about Africa; *The Color Curtain* (1956), about Asia; and *Pagan Spain* (1957). *White Man, Listen!* (1957) is a collection of lectures on racial injustice.

Wright, S. Fowler See SCIENCE FICTION.

Wright, Stephen 1946– American. He explores the surreal, demented side of American life in *Meditations in Green* (1983), about the Vietnam War, *M31: A Family Romance* (1988), about a couple who believe they are descended from aliens, and *Going Native* (1994), about a suburbanite who takes to the road.

Wuthering Heights The only novel by EMILY BRONTË, published in 1847. Its complex plot centres on the remote farmhouse of Wuthering Heights on the Yorkshire moors, and on two generations of the Earnshaw family.

The story is narrated by Lockwood, a visiting gentleman, and Mrs Dean, servant to the Earnshaws. Heathcliff, a foundling from Liverpool, is brought to the Heights by Mr Earnshaw to be treated like his own children, Catherine and Hindley. But after Earnshaw's death Hindley bullies and degrades Heathcliff. He leaves because Catherine, despite returning his love, would find it humiliating to marry him. She chooses the genteel Edgar Linton of neighbouring Thrushcross Grange instead. Heathcliff returns to wreak vengeance on his tormentors. Weakened by his accusations of betrayal, Catherine dies after giving birth to a girl, another Catherine. Heathcliff marries Edgar's sister Isabella and mistreats her until she runs away. He destroys Hindley, a drunkard and gambler, and gains control of the Heights. To secure the Linton family property he forces a marriage between young Catherine and Linton, his sickly son by Isabella. When Linton dies the young widow develops an interest in Hareton, Hindley's son, whom Heathcliff has brought up in brutish ignorance. By now, all passion spent, Heathcliff longs only for union with Catherine. He dies, leaving young Catherine and Hareton with hopes of a richer life.

The novel's stern power, which shocked contemporaries but impressed later generations, owes much to the enigmatic portrait of Heathcliff. Hardly less remarkable is the way that the tortuous, violent plot is given solidity by the precisely realized Yorkshire locations and subtlety by the shifting narrative viewpoints.

Wyndham, John [Harris, John Wyndham Parkes Lucas Beynon] 1903–69 English. He used various combinations of his given names in different phases of his career. He is best known for his post-war SCIENCE FICTION novels: *The Day of the Triffids* (1951), *The Kraken Wakes* (1953), *The Chrysalids* (1955), *The Midwich Cuckoos* (1957) and *The Trouble with Lichen* (1960). The best of his short fiction is in *Consider Her Ways and Others* (1961). Concentrating on the reactions of ordinary people to terrible circumstances which plunge them into a struggle for survival, his work bridged traditional British scientific romance and the more varied science fiction which has replaced it.

Yates, Dornford [Mercer, Cecil William] 1885–1960 English. His novels, almost invariably sustained by gently farcical plots and centred on an elegant leisured society, found a huge popular readership in the 1920s and 1930s. Books about Berry Pleydell and his circle include *Berry and Co.* (1921), *Jonah and Co.* (1922) and *Maiden Stakes* (1929). His 'Chandos' thrillers include *Blind Corner* (1927) and *Perishable Goods* (1928).

Yates, Edmund (Hodgson) 1831–94 English. A protégé of CHARLES DICKENS, he contributed to *Household Words* and *All the Year Round*. An offensive article about WILLIAM MAKEPEACE THACKERAY which he wrote soon after becoming the first editor of *Town Talk* in 1858 led to his expulsion from the Garrick Club, as well as worsening the rift between Thackeray and Dickens. The incident did not quench Yates's journalistic energy or his appetite for literary society, duly recorded in *Recollections and Experiences* (1884). His first novel, *Broken To Harness* (1865), exploited his familiarity with the fashionable world; *Running the Gauntlet* (1865) and *Black Sheep* (1867) catered to the craze for the SENSATION NOVEL.

Years, The A novel by VIRGINIA WOOLF, published in 1937. Unlike her other late works, it is a conventional family saga, chronicling the lives of the Pargiters from 1880 to the 1930s. At the beginning, Colonel Pargiter's wife, Rose, is dying and their seven children live under the oppressive weight of her illness. Subsequent chapters trace the lives of each of the children in a series of separate but connected episodes, which include some vivid descriptions of London life.

Yeast: A Problem A novel by CHARLES KINGSLEY, serialized in 1848 and published in book form in 1850. It is unashamedly a novel of ideas, in which Lancelot Smith, a gentleman and heedless atheist, learns about life from Paul Tregarva, one of the 'Dissenting poor'. The picture of rural degradation is vivid and the descriptions of the poor memorable. Kingsley deplores the waste of sewage, which fouls rivers when it should be fertilizing fields, attacks the game laws and defends the 'true idea of Protestantism' against the lure of Roman Catholicism. Though claiming to avoid taking sides, he preaches that art is a mere self-indulgence when political action (reformist, not revolutionary) is needed.

Yellowplush Papers, The Comic sketches by WILLIAM MAKEPEACE THACKERAY, serialized as *The Yellowplush Correspondence* in 1837–40 and reprinted under its present title in *Comic Tales and Sketches* (1841). Charles James Yellowplush, a footman, writes his memoirs in cockney idiom. His first master is a respectable gentleman who turns out to be a crossing-sweeper; his second is a card-sharping aristocrat, the Hon. Algernon Deuceace.

Yemassee, The: A Romance of Carolina A novel by WILLIAM GILMORE SIMMS, published in 1835. It is based on the 1715 uprising of the Yemassee Indians. Chief Sanutee attacks the colonists, whose defence is led by Gabriel Harrison. The Indians are helped by Chorley, a renegade English officer, but betrayed by Sanutee's son, Occonestoga; both men are killed. Harrison successfully proposes to Bess Matthews and then reveals that he is really Charles Craven, governor of Carolina. He leaves Hugh Grayson in charge of the local forces and travels to Charleston to organize the force which finally destroys the Yemassee. The book ends with Sanutee's death.

Yezierska, Anzia *c.* 1885–1970 Born in Russian Poland, she emigrated with her family to the USA in the 1890s. She dealt realistically with the lives of ghetto immigrants in collections of stories such as *Hungry Hearts* (1920) and *Children of Loneliness* (1923) and in novels such as *Salome of the Tenements* (1922), *Bread Givers* (1925), *Arrogant Beggar* (1927) and *All I Could Never Be* (1932). *Red Ribbon on a White Horse* (1950) is her autobiography.

Yonge, Charlotte M(ary) 1823–1901 English. She lived all her life in Otterbourne, Hampshire, deeply influenced by John Keble, vicar of neighbouring Hursley. Tirelessly energetic, she edited a girls' magazine, *The Monthly Packet*, for nearly 50 years and produced 160 books, including biographies of Bishop Patterson (1874) and HANNAH MORE (1888), histories and textbooks as well as fiction aimed at young female readers. Success first came with THE HEIR OF REDCLYFFE (1853), about the blameless Sir Guy Morville. THE DAISY CHAIN (1856) deals with the widowed Dr May's large family, whose fortunes are followed in several later volumes. The authentic home and family background makes these books an excellent source of information about Victorian middle-class life. Historical romances include *The Little Duke* (1854), *The Lances of Lynwood* (1855), *The Prince and the Page* (1865) and *The Caged Lion* (1870).

Yorke, Henry Vincent See GREEN, HENRY.

Young, Francis Brett 1884–1954 English. He is best remembered for *Portrait of Clare* (1927) and *My Brother Jonathan* (1928), set in the west Midlands. *They Seek a Country* (1937) and *The City of*

Gold (1939) are ambitious novels dealing with the history of South Africa, where Young retired after World War II. *The Island* (1944), written in response to the Battle of Britain, is a verse history of England, using verse forms appropriate to each period.

Zameenzad, Adam Born in Nairobi to parents from Pakistan, he has laid claim to various dates of birth, of which the latest is 1954. Widely travelled and, at one time or another, an adherent of most of the world's major religions, he gleefully juxtaposes East and West in his writing. The clerkly protagonist of his first novel, *The Thirteenth House* (1987), belongs to Karachi's desperately impoverished underclass. *My Friend Matt and Hena the Whore* (1988), about starvation in Africa, began an indictment of avoidable suffering reiterated in the slimly elegant *Love Bones and Water* (1989) and the sprawling, flamboyant *Cyrus Cyrus* (1990), which moves from the banks of the Ganges to the world of illegal immigrants in Britain.

Zangwill, Israel 1864–1926 English. Of Russian-Jewish descent, he captured the stark reality of immigrant life in London in *Children of the Ghetto* (1892), *Ghetto Tragedies* (1893), *The Kings of Shnorrers* (1894) and *The Mantle of Elijah* (1900), which established him as a leading figure and powerful spokesman in the struggle for Jewish rights. *The Melting Pot* (1909), the best known of his plays, dealt with a similar theme, as did various non-fictional works, including *The War for the World* (1916) and *The Voice of Jerusalem* (1920). *The Big Bow Mystery* (1892) is a canny venture into DETECTIVE FICTION.

Zanoni A novel by EDWARD BULWER LYTTON, published in 1842, and set partly during the French Revolution. The hero is a master of the occult arts who possesses the secret of eternal life. His superhuman powers begin to fail him when he falls in love. Realizing that the affections of the heart can lead to a higher spiritual state than the abstractions of the intellect, he forsakes his immortality, marries the woman, and eventually dies in her place on the guillotine. His sacrifice prefigures the ending of DICKENS's *A TALE OF TWO CITIES*.

Zelazny, Roger See SCIENCE FICTION.

Zen and the Art of Motorcycle Maintenance See PIRSIG, ROBERT.

Zuleika Dobson*: or, *An Oxford Love Story A novel by MAX BEERBOHM, published in 1911. He preferred to call it a 'fantasy' rather than a satire. When Zuleika visits her grandfather, the Warden of Judas College, during Eights Week her beauty devastates the undergraduates, even the splendid Duke of Dorset. She remains disappointed in her quest for a man 'who would not bow down to her'. The Duke drowns himself, followed by the entire undergraduate population except the pedestrian Noaks. At the end of the novel Zuleika consults the train timetable to Cambridge.

Suggested reading

The distinction between 'Critical and Theoretical Works' and 'Histories, Surveys and Thematic Studies', used to divide the lists below, is admittedly rough and ready but should at least give initial guidance. To keep them within manageable proportions, the lists exclude: studies of individual writers (except for rare cases like Genette's *Narrative Discourse*, whose nominal subject is Proust though his argument concerns the theory of narrative); articles published in journals; and multi-volume series comprehending literary history, though the relevant volumes of the Longman Literature in English series, edited by David Carroll and Michael Wheeler, are to be recommended.

Critical and Theoretical Works

Allott, Miriam (editor). *Novelists on the Novel*. 1959.

Alter, Robert. *Partial Magic: The Novel as a Self-Conscious Genre*. 1975.

Auerbach, Eric. *Mimesis: The Representation of Reality in Western Literature*. 1946; translated by Willard Trask, 1953.

Bakhtin, Mikhail. *The Dialogic Imagination: Four Essays*. 1975; translated by Caryl Emerson and Michael Holquist, and edited by Michael Holquist, 1981.

Bal, Mieke. *Narratology: Introduction to the Theory of Narrative*. 1977; second edition, 1980; translated by Christine van Boheemen, 1985.

Banfield, Ann. *Unspeakable Sentences: Narration and Representation in the Language of Fiction*. 1982.

Barthes, Roland. *S/Z*. 1970; translated by Richard Miller, 1974.

Booth, Wayne C. *The Company We Keep: An Ethics of Fiction*. 1989.

Booth, Wayne C. *The Rhetoric of Fiction*. 1961; second edition 1983.

Brodsky, Claudia J. *Imposition of Form: Studies in Narrative Representation*. 1987.

Brooke-Rose, Christine. *A Rhetoric of the Unreal: Studies in Narrative and Structure, Especially of the Fantastic*. 1981.

Brooks, Cleanth, and Warren, Robert Penn. *Understanding Fiction*. 1943.

Brooks, Peter. *Reading for the Plot: Design and Intention in Narrative*. 1984.

Champigny, Robert. *Ontology of the Narrative*. 1972.

Chatman, Seymour. *Story and Discourse: Narrative Structure in Fiction and Film*. 1978.

Cohn, Dorrit. *Transparent Minds: Narrative Modes for Presenting Consciousness in Fiction*. 1978.

Culler, Jonathan. *On Deconstruction: Theory and Criticism After Structuralism*. 1983.

Culler, Jonathan. *Structuralist Poetics: Structuralism, Linguistics and the Study of Literature*. 1975.

Davis, Leonard J. *Resisting Novels: Ideology and Fiction*. 1987.

Eco, Umberto. *The Role of the Reader: Explorations in the Semiotics of Texts*. 1979.

Forster, E. M. *Aspects of the Novel*. 1927.

Fowler, Roger. *Linguistics and the Novel*. 1977.

Frye, Northrop. *The Anatomy of Criticism*. 1957.

Frye, Northrop. *The Secular Scripture: A Study of the Structure of Romance*. 1976.

Gardner, John. *On Moral Fiction*. 1978.

Genette, Gérard. *Narrative Discourse: An Essay on Method*. 1972; translated by Jane E. Lewin, 1980.

Genette, Gérard. *Narrative Discourse Revisited*. 1983; translated by Jane E. Lewin, 1988.

Hardy, Barbara. *The Appropriate Form: An Essay on the Novel*. 1964.

Hardy, Barbara. *Tellers and Listeners: The Narrative Imagination*. 1975.

Harvey, W. J. *Character and the Novel*. 1965.

Hochman, Baruch. *Character in Literature*. 1985.

Iser, Wolfgang. *The Act of Reading: A Theory of Aesthetic Response*. 1976; translated 1978.

Iser, Wolfgang. *The Implied Reader: Patterns of Communication in Prose Fiction from Bunyan to Beckett*. 1974.

James, Henry. *The Art of the Novel: Critical Prefaces of Henry James*. Edited by R. P. Blackmur. 1934.

Jameson, Frederic. *The Political Unconscious: Narrative as a Socially Symbolic Act*. 1981.

Kahler, Erich. *The Inward Turn of Narrative*. 1970; translated by Richard and Clara Winston, 1973.

Kellogg, Robert, and Scholes, Robert. *The Nature of Narrative*. 1966.

Kermode, Frank. *Essays on Fiction 1971–82* (US title: *The Art of Telling: Essays on Fiction*). 1983.

Kermode, Frank. *The Genesis of Secrecy: On the Interpretation of Narrative*. 1979.

Kermode, Frank. *The Sense of an Ending: Studies in the Theory of Fiction*. 1967.

Kundera, Milan. *The Art of the Novel*. 1986; translated by Linda Asher, 1988.

Lawrence, D. H. *Phoenix*. Edited by Edward D. McDonald. 1936.

Leavis, F. R. *The Great Tradition: George Eliot, Henry James, Joseph Conrad*. 1948.

Lodge, David. *After Bakhtin: Essays on Fiction and Criticism*. 1990.

Lodge, David. *The Art of Fiction: Illustrated from Classic and Modern Texts*. 1992.

Lodge, David. *Language of Fiction: Essays in Criticism and Verbal Analysis of the English Novel*. 1966; second edition 1984.

Lodge, David. *The Novelist at the Crossroads and Other Essays on Fiction and Criticism*. 1971.

Lodge, David. *Working with Structuralism: Essays on Nineteenth- and Twentieth-Century Literature*. 1981.

Lubbock, Percy. *The Craft of Fiction*. 1921.

Lukács, György (Georg). *The Theory of the Novel: A Historical-Philosophical Essay on the Forms of Great Epic Literature*. 1920; translated by Anna Bostock, 1971.

Martin, Wallace. *Recent Theories of Narrative*. 1986.

Miller, D. A. *Narrative and Its Discontents: Problems of Closure in the Traditional Novel*. 1981.

Miller, J. Hillis. *Ariadne's Thread: Story Lines*. 1992.

Miller, J. Hillis. *Fiction and Repetition: Seven English Novels*. 1982.

Pascal, Roy. *The Dual Voice: Free Indirect Speech and Its Functioning in the Nineteenth-Century European Novel*. 1977.

Phelan, James. *Reading People, Reading Plots: Character, Progression, and the Interpretation of Narrative*. 1989.

Phelan, James. *Worlds from Words: A Theory of Language in Fiction*. 1981.

Prince, Gerald. *A Grammar of Stories: An Introduction*. 1973.

Prince, Gerald. *Narratology: The Form and Function of Narrative*. 1982.

Rabinowitz, Peter. *Before Reading: Narrative Conventions and the Politics of Interpretation*. 1987.

Ricoeur, Paul. *Time and Narrative*. 3 volumes. 1983, 1984 and 1985; translated by Kathleen McLaughlin and David Pellauer, 1984, 1985 and 1988.

Rimmon-Kenan, Shlomith. *Narrative Fiction: Contemporary Poetics*. 1983.

Springer, Mary Doyle. *A Rhetoric of Literary Character*. 1978.

Sternberg, Meir. *Expositional Modes and Temporal Ordering in Fiction*. 1978.

Sturgess, Philip J. M. *Narrativity: Theory and Practice*. 1992.

Suleiman, Susan R. and Crosman, Inge (editors). *The Reader in the Text: Essays on Audience and Interpretation*. 1980.

Todorov, Tzvetan. *The Poetics of Prose*. 1971; translated by Richard Howard, 1977.

Tomkins, Jane (editor). *Reader-Response Criticism: From Formalism to Post-Structuralism*. 1980.

Torgovnick, Marianna. *Closure in the Novel*. 1981.

Trilling, Lionel. *The Liberal Imagination: Essays on Literature and Society*. 1950.

Van Ghent, Dorothy. *The English Novel: Form and Function*. 1953.

Woolf, Virginia. *The Common Reader*. 1925.

Woolf, Virginia. *The Second Common Reader*. 1932.

Histories, Surveys and Thematic Studies

Abbott, H. Porter. *Diary Fiction*. 1984.

Adams, Percy G. *Travel Literature and the Evolution of the Novel*. 1983.

Aldiss, Brian W. *Billion-Year Spree: The History of Science Fiction*. 1973; revised, with David Wingrove, as *Trillion-Year Spree*, 1986.

Aldridge, John W. *The American Novel and the Way We Live Now*. 1983.

Alexander, Marguerite. *Flights from Realism: Themes and Strategies in Postmodernist British and American Fiction*. 1990.

Allen, Walter. *The English Novel: A Short Critical History*. 1954.

Altick, Richard D. *The English Common Reader: A Social History of the Mass Reading Public, 1800–1900*. 1957.

Altman, Janet. *Epistolarity: Approaches to a Form*. 1983.

Ardis, Ann. *New Women, New Novels: Feminism and Early Modernism*. 1990.

Armstrong, Nancy. *Desire and Domestic Fiction: A Political History of the Novel*. 1987.

Ashcroft, Bill; Griffiths, Gareth; and Tiffin, Helen. *The Empire Writes Back*. 1989.

Baker, Houston A., Jr. *Blues, Ideology and Afro-American Literature: A Vernacular Theory.* 1985.

Beatson, Peter. *The Healing Tongue: Themes in Contemporary Maori Literature.* 1989.

Beer, Gillian. *Darwin's Plots: Evolutionary Narrative in Darwin, George Eliot and Nineteenth-Century Fiction.* 1983.

Bender, John. *Imagining the Penitentiary: Fiction and the Architecture of Mind in Eighteenth-Century England.* 1987.

Berger, Morroe. *Real and Imagined Worlds: The Novel and Social Science.* 1977.

Berthoff, Warner. *A Literature Without Qualities: American Writing Since 1945.* 1979.

Bharucha, Nilufer and Sarang, Vilas. *Indian-English Fiction 1980–1990: An Assessment.* 1994.

Bradbury, Malcolm. *The Modern American Novel.* 1983; revised edition, 1990.

Bradbury, Malcolm. *The Modern British Novel.* 1993.

Bradbury, Malcolm. *Possibilities: Essays on the State of the Novel.* 1973.

Brooks, Peter. *Body Work: Objects of Desire in Modern Narrative.* 1993.

Buckley, Jerome Hamilton. *Season of Youth: The Bildungsroman from Dickens to Golding.* 1974.

Castle, Terry. *Masquerade and Civilization: The Carnivalesque in Eighteenth-Century English Culture and Fiction.* 1986.

Cazamian, Louis. *The Social Novel in England, 1830–50.* 1903; translated by Martin Fido, 1973.

Chapman, Michael. *Southern African Literatures.* 1996.

Chase, Richard. *The American Novel and Its Tradition.* 1957.

Cheung, King-Kok (editor). *An Interethnic Companion to Asian American Literature.* 1997.

Coetzee, J. M. *White Writing: On the Culture of Letters in South Africa.* 1988.

Connor, Steven. *The English Novel in History, 1950–1995.* 1996.

Crawford, Robert. *Devolving English Literature.* 1992.

Davidson, Cathy N. *Revolution and the Word: The Rise of the Novel in America.* 1986.

Davis, Leonard J. *Factual Fictions: The Origins of the English Novel.* 1983.

Day, Geoffrey. *From Fiction to the Novel.* 1987.

Du Plessis, Rachel. *Writing Beyond the Ending: Narrative Strategies of Twentieth-Century Women Writers.* 1985.

Fetterley, Judith. *The Resisting Reader: A Feminist Approach to American Fiction.* 1978.

Fiedler, Leslie A. *Love and Death in the American Novel.* 1960; second edition, 1966.

Fleishman, Avrom. *The English Historical Novel: Walter Scott to Virginia Woolf.* 1971.

Flint, Kate. *The Woman Reader 1837–1914.* 1993.

Foley, Barbara. *Telling the Truth: The Theory and Practice of Documentary Fiction.* 1986.

Friedman, Edward. *The Antiheroine's Voice: Narrative Discourse and Transformations of the Picaresque.* 1987.

Frye, Joanne S. *Living Stories, Telling Lives: Women and the Novel in Contemporary Experience.* 1986.

Gates, Henry Louis, Jr. *The Signifying Monkey: A Theory of Afro-American Literary Criticism.* 1988.

Gilbert, Sandra and Gubar, Susan. *The Madwoman in the Attic: The Woman Writer and the Nineteenth-Century Literary Imagination.* 1979.

Goldie, Terry. *Fear and Loathing: The Image of the Indigene in Canadian, Australian and New Zealand Literatures.* 1989.

Goodwin, Ken. *A History of Australian Literature.* 1986.

Greiner, Donald J. *Women Enter the Wilderness: Male Bonding and the American Novel of the 1980s.* 1991.

Gunn, Daniel. *Psychoanalysis and Fiction: An Exploration of Literary and Psychoanalytic Borders.* 1988.

Hassan, Ihab. *The Dismemberment of Orpheus: Toward a Postmodern Literature.* 1971; second edition, 1982.

Heiserman, Arthur. *The Novel Before the Novel: Essays and Discussions about the Beginnings of Prose Fiction in the West.* 1977.

Henderson, Harry B. *Versions of the Past: The Historical Imagination in American Fiction.* 1974.

Hollingsworth, Keith. *The Newgate Novel, 1830–47: Bulwer, Ainsworth, Dickens and Thackeray.* 1963.

Hollowell, John. *Fact and Fiction: The New Journalism and the Nonfiction Novel.* 1977.

Hughes, Winifred. *The Maniac in the Cellar: Sensation Novels of the 1860s.* 1980.

Humphrey, Robert. *Stream of Consciousness in the Modern Novel.* 1954.

Hunter, Paul J. *Before Novels: The Cultural Contexts of Eighteenth-Century English Fiction.* 1990.

Hutcheon, Linda. *Narcissistic Narrative: The Metafictional Paradox.* 1980.

Hutcheon, Linda. *A Poetics of Postmodernism: History, Theory, Fiction.* 1988.

James, Louis. *Fiction for the Working Man 1830–50: A Study of the Literature Produced for the Working Classes in Early Victorian Urban England.* 1963.

Jayasuriya, Wilfred. *Sri Lanka's Modern English Literature.* 1994.

Josipovici, Gabriel. *The World and the Book: A Study of Modern Fiction.* 1971.

Karl, Frederick. *American Fictions, 1940–1980: A Comprehensive History and Critical Evaluation.* 1985.

Kauffman, Linda S. *Discourses of Desire: Gender, Genre, and Epistolary Fictions*. 1986.

Kelly, Gary. *The English Jacobin Novel, 1780–1805*. 1976.

Kiberd, Declan. *Inventing Ireland: The Literature of the Modern Nation*. 1995.

Kiely, Robert. *The Romantic Novel in England*. 1972.

King, Bruce (editor). *Introduction to West Indian Literature*. Second edition, 1996.

Klinkowitz, Jerome. *Literary Disruptions: The Making of a Post-Contemporary American Fiction*. 1975; second edition, 1980.

Klinkowitz, Jerome. *Literary Subversions: New American Fiction and the Practice of Criticism*. 1985.

Klinkowitz, Jerome. *The Self-Apparent Word: Fiction as Language/ Language as Fiction*. 1984.

Lattin, Vernon E. *Contemporary Chicano Fiction: A Critical Survey*. 1985.

Lawrence, D. H. *Studies in Classic American Literature*. 1923.

Leavis, Q. D. *Fiction and the Reading Public*. 1932.

Levin, Harry. *The Power of Blackness: Poe, Melville, Hawthorne*. 1958.

Levine, George. *The Realistic Imagination: English Fiction from 'Frankenstein' to 'Lady Chatterley's Lover'*. 1981.

Lim, Shirley Geok-lin. *Writing South East Asia in English*. 1994.

Lukács, György (Georg). *The Historical Novel*. 1937; translated by Hannah and Stanley Mitchell, 1962.

McKeon, Michael. *The Origins of the English Novel, 1600–1740*. 1987.

Maltby, Paul. *Dissident Postmodernists: Barthelme, Coover, Pynchon*. 1991.

Miller, J. Hillis. *The Form of Victorian Fiction*. 1968.

Moss, John. *A Reader's Guide to the Canadian Novel*. 1987.

Naik, M. A. *A History of Indian English Literature*. 1982.

Narogin, Mudrooroo. *The Indigenous Literature of Australia*. 1997.

Nelson, Emmanuel S. *Writers of the Indian Diaspora*. 1993.

O'Donnell, Patrick. *Passionate Doubts: Designs of Interpretation in Contemporary American Fiction*. 1986.

Owomeyala, Oyekan (editor). *History of Twentieth-Century African Literatures*. 1993.

Paulson, Ronald. *Satire and the Novel in Eighteenth-Century England*. 1967.

Perosa, Sergio. *American Theories of the Novel: 1793–1903*. 1985.

Peterson, Carla L. *The Determined Reader: Gender and Culture in the Novel from Napoleon to Victoria*. 1986.

Pizer, Donald (editor). *The Cambridge Companion to American Realism and Naturalism*. 1995.

Pryse, Marjorie, and Spillers, Hortense (editors). *Conjuring: Black Women, Fiction and Literary Tradition*. 1985.

Punter, David. *The Literature of Terror: A History of Gothic Fictions from 1765 to the Present Day*. 1980.

Rahman, Tariq. *A History of Pakistani Literature in English*. 1991.

Ramchand, Kenneth. *The West Indian Novel and Its Background*. Second edition, 1983.

Reed, Walter L. *An Exemplary History of the Novel: The Quixotic Versus the Picaresque*. 1981.

Reising, Russell J. *The Unusable Past: Theory and Study of American Literature*. 1986.

Richetti, John (editor). *The Cambridge Companion to the Eighteenth-Century Novel*. 1996.

Safer, Elaine B. *The Contemporary American Comic Epic: The Novels of Barth, Pynchon, Gaddis, and Kesey*. 1989.

Shechner, Mark. *After the Revolution: Studies in the Contemporary Jewish American Imagination*. 1987.

Showalter, Elaine. *A Literature of Their Own: British Women Novelists from Brontë to Lessing*. 1977.

Skinner, John. *The Stepmother Tongue: An Introduction to New Anglophone Fiction*. 1998.

Spacks, Patricia Meyer. *Desire and Truth: Functions of Plot in Eighteenth-Century England*. 1990.

Spacks, Patricia Meyer. *Imagining a Self: Autobiography and the Novel in Eighteenth-Century England*. 1976.

Spencer, Jane. *The Rise of the Woman Novelist: From Aphra Behn to Jane Austen*. 1986.

Stang, Richard. *The Theory of the Novel in England, 1850–1870*. 1959.

Sturm, Terry (editor). *The Oxford History of New Zealand Literature in English*. 1991.

Subramani. *South Pacific Literature: Myth to Fabulation*. 1985.

Symons, Julian. *Bloody Murder: From the Detective Story to the Crime Novel* (US title: *Mortal Consequences*). 1972; third edition, 1992.

Tanner, Tony. *City of Words: American Fiction 1950–1970*. 1971.

Taylor, D. J. *After the War: The Novel and English Society Since 1945*. 1993.

Tillotson, Kathleen. *Novels of the Eighteen-Forties*. 1954.

Tillyard, E. M. *The Epic Strain in the English Novel*. 1958.

Tomkins, Jane. *Sensational Designs: The Cultural Work of American Fiction, 1790–1860*. 1985.

Trotter, David. *The English Novel in History, 1895–1920*. 1993.

Valeros, B. Florentino and Gruenberg, Estrelita V. *Filipino Writers in English*. 1987.

Voss, Arthur. *The American Short Story*. 1973.

Wallace, Gavin and Stevenson, Randall (editors). *The Scottish Novel Since the Seventies*. 1993.
Warhol, Robyn. *Gendered Intervention: Narrative Discourse in the Victorian Novel*. 1989.
Watt, Ian. *The Rise of the Novel: Studies in Defoe, Richardson and Fielding*. 1957.
Weisenburger, Steven. *Fables of Subversion: Satire and the American Novel 1930–1980*. 1995.
Wheeler, Michael. *The Art of Allusion in Victorian Fiction*. 1979.
Wiget, Andrew. *Native American Literature*. 1985.
Wilde, Alan. *Middle Grounds: Studies in Contemporary American Fiction*. 1987.
Williams, Ioan (editor). *Novel and Romance 1700–1800: A Documentary Record*. 1970.
Williams, Raymond. *The English Novel from Dickens to Lawrence*. 1970.
Witalec, Jane (editor). *Native American Literature*. 1994.

Selected literary prizes

Bold denotes an entry in the Guide

Booker Prize (United Kingdom and Commonwealth)

1997	Arundhati Roy	*The God of Small Things*
1996	**Graham Swift**	*Last Orders*
1995	**Pat Barker**	*The Ghost Road*
1994	**James Kelman**	*How Late It Was, How Late*
1993	**Roddy Doyle**	*Paddy Clarke Ha Ha Ha*
1992	**Michael Ondaatje**	*The English Patient*
	Barry Unsworth	*Sacred Hunger*
1991	**Ben Okri**	*The Famished Road*
1990	**A. S. Byatt**	*Possession*
1989	**Kazuo Ishiguro**	*The Remains of the Day*
1988	**Peter Carey**	*Oscar and Lucinda*
1987	**Penelope Lively**	*Moon Tiger*
1986	**Kingsley Amis**	*The Old Devils*
1985	**Keri Hulme**	*The Bone People*
1984	**Anita Brookner**	*Hôtel du Lac*
1983	**J. M. Coetzee**	*Life and Times of Michael K*
1982	**Thomas Keneally**	*Schindler's Ark*
1981	**Salman Rushdie**	*Midnight's Children*
1980	**William Golding**	*Rites of Passage*
1979	**Penelope Fitzgerald**	*Offshore*
1978	**Iris Murdoch**	*The Sea, The Sea*
1977	**Paul Scott**	*Staying On*
1976	**David Storey**	*Saville*
1975	**Ruth Prawer Jhabvala**	*Heat and Dust*
1974	**Nadine Gordimer**	*The Conservationist*
	Stanley Middleton	*Holiday*
1973	**J. G. Farrell**	*The Siege of Krishnapur*
1972	**John Berger**	*G*
1971	**V. S. Naipaul**	*In a Free State*
1970	**Bernice Rubens**	*The Elected Member*
1969	**P. H. Newby**	*Something to Answer For*

Commonwealth Writers Prize

From 1989 entries were divided into two different categories. The overall winner is cited first; the winner of the prize for the best first book is marked with an asterisk.

1997	**Earl Lovelace** (Trinidad)	*Salt*
	*Anne-Marie MacDonald (Canada)	*Fall on Your Knees*
1996	**Rohinton Mistry** (Canada)	*A Fine Balance*
	*Vikram Chandra (India)	*Red Earth and Pouring Rain*
1995	**Louis de Bernières** (UK)	*Captain Corelli's Mandolin*
	*Adib Khan (Australia)	*Seasonal Adjustments*
1994	**Vikram Seth** (India)	*A Suitable Boy*
	*Keith Oatley (UK)	*The Case of Emily V*
1993	Alex Miller (Australia)	*The Ancestor Game*
	*Githa Hariharan (India)	*The Thousand Faces of Night*
1992	Rohinton Mistry (Canada)	*Such a Long Journey*
	*Robert Antoni (Bahamas)	*Divina Trace*
1991	**David Malouf** (Australia)	*The Great World*
	*Pauline Melville (Guyana)	*Shape-Shifter*
1990	**Mordecai Richler** (Canada)	*Solomon Gursky Was Here*
	*John Cranna (New Zealand)	*Visitors*

1989	**Janet Frame** (New Zealand)	*The Carpathians*
	*Bonnie Burnard (Canada)	*Women of Influence*
1988	**Festus Iyayi** (Nigeria)	*Heroes*
	Runner-up: George Turner (Australia)	*The Sea and the Summer*
1987	**Olive Senior** (Jamaica)	*Summer Lightning*
	Runner-up:	**Witi Ihimaera** (New Zealand)
		The Matriarch

Governor General's Award (Canada)

1997	**Jane Urquhart**	*The Underpainter*
1996	**Guy Vanderhaeghe**	*The Englishman's Boy*
1995	Greg Hollingshead	*The Roaring Girl*
1994	**Rudy Wiebe**	*A Discovery of Strangers*
1993	**Carol Shields**	*The Stone Diaries*
1992	**Michael Ondaatje**	***The English Patient***
1991	**Rohinton Mistry**	***Such a Long Journey***
1990	**Nino Ricci**	*Lives of the Saints*
1989	Paul Quarrington	*Whale Music*
1988	**David Adams Richards**	*Nights Below Station Street*
1987	M. T. Kelly	*A Dream Like Mine*
1986	**Alice Munro**	*The Progress of Love*
1985	**Margaret Atwood**	***The Handmaid's Tale***
1984	Josef Skvorecký	*The Engineer of Human Souls*
1983	Leon Rooke	*Shakespeare's Dog*
1982	Guy Vanderhaeghe	*Man Descending*
1981	**Mavis Gallant**	*Home Truths: Selected Canadian Stories*
1980	**George Bowering**	*Burning Water*
1979	**Jack Hodgins**	*The Resurrection of Joseph Bourne*
1978	Alice Munro	*Who Do You Think You Are?*
1977	**Timothy Findley**	*The Wars*
1976	**Marian Engel**	*Bear*
1975	**Brian Moore**	*The Great Victorian Collection*
1974	**Margaret Laurence**	***The Diviners***
1973	Rudy Wiebe	*The Temptations of Big Bear*
1972	**Robertson Davies**	*The Manticore* [in ***The Deptford Trilogy***]
1971	**Mordecai Richler**	*St Urbain's Horseman*
1970	Dave Godfrey	*The New Ancestors*
1969	**Robert Kroetsch**	*The Studhorse Man*
1968	Alice Munro	*Dance of the Happy Shades*
	Mordecai Richler	*Cocksure and Hunting Tigers Under Glass* (in non-fiction category)
1967	no award	
1966	Margaret Laurence	*A Jest of God*
1965	no award	
1964	Douglas LePan	*The Deserter*
1963	**Hugh Garner**	*Hugh Garner's Best Stories*
1962	Kildare Dobbs	*Running to Paradise*
1961	**Malcolm Lowry**	*Hear Us, O Lord, from Heaven Thy Dwelling Place*
1960	Brian Moore	*The Luck of Ginger Coffey*
1959	**Hugh MacLennan**	*The Watch that Ends the Night*
1958	Colin McDougall	*Execution*
1957	Gabrielle Roy	*Street of Riches* (translation)
1956	**Adele Wiseman**	*The Sacrifice*
1955	Lionel Shapiro	*The Sixth of June*
1954	Igor Gouzenko	*The Fall of a Titan*
1953	David Walker	*Digby*
1952	David Walker	*The Pillar*
1951	**Morley Callaghan**	*The Loved and the Lost*
1950	Germaine Guèvremont	*The Outlander* (translation)
1949	Philip Child	*Mr Ames Against Time*
1948	Hugh MacLennan	*The Precipice*
1947	Gabrielle Roy	*The Tin Flute* (translation)
1946	Winifred Brambrick	*Continental Revue*
1945	Hugh MacLennan	*Two Solitudes*
1944	Gwethalyn Graham	*Earth and High Heaven*
1943	Thomas H. Raddall	*The Pied Piper of Dipper Creek*

1942	G. Herbert Sallans	*Little Man*
1941	Alan Sullivan	*Three Came to Ville Marie*
1940	Ringuet (pseud.)	*Thirty Acres* (translation)
1939	Franklin D. McDowell	*The Champlain Road*
1938	Gwethalyn Graham	*Swiss Sonata*
1937	Laura G. Salverson	*The Dark Weaver*
1936	Bertram Brooker	*Think of the Earth*

Hawthornden Prize (United Kingdom)

It is awarded annually to the best work of 'imaginative literature'. The following works of fiction have won the prize.

1997	John Lanchester	*The Debt to Pleasure*
1996	**Hilary Mantel**	*An Experiment in Love*
1994	Tim Pears	*In The Place of Fallen Leaves*
1993	Andrew Barrow	*The Tap Dancer*
1992	Ferdinand Mount	*Of Love and Asthma*
1987–84	no award	
1983	Jonathan Keates	*Allegro Postillions*
1982	**Timothy Mo**	*Sour Sweet*
1979	P. S. Rushforth	*Kindergarten*
1978	David Cook	*Walter*
1976	**Robert Nye**	*Falstaff*
1975	**David Lodge**	*Changing Places*
1973–1		no award
1970	**Piers Paul Read**	*Monk Dawson*
1967	**Michael Frayn**	*The Russian Interpreter*
1966	no award	
1965	**William Trevor**	*The Old Boys*
1964	**V. S. Naipaul**	*Mr Stone and the Knights Companions*
1962	Robert Shaw	*The Sun Doctor*
1960	**Alan Sillitoe**	*The Loneliness of the Long-Distance Runner*
1959	no award	
1945–57	no award	
1942	John Llewellyn Rhys	*England is My Village*
1941	**Graham Greene**	***The Power and the Glory***
1938	**David Jones**	*In Parenthesis*
1937	Ruth Pitter	*A Trophy of Arms*
1935	**Robert Graves**	*I, Claudius*
1934	**James Hilton**	*Lost Horizon*
1932	**Charles Morgan**	*The Fountain*
1931	Kate O'Brien	*Without My Cloak*
1930	Geoffrey Dennis	*The End of the World*
1928	Siegfried Sassoon	*Memoirs of a Fox-Hunting Man*
1927	**Henry Williamson**	*Tarka the Otter*
1924	**R. H. Mottram**	*The Spanish Farm*
1923	**David Garnett**	*Lady into Fox*
1921	Romer Wilson	*The Death of Society*

James Tait Black Memorial Prize (United Kingdom)

1996	**Graham Swift**	*Last Orders*
	Alice Thompson	*Justine*
1995	Christopher Priest	*The Prestige*
1994	Alan Hollinghurst	*The Folding Star*
1993	**Caryl Phillips**	***Crossing the River***
1992	**Rose Tremain**	*Sacred Country*
1991	**Iain Sinclair**	*Downriver*
1990	**William Boyd**	*Brazzaville Beach*
1989	**James Kelman**	*A Disaffection*
1988	**Piers Paul Read**	*A Season in the West*
1987	**George Mackay Brown**	*The Golden Bird: Two Orkney Stories*
1986	Jenny Joseph	*Persephone*
1985	Robert Edric	*Winter Garden*
1984	**J. G. Ballard**	*Empire of the Sun*
	Angela Carter	*Nights at the Circus*
1983	Jonathan Keates	*Allegro Postillions*
1982	**Bruce Chatwin**	*On the Black Hill*
1981	**Salman Rushdie**	***Midnight's Children***

	Paul Theroux	*The Mosquito Coast*
1980	**J. M. Coetzee**	*Waiting for the Barbarians*
1979	**William Golding**	*Darkness Visible*
1978	**Maurice Gee**	*Plumb*
1977	**John Le Carré**	*The Honourable Schoolboy*
1976	**John Banville**	*Doctor Copernicus*
1975	**Brian Moore**	*The Great Victorian Collection*
1974	**Lawrence Durrell**	*Monsieur, Or The Prince of Darkness*
1973	**Iris Murdoch**	*The Black Prince*
1972	**John Berger**	*G*
1971	**Nadine Gordimer**	*A Guest of Honour*
1970	Lily Powell	*The Birds of Paradise*
1969	**Elizabeth Bowen**	*Eva Trout*
1968	Maggie Ross	*The Gasteropod*
1967	**Margaret Drabble**	*Jerusalem the Golden*
1966	**Christine Brooke-Rose**	*Such*
	Aidan Higgins	*Langrishe, Go Down*
1965	**Muriel Spark**	*The Mandelbaum Gate*
1964	Frank Tuohy	*The Ice Saints*
1963	Gerda Charles	*A Slanting Light*
1962	Ronald Hardy	*Act of Destruction*
1961	**Jennifer Dawson**	*The Ha-Ha*
1960	**Rex Warner**	*Imperial Caesar*
1959	Morris West	*The Devil's Advocate*
1958	**Angus Wilson**	*The Middle Age of Mrs Eliot*
1957	**Anthony Powell**	*At Lady Molly's* [in **A Dance to the Music of Time**]
1956	**Rose Macaulay**	*The Towers of Trebizond*
1955	**Ivy Compton-Burnett**	*Mother and Son*
1954	**C. P. Snow**	*The New Men* and *The Masters*
1953	**Margaret Kennedy**	*Troy Chimneys*
1952	**Evelyn Waugh**	*Men at Arms* [in **Sword of Honour**]
1951	W. C. Chapman-Mortimer	*Father Goose*
1950	Robert Henriquez	*Along the Valley*
1949	Emma Smith	*The Far Cry*
1948	**Graham Greene**	**The Heart of the Matter**
1947	**L. P. Hartley**	*Eustace and Hilda*
1946	G. Oliver Onions	*Poor Man's Tapestry*
1945	**L. A. G. Strong**	*Travellers*
1944	**Forrest Reid**	*Young Tom*
1943	**Mary Lavin**	*Tales From Bective Bridge*
1942	Arthur Waley	*Monkey by Wu Cheng-en*
1941	**Joyce Cary**	*A House of Children*
1940	**Charles Morgan**	*The Voyage*
1939	**Aldous Huxley**	*After Many a Summer Dies the Swan*
1938	**C. S. Forester**	*A Ship of the Line* and *Flying Colours*
1937	**Neil M. Gunn**	*Highland River*
1936	**Winifred Holtby**	*South Riding*
1935	**L. H. Myers**	*The Root and the Flower*
1934	**Robert Graves**	*I, Claudius* and *Claudius the God*
1933	A. G. Macdonell	*England, Their England*
1932	Helen Simpson	*Boomerang*
1931	Kate O'Brien	*Without My Cloak*
1930	E. H. Young	*Miss Mole*
1929	**J. B. Priestley**	*The Good Companions*
1928	Siegfried Sassoon	*Memoirs of a Fox-Hunting Man*
1927	**Francis Brett Young**	*Portrait of Clare*
1926	**Radclyffe Hall**	*Adam's Breed*
1925	**Liam O'Flaherty**	*The Informer*
1924	**E. M. Forster**	**A Passage to India**
1923	**Arnold Bennett**	**Riceyman Steps**
1922	**David Garnett**	*Lady Into Fox*
1921	Walter de la Mare	*Memoirs of a Midget*
1920	**D. H. Lawrence**	*The Lost Girl*
1919	**Hugh Walpole**	*The Secret City*

Miles Franklin Award (Australia)

1997	**David Foster**	*The Glade Within the Grove*
1996	**Christopher Koch**	*Highways to a War*
1995	Helen 'Demidenko' [Darville]	*The Hand That Signed the Paper*
1994	**Rodney Hall**	*The Grisly Wife*
1993	Alex Miller	*The Ancestor Game*
1992	**Tim Winton**	*Cloudstreet*
1991	**David Malouf**	*The Great World*
1990	Tom Flood	*Oceana Fine*
1989	**Peter Carey**	***Oscar and Lucinda***
*1987	Glenda Adams	*Dancing on Coral*
1986	**Elizabeth Jolley**	*The Well*
1985	Christopher Koch	*The Doubleman*
1984	Tim Winton	*Shallows*
1983	no award	
1982	Rodney Hall	*Just Relations*
1981	Peter Carey	*Bliss*
1980	**Jessica Anderson**	*The Impersonators*
1979	**David Ireland**	*A Woman of the Future*
1978	Jessica Anderson	*Tirra Lirra by the River*
1977	**Ruth Park**	*Swords and Crowns and Rings*
1976	David Ireland	*The Glass Canoe*
1975	**Xavier Herbert**	*Poor Fellow My Country*
1974	Ronald McKie	*The Mango Tree*
1973	no award	
1972	**Thea Astley**	*The Acolyte*
1971	David Ireland	*The Unknown Industrial Prisoner*
1970	Dal Stivens	*A Horse of Air*
1969	George Johnston	*Clean Straw for Nothing*
1968	**Thomas Keneally**	*Three Cheers for the Paraclete*
1967	Thomas Keneally	*Bring Larks and Heroes*
1966	**Peter Mathers**	*Trap*
1965	Thea Astley	*The Slow Natives*
1964	George Johnston	*My Brother Jack*
1963	Sumner Lock Elliott	*Careful, He Might Hear You*
1962	Thea Astley	*The Well Dressed Explorer*
	George Turner	*The Cupboard Under the Stairs*
1961	**Patrick White**	*Riders in the Chariot*
1960	Elizabeth O'Conner	*The Irishman*
1959	**Vance Palmer**	*The Big Fellow*
1958	**Randolph Stow**	*To the Islands*
1957	Patrick White	***Voss***

*The year of the award was changed to the year granted rather than the year published, thus no 1988

Montana New Zealand Book Award (New Zealand)

The winner of the best first book is marked with an asterisk.

1997	**Alan Duff**	*What Becomes of the Broken Hearted?*
	*Dominic Sheehan	*Finding Home*
1996	Sheridan Keith	*Zoology*
	*Emily Perkins	*Not Her Real Name*

The Montana New Zealand Book Awards were created in 1996 by merging the New Zealand Book Awards and the Montana Awards

New Zealand Book Award

1995	**C . K. Stead**	*The Singing Wakapapa*
1994	**Damien Wilkins**	*The Miserables*
1993	Fiona Farrell	*The Skinny Louie Book*
1992	Peter Wells	*Dangerous Desires*
1991	**Maurice Gee**	*The Burning Boy*
1990	John Cranna	*Visitors*
1989	**Janet Frame**	*The Carpathians*
1988	**Fiona Kidman**	*The Book of Secrets*
1987	**Patricia Grace**	*Potiki*
1986	Peter Hooper	*People of the Long Water*

1985	**Marilyn Duckworth**	*Disorderly Conduct*
1984	**Keri Hulme**	***The Bone People***
1983	Sue McCauley	*Other Halves*
1982	Maurice Gee	*Meg*
	Vincent O'Sullivan	*Dandy Edison for Lunch*
1981	**Maurice Shadbolt**	*The Lovelock Version*
1980	Janet Frame	*Living in the Maniototo*
1979	Maurice Gee	*Plumb*
1978	M. K. Joseph	*The Time of Achamoth*
1977	**Ian Wedde**	*Dick Seddon's Great Dive*
1976	Maurice Gee	*A Glorious Morning Comrade*
	O. E. Middleton	*Selected Stories*

Montana Book Awards

| 1995 | **Witi Ihimaera** | *Bulibasha* |
| 1994 | Vincent O'Sullivan | *Let the River Stand* |

Before 1994 the Montana Awards were known as the Goodman Fielder Wattie Book Awards

Goodman Fielder Wattie Award

1993	Maurice Gee	*Going West*
1992	**Barbara Anderson**	*Portrait of the Artist's Wife*
1991	Alan Duff	*Once Were Warriors*
1988	**Steven Eldred-Grigg**	*Oracles and Miracles*
1987	Maurice Shadbolt	*Season of the Jew*
1986	Keri Hulme	*Te Kaihau: The Windeater*
	Patricia Grace	*Potiki*
	Witi Ihimaera	*The Matriarch*
1982	Sue McCauley	*Other Halves*
1981	Maurice Shadbolt	*The Lovelock Version*
1980	Albert Wendt	*Leaves of the Banyan Tree*
1979	Maurice Gee	*Plumb*
1978	Vincent O'Sullivan	*The Boy, The Bridge, The River*
1976	M. K. Joseph	*A Soldier's Tale*
1975	Noel Hilliard	*Maori Woman*
1974	Witi Ihimaera	*Tangi*
1973	Witi Ihimaera	*Pounamu, Pounamu*
	Janet Frame	*Daughter Buffalo*
	Maurice Shadbolt	*Strangers and Journeys*
1972	C. K. Stead	*Smith's Dream*

National Book Awards: Fiction (USA)

1996	Andrea Barrett	*Ship Fever and Other Stories*
1995	**Philip Roth**	*Sabbath's Theater*
1994	**William Gaddis**	*Frolic of His Own*
1993	**E. Annie Proulx**	*The Shipping News*
1992	**Cormac McCarthy**	*All the Pretty Horses*
1991	Norman Rush	*Mating*
1990	**Charles Johnson**	*Middle Passage*
1989	John Casey	*Spartina*
1988	Pete Dexter	*Paris Trout*
1987	Larry Heinemann	*Paco's Story*
1986	**E. L. Doctorow**	*World's Fair*
1985	**Don DeLillo**	*White Noise*
1984	**Ellen Gilchrist**	*Victory Over Japan*
1983	**Alice Walker**	*The Color Purple*
1982	**John Updike**	*Rabbit is Rich* [in the **Rabbit tetralogy**]
1981	**Wright Morris**	*Plains Song*
1980	**William Styron**	*Sophie's Choice*
1979	**Tim O'Brien**	*Going After Cacciato*
1978	Mary Lee Settle	*Blood Ties*
1977	**Wallace Stegner**	*The Spectator Bird*
1976	William Gaddis	*JR*
1975	**Robert Stone**	*Dog Soldiers*
	Thomas Williams	*The Hair of Harold Roux*
1974	**Thomas Pynchon**	***Gravity's Rainbow***
	Isaac Bashevis Singer	*A Crown of Feathers*

1973	**John Barth**	*Chimera*
1972	**Flannery O'Connor**	*The Complete Stories*
1971	**Saul Bellow**	*Mr Sammler's Planet*
1970	**Joyce Carol Oates**	*Them*
1969	**Jerzy Kosinski**	*Steps*
1968	**Thornton Wilder**	*The Eighth Day*
1967	**Bernard Malamud**	*The Fixer*
1966	Katherine Anne Porter	*The Collected Stories*
1965	Saul Bellow	**Herzog**
1964	John Updike	*The Centaur*
1963	J. F. Powers	*Morte D'Urban*
1962	**Walker Percy**	*The Moviegoer*
1961	Conrad Richter	*The Waters of Kronos*
1960	Philip Roth	*Goodbye, Columbus*
1959	Bernard Malamud	*The Magic Barrel*
1958	**John Cheever**	*The Wapshot Chronicle*
1957	Wright Morris	*Field of Vision*
1956	**John O'Hara**	*Ten North Frederick*
1955	**William Faulkner**	*A Fable*
1954	Saul Bellow	**The Adventures of Augie March**
1953	**Ralph Ellison**	**Invisible Man**
1952	**James Jones**	*From Here to Eternity*
1951	William Faulkner	*Collected Stories*
1950	**Nelson Algren**	*The Man With the Golden Arm*

National Book Critics Circle Award: Fiction (USA only to 1997)

1997	**Penelope Fitzgerald**	*The Blue Flower*
1996	Gina Berriault	*Women in Their Beds*
1995	**Stanley Elkin**	*Mrs Ted Bliss*
1994	**Carol Shields**	*The Stone Diaries*
1993	**Ernest J. Gaines**	*A Lesson Before Dying*
1992	**Cormac McCarthy**	*All the Pretty Horses*
1991	**Jane Smiley**	*A Thousand Acres*
1990	**John Updike**	*Rabbit at Rest* [in the **Rabbit tetralogy**]
1989	**E. L. Doctorow**	*Billy Bathgate*
1988	Bharati Mukherjee	*The Middleman and Other Stories*
1987	**Philip Roth**	*The Counterlife*
1986	Reynolds Price	*Kate Vaiden*
1985	**Anne Tyler**	*The Accidental Tourist*
1984	**Louise Erdrich**	*Love Medicine*
1983	**William Kennedy**	*Ironweed*
1982	Stanley Elkin	*George Mills*
1981	John Updike	*Rabbit is Rich* [in the **Rabbit tetralogy**]
1980	**Shirley Hazzard**	*The Transit of Venus*
1979	Thomas Flanagan	*The Year of the French*
1978	**John Cheever**	*The Stories of John Cheever*
1977	**Toni Morrison**	*Song of Solomon*
1976	**John Gardner**	*October Light*

Nobel Prize: English-language writers (all nationalities)

1993	**Toni Morrison** (USA)
1991	**Nadine Gordimer** (South Africa)
1986	**Wole Soyinka** (Nigeria)
1983	**William Golding** (United Kingdom)
1976	**Saul Bellow** (USA)
1973	**Patrick White** (Australia)
1969	**Samuel Beckett** (Ireland/France)
1962	**John Steinbeck** (USA)
1954	**Ernest Hemingway** (USA)
1953	Sir Winston Churchill (UK)
1949	**William Faulkner** (USA)
1938	**Pearl S. Buck** (USA)
1932	**John Galsworthy** (United Kingdom)
1930	**Sinclair Lewis** (USA)
1925	**George Bernard Shaw** (United Kingdom)
1907	**Rudyard Kipling** (United Kingdom)

Noma Award for Publishing in Africa: Fiction

1992	**Charles Mungoshi**	*One Day, Long Ago*
1989	**Chenjerai Hove**	*Bones*

Orange Prize (women novelists of all nationalities)

1997	Carol Shields	*Larry's Party*
1996	Anne Michael	*Fugitive Pieces*
1995	**Helen Dunmore**	*A Spell of Winter*

PEN/Faulkner Award for Fiction (USA)

1997	Gina Berriault	*Women in Their Beds*
1996	**Richard Ford**	*Independence Day*
1995	David Guterson	*Snow Falling on Cedars*
1994	**Philip Roth**	*Operation Shylock*
1993	**E. Annie Proulx**	*Postcards*
1992	**Don DeLillo**	*Mao II*
1991	**John Edgar Wideman**	*Philadelphia Fire*
1990	**E. L. Doctorow**	*Billy Bathgate*
1989	James Salter	*Dusk*
1988	**T. Coraghessan Boyle**	*World's End*
1987	Richard Wiley	*Soldiers in Hiding*
1986	**Peter Taylor**	*The Old Forest*
1985	Tobias Wolff	*The Barracks Thief*
1984	John Edgar Wideman	*Sent For You Yesterday*
1983	Toby Olson	*Seaview*
1982	David Bradley	*The Chaneysville Incident*
1981	**Walter Abish**	*How German is It?*

Pulitzer Prize: Fiction (USA)

1997	**Stephen Millhauser**	*Martin Dressler*
1996	**Richard Ford**	*Independence Day*
1995	**Carol Shields**	*The Stone Diaries*
1994	**E. Annie Proulx**	*The Shipping News*
1993	**Robert Olen Butler**	*Good Scent From Strange Mountain*
1992	**Jane Smiley**	*A Thousand Acres*
1991	**John Updike**	*Rabbit at Rest* [in the ***Rabbit* tetralogy**]
1990	**Oscar Hijuelos**	*The Mambo Kings Play Songs of Love*
1989	**Anne Tyler**	*Breathing Lessons*
1988	**Toni Morrison**	*Beloved*
1987	**Peter Taylor**	*A Summons to Memphis*
1986	**Larry McMurtry**	*Lonesome Dove*
1985	**Alison Lurie**	*Foreign Affairs*
1984	**William Kennedy**	*Ironweed*
1983	**Alice Walker**	*The Color Purple*
1982	John Updike	*Rabbit is Rich*
1981	**John Kennedy Toole**	*A Confederacy of Dunces*
1980	**Norman Mailer**	***The Executioner's Song***
1979	**John Cheever**	*The Stories of John Cheever*
1978	James Alan McPherson	*Elbow Room*
1977	no award	
1976	**Saul Bellow**	*Humboldt's Gift*
1975	Michael Shaara	*The Killer Angels*
1974	**Thomas Pynchon**	***Gravity's Rainbow***
1973	**Eudora Welty**	*The Optimist's Daughter*
1972	**Wallace Stegner**	*Angle of Repose*
1971	no award	
1970	**Jean Stafford**	*Collected Stories*
1969	**N. Scott Momaday**	*House Made of Dawn*
1968	**William Styron**	*The Confessions of Nat Turner*
1967	**Bernard Malamud**	*The Fixer*
1966	**Katherine Anne Porter**	*Collected Stories of Katherine Anne Porter*
1965	Shirley Ann Grau	*The Keepers of the House*
1964	no award	
1963	**William Faulkner**	*The Reivers*
1962	Edwin O'Connor	*The Edge of Sadness*
1961	**Harper Lee**	*To Kill a Mockingbird*
1960	Allen Drury	*Advise and Consent*

1959	Robert Lewis Taylor	*The Travels of Jaimie McPheeters*
1958	**James Agee**	*A Death in the Family*
1957	no award	
1956	MacKinlay Kantor	*Andersonville*
1955	William Faulkner	*A Fable*
1954	no award	
1953	**Ernest Hemingway**	*The Old Man and the Sea*
1952	Herman Wouk	*The Caine Mutiny*
1951	Conrad Richter	*The Town*
1950	A. B. Guthrie Jr	*The Way West*
1949	**James Gould Cozzens**	*Guard of Honor*
1948	**James A. Michener**	*Tales of the South Pacific*
1947	**Robert Penn Warren**	*All the King's Men*
1946	no award	
1945	**John Hersey**	*A Bell for Adano*
1944	Martin Flavin	*Journey in the Dark*
1943	**Upton Sinclair**	*Dragon's Teeth*
1942	**Ellen Glasgow**	*In This Our Life*
1941	no award	
1940	**John Steinbeck**	**The Grapes of Wrath**
1939	Marjorie Rawlings	*The Yearling*
1938	**John P. Marquand**	*The Late George Apley*
1937	**Margaret Mitchell**	**Gone With The Wind**
1936	Harold L. Davis	*Honey in the Horn*
1935	Josephine Johnson	*Now in November*
1934	Caroline Miller	*Lamb in His Bosom*
1933	T. S. Stribling	*The Store*
1932	**Pearl S. Buck**	*The Good Earth*
1931	Margaret Ayer Barnes	*Years of Grace*
1930	Oliver La Farge	*Laughing Boys*
1929	Julia Peterkin	*Scarlet Sister Mary*
1928	**Thornton Wilder**	*The Bridge of San Luis Rey*
1927	**Louis Bromfield**	*Early Autumn*
1926	**Sinclair Lewis**	*Arrowsmith*
1925	Edna Ferber	*So Big*
1924	Margaret Wilson	*The Able McLaughlins*
1923	**Willa Cather**	*One of Ours*
1922	**Booth Tarkington**	*Alice Adams*
1921	**Edith Wharton**	**The Age of Innocence**
1920	no award	
1919	Booth Tarkington	*The Magnificent Ambersons*
1918	Ernest Poole	*His Family*

Sahitya Akademi Prize (India)

It is awarded annually to literary works in any of twenty-two languages. The following works of fiction in English have won the prize.

1992	Ruskin Bond	*Our Trees Still Grow in Dehra*
1991	**I. Allan Sealy**	**The Trotter-Nama**
1990	**Shashi Deshpande**	*That Long Silence*
1989	**Amitav Ghosh**	**The Shadow Lines**
1988	**Vikram Seth**	*The Golden Gate*
1986	**Nayantara Sahgal**	**Rich Like Us**
1982	**Arun Joshi**	*The Last Labyrinth*
1978	**Anita Desai**	*Fire on the Mountain*
1977	**Chaman Nahal**	**Azadi**
1971	**Mulk Raj Anand**	*Morning Face*
1967	**Bhabani Bhattacharya**	*Shadow from Ladakh*
1963	**Rajo Rao**	**The Serpent and the Rope**
1960	**R. K. Narayan**	*The Guide*

Somerset Maugham Awards (United Kingdom)

It is awarded annually to up to four works of any type, except drama. The following works of fiction have won the award.

1997	Rhidian Brook	*The Testimony of Taliesin Jones*
	Kate Clanchy	*Slattern*
	Philip Hensher	*Kitchen Venom*
1996	Alan Warner	*Morvern Callar*

1994	A. L. Kennedy	*Looking for the Possible Dance*
1993	Duncan McLean	*Bucket of Tongues'*
1992	Lawrence Norfolk	*Lempriére's Dictionary*
1991	Peter Benson	*The Other Occupant*
	Lesley Glaister	*Honour Thy Father*
	Helen Simpson	*Four Bare Legs in a Bed*
1990	Sam North	*The Automatic Man*
	Nicholas Shakespeare	*The Vision of Elena Silves*
1989	Alan Hollinghurst	*The Swimming Pool Library*
	Deirdre Madden	*The Birds of the Innocent Wood*
1988	Matthew Kneale	*Whore Banquets*
1987	Stephen Gregory	*The Cormorant*
	Janni Howker	*Isaac Campion*
1986	**Tim Parks**	*Tongues of Flame*
1985	**Jane Rogers**	*Her Living Image*
1984	**Peter Ackroyd**	*The Last Testament of Oscar Wilde*
1983	Lisa St Aubin de Teran	*Keepers of the House*
1982	**William Boyd**	*A Good Man in Africa*
	Adam Mars-Jones	*Lantern Lecture*
1981	**Julian Barnes**	*Metroland*
	Clive Sinclair	*Hearts of Gold*
	A. N. Wilson	*The Healing Art*
1979	Helen Hodgman	*Jack & Jill*
	Sara Maitland	*Daughter of Jerusalem*
1978	**Nigel Williams**	*My Life Closed Twice*
1976	Dominic Cooper	*The Dead of Winter*
	Ian McEwan	*First Love, Last Rites*
1975	no award	
1974	**Martin Amis**	*The Rachel Papers*
1973	Peter Prince	*Play Things*
	Jonathan Street	*Prudence Dictates*
1972	Gillian Tindall	*Fly Away Home*
1971	**Susan Hill**	*I'm the King of the Castle*
	Michael Hastings	*Tussy is Me*
1970	Jane Gaskell	*A Sweet, Sweet Summer*
	Piers Paul Read	*Monk Dawson*
1968	**Paul Bailey**	*At the Jerusalem*
1967	**B. S. Johnson**	*Trawl*
1966	**Michael Frayn**	*The Tin Men*
	Julian Mitchell	*The White Feather*
1965	Peter Everett	*Negatives*
1964	**Dan Jacobson**	*Time of Arrival*
	John Le Carré	*The Spy Who Came in from the Cold*
1963	**David Storey**	*Flight into Camden*
1961	**V. S. Naipaul**	*Miguel Street*
1957	**George Lamming**	***In the Castle of My Skin***
1955	**Kingsley Amis**	***Lucky Jim***
1954	**Doris Lessing**	*Five Short Novels*
1953	Emyr Humphreys	*Hear and Forgive*
1952	**Francis King**	*The Dividing Stream*
1951	Roland Camberton	*Scamp*
1950	Nigel Kneale	*Tomato Cain and Other Stories*
1948	**P. H. Newby**	*Journey to the Interior*
1947	**A. L. Barker**	*Innocents*

Whitbread Award (United Kingdom)

1997	Pauline Melville	*The Ventriloquist's Tale*
1996	**Beryl Bainbridge**	*Every Man for Himself*
1995	**Salman Rushdie**	*The Moor's Last Sigh*
1994	**William Trevor**	***Felicia's Journey***
1993	**Joan Brady**	*Theory of War*
1992	**Alasdair Gray**	*Poor Things*
1991	**Jane Gardam**	*The Queen of the Tambourine*
1990	**Nicholas Mosley**	*Hopeful Monsters*
1989	Lindsay Clarke	*The Chymical Wedding*
1988	Salman Rushdie	***The Satanic Verses***
1987	**Ian McEwan**	*The Child in Time*

1986	**Kazuo Ishiguro**	*An Artist of the Floating World*
1985	**Peter Ackroyd**	*Hawksmoor*
1984	**Christopher Hope**	*Kruger's Alp*
1983	William Trevor	*Fools of Fortune*
1982	**John Wain**	*Young Shoulders*
1981	Maurice Leitch	*Silver's City*
1980	**David Lodge**	*How Far Can You Go?*
1979	**Jennifer Johnston**	*The Old Jest*
1978	**Paul Theroux**	*Picture Palace*